# Collins
## Children's
### Dictionary

## Published by Collins

An imprint of HarperCollins Publishers
Westerhill Road
Bishopbriggs
Glasgow G64 2QT

HarperCollins Publishers
Macken House, 39/40 Mayor Street Upper,
Dublin 1, D01 C9W8, Ireland

First Edition 2018

10 9 8 7

Text © HarperCollins Publishers 2018
Illustrations © Maria Herbert-Liew 2018

ISBN 978-0-00-827117-6

Collins® is a registered trademark of
HarperCollins Publishers Limited

www.collins.co.uk/dictionaries

Typeset by QBS Learning

Printed in India by Replika Press Pvt. Ltd.

A catalogue record for this book is available
from the British Library.

If you would like to comment on any
aspect of this book, please contact us
at the given address or e-mail
dictionaries@harpercollins.co.uk.

## Acknowledgements

We would like to thank those authors and
publishers who kindly gave permission for
copyright material to be used in the Collins
Corpus. We would also like to thank Times
Newspapers Ltd for providing valuable data.

**Managing Editors:**
Maree Airlie
Mary O'Neill

**Contributors:**
Lucy Hollingworth
Lynne Tarvit

**Artwork and Design:**
Maria Herbert-Liew

**For the Publisher:**
Kerry Ferguson
Michelle Fullerton
Laura Waddell

# Contents

# How to use this dictionary

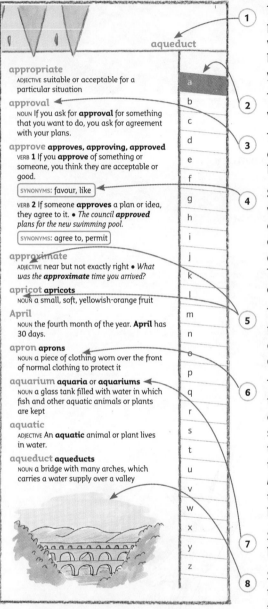

**appropriate**
ADJECTIVE suitable or acceptable for a particular situation

**approval**
NOUN If you ask for **approval** for something that you want to do, you ask for agreement with your plans.

**approve** approves, approving, approved
VERB **1** If you **approve** of something or someone, you think they are acceptable or good.

SYNONYMS: favour, like

VERB **2** If someone **approves** a plan or idea, they agree to it. • The council **approved** plans for the new swimming pool.

SYNONYMS: agree to, permit

**approximate**
ADJECTIVE near but not exactly right • What was the **approximate** time you arrived?

**apricot** apricots
NOUN a small, soft, yellowish-orange fruit

**April**
NOUN the fourth month of the year. **April** has 30 days.

**apron** aprons
NOUN a piece of clothing worn over the front of normal clothing to protect it

**aquarium** aquaria or aquariums
NOUN a glass tank filled with water in which fish and other aquatic animals or plants are kept

**aquatic**
ADJECTIVE An **aquatic** animal or plant lives in water.

**aqueduct** aqueducts
NOUN a bridge with many arches, which carries a water supply over a valley

aqueduct

a b c d e f g h i j k l m n o p q r s t u v w x y z

1. The **guide word** on a left-hand page tells you the first word you will find on the page. On a right-hand page, the guide word tells you the last word on the page.

2. The **alphabet line** shows you which letter you are in.

3. The **headword** is the word you are looking up. Headwords are blue and in alphabetical order.

4. **Synonyms** are given for some words. These are words with a similar meaning that you can use instead. **Antonyms** are given for some words. These are words that have the opposite meaning.

5. The **word class** tells you if the headword is, for example, a noun, verb, adjective, adverb or pronoun.

6. The **definition** tells you what the word means. Sometimes definitions include a label, such *formal* or *informal*. *Formal* tells you that a word is used in serious writing and speech. *Informal* tells you that a word is used in a more relaxed way, between family and friends.

7. Some words or word forms can have more than one spelling.

8. Sometimes an **illustration** is included to give you more information.

**9** Sometimes there is an **example** to show how the word is used.

**10** If there is useful information about a word at an **illustration** elsewhere in the book, a note tells you where to find it.

**11** A **pronunciation tip** shows you how to say a difficult word. A **language tip** helps you with the spelling of words or the way they are used.

**12** There can be **other forms** of the word after the headword. These might be the plural of a noun, tenses of a verb, or comparative and superlative forms of an adjective.

**13** A **word history** tells you where a word originally came from.

---

**nuclear**
ADJECTIVE relating to the energy produced when atoms are split • *We live near a **nuclear** power station.*

**nucleus nuclei**
NOUN **1** the central part of an atom or a cell
→ Have a look at the illustration for **atom**
NOUN **2** the important or central part of something • *We still have the **nucleus** of the team.*

PRONUNCIATION TIP
The singular is pronounced **nyoo**-clee-us. The plural is pronounced **nyoo**-clee-eye.

**nude nudes**
ADJECTIVE **1** If someone is **nude**, they are naked.
NOUN **2** A **nude** is a picture or statue of a naked person.

**nudge nudges, nudging, nudged**
VERB **1** If you **nudge** someone, you push them gently with your elbow to get their attention or to make them move.
NOUN **2** a gentle push with your elbow

**nugget nuggets**
NOUN a small rough lump of something, especially gold

**nuisance nuisances**
NOUN someone or something that is annoying or causing problems

**numb**
ADJECTIVE unable to feel anything • *I was so cold my hands and feet felt **numb**.*

WORD HISTORY
from Middle English *nomen* meaning paralysed

**number numbers, numbering, numbered**
NOUN **1** a word or symbol used for counting or calculating
NOUN **2** the series of numbers that you dial when you phone someone
VERB **3** If you **number** something, you give it a number, usually in a sequence. • *Please **number** each page you write on.*

**number bond number bonds**
NOUN any pair of numbers that add together to make up another number

**numeracy**
NOUN the ability to do arithmetic

# Word classes

Each word in this dictionary belongs to a particular word class, for example, nouns, verbs or adjectives. To find out more about each of these word classes, look at pages 460–462 in the **Word Wizard**.

## Nouns

A **noun** is a word that is used for talking about a person or thing. **Nouns** are sometimes called "naming words" because they are often the names of people, places, things and ideas. Examples of nouns are **book**, **child** and **smile**.

## Adjectives

An **adjective** is a word that tells you more about a person or thing. **Adjectives** are often called "describing words" because they describe what something looks, feels or smells like. Examples of adjectives are **happy**, **green** and **cloudy**.

## Verbs

A **verb** is a word that you use for saying what someone or something does. **Verbs** are often called "doing words" because they talk about an action that someone or something is doing. Examples of verbs are **walk**, **speak** and **look**.

## Adverbs

An **adverb** is a word that tells you more about how someone does something. Examples of adverbs are **slowly**, **loudly** and **hungrily**.

## Pronouns

A **pronoun** is a word you use instead of a noun, to refer to someone or something. Examples of pronouns are **he**, **it** and **their**.

## Prepositions

A **preposition** is a word that links a noun, pronoun or noun phrase to some other word in the sentence. Examples of prepositions are **under**, **in** and **with**.

## Conjunctions

A **conjunction** is a word that links two words or phrases or two parts of a sentence. Examples of conjunctions are **and**, **but** and **because**.

## Determiners

A **determiner** is a specific word you use before a noun and/or an adjective. Examples of determiners are **a**, **the** and **some**.

**a or an**

ADJECTIVE **A** and **an** are used when you talk about one of something. **A** is used when the next sound is a consonant: *a car, a dog*. **An** is used when the next sound is a vowel (a, e, i, o or u): *an apple, an elephant*.

**abacus abacuses**

NOUN a frame with beads that slide along rods, used for counting

---

**WORD HISTORY**

from Greek *abax* meaning board covered with sand for doing sums on

---

**abandon abandons, abandoning, abandoned**

VERB If you **abandon** someone or something, you leave them or give them up for good. • *He abandoned all hope of catching the train on time.*

**abbey abbeys**

NOUN a church with buildings attached to it in which monks or nuns live

**abbreviation abbreviations**

NOUN a short form of a word or phrase • *N is an abbreviation for North.*

**abdomen abdomens**

NOUN **1** the front part of your body below your chest, containing your stomach and intestines
NOUN **2** the back part of the body of an insect or spider

→ Have a look at the illustrations for **insect** and **spider**

**abdominal**

ADJECTIVE **Abdominal** describes something that is in the front part of your body below your chest, where your stomach and intestines are. • *abdominal pain*

**ability abilities**

NOUN If you have **ability**, you have the intelligence and skill to do things.

**able**

ADJECTIVE If you are **able** to do something, you can do it.

ANTONYM: unable

**abnormal**

ADJECTIVE not normal or usual

**aboard**

PREPOSITION **1** If you are **aboard** a plane or a ship you are on it. • *The captain invited us aboard his boat.*
ADVERB **2** If you go **aboard** a plane or a ship, you go onto it. • *It took two hours to bring all the passengers aboard.*

**Aborigine Aborigines**

NOUN someone descended from the people who were living in Australia before the European settlers arrived

**about**

PREPOSITION **1** If you talk or write **about** a particular thing, you say things that are to do with that subject. • *a book about London*
ADVERB **2** You say **about** in front of a number to show it is not exact. • *He arrived about two o'clock.*
PHRASE **3** If you are **about to** do something, you are just going to do it. • *He was about to leave.*

**above**

PREPOSITION **1** If one thing is above another, it is higher up. • *The plane was flying above the clouds.*

ANTONYM: below

PREPOSITION **2** If something is **above** a particular amount or level, it is more than it. • *above average intelligence*

ANTONYM: below

**abroad**

ADVERB If you go **abroad**, you go to another country.

**abscess abscesses**

NOUN a painful swelling on the body, which contains pus

**abseil abseils, abseiling, abseiled**

VERB If you **abseil** down a rock face, you use ropes to go down it.

A
B
C
D
E
F
G
H
I
J
K
L
M
N
O
P
Q
R
S
T
U
V
W
X
Y
Z

### absent

ADJECTIVE If you are **absent** from a place, you are not there.

ANTONYM: present

### absolute

ADJECTIVE **1** total and complete • *absolute darkness*

ADJECTIVE **2** having total power • *an **absolute** ruler*

### absolutely

ADVERB If you are **absolutely** sure about something, you are completely sure of it.

### absorb absorbs, absorbing, absorbed

VERB If something **absorbs** liquid or gas, it soaks it up. • *Plants **absorb** moisture from the soil.*

### absorbent

ADJECTIVE If something is **absorbent**, it soaks up liquids easily.

### abstract

ADJECTIVE **1** An **abstract** idea is based on thoughts and ideas rather than on real objects or happenings, for example *bravery* and *happiness*.

ADJECTIVE **2 Abstract** art uses shapes rather than images of people or objects.

ADJECTIVE **3** In grammar, **abstract** nouns refer to qualities or ideas, rather than real objects, for example *happiness*.

### absurd

ADJECTIVE Something that is **absurd** is stupid or ridiculous.

### abundant

ADJECTIVE present in large amounts • *There is **abundant** wildlife, including a pride of lions.*

### abuse abuses, abusing, abused

NOUN **1** cruel treatment of someone

NOUN **2** rude and unkind remarks

VERB **3** To **abuse** someone is to treat them cruelly.

VERB **4** If you **abuse** someone, you speak to them in a rude and insulting way.

### abysmal

ADJECTIVE very bad

### academic academics

ADJECTIVE **1 Academic** work is done in school, college and university.

NOUN **2** someone who teaches or does research in a college or university

### academy academies

NOUN **1** a school or college, usually one that specialises in a particular subject

• *the Royal **Academy** of Arts*

NOUN **2** an organisation of scientists, writers, artists or musicians

### accelerate accelerates, accelerating, accelerated

VERB To **accelerate** is to speed up.

ANTONYM: decelerate

### acceleration

NOUN the rate at which the speed of something increases

### accent accents

NOUN a way of pronouncing a language

• *She had an Australian **accent**.*

### accept accepts, accepting, accepted

VERB **1** If you **accept** something, you say yes to it or you take it from someone.

• *She **accepted** our invitation to the party.*

VERB **2** If you **accept** a situation, you realise that it cannot be changed. • *I **accepted** that I would have to work hard before my exams.*

### acceptable

ADJECTIVE satisfactory • *These are all **acceptable** answers.*

### access

NOUN If you have **access** to a place, you may enter it. If you have **access** to a thing, you may use it.

### accessible

ADJECTIVE **1** easy to reach or to see • *The beach was **accessible** by a narrow path.*

ADJECTIVE **2** Books that are **accessible** are easy to understand.

### accident accidents

NOUN **1** something that happens suddenly or unexpectedly, causing people to be hurt or killed

PHRASE **2** Something that happens **by accident** has not been planned. • *We met **by accident** in the supermarket.*

### accidental

ADJECTIVE Something that is **accidental** has not been planned.

### accidentally

ADVERB If you do something **accidentally**, you do not plan to do it.

**accommodate** **accommodates, accommodating, accommodated**
VERB If you **accommodate** someone, you provide them with a place to sleep, live or work.

**accommodation**
NOUN a place where you can live, work or sleep

**accompany** **accompanies, accompanying, accompanied**
VERB 1 If you **accompany** someone, you go with them.
VERB 2 If you **accompany** a singer, you play an instrument while they sing.

**accomplice** **accomplices**
NOUN a person who helps someone else to commit a crime

**accomplish** **accomplishes, accomplishing, accomplished**
VERB If you **accomplish** something, you succeed in doing it.

**according to**
PREPOSITION If something is true **according to** a particular person, that person says that it is true. ● *According to* my grandad, that castle is haunted.

**account** **accounts, accounting, accounted**
NOUN 1 a written or spoken report of something
NOUN 2 money that you keep at a bank
PHRASE 3 **On account of** means because of.
● *He couldn't play football, on account of a sore throat.*

**account for**
VERB To **account for** something is to explain it.

**accountant** **accountants**
NOUN someone whose job is to look after the financial affairs of people and companies

**accumulate** **accumulates, accumulating, accumulated**
VERB If things **accumulate**, or if you **accumulate** things, they collect over a period of time. ● *While they were away, a large pile of letters accumulated on the doormat.*

**accuracy**
NOUN the quality of being absolutely correct

**accurate**
ADJECTIVE absolutely correct

**accusation** **accusations**
NOUN An **accusation** is when you say that someone has done something wrong.

**accuse** **accuses, accusing, accused**
VERB If you **accuse** someone of doing something wrong, you say they have done it.

**ace** **aces**
NOUN 1 In a pack of cards, the **ace** is a card with a single symbol on it.
NOUN 2 In tennis, an **ace** is a serve that the other player is unable to return.
ADJECTIVE 3 (*informal*) good or skilful ● *an ace squash player*

**ache** **aches, aching, ached**
NOUN 1 a continuous, dull pain
VERB 2 If a part of your body **aches**, you feel a continuous, dull pain there.

**achieve** **achieves, achieving, achieved**
VERB If you **achieve** something, you are successful at doing it or at making it happen.

LANGUAGE TIP
The *i* comes before the *e* in *achieve* and *achievement*.

**achievement** **achievements**
NOUN something which someone has been successful in doing or making happen, especially after a lot of effort

**acid** **acids**
NOUN 1 a chemical substance. Strong **acids** can damage skin, cloth and metal, for example sulphuric **acid**. Other **acids**, such as those found in citrus fruit and vinegar, are harmless.

ANTONYM: alkali

ADJECTIVE 2 If something has an **acid** taste, it tastes sharp or bitter.

ANTONYM: alkaline

WORD HISTORY
from Latin *acidus* meaning sour

**acid rain**
NOUN rain that has been polluted by the burning of fossil fuels, such as coal and oil

**acknowledge** acknowledges, acknowledging, acknowledged
VERB **1** If you **acknowledge** a fact or a situation, you admit that it is true.
VERB **2** If you **acknowledge** someone, you show that you have seen and recognised them, by waving or saying *hello*.
VERB **3** If you **acknowledge** a message or a letter, you tell the person who sent it that you have received it.

**acne**
NOUN a skin condition that causes spots on the face and neck. **Acne** is common among teenagers.

**acorn** acorns
NOUN a nut that grows on oak trees

**acquaintance** acquaintances
NOUN someone you know slightly but not well

**acre** acres
NOUN a unit for measuring land. One **acre** is equal to 4840 square yards or about 4047 square metres.

**acrobat** acrobats
NOUN an entertainer who performs difficult gymnastic acts

WORD HISTORY
from Greek *akrobates* meaning someone who walks on tiptoe

**acrobatic**
ADJECTIVE involving difficult gymnastic acts

**acrobatics**
PLURAL NOUN difficult gymnastic acts

**acronym** acronyms
NOUN a word made up of the initial letters of a phrase. NATO is an **acronym**, and stands for North Atlantic Treaty Organization.

**across**
PREPOSITION **1** If you go **across** a place, you go from one side of it to the other. • *We walked across Hyde Park.*
PREPOSITION **2** Something that is situated **across** a road or river is on the other side of it.

**act** acts, acting, acted
VERB **1** If you **act**, you do something.
• *We have to act quickly in an emergency.*
VERB **2** If you **act** in a particular way, you behave in that way. • *You're acting like a baby.*
VERB **3** If you **act** in a play or film, you play a role in it.

NOUN **4** a single thing someone does
• *The rescue was a brave act.*
NOUN **5** An **Act** of Parliament is a law passed by the government.
NOUN **6** Stage plays are divided into parts called **acts**.

**action** actions
NOUN **1** something you do for a particular purpose
NOUN **2** a physical movement, such as jumping

**active**
ADJECTIVE **1** Someone who is **active** moves around a lot or does a lot of things.
ADJECTIVE **2** In grammar the **active**, or the **active** voice, is the form of the verb in which the subject of the sentence is the person or thing doing the action, rather than having it done to them. For example, the sentence *The dog bit Ben* is in the **active** voice. In the passive voice the subject has the thing done to them: *Ben was bitten by the dog.*

ANTONYM: passive

**activity** activities
NOUN **1** a situation in which a lot of things are happening at the same time • *There was a great deal of activity in the hall as we got ready for the school play.*
NOUN **2** something you do for pleasure, such as gymnastics or music

**actor** actors
NOUN a man or woman whose job is performing in plays or films

**actress** actresses
NOUN a woman whose profession is acting

**actual**
ADJECTIVE real, rather than imaginary or guessed at • *You guessed I was eleven – my actual age is twelve.*

**actually**
ADVERB **1** You use **actually** to show that something is real or true. • *Mum told me what actually happened.*
ADVERB **2** You use **actually** to politely tell someone that they are wrong. • *No, I'm not eight. I'm nine, actually.*

**acute**

ADJECTIVE **1** severe or intense ● *She had an* ***acute*** *pain in her arm.*

ADJECTIVE **2** In mathematics, an **acute** angle measures less than 90 degrees.

ADJECTIVE **3** Someone who is **acute** is intelligent.

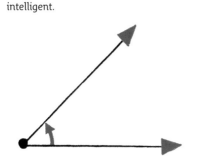

**AD**

ADJECTIVE You use **AD** in dates to show the number of years after the birth of Jesus Christ.

**WORD HISTORY**

an abbreviation of the Latin *Anno Domini* meaning the year of Our Lord

**adapt adapts, adapting, adapted**

VERB **1** If you **adapt** to something, you get used to it.

VERB **2** If you **adapt** something, you change it so that it can be used in a new way.

**adaptable**

ADJECTIVE If you are **adaptable**, you change easily in a new situation or to suit new circumstances.

**adaptation**

NOUN the act of changing something to make it suitable for a new purpose or situation ● *Most living creatures are capable of* ***adaptation*** *when they need to be.*

**add adds, adding, added**

VERB **1** If you **add** something to a number of things, you put it with those things. ● *Each girl* ***added*** *more wood to the pile.*

VERB **2** If you **add** numbers together, or **add** them up, you work out the total. ● *Two and three* ***added*** *together are five (2 + 3 = 5).*

**adder adders**

NOUN a small, poisonous snake

**addicted**

ADJECTIVE If you are **addicted** to something, you cannot stop doing it or wanting it.

**addiction addictions**

NOUN If you have an **addiction** to something, you cannot stop doing it or wanting it.

**addition additions**

NOUN **1** the process of adding two or more numbers together

NOUN **2** something that is added to something else ● *The* ***addition*** *of sugar would improve the taste of these plums.*

**additional**

ADJECTIVE extra or more

**additive additives**

NOUN something that is added to something else, such as food

**address addresses, addressing, addressed**

NOUN **1** Your **address** is the number of the house where you live, together with the name of the street and the town or village.

VERB **2** If someone **addresses** a letter to you, they write your name and address on it.

VERB **3** If you **address** a group of people, you speak to them formally.

**LANGUAGE TIP**

There are two *d*s and two *ss* in *address*.

**adenoids**

PLURAL NOUN small lumps of flesh at the back of the throat

**adequate**

ADJECTIVE just enough for what is needed

SYNONYMS: enough, satisfactory, sufficient

**adhesive adhesives**

NOUN **1** a substance used to stick things together, such as glue

ADJECTIVE **2** If something is **adhesive**, it sticks to other things.

**adjacent**

PREPOSITION If one thing is **adjacent** to another, the two things are next to each other.

**adjective adjectives**

NOUN a word that adds to the description of a noun. For example, *large* and *old* are both **adjectives**.

a
b
c
d
e
f
g
h
i
j
k
l
m
n
o
p
q
r
s
t
u
v
w
x
y
z

**11**

## adjust adjusts, adjusting, adjusted
VERB **1** If you **adjust** something, you change its position or alter it in some other way.
● *She adjusted her pillow to make herself more comfortable.*
VERB **2** If you **adjust** to a new situation, you get used to it.

## adjustment adjustments
NOUN **1** a small change that you make to something ● *By making adjustments to your diet, you can improve your health.*
NOUN **2** **Adjustment** is when you get used to a new situation.

## administration administrations
NOUN the work of managing and supervising an organisation

## admiral admirals
NOUN a senior officer in the navy

## admire admires, admiring, admired
VERB If you **admire** someone or something, you respect and approve of them.

## admirer admirers
NOUN someone who respects and approves of someone or something

## admission admissions
NOUN **1** If you are allowed **admission** to a place, you may go into it.
NOUN **2** If you make an **admission**, you confess to something or agree that it is true.

## admit admits, admitting, admitted
VERB **1** If you **admit** something, you agree that it is true.
VERB **2** If you **admit** to something, you agree that you did something you shouldn't have done.
VERB **3** To **admit** someone or something to a place is to allow them to enter it.

## admittance
NOUN the right to enter somewhere
● *There will be no admittance to the party after eight o'clock.*

## adolescent adolescents
NOUN a young person who is no longer a child, but is not yet an adult

**WORD HISTORY**
from Latin *adolescere* meaning to grow up

## adopt adopts, adopting, adopted
VERB If someone **adopts** a child, they take them into their family as their son or daughter by a legal process.

**WORD HISTORY**
from Latin *adoptare* meaning to choose for oneself

## adorable
ADJECTIVE loveable and attractive

## adoration
NOUN a feeling of deep love and admiration for someone

## adore adores, adoring, adored
VERB If you **adore** someone, you feel deep love and admiration for them.

## adult adults
NOUN a mature and fully developed person or animal

## advance advances, advancing, advanced
VERB **1** To **advance** is to move forward.
NOUN **2** An **advance** is progress in something. ● *There have been many scientific advances in the past century.*
PHRASE **3** If you do something **in advance** of something, you do it beforehand.
● *We booked our holiday well in advance.*

## advanced
ADJECTIVE If something is **advanced**, it is at a high level, or ahead in development or progress. ● *The children in the top group do advanced maths exercises.*

## advantage advantages
NOUN **1** a benefit, or something that puts you in a better position ● *The advantage of email is that it is quicker than the post.*
PHRASE **2** If you **take advantage** of someone, you treat them unfairly for your own benefit.
PHRASE **3** If you **take advantage** of something, you make use of it.

## adventure adventures
NOUN something that is exciting, and perhaps even dangerous

## adverb adverbs
NOUN a word that tells you how, when, where or why something happens or something is done. For example, she walked *slowly*, he came *yesterday*, they live *here*.

**WORD HISTORY**
from Latin *adverbium* meaning added word

## advert adverts
NOUN an abbreviation for *advertisement*

A
B
C
D
E
F
G
H
I
J
K
L
M
N
O
P
Q
R
S
T
U
V
W
X
Y
Z

**advertise advertises, advertising, advertised**
VERB If you **advertise** something, you tell people about it online, in a newspaper, on a poster or on TV.

**advertisement advertisements**
NOUN a notice in a newspaper, on a poster, on TV or on the internet, about something such as a product, event or job

**advice**
NOUN a suggestion from someone about what you should do

**LANGUAGE TIP**
The noun *advice* ends in *ce*.

**advisable**
ADJECTIVE If it is **advisable** to do something, it is a sensible thing to do and will probably give the results that you want. • *It is* **advisable** *to wear a helmet when cycling.*

**advise advises, advising, advised**
VERB If you **advise** someone to do something, you tell them you think they should do it.

**LANGUAGE TIP**
The verb *advise* ends in *se*.

**aerial aerials**
NOUN **1** a piece of wire for receiving television or radio signals
ADJECTIVE **2** happening in the air • *We watched the* **aerial** *displays at the RAF airshow.*

**aero-**
PREFIX to do with the air, for example **aero**plane

**WORD HISTORY**
from Greek *aer* meaning air

**aeroplane aeroplanes**
NOUN a vehicle with wings and engines that enable it to fly
→ Have a look at the illustration

**aerosol aerosols**
NOUN a small, metal container in which liquid is kept under pressure so that it can be forced out as a spray

**affair affairs**
NOUN **1** an event or series of events
• *The wedding was a happy* **affair**.
NOUN **2** If something is your own **affair**, then it is your concern only.

**affect affects, affecting, affected**
VERB When something **affects** someone or something, it causes them to change.
• *Computers* **affect** *our lives in many ways.*

**affection**
NOUN a feeling of love and fondness for someone

**affectionate**
ADJECTIVE showing that you love or like someone • *He was a very* **affectionate** *child.*

**affluent**
ADJECTIVE People who are **affluent** have a lot of money and possessions.

a
b
c
d
e
f
g
h
i
j
k
l
m
n
o
p
q
r
s
t
u
v
w
x
y
z

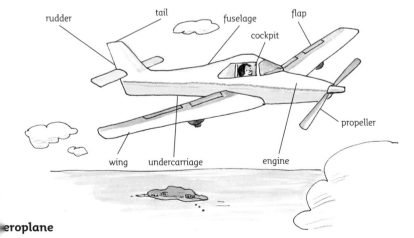

rudder  tail  fuselage  flap  cockpit  propeller  engine  undercarriage  wing

**aeroplane**

## afford affords, affording, afforded
VERB **1** If you can **afford** something, you have enough money to pay for it.
VERB **2** If you can **afford** to relax, you feel you have done enough work for the moment, and have time to take things easy.

## afloat
ADVERB If something or someone is **afloat**, they are floating.

## afraid
ADJECTIVE **1** If you are **afraid**, you are frightened.

SYNONYM: scared

ADJECTIVE **2** If you are **afraid** something might happen, you worry that it might happen.

## after
PREPOSITION **1** later than a particular time, date or event • She left just **after** breakfast.

ANTONYM: before

PREPOSITION **2** If you come **after** someone or something, you are behind them and following them. • They ran **after** her.
ADVERB **3** later • Soon **after**, he went to work.

## afternoon afternoons
NOUN the part of the day between twelve noon and about six o'clock

## afterwards
ADVERB after an event or time • We went swimming, and **afterwards** we had an ice cream.

## again
ADVERB happening one more time • The film was so good that we went to see it **again**.

SYNONYM: once more

## against
PREPOSITION **1** touching and resting on • He leaned the ladder **against** the wall.
PREPOSITION **2** in opposition to • France played **against** England.

ANTONYM: for

## age ages, ageing or aging, aged
NOUN **1** The **age** of something or someone is the number of years they have lived or existed.
NOUN **2** a particular period in history • the Iron **Age**

PLURAL NOUN **3** (informal) **Ages** means a very long time. • He's been talking for **ages**.
VERB **4** To **age** is to grow old or to appear older.

LANGUAGE TIP
*Ageing* and *aging* are both correct spellings

## agency agencies
NOUN an organisation or business that provides special services • detective **agency** • advertising **agency**

## agenda agendas
NOUN a list of items to be discussed at a meeting

## agent agents
NOUN **1** someone who does business or arranges things for other people • a travel **agent**
NOUN **2** someone who works for their country's secret service

## aggravate aggravates, aggravating, aggravated
VERB **1** If you **aggravate** something, you make it worse.
VERB **2** (informal) If you **aggravate** someone you annoy them.

## aggressive
ADJECTIVE full of hostility and violence • Some breeds of dog are more **aggressive** than others.

SYNONYMS: belligerent, hostile

## agile
ADJECTIVE able to move quickly and easily • He is as **agile** as a cat.

## agility
NOUN the ability to move quickly and easily

## agitated
ADJECTIVE worried and anxious

## ago
ADVERB in the past • She bought her flat three years **ago**.

## agony
NOUN very great physical or mental pain

SYNONYMS: suffering, torment

## agree agrees, agreeing, agreed
VERB **1** If you **agree** with someone, you have the same opinion as they do.
VERB **2** If you **agree** to do something, you say you will do it.

## agreeable

ADJECTIVE **1** pleasant or enjoyable

ADJECTIVE **2** If you are **agreeable** to something, you are willing to allow it or to do it.

## agreement agreements

NOUN If you reach an **agreement** with one or more people, you make a decision with them or come to an arrangement with them.

## agriculture

NOUN farming

## ahead

ADVERB **1** in front ● *He looked **ahead** as he cycled down the road.*

ADVERB **2** more advanced than someone or something else ● *Some countries are **ahead** of others in space travel.*

ADVERB **3** in the future ● *I can't think that far **ahead**.*

## aid aids

NOUN **1** money, equipment or services provided for people in need

NOUN **2** something that makes a job easier ● *The whiteboard is a useful teaching **aid**.*

## ailment ailments

NOUN a minor illness

## aim aims, aiming, aimed

VERB **1** If you **aim** at something, you point a weapon at it.

VERB **2** If you **aim** to do something, you are planning to do it.

SYNONYMS: intend, mean

NOUN **3** Your **aim** is what you intend to achieve. ● *The **aim** of the jumble sale is to raise money for charity.*

SYNONYMS: goal, objective

## aimless

ADJECTIVE If you are **aimless**, you have no clear purpose or sense of direction.

## air

NOUN **1** the mixture of oxygen and other gases that we breathe and that forms the Earth's atmosphere

NOUN **2** the space around things or above the ground ● *The balloons floated up into the **air**.*

NOUN **3** used to refer to travel in aircraft ● *My uncle often travels by **air**.*

## air conditioning

NOUN a way of keeping cool, fresh air in a building or car

## aircraft

NOUN any vehicle that can fly

## air force air forces

NOUN the part of a country's armed services that fights using aircraft

## airline airlines

NOUN a company that provides air travel

## airmail

NOUN the system of sending letters and parcels by air ● *He sent letters from Hong Kong to Britain by **airmail**.*

## airport airports

NOUN a place where people go to catch aeroplanes

## airtight

ADJECTIVE If something is **airtight**, no air can get in or out.

## aisle aisles

NOUN a long, narrow gap that people can walk along between rows of seats or shelves ● *The ticket collector was coming down the **aisle**.*

## ajar

ADJECTIVE A door or window that is **ajar** is slightly open.

## alarm alarms, alarming, alarmed

NOUN **1** a feeling of fear and worry ● *The cat sprang back in **alarm**.*

NOUN **2** an automatic device used to warn people of something ● *The burglar **alarm** went off accidentally.*

VERB **3** If something **alarms** you, it makes you worried and anxious.

## album albums

NOUN **1** a recording with a collection of songs on it

NOUN **2** a book in which you keep a collection of things, such as photographs or stamps

## alcohol

NOUN the name for drinks such as beer, wine and spirits

## alert alerts, alerting, alerted

ADJECTIVE **1** If you are **alert**, you are paying full attention to what is happening.

SYNONYMS: vigilant, watchful

VERB **2** If you **alert** someone to a problem or danger, you warn them of it.

## algebra
NOUN a branch of mathematics in which symbols and letters are used to represent unknown numbers

**WORD HISTORY**
from Arabic *aljabr* meaning reunion

## alias **aliases**
NOUN a false name

## alibi **alibis**
NOUN If you have an **alibi**, you have evidence proving you were somewhere else when a crime was committed.

## alien **aliens**
NOUN **1** In science fiction, an **alien** is a creature from outer space.
ADJECTIVE **2** Something that is **alien** to you seems strange because it is not part of your normal experience. • *The desert is an **alien** environment to many people.*

**WORD HISTORY**
from Latin *alienus* meaning foreign

## alight **alights, alighting, alighted**
ADJECTIVE **1** Something that is **alight** is burning.
VERB **2** If something **alights** somewhere, it lands there.

## alike
ADJECTIVE **1** Things that are **alike** are very similar in some way.
ADVERB **2** If people or things are treated **alike**, they are treated the same.

## alive
ADJECTIVE If someone or something is **alive**, they are living.

## alkali **alkalis**
NOUN a chemical substance sometimes used in cleaning materials. **Alkalis** can neutralise acids.

ANTONYM: acid

## alkaline
ADJECTIVE If something is **alkaline**, it is made up of an alkali.

ANTONYM: acid

## all
ADJECTIVE **1** used for talking about the whole of something • *He ate **all** the chocolate.*
ADVERB **2** completely • *I went away and left her **all** alone.*

ADVERB **3** used to show that both sides in a game or contest have the same score
• *The final score was three points **all**.*

## Allah
PROPER NOUN **Allah** is the being worshipped by Muslims as the creator and ruler of the world

## allege **alleges, alleging, alleged**
VERB If you **allege** that something is true, you say it's true, but you cannot prove it.

## allergic
ADJECTIVE If you are **allergic** to something, it makes you ill to eat or touch it.
• *I'm **allergic** to peanuts.*

## allergy **allergies**
NOUN If you have an **allergy** to something, it makes you ill to eat or touch it.

## alley **alleys**
NOUN a narrow street or passageway between buildings

## alliance **alliances**
NOUN a group of countries, organisations or people who have similar aims and who work together to achieve them

## alligator **alligators**
NOUN a large, scaly reptile, similar to a crocodile

**WORD HISTORY**
from Spanish *el lagarto* meaning lizard

## alliteration
NOUN the use of several words together that begin with the same letter or sound. For example, *the slithery snake slid silently across the sand.*

## allotment **allotments**
NOUN a piece of land that people rent to grow fruit and vegetables on

## allow **allows, allowing, allowed**
VERB If someone **allows** you to do something, they let you do it.

## all right
ADJECTIVE **1** If something is **all right**, it is satisfactory, but not especially good.
• *Do you like mushrooms? They're **all right**.*
ADJECTIVE **2** If someone is **all right**, they are safe and not harmed.
ADJECTIVE **3** You say **all right** if you agree to something. • *Will you help? **All right**.*

## ally allies
NOUN a person or a country that helps and supports another

SYNONYMS: friend, partner

## almond almonds
NOUN an oval edible nut, cream in colour

## almost
ADVERB very nearly • I have **almost** as many points as you.

SYNONYMS: just about, practically

## alone
ADJECTIVE not with other people or things

## along
PREPOSITION **1** moving forward • We strolled **along** the road.
PREPOSITION **2** from one end of something to the other • The cupboards stretched **along** the wall.

## alongside
PREPOSITION next to something • We tied our boat **alongside** the jetty.

## aloud
ADVERB When you read **aloud**, you read so that people can hear you.

## alphabet alphabets
NOUN all the letters used to write words in a language. The letters of an **alphabet** are written in a special order.

## alphabetical
ADJECTIVE If something is in **alphabetical** order, it is arranged according to the order of the letters of the alphabet.

## alphabetically
ADVERB If something is arranged **alphabetically**, it is arranged according to the order of the letters of the alphabet.

## already
ADVERB If you have done something **already**, you did it earlier. • Josh has **already** gone to bed.

## also
ADVERB in addition to something that has just been mentioned • I bought an ice cream, and I **also** bought a drink.

## altar altars
NOUN a holy table in a church or temple

## alter alters, altering, altered
VERB If something **alters**, or if you **alter** it, it changes.

## alternate alternates, alternating, alternated
ADJECTIVE **1** If something happens on **alternate** days, it happens on one in every two days.
VERB **2** If two things **alternate**, they regularly happen one after the other.

PRONUNCIATION TIP
The adjective is pronounced ol-**ter**-nut. The verb is pronounced **ol**-ter-nayt.

## alternative alternatives
NOUN something you can do or have instead of something else • Is there an **alternative** to meat on the menu?

## although
CONJUNCTION in spite of the fact that • He wasn't well-known in America, **although** he had made a film there.

## altitude altitudes
NOUN height above sea level • The mountain range reaches an **altitude** of 1330 metres.

## altogether
ADVERB **1** completely or entirely • The car got slower, then stopped **altogether**.
ADVERB **2** in total when used of amounts • I have two cats and two rabbits. That's four pets **altogether**.

## aluminium
NOUN a silvery-white, lightweight metal

## always
ADVERB **1** all the time • He's **always** late.
ADVERB **2** forever • I'll **always** remember this day.

## a.m.
**a.m.** is used to show times in the morning

WORD HISTORY
an abbreviation of the Latin ante meridiem meaning before noon

## am
VERB a present tense of **be**

## amateur amateurs
NOUN someone who does something without being paid for it • He began playing football as an **amateur**, but now he is a professional.

## amaze amazes, amazing, amazed
VERB If something **amazes** you, it surprises you very much.

SYNONYMS: astonish, astound

## amazement
NOUN the feeling of being very surprised

**17**

a b c d e f g h i j k l m n o p q r s t u v w x y z

**amazing**

ADJECTIVE If something is **amazing**, it is very surprising.

**ambassador ambassadors**

NOUN a person sent to a foreign country as the representative of their own government

**amber**

NOUN **1** a hard, yellowish-brown substance from trees, used in making jewellery

NOUN **2** an orange-brown colour

ADJECTIVE **3** having an orange-brown colour

**ambiguous**

ADJECTIVE If something is **ambiguous**, it can have more than one meaning.

**ambition ambitions**

NOUN If you have an **ambition** to do something, you want very much to do it.

**amble ambles, ambling, ambled**

VERB If you **amble**, you walk along in a slow, relaxed way.

**ambulance ambulances**

NOUN a vehicle for taking sick and injured people to hospital

**ambush ambushes, ambushing, ambushed**

NOUN **1** a surprise attack

VERB **2** If one group of people **ambushes** another, they hide and lie in wait, and then make a surprise attack.

**ammonia**

NOUN a strong-smelling, colourless liquid or gas, often used in cleaning substances

**ammunition**

NOUN anything that can be fired from a gun or other weapon, for example bullets and shells

**amoeba amoebas or amoebae**

NOUN a tiny living organism that has only one cell. An **amoeba** reproduces by dividing into two.

**among** or **amongst**

PREPOSITION **1** surrounded by

PREPOSITION **2** in the company of • *He was **among** friends.*

PREPOSITION **3** between more than two • *The money will be divided **among** seven charities.*

**amount amounts**

NOUN how much there is of something • *You need a large **amount** of flour for this recipe.*

**amphibian amphibians**

NOUN an animal that lives partly on land and partly in water, for example a frog or a newt

**amphibious**

ADJECTIVE An **amphibious** animal lives partly on land and partly in water.

**amphitheatre amphitheatres**

NOUN a large open area, often in the shape of a semicircle, surrounded by rows of seats sloping upwards

**amplifier amplifiers**

NOUN a piece of equipment that makes sounds louder

**amplify amplifies, amplifying, amplified**

VERB If you **amplify** a sound, you make it louder.

**amputate amputates, amputating, amputated**

VERB If a surgeon **amputates** part of the body, such as an arm or a leg, they cut it off.

**amputation amputations**

NOUN **1 Amputation** is cutting off part of the body such as an arm or a leg.

NOUN **2** an operation to cut off part of the body, such as an arm or a leg • *The surgeon had performed about 20 **amputations**.*

**amuse amuses, amusing, amused**

VERB **1** If something **amuses** you, you think it is funny.

VERB **2** If you **amuse** yourself, you find things to do that stop you from being bored.

**amused**

ADJECTIVE If you are **amused**, you think something is funny.

**amusement amusements**

NOUN **1** the feeling you have when you think that something is funny or when something gives you pleasure

NOUN **2** a mechanical device used for entertainment, at a fair for example

**amusing**

ADJECTIVE funny and making you smile or laugh • *an **amusing** story*

**an**

ADJECTIVE **An** is used instead of *a* in front of words that begin with the vowels a, e, i, o, or u. • *an apple* • *an egg*

**anaemia**

NOUN a medical condition in which there are too few red cells in your blood. It makes you feel tired and look pale.

## anaemic

ADJECTIVE If you are **anaemic**, you have a medical condition in which there are too few red cells in your blood. It makes you feel tired and look pale.

## anaesthetic anaesthetics; also spelt anesthetic

NOUN a substance that stops you feeling pain. A general **anaesthetic** stops you from feeling pain in the whole of your body by putting you to sleep. A local **anaesthetic** makes just one part of your body go numb.

## anagram anagrams

NOUN a word or phrase formed by changing the order of the letters of another word or phrase. For example, *draw* is an **anagram** of *ward* and *dear* is an **anagram** of *read*.

## analogue

ADJECTIVE An **analogue** watch or clock shows the time with pointers that move round a dial.

ANTONYM: digital

## analogy analogies

NOUN a comparison between two things that are similar in some ways

## analyse analyses, analysing, analysed

VERB If you **analyse** something, you investigate it carefully to understand it or to find out what it consists of.

## anatomical

ADJECTIVE **Anatomical** describes things that are to do with the structure of human and animal bodies.

## anatomy anatomies

NOUN the study of the structure of human and animal bodies to find out how they work

## ancestor ancestors

NOUN a member of your family who lived many years ago • *He could trace his* **ancestors** *back 700 years.*

WORD HISTORY
from Latin *antecessor* meaning one who goes before

## anchor anchors, anchoring, anchored

NOUN **1** a heavy, hooked object at the end of a chain. It is dropped from a boat into the water to keep the boat from floating away.

→ Have a look at the illustration for **ship**

VERB **2** If you **anchor** something, you hold it down firmly.

## ancient

ADJECTIVE Things that are **ancient** existed or happened a very long time ago.

ANTONYM: modern

## and

CONJUNCTION You use **and** to link two or more parts of a sentence together. • *Let's go to the cinema* **and** *then have pizza*

## anecdote anecdotes

NOUN a short, sometimes entertaining story about a person or an event

## angel angels

NOUN a being who, some people believe, lives in heaven and acts as a messenger for God

WORD HISTORY
from Greek *angelos* meaning messenger

## anger

NOUN the strong feeling you get about something unfair or cruel

SYNONYMS: fury, rage, wrath

## angle angles

NOUN **1** the distance between two lines at the point where they join together. **Angles** are measured in degrees. • *an* **angle** *of 90 degrees*
NOUN **2** the direction from which you look at something • *He painted pictures of the garden from all* **angles**.

## angry angrier, angriest

ADJECTIVE very annoyed

SYNONYMS: furious, cross

## anguish

NOUN great suffering

## animal animals

NOUN any living being that is not a plant

## animated

ADJECTIVE **Animated** films are made with drawings that seem to move when you watch them.

a
b
c
d
e
f
g
h
i
j
k
l
m
n
o
p
q
r
s
t
u
v
w
x
y
z

**19**

**animation** animations
NOUN **1** a way of making films using drawings that seem to move when you watch them
NOUN **2** a film made using drawings that seem to move when you watch them

**ankle** ankles
NOUN the joint that connects your foot to your leg

**annihilate** annihilates, annihilating, annihilated
VERB If someone or something **annihilates** someone or something else, they destroy them completely.

**anniversary** anniversaries
NOUN a date that is remembered because something special happened on that date in a previous year • *We celebrated Mum and Dad's twelfth wedding **anniversary**.*

**announce** announces, announcing, announced
VERB If you **announce** something, you tell people about it publicly or officially. • *They **announced** the team on Friday morning.*

SYNONYM: make known

**announcement** announcements
NOUN something that you tell people in a speech or official statement • *I have an **announcement** to make.*

**annoy** annoys, annoying, annoyed
VERB If someone or something **annoys** you, they make you angry or impatient.

SYNONYMS: bother, irritate

**annoyance** annoyances
NOUN **1** something that makes you slightly angry or impatient
NOUN **2** the feeling of being slightly angry or impatient

**annual** annuals
ADJECTIVE **1** happening once a year
• *our **annual** sports day*
NOUN **2** a book that is published once a year for children

**anonymous**
ADJECTIVE If something is **anonymous**, nobody knows who is responsible for it. • *The charity received an **anonymous** donation.*

**anorak** anoraks
NOUN a warm, waterproof jacket, usually with a hood

WORD HISTORY
an Inuit word

**anorexia**
NOUN a psychological illness in which the person refuses to eat

WORD HISTORY
from Greek *an* + *orexis* meaning no appetite

**another**
PRONOUN **1** one more person or thing • *You've finished your cake – would you like **another**?*
ADJECTIVE **2** used to talk about one more person or thing • *I need **another** pencil.*

**answer** answers, answering, answered
VERB **1** If you **answer** someone, you reply to them in speech or writing.
NOUN **2** the reply you give when you answer someone • *I received an **answer** to my letter.*
NOUN **3** a solution to a problem

**ant** ants
NOUN **Ants** are small insects that live in large groups.

**antagonise** antagonises, antagonising, antagonised; also spelt **antagonize**
VERB If you **antagonise** someone, you upset them and make them feel angry.

**Antarctic**
NOUN The **Antarctic** is the area around the South Pole.

→ Have a look at the illustration for **equator**

**antelope** antelopes
NOUN a hoofed animal, similar to a deer

**antenna** antennae or antennas
NOUN **1** one of the two long, thin parts attached to the head of an insect or other animal, which it uses to feel with. The plural is **antennae**.

→ Have a look at the illustration for **insect**

NOUN **2** In Australian, New Zealand and American English, an **antenna** is a radio or television aerial. The plural is **antennas**.

**anthem** anthems
NOUN usually a song of celebration, and sometimes a religious song

**anther anthers**

NOUN the part of the stamen in a flower where the pollen matures

**anthology anthologies**

NOUN a collection of writings by various authors, published in one book

WORD HISTORY

from Greek *anthologia* meaning flower gathering

**anti-**

PREFIX against or opposite • *an **anti**malaria tablet*

ANTONYM: pro-

**antibiotic antibiotics**

NOUN a drug or chemical used in medicine to kill bacteria and cure infections

**anticipate anticipates, anticipating, anticipated**

VERB If you **anticipate** an event, you are expecting it and are getting prepared for it.

**anticipation**

NOUN **1** If you do something in **anticipation** of something else, you do it because you think that thing will happen. • *Shops have taken on more staff in **anticipation** of the Christmas shopping rush.*

NOUN **2** a feeling of excitement about something that is going to happen

**anticlimax anticlimaxes**

NOUN If something is an **anticlimax**, it disappoints you because it is not as exciting as you expected, or because it occurs after something that was more exciting.

**anticlockwise**

ADVERB in the opposite direction to the hands of a clock

SYNONYM: vertex

**antidote antidotes**

NOUN a chemical substance that works against the effects of a poison

**antique antiques**

NOUN an object from the past that is collected because of its value or beauty

**antiseptic**

ADJECTIVE Something that is **antiseptic** can kill some germs.

**antler antlers**

NOUN **Antlers** are the branched horns on the top of a male deer's head.

**antonym antonyms**

NOUN a word that means the opposite of another word • *Happy is the **antonym** of sad.*

**anxiety anxieties**

NOUN a feeling of nervousness or worry

**anxious**

ADJECTIVE **1** If you are **anxious**, you are nervous or worried.

ADJECTIVE **2** If you are **anxious** to do something, you very much want to do it. • *She was **anxious** to pass her ballet exam.*

**any**

ADJECTIVE **1** one, some or several • *Have you **any** sausages?*

ADJECTIVE **2** even the smallest amount or even one • *She can't eat nuts of **any** kind.*

ADJECTIVE **3** no matter which or what • *I'm so thirsty, **any** drink will do.*

PRONOUN **4** one, some or several • *I need new clothes but I can't afford **any**.*

**anybody**

PRONOUN any person

**anyhow**

ADVERB **1** in any case • *It's still early, but I'm going to bed **anyhow**.*

ADVERB **2** in a careless way • *They were all shoved in **anyhow**.*

**anyone**

PRONOUN any person • *I won't tell **anyone**.*

**anything**

PRONOUN any object, event, situation or action • *Can you see **anything**?*

**anyway**

ADVERB in any case • *It's raining, but I'm going out **anyway**.*

**anywhere**

ADVERB in, at or to any place • *Can you see him **anywhere**?* • *We haven't got **anywhere** to play.*

**apart**

ADVERB **1** When something is **apart** from something else, there is a space or a distance between them. • *The gliders landed about seventy metres **apart**.*

ADVERB **2** If you take something **apart**, you separate it into pieces.

a
b
c
d
e
f
g
h
i
j
k
l
m
n
o
p
q
r
s
t
u
v
w
x
y
z

**21**

**apartment apartments**
NOUN a set of rooms for living in, usually on one floor of a building

**apatosaurus apatosauruses**
NOUN a very large, plant-eating dinosaur

**ape apes, aping, aped**
NOUN **1** a large animal similar to a monkey, but without a tail. **Apes** include chimpanzees and gorillas.
VERB **2** If you **ape** someone's speech or behaviour, you imitate it.

**apex apexes** or **apices**
NOUN The **apex** of something is its pointed top. • the **apex** of a cone

SYNONYM: vertex

**apologise apologises, apologising, apologised**; also spelt **apologize**
VERB When you **apologise** to someone, you say you are sorry for something you have said or done.

**apology apologies**
NOUN An **apology** is when you say sorry to someone, for something you have said or done.

**apostrophe apostrophes**
NOUN **1** a punctuation mark (') used to show that one or more letters have been missed out of a word, for example *he's* for *he is*
NOUN **2 Apostrophes** are also used with *-s* at the end of a noun to show that what follows belongs to or relates to the noun. If the noun already has an *-s* at the end, for example because it is plural, the **apostrophe** comes after the *-s*. For example, *my brother's books* (one brother), *my brothers' books* (more than one brother).

**app apps**
NOUN a computer program with one main purpose, especially one that you use on your mobile phone

**apparatus**
NOUN the equipment used for a particular task • *The firefighters wore breathing **apparatus**.*

**apparent**
ADJECTIVE **1** An **apparent** situation seems to exist, although you cannot be certain of it.
ADJECTIVE **2** clear and obvious • *It was **apparent** they would get on well together.*

**apparently**
ADVERB You use **apparently** to say what seems to be true, although you cannot be certain of it. • *He was lying on the sofa, **apparently** asleep.*

**appeal appeals, appealing, appealed**
VERB **1** If you **appeal** for something, you make an urgent request for it. • *The police **appealed** for witnesses to come forward.*
VERB **2** If something or someone **appeals** to you, you find them attractive or interesting.
NOUN **3** a formal or serious request • *an **appeal** for funds to help people in need*

**appear appears, appearing, appeared**
VERB **1** When something **appears**, it moves from somewhere you could not see to somewhere you can see it. • *The sun **appeared** from behind the clouds.*
VERB **2** If something **appears** to be a certain way, it seems or looks that way.

**appearance appearances**
NOUN **1** Someone's or something's **appearance** is the way they look to other people.
NOUN **2** If a person makes an **appearance** in a film or a show, they take part in it.
NOUN **3** The **appearance** of something is the time it begins to exist.

**appendicitis**
NOUN a painful illness in which a person's appendix becomes infected

**appendix appendices** or **appendixes**
NOUN **1** Your **appendix** is a small, closed tube forming part of your digestive system.
NOUN **2** extra information that comes at the end of a book

LANGUAGE TIP
When *appendix* means the body part, the plural is *appendixes*. When it means the part of a book, the plural is *appendices*.

**appetising**; also spelt **appetizing**
ADJECTIVE When food is **appetising**, it looks or smells good and you want to eat it.

**appetite appetites**
NOUN a desire to eat

WORD HISTORY
from Latin *appetere* meaning to desire

**applause**
NOUN the sound of people clapping to show their enjoyment or approval of something

**apple** **apples**
NOUN a round fruit with smooth skin and firm white flesh

**appliance** **appliances**
NOUN any machine in your home that you use to do a job like cleaning or cooking. For example, a toaster is a kitchen **appliance**.

**application** **applications**
NOUN **1** If you make an **application** for something, you make a formal request, usually in writing.
NOUN **2** a piece of software designed to carry out a particular task on a computer

**apply** **applies, applying, applied**
VERB **1** If you **apply** for something, you ask for it formally, usually by writing a letter or an email. • *My brother is **applying** for jobs.*
VERB **2** If you **apply** something to a surface, you put it on or rub it into the surface. • *She **applied** sun cream to her face.*
VERB **3** If you **apply** yourself to a task, you give it all of your attention.

**appoint** **appoints, appointing, appointed**
VERB If a person **appoints** someone to a job or position, they formally choose them for it. • *The teacher **appointed** Sunita as team captain.*

**appointment** **appointments**
NOUN an arrangement you have with someone to meet them

**appreciate** **appreciates, appreciating, appreciated**
VERB If you **appreciate** something that someone has done for you, you are grateful to them for it.

**apprehensive**
ADJECTIVE If you are **apprehensive** about something, you feel worried and unsure about it.

**apprentice** **apprentices**
NOUN someone who works with another person for a length of time to learn that person's job or skill

**approach** **approaches, approaching, approached**
VERB If you **approach** something, you come near or nearer to it.

**appropriate**
ADJECTIVE suitable or acceptable for a particular situation

**approval**
NOUN If you ask for **approval** for something that you want to do, you ask for agreement with your plans.

**approve** **approves, approving, approved**
VERB **1** If you **approve** of something or someone, you think they are acceptable or good.

SYNONYMS: favour, like

VERB **2** If someone **approves** a plan or idea, they agree to it. • *The council **approved** plans for the new swimming pool.*

SYNONYMS: agree to, permit

**approximate**
ADJECTIVE near but not exactly right • *What was the **approximate** time you arrived?*

**apricot** **apricots**
NOUN a small, soft, yellowish-orange fruit

**April**
NOUN the fourth month of the year. **April** has 30 days.

**apron** **aprons**
NOUN a piece of clothing worn over the front of normal clothing to protect it

**aquarium** **aquaria** or **aquariums**
NOUN a glass tank filled with water in which fish and other aquatic animals or plants are kept

**aquatic**
ADJECTIVE An **aquatic** animal or plant lives in water.

**aqueduct** **aqueducts**
NOUN a bridge with many arches, which carries a water supply over a valley

a
b
c
d
e
f
g
h
i
j
k
l
m
n
o
p
q
r
s
t
u
v
w
x
y
z

23

A
B
C
D
E
F
G
H
I
J
K
L
M
N
O
P
Q
R
S
T
U
V
W
X
Y
Z

**arable**
ADJECTIVE **Arable** land is used for growing crops.

**arc arcs**
NOUN **1** a smoothly curving line
NOUN **2** In geometry, an **arc** is a section of the circumference of a circle.

**arcade arcades**
NOUN a covered passageway where there are shops or market stalls

**arch arches, arching, arched**
NOUN **1** a structure that has a curved top, supported on either side by a pillar or wall
VERB **2** If something **arches**, or if you **arch** it, it forms a curved line or shape. • *The cat **arched** its back.*

**archaeology**; also spelt **archeology**
NOUN the study of the past by digging up and examining the remains of things such as buildings, tools and pots

**WORD HISTORY**
from Greek *arkhaios* meaning ancient

**archbishop archbishops**
NOUN a bishop of the highest rank in a Christian Church • *the **Archbishop** of Canterbury*

**archery**
NOUN a sport in which people shoot at a target with a bow and arrow

**architect architects**
NOUN a person who designs buildings

**architecture**
NOUN the art or practice of designing buildings

**arctic**
NOUN **1** The **Arctic** is the area around the North Pole.

→ Have a look at the illustration for **equator**

ADJECTIVE **2** very cold indeed • *You need specially warm clothes for **arctic** conditions.*

**are**
VERB a present tense of **be**

**area areas**
NOUN **1** a particular part of a place, country, or the world • *a built-up **area** of the city*

SYNONYMS: district, region, zone

NOUN **2** the measurement of a flat surface • *The **area** of the playground is 1500 square metres.*

**arena arenas**
NOUN a place where sports and other public events take place

**WORD HISTORY**
from Latin *harena* meaning sand, because of the sandy centre of an amphitheatre where gladiators fought

**aren't**
VERB a contraction of *are not*

**argue argues, arguing, argued**
VERB **1** If you **argue** with someone about something, you disagree with them about it, sometimes in an angry way.
VERB **2** If you **argue** that something is true, you give reasons why you think that it is.

**argument arguments**
NOUN a talk between people who do not agree

**arid**
ADJECTIVE **Arid** land is very dry because there has been very little rain.

ANTONYM: fertile

**arise arises, arising, arose, arisen**
VERB When something such as an opportunity or a problem **arises**, it begins to exist.

**aristocracy**
NOUN The **aristocracy** are people whose families have a high social rank, and who have a title such as Lord or Lady.

**aristocrat aristocrats**
NOUN someone whose family has a high social rank, and who has a title such as Lord or Lady

**arithmetic**
NOUN the part of mathematics that is to do with the addition, subtraction, multiplication and division of numbers

**WORD HISTORY**
from Greek *arithmos* meaning number

**arm arms, arming, armed**
NOUN **1** the part of your body between your shoulder and your wrist
PLURAL NOUN **2 Arms** are weapons used in a war.
VERB **3** If a country **arms** itself, it prepares for war.

**armada armadas**
NOUN a large fleet of warships • *The Spanish **Armada** was the fleet sent to destroy the English in 1588.*

**armchair** armchairs

NOUN a large chair with a support on each side for your arms

**armistice** armistices

NOUN In war, an **armistice** is an agreement to stop fighting.

**armour**

NOUN **1** In the past, **armour** was metal clothing worn for protection in battle.
NOUN **2** In modern warfare, tanks are often referred to as **armour**.

**army** armies

NOUN a large group of soldiers who are trained to fight on land

**aroma** aromas

NOUN a strong, pleasant smell

WORD HISTORY
a Greek word meaning spice

**around**

PREPOSITION **1** situated at various points in a place or area • There are several post boxes **around** the town.
PREPOSITION **2** from place to place inside an area • We walked **around** the stalls at the summer fair.
PREPOSITION **3** surrounding or encircling a place or object • We were sitting **around** the table.
PREPOSITION **4** at approximately the time or place mentioned • The jumble sale began **around** noon.

**arrange** arranges, arranging, arranged

VERB **1** If you **arrange** to do something, or **arrange** something for someone, you make plans for it or make it possible.
• I **arranged** to meet him later. • Dad **arranged** a trip to the circus for us.
VERB **2** If you **arrange** objects, you set them out in a particular way. • We **arranged** the books in alphabetical order.

**array** arrays

NOUN **1** a large number of different things displayed together
NOUN **2** a mathematical way of grouping

**arrest** arrests, arresting, arrested

VERB **1** If the police **arrest** someone, they take them to a police station because they believe they may have committed a crime.
NOUN **2** An **arrest** is the act of arresting someone.

**arrival** arrivals

NOUN **1** **Arrival** is when you reach a place at the end of your journey. • On their **arrival** in London, they went straight to the hotel.
NOUN **2** someone or something that has just come to a place

**arrive** arrives, arriving, arrived

VERB **1** When you **arrive** at a place, you reach it at the end of your journey.
VERB **2** When you **arrive** at a decision you make up your mind.

**arrogant**

ADJECTIVE **Arrogant** people behave as if they are better than other people.

**arrow** arrows

NOUN a long, thin weapon with a sharp point at one end, shot from a bow

**arsenal** arsenals

NOUN a place where weapons and ammunition are stored or produced

**arsenic**

NOUN a strong, dangerous poison that can kill

**arson**

NOUN the crime of deliberately setting fire to something, especially a building

**art** arts

NOUN **1** the creation of objects, such as paintings and sculptures, that are thought to be beautiful or that express a particular idea • He wanted to take **art** classes to learn how to draw and paint well.
NOUN **2** **Art** is also used to refer to the objects themselves. • We saw lots of interesting paintings and sculptures at the **art** exhibition.
NOUN **3** something that needs special skills or ability • I would like to master the **art** of sewing.

**artery** arteries

NOUN the tubes that carry blood from your heart to the rest of your body

**arthritis**

NOUN a condition in which the joints in someone's body become painful, and sometimes swollen

**article** articles

NOUN **1** a piece of writing in a newspaper or magazine
NOUN **2** a particular item • an **article** of clothing

## artificial

ADJECTIVE Something **artificial** is created by people rather than occurring naturally.

ANTONYM: natural

## artillery

NOUN **1 Artillery** consists of large, powerful guns and rockets.

NOUN **2** The **artillery** is the branch of an army that uses these weapons.

## artist artists

NOUN a person who draws or paints or produces other works of art

## as

CONJUNCTION **1** at the same time that • *We watched television **as** we ate our sandwiches.*

CONJUNCTION **2** because • ***As** I like school I get there early.*

PHRASE **3** You use **as if** or **as though** when you are giving an explanation for something. • *Shane walked past **as if** he didn't know me.*

## ascend ascends, ascending, ascended

VERB (*formal*) If someone or something **ascends**, they move or lead upwards. • *We **ascended** the stairs to the second floor.*

ANTONYM: descend

## ash ashes

NOUN the grey or black powdery remains of anything that has been burnt • *We put the **ashes** from the bonfire on the compost heap.*

→ Have a look at the illustration for **volcano**

## ashamed

ADJECTIVE **1** If you are **ashamed**, you feel embarrassed or guilty.

ADJECTIVE **2** If you are **ashamed** of someone, you feel embarrassed to be connected with them.

## ashore

ADVERB If someone or something comes **ashore**, they come on to the land from the sea or a river.

## aside

ADVERB If you move something **aside**, you move it to one side. • *She closed the book and laid it **aside**.*

## ask asks, asking, asked

VERB **1** If you **ask** someone something, you put a question to them.

VERB **2** If you **ask** someone to do something, you tell them you want them to do it. • *We **asked** him to do his card trick.*

VERB **3** If you **ask** for something, you say you would like to have it. • *She **asked** for a drink of water.*

VERB **4** If you **ask** someone to come or go somewhere, you invite them there.

## asleep

ADJECTIVE If you are **asleep**, your eyes are closed and your whole body is resting. • *The cat was **asleep** under the bed.*

## aspect aspects

NOUN one of many ways of seeing or thinking about something

## aspirin aspirins

NOUN a small white tablet of this drug

## ass asses

NOUN another word for **donkey**

## assassinate assassinates, assassinating, assassinated

VERB If someone **assassinates** an important person, they murder them.

## assassination assassinations

NOUN An **assassination** is when someone murders an important person.

## assault assaults

NOUN a violent attack on someone

WORD HISTORY
from Latin *assalire* meaning to leap upon

## assemble assembles, assembling, assembled

VERB **1** If people **assemble**, they gather together. • *We **assembled** in the playground to watch the display.*

VERB **2** If you **assemble** something, you fit the parts of it together. • *It took us ages to **assemble** the model car.*

## assembly assemblies

NOUN a group of people who have gathered together for a particular purpose • *The headteacher made the announcement during a school **assembly**.*

## assess assesses, assessing, assessed

VERB If you **assess** something, you consider it carefully and make a judgement about it • *She tried to **assess** how much further they had to walk.*

SYNONYMS: judge, size up

**asset assets**
NOUN **1** If someone or something is an **asset**, they are useful or helpful. • *He's an **asset** to the school.*
NOUN **2** The **assets** of a person or a company are all the things they own that could be sold to raise money.

**assignment assignments**
NOUN a job you are given to do

**assist assists, assisting, assisted**
VERB If you **assist** someone, you help them to do something.

**assistant assistants**
NOUN someone who helps another person to do their job

**associate associates, associating, associated**
VERB **1** If you **associate** with someone, you spend time with them.
VERB **2** If you **associate** one thing with another, you make a connection between them.

**association associations**
NOUN **1** an organisation for people who have similar interests, jobs or aims
NOUN **2** An **association** between two things is a link you make in your mind between them.

**assorted**
ADJECTIVE **Assorted** things are a mixture of various sorts of something. They may be different colours, sizes and shapes.

**assortment assortments**
NOUN a group of similar things that are different sizes, shapes and colours • *There was an amazing **assortment** of toys in the shop.*

**assume assumes, assuming, assumed**
VERB **1** If you **assume** that something is true, you believe it, even if you have not thought carefully about it.
VERB **2** If you **assume** responsibility for something, you decide to do it. • *I **assumed** responsibility for feeding the hamster.*

**assure assures, assuring, assured**
VERB If you **assure** someone of something, you say something to make them less worried about it. • *I **assured** him that I wouldn't be late.*

**asterisk asterisks**
NOUN a symbol (*) used in writing and printing to draw attention to something that is explained somewhere else, usually at the bottom of the page

**asteroid asteroids**
NOUN one of the large number of rocks that move around the sun between the orbits of Jupiter and Mars in an area called the asteroid belt

**asthma**
NOUN a condition of the chest that causes wheezing and difficulty in breathing

WORD HISTORY
from Greek *azein* meaning to breathe hard

**asthmatic**
ADJECTIVE Someone who is **asthmatic** has a condition of the chest that causes wheezing and difficulty in breathing.

**astonish astonishes, astonishing, astonished**
VERB If something **astonishes** you, it surprises you very much.

**astonished**
ADJECTIVE very surprised

**astonishing**
ADJECTIVE very surprising

**astonishingly**
ADVERB in a way that is very surprising

**astonishment**
NOUN **Astonishment** is when you are very surprised.

**astrology**
NOUN the study of the sun, moon and stars in the belief that their movements can influence people's lives

**astronaut astronauts**
NOUN a person who operates a spacecraft

WORD HISTORY
from Greek *astron* meaning star and *nautes* meaning sailor

**astronomer astronomers**
NOUN someone who studies stars and planets

**astronomy**
NOUN the scientific study of stars and planets

**at**
PREPOSITION **1** where someone or something is • *John waited for me **at** the bus stop.*
PREPOSITION **2** the direction something is going in • *I threw the snowball **at** my brother.*
PREPOSITION **3** when something happens • *The party starts **at** six o'clock.*

**ate**
VERB the past tense of **eat**

**atheist atheists**
NOUN someone who does not believe in any form of God

**athlete athletes**
NOUN a person who is very good at sport and who takes part in sporting competitions

**athletic**
ADJECTIVE physically fit and strong

**athletics**
NOUN sporting events such as running, long jump and discus

**Atlantic**
NOUN the ocean that separates North and South America from Europe and Africa

**atlas atlases**
NOUN a book of maps

**WORD HISTORY**
from the giant *Atlas* in Greek mythology, who supported the sky on his shoulders

**atmosphere atmospheres**
NOUN **1** gases that surround a planet
→ Have a look at the illustration for **greenhouse effect**
NOUN **2** the general mood of a place • *There was a friendly atmosphere at the party.*

**atom atoms**
NOUN the smallest part of an element that can take part in a chemical reaction

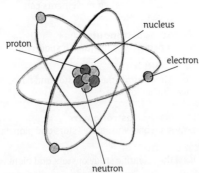

nucleus
proton
electron
neutron

**atrocity atrocities**
NOUN an extremely shocking and cruel act

**attach attaches, attaching, attached**
VERB If you **attach** something to something else, you join or fasten the two things together.

**attached**
ADJECTIVE If you are **attached** to someone, you are very fond of them.

**attachment attachments**
NOUN **1** a feeling of love and affection for someone
NOUN **2** a file attached to an email

**attack attacks, attacking, attacked**
VERB **1** If someone **attacks** another person or animal, they use violence in order to hurt or kill them. • *The lion attacked the zebra in order to kill it for food.*
VERB **2** In a game such as football or hockey, players **attack** to get the ball into a position from which a goal can be scored.
NOUN **3** violent, physical action against someone

**attempt attempts, attempting, attempted**
VERB **1** If you **attempt** to do something, you try to do it.
NOUN **2** the act of trying to do something • *He made a brave attempt to help.*

**attend attends, attending, attended**
VERB **1** If you **attend** school, church or hospital, you go there regularly.
VERB **2** If you **attend** an event, you are present at it.

**attend to**
VERB If you **attend to** something, you deal with it. • *We should attend to our homework before going to the park.*

**attendant attendants**
NOUN someone whose job is to help people in a place such as a cloakroom or swimming pool

**attention**
NOUN the thought or care that you give to someone or something • *I paid a lot of attention to my homework.*

**attentive**
ADJECTIVE When you are **attentive**, you pay close attention.

**attic attics**
NOUN a room at the top of a house immediately below the roof

**attitude attitudes**
NOUN the way you think about someone or something and behave towards them
• *I'm not going in that shop again. I don't like their attitude.*

A B C D E F G H I J K L M N O P Q R S T U V W X Y Z

**attract attracts, attracting, attracted**
VERB **1** If something **attracts** people, it interests them and makes them want to go to it.
VERB **2** If someone **attracts** you, you like them and are interested in them.
VERB **3** When magnetic materials are **attracted** to a magnet, they are pulled towards it.

**attraction attractions**
NOUN **1** If you feel an **attraction** for someone, you like them very much.
NOUN **2** somewhere people like to visit for interest or pleasure, such as a fun fair or a stately home
NOUN **3** A force of **attraction** pulls magnetic materials towards a magnet.

**attractive**
ADJECTIVE **1** Someone who is **attractive** is good looking or has an exciting personality.
ADJECTIVE **2** If something is **attractive**, it is interesting.

**aubergine aubergines**
NOUN a dark purple, pear-shaped vegetable. It is also called an eggplant.

**auburn**
ADJECTIVE a red-brown hair colour

**auction auctions, auctioning, auctioned**
NOUN **1** a public sale in which goods are sold to the person who offers the highest price
VERB **2** to sell something in an auction

**audible**
ADJECTIVE If something is **audible**, you can hear it.

**audience audiences**
NOUN **1** the group of people who are watching or listening to a performance
NOUN **2** a private or formal meeting with an important person ● *The winners of the bravery awards had an* **audience** *with the Queen.*

**audition auditions**
NOUN a short performance by an actor or musician, so that a director can decide whether they are suitable for a part in a play or a film, or for a place in an orchestra

**auditorium auditoriums or auditoria**
NOUN the part of a theatre or concert hall where the audience sits

**August**
NOUN the eighth month of the year. **August** has 31 days.

**aunt aunts**
NOUN Your **aunt** is the sister of your mother or father, or the wife of your uncle.

**author authors**
NOUN The **author** of a book is the person who wrote it.

**authorisation**; also spelt **authorization**
NOUN **Authorisation** is when someone gives official permission for something.

**authorise authorises, authorising, authorised**; also spelt **authorize**
VERB If someone **authorises** something, they give official permission for it.

**authority authorities**
NOUN **1** the power to tell other people what to do ● *The teacher had the* **authority** *to give me detention.*
NOUN **2** an organisation that controls public interests ● *the local health* **authority**
NOUN **3** Someone who is an **authority** on something, knows a lot about it.

**autism**
NOUN a condition that makes it difficult to communicate in the way most people expect

**autistic**
ADJECTIVE An **autistic** person has a condition that makes it difficult to communicate in the way most people expect.

**auto-**
PREFIX **1** self or same ● **auto**biography
PREFIX **2** self-propelling ● **auto**matic car

**autobiography autobiographies**
NOUN an account of someone's life that they have written themselves

**autograph autographs**
NOUN the signature of a famous person

**WORD HISTORY**
from Greek *auto* meaning self and *graphos* meaning written

**automatic automatics**
ADJECTIVE **1** An **automatic** machine is programmed to perform tasks without needing a person to operate it.
NOUN **2** a car in which the gears change automatically as the car's speed changes

**autumn autumns**
NOUN the season between summer and winter, when the leaves fall off the trees ● *I love the golden colours of the trees in* **autumn**.

29

## available

ADJECTIVE **1** If something is **available**, it is easy to get or to buy.
ADJECTIVE **2** A person who is **available** is ready for work or free to talk to.

## avalanche **avalanches**

NOUN a huge mass of snow and ice that falls down a mountainside

## avatar **avatars**

NOUN an image that represents you on the screen in an online game or chatroom

## avenue **avenues**

NOUN a street, especially one with trees along it

## average **averages**

NOUN **1** a result obtained by adding several amounts together and then dividing the total by the number of different amounts • *If I shared 36 sweets between four children, the **average** would be nine sweets per child.*
ADJECTIVE **2** standard or usual • *The **average** teenager is interested in pop music.*

> SYNONYMS: normal, ordinary, typical

PHRASE **3** You say **on average** when mentioning what usually happens in a situation. • *Men are, **on average**, taller than women.*

## aviary **aviaries**

NOUN a large cage or group of cages in which birds are kept

## aviation

NOUN the science of flying aircraft

## avocado **avocados**

NOUN a pear-shaped fruit with dark green skin, soft greenish-yellow flesh, and a large stone

## avoid **avoids, avoiding, avoided**

VERB **1** If you **avoid** someone or something, you keep away from them. • *To **avoid** him, she went home the other way.*
VERB **2** If you **avoid** doing something, you make an effort not to do it.

> SYNONYMS: dodge, shirk

## awake

ADJECTIVE Someone who is **awake** is not sleeping.

## award **awards, awarding, awarded**

NOUN **1** a prize or certificate for doing something well
VERB **2** If someone **awards** you something, they give it to you formally or officially.
• *He was **awarded** the prize for fastest runner.*

## aware

ADJECTIVE **1** If you are **aware** of something, you know about it. • *They are **aware** of the danger.*
ADJECTIVE **2** If you are **aware** of something, you can see, hear, smell or feel it.

## away

ADVERB **1** moving from a place • *I saw them walk **away** from the house.*
ADVERB **2** at a distance from a place • *The nearest supermarket is 12 kilometres **away**.*
ADVERB **3** in its proper place • *He put his clothes **away**.*
ADVERB **4** not at home, school or work • *My friend's been **away** from school for a week.*

## awe

NOUN (*formal*) a feeling of great respect mixed with amazement, and sometimes slight fear • *Looking up at the mountains, we felt a sense of **awe**.*

## awful

ADJECTIVE very unpleasant or very bad • *Isn't the weather **awful**?*

> SYNONYMS: dreadful, terrible

## awkward

ADJECTIVE **1** difficult to deal with • *an **awkward** situation*
ADJECTIVE **2** clumsy and uncomfortable • *The large bag was **awkward** to carry.*

**WORD HISTORY**
from Old Norse *ofugr* meaning turned the wrong way

## axe **axes**

NOUN a tool with a handle and a sharp blade, used for chopping wood

## axis **axes**

NOUN **1** an imaginary line through the middle of something, around which it moves • *The Earth turns on its **axis**.*
NOUN **2** one of the two sides of a graph, the x-**axis** or the y-**axis**

## axle **axles**

NOUN the long bar that connects a pair of wheels on a vehicle

A B C D E F G H I J K L M N O P Q R S T U V W X Y Z

# Bb

**babble** **babbles, babbling, babbled**
VERB If someone **babbles**, they talk in a quick and confused way that is difficult to understand.

**baboon** **baboons**
NOUN an African monkey with a pointed face, large teeth and a long tail

**baby** **babies**
NOUN a child in the first year or two of its life

**baby-sit** **baby-sits, baby-sitting, baby-sat**
VERB If you **baby-sit** for someone, you look after their children while they are out.

**bachelor** **bachelors**
NOUN a man who has never been married

**back** **backs, backing, backed**
ADVERB **1** When people or things move **back**, they move in the opposite direction to the one they are facing.
ADVERB **2** When you go **back** to a place or situation, you return to it. ● *She went **back** to sleep.*
NOUN **3** the rear part of your body
ADJECTIVE **4** The **back** parts of something are the ones at the rear. ● *the dog's **back** legs*
VERB **5** If a building **backs** on to something, the back of it faces in that direction.

**backbone** **backbones**
NOUN the column of linked bones along the middle of the back of a human and other vertebrates

**background** **backgrounds**
NOUN **1** the things in a picture or scene that are less noticeable than the main things
NOUN **2** the kind of home you come from, and your education and experience

**backstroke**
NOUN a style of swimming movement on your back

**backward**
ADJECTIVE If you take a **backward** look, you look behind you.

**backwards**
ADVERB **1** If you move **backwards**, you move to a place behind you.
ADVERB **2** If you do something **backwards**, you do it opposite to the usual way. ● *He told them to count **backwards** from 20 to 5.*

**bacon**
NOUN meat from the back or sides of a pig, which has been salted or smoked

**bacteria**
PLURAL NOUN very tiny organisms that can cause diseases

**WORD HISTORY**
from Greek *bakterion* meaning little rod; some bacteria are rod-shaped

**bacterial**
ADJECTIVE involving or caused by very tiny organisms that can cause diseases
● ***bacterial*** *infections*

**bad** **worse, worst**
ADJECTIVE **1** **Bad** things are harmful or upsetting. ● *I have some **bad** news.*

SYNONYMS: distressing, grave, terrible

ADJECTIVE **2** not enough or of poor quality
● *The food was **worse** than usual.*
ADJECTIVE **3** **Bad** food is not fresh.

SYNONYMS: rotten, decayed

**badge** **badges**
NOUN a piece of plastic or metal with a design or message on it that you can pin to your clothes

**badger** **badgers, badgering, badgered**
NOUN **1** a nocturnal mammal that has a white head with two black stripes on it
VERB **2** If you **badger** someone, you keep asking them questions or pestering them to do something.

**badly** **worse, worst**
ADVERB **1** not well or poorly ● *The script was **badly** written.*
ADVERB **2** seriously ● *She was **badly** hurt in the accident.*

**badminton**
NOUN a game in which two or four players use rackets to hit a feathered object, called a shuttlecock, over a high net

a
b
c
d
e
f
g
h
i
j
k
l
m
n
o
p
q
r
s
t
u
v
w
x
y
z

**31**

## bag bags
NOUN a container for carrying things in

**WORD HISTORY**
From Old Norse *baggi* meaning bundle

## baggage
NOUN Your **baggage** is all the suitcases, holdalls and bags that you take with you when you travel.

## bagpipes
PLURAL NOUN a musical instrument played by squeezing air out of a leather bag and through pipes

## baguette baguettes
NOUN a long, thin French loaf of bread

## bail bails
NOUN 1 a sum of money paid to a court to allow an accused person to go free until the time of the trial • *The accused man was released on **bail**.*
NOUN 2 In cricket, the **bails** are the two small pieces of wood placed on top of the stumps to form the wicket.

## bait baits, baiting, baited
NOUN 1 a small amount of food placed on a hook, or in a trap, to attract and catch a fish or wild animal
VERB 2 If you **bait** a hook or a trap, you put some food on it to catch a fish or wild animal.

## bake bakes, baking, baked
VERB 1 When you **bake** food, you cook it in an oven without using extra liquid or fat.
VERB 2 If you **bake** earth or clay, you heat it until it becomes hard.

## baker bakers
NOUN a person who makes and sells bread and cakes

## balance balances, balancing, balanced
VERB 1 When someone or something **balances**, they remain steady and do not fall over.
VERB 2 used in mathematics when weighing and comparing two weights. If two weights are equal, they **balance**.
NOUN 3 the state of being upright and steady • *She lost her **balance** and fell.*
NOUN 4 the amount of money in someone's bank account

## balcony balconies
NOUN 1 a platform on the outside of a building, with a wall or railing round it
NOUN 2 an area of upstairs seats in a theatre or cinema

## bald balder, baldest
ADJECTIVE A **bald** person has little or no hair on their head.

**WORD HISTORY**
from Middle English *ballede* meaning having a white patch

## bale bales, baling, baled
NOUN 1 a large bundle of something, such as paper or hay, tied tightly
VERB 2 If you **bale** water from a boat, you remove it using a container.

**LANGUAGE TIP**
In meaning 2, the spelling *bail* can also be used.

## ball balls
NOUN 1 a round object used in games such as tennis, football, and hockey
NOUN 2 The **ball** of your foot or thumb is the rounded part where your toes join your foot or your thumb joins your hand.

## ballad ballads
NOUN 1 a long song or poem that tells a story
NOUN 2 a slow, romantic pop song

## ballerina ballerinas
NOUN a female ballet dancer

## ballet
NOUN a type of artistic dancing based on precise steps

**WORD HISTORY**
from Italian *balletto* meaning little dance

## balloon balloons
NOUN 1 a small bag made of thin rubber that you blow into until it becomes larger. **Balloons** are often used as party decorations.
NOUN 2 a large, strong bag filled with gas or hot air, that travels through the air carrying passengers in a basket underneath it • *They went on a hot-air **balloon** flight over the city.*

## ballpoint ballpoints
NOUN a pen with a small, metal ball at the writing point

## bamboo
NOUN a tall tropical grass with hard, hollow stems used for making furniture

**ban bans, banning, banned**

VERB **1** If you **ban** something, you forbid it to be done.

SYNONYMS: forbid, prohibit

NOUN **2** If there is a **ban** on something, it is not allowed.

**banana bananas**

NOUN a long, curved fruit with a yellow skin

**band bands**

NOUN **1** a group of musicians who play jazz or pop music together

NOUN **2** a group of people who share a common purpose

NOUN **3** a narrow strip of something used to hold things together • *She tied her hair back with an elastic* **band**.

**bandage bandages**

NOUN a strip of cloth wrapped round a wound to protect it

**bang bangs, banging, banged**

NOUN **1** a sudden, short, loud noise

NOUN **2** a hard, painful bump against something

VERB **3** If you **bang** something, you hit it or put it down violently so that it makes a loud noise.

VERB **4** If you **bang** a part of your body against something, you accidentally bump it.

**banish banishes, banishing, banished**

VERB **1** If someone is **banished**, they are sent away and never allowed to return.

VERB **2** If you **banish** something from your thoughts, you try not to think about it.

**banishment**

NOUN **Banishment** is when someone is sent away and never allowed to return.

**banister banisters**

NOUN a rail supported by posts up the side of a staircase

**banjo banjos or banjoes**

NOUN a musical instrument, like a small guitar with a round body

**bank banks, banking, banked**

NOUN **1** a business that looks after people's money

NOUN **2** the raised ground along the edge of a river or lake

**bank on**

VERB If you **bank on** something happening, you rely on it. • *I know we said we'd go swimming, but don't* **bank on** *it.*

**banner banners**

NOUN **1** a long strip of cloth with a message or slogan on it • *We saw* **banners** *advertising the fair.*

ADJECTIVE **2** A **banner** headline is a headline printed right across the page of a newspaper.

**banquet banquets**

NOUN a grand, formal dinner, often followed by speeches

WORD HISTORY

from Old French *banquet*, originally meaning little bench

**baptise baptises, baptising, baptised;** also spelt **baptize**

VERB When a church official **baptises** someone, they sprinkle water on them, or immerse them in water, as a sign that they have become a Christian.

**baptism baptisms**

NOUN the ceremony in which someone has water sprinkled on them, or they are immersed in water, as a sign that they have become a Christian

**bar bars, barring, barred**

NOUN **1** a long, straight piece of metal • *There were* **bars** *on the windows.*

VERB **2** If you **bar** a door or a window, you put a bar across it to fasten it.

VERB **3** If you **bar** someone's way, you stop them going somewhere by standing in front of them.

NOUN **4** a counter or room where alcoholic drinks are served

NOUN **5** a piece of something made in a rectangular shape • *a* **bar** *of soap* • *a chocolate* **bar**

**barbecue barbecues**

NOUN **1** a grill with a charcoal fire on which you cook food, usually outdoors

NOUN **2** an outdoor party where you eat food cooked on a barbecue • *We were invited to their annual* **barbecue**.

WORD HISTORY

from a Caribbean word meaning framework

a
b
c
d
e
f
g
h
i
j
k
l
m
n
o
p
q
r
s
t
u
v
w
x
y
z

**33**

### barber **barbers**

NOUN a person who cuts men's hair

### bar chart **bar charts**

NOUN a kind of graph where the information is shown in rows or bars

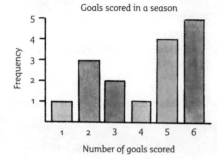

Goals scored in a season

### bar code **bar codes**

NOUN a pattern of lines and numbers on something that is for sale, so that the price can be read by a machine

### bare **barer, barest**

ADJECTIVE **1** If a part of your body is **bare**, it is not covered by any clothing. • *bare feet*

SYNONYMS: naked, uncovered

ADJECTIVE **2** If something is **bare**, it is not covered or decorated with anything.
• *bare wooden floors*

ADJECTIVE **3** The **bare** minimum, or the **bare** essentials, means the very least that is needed.

### barely

ADVERB If you **barely** manage to do something, you only just succeed in doing it.

### bargain **bargains, bargaining, bargained**

NOUN **1** an agreement in which two people or groups discuss and agree what each will do, pay or receive

NOUN **2** something that is sold at a low price and that is good value • *The apples are a bargain at this price.*

VERB **3** When people **bargain** with each other, they discuss and agree terms about what each will do, pay or receive.

### barge **barges, barging, barged**

NOUN **1** a boat with a flat bottom used for carrying heavy loads, especially on canals

VERB **2** (*informal*) If you **barge** into a place, you push into it in a rough or rude way.

### bark **barks, barking, barked**

VERB **1** When a dog **barks**, it makes a short loud noise, once or several times.

NOUN **2** the tough material that covers the outside of a tree

### barley

NOUN a cereal that is grown for food and is also used for making beer and whisky

### bar mitzvah

NOUN A Jewish boy's **bar mitzvah** is a ceremony that takes place on his 13th birthday, after which he is regarded as an adult.

### barn **barns**

NOUN a large farm building used for storing crops or animal food

WORD HISTORY
from Old English *beren* meaning barley roo?

### barnacle **barnacles**

NOUN a small shellfish that fixes itself to rocks and to the bottom of boats

### barometer **barometers**

NOUN an instrument that measures air pressure and shows when the weather is changing

### barrel **barrels**

NOUN **1** a wooden container with rounded sides and flat ends

NOUN **2** The **barrel** of a gun is the long tube through which the bullet is fired.

### barricade **barricades, barricading, barricaded**

NOUN **1** a temporary barrier put up to stop people getting past

VERB **2** If you **barricade** yourself inside a room or building, you put something heavy against the door to stop people getting in.

WORD HISTORY
from Old French *barriquer* meaning to bloc? with barrels

### barrier **barriers**

NOUN a fence or wall that prevents people o? animals getting from one area to another

### barrister **barristers**

NOUN a lawyer who is qualified to represent people in the higher courts

**arrow barrows**

NOUN **1** another word for **wheelbarrow**

NOUN **2** a large cart from which fruit or other goods are sold in the street

**ase bases, basing, based**

NOUN **1** the lowest part of something
• *The waves crashed at the **base** of the cliffs.*

NOUN **2** The **base** of a triangle or a square-shaped pyramid is the bottom.

NOUN **3** a place where part of an army, navy or air force works from

VERB **4** If you **base** one thing on another, you develop the first thing from it. • *She **based** the film on a true story.*

VERB **5** If you are **based** somewhere, you live there or work from there. • *My dad is **based** in Cardiff, but spends a lot of time abroad.*

**aseball**

NOUN a team game played with a bat and a ball. It is popular in the USA.

**asement basements**

NOUN a room or set of rooms below the level of the street • *My aunt lives in the **basement** of our house.*

**asic**

ADJECTIVE **1** The **basic** aspects of something are the most necessary ones. • *The **basic** ingredients of bread are flour, yeast and water.*

ADJECTIVE **2** having only the essentials, and no extras or luxuries

**asically**

ADVERB You use **basically** to give the most important facts or reasons, or to give a simple explanation. • ***Basically**, you have two choices.*

**asin basins**

NOUN **1** a round, wide container which is open at the top

NOUN **2** A river **basin** is a bowl of land from which water runs into the river.

**asis bases**

NOUN If something is the **basis** of something else, it is the main principle on which that thing is based, and from which other points and ideas can be developed.

**ask basks, basking, basked**

VERB If you **bask** in hot weather, you lie in the sun and enjoy the warmth.

**basket baskets**

NOUN a container made of thin strips of wood or metal woven together • *a shopping **basket***

**basketball**

NOUN a game in which two teams try to score goals by throwing a large ball through one of two circular nets that are suspended high up at each end of the **basketball** court

**bass basses**

NOUN **1** a man with a very deep singing voice

ADJECTIVE **2** In music, a **bass** instrument produces a very deep sound. • *a **bass** guitar*

**bassoon bassoons**

NOUN a large woodwind instrument

**bat bats, batting, batted**

NOUN **1** a specially shaped piece of wood with a handle, used for hitting a ball in games such as table tennis or cricket

NOUN **2** a small mammal with leathery wings. **Bats** fly at night and sleep hanging upside down.

VERB **3** If you are **batting** in cricket, baseball or rounders, it is your turn to hit the ball.

**batch batches**

NOUN A **batch** of things is a group of things that are all the same or are being dealt with at the same time. • *They delivered the first **batch** of books at the start of term.*

**bath baths**

NOUN a long container that you fill with water and sit in to wash yourself

**bathe bathes, bathing, bathed**

VERB When you **bathe** in a sea, river or lake, you swim or play there.

**bathroom bathrooms**

NOUN a room with a bath or shower, a washbasin and often a toilet in it

**bat mitzvah**

NOUN A Jewish girls's **bat mitzvah** is a ceremony that usually takes place on her 12th birthday, after which she is regarded as an adult.

**baton batons**

NOUN **1** a light, thin stick that a conductor uses to direct an orchestra or choir

NOUN **2** a short stick passed from one runner to another at the changeover in a relay race

**battalion battalions**

NOUN an army unit consisting of three or more companies

a
b
c
d
e
f
g
h
i
j
k
l
m
n
o
p
q
r
s
t
u
v
w
x
y
z

**35**

## batter batters, battering, battered

NOUN **1** a mixture of flour, eggs and milk, used to make pancakes, or to coat food before frying it

VERB **2** When someone or something **batters** someone or something, they hit them many times. • *The waves **battered** the sides of the ship.*

## battery batteries

NOUN a device for storing energy and producing electricity, for example in a torch or a car

## battle battles

NOUN **1** a fight between armed forces

NOUN **2** a struggle between two people or groups with different aims

## battlefield battlefields

NOUN a place where a battle has been fought or is being fought

## battlements

PLURAL NOUN the top part of a castle where there are openings through which arrows or guns could be fired

→ Have a look at the illustration for **castle**

## battleship battleships

NOUN a large fighting ship carrying powerful guns

## bawl bawls, bawling, bawled

VERB If someone **bawls**, they shout or cry loudly.

## bay bays, baying, bayed

NOUN **1** part of the coastline where the land curves

NOUN **2** a space or an area used for a particular purpose • *a loading **bay***

NOUN **3** a tree with dark green leaves. The leaves are used for flavouring food.

VERB **4** When a dog or a wolf **bays**, it makes a deep, howling sound.

PHRASE **5** If you keep something **at bay**, you stop it hurting you. • *Try eating an orange to keep a cold **at bay**.*

## bayonet bayonets

NOUN a sharp blade that can be fixed to the end of a rifle

## bazaar bazaars

NOUN **1** an area with many small shops and stalls, especially in Eastern countries

NOUN **2** a sale to raise money for charity • *a Christmas **bazaar***

**WORD HISTORY**
from Persian *bazar* meaning market

## BC

ADJECTIVE You use **BC** to show the dates before the birth of Jesus Christ. It is an abbreviation for *before Christ*.

## BCE

ADJECTIVE You use **BCE** in dates to show the number of years or centuries before the year in which Jesus Christ is believed to have been born. **BCE** is an abbreviation for *before the Common Era*.

## be am, is, are; being; was, were; been

VERB **1** You can use **be** with the present participle of other verbs. • *Look! I **am** riding on my own!*

VERB **2** You can also use **be** to say that something will happen. • *I will **be** nine in November.*

VERB **3** You use **be** to say more about something or somebody. • *His name **is** Tom*

## beach beaches

NOUN an area of sand or pebbles beside the sea

## beacon beacons

NOUN In the past, a **beacon** was a light or fire on a hill, which acted as a signal or warning

## bead beads

NOUN **1** a small, shaped piece of glass, stone or wood with a hole through the middle. **Beads** are strung together to make necklaces or bracelets.

NOUN **2** a drop of liquid • ***beads** of perspiration*

## beak beaks

NOUN the hard part of a bird's mouth that sticks out. It is used for pecking up food and for carrying things such as twigs.

→ Have a look at the illustration for **bird**

## beam beams, beaming, beamed

NOUN **1** a long, thick bar of wood or metal, especially one that supports a roof

NOUN **2** a band of light that shines from something such as a torch or the sun

VERB **3** If you **beam**, you smile broadly.

## bean beans

NOUN the seed or pod of a plant, eaten as a vegetable or used for other purposes • *runner **beans*** • *coffee **beans*** • *soya **beans***

**bear bears, bearing, bore, borne**
NOUN **1** a large, strong, wild mammal with thick fur and sharp claws • polar **bear**
• grizzly **bear**
VERB **2** If someone or something **bears** something, they carry it or support its weight. • The ice wasn't thick enough to **bear** their weight.
VERB **3** If something **bears** a mark or typical feature, it has it. • The room **bore** all the signs of a violent struggle.
VERB **4** If you **bear** something difficult, you accept it and are able to deal with it.
• The loneliness was hard to **bear**.

**beard beards**
NOUN the hair that grows on the lower part of a man's face

**bearing bearings**
NOUN **Bearings** are used to work out the position of things or places by measuring the angle of the item, sometimes using a compass.

**beast beasts**
NOUN **1** an old-fashioned word for a large, wild animal
NOUN **2** (informal) If you call someone a **beast**, you mean that they are cruel or spiteful.

**beat beats, beating, beat, beaten**
VERB **1** If someone or something **beats** someone or something else, they hit them hard and repeatedly. • The rain was **beating** against the window.
VERB **2** If you **beat** someone in a race or game, you defeat them or do better than them.
VERB **3** When your heart **beats**, it pumps blood with a regular rhythm.
NOUN **4** the main pulse of a piece of music or poetry

**beautiful**
ADJECTIVE very attractive or pleasing

SYNONYM: lovely

**beauty beauties**
NOUN **1** the quality of being beautiful
• the **beauty** of the stars on a clear night
NOUN **2** The **beauty** of an idea or a plan is what makes it attractive or worth doing.
• The **beauty** of going in September is that the sea will be warmer for swimming.

**beaver beavers**
NOUN a mammal with a big, flat tail and webbed hind feet. **Beavers** build dams.

**because**
CONJUNCTION **1 Because** is used with other words to give the reason for something.
• I went home **because** I was tired.
PHRASE **2 Because of** is used with a noun that gives the reason for something. • I had to stay late **because of** detention.

**beckon beckons, beckoning, beckoned**
VERB If you **beckon** to someone, you make a sign to them with your hand, asking them to come to you.

**become becomes, becoming, became, become**
VERB If someone or something **becomes** something else, they start feeling or being that thing. • I **became** more and more angry.

WORD HISTORY
from Old English becuman meaning to happen

**bed beds**
NOUN **1** a piece of furniture that you lie on when you sleep
NOUN **2** an area of ground in a garden which has been dug and prepared for planting
NOUN **3** The **bed** of the sea or a river is the bottom of it.

**bedraggled**
ADJECTIVE If a person or animal is **bedraggled**, they are wet, dirty and messy.

**bedroom bedrooms**
NOUN a room for sleeping in

**bedtime bedtimes**
NOUN the time when you go to bed

**bee bees**
NOUN a winged insect, some species of which make honey. Many types of **bee** live in large groups.

**beech beeches**
NOUN a tree with a smooth, grey trunk and shiny leaves

**beef**
NOUN the meat of a cow, bull or ox

**beehive beehives**
NOUN a specially designed structure in which bees are kept so that their honey can be collected

**been**
VERB the past participle of **be**

**beer beers**
NOUN an alcoholic drink made from malt and flavoured with hops

**beetle beetles**
NOUN a flying insect with hard wing cases that cover its body when it is not flying

WORD HISTORY
from Old English *bitan* meaning to bite

**beetroot beetroots**
NOUN a round, dark red root vegetable

**before**
PREPOSITION **1** If something happens **before** something else, it happens earlier than that. • *Annie was born a few minutes **before** midnight.*

ANTONYM: after

CONJUNCTION **2** used to show that something happens before something else • *Can I see you **before** you go?*

ANTONYM: after

ADVERB **3** If you have done something **before**, you have done it at an earlier time. • *I have been here **before**.*

**beg begs, begging, begged**
VERB **1** When people **beg**, they ask for food or money, because they are very poor.
VERB **2** If you **beg** someone to do something, you ask them very anxiously to do it.
• *David **begged** his dad to take him to the cinema.*

**began**
VERB the past tense of **begin**

**begin begins, beginning, began, begun**
VERB If you **begin** something, you start it.

**beginner beginners**
NOUN someone who has just started to learn something

SYNONYM: learner

**beginning beginnings**
NOUN The **beginning** of something is when or where it starts.

**begun**
VERB the past participle of **begin**

**behalf**
PHRASE If you do something **on behalf of** someone or something, you do it for them or in their name. • *We did the sponsored swim **on behalf of** various charities.*

**behave behaves, behaving, behaved**
VERB **1** If you **behave** in a particular way, you act in that way. • *He knew that he'd **behaved** badly.*
VERB **2** If you **behave** yourself, you act correctly or properly.

**behind**
PREPOSITION **1** at the back of • *The moon disappeared **behind** a cloud.*
PREPOSITION **2** supporting someone • *The whole school was **behind** him in the competition.*
ADVERB **3** If you stay **behind**, you remain after other people have gone.
ADVERB **4** If you leave something **behind**, you do not take it with you.

**beige**
ADJECTIVE having a cream-brown colour

**being**
VERB the present participle of **be**

**belch belches, belching, belched**
VERB **1** If you **belch**, you make a sudden noise in your throat because air has risen up from your stomach.
VERB **2** If something **belches** smoke or fire, it sends it out in large amounts. • *Smoke **belched** from the factory chimneys.*
NOUN **3** the noise you make when you belch

**belief beliefs**
NOUN If you have a **belief** in something, you are certain that it is right or true.

**believe believes, believing, believed**
VERB **1** If you **believe** that something is true, you think that it is true.
VERB **2** If you **believe** someone, you accept that they are telling the truth.

**bell bells**
NOUN **1** a cup-shaped metal object with a piece inside it called a clapper that hits the side and makes a ringing sound
NOUN **2** an electrical device that you can ring or buzz to get attention

**bellow bellows, bellowing, bellowed**
VERB If a human or other animal **bellows**, they shout very loudly or make a very loud, deep noise like a roar.

**belly bellies**
NOUN the part of a human or other animal's body, especially the stomach, that holds and digests food

→ Have a look at the illustration for **bird**

**belong belongs, belonging, belonged**
VERB **1** If something **belongs** to you, it is yours and you own it.
VERB **2** If you **belong** to a group, you are a member of it.
VERB **3** If something **belongs** in a particular place, that is where it should be. • *That book belongs on the top shelf.*

**belongings**
PLURAL NOUN Your **belongings** are all the things that you own.

**below**
PREPOSITION **1** If something is **below** something else, it is in a lower position.
• *We could hear music coming up from the flat two floors below ours.*

ANTONYM: above

PREPOSITION **2** If something is **below** a particular amount or level, it is less than it.
• **below** *average rainfall*

ANTONYM: above

**belt belts**
NOUN a strip of leather or cloth that you fasten round your waist to hold your trousers or skirt up

**bench benches**
NOUN a long seat that two or more people can sit on

**bend bends, bending, bent**
VERB **1** When you **bend** something, you use force to make it curved or angular.
VERB **2** When you **bend**, you move your head and shoulders forwards and downwards.
• *I bent over to pick up my glasses.*
NOUN **3** a curved part of something • *a bend in the road*

**beneath**
PREPOSITION (*formal*) underneath • *There is a car park beneath the shopping centre.*

**benefit benefits, benefiting, benefited**
NOUN **1** the advantage that something brings to people • *the benefit of a good education*
VERB **2** If you **benefit** from something, it helps you. • *He'll benefit from some extra tuition.*

WORD HISTORY
from Latin *benefactum* meaning good deed

**bent**
ADJECTIVE curved or twisted out of shape

**bereaved**
ADJECTIVE (*formal*) You say that someone is **bereaved** when a close relative of theirs has recently died.

**bereavement bereavements**
NOUN (*formal*) **Bereavement** is when a close relative has recently died.

**berry berries**
NOUN a small, round fruit that grows on bushes or trees

**berserk**
ADVERB If somebody goes **berserk**, they lose control of themselves and become extremely violent.

WORD HISTORY
from Icelandic *berserkr* meaning a Viking who wore a shirt made from the skin of a bear and who worked himself into a mad frenzy before going into battle

**berth berths**
NOUN **1** a space in a harbour where a ship stays when it is being loaded or unloaded
NOUN **2** In a boat or caravan, a **berth** is a bed.
PHRASE **3** If you give someone or something **a wide berth**, you avoid them because they are unpleasant or dangerous.

**beside**
PREPOSITION If one thing is **beside** another thing, it is next to it.

**besides**
ADVERB also or in addition to • *The trip is far too expensive. Besides, I don't want to go away for two days.*

**best**
ADJECTIVE **1** the superlative of *good* • *That was one of the best films I've ever seen.*

ANTONYM: worst

ADVERB **2** the superlative of *good* or *well*
• *I did best in maths in my class.*

ANTONYM: worst

ADVERB **3** The thing that you like **best** is the thing that you prefer to everything else.

39

**bet** bets, betting, bet

VERB **1** If you **bet** on the result of an event, you will win money if what you bet on happens, and lose money if it does not.
VERB **2** If you say that you **bet** something happens or is the case, you mean you are sure of it • *I **bet** you were good at sports when you were at school.*

**betray** betrays, betraying, betrayed

VERB If you **betray** someone who trusts you, you tell people something secret about them.

**better**

ADJECTIVE **1** the comparative of *good* • *This book is **better** than her last one.*

ANTONYM: worse

ADJECTIVE **2** If you are **better** after an illness, you are no longer ill.

SYNONYM: cured

ADVERB **3** the comparative of *well* • *I am feeling **better** today.*

ANTONYM: worse

**between**

PREPOSITION **1** If something is **between** two other things, it is situated or happens in the space or time that separates them. • *He was head teacher **between** 1989 and 2000.*
PREPOSITION **2** A relationship or a difference **between** two people or two things is one that involves them both. • *the difference **between** frogs and toads*

**beware**

VERB If you tell someone to **beware** of something, you are warning them that it might be dangerous or harmful.

**bewilder** bewilders, bewildering, bewildered

VERB If something **bewilders** you, it confuses and muddles you so that you can't understand.

**bewilderment**

NOUN a feeling of being confused, muddled and not able to understand something

**beyond**

PREPOSITION **1** If something is **beyond** a certain place, it is on the other side of it. • ***Beyond** the mountains was the secret valley.*
PREPOSITION **2** If something is **beyond** you, you cannot do it or understand it.

**bi-**

PREFIX added to a word to mean two or twice. For example, someone who is **bi**lingual can speak two languages.

**bib** bibs

NOUN a piece of cloth or plastic put under a baby's chin to protect its clothes from stains

**Bible** Bibles

NOUN the sacred book of the Christian religion • *I read about Noah and the Ark in the **Bible**.*

**bibliography** bibliographies

NOUN a list of books or articles

**bicycle** bicycles

NOUN a two-wheeled vehicle that you ride by pushing two pedals with your feet

→ Have a look at the illustration

**bid** bids, bidding, bid

VERB If you **bid** for something, you offer to buy it for a certain sum of money. • *He **bid** for an old bike at the auction.*

**big** bigger, biggest

ADJECTIVE large or important

ANTONYMS: small, tiny, little

**bike** bikes

NOUN an abbreviation for *bicycle*

**bikini** bikinis

NOUN a small, two-piece swimming costume worn by women

**bilingual**

ADJECTIVE involving or using two languages • ***bilingual** street signs*

WORD HISTORY
from Latin *bis* meaning two and *lingua* meaning tongue

**bill** bills

NOUN **1** a written statement of how much is owed for goods or services • *a phone **bill***
NOUN **2** a formal statement of a proposed new law that is discussed and then voted on in Parliament
NOUN **3** A **bill** can be a piece of paper money. • *a dollar **bill***
NOUN **4** A bird's **bill** is its beak.

**billiards**

NOUN a game in which a long stick called a cue is used to move balls on a table

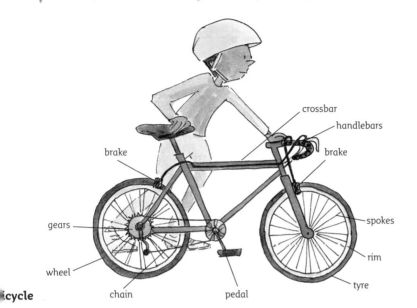

**bicycle**

crossbar

handlebars

brake

brake

gears

spokes

wheel

rim

chain

pedal

tyre

**billion billions**

NOUN a thousand million. You can write one **billion** like this: 1,000,000,000.

**billow billows, billowing, billowed**

VERB **1** When things made of cloth **billow**, they swell out and flap slowly in the wind.
• *The sails **billowed** in the light breeze.*
VERB **2** When smoke or cloud **billows**, it spreads upwards and outwards.

**billy goat billy goats**

NOUN a male goat

**bin bins**

NOUN a container, especially one that you put rubbish in

**binary**

ADJECTIVE The **binary** system is a number system used when working with computers. It uses only two digits, 0 and 1.

**bind binds, binding, bound**

VERB **1** If you **bind** something, you tie rope or string round it so that it is held firmly.
VERB **2** If you **bind** a wound, you wrap bandages round it.
VERB **3** When a book is **bound**, the pages are joined together and a cover is put on.

**bingo**

NOUN a game in which players aim to match the numbers that someone calls out with the numbers on the card they have been given

**binoculars**

PLURAL NOUN an instrument with lenses for both eyes, which you look through in order to see objects far away • *They used **binoculars** for bird watching.*

**biodegradable**

ADJECTIVE **Biodegradable** materials can be broken down naturally, and so they are not dangerous to the environment.

**biography biographies**

NOUN the history of someone's life, written by someone else • *a **biography** of the late prime minister*

**biology**

NOUN the study of living things

WORD HISTORY
from Greek *bios* + *logos* meaning life study

**birch birches**

NOUN a tall, deciduous tree with thin branches and thin bark

## bird birds

NOUN an egg-laying animal with feathers, two wings, two legs and a beak

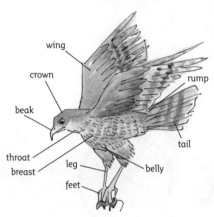

wing

crown

rump

beak

throat

breast

leg

feet

belly

tail

## birth births

NOUN Your **birth** was when you were born.

## birthday birthdays

NOUN Your **birthday** is the anniversary of the date on which you were born.

## birthmark birthmarks

NOUN a mark on your skin that has been there since you were born

## biscuit biscuits

NOUN a small, flat cake that is crisp and usually sweet

## bisect bisects, bisecting, bisected

VERB to divide a line or an area in half

## bishop bishops

NOUN a high-ranking clergyman in some Christian Churches

## bison

NOUN a large, hairy animal, related to cattle, with a large head and shoulders. **Bison** used to be very common on the prairies in North America, but they are now almost extinct.

## bit bits

VERB **1** the past tense of **bite** • She **bit** into the toast.

NOUN **2** A **bit** of something is a small amount of it.

PHRASE **3** (*informal*) **A bit** means slightly or to a small extent. • That's **a bit** difficult.

## bitch bitches

NOUN a female dog

## bite bites, biting, bit, bitten

VERB If you **bite** something, you cut into it with your teeth.

## bitter bitterest

ADJECTIVE **1** A **bitter** taste is sharp and unpleasant.

ADJECTIVE **2** A **bitter** wind is extremely cold.

ADJECTIVE **3** If you are **bitter** about something you feel angry and resentful.

## bizarre

ADJECTIVE very strange and weird

SYNONYMS: odd, peculiar

## black blacker, blackest

NOUN **1** the darkest possible colour, like the sky at night when there is no light

ADJECTIVE **2** having the darkest possible colour

## blackberry blackberries

NOUN a small, soft black fruit that grows on brambles

## blackbird blackbirds

NOUN a common European bird, the male of which has black feathers and a yellow beak

## blackboard blackboards

NOUN a dark-coloured board which people can write on using chalk

## blackcurrant blackcurrants

NOUN **Blackcurrants** are very small, dark, purple fruits that grow in bunches on bushes

## black hole black holes

NOUN the empty space made by the collapse of a star

## blacksmith blacksmiths

NOUN a person whose job is making things out of metal, and making and fitting horseshoes

## bladder bladders

NOUN the part of your body where urine is held until it leaves your body

## blade blades

NOUN **1** the sharp part of a knife, axe or saw

NOUN **2** a single piece of grass

NOUN **3** the long, flat parts that turn round on a windmill, fan or propeller

→ Have a look at the illustration for **turbine**

**blame** blames, blaming, blamed
VERB If someone **blames** a person for something bad that has happened, they believe that person caused it.

SYNONYM: accuse

**blank** blanker, blankest
ADJECTIVE 1 Something that is **blank** has nothing on it. • *a blank sheet of paper*
ADJECTIVE 2 If you look **blank**, your face shows no feeling or interest.

**blanket** blankets
NOUN a large rectangle of thick cloth that is put on a bed to keep people warm

WORD HISTORY
from Old French *blancquete* meaning little white thing

**blare** blares, blaring, blared
VERB to make a loud, unpleasant noise • *The radio blared from the flat below.*

**blast** blasts, blasting, blasted
VERB 1 When people **blast** a hole in something, they make a hole with an explosion. • *They're using dynamite to blast away rocks.*
NOUN 2 a big explosion, especially one caused by a bomb

**blaze** blazes, blazing, blazed
NOUN 1 a large, hot fire
VERB 2 If something **blazes**, it burns or shines brightly. • *The fire blazed in the fireplace.*

**blazer** blazers
NOUN a kind of jacket, often in the colours of a school or sports team

**bleach** bleaches, bleaching, bleached
NOUN 1 a chemical that is used to make material white or to clean thoroughly and kill germs
VERB 2 If you **bleach** material or hair, you make it white, usually by using a chemical.

**bleak** bleaker, bleakest
ADJECTIVE 1 If a place is **bleak**, it is cold, bare and exposed to the wind. • *a bleak mountain top*
ADJECTIVE 2 If a situation is **bleak**, it is bad and seems unlikely to improve.

**bleat** bleats, bleating, bleated
VERB When sheep or goats **bleat**, they make a high-pitched cry.

**bleed** bleeds, bleeding, bled
VERB When you **bleed**, you lose blood as a result of an injury. • *My hand bled a lot after I cut it.*

**blend** blends, blending, blended
VERB 1 When you **blend** substances, you mix them together to form a single substance. • *Blend the butter with the sugar.*
VERB 2 When colours or sounds **blend**, they combine in a pleasing way.

**bless** blesses, blessing, blessed or blest
VERB When a priest or vicar **blesses** people or things, they ask God to give his protection to them.

WORD HISTORY
from Old English *bloedsian* meaning to sprinkle with sacrificial blood

**blew**
VERB the past tense of **blow**

**blind** blinds, blinding, blinded
ADJECTIVE 1 Someone who is **blind** cannot see.
VERB 2 If something **blinds** you, it stops you seeing, either for a short time or permanently.
NOUN 3 a roll of cloth or paper that you pull down over a window to keep out the light

**blindfold** blindfolds
NOUN a strip of cloth tied over someone's eyes to stop them seeing

**blink** blinks, blinking, blinked
VERB When you **blink**, you close your eyes quickly for a moment.

**bliss**
NOUN a state of complete happiness

**blister** blisters
NOUN a small bubble on your skin containing watery liquid, caused by a burn or rubbing

**blizzard** blizzards
NOUN a heavy snowstorm with strong winds

**bloated**
ADJECTIVE Something that is **bloated** is much larger than normal, often because there is a lot of liquid or gas inside it.

43

**block** blocks, blocking, blocked

NOUN **1** a large building containing flats or offices

NOUN **2** In a town, a **block** is an area of land with streets on all its sides.

NOUN **3** a large, rectangular, three-dimensional piece of something • *Elizabeth carves animals from **blocks** of wood.*

VERB **4** If someone or something **blocks** a road or channel, they put something across it so that nothing can get through.

SYNONYM: obstruct

**block capitals**

PLURAL NOUN large upper-case letters. THESE ARE BLOCK CAPITALS.

**block graph** block graphs

NOUN another name for **bar chart**

**blog** blogs, blogging, blogged

NOUN **1** a person's online diary that they put on the internet so that other people can read it

VERB **2** If you **blog** about something, you write about it in a blog. • *He **blogs** about cooking and restaurants.*

**blogger** bloggers

NOUN a person who writes an online diary that they put on the internet so that other people can read it

**blonde** blondes

ADJECTIVE **1** **Blonde** hair is pale yellow in colour. The spelling **blond** is used when referring to men.

NOUN **2** A **blonde** or **blond** is a person with pale yellow hair.

**blood**

NOUN the red liquid that is pumped by the heart round the bodies of human beings and other vertebrates

**bloodstream**

NOUN the flow of blood through your body

**bloodthirsty**

ADJECTIVE Someone who is **bloodthirsty** enjoys using or watching violence.

**bloom** blooms, blooming, bloomed

NOUN **1** a flower on a plant

VERB **2** When a plant **blooms**, it produces flowers.

**blossom** blossoms, blossoming, blossomed

NOUN **1** all the flowers that appear on a tree before the fruit

VERB **2** When a tree **blossoms**, it produces flowers.

**blot** blots

NOUN a mark made by a drop of liquid, especially ink

**blouse** blouses

NOUN a light shirt, worn by a girl or a woma

**blow** blows, blowing, blew, blown

VERB **1** When the wind **blows**, the air move

VERB **2** If you **blow**, you send a stream of ai from your mouth.

VERB **3** If you **blow** your nose, you force air out of it through your nostrils in order to clear it.

NOUN **4** If you receive a **blow**, someone or something hits you.

**blow up**

VERB **1** If something **blows up**, it is destroyed by an explosion.

VERB **2** If you **blow up** a balloon or a tyre you fill it with air.

**blubber**

NOUN the layer of fat beneath the skin of animals such as whales and seals that protects them from the cold

**blue** bluer, bluest

NOUN **1** the colour of the sky on a clear, sunny day

ADJECTIVE **2** having the colour of the sky on a clear, sunny day

**bluebell** bluebells

NOUN a woodland plant with blue, bell-shaped flowers

**bluff** bluffs, bluffing, bluffed

NOUN **1** an attempt to make someone believ that you will do something when you do n really intend to do it

VERB **2** If you are **bluffing**, you are trying to make someone believe that you are in a strong position when you are not.

NOUN **3** a steep cliff or river bank

WORD HISTORY

from Dutch *bluffen* meaning to boast

**blunder** blunders, blundering, blundered

NOUN **1** a silly mistake

VERB **2** If you **blunder**, you make a silly mistake.

**blunt** blunter, bluntest

ADJECTIVE **1** A **blunt** object has a rounded point or edge, rather than a sharp one.
● *My pencil was **blunt** so I could not write with it.*

ADJECTIVE **2** If you are **blunt**, you say exactly what you think, without trying to be polite.

SYNONYMS: outspoken, straightforward

**blur**

NOUN If something is a **blur**, you can't see it clearly. ● *The mountain was a **blur** through the mist.*

**blurb** blurbs

NOUN the description of a book printed on the back cover

**blurt out** blurts out, blurting out, blurted out

VERB If you **blurt out** something, you say it suddenly, after trying to keep it a secret.

**blush** blushes, blushing, blushed

VERB If you **blush**, your face becomes red, because you are embarrassed or ashamed.

**WORD HISTORY**

from Old English *blyscan* meaning to glow

**boa** boas

NOUN a large snake that kills its prey by coiling round it and crushing it

**boar** boars

NOUN **1** a male wild pig
NOUN **2** a male domestic pig used for breeding

**board** boards, boarding, boarded

NOUN **1** a long, flat piece of wood
NOUN **2** a flat piece of wood, plastic or cardboard, which is used for a particular purpose ● *a chess**board*** ● *a surf**board***
NOUN **3** the group of people who control a company or organisation ● *My mum is on the **board** of governors.*
NOUN **4** the meals provided when you stay in a hotel or guesthouse ● *The price includes full **board**.*
VERB **5** If you **board** a ship or aircraft, you get on it or in it.
PHRASE **6** If you are **on board** a ship or aircraft, you are on it or in it.

**LANGUAGE TIP**

Do not confuse *board* with *bored*.

**boarder** boarders

NOUN **1** a pupil who lives at school during term
NOUN **2** a lodger

**boast** boasts, boasting, boasted

VERB If you **boast**, you talk proudly about what you have or what you can do.

SYNONYM: brag

**boat** boats

NOUN a small vehicle for travelling across water

**body** bodies

NOUN **1** Your **body** is all of you, from your head to your feet.
NOUN **2** You can say **body** when you mean just the main part of a human or other animal, not counting head, arms and legs.

**bodyguard** bodyguards

NOUN a person employed to protect someone

**bog** bogs

NOUN an area of wet, spongy ground

**boil** boils, boiling, boiled

VERB **1** When a hot liquid **boils**, or when you **boil** it, it starts to bubble and to give off steam.
VERB **2** When you **boil** food, you cook it in boiling water.

**boiler** boilers

NOUN a piece of equipment that burns fuel to provide hot water

**boiling point**

NOUN the temperature at which a liquid starts to change into steam or vapour

**boisterous**

ADJECTIVE Someone who is **boisterous** is noisy and lively.

SYNONYMS: loud, rowdy

**bold** bolder, boldest

ADJECTIVE **1** brave or confident ● *He was **bold** enough to ask for her autograph.*
ADJECTIVE **2** clear and noticeable ● *The sign was painted in **bold** colours.*

**WORD HISTORY**

from Old Norse *ballr* meaning dangerous or terrible

**bollard** bollards

NOUN a short, thick post used to stop vehicles from entering a road

a
b
c
d
e
f
g
h
i
j
k
l
m
n
o
p
q
r
s
t
u
v
w
x
y
z

**45**

**bolt** **bolts, bolting, bolted**
NOUN **1** a metal object that screws into a nut and is used to fasten things together
VERB **2** If you **bolt** one thing to another, you fasten them together using a bolt.
• They **bolted** the chair to the floor.
VERB **3** If you **bolt** a door or window, you slide a metal bar across in order to fasten it.

**bomb** **bombs, bombing, bombed**
NOUN **1** a container filled with material that explodes when it hits something or when it is set off by a timer
VERB **2** If you **bomb** something, you attack it with a bomb.

WORD HISTORY
from Greek bombos meaning a booming sound

**bond** **bonds**
NOUN a close relationship between people
• the **bond** between mothers and babies

**bone** **bones**
NOUN the hard parts that form the internal framework of a person's or animal's body

**bonfire** **bonfires**
NOUN a large fire made outdoors, to burn rubbish or to celebrate something

WORD HISTORY
from bone + fire – bones were used as fuel in the Middle Ages

**bonnet** **bonnets**
NOUN **1** the metal cover over a car's engine
→ Have a look at the illustration for **car**
NOUN **2** a baby's or woman's hat tied under the chin

**bonus** **bonuses**
NOUN **1** an amount of money added to a person's usual pay
NOUN **2** a good thing that you get in addition to something else

**bony** **bonier, boniest**
ADJECTIVE **Bony** people or animals are very thin, with not much flesh covering their bones.

**book** **books, booking, booked**
NOUN **1** a number of pages held together inside a cover
VERB **2** When you **book** something, you arrange to have it or use it at a particular time. • Mum **booked** two rooms at the hotel.

**bookcase** **bookcases**
NOUN a piece of furniture where you keep books

**booklet** **booklets**
NOUN a thin book with a paper cover

**boom** **booms, booming, boomed**
NOUN **1** a deep, echoing sound
NOUN **2** a fast increase in something
• There has been a **boom** in the sale of sun cream this summer.
VERB **3** If something **booms**, it makes a loud booming sound. • We heard the foghorn **boom** in the distance.

**boomerang** **boomerangs**
NOUN a curved, wooden missile that can be thrown so that it returns to the thrower. **Boomerangs** were traditionally used as weapons by Australian Aborigines.

**boost** **boosts, boosting, boosted**
VERB If someone **boosts** something, they improve or increase it. • The teacher **boosted** Juliet's confidence when she praised her story.

**boot** **boots**
NOUN **1** strong shoes that come up over your ankle, and sometimes your calf
NOUN **2** the covered space in a car, usually at the back, for carrying things in
→ Have a look at the illustration for **car**

**booth** **booths**
NOUN **1** a small, partly-enclosed area
• a phone **booth**
NOUN **2** a stall where you can buy things, for example at a market or a fair

**border** **borders**
NOUN **1** the dividing line between two countries
NOUN **2** a strip or band round the edge of something
NOUN **3** flower beds round the edges of a garden

**borderline** **borderlines**
NOUN If someone or something is on the **borderline**, they are on the division between two different categories.

**bore** **bores, boring, bored**
VERB **1** If something **bores** you, you find it dull and uninteresting.
VERB **2** If you **bore** a hole in something, you make it using a tool such as a drill.
VERB **3** the past tense of **bear**
NOUN **4** someone or something that bores you

A
B
C
D
E
F
G
H
I
J
K
L
M
N
O
P
Q
R
S
T
U
V
W
X
Y
Z

**bored**
ADJECTIVE If you are **bored**, you are miserable because you have nothing interesting to do.

**LANGUAGE TIP**
Do not confuse *bored* with *board*.

**boring**
ADJECTIVE dull and uninteresting

ANTONYM: interesting

**born**
VERB When an animal such as a human baby is **born**, it comes out of its mother's body and starts to live.

**borrow** borrows, borrowing, borrowed
VERB If you **borrow** something that belongs to someone else, they let you have it for a period of time. ● *I **borrowed** a book from my friend.*

**boss** bosses, bossing, bossed
NOUN **1** Someone's **boss** is the person in charge of the place where they work.
VERB **2** If someone **bosses** you, they keep telling you what to do.

**bossy** bossier, bossiest
ADJECTIVE If you are **bossy**, you like to order other people around.

**botany**
NOUN the study and classification of plants

**both**
ADJECTIVE **1 Both** is used to refer to two things or two people. ● *Stand up straight with **both** arms at your sides.*
PRONOUN **2 Both** is used when saying something about two things or two people. ● *You can **both** come to my party.*

**bother** bothers, bothering, bothered
VERB **1** If you don't **bother** to do something, you don't do it because it takes too much effort or it's not important.
VERB **2** If something **bothers** you, you are worried about it.
VERB **3** If you are not **bothered** about something, you don't care about it.
VERB **4** If you **bother** someone, you interrupt them when they are busy.
NOUN **5** trouble, fuss or difficulty ● *Mum's having a bit of **bother** with the car.*

**bottle** bottles, bottling, bottled
NOUN **1** a glass or plastic container for keeping liquids in
VERB **2** If you **bottle** something, you put it in a bottle to store it.

**bottom** bottoms
NOUN **1** the lowest part of something ● *It sank to the **bottom** of the pond.*
NOUN **2** Your **bottom** is the part of your body that you sit on.

**bottomless**
ADJECTIVE If something is **bottomless**, it has no bottom or it is very deep.

**bough** boughs
NOUN a large branch of a tree

**PRONUNCIATION TIP**
This word rhymes with "cow".

**bought**
VERB the past tense and past participle of **buy**

**LANGUAGE TIP**
Do not confuse *bought* with *brought*.

**boulder** boulders
NOUN a large, rounded rock

**bounce** bounces, bouncing, bounced
VERB When an object **bounces**, it springs back from something after hitting it.
● *The ball **bounced** high off the ground.*

**bound** bounds, bounding, bounded
ADJECTIVE **1** If you say that something is **bound** to happen, you mean that it is certain to happen. ● *He's **bound** to find out.*
NOUN **2** a large leap
VERB **3** When humans or other animals **bound**, they move quickly with large leaps.

**boundary** boundaries
NOUN the limit of an area

**bouquet** bouquets
NOUN an attractively arranged bunch of flowers

**bout** bouts
NOUN **1** something that lasts for a short period of time ● *I had a **bout** of flu.*
NOUN **2** a boxing or wrestling match

**boutique** boutiques
NOUN a small shop that sells fashionable clothes

a
b
c
d
e
f
g
h
i
j
k
l
m
n
o
p
q
r
s
t
u
v
w
x
y
z

**47**

## bow **bows, bowing, bowed**
VERB **1** When you **bow**, you bend your body or lower your head as a sign of respect or greeting.
NOUN **2** the movement you make when you bow
NOUN **3** the front part of a ship
→ Have a look at the illustration for **ship**
NOUN **4** a knot with two loops and two loose ends • *The ribbon was tied in a bow*.
NOUN **5** a long, thin piece of wood with horsehair strings stretched along it, used to play some stringed instruments, such as the violin and the cello
NOUN **6** a long, flexible piece of wood used for shooting arrows

PRONUNCIATION TIP
Meanings 1, 2 and 3 rhyme with "now". Meanings 4, 5 and 6 rhyme with "low".

## bowel **bowels**
NOUN the tubes leading from your stomach, through which waste passes before it leaves your body

WORD HISTORY
from Latin *botellus* meaning little sausage

## bowl **bowls, bowling, bowled**
NOUN **1** a round container with a wide, uncovered top, used for holding liquid or for serving food • *a bowl of soup*
NOUN **2** the hollow, rounded part of something • *a toilet bowl*
VERB **3** When you **bowl** in cricket and rounders, you throw the ball towards the batsman.

## bowling
NOUN a game in which you roll a heavy ball down a narrow track towards a set of wooden objects called pins, and try to knock them down

## bowls
NOUN a game in which the players try to roll large wooden balls as near as possible to a small ball

## box **boxes, boxing, boxed**
NOUN **1** a container with a firm base and sides, and usually a lid
VERB **2** If someone **boxes**, they fight according to special rules.

## boxer **boxers**
NOUN **1** a person who boxes
NOUN **2** a medium-sized, smooth-haired dog with a flat face

## Boxing Day
NOUN the day after Christmas Day

## boy **boys**
NOUN a male child

## boyfriend **boyfriends**
NOUN Someone's **boyfriend** is the man or boy with whom they are having a romantic relationship.

## bra **bras**
NOUN a piece of underwear worn by a woma to support her breasts

## brace **braces, bracing, braced**
NOUN **1** an object fixed to something to straighten or support it • *I wore a brace on my teeth for two years*.
PLURAL NOUN **2 Braces** are elastic straps wor over the shoulders to hold trousers up.
VERB **3** If you **brace** yourself, you stiffen your body to steady yourself. • *We braced ourselves as the bus went round the corner*.
VERB **4** If you **brace** yourself for something unpleasant, you prepare yourself to deal with it.

## bracelet **bracelets**
NOUN a chain or band worn around someone's wrist as an ornament

WORD HISTORY
from Old French *bracel* meaning little arm

## bracken
NOUN a plant like a large fern that grows on hills and in woods

## bracket **brackets**
NOUN a pair of written marks, ( ), { } or [ ], placed round a word or sentence that is no part of the main text, or to show that the items inside the **brackets** belong together

## brag **brags, bragging, bragged**
VERB If you **brag**, you boast about something.

## Braille
NOUN a system of printing for blind people i which letters are represented by raised dot that can be felt with the fingers

**brain brains**
NOUN the organ inside your head that controls your body and enables you to think and feel

→ Have a look at the illustration for **organ**

**brainstorm brainstorms**
NOUN **1** a clever idea that you think of suddenly
NOUN **2** If you have a **brainstorm**, you become confused and cannot think clearly.

**brainy brainier, brainiest**
ADJECTIVE clever and good at learning things

**brake brakes, braking, braked**
NOUN **1** a device for making a vehicle stop or slow down

→ Have a look at the illustration for **bicycle**

VERB **2** When drivers **brake**, they make a vehicle stop or slow down by using its brakes.

**bramble brambles**
NOUN a wild, trailing bush with thorns, which produces blackberries

**branch branches, branching, branched**
NOUN **1** part of a tree that grows out from the trunk
NOUN **2** A **branch** of a business or organisation is one of its offices or shops.
VERB **3** A road that **branches** off from another road splits off from it to lead in a different direction.

**brand brands**
NOUN a particular kind or make of something

**brandy**
NOUN a strong, alcoholic drink, often drunk after a meal

WORD HISTORY
from Dutch *brandewijn* meaning burnt wine

**brass**
NOUN **1** a yellow-coloured metal made from copper and zinc
ADJECTIVE **2** **Brass** instruments are musical instruments such as trumpets and trombones, made of metal.

**brave braver, bravest; braves, braving, braved**
ADJECTIVE **1** A **brave** person is willing to do dangerous things and does not show any fear.

SYNONYMS: courageous, daring

VERB **2** If you **brave** an unpleasant or dangerous situation, you face up to it in order to do something. ● We **braved** the snow to go to the party.

WORD HISTORY
from Italian *bravo* meaning courageous or wild

**brawl brawls, brawling, brawled**
NOUN **1** a rough fight
VERB **2** When people **brawl**, they take part in a rough fight.

**bread**
NOUN a very common food made from flour, and baked in an oven

**breadth breadths**
NOUN the distance between two sides of something ● I can swim the **breadth** of the pool.

**break breaks, breaking, broke, broken**
VERB **1** When an object **breaks**, or when you **break** it, it becomes damaged or separates into pieces.
VERB **2** If you **break** a rule or promise, you fail to keep it.
VERB **3** To **break** a record means to do better than the previous recorded best. ● She **broke** the record for the long jump.
NOUN **4** a short period during which you rest or do something different

**break down**
VERB When a machine or a vehicle **breaks down**, it stops working.

**break up**
VERB When schools **break up**, the term ends. ● We **break up** on Thursday.

**breakable**
ADJECTIVE easy to break

**breakdown breakdowns**
NOUN If there is a **breakdown** in a system, it stops working.

**breakfast breakfasts**
NOUN the first meal of the day

**breast breasts**
NOUN A woman's **breasts** are the two soft, fleshy parts on her chest, which produce milk after she has had a baby.

a
b
c
d
e
f
g
h
i
j
k
l
m
n
o
p
q
r
s
t
u
v
w
x
y
z

**49**

A
B
C
D
E
F
G
H
I
J
K
L
M
N
O
P
Q
R
S
T
U
V
W
X
Y
Z

50

tower

main cable

suspension cable

deck

**bridge**

**breast-feed breast-feeds, breast-feeding, breast-fed**
VERB If a woman **breast-feeds** her baby, she feeds it with milk from her breasts.

**breath breaths**
NOUN **1** the air you take into your lungs and let out again when you breathe • *He took a deep breath before jumping into the pool.*
PHRASE **2** If you are **out of breath**, you are breathing with difficulty after doing something energetic.

**breathe breathes, breathing, breathed**
VERB When you **breathe**, you take air into your lungs and let it out again.

**breathless**
ADJECTIVE If you are **breathless**, you are breathing very fast or with difficulty.

**breed breeds, breeding, bred**
NOUN **1** a particular type of animal. For example, an Alsatian is a **breed** of dog.
VERB **2** Someone who **breeds** animals or plants keeps them in order to produce more animals or plants with particular qualities.
VERB **3** When animals **breed**, they produce young.

SYNONYM: reproduce

**breeze breezes**
NOUN a gentle wind

**breezy breezier, breeziest**
ADJECTIVE If the weather is **breezy**, there is a gentle wind.

**brewery breweries**
NOUN a place where beer is made, or a company that makes beer

**bribe bribes, bribing, bribed**
NOUN **1** a gift or money given to someone to persuade them to allow you to do somethin
VERB **2** If someone **bribes** someone else, the give them a bribe.

**brick bricks**
NOUN a rectangular block of baked clay used in building

**bride brides**
NOUN a woman who is getting married or who has just got married

**bridegroom bridegrooms**
NOUN a man who is getting married or who has just got married

**bridesmaid bridesmaids**
NOUN a woman or girl who helps a bride on her wedding day

**bridge bridges**
NOUN **1** a structure built over a river, road or railway so that vehicles and people can cros
NOUN **2** a card game for four players

**bridle** **bridles**

NOUN a set of straps round a horse's head and mouth, which the rider uses to control the horse

**brief** **briefer, briefest; briefs, briefing, briefed**

ADJECTIVE **1** Something that is **brief** lasts only a short time. • We only had time for a **brief** visit.

VERB **2** When you **brief** someone on a task, you give them all the necessary instructions or information about it.

**briefcase** **briefcases**

NOUN a small, flat case for carrying papers

**bright** **brighter, brightest**

ADJECTIVE **1** strong and startling • a **bright** light

SYNONYMS: brilliant, dazzling

ADJECTIVE **2** clever • That's a **bright** idea.

SYNONYMS: intelligent, quick

**brighten** **brightens, brightening, brightened**

VERB If something **brightens**, it becomes brighter.

**brighten up**

VERB If you **brighten up** something, you make it look brighter and more attractive.

**brilliant**

ADJECTIVE **1** A **brilliant** person is extremely clever.

ADJECTIVE **2** (informal) Something that is **brilliant** is extremely good or enjoyable.

ADJECTIVE **3** A **brilliant** colour or light is extremely bright.

**brim** **brims**

NOUN **1** the wide part of a hat that sticks outwards from the head

NOUN **2** If a container is filled to the **brim**, it is filled right to the top.

**bring** **brings, bringing, brought**

VERB If you **bring** something or someone with you when you go to a place, you take them with you.

**bring up**

VERB When someone **brings up** children, they look after them while they grow up.

**brink**

NOUN **1** the edge of a deep hole, cliff or ravine

PHRASE **2** If you are **on the brink** of something, you are about to do it. • They were **on the brink** of discovering a cure for the common cold.

**brisk** **brisker, briskest**

ADJECTIVE **1** quick and energetic • a **brisk** walk

ADJECTIVE **2** If someone's manner is **brisk**, it shows that they want to get things done quickly and efficiently.

**bristle** **bristles, bristling, bristled**

NOUN **1** **Bristles** are strong animal hairs used to make brushes.

VERB **2** If the hairs on an animal's body **bristle**, they rise up because it is frightened.

**bristly** **bristlier, bristliest**

ADJECTIVE Something that is **bristly** is covered with or has short, stiff hairs. • a **bristly** moustache

**brittle**

ADJECTIVE An object that is **brittle** is hard but breaks easily.

**broad** **broader, broadest**

ADJECTIVE **1** A **broad** river is wide.

ADJECTIVE **2** The **broad** outline of a story gives the main points, but no details.

**broadband**

NOUN **Broadband** is a type of very fast internet connection that allows many messages to be sent at the same time. • What is the **broadband** speed like here?

**broadcast** **broadcasts, broadcasting, broadcast**

NOUN **1** a programme or announcement on radio or television

VERB **2** When someone **broadcasts** something, they send it out by radio waves, so that it can be seen on television or heard on radio.

**broadsheet** **broadsheets**

NOUN a newspaper that is usually printed on large sheets of paper, and which is considered to be more serious than some other newspapers

a
b
c
d
e
f
g
h
i
j
k
l
m
n
o
p
q
r
s
t
u
v
w
x
y
z

**51**

A
B
C
D
E
F
G
H
I
J
K
L
M
N
O
P
Q
R
S
T
U
V
W
X
Y
Z

**broccoli**

NOUN a vegetable with green stalks and green or purple flower buds

**brochure brochures**

NOUN a booklet that gives information about a product or a service • holiday **brochure**

**broke**

VERB **1** the past tense of **break**

ADJECTIVE **2** (informal) If you are **broke**, you have no money.

**broken**

ADJECTIVE A **broken** object is damaged in some way.

**bronchitis**

NOUN an illness in which the tubes connecting your windpipe to your lungs become infected, making you cough

**bronze**

NOUN a yellowish-brown metal that is a mixture of copper and tin

**brooch brooches**

NOUN a piece of jewellery with a pin at the back for attaching to clothes

**PRONUNCIATION TIP**

This word rhymes with "coach".

**brood broods, brooding, brooded**

NOUN **1** a family of baby birds

VERB **2** If you **brood** about something, you are worried about it and can't stop thinking about it.

**brook brooks**

NOUN a stream

**broom brooms**

NOUN a long-handled brush

**brother brothers**

NOUN Your **brother** is a boy or man who has the same parents as you.

**brother-in-law brothers-in-law**

NOUN Someone's **brother-in-law** is the brother of their husband or wife, or the husband of one of their siblings.

**brought**

VERB the past tense and past participle of **bring**

**LANGUAGE TIP**

Do not confuse brought with bought.

**brown browner, brownest**

NOUN **1** the colour of earth or wood

ADJECTIVE **2** having the colour of earth or wood

**Brownie Brownies**

NOUN a junior member of the Girl Guides

**bruise bruises, bruising, bruised**

NOUN **1** a purple mark that appears on your skin after something has hit it

VERB **2** If something **bruises** you, it hits you so that a bruise appears on your skin.

**brunette brunettes**

NOUN a girl or a woman with dark brown hair

**brush brushes, brushing, brushed**

NOUN **1** an object with bristles. There are **brushes** for cleaning things, painting or tidying your hair.

VERB **2** If you **brush** something, you clean it or tidy it with a brush.

**Brussels sprout Brussels sprouts**

NOUN a vegetable that looks like a tiny cabbage

**brutal**

ADJECTIVE **Brutal** behaviour is violent and cruel

**brutality**

NOUN violent and cruel behaviour

**bubble bubbles, bubbling, bubbled**

NOUN **1** a ball of air in a liquid

VERB **2** When a liquid **bubbles**, bubbles form in it.

**buck bucks, bucking, bucked**

NOUN **1** the male of various animals, including deer and rabbits

VERB **2** If a horse **bucks**, it jumps into the air with all four feet off the ground.

**bucket buckets**

NOUN a deep, round container with an open top and a handle

**buckle buckles, buckling, buckled**

NOUN **1** a fastening on the end of a belt or strap

VERB **2** If you **buckle** a belt or strap, you fasten it.

VERB **3** If metal **buckles**, it crumples up.

**bud buds**

NOUN a small, tight swelling on a tree or plant, which develops into a flower or leaf

**Buddhism**

NOUN a religion based on the teachings of Buddha, who taught in India in the fifth century. In **Buddhism**, people believe that the way to end suffering is by overcoming our desires.

**Buddhist Buddhists**
NOUN a person whose religion is Buddhism

**budgerigar budgerigars**
NOUN a small, brightly-coloured pet bird. **Budgerigars** originated in Australia.

**budget budgets, budgeting, budgeted**
NOUN 1 a plan showing how much money will be available and how it will be spent
VERB 2 If you **budget** for something, you plan how you use your money carefully, so as to be able to afford what you want.

**buffalo buffaloes**
NOUN 1 a wild animal like a large cow with long curved horns
NOUN 2 another word for **bison**

**buffet buffets**
NOUN 1 a café at a station or on a train
NOUN 2 a meal at which people serve themselves

**bug bugs, bugging, bugged**
NOUN 1 a small insect, especially one that causes damage
NOUN 2 an infection or virus that makes you ill
NOUN 3 a small error in a computer programme that stops it working properly
VERB 4 If a place is **bugged**, tiny microphones are hidden there to pick up what people are saying.

**bugle bugles**
NOUN a simple brass musical instrument that looks like a small trumpet

**build builds, building, built**
VERB If you **build** something, you make it from all its parts.

**builder builders**
NOUN a person whose job is to build buildings

**building buildings**
NOUN a structure with walls and a roof

**bulb bulbs**
NOUN 1 the glass part of an electric lamp
NOUN 2 an onion-shaped root from which a flower or plant grows. Tulips and daffodils are grown from **bulbs**.

**bulge bulges, bulging, bulged**
VERB 1 If something **bulges**, it swells out.
NOUN 2 a lump on a normally flat surface

**bulk bulks**
NOUN 1 a large mass of something
PHRASE 2 If you buy something **in bulk**, you buy it in large quantities.

**bulky bulkier, bulkiest**
ADJECTIVE Something that is **bulky** is large and heavy and sometimes difficult to move.

**bull bulls**
NOUN the male of some animal species including cattle, elephants and whales

**bulldozer bulldozers**
NOUN a powerful tractor with a broad blade in front, which is used for moving earth or knocking things down

**bullet bullets**
NOUN a small piece of metal fired from a gun

**bulletin bulletins**
NOUN a short news report on radio or television

**bullion**
NOUN gold or silver bars

**bullock bullocks**
NOUN a young male bull that is reared for meat

**bully bullies, bullying, bullied**
NOUN 1 someone who tries to hurt or frighten other people, often repeatedly
VERB 2 If someone **bullies** you into doing something, they make you do it by using force or threats.

**bump bumps, bumping, bumped**
VERB 1 If you **bump** into something, you knock into it accidentally.
NOUN 2 a soft noise made by something knocking into something else
NOUN 3 a raised, uneven part of a surface

SYNONYMS: bulge, lump

**bumper bumpers**
NOUN a bar on the front or back of a vehicle that protects it if it bumps into something

a
b
c
d
e
f
g
h
i
j
k
l
m
n
o
p
q
r
s
t
u
v
w
x
y
z

A
**B**
C
D
E
F
G
H
I
J
K
L
M
N
O
P
Q
R
S
T
U
V
W
X
Y
Z

**bumpy bumpier, bumpiest**
ADJECTIVE Something that is **bumpy** has a rough, uneven surface. • *a bumpy road*

**bun buns**
NOUN a small, round bread roll or cake

**bunch bunches**
NOUN a group of things together • *a bunch of flowers*

**bundle bundles, bundling, bundled**
NOUN 1 a number of things tied together or wrapped up in a cloth
VERB 2 If you **bundle** someone or something somewhere, you push them there quickly and roughly.

**bungalow bungalows**
NOUN a one-storey house

**WORD HISTORY**
from Hindi *bangla* meaning house

**bunk bunks**
NOUN a bed fixed to a wall in a ship or caravan

**bunk beds**
PLURAL NOUN two beds fixed together, one above the other

**buoy buoys**
NOUN a floating object anchored to the bottom of the sea, marking a channel or warning of danger

**buoyancy**
NOUN Something that has **buoyancy** is able to float in liquid or in the air.

**buoyant**
ADJECTIVE 1 Something that is **buoyant** is able to float.
ADJECTIVE 2 Someone who is **buoyant** is lively and cheerful.

**burden burdens**
NOUN a heavy load

**burger burgers**
NOUN a flat fried cake of meat, vegetables or cheese, served in a bread roll

**burglar burglars**
NOUN someone who breaks into buildings and steals things

**burglary burglaries**
NOUN the crime of breaking into buildings and stealing things

**burgle burgles, burgling, burgled**
VERB If a building is **burgled**, someone breaks into it and steals things.

**burn burns, burning, burned** or **burnt**
VERB 1 If something is **burning**, it is on fire.
VERB 2 To **burn** something means to damage or destroy it with fire.
VERB 3 People often **burn** fuel, such as coal, to keep warm.
NOUN 4 A **burn** is an injury caused by fire or by something hot.

**LANGUAGE TIP**
You can write either *burned* or *burnt* as the past form of *burn*.

**burqa burqas**; also spelt **burka**
NOUN a long garment worn by some Muslim women in public, covering everything except the eyes

**PRONUNCIATION TIP**
This word is pronounced **bur**-ka.

**burrow burrows, burrowing, burrowed**
NOUN 1 a tunnel or hole in the ground dug by a small animal
VERB 2 When an animal **burrows**, it digs a burrow.

**burst bursts, bursting, burst**
VERB 1 When something **bursts**, or when you **burst** it, it splits open suddenly.
VERB 2 When you **burst** into a room, you enter suddenly and with force.
NOUN 3 A **burst** of something is a sudden short period of it. • *a burst of applause*

**bury buries, burying, buried**
VERB 1 If you **bury** something, you put it in a hole in the ground and cover it with earth.
VERB 2 If something is **buried** under something, it is covered by it. • *My trainers were buried under a pile of clothes.*

**bus buses**
NOUN a large motor vehicle that carries passengers

**WORD HISTORY**
from Latin *omnibus* meaning for all

**bush bushes**
NOUN 1 a large plant, smaller than a tree and with a lot of woody branches
NOUN 2 In Australia and South Africa, an uncultivated area outside a town or city is called the **bush**.
NOUN 3 In New Zealand, the **bush** is land covered by rainforest.

**bushy** bushier, bushiest
ADJECTIVE **Bushy** hair or fur grows very thickly.
• *My dad has **bushy** eyebrows.*

**business** businesses
NOUN **1** work relating to the buying and selling of goods and services
NOUN **2** an organisation that produces or sells goods, or provides a service

SYNONYMS: company, firm, organization

**busker** buskers
NOUN someone who sings or plays music in public places for money

**bus stop** bus stops
NOUN a place where the bus stops regularly for passengers to get on or off, usually marked with a sign

**busy** busier, busiest
ADJECTIVE **1** If you are **busy**, you are doing something and are not free to do anything else. • *She was too **busy** to come to the cinema with us.*
ADJECTIVE **2** A **busy** place is full of people doing things or moving about.

**but**
CONJUNCTION **1** used to introduce an idea that is opposite to what has gone before • *I love cooking, **but** I hate washing up afterwards.*
CONJUNCTION **2** used when you apologise for something • *Sorry, **but** I can't come to play tomorrow.*
PREPOSITION **3** except • *There was nothing to eat **but** potatoes.*

**butcher** butchers
NOUN a shopkeeper who prepares and sells meat

**butter**
NOUN a soft, fatty food made from cream, which is spread on bread and used in cooking

**buttercup** buttercups
NOUN a wild plant with bright yellow flowers

**butterfly** butterflies
NOUN a type of insect with large, colourful wings. **Butterflies** develop from caterpillars.
→ Have a look at the illustration for **life cycle**

**buttocks**
PLURAL NOUN Your **buttocks** are the part of your body that you sit on.

WORD HISTORY
from Old English *buttuc* meaning rounded slope

**button** buttons, buttoning, buttoned
NOUN **1** a small, hard round object sewn on to clothing such as shirts • *My new jeans fasten with **buttons** instead of a zip.*
NOUN **2** a small object on a piece of equipment that you press to make it work • *You must push the **button** down to switch the video on.*
VERB **3** If you **button** a garment, you fasten it using its buttons.

**buy** buys, buying, bought
VERB If you **buy** something, you get it by paying money for it.

**buzz** buzzes, buzzing, buzzed
VERB If something **buzzes**, it makes a humming sound, like a bee.

**buzzer** buzzers
NOUN a device that makes a buzzing sound. **Buzzers** are used to attract attention. • *I pressed the door **buzzer** but nobody was home.*

**by**
PREPOSITION **1** used to show who or what has done something • *The announcement was made **by** the head teacher.*
PREPOSITION **2** used to show how something is done • *He cheered us up **by** taking us to the cinema.*
PREPOSITION **3** next to or near to • *They live **by** the park.*
PREPOSITION **4** before a particular time • *We should finish **by** tea time.*
PREPOSITION **5** going past • *We drove **by** her house.*
ADVERB **6** past • *They would always say hello as they walked **by**.*

**bypass** bypasses
NOUN a road that takes traffic around the edge of a town instead of through the middle • *The centre of town is much quieter since they built the **bypass**.*

**byte** bytes
NOUN a unit of storage in a computer

# Cc

**cab** cabs
NOUN **1** a taxi
NOUN **2** The **cab** is where the driver sits in a lorry, bus or train.

**cabbage** cabbages
NOUN a large, green, leafy vegetable

**cabin** cabins
NOUN **1** a room in a ship where a passenger sleeps
NOUN **2** a small wooden house, usually in the country

**cabinet** cabinets
NOUN **1** a small cupboard • *a medicine cabinet*
NOUN **2** The **cabinet** in a government is a group of ministers who advise the leader and decide policies.

**cable** cables
NOUN **1** a strong, thick rope or chain
→ Have a look at the illustration for **bridge**
NOUN **2** a bundle of wires with a rubber covering, which carries electricity

**cable television**
NOUN a television service that comes through underground wires

**cactus** cacti or cactuses
NOUN a thick, fleshy plant that grows in deserts. **Cactuses** are usually covered in spikes.

**cadet** cadets
NOUN a young person being trained in the armed forces or police

**café** cafés
NOUN a place where you can buy light meals and drinks

WORD HISTORY
from the French *café* meaning coffee or coffee house

**caffeine**; also spelt **caffein**
NOUN a chemical in coffee and tea that makes you more active

**cage** cages
NOUN a box or room made with bars, in which birds or animals are kept

**cake** cakes, caking, caked
NOUN **1** a sweet food made from eggs, flour, butter and sugar
NOUN **2** a block of a hard substance such as soap
VERB **3** If something is **caked**, it becomes covered with a solid layer of something else
• *My shoes were **caked** in mud.*

**calamity** calamities
NOUN something terrible that happens, causing destruction and misery
• *The earthquake was a terrible **calamity**.*

SYNONYMS: disaster, catastrophe

**calcium**
NOUN a soft white mineral found in bones and teeth and in some foods. Milk and cheese are good sources of **calcium**.

**calculate** calculates, calculating, calculated
VERB If you **calculate** something, you work it out, usually by doing some arithmetic.
• *We **calculated** how much money we had raised from the sponsored walk.*

WORD HISTORY
from Latin *calculus* meaning stone or pebble, which the Romans used for counting

**calculation** calculations
NOUN something that you think about carefully and work out mathematically, or that you do on a machine such as a calculator

**calculator** calculators
NOUN a small electronic machine used for doing mathematical calculations

**calendar** calendars
NOUN a chart, usually organised month by month, showing the date of each day in a particular year • *We marked the end of term on the **calendar** in red.*

**calf** calves
NOUN **1** a young cow
NOUN **2** Your **calves** are the backs of your legs between your knees and ankles.

**call** calls, calling, called

VERB **1** If you **call** someone or something a particular name, that is their name. • *I will call my cat Pip.* • *That type of machine is called a combine harvester.*

VERB **2** If you **call** someone, you phone them.

VERB **3** If you **call** someone, you shout their name loudly.

NOUN **4** A **call** is a shout or a cry. • *We heard a call for help.*

**call off**

VERB If something is **called off** it is cancelled. • *The party was called off.*

**call on**

VERB If you **call on** someone, you pay them a short visit.

**calm** calmer, calmest

ADJECTIVE **1** Someone who is **calm** is quiet and does not show any worry or excitement.

ADJECTIVE **2** If the sea is **calm**, the water is not moving very much.

**calorie** calories

NOUN The amount of energy that food gives you is measured in **calories**.

**came**

VERB the past tense of **come**

**camel** camels

NOUN a large mammal with either one or two humps on its back. **Camels** live in hot desert areas and are used for carrying people and things.

**camera** cameras

NOUN a piece of equipment used for taking photographs or for filming

**camouflage** camouflages, camouflaging, camouflaged

NOUN **1** a way of avoiding being seen by having the same colour or appearance as the surroundings

VERB **2** To **camouflage** something is to hide it by giving it the same colour or appearance as its surroundings.

**camp** camps, camping, camped

NOUN **1** a place where people live in tents or stay in tents for a holiday

VERB **2** If you **camp**, you stay in a tent.

NOUN **3** a collection of buildings for soldiers or prisoners

**campaign** campaigns, campaigning, campaigned

VERB **1** When people **campaign**, they take action in order to achieve something. • *She campaigned against the export of live animals.*

NOUN **2** a series of actions that a group of people does in order to achieve something • *Parents began a campaign to save the school from closure.*

**camper** campers

NOUN someone who is staying in a tent for a holiday

**can** could; cans

VERB **1** If someone says you **can** do something, you are allowed to do it.

VERB **2** If you **can** do something, you are able to do it. • *I can say "hello" in French.*

NOUN **3** a metal container, often sealed, with food or drink inside

**canal** canals

NOUN a long, narrow, man-made stretch of water

**canary** canaries

NOUN a yellow songbird

**cancel** cancels, cancelling, cancelled

VERB If you **cancel** something that has been arranged, you stop it from happening. • *They cancelled the school trip.*

**cancer** cancers

NOUN a serious disease in which abnormal cells in a part of the body increase rapidly, causing growths

**candidate** candidates

NOUN a person who is being considered for a job

**candle** candles

NOUN a stick of hard wax with a piece of string called a wick through the middle. You light the wick to produce a flame.

**cane** canes

NOUN **1** the long, hollow stem of a plant such as bamboo

NOUN **2** strips of cane used for weaving baskets and other containers

NOUN **3** a long, narrow stick used to support plants

**canine** canines

ADJECTIVE **1** relating to dogs

NOUN **2** A **canine** is one of the pointed teeth near the front of the mouth in humans and some animals.

→ Have a look at the illustration for **teeth**

**cannibal** cannibals

NOUN a person who eats human flesh

**cannon** cannons or cannon

NOUN a large gun, usually on wheels, which fires heavy iron balls

**cannot**

VERB the same as *can not*

**canoe** canoes

NOUN a small, narrow boat that you row using a paddle

**can't**

VERB a contraction of *cannot*

**canteen** canteens

NOUN a place to eat in a school or workplace

**canvas** canvases

NOUN **1** strong, heavy cloth used for making things such as sails and tents
NOUN **2** a piece of canvas on which an artist does a painting

**canyon** canyons

NOUN a narrow river valley with steep sides

**cap** caps

NOUN **1** a soft, flat hat, often with a peak at the front
NOUN **2** a bottle top
NOUN **3** a small explosive used in toy guns

**capable**

ADJECTIVE **1** If you are **capable** of doing something, you are able to do it.
ADJECTIVE **2** Someone who is **capable** is able to do something well.

**capacity** capacities

NOUN the maximum amount that something can hold or produce ● *The arena has a seating* **capacity** *of two thousand.*

**capital** capitals

NOUN **1** The **capital** of a country is the city where the government meets. ● *Paris is the* **capital** *of France.*

NOUN **2** A **capital**, or a **capital** letter, is a larger, upper-case letter used at the beginning of a sentence or a name: **C**arol, **T**im.

**capsize** capsizes, capsizing, capsized

VERB If a boat **capsizes**, it turns upside down

**capsule** capsules

NOUN **1** a small container with medicine inside, which you swallow
NOUN **2** the part of a spacecraft in which astronauts travel

---

**WORD HISTORY**

from Latin *capsula* meaning little box

**captain** captains

NOUN **1** the officer in charge of a ship or aeroplane
NOUN **2** the leader of a sports team

**caption** captions

NOUN a title printed underneath a picture or a photograph

**captive** captives

NOUN someone who is locked up and kept prisoner

**capture** captures, capturing, captured

VERB If someone **captures** someone or something, they take them prisoner.

**car** cars

NOUN **1** a four-wheeled road vehicle with an engine and room to carry a few passengers

→ Have a look at the illustration

NOUN **2** a railway carriage used for a particular purpose ● *the buffet* **car**

**caravan** caravans

NOUN **1** a vehicle pulled by a car in which people live or spend their holidays
NOUN **2** a group of people and animals travelling together, usually across a desert

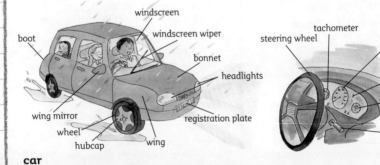

windscreen
windscreen wiper
boot
bonnet
headlights
wing mirror
wheel
hubcap
wing
registration plate

tachometer
steering wheel
speedometer
warning l
fuel gauge
indicator

**arbohydrate carbohydrates**
NOUN a substance that gives you energy. It is found in foods like sugar and bread.

**arbon**
NOUN a chemical found in coal, diamonds and graphite. All living things contain **carbon**.

**arbon dioxide**
NOUN the gas that human beings and other animals breathe out

**arbon footprint carbon footprints**
NOUN the amount of carbon monoxide produced by a person, company or country

**arbon monoxide**
NOUN a poisonous gas that is produced especially by the engines of vehicles

**ard cards**
NOUN **1** a piece of stiff paper or plastic with a message or information on it • *birthday* **card** • *credit* **card**
NOUN **2** When you play **cards**, you play a game using special playing cards.
NOUN **3** strong, stiff paper

**ardboard**
NOUN thick, stiff paper, which is stronger than card

**ardigan cardigans**
NOUN a knitted jacket that fastens up the front

**ardinal**
ADJECTIVE A **cardinal** number is a number such as 1, 3, or 10 that tells you how many things there are in a group but not what order they are in.

**are cares, caring, cared**
VERB **1** If you **care** about something or someone, you are concerned about them and interested in them.
VERB **2** If you **care** for a person or an animal, you look after them.
NOUN **3** worry or trouble • *She didn't have a* **care** *in the world.*
NOUN **4** If you do something with **care**, you concentrate very hard on it so that you don't make mistakes. • *He wrote the phone number down with great* **care**.
PHRASE **5** If you **take care of** a person or an animal, you look after them. • *Shakira said she would* **take care of** *the hamsters while we were on holiday.*

**areer careers**
NOUN Your **career** is the series of jobs you have in life, often in the same occupation. • *a teaching* **career**

**careful**
ADJECTIVE behaving sensibly and with care
ANTONYM: careless

**carefully**
ADVERB behaving in a sensible way and with care
ANTONYM: carelessly

**careless**
ADJECTIVE not paying attention to what you are doing
SYNONYMS: slapdash, sloppy
ANTONYM: careful

**carelessly**
ADJECTIVE without paying attention to what you are doing
ANTONYM: carefully

**carelessness**
NOUN **Carelessness** is when you do not pay attention to what you are doing.
ANTONYM: carefulness

**caretaker caretakers**
NOUN a person who looks after a large building such as a school

**cargo cargoes**
NOUN goods carried on a ship or plane

**Caribbean**
NOUN **1** the large sea between Central America and South America
ADJECTIVE **2** relating to the **Caribbean** Sea or the islands in it • *I love* **Caribbean** *food.*

**carnation carnations**
NOUN a plant with thin leaves and scented white, pink or red flowers

**carnival carnivals**
NOUN a public festival with music, processions and dancing

**carnivore carnivores**
NOUN an animal that eats meat

**carnivorous**
ADJECTIVE A **carnivorous** animal eats meat.

**carol carols**
NOUN a religious song usually sung at Christmas time

a b c d e f g h i j k l m n o p q r s t u v w x y z

**59**

**carpenter carpenters**
NOUN a person who makes and repairs wooden things

**carpentry**
NOUN the work of making and repairing wooden things

**carpet carpets**
NOUN a thick floor covering usually made of material like wool

**carriage carriages**
NOUN 1 one of the separate sections of a passenger train
NOUN 2 an old-fashioned vehicle for carrying passengers, usually pulled by horses

**Carroll diagram Carroll diagrams**
NOUN a way of sorting and displaying information in the form of a grid

Girls and boys that have black hair

**carrot carrots**
NOUN a long, thin, orange-coloured root vegetable

**carry carries, carrying, carried**
VERB 1 If you **carry** something, you hold it and take it somewhere.
VERB 2 When a vehicle **carries** people, they travel in it.
VERB 3 If people or animals **carry** a germ or a disease, they can pass it on to others.
VERB 4 If a sound **carries** it can be heard a long way off. ● *Their voices **carried** across the valley.*

**cart carts**
NOUN a vehicle with wheels, used for carrying things and usually pulled by horses or cattle

**carton cartons**
NOUN a cardboard or plastic container

**cartoon cartoons**
NOUN 1 a humorous drawing in a newspaper comic or magazine
NOUN 2 a film in which all the characters an scenes are drawn

**cartridge cartridges**
NOUN 1 a tube containing a bullet and an explosive substance, used in guns
NOUN 2 a small plastic container filled with ink that you put in a pen or a printer

**cartwheel cartwheels**
NOUN an acrobatic movement in which you lift both arms in the air then throw yoursel sideways on to one hand, swinging your body around in a circle with your legs straight until you land on your feet again

**carve carves, carving, carved**
VERB If you **carve** something, you shape it c slice it with a knife.

**cascade cascades, cascading, cascade**
NOUN 1 a small waterfall or group of waterfalls flowing down a rocky hillside
VERB 2 When water **cascades**, it flows very fast down a hillside or over rocks.

**case cases**
NOUN 1 a box for keeping or carrying things in
NOUN 2 a particular situation or event
● *a bad **case** of measles*
NOUN 3 A crime that the police are investigating is called a **case**.
NOUN 4 If something is written in lower **cas** it is written in small letters. If it is written i upper **case**, it is written in capital letters.

**cash**
NOUN money in notes and coins

**cashier cashiers**
NOUN the person who deals with money in place such as a shop or a bank

**casserole casseroles**
NOUN 1 a stew made with meat, vegetables or fish that is baked in the oven
NOUN 2 a dish with a lid, which is used for cooking

**cast casts, casting, cast**
NOUN 1 all the people who act in a play or film
NOUN 2 an object made by pouring a liquid such as plaster into a container and leavir it to harden
VERB 3 If an object **casts** a shadow on to a place, it makes a shadow fall there.

**astaway castaways**

NOUN someone who has been shipwrecked but manages to survive on a lonely shore or an island

**astle castles**

NOUN a large building with walls or ditches round it to protect it from attack

→ Have a look at the illustration

---

WORD HISTORY
from Latin *castellum* meaning small fort

---

**asual**

ADJECTIVE **1** happening by chance and without planning • *I made a casual remark.*
ADJECTIVE **2 Casual** clothes are suitable for informal occasions.

**asualty casualties**

NOUN a person killed or injured in an accident or a war • *There were many casualties after the motorway crash.*

**at cats**

NOUN a small, furry mammal with whiskers, a tail and sharp claws, often kept as a pet

**atalogue catalogues**

NOUN a list of things, such as the goods you can buy from a company, the objects in a museum, or the books in a library • *All the products are shown in their new catalogue.*

**atalyst catalysts**

NOUN a substance that causes a chemical reaction to take place more quickly

**atastrophe catastrophes**

NOUN a terrible disaster

**catastrophic**

ADJECTIVE Something that is **catastrophic** is extremely bad and causes a lot of damage, suffering or problems. • *catastrophic floods*

**catch catches, catching, caught**

VERB **1** If you **catch** an object that is moving through the air, you grasp it with your hands.
VERB **2** If you **catch** a person or animal, you capture them. • *The police caught the thief.*
VERB **3** If you **catch** a bus, train or plane, you get on it and travel somewhere.
VERB **4** If you **catch** a cold or a disease, you become ill with it.
NOUN **5** a hook that fastens or locks a door or window

**catching**

ADJECTIVE If a disease or illness is **catching**, it spreads very quickly. • *Measles is catching.*

**catchy catchier, catchiest**

ADJECTIVE Something that is **catchy**, such as a tune, is pleasant and easy to remember.

**category categories**

NOUN a group of things that have something in common

**caterpillar caterpillars**

NOUN the larva of a butterfly or moth. **Caterpillars** look like small, coloured worms and feed on plants.

→ Have a look at the illustration for **life cycle**

**cathedral cathedrals**

NOUN an important church with a bishop in charge of it • *Canterbury Cathedral*

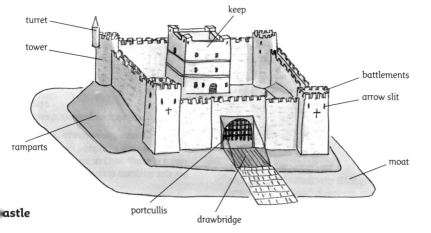

turret
tower
keep
battlements
arrow slit
ramparts
moat
**astle**
portcullis
drawbridge

**Catholic** Catholics
NOUN **1** a Roman **Catholic**
ADJECTIVE **2** belonging to the Roman **Catholic** religion

**cattle**
PLURAL NOUN cows and bulls kept by farmers

**caught**
VERB the past tense of **catch**

**cauldron** cauldrons
NOUN a large, round metal cooking pot, especially one that sits over a fire

WORD HISTORY
from Latin *caldarium* meaning hot bath

**cauliflower** cauliflowers
NOUN a large, round, white vegetable surrounded by green leaves

**cause** causes, causing, caused
VERB **1** To **cause** something means to make it happen.
NOUN **2** The **cause** of something is the thing that makes it happen. • *The cause of the explosion was a gas leak.*

**cautious**
ADJECTIVE Someone who is **cautious** acts carefully in order to avoid danger or disappointment.

**cavalry**
NOUN The **cavalry** is the part of an army that fights on horseback or in armoured vehicles such as tanks.

**cave** caves, caving, caved
NOUN a large hole in the side of a cliff or under the ground
**cave in**
VERB If a roof **caves in**, it collapses inwards.

**caveman** cavemen
NOUN **Cavemen** were men who lived in caves in prehistoric times.

**cavewoman** cavewomen
NOUN **Cavewomen** were women who lived in caves in prehistoric times.

**cavity** cavities
NOUN a small hole in something solid
• *There were cavities in his back teeth.*

**CD**
NOUN an abbreviation for *compact disc*

**CD-ROM**
NOUN a way of storing video, sound or text on a compact disc that can be played on a computer. **CD-ROM** is an abbreviation for *compact disc read-only memory.*

**CE**
ADJECTIVE You use **CE** in dates to show the number of years or centuries after the year in which Jesus Christ is believed to have been born. **CE** is an abbreviation for *Common Era.*

**cease** ceases, ceasing, ceased
VERB **1** If something **ceases**, it stops.
VERB **2** If you **cease** doing something, you stop doing it.

**ceiling** ceilings
NOUN the roof inside a room

**celebrate** celebrates, celebrating, celebrated
VERB If you **celebrate** something, you do something special and enjoyable because it. • *We felt like celebrating the end of exam*

**celebration** celebrations
NOUN a party or special event that you have because something good has happened
• *All the family were there for my grandma's 60th birthday celebration.*

**celebrity** celebrities
NOUN a famous person

**celery**
NOUN a vegetable with long, pale green stalks

**celestial**
ADJECTIVE relating to the sky • *She was fascinated by stars and other celestial objec*

**cell** cells
NOUN **1** In biology, a **cell** is the smallest pa of an animal or plant that can exist by itse Humans, animals and plants are made up of millions of **cells**.
NOUN **2** a small room in a prison or police station where a prisoner is locked up
NOUN **3** In physics, a **cell** is a device that produces electrical energy by chemical reaction.

**cellar** cellars
NOUN a room underneath a building

**cellist** cellists
NOUN someone who plays a cello

PRONUNCIATION TIP
This word is pronounced **chell**-ist.

A B C D E F G H I J K L M N O P Q R S T U V W X Y Z

**ello cellos**

NOUN a large, stringed musical instrument that you play sitting down

---

PRONUNCIATION TIP
This word is pronounced **chell**-oh.

---

**elsius**

NOUN a scale for measuring temperature in which water freezes at 0 degrees (0 °C) and boils at 100 degrees (100 °C)

---

WORD HISTORY
named after Anders *Celsius* (1701–1744) who invented it

---

**ement**

NOUN a grey powder that is mixed with sand and water to make concrete

**emetery cemeteries**

NOUN an area of land where dead people are buried

**nsus censuses**

NOUN an official survey of the population of a country

**nt cents**

NOUN In some countries a **cent** is a unit of currency.

**ntenary centenaries**

NOUN the hundredth anniversary of something

**ntigrade**

NOUN another word for **Celsius**

**ntilitre centilitres**

NOUN a unit of volume (cl). One **centilitre** is equal to ten millilitres (ml) and is the same as a cubic centimetre (cc).

**ntimetre centimetres**

NOUN a unit of length (cm). One **centimetre** is equal to ten millimetres (mm).

**ntipede centipedes**

NOUN a long, thin creature with many pairs of legs

---

WORD HISTORY
from Latin *centum* + *pedes* meaning a hundred feet

---

**ntral**

ADJECTIVE **1** Something **central** is in the middle.

ADJECTIVE **2** An idea that is **central** is the main idea.

**central heating**

NOUN a heating system in which water or air is heated and passed round a building through pipes and radiators

**centre centres**

NOUN **1** the middle of an object or area

NOUN **2** a building where people go for activities, meetings or help ● *We played badminton at the sports centre.*

**century centuries**

NOUN a period of one hundred years

**ceramic ceramics**

NOUN **1** a hard material made by baking clay at very high temperatures

PLURAL NOUN **2 Ceramics** are objects made out of clay.

**cereal cereals**

NOUN **1** a food made from grain, often eaten with milk for breakfast

NOUN **2** a plant that produces edible grain, such as wheat, oats, barley and rye

**ceremony ceremonies**

NOUN a formal event such as a wedding or prizegiving

**certain**

ADJECTIVE **1** If you are **certain** about something, you are sure it is true. ● *She is certain she wants to be a vet.*

ADJECTIVE **2** You use **certain** to refer to a particular person, place or thing. ● *I like certain animals, for example cats and dogs.*

**certainly**

ADVERB without any doubt ● *"Will you be at the party?" "I certainly will."*

**certificate certificates**

NOUN an official piece of paper that proves that something took place ● *a birth certificate*

**chaffinch chaffinches**

NOUN a small European bird with black and white wings

**chain chains**

NOUN **1** a number of metal rings linked together in a line

→ Have a look at the illustration for **bicycle**

NOUN **2** a number of things in a series or connected to each other ● *a chain of shops* ● *a chain of events*

**chair chairs**

NOUN a seat for one person to sit on, with a back and four legs

## chalet chalets

NOUN a small wooden house with a sloping roof, especially found in mountain areas or holiday camps

## chalk

NOUN a soft, white rock. Small sticks of **chalk** are used for writing or drawing with.

## chalky chalkier, chalkiest

ADJECTIVE looking, feeling or tasting like chalk

## challenge challenges, challenging, challenged

NOUN **1** something new and exciting that needs a lot of effort • *Learning how to cook is a new **challenge** for me.*
VERB **2** If someone **challenges** you, they suggest that you compete with them. • *She **challenged** me to a game of table tennis.*

## challenging

ADJECTIVE If you find something **challenging**, you find it quite difficult.

## chameleon chameleons

NOUN a lizard that is able to change the colour of its skin to match the colour of its surroundings

### WORD HISTORY

from Greek *khamai* + *leon* meaning ground lion

## champagne champagnes

NOUN a sparkling white wine made in France

## champion champions

NOUN a person who wins a competition

## championship championships

NOUN a competition to find the best player or players of a particular sport

## chance chances

NOUN **1** how possible or likely something is
• *I think we've got a good **chance** of winning.*
NOUN **2** an opportunity to do something
• *This is your **chance** to be a TV star!*
NOUN **3** a possibility that something dangerous or unpleasant may happen
PHRASE **4** Something that happens **by chance** happens unexpectedly, without being planned.

## chancellor chancellors

NOUN the head of government in some European countries

## Chancellor of the Exchequer

NOUN the government minister in charge of finance and taxes in the UK

## change changes, changing, changed

NOUN **1** money you get back when you pay for something with more money than it costs
VERB **2** When something **changes**, or you **change** it, it becomes different. • *The win* **changed** *direction.*

## channel channels

NOUN **1** a wavelength on which television programmes are broadcast. **Channel** can also mean the television station itself.
NOUN **2** a passage for water or other liquid
NOUN **3** The **Channel**, or the English **Channel**, is the stretch of sea between England and France.

## chaos

NOUN a state of complete disorder
• *The demonstration ended in **chaos**.*

## chaotic

ADJECTIVE A **chaotic** situation is one that is completely disorganised and confusing.
• *There were **chaotic** scenes at the airport when hundreds of flights were cancelled.*

## chapel chapels

NOUN **1** a section of a church or cathedral with its own altar
NOUN **2** a type of small church

## chapter chapters

NOUN one of the parts into which a book is divided

## character characters

NOUN **1** all the qualities that make a person or a place special • *She has a gentle* **character**.
NOUN **2** The **characters** in a film, play or book are the people in it.

## characteristic characteristics

NOUN **1** a special quality about a person, place or thing
ADJECTIVE **2** typical of a place or person • *Noi and traffic fumes are **characteristic** of cities*

## charades

NOUN a party game where one team guesses what the other team is acting out

## charcoal

NOUN burnt wood used as a fuel. **Charcoa** is also used for drawing.

**charge charges, charging, charged**

VERB **1** If someone **charges** you money, they ask you to pay for something you have bought or received.

VERB **2** If someone **charges** an electronic device, they put electricity into its battery. • Alex forgot to **charge** his mobile phone.

VERB **3** If someone **charges** somewhere, they rush in that direction. • She **charged** into the room.

PHRASE **4** If you are **in charge of** someone or something, you are responsible for them. • I left him **in charge of** the shop while I went out.

**chariot chariots**

NOUN a two-wheeled open vehicle pulled by horses in ancient times

**charity charities**

NOUN **1** an organisation that raises money to help people in need

NOUN **2** money or other help given to people in need

**charm charms, charming, charmed**

NOUN **1** something you wear for good luck

NOUN **2** the quality of being attractive and pleasant

VERB **3** If you **charm** someone, you use your charm to please them.

**chart charts**

NOUN a diagram or table showing information

**chase chases, chasing, chased**

VERB If you **chase** someone, you run after them or follow them in order to catch them or make them leave a place.

**chat chats, chatting, chatted**

NOUN **1** a friendly talk with someone

VERB **2** When people **chat**, they talk to each other in a friendly way about things that are not very important.

VERB **3** When people **chat**, they send each other short messages on the internet or on their phones.

**chatroom chatrooms**

NOUN an internet site where users have discussions with each other

**chatter chatters, chattering, chattered**

VERB **1** When people **chatter**, they talk about unimportant things.

VERB **2** If your teeth **chatter**, they knock together and make a clicking noise because you are cold.

**chatty chattier, chattiest**

ADJECTIVE Someone who is **chatty** likes to talk to people.

**chauffeur chauffeurs**

NOUN a person whose job is to drive another person's car • He had a **chauffeur** to drive him everywhere.

**cheap cheaper, cheapest**

ADJECTIVE **1** Something that is **cheap** costs very little money.

ADJECTIVE **2 Cheap** sometimes means of poor quality.

**cheat cheats, cheating, cheated**

VERB If someone **cheats** in a game or exam, they break the rules in order to do better.

**check checks, checking, checked**

VERB **1** If you **check** something, you examine it to make sure that everything is all right. • **Check** your work carefully when you finish.

NOUN **2** an inspection to make sure that everything is all right

NOUN **3 Checks** are different coloured squares that form a pattern.

**checkout checkouts**

NOUN the place in a supermarket where you pay for your goods

**cheek cheeks**

NOUN **1** Your **cheeks** are the sides of your face below your eyes.

NOUN **2** speech or behaviour that is rude and disrespectful • Their grandparents won't stand any **cheek** from them.

**cheekily**

ADVERB in a way that is rude and disrespectful, but can be slightly amusing

**cheeky cheekier, cheekiest**

ADJECTIVE speaking or behaving in a way that is rude and disrespectful, but can be slightly amusing

**cheer cheers, cheering, cheered**

VERB When people **cheer**, they shout loudly and happily. • We **cheered** our team when they won.

**cheerful**

ADJECTIVE A **cheerful** person is happy.

**cheerfully**

ADVERB in a happy way

**cheese cheeses**

NOUN a solid savoury food made from milk

a b c d e f g h i j k l m n o p q r s t u v w x y z

**65**

**cheetah cheetahs**

NOUN a wild mammal like a large cat with black spots, mainly found in Africa

WORD HISTORY
from Sanskrit *citra* + *kaya* meaning speckled body

**chef chefs**

NOUN a head cook in a restaurant or hotel

WORD HISTORY
from French *chef* meaning head

**chemical chemicals**

NOUN 1 a substance made by the use of chemistry • Dangerous **chemicals** should be handled carefully.
ADJECTIVE 2 involved in chemistry or using chemicals • a **chemical** reaction

**chemist chemists**

NOUN a shop that sells medicines and cosmetics

**chemistry**

NOUN the scientific study of substances and the ways in which they change when they are combined

**cheque cheques**

NOUN a personalised printed piece of paper that people can use to pay for things

**cherry cherries**

NOUN a small, juicy fruit with a red, yellow or black skin and a hard stone in the centre

**chess**

NOUN a game played on a board with 64 squares. Each player has 16 pieces.

**chest chests**

NOUN 1 the front part of your body between your shoulders and your waist
NOUN 2 a large wooden box used for storing things

**chestnut chestnuts**

NOUN 1 a reddish-brown nut that grows inside a prickly, green outer covering
NOUN 2 the tree that produces these nuts
ADJECTIVE 3 Something that is **chestnut** is reddish-brown in colour.

**chew chews, chewing, chewed**

VERB When you **chew** something, you use your teeth to break it up in your mouth before swallowing it.

**chewing gum**

NOUN a kind of sweet that you chew for a long time, but which you do not swallow

**chick chicks**

NOUN a young bird

**chicken chickens**

NOUN a bird kept on a farm for its eggs and meat; also the meat of this bird

**chickenpox**

NOUN an illness that causes a fever and blister-like spots to appear on the skin

**chief chiefs**

NOUN 1 the leader of a group or organisatio
ADJECTIVE 2 main or most important

**chilblain chilblains**

NOUN a sore, itchy swelling on a finger or to which causes discomfort in cold weather

**child children**

NOUN 1 a young person who is not yet an adult

SYNONYMS: kid, youngster

NOUN 2 Someone's **child** is their son or daughter.

**childhood childhoods**

NOUN Your **childhood** is the time when yo are a child.

**childish**

ADJECTIVE If someone is **childish**, they are n acting in an adult way.

ANTONYM: adult

**childminder childminders**

NOUN a person who is paid to look after children while their parents are at work

**children**

PLURAL NOUN the plural of **child**

**chill chills, chilling, chilled**

VERB 1 When you **chill** something, you ma it cold. • **Chill** the orange juice before you drink it.
NOUN 2 a feverish cold
NOUN 3 a feeling of cold • the **chill** of early morning

**chilli chillies**

NOUN the red or green seed pod of a type o pepper that has a very hot, spicy taste

**chilly chillier, chilliest**

ADJECTIVE 1 **Chilly** weather is rather cold.
ADJECTIVE 2 If people behave in a **chilly** way they are not very friendly.

A
B
C
D
E
F
G
H
I
J
K
L
M
N
O
P
Q
R
S
T
U
V
W
X
Y
Z

**ime chimes, chiming, chimed**
VERB **1** When a bell **chimes**, it makes a clear ringing sound.
NOUN **2 Chimes** are a set of bells or other objects that make ringing sounds.

**imney chimneys**
NOUN a pipe above a fireplace or furnace through which smoke from the fire can escape

**impanzee chimpanzees**
NOUN a small ape with dark fur that lives in forests in Africa

**in chins**
NOUN the part of your face below your mouth

**ina**
NOUN plates, cups, saucers and other dishes that are made from fine clay

**ink chinks**
NOUN **1** a small, narrow opening • *a chink in the fence*
NOUN **2** a small ringing sound, like glasses touching each other

**ip chips, chipping, chipped**
NOUN **1 Chips** are thin strips of fried potato.
NOUN **2** a tiny piece of silicon inside a computer, which is used to form electronic circuits • *computer chips*
VERB **3** If you **chip** an object, you break a small piece off it.

**irp chirps, chirping, chirped**
VERB When a bird **chirps**, it makes a short, high-pitched sound.

**isel chisels, chiselling, chiselled**
NOUN **1** a tool with a long metal blade and a sharp edge at the end. **Chisels** are used for cutting and shaping wood, stone or metal.
VERB **2** If you **chisel** wood, stone or metal, you cut or shape it using a chisel.

**lorine**
NOUN a poisonous greenish-yellow gas with a strong, unpleasant smell. It is used to disinfect water and to make bleach.

**ocolate chocolates**
NOUN a sweet food made from cocoa beans

**WORD HISTORY**
from Aztec *xococ* + *atl* meaning bitter water

**choice choices**
NOUN **1** a range of different things that are available to choose from

> SYNONYMS: range, variety

NOUN **2** something that you choose • *You made a good choice when you bought this book.*

**choir choirs**
NOUN a group of singers, for example in a church

**choke chokes, choking, choked**
VERB If you **choke** on something, it prevents you from breathing properly. • *He choked on a fish bone.*

**cholesterol**
NOUN a substance found in all animal fats, tissues and blood

**choose chooses, choosing, chose, chosen**
VERB If you **choose** something, you decide to have it or do it.

> SYNONYMS: pick, select

**chop chops, chopping, chopped**
VERB **1** If you **chop** something, you cut it with quick, heavy strokes using an axe or a knife. • *Mum chopped the logs for firewood.*
NOUN **2** a small piece of pork or lamb that contains a bone • *We had chops and broccoli for dinner.*

**choppy**
ADJECTIVE When the sea or a stretch of water is **choppy**, there are a lot of waves on it because it is windy.

**chopstick chopsticks**
NOUN **Chopsticks** are a pair of thin sticks used for eating Chinese and Japanese food.

**choral**
ADJECTIVE for a choir

**chord chords**
NOUN a group of three or more musical notes played together

**chore chores**
NOUN an uninteresting job that has to be done

**chorus choruses**
NOUN **1** a part of a song that is repeated after each verse
NOUN **2** a large group of singers

**67**

A
B
C
D
E
F
G
H
I
J
K
L
M
N
O
P
Q
R
S
T
U
V
W
X
Y
Z

**chose**
VERB the past tense of **choose**

**chosen**
VERB **1** the past participle of **choose**
VERB **2** When you are **chosen**, you are picked to do something. • *I was **chosen** for the volleyball team.*

**christen christens, christening, christened**
VERB When a priest **christens** someone, they name them in a ceremony where water is poured over their head as a sign that they are a member of the Christian church.

**christening christenings**
NOUN a ceremony in which a person becomes a member of the Christian church

**Christian Christians**
NOUN a person who believes in Jesus Christ and his teachings

**Christianity**
NOUN a religion based on Jesus Christ and his teachings

**Christmas Christmases**
NOUN a Christian festival held on December 25th to celebrate the birth of Jesus Christ

**chrome**
NOUN metal plated with chromium, a hard, silver-grey metal

**chromosome chromosomes**
NOUN the part of a cell in living things that contains the genes that determine what characteristics the animal or plant will have

**chronic**
ADJECTIVE lasting a very long time or never stopping • *He suffers from **chronic** hay fever.*

**chronological**
ADJECTIVE arranged in the order in which things happened • *Tell me the whole story in **chronological** order.*

**chrysalis chrysalises**
NOUN a butterfly or moth when it is developing from being a caterpillar to being a fully grown adult

→ Have a look at the illustration for **life cycle**

**chrysanthemum chrysanthemums**
NOUN a plant with large, brightly-coloured flowers

**chuckle chuckles, chuckling, chuckles**
VERB When you **chuckle**, you laugh quietly. • *They were **chuckling** quietly to themselves.*

**chunk chunks**
NOUN a thick piece of something

SYNONYMS: hunk, lump, piece

**chunky chunkier, chunkiest**
ADJECTIVE large and thick • *a **chunky** silver necklace*

**church churches**
NOUN a building where Christians go for religious services and worship

**churchyard churchyards**
NOUN an area of land around a church, oft used as a graveyard

**churn churns, churning, churned**
NOUN **1** a container used for making milk c cream into butter
VERB **2** When you **churn** something, you s it vigorously, for example when making m into butter.

**churn out**
VERB If you **churn out** something, you produce it quickly in large numbers.
• *They **churned out** hundreds of leaflets advertising the dance.*

**chutney**
NOUN a strong-tasting, thick sauce made from fruit, vinegar and spices

**cider**
NOUN an alcoholic drink made from apples

**cigar cigars**
NOUN a roll of dried tobacco leaves, which people smoke

**cigarette cigarettes**
NOUN a thin tube of paper containing tobacco, which people smoke

**cinder cinders**
NOUN **Cinders** are small pieces of burnt material left after something such as woc or coal has burned.

**cinema cinemas**
NOUN a place where people go to watch films • *Every Saturday night they used to go the **cinema**.*

**circle circles, circling, circled**
NOUN **1** a regular, two-dimensional round shape. Every point on the edge is the same distance from the centre.
VERB **2** to move around in a circle • *We stood and watched as the gulls **circled** overhead.*

**circuit circuits**
NOUN **1** the path of an electric current
NOUN **2** a racecourse
NOUN **3** A training **circuit** is a course of physical activities.

**circular**
ADJECTIVE having the shape of a circle

**circulation circulations**
NOUN **1** the movement of blood around a body
NOUN **2** the number of copies of a newspaper or magazine that are sold each time it is issued

**circulatory system**
NOUN Your **circulatory system** is the system that moves blood around your body.

**circumference circumferences**
NOUN the outer line or edge of a circle. The length of this line is also called the **circumference**.

**circumstance circumstances**
NOUN The **circumstances** of a situation or event are the conditions that affect what happens. • *He did well under difficult **circumstances**.*

**circus circuses**
NOUN a travelling show performed in a large tent, with performers such as clowns and acrobats

**cistern cisterns**
NOUN a tank in which water is stored, such as in the roof of a house, or above a toilet

**citizen citizens**
NOUN The **citizens** of a country or city are the people who live in it or belong to it.

**citrus fruit citrus fruits**
NOUN **Citrus fruits** are juicy, sharp-tasting fruits such as oranges, lemons and grapefruit.

**city cities**
NOUN a large town where many people live and work

**civil**
ADJECTIVE **1** relating to the citizens of a place
ADJECTIVE **2** Someone who is **civil** is polite.

**civilian civilians**
NOUN a person who is not in the armed forces

**civilisation civilisations**; also spelt **civilization**
NOUN **1** a large group of people with a high level of organisation and culture • *We're learning about the ancient **civilisations** of Greece, Rome and Egypt.*
NOUN **2** a highly developed and organised way of life

**civilised**; also spelt **civilized**
ADJECTIVE **1** A **civilised** society is one with a highly developed social organisation and a comfortable way of life.
ADJECTIVE **2** A **civilised** person is polite and reasonable.

**civil war civil wars**
NOUN a war between groups of people who live in the same country

**cl**
an abbreviation for *centilitre*

**claim claims, claiming, claimed**
VERB **1** If you **claim** that something is the case, you say that it is so.
VERB **2** If you **claim** something, you ask for it because you believe you have a right to it.

**clamber clambers, clambering, clambered**
VERB If you **clamber** somewhere, you climb there with difficulty. • *We **clambered** over the rocks to get to the beach.*

**clammy** clammier, clammiest
ADJECTIVE unpleasantly damp and sticky
• *The weather was very* **clammy**.

**clamp** clamps, clamping, clamped
NOUN **1** a device that holds something firmly in place
VERB **2** When you **clamp** one thing to another, you fasten them together with a clamp.

**clan** clans
NOUN a group of families related to each other by being descended from the same ancestor

**clang** clangs, clanging, clanged
VERB When something made of metal **clangs**, or when you **clang** it, it makes a loud, ringing sound.

**clank** clanks, clanking, clanked
VERB When something **clanks**, it makes a loud, metallic sound.

**clap** claps, clapping, clapped
VERB **1** When you **clap**, you hit your hands together loudly to show that you have enjoyed something or that you approve of something.
NOUN **2** a sudden loud noise of thunder

**clarify** clarifies, clarifying, clarified
VERB If you **clarify** something, you make it clear and easier to understand.

**clarinet** clarinets
NOUN a woodwind instrument with a straight tube and a single reed in its mouthpiece

**clarity**
NOUN The **clarity** of something is its clearness. • *The* **clarity** *of the water made me think it was very clean.*

**clash** clashes, clashing, clashed
VERB **1** Colours or ideas that **clash** are so different that they do not go together.
• *Debbie's red shirt* **clashed** *with her green shorts.*
VERB **2** If one event **clashes** with another, they happen at the same time, so you cannot go to both.
VERB **3** If people **clash** with each other, they fight or argue.

**clasp** clasps, clasping, clasped
VERB **1** If you **clasp** something, you hold it tightly.
NOUN **2** a fastening such as a hook or a catch

**class** classes
NOUN **1** a group of pupils or students taught together, or a lesson that they have together

NOUN **2** A **class** of people or things is a gro of them of a particular type. • *Beetles and ants belong to different* **classes** *of insect.*

SYNONYMS: group, kind, type

**classic**
ADJECTIVE Something described as **classic** is considered a high quality example of something. • *He has a* **classic** *car.*

**classical**
ADJECTIVE **1** traditional in style and content
• **classical** *ballet*
ADJECTIVE **2** **Classical** music is serious mus thought to be of lasting value.

**classification** classifications
NOUN the process of arranging things into groups with something in common

**classify** classifies, classifying, classifi
VERB to arrange things into groups with something in common • *We* **classified** *the foods into three groups: fruits, vegetables an meats.*

**classroom** classrooms
NOUN a room in a school where lessons ta place

**clatter** clatters, clattering, clattered
VERB **1** When things **clatter**, they hit each other with a loud, rattling noise.
NOUN **2** a loud noise made by hard things hitting against each other • *There was a gr* **clatter** *when the waitress dropped the tray.*

**clause** clauses
NOUN In grammar, a **clause** is a group of words with a subject and a verb, which mc be a complete sentence or part of a senten

**claw** claws, clawing, clawed
NOUN **1** An animal's **claws** are the hard, curved nails at the end of its feet.
NOUN **2** The **claws** of a crab or a lobster ar the two jointed parts at the end of the leg used for holding things.
VERB **3** If an animal **claws** something, it di its claws into it.

**clay**
NOUN a type of earth that is soft and sticky when wet and hard when baked dry. It is used to make pottery and bricks.

**clean** cleaner, cleanest; cleans, cleaning, cleaned
ADJECTIVE **1** free from dirt or unwanted mark
VERB **2** to remove dirt from something

**ear clearer, clearest; clears, clearing, cleared**

ADJECTIVE **1** easy to understand, see or hear • *The instructions on the packet were very clear*.

ADJECTIVE **2** easy to see through • *a clear liquid*

ANTONYM: opaque

VERB **3** To **clear** unwanted things from a place is to remove them. • *We cleared the dirty dishes from the table.*

VERB **4** If you **clear** a fence or other obstacle, you jump over it without touching it.

**clear up**

VERB When you **clear up** a place, you tidy it and put things away.

**early**

ADVERB **1** in a way that people can easily understand, see or hear • *He spoke loudly and clearly.*

ADVERB **2** obviously and without any doubt • *Clearly, the answer has to be no.*

**ef clefs**

NOUN a symbol at the beginning of a line of music that shows the pitch of the notes

**ench clenches, clenching, clenched**

VERB **1** When you **clench** your fist, you curl your fingers up tightly.

VERB **2** When you **clench** your teeth, you squeeze them together tightly, either in pain or in anger.

**erk clerks**

NOUN a person who keeps records or accounts in an office, bank or law court

**ever cleverer, cleverest**

ADJECTIVE **1** intelligent and quick to understand things

SYNONYMS: bright, intelligent, smart

ADJECTIVE **2** very effective or skilful • *We came up with a clever plan.*

**iché clichés**

NOUN an idea or phrase that is no longer effective because it has been used so much. For example, *in this day and age* and *over the moon*.

**ick clicks, clicking, clicked**

VERB **1** When something **clicks** or when you **click** it, it makes a short snapping sound.

VERB **2** If you **click** on an area of a computer screen, you point the cursor at that area and press one of the buttons on the mouse in order to make something happen. If you

double-**click**, you press it quickly twice. • *Click on the link at the top of the page.*

NOUN **3** a sound of something clicking

**client clients**

NOUN someone who pays a professional person or company for a service

**cliff cliffs**

NOUN a high area of land with a very steep side, usually next to the sea

**cliffhanger cliffhangers**

NOUN a very exciting or frightening situation, usually in a television or radio serial, where you are left not knowing what is going to happen next

**climate climates**

NOUN the general weather conditions that are typical of a place

**climate change**

NOUN changes in the Earth's climate, especially the rise in temperature caused by high levels of pollution

**climax climaxes**

NOUN the most exciting moment of something, usually near the end

**climb climbs, climbing, climbed**

VERB **1** If you **climb** something, such as a tree, mountain or ladder, you move towards the top of it.

VERB **2** If you **climb** somewhere, you move there with difficulty. • *We climbed over the high wall.*

NOUN **3** a movement upwards • *I was tired after the long climb to the top of the hill.*

**climber climbers**

NOUN someone who climbs rocks or mountains

**cling clings, clinging, clung**

VERB If you **cling** to something, you hold on to it tightly.

**clinic clinics**

NOUN a place where people go for medical advice or treatment

**clip clips, clipping, clipped**

NOUN **1** a small metal or plastic object used for holding things together

NOUN **2** a short piece of a film shown by itself

VERB **3** If you **clip** something, you cut bits from it to shape it.

**clipboard clipboards**

NOUN a stiff piece of board or plastic, with a clip at the top to keep papers in place

a
b
c
d
e
f
g
h
i
j
k
l
m
n
o
p
q
r
s
t
u
v
w
x
y
z

**71**

## clippers

PLURAL NOUN a tool used for cutting
• hedge **clippers**

## cloak cloaks, cloaking, cloaked

NOUN **1** a wide, loose coat without sleeves
VERB **2** If something **cloaks** something else, it covers or hides it. • *The mist **cloaked** the land.*

## cloakroom cloakrooms

NOUN **1** a room where you can leave coats and luggage for a while
NOUN **2** a room with toilets and washbasins in a public building

## clock clocks

NOUN an instrument that measures and shows the time

## clockwise

ADVERB in the same direction as the hands on a clock

ANTONYM: anticlockwise

## clockwork

NOUN **1** Toys that move by **clockwork** are wound up with a key.
PHRASE **2** If something goes **like clockwork**, it happens with no problems or delays.

## clog clogs, clogging, clogged

VERB **1** When something is **clogged**, or when you **clog** something up, it becomes blocked and doesn't work properly or doesn't allow things to move freely. • *The traffic was **clogging** the roads.*
NOUN **2** a shoe made entirely of wood, originally from the Netherlands

## clone clones

NOUN an animal or plant that is an identical copy of another animal or plant

## close closes, closing, closed; closer, closest

VERB **1** If you **close** something, you move it so that it is no longer open. • *He **closed** the door behind him.*
VERB **2** If a shop or other building **closes** at a certain time, it does not do business after that time.
ADJECTIVE **3** Something that is **close** to something else is near to it.

SYNONYMS: near, nearby

ADJECTIVE **4** People who are **close** are very friendly with each other and know each other well.

ADJECTIVE **5** If the weather is **close**, it is uncomfortably warm and stuffy.
NOUN **6** a street that is closed at one end
• *We live in Park **Close**.*

PRONUNCIATION TIP

Meanings 1 and 2 are pronounced **klohz**. Meanings 3, 4, 5 and 6 are pronounced **klohss**.

## closely

ADVERB **1** very carefully • *She was watching him **closely**.*
ADVERB **2** to a very large degree • *We work **closely** with other schools.*
ADVERB **3** without much time or distance between two people or things • *She came into the room, **closely** followed by a young boy.*

PRONUNCIATION TIP

This word is pronounced **klohss**-li.

## close-up close-ups

NOUN A **close-up** in a film or a photograph is taken at very close range and shows things in great detail.

PRONUNCIATION TIP

This word is pronounced **klohss**-up.

## clot clots

NOUN a sticky lump that forms when a liquid such as blood dries up or becomes thick

## cloth cloths

NOUN **1** fabric made by a process such as weaving
NOUN **2** a piece of material used for wiping protecting things

## clothes

PLURAL NOUN things people wear on their bodies

## cloud clouds

NOUN **1** a mass of water vapour that is seen as a white or grey patch in the sky • *The s went behind a **cloud**.*
NOUN **2** A **cloud** of smoke or dust is a mass of it floating in the air.
NOUN **3** **Cloud** computing is when data an programs are stored and accessed over th internet instead of through your computer hard drive.

**oudy cloudier, cloudiest**
ADJECTIVE **1** full of clouds • The sky was **cloudy**.

SYNONYMS: dull, overcast

ADJECTIVE **2** difficult to see through • a **cloudy** liquid

SYNONYM: murky

**over**
NOUN a small plant with leaves made up of three similar parts

**own clowns**
NOUN a circus performer who wears funny clothes and make-up and does silly things to make people laugh

**ub clubs**
NOUN **1** a group of people with similar interests, who meet regularly. The place where they meet is also called a **club**. • a youth **club**
NOUN **2** a team that competes in sports competitions

**ue clues**
NOUN something that helps solve a problem or mystery • Police have found **clues** to the robbery.

**ueless**
ADJECTIVE (informal) If you say that someone is **clueless**, you think they are stupid and not able to do things properly.

**ump clumps**
NOUN a small group of things growing or standing close together • a **clump** of trees

**umsily**
ADVERB in and awkward and careless way

**umsy clumsier, clumsiest**
ADJECTIVE moving awkwardly and carelessly

SYNONYMS: awkward, ungainly

**ung**
VERB the past tense and past participle of **cling**

**uster clusters, clustering, clustered**
NOUN **1** a group of things together • There is a **cluster** of houses by the lake.
VERB **2** If people **cluster** together, they stay together in a close group.

WORD HISTORY
from Old English clyster meaning bunch of grapes

**utch clutches, clutching, clutched**
VERB If you **clutch** something, you hold it tightly or seize it.

**clutter clutters, cluttering, cluttered**
NOUN **1** an untidy mess
VERB **2** Things that **clutter** a place fill it and make it untidy.

**cm**
an abbreviation for centimetre

**coach coaches, coaching, coached**
NOUN **1** a large bus that takes passengers on long journeys
NOUN **2** a section of a train that carries passengers
VERB **3** If someone **coaches** you, they help you to get better at a sport or a subject.

SYNONYMS: instruct, train

NOUN **4** someone who coaches a person or sports team

**coal**
NOUN a hard, black rock taken from under the ground and burned as a fuel

**coarse coarser, coarsest**
ADJECTIVE **1** Something that is **coarse** is rough in texture.
ADJECTIVE **2** Someone who is **coarse** talks or behaves in a rude, offensive way.

**coarseness**
NOUN **1** the quality that something has when it feels rough
NOUN **2** **Coarseness** is when someone talks or behaves in a rude, offensive way.

**coast coasts, coasting, coasted**
NOUN **1** the edge of the land where it meets the sea
VERB **2** If a vehicle **coasts** somewhere, it moves there with the engine switched off. • The car **coasted** quietly down the hill.

**coastal**
ADJECTIVE on the edge of the land where it meets the sea • **coastal** villages

**coastguard coastguards**
NOUN an official who watches the sea near a coast to get help for sailors when they need it

**coat coats, coating, coated**
NOUN **1** a piece of outdoor clothing with sleeves, which you wear over other clothes
NOUN **2** An animal's **coat** is the fur or hair on its body.
NOUN **3** A **coat** of paint or varnish is a layer of it.
VERB **4** If you **coat** something, you cover it with a thin layer of something. • We **coated** the biscuits with chocolate.

73

**coating** coatings
NOUN a thin layer of something spread over a surface

**coax** coaxes, coaxing, coaxed
VERB If you **coax** someone to do something, you persuade them gently to do it.

**cobble** cobbles
NOUN **Cobbles** or cobblestones are stones with a rounded surface that were used in the past for making roads.

**cobra** cobras
NOUN a type of large poisonous snake from Africa and Asia

**cobweb** cobwebs
NOUN the very thin net that a spider spins to catch insects

**cock** cocks
NOUN an adult male chicken, or any other male bird

**cockerel** cockerels
NOUN a young cock

**cockle** cockles
NOUN a type of small, edible shellfish

**Cockney** Cockneys
NOUN someone who was born in the East End of London

**cockpit** cockpits
NOUN **1** the area in a plane where the pilot sits in control

→ Have a look at the illustration for **aeroplane**

NOUN **2** the driver's compartment in a racing car

**cockroach** cockroaches
NOUN a large, dark-coloured insect often found in dirty rooms

WORD HISTORY
from Spanish *cucaracha*

**cocky** cockier, cockiest
ADJECTIVE (*informal*) If you are **cocky**, you are sure of yourself and sometimes rather cheeky.

**cocoa**
NOUN **1** a brown powder made from the seeds of a tropical tree and used for making chocolate
NOUN **2** a hot drink made from this powder

**coconut** coconuts
NOUN a very large nut with white flesh, mil juice, and a hard hairy shell

**cocoon** cocoons
NOUN a silky covering over the larvae of moths and some other insects

**cod**
NOUN a large, edible fish

LANGUAGE TIP
The plural of *cod* is *cod*.

**code** codes
NOUN **1** a system of replacing the letters or words in a message with other letters or words, so that nobody can understand the message unless they know the system
● *They wrote messages in* **code**.
NOUN **2** a group of numbers and letters use to identify something ● *the area* **code** *for Falmouth*
NOUN **3** the set of instructions in a compute program
VERB **4** When you **code**, you write the instructions in a computer program.

**coeducation**
NOUN **Coeducation** is a system where girls and boys are taught together at the same school.

**coffee**
NOUN **1** a powder made by roasting and grinding the beans of the coffee plant
NOUN **2** a hot drink made from coffee

**coffin** coffins
NOUN a box in which a dead body is buried cremated

**cog** cogs
NOUN a wheel with teeth, which turns another wheel or part of a machine

**coil** coils, coiling, coiled
NOUN **1** a length of rope or wire wound into series of loops
NOUN **2** A single loop is also called a **coil**.
VERB **3** If something **coils**, or if you **coil** it, it winds into a series of loops. ● *The snake* **coiled** *around the branch.*

**coin** coins, coining, coined
NOUN **1** a small metal disc used as money
VERB **2** If you **coin** a word or a phrase, you invent it.

**coinage**
NOUN the coins that are used in a particula country

**coincide coincides, coinciding, coincided**
VERB When two things **coincide**, they happen at the same time. • *Auntie's visit coincided with my birthday.*

**coincidence coincidences**
NOUN what happens when two or more things occur at the same time by chance

**coke**
NOUN a grey fuel produced from coal

**cola colas**
NOUN a sweet, brown fizzy drink

**colander colanders**
NOUN a bowl-shaped container with holes in it, used for washing or draining food

**cold colder, coldest; colds**
ADJECTIVE 1 If something is **cold**, it has a very low temperature.
ADJECTIVE 2 If the weather is **cold**, the air temperature is very low.
NOUN 3 a minor illness that makes you sneeze and cough, and sometimes gives you a sore throat

**cold-blooded**
ADJECTIVE 1 A **cold-blooded** animal has a body temperature that changes according to the surrounding temperature.
ADJECTIVE 2 Someone who is **cold-blooded** does not show any pity.

**coleslaw**
NOUN a salad of chopped cabbage and other vegetables in mayonnaise

**collaborate collaborates, collaborating, collaborated**
VERB When people **collaborate**, they work together to produce something. • *The two schools collaborated to produce a play.*

**collaboration**
NOUN **Collaboration** is when people work together to produce something.

**collaborator collaborators**
NOUN someone who works together with someone else to produce something.

**collage collages**
NOUN a picture made by sticking pieces of paper or cloth on to a surface

**collapse collapses, collapsing, collapsed**
VERB 1 If something such as a building **collapses**, it falls down suddenly.
VERB 2 If a person **collapses**, they fall down suddenly because they are ill.

**collapsible**
ADJECTIVE A **collapsible** object can be folded flat when it is not in use. • *collapsible chairs*

**collar collars**
NOUN 1 the part around the neck of something, such as a coat or shirt
NOUN 2 a leather band round the neck of a dog or cat

**colleague colleagues**
NOUN A person's **colleagues** are the people they work with.

**collect collects, collecting, collected**
VERB 1 If you **collect** things, you gather them together for a special purpose or as a hobby.
VERB 2 If you **collect** someone or something from a place, you call there and take them away. • *We collected Ali from school.*
VERB 3 When things **collect** in a place, they gather there over a period of time. • *Dust collects in corners.*

**collection collections**
NOUN 1 a group of things you have gathered over a period of time • *a stamp collection*
NOUN 2 the organised collecting of money, for example for charity, or the money collected

**collective noun collective nouns**
NOUN a noun that refers to a group of people or things. For example, a flock, a herd and a shoal are all **collective nouns**.

**college colleges**
NOUN a place where students study after they have left school

**collide collides, colliding, collided**
VERB If a moving object **collides** with something, it hits it. • *They collided with each other as they rushed through the door.*

**collision collisions**
NOUN A **collision** is when a moving object hits something.

SYNONYM: crash

**colon colons**
NOUN 1 the punctuation mark (:). It is used to introduce a list, a quotation or an explanation of a statement. • *We need to buy several things: bread, milk, fruit and toothpaste.*
NOUN 2 part of your intestine

→ Have a look at the illustration for **stomach**

**colonel colonels**
NOUN an army officer with a fairly high rank

a
b
c
d
e
f
g
h
i
j
k
l
m
n
o
p
q
r
s
t
u
v
w
x
y
z

A
B
C
D
E
F
G
H
I
J
K
L
M
N
O
P
Q
R
S
T
U
V
W
X
Y
Z

**colony colonies**

NOUN **1** a country that is controlled by another country

NOUN **2** a group of people or animals living together

**colossal**

ADJECTIVE very large indeed

WORD HISTORY
from Greek *kolossos* meaning huge statue

**colour colours**

NOUN the appearance something has as a result of reflecting light • *Red, blue and yellow are the primary **colours**.*

**colour blind**

ADJECTIVE Someone who is **colour blind** is not able to see the difference between certain colours.

**colourful**

ADJECTIVE **1** Something that is **colourful** has a lot of different colours or bright colours.

ANTONYMS: dull, colourless

ADJECTIVE **2** A **colourful** story is very exciting and interesting.

ANTONYMS: dull, boring

**colourless**

ADJECTIVE **1** without colour

ANTONYM: colourful

ADJECTIVE **2** dull and uninteresting

**colt colts**

NOUN a young male horse

**column columns**

NOUN **1** a tall, solid, upright cylinder, especially one supporting part of a building

NOUN **2** In a newspaper or magazine, a **column** is a vertical section of writing.

NOUN **3** a group of people or vehicles moving in a long line

**coma comas**

NOUN a state of deep unconsciousness

**comb combs, combing, combed**

NOUN **1** a flat object with long, thin, pointed parts, which you use for tidying your hair

VERB **2** When you **comb** your hair, you tidy it with a comb.

**combat combats, combating, combat**

NOUN **1** fighting • *In the Falklands War man soldiers had to take part in armed **combat**.*

VERB **2** If someone **combats** something, th try to stop it happening. • *We need new we to **combat** crime.*

**combination combinations**

NOUN **1** a mixture of things • *Fatima won th competition through a **combination** of skill and determination.*

NOUN **2** a series of numbers or letters used open a special lock

**combine combines, combining, combined**

VERB If you **combine** things, you mix them together. • ***Combine** the butter and sugar, then add the eggs.* • *The book **combines** adventure and mystery.*

**combine harvester combine harvesters**

NOUN a large machine used on farms to cu sort and clean grain

**combustion**

NOUN the process of burning

**come comes, coming, came**

VERB **1** If you **come** to a place, you move o arrive there.

VERB **2** If something **comes** to a particular point, it reaches that point. • *The water **came** up to her waist.*

VERB **3** When a particular time **comes**, it happens. • *Spring **came** early this year.*

**comedian comedians**

NOUN an entertainer whose job is to make people laugh

**comedy comedies**

NOUN a play, film, or television programme that is intended to make people laugh

**comet comets**

NOUN an object that travels around the sun leaving a bright trail behind it

WORD HISTORY
from Greek *kometes* meaning long-haired

**comfort comforts, comforting, comforted**

NOUN **1** the state of being pleasantly relaxe

NOUN **2** a feeling of relief from worry or unhappiness • *It's a **comfort** to me to know that they are safe.*

VERB **3** If you **comfort** someone, you make them less worried or unhappy.

**omfortable**

ADJECTIVE **1** If you are **comfortable**, you are at ease and relaxed.

ADJECTIVE **2** Something that is **comfortable** makes you feel relaxed. ● *a comfortable chair*

**omfortably**

ADVERB in a way that makes someone feel relaxed and without pain ● *He was sitting comfortably in a chair.*

**omic comics**

NOUN **1** a magazine that contains stories told in pictures

ADJECTIVE **2** funny ● *a comic song*

**omma commas**

NOUN the punctuation mark (,). It can show a short pause, or it can separate items in a list or words in speech marks from the rest of the sentence.

**ommand commands, commanding, commanded**

NOUN **1** an order to do something

VERB **2** If you **command** someone to do something, you order them to do it.

**ommandment commandments**

NOUN one of the ten rules of behaviour that, according to the Bible, people should obey

**ommemorate commemorates, commemorating, commemorated**

VERB If you **commemorate** something, you do something special to show that you remember it. ● *On Remembrance Day we commemorate all the people who died in the two World Wars.*

**omment comments, commenting, commented**

NOUN **1** a remark about something

VERB **2** If you **comment** on something, you make a remark about it.

**ommentary commentaries**

NOUN a description of an event that is broadcast on radio or television while the event is happening ● *The commentary on the match was on the radio.*

**ommentator commentators**

NOUN someone who gives a radio or television commentary

**ommerce**

NOUN the buying and selling of goods

**ommercial commercials**

NOUN **1** an advertisement on television or radio

ADJECTIVE **2 Commercial** activities involve producing large amounts of goods to sell and make money.

**commit commits, committing, committed**

VERB When someone **commits** a crime or sin, they do it. ● *The police know who committed the burglary.*

**committee committees**

NOUN a group of people who make decisions on behalf of a larger group

**common commoner, commonest; commons**

ADJECTIVE **1** Something that is **common** exists in large numbers or happens often.

NOUN **2** an area of grassy land where everyone can go

ADJECTIVE **3** If something is **common** to two or more people, they all have it or use it. ● *We had a common interest in butterflies.*

PHRASE **4** If two things or people have something **in common**, they both have it. ● *Sarah and I have a lot in common.*

**common noun common nouns**

NOUN **Common nouns** name things in general. They begin with lower-case letters: *girl, boy, animal, picture.*

**common sense**

NOUN knowing how to behave sensibly in any situation

**Commonwealth**

NOUN The **Commonwealth** is a group of countries that used to be ruled by Britain.

**commotion**

NOUN a lot of noise and excitement

**communal**

ADJECTIVE shared by a group of people ● *The shop had communal changing rooms.*

**communicate communicates, communicating, communicated**

VERB When people **communicate**, they exchange information, usually by talking or writing to each other.

**communication communications**

NOUN **1** the act of exchanging information, usually by talking, writing or, in the case of animals, making sounds ● *the communication of ideas*

PLURAL NOUN **2 Communications** are electrical or radio systems that allow people to broadcast or communicate information.

a
b
c
d
e
f
g
h
i
j
k
l
m
n
o
p
q
r
s
t
u
v
w
x
y
z

**77**

## communion

NOUN **1** a Christian religious service in which people share holy bread and wine

NOUN **2** the sharing of thoughts and feelings

## community **communities**

NOUN all the people living in a particular area

## commuter **commuters**

NOUN a person who travels to work every day

## compact

ADJECTIVE Something that is **compact** takes up very little space, or no more space than is necessary.

## compact disc **compact discs**

NOUN a small plastic disc on which sound, especially music, is recorded. **Compact discs** can also be used to store information which can be read by a computer.

## companion **companions**

NOUN someone you travel or spend time with

## company **companies**

NOUN **1** a business that sells goods or provides a service

NOUN **2** If you have **company**, you have a friend or visitor with you.

PHRASE **3** If you **keep someone company**, you spend time with them.

## comparative **comparatives**

ADJECTIVE **1** You use **comparative** to show that something is true only when compared with something else. • *The group of tourists watched the lions from the comparative safety of their truck.*

NOUN **2** In grammar, the **comparative** is the form of an adjective or adverb that shows an increase in size, quality or amount. It is usually formed by adding *-er* to a word, for example, *bigger, faster,* or by putting *more* before the word, for example, *more difficult.*

## comparatively

ADVERB You use **comparatively** to show that something is true only when compared with something else. • *Some children find it hard to make friends, while others find it comparatively easy.*

## compare **compares, comparing, compared**

VERB When you **compare** things, you see in what ways they are different or similar. • *We compared our hair to see whose was longest.*

## comparison **comparisons**

NOUN When you make a **comparison**, you consider two things together and decide in what ways they are different or imilar.

## compartment **compartments**

NOUN **1** a section of a railway carriage

NOUN **2** one of the separate sections of something such as a bag or a box

## compass **compasses**

NOUN **1** an instrument with a magnetic needle that always points north. You use a **compass** to find your way.

→ Have a look at the illustration for **compass point**

PLURAL NOUN **2 Compasses** are a hinged instrument for drawing circles.

## compassion

NOUN pity and sympathy for someone who suffering

## compassionate

ADJECTIVE showing pity and sympathy for someone who is suffering

## compass point **compass points**

NOUN one of the 32 marks on the dial of a compass that show direction • *North, sout east and west are compass points.*

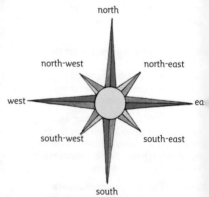

## compatible

ADJECTIVE **1** If people or things are **compatible**, they can live or work together uccessfully.

ADJECTIVE **2** If two or more devices are **compatible**, they can be used together.

**ompel compels, compelling, compelled**
VERB **1** If you **compel** someone to do something, you force them to do it.
ADJECTIVE **2** A **compelling** story or event is extremely interesting.
ADJECTIVE **3** A **compelling** argument or reason makes you believe that something is true.

**ompensate compensates, compensating, compensated**
VERB **1** To **compensate** someone means to give them money to replace something that has been lost or damaged.
VERB **2** If one thing **compensates** for another, it cancels out the bad effects of it.
● *The trip to Blackpool* **compensated** *for her missing the school outing.*

**ompete competes, competing, competed**
VERB **1** If you **compete** in a contest or game, you take part in it.
VERB **2** If you **compete**, you try to do better than others.

**ompetent**
ADJECTIVE Someone who is **competent** at something can do it satisfactorily. ● *He is a* **competent** *nurse.*

**ompetition competitions**
NOUN an event in which people take part to find out who is the best at something

**ompile compiles, compiling, compiled**
VERB When you **compile** information, you collect it and put it together.

**omplain complains, complaining, complained**
VERB **1** If you **complain**, you say that you are not happy about something. ● *The neighbours* **complained** *about the noise.*
VERB **2** If you **complain** of pain or illness, you say that you have it.

**omplaint complaints**
NOUN **1** If you make a **complaint**, you say that you are not happy about something.
● *The magazine received several* **complaints** *from readers about the picture.*
NOUN **2** an illness that affects a particular part of your body ● *a skin* **complaint**

**omplement complements, complementing, complemented**
VERB **1** If one thing **complements** another, the two things go well together. ● *Her piano music* **complements** *the poem.*

NOUN **2** In grammar, a **complement** is a word or phrase that gives information about the subject or object of a sentence. For example, in the sentence *Rover is a dog*, *is a dog* is the **complement**.

---

LANGUAGE TIP
Do not confuse *complement* with *compliment*.

---

**complete completes, completing, completed**
VERB **1** If you **complete** something, you finish it. ● *She has just* **completed** *her third short story.*
ADJECTIVE **2** If something is **complete**, none of it is missing.

**completely**
ADVERB totally

SYNONYM: utterly

**complex complexes**
ADJECTIVE **1 Complex** things have many different parts and are hard to understand.
NOUN **2** a group of buildings used for a particular purpose, such a sports **complex**

**complexion complexions**
NOUN the quality of the skin on your face

**complicated**
ADJECTIVE Something that is **complicated** is hard to understand.

**complication complications**
NOUN something that makes a situation more difficult to deal with

**compliment compliments**
NOUN If you pay someone a **compliment**, you tell them you admire or like something about them.

---

LANGUAGE TIP
Do not confuse *compliment* with *complement*.

---

**component components**
NOUN The **components** of something are the parts it is made of.

**compose composes, composing, composed**
VERB **1** If you **compose** a piece of music, a letter or a speech, you write it.
VERB **2** If something is **composed** of particular things or people, it is made up of them.

**composer composers**
NOUN someone who writes music

a
b
c
d
e
f
g
h
i
j
k
l
m
n
o
p
q
r
s
t
u
v
w
x
y
z

A
B
C
D
E
F
G
H
I
J
K
L
M
N
O
P
Q
R
S
T
U
V
W
X
Y
Z

## composition compositions

NOUN **1** a piece of music or writing

NOUN **2** the things that something is made up of ● *The* **composition** *of the two liquids is very different.*

## compost

NOUN a mixture of rotted plants and manure that gardeners add to the soil to help plants grow

## compound compounds

NOUN a substance that consists of two or more chemical elements ● *Water is a* **compound** *made up of hydrogen and oxygen.*

## compound word compound words

NOUN a word with a single meaning, but made up of two or more words. For example, *gingerbread*, *housework* and *teapot* are all **compound words**.

## comprehend comprehends, comprehending, comprehended

VERB If you **comprehend** something, you understand it.

## comprehensive comprehensives

ADJECTIVE **1** Something that is **comprehensive** includes everything that you need to know.

NOUN **2** a school where children of all abilities are taught together ● *She goes to the local* **comprehensive**.

## compress compresses, compressing, compressed

VERB If you **compress** something, you squeeze it or shorten it. ● *She* **compressed** *her story into one page.*

## compromise compromises, compromising, compromised

NOUN **1** an agreement in which people accept less than they really wanted ● *We will need to reach a* **compromise** *between what we both want.*

VERB **2** When people **compromise**, they settle for less than they really wanted.

## compulsory

ADJECTIVE If something is **compulsory**, you have to do it.

ANTONYM: optional

## computer computers

NOUN an electronic machine that stores information and makes calculations

screen

keyboard

trackpad

USB p

mouse

## computerise computerises, computerising, computerised; also spe computerize

VERB When a system or process is **computerised**, such as train timetables or bank accounts, the work is done by computers.

## comrade comrades

NOUN a companion, especially in battle

## con cons, conning, conned

VERB **1** If someone **cons** you, or you are **conned**, you are tricked into doing something. ● *He* **conned** *me into buying the tickets.*

NOUN **2** a trick that makes you believe or do something that you would not normally believe or do

## concave

ADJECTIVE A **concave** surface curves inwards, rather than being level or bulging outwards.

ANTONYM: convex

## conceal conceals, concealing, concealed

VERB If you **conceal** something, you hide it.

## conceited

ADJECTIVE Someone who is **conceited** is too proud of their appearance or abilities.

SYNONYMS: bigheaded, self-important

**onceive conceives, conceiving, conceived**
VERB 1 If you can't **conceive** of something, you can't imagine it or believe it.
• He couldn't **conceive** of anything more fun than surfing.
VERB 2 If you **conceive** something such as a plan, you think of it and work out how it could be done. • Alex **conceived** the idea while eating his lunch.
VERB 3 When a woman **conceives**, she becomes pregnant.

**oncentrate concentrates, concentrating, concentrated**
VERB 1 If you **concentrate** on something, you give it all your attention. • I need to **concentrate** on my homework.
VERB 2 When something is **concentrated** in one place, it is all there rather than in several places. • The shops were **concentrated** in the town centre.

**oncentrated**
ADJECTIVE A **concentrated** liquid has been made stronger by having water removed from it. • **concentrated** orange juice

**oncentration concentrations**
NOUN 1 the ability to give your full attention to something you do or hear
NOUN 2 A **concentration** of something is a large amount of it in one place.

**oncentric**
ADJECTIVE **Concentric** circles have the same centre.

**oncept concepts**
NOUN an abstract or general idea

**onception conceptions**
NOUN the idea you have of something

**oncern concerns, concerning, concerned**
NOUN 1 worry about something or someone
NOUN 2 If something is your **concern**, it is your duty or responsibility.
VERB 3 If something **concerns** you or if you are **concerned** about it, it worries you.

**oncerned**
ADJECTIVE worried about something or someone

**oncerning**
PREPOSITION You use **concerning** to show what something is about. • an article **concerning** fox hunting

**concert concerts**
NOUN a public performance by musicians

**concession concessions**
NOUN If you make a **concession**, you agree to let someone have or do something.

**concise**
ADJECTIVE giving all the necessary information using as few words as possible • a **concise** explanation

SYNONYMS: brief, short

**conclude concludes, concluding, concluded**
VERB 1 If you **conclude** something, you examine the facts and decide what your opinion is. • We **concluded** that the letter was a fake.
VERB 2 When you **conclude** something, you finish it.

**conclusion conclusions**
NOUN 1 the end of something
NOUN 2 a final decision about something
• We wanted to go for a swim in the sea, but we came to the **conclusion** that it was too cold.

**concrete**
NOUN 1 a building material made by mixing cement, sand and water
ADJECTIVE 2 real and physical, rather than abstract • He had no **concrete** evidence.

**concussed**
ADJECTIVE If you are **concussed**, you are unconscious or feel confused and sick because something has hit your head.

**concussion**
NOUN damage to the brain caused by something hitting your head, which makes you unconscious, confused or sick for a short time

**condemn condemns, condemning, condemned**
VERB 1 If you **condemn** something, you say it is bad and unacceptable.
VERB 2 If someone is **condemned** to a punishment, they are given it. • The burglar was **condemned** to five years in prison.

**condensation**
NOUN a coating of tiny drops of liquid formed on a cold surface by steam or vapour

→ Have a look at the illustration for **water cycle**

a
b
c
d
e
f
g
h
i
j
k
l
m
n
o
p
q
r
s
t
u
v
w
x
y
z

**81**

## condense condenses, condensing, condensed

VERB **1** If you **condense** a piece of writing or a speech, you shorten it.

VERB **2** When a gas or vapour **condenses**, it changes into a liquid.

## condition conditions

NOUN **1** the state someone or something is in • *The antique clock was still in good* ***condition***.

NOUN **2** something that must happen in order for something else to be possible • *I can go swimming on Saturday on the* ***condition*** *that I do my homework first.*

## conduct conducts, conducting, conducted

NOUN **1** behaviour • *He won a prize for good* ***conduct*** *in school.*

VERB **2** When you **conduct** an activity, you carry it out. • *I decided to* ***conduct*** *an experiment.*

VERB **3** When someone **conducts** an orchestra, a band or a choir, they direct it in a piece of music.

VERB **4** If something **conducts** heat or electricity, heat or electricity can pass along it. • *Copper* ***conducts*** *electricity well.*

### PRONUNCIATION TIP
The noun is pronounced **kon**-duct. The verb is pronounced kon-**duct**.

## conductivity
NOUN the ability of a substance to conduct heat or electricity

## conductor conductors
NOUN **1** someone who conducts an orchestra or choir

NOUN **2** someone who moves round a bus or train selling and checking tickets

NOUN **3** a substance that conducts heat or electricity

## cone cones
NOUN **1** a regular three-dimensional shape with a circular base and a point at the top

NOUN **2** the fruit of a fir or pine tree

## conference conferences
NOUN a meeting at which formal discussion take place

## confess confesses, confessing, confessed
VERB If you **confess** to something, you admit that you did it.

## confession confessions
NOUN **1** If you make a **confession**, you admit that you have done something wrong.

SYNONYM: admission

NOUN **2** the act of confessing something, especially as a religious act, where people confess their sins to a priest

## confetti
NOUN small pieces of coloured paper thrown over the newly married couple at a wedding

### WORD HISTORY
from Italian *confetto* meaning a sweet

## confide confides, confiding, confided
VERB If you **confide** in or to someone, you tell them a secret.

## confidence
NOUN **1** If you have **confidence** in someone, you feel you can trust them.

NOUN **2** Someone who has **confidence** is sure of their own abilities or qualities.

## confident
ADJECTIVE **1** If you are **confident** about something, you are sure it will happen the way you want it to.

ADJECTIVE **2** Someone who is **confident** is very sure of themselves and their own abilities.

## confidential
ADJECTIVE **Confidential** information is meant to be kept secret.

**onfine confines, confining, confined**
VERB **1** If someone **confines** you to a place, you can't leave it. ● *The doctor confined Debbie to bed for two weeks as she had pneumonia.*
VERB **2** If you **confine** yourself to doing something, you do only that thing. ● *On their trip abroad, they confined themselves to drinking bottled water.*

**onfirm confirms, confirming, confirmed**
VERB **1** If you **confirm** something, you say or show that it is true. ● *The teacher confirmed that we had all passed our spelling test.*
VERB **2** If you **confirm** an arrangement or appointment, you say it is definite. ● *Dad confirmed our holiday booking.*

**onfirmation confirmations**
NOUN **1 Confirmation** is when something is said to be definite or shown to be true.
NOUN **2** a ceremony that confirms a baptised person as a Christian and allows them to belong fully to the church

**onfiscate confiscates, confiscating, confiscated**
VERB If someone **confiscates** something, they take it away from someone as a punishment.

**WORD HISTORY**
from Latin *confiscare* meaning to seize for the public treasury

**onfiscation**
NOUN **Confiscation** is when someone takes something away from someone else as a punishment.

**onflict conflicts, conflicting, conflicted**
NOUN **1** disagreement and argument
NOUN **2** a war or battle
VERB **3** When two ideas or interests **conflict**, they are different and it seems impossible for them both to be true.

**onform conforms, conforming, conformed**
VERB **1** If you **conform**, you behave the way people expect you to.
VERB **2** If something **conforms** to a law or to someone's wishes, it does what is required or wanted.

**onfront confronts, confronting, confronted**
VERB **1** If you are **confronted** with a problem or task, you have to deal with it.

VERB **2** If you **confront** someone, you meet them face to face, especially when you are going to fight or argue with them.

**confrontation confrontations**
NOUN a serious dispute between two people or groups of people who come face to face

**confuse confuses, confusing, confused**
VERB **1** If you **confuse** two people or things, you mix them up and are not sure which is which.
VERB **2** If you **confuse** someone, you make them uncertain about what is happening or what to do.

**confusion**
NOUN **1 Confusion** is when you mix up people or things and are not sure which is which. ● *The teacher calls me "Sam" to avoid confusion with the other Samuel in the class.*
NOUN **2** the feeling of being uncertain about what is happening or what to do

**congested**
ADJECTIVE **1** When a road is **congested**, it is so full of traffic that normal movement is impossible.
ADJECTIVE **2** If your nose is **congested**, it is blocked and you cannot breathe properly.

**congestion**
NOUN **1** There is **congestion** when a road is so full of traffic that normal movement is impossible.
NOUN **2 Congestion** is when your nose is blocked and you cannot breathe properly.

**congratulate congratulates, congratulating, congratulated**
VERB If you **congratulate** someone, you say that you're pleased about something good that has happened to them, or praise them for something they have done.
● *He congratulated us on winning the competition.*

**congratulations**
INTERJECTION You say **congratulations** to someone when you are pleased about something good that has happened to them or to praise them for something they have done.

**congregation congregations**
NOUN the people attending a service in a church.

a
b
c
d
e
f
g
h
i
j
k
l
m
n
o
p
q
r
s
t
u
v
w
x
y
z

**83**

A
B
C
D
E
F
G
H
I
J
K
L
M
N
O
P
Q
R
S
T
U
V
W
X
Y
Z

## congruent

ADJECTIVE In mathematics, things that are **congruent** are exactly the same size and shape, and would fit exactly on top of each other. • *congruent* triangles

## conifer conifers

NOUN any type of evergreen tree that produces cones

## coniferous

ADJECTIVE A **coniferous** tree is any type of evergreen tree that produces cones.

## conjunction conjunctions

NOUN In grammar, a **conjunction** is a word that links two other words or two clauses, such as *and*, *but*, *or*, *while* and *that*. For example: "I love bacon *and* eggs." "I'm happy, *but* my brother is not".

## conjurer conjurers

NOUN someone who entertains people by doing magic tricks

## conker conkers

NOUN a brown nut from a horse chestnut tree

## connect connects, connecting, connected

VERB 1 If you **connect** two things, you join them together.
VERB 2 If one thing or person is **connected** with another, there is a link between them.

## connection connections

NOUN 1 the point where two things are joined together
NOUN 2 a relationship between two people, groups or things
NOUN 3 If you make a **connection** at a station or airport, you continue your journey by catching another train, bus or plane. • *Our train was late, so we missed our **connection**.*

## connective connectives

NOUN a word that connects phrases, clauses or words together

## conquer conquers, conquering, conquered

VERB 1 If you **conquer** something difficult or dangerous, you succeed in controlling it. • *She **conquered** her fear of spiders.*
VERB 2 to take control of a country by force

## conqueror conquerors

NOUN someone who takes control of a country by force

## conscience

NOUN Your **conscience** is the part of your mind that tells you what is right or wrong.

## conscientious

ADJECTIVE Someone who is **conscientious** takes great care over their work.

## conscious

ADJECTIVE 1 Someone who is **conscious** is awake, rather than asleep or unconscious.
ADJECTIVE 2 If you are **conscious** of something, you are aware of it.
ADJECTIVE 3 A **conscious** action or effort is done deliberately.

## consecutive

ADJECTIVE 1 **Consecutive** events or periods of time happen one after the other. • *We had eight **consecutive** days of rain.*
ADJECTIVE 2 **Consecutive** numbers follow each other in order. For example, 1, 2, 3, 4 are **consecutive** numbers.

## consent consents, consenting, consented

NOUN 1 permission to do something
NOUN 2 agreement between two or more people • *By common **consent** we went to France for the holiday.*
VERB 3 If you **consent** to something, you agree to do it or allow it to happen.

## consequence consequences

NOUN result or effect

## conservation

NOUN work done to protect the environment or things such as old buildings, and prevent them from being damaged or destroyed

## conservationist conservationists

NOUN someone whose job is to protect the environment or things such as old buildings

## conservative conservatives

NOUN 1 a member or supporter of the **Conservative** Party in Britain
ADJECTIVE 2 Someone who is **conservative** does not like change or new ideas.
ADJECTIVE 3 A **conservative** estimate or guess is a cautious or moderate one.

## conservatory conservatories

NOUN a room with glass walls and a glass roof in which plants are kept

## conserve conserves, conserving, conserved

VERB 1 If you **conserve** a supply of something, you make it last as long as possible. • *I switched off my torch to **conserve** the battery.*
VERB 2 If you **conserve** something, you keep it as it is and do not change it. • *We should **conserve** this old building.*

**consider** **considers, considering, considered**
VERB If you **consider** something, you think about it carefully.

**considerable**
ADJECTIVE A **considerable** amount of something is a lot of it.

**considerate**
ADJECTIVE Someone who is **considerate** thinks of other people's needs and feelings.

**consideration** **considerations**
NOUN 1 careful thought about something
NOUN 2 something that should be thought about when you are planning or deciding something
NOUN 3 Someone who shows **consideration** pays attention to the needs and feelings of other people.

**consist** **consists, consisting, consisted**
VERB Something that **consists** of certain things is made up of them. • *This bread* *consists of flour, yeast and water.*

**consistent**
ADJECTIVE Something that is **consistent** does not change.

**console** **consoles, consoling, consoled**
VERB 1 If you **console** someone who is unhappy, you comfort them and cheer them up.
NOUN 2 a panel with switches or knobs for operating a machine

PRONUNCIATION TIP
The verb is pronounced kon-**sole**. The noun is pronounced **kon**-sole.

**consonant** **consonants**
NOUN all the letters of the alphabet that are not vowels

**conspicuous**
ADJECTIVE If something is **conspicuous**, you can see or notice it very easily.

**conspiracy** **conspiracies**
NOUN an illegal plan made in secret by a group of people

**constable** **constables**
NOUN a police officer of the lowest rank

**constant**
ADJECTIVE 1 Something that is **constant** happens all the time or is always there.
• *We could hear the* **constant** *sound of the waves pounding the shore.*

ADJECTIVE 2 If an amount or level is **constant**, it stays the same.

**constellation** **constellations**
NOUN a group of stars

**constipated**
ADJECTIVE Someone who is **constipated** is suffering from constipation.

**constipation**
NOUN a condition that affects your bowels so that you find it difficult to go to the lavatory

**constitution** **constitutions**
NOUN 1 The **constitution** of a country is the system of laws and principles by which it is governed.
NOUN 2 Your **constitution** is your health.

**construct** **constructs, constructing, constructed**
VERB If you **construct** something, you build or make it.

**construction** **constructions**
NOUN 1 the process of building or making something
NOUN 2 something built or made

**constructive**
ADJECTIVE helpful • *The tennis coach made some* **constructive** *comments about my backhand.*

**consult** **consults, consulting, consulted**
VERB 1 If you **consult** someone, you ask for their opinion or advice.
VERB 2 If you **consult** a book or map, you look at it for information.

**consultant** **consultants**
NOUN an experienced doctor who specialises in one type of medicine • *a* **consultant** *heart surgeon*

**consume** **consumes, consuming, consumed**
VERB 1 If you **consume** something, you eat or drink it.
VERB 2 To **consume** fuel or energy is to use it up.

**consumer** **consumers**
NOUN someone who buys things or uses services • *magazines aimed at teenage* **consumers**

**consumption**
NOUN The **consumption** of fuel or food is the using of it, or the amount used.
• *The* **consumption** *of ice cream rises in hot weather.*

a
b
c
d
e
f
g
h
i
j
k
l
m
n
o
p
q
r
s
t
u
v
w
x
y
z

85

A
B
C
D
E
F
G
H
I
J
K
L
M
N
O
P
Q
R
S
T
U
V
W
X
Y
Z

**contact** **contacts, contacting, contacted**
NOUN **1** If you are in **contact** with someone, you talk or write to them regularly. • *I am in* **contact** *with a pen pal in France.*
NOUN **2** When things are in **contact**, they are touching each other.
VERB **3** If you **contact** someone, you phone them or write to them.

**contact lens** **contact lenses**
NOUN small plastic lenses that you put in your eyes instead of wearing glasses, to help you see better

**contagious**
ADJECTIVE A **contagious** disease can be caught by touching people or things infected with it. • *Measles is* **contagious**.

**contain** **contains, containing, contained**
VERB **1** If a substance **contains** something, that thing is a part of it.
VERB **2** The things a box or room **contains** are the things inside it.

**container** **containers**
NOUN something that you keep things in, such as a box or a jar

**contaminate** **contaminates, contaminating, contaminated**
VERB If dirt, chemicals or radiation **contaminate** something, they make it impure and harmful.

**contamination**
NOUN **Contamination** is dirt, chemicals or radiation that make something impure and harmful.

**contemplate** **contemplates, contemplating, contemplated**
VERB **1** If you **contemplate**, you think very carefully about something. • *She* **contemplated** *what she would do at the weekend.*
VERB **2** If you **contemplate** something, you look at it for a long time.

**contemporary**
ADJECTIVE **1** produced or happening now
ADJECTIVE **2** A **contemporary** work is one that was written at the time of the events it describes.

**contempt**
NOUN If you treat someone with **contempt**, you show no respect for them at all.

**content**
ADJECTIVE **1** If you are **content**, you are happy and satisfied with your life.
ADJECTIVE **2** If you are **content** to do something, you are willing to do it.

PRONUNCIATION TIP
This word is pronounced kon-**tent**.

**contents**
PLURAL NOUN **1** The **contents** of something like a box or a book are the things in it.
PLURAL NOUN **2** The **contents** page of a book tells you what is in it.

PRONUNCIATION TIP
This word is pronounced **kon**-tents.

**contest** **contests**
NOUN a competition or game

**contestant** **contestants**
NOUN someone who takes part in a competitio

SYNONYMS: competitor, player

**context** **contexts**
NOUN The **context** of a word or sentence is the words or sentences that come before and after it, which help to make the meaning clear.

**continent** **continents**
NOUN **1** a very large area of land, such as Africa or Asia
NOUN **2** In Britain, the mainland of Europe i sometimes called the **Continent**.

→ Have a look at the illustration

WORD HISTORY
from Latin *terra continens* meaning continuous land

**continental**
ADJECTIVE In Britain, **continental** means on belonging to or typical of the mainland of Europe. • **continental** *breakfast*

**continual**
ADJECTIVE happening again and again • *Mur. had a* **continual** *stream of phone calls.*

**continue** **continues, continuing, continued**
VERB **1** If you **continue** to do something, yc keep doing it.
VERB **2** If something **continues**, it does not stop.
VERB **3** You say something **continues** whe it starts again after stopping. • *She paused for a moment, then* **continued**.

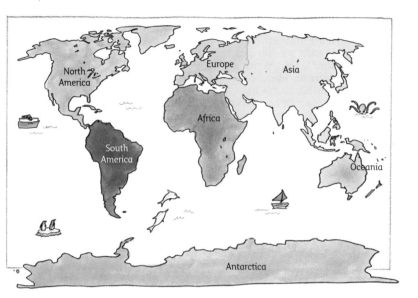

**ontinents**

**ontinuous**

ADJECTIVE happening all the time without stopping • *The television made a* **continuous** *buzzing noise.*

**ontour contours**

NOUN **1** The **contour** of something is its general shape or outline.

NOUN **2** On a map, a **contour** is a line joining points of equal height.

→ Have a look at the illustrations for **map** and **weather**

**ontract contracts, contracting, contracted**

NOUN **1** a legal agreement about the sale of something or work done for money • *He was given a two-year* **contract***.*

VERB **2** When something **contracts**, it gets smaller or shorter. • *Metals* **contract** *with cold and expand with heat.*

ANTONYM: expand

**PRONUNCIATION TIP**
The noun is pronounced **kon**-tract. The verb is pronounced kon-**tract**.

**ontraction contractions**

NOUN a shortened form of a word or words,

often marked by an apostrophe • *"I've" is a* **contraction** *of "I have".*

**contradict contradicts, contradicting, contradicted**

VERB If you **contradict** someone, you say that what they have just said is wrong.

**contradiction contradictions**

NOUN a difference between two statements that means they cannot both be true

**contrary**

ADJECTIVE **1 Contrary** ideas, opinions or attitudes are completely different from each other.

PHRASE **2 On the contrary** is used to contradict something that has just been said.

**contrast contrasts, contrasting, contrasted**

NOUN **1** a great difference between things • *the* **contrast** *between town and country*

VERB **2** If you **contrast** things, you describe or emphasise the differences between them.

**PRONUNCIATION TIP**
The noun is pronounced **kon**-trast. The verb is pronounced kon-**trast**.

## contribute contributes, contributing, contributed

VERB **1** If you **contribute** to something, you do something to make it successful. • *Everyone **contributed** to the class project.*

VERB **2** If you **contribute** money to something, you help to pay for it. • *We **contributed** some money to the appeal for the homeless.*

SYNONYMS: donate, give

## contribution contributions

NOUN **1** If you make a **contribution** to something, you do something to make it successful.

NOUN **2** an amount of money that you give to help pay for something

## control controls, controlling, controlled

NOUN **1** If you have **control** over something, you are able to make it work the way you want it to.

NOUN **2** The **controls** on a machine are the knobs or other devices used to work it.

VERB **3** If someone **controls** a country or an organisation, they make the decisions about how it is run.

VERB **4** If someone **controls** something such as a machine, they make it work the way they want it to.

PHRASE **5** If something is **out of control**, nobody has any power over it. • *The fire was **out of control**.*

## controversial

ADJECTIVE Something that is **controversial** causes a lot of discussion and argument, because many people disapprove of it. • *The film was **controversial**.*

## controversy controversies

NOUN discussion and argument because many people disapprove of something

## convalescent convalescents

NOUN someone who is resting while recovering from an illness

## convenience

NOUN The **convenience** of something is how easy it is to use or do.

## convenient

ADJECTIVE If something is **convenient**, it is easy to use or it makes something easy to do. • *It's **convenient** living close to the bus stop.*

## convent convents

NOUN **1** a building where nuns live

NOUN **2** a school run by nuns

## conventional

ADJECTIVE Someone who is **conventional** thinks or behaves in an ordinary and accepted way.

## converge converges, converging, converged

VERB When things meet or join at a particular place, they **converge**. • *The road converge after three kilometres.*

## conversation conversations

NOUN When people have a **conversation**, they talk to each other.

## convert converts, converting, converted

VERB **1** If you **convert** something, it changes from one thing to another. • *Dad converted the loft into a workshop.*

VERB **2** If someone **converts** you, they persuade you to change your religious or political beliefs.

VERB **3** In mathematics, **convert** means to change a number from one form to another. These are equal to each other. For example you can **convert** a fraction to a decimal ($\frac{1}{2}$ = 0.5).

## convex

ADJECTIVE A **convex** surface bulges outwards, rather than being level or curving inwards.

ANTONYM: concave

## convey conveys, conveying, conveyed

VERB **1** If someone **conveys** people or things to a place, they take them there.

VERB **2** If you **convey** information, ideas or feelings, you tell people about them.

## conveyor belt conveyor belts

NOUN a moving strip used in factories for moving objects along

## convict convicts, convicting, convicted

VERB **1** If a law court **convicts** someone of crime, it says they are guilty of it.

NOUN **2** someone serving a prison sentence

### PRONUNCIATION TIP

The verb is pronounced kon-**vict**. The noun is pronounced **kon**-vict.

**convince** convinces, convincing, convinced
VERB If you **convince** someone of something, you persuade them to do it or that it is true. ● *I* **convinced** *mum and dad to let me go on the school trip.*

**convoy** convoys
NOUN a group of ships or vehicles travelling together

**cook** cooks, cooking, cooked
VERB 1 When you **cook**, you prepare food for eating by boiling, baking or frying it.
NOUN 2 a person whose job is to prepare food

**cooker** cookers
NOUN an apparatus for cooking food

**cookery**
NOUN the art of preparing and cooking food

**cookie** cookies
NOUN 1 a sweet biscuit ● *a chocolate* **cookie**
NOUN 2 a small file placed on a user's computer by a website ● *This website uses* **cookies**.

**cool** cooler, coolest; cools, cooling, cooled
ADJECTIVE 1 Something **cool** has a low temperature but is not cold.
ADJECTIVE 2 If you are **cool** in a difficult situation, you stay calm.
VERB 3 When something **cools**, it becomes less warm.

**cooperate** cooperates, cooperating, cooperated
VERB 1 When people **cooperate**, they work or act together.
VERB 2 If you **cooperate**, you do what someone asks you to do.

**cooperative** cooperatives
ADJECTIVE 1 A **cooperative** person does what they are asked to do willingly and cheerfully.
NOUN 2 a business or organisation run by the people who work for it, and who share its profits

**coordinates**
PLURAL NOUN a pair of numbers or letters that tell you exactly where a point is on a grid, map or graph

**cop** cops
NOUN (*informal*) a police officer

**cope** copes, coping, coped
VERB If you **cope**, you are able to do something even if the circumstances are difficult. ● *I managed to* **cope** *with my*

homework and with looking after my little brother at the same time.

**copper**
NOUN a soft, reddish-brown metal

**copy** copies, copying, copied
NOUN 1 something made to look like something else ● *a* **copy** *of a famous painting*
NOUN 2 A **copy** of a book, newspaper or record is one of many identical ones produced at the same time. ● *a* **copy** *of today's newspaper*
VERB 3 If you **copy** what someone does, you do the same thing.
VERB 4 If you **copy** something, you make a copy of it.

**copyright** copyrights
NOUN If someone has the **copyright** on a piece of writing or music, it cannot be copied or performed without their permission.

**coral** corals
NOUN a hard substance that forms in the sea from the skeletons of tiny animals called **corals**

**cord** cords
NOUN 1 strong, thick string
NOUN 2 electrical wire covered in rubber or plastic

**corduroy**
NOUN heavy, ribbed cloth made of cotton

**core** cores
NOUN the most central part of an object or place ● *an apple* **core** ● *the Earth's* **core**
→ Have a look at the illustration for **earth**

**cork** corks
NOUN 1 a soft, light substance that forms the bark of a Mediterranean tree
NOUN 2 a piece of **cork** pushed into the end of a bottle to close it

**corkscrew** corkscrews
NOUN a device for pulling corks out of bottles

**corn**
NOUN 1 crops such as wheat and barley
NOUN 2 the seeds of these crops

**corner** corners, cornering, cornered
NOUN 1 the point where two sides or edges of something meet ● *The TV was in the* **corner** *of the room.*
VERB 2 If someone **corners** a person or animal, they get them into a place they can't escape from. ● *The police* **cornered** *the thief.*

a
b
c
d
e
f
g
h
i
j
k
l
m
n
o
p
q
r
s
t
u
v
w
x
y
z

A
B
C
D
E
F
G
H
I
J
K
L
M
N
O
P
Q
R
S
T
U
V
W
X
Y
Z

**cornet cornets**
NOUN a small, brass instrument used in brass and military bands

**coronation coronations**
NOUN the ceremony at which a king or queen is crowned

**coroner coroners**
NOUN an official who investigates the deaths of people who have died in a violent or unusual way

**corporal corporals**
NOUN an officer of low rank in the army or air force

**corporal punishment**
NOUN punishing of people by beating them

**corps**
NOUN part of an army with special duties
• the Medical **Corps**

PRONUNCIATION TIP
This word is pronounced **kor**.

**corpse corpses**
NOUN a dead body

**correct corrects, correcting, corrected**
ADJECTIVE 1 If something is **correct**, there are no mistakes in it.
VERB 2 If you **correct** something that is wrong, you make it right. • She **corrected** my maths homework.

**correction corrections**
NOUN a change that you make in order to make something right

**correspond corresponds, corresponding, corresponded**
VERB 1 If one thing **corresponds** with another, it is similar to it or it matches it in some way.
VERB 2 If numbers or amounts **correspond**, they are the same.
VERB 3 When people **correspond**, they write to each other.

**correspondence**
NOUN 1 letters or the writing of letters
NOUN 2 If there is a **correspondence** between two things, there is a similarity between them.

**correspondent correspondents**
NOUN 1 a newspaper, radio or television reporter
NOUN 2 someone who writes letters

**corridor corridors**
NOUN a long passage in a building, with doors and rooms on one or both sides

WORD HISTORY
from Old Italian corridore meaning place fo running

**corrode corrodes, corroding, corroded**
VERB When something **corrodes**, it is eaten away. When iron and steel are **corroded**, rust is formed.

**corrosion**
NOUN a process in which metal becomes rusty or damaged by water or chemicals

**corrosive**
ADJECTIVE A **corrosive** substance can damage or destroy solid materials such as metal or plastic.

**corrugated**
ADJECTIVE **Corrugated** metal or cardboard has parallel folds to make it stronger.

**corrupt corrupts, corrupting, corrupted**
ADJECTIVE 1 People who are **corrupt** act dishonestly or illegally in return for money or power.

SYNONYM: dishonest

VERB 2 If you **corrupt** someone, you make them dishonest.
VERB 3 If a bug in a computer spoils files, it **corrupts** them.

**cosmetics**
PLURAL NOUN lipstick, face powder and other make-up

**cosmic**
ADJECTIVE belonging to or relating to the whole universe

**cosmos**
NOUN the universe

**cost costs, costing, cost**
NOUN 1 the amount of money needed to bu do or make something
VERB 2 You use **cost** to talk about the amount of money you have to pay for things. • You can't have that – it **costs** too much.

**costume costumes**
NOUN 1 a set of clothes worn by an actor
NOUN 2 the clothing worn in a particular place or during a particular period

**cosy cosier, cosiest**
ADJECTIVE warm and comfortable

**cot cots**
NOUN a small bed for a baby, with bars or panels round it to stop the baby falling out

**cottage cottages**
NOUN a small house, especially in the country

**cotton**
NOUN 1 cloth made from the soft fibres of the **cotton** plant • a **cotton** shirt
NOUN 2 thread used for sewing • a needle and **cotton**

**couch couches**
NOUN a long, soft piece of furniture for sitting or lying on

**cough coughs, coughing, coughed**
VERB When you **cough**, you force air out of your throat with a sudden harsh noise.

**could**
VERB 1 the past tense of **can**
VERB 2 You use **could** to say that something might happen or might be true. • It **could** rain later.
VERB 3 You use **could** when you are asking for something politely. • **Could** you tell me the way to the station, please?

**couldn't**
VERB a contraction of could not

**council councils**
NOUN a group of people elected to look after something, especially the affairs of a town, district or county

**counsel counsels, counselling, counselled**
NOUN 1 advice
VERB 2 If someone **counsels** people, they give them advice about their problems.

**count counts, counting, counted**
VERB 1 When you **count**, you say all the numbers in order up to a particular number.
VERB 2 If you **count**, or **count** up, all the things in a group, you add them up to see how many there are.
PHRASE 3 If you **keep count** of something, you keep a record of how often it happens.
• Who's **keeping count** of the score?
PHRASE 4 If you **lose count** of something, you cannot remember how often it has happened.

**count on**
VERB If you can **count** on someone or something, you can rely on them. • You can **count** on me to help.

**counter counters**
NOUN 1 a long, flat surface in a shop, over which goods are sold
NOUN 2 a small, flat, round object used in board games

**counterfeit counterfeits, counterfeiting, counterfeited**
ADJECTIVE 1 **Counterfeit** things are not genuine, but have been made to look genuine in order to deceive people.
• **counterfeit** money
VERB 2 If someone **counterfeits** something, they make an exact copy of it in order to trick people.

PRONUNCIATION TIP
This word is pronounced **kown**-ter-fit.

**countless**
ADJECTIVE too many to count

**country countries**
NOUN 1 one of the political areas the world is divided into
NOUN 2 land away from towns and cities
• It is peaceful living in the **country**.

**countryside**
NOUN land away from towns and cities

**county counties**
NOUN a region with its own local government
• The **county** of Lincolnshire is in the east of England.

**coup coups**
NOUN a group of people taking power in a country

PRONUNCIATION TIP
This word is pronounced **koo**.

**couple couples**
NOUN 1 two people who are married or having a romantic relationship
NOUN 2 A **couple** of things or people means two of them, or not very many.

**couplet couplets**
NOUN two lines of poetry together that usually rhyme

**coupon coupons**
NOUN 1 a piece of printed paper that entitles you to pay less than usual for something
NOUN 2 a form you fill in to ask for information or to enter a competition

a
b
c
d
e
f
g
h
i
j
k
l
m
n
o
p
q
r
s
t
u
v
w
x
y
z

**91**

**courage**

NOUN the quality shown by people who do things that they know are dangerous or difficult • *She showed great* **courage** *in her efforts to save them from the burning house.*

**courageous**

ADJECTIVE Someone who is **courageous** is willing to do things that they know are dangerous or difficult.

**courageously**

ADVERB in a way that shows you are willing to do things that you know are dangerous or difficult

**courgette courgettes**

NOUN a long vegetable with dark green or yellow skin

**courier couriers**

NOUN **1** someone employed by a travel company to look after people on holiday
NOUN **2** someone employed to deliver letters and parcels quickly

**course courses**

NOUN **1** a series of lessons or lectures
NOUN **2** a piece of land where races take place or golf is played
NOUN **3** the route something such as a ship or a river takes • *The captain changed* **course** *to avoid the storm.*
NOUN **4** one of the parts of a meal • *The first* **course** *was soup.*
PHRASE **5** If you say **of course**, you are showing that you are absolutely sure about something. • **Of course** *she wouldn't do a thing like that.*

**court courts**

NOUN **1** a place where legal matters are decided by a judge and jury or a magistrate. The judge and jury or magistrate can also be referred to as the **court**. • *He is due to appear in* **court** *next week.* • *The* **court** *awarded him ten thousand pounds in compensation.*
NOUN **2** a place where a game such as tennis or badminton is played
NOUN **3** the place where a king or queen lives and works

**courteous**

ADJECTIVE **Courteous** behaviour is polite and considerate.

**courtyard courtyards**

NOUN a flat area of ground surrounded by buildings or walls

**cousin cousins**

NOUN Your **cousin** is the child of your uncle or aunt.

**cove coves**

NOUN a small bay on the coast

**cover covers, covering, covered**

VERB **1** If you **cover** something, you put something else over it to protect it or hide
VERB **2** If something **covers** something else it forms a layer over it.
VERB **3** If you **cover** a particular distance, you travel that distance.
VERB **4** If you **cover** a subject, you discuss it in a lesson, course or book. • *We* **covered** *the Vikings in today's lesson.*
NOUN **5** something put over an object to protect it or keep it warm
NOUN **6** The **cover** of a book or magazine is its outside.
NOUN **7** **Cover** is trees, rocks or other places where you can shelter or hide. • *When it started raining they ran for* **cover**.

**coverage**

NOUN The **coverage** of something in the news is the reporting of it. • *There was complete* **coverage** *of the Wimbledon finals on television.*

**cow cows**

NOUN a large female mammal kept on farms for its milk and meat

**coward cowards**

NOUN a person who is easily frightened and avoids dangerous situations

**cowardice**

NOUN the quality shown by someone who is easily frightened and avoids dangerous situations

**cowboy cowboys**

NOUN a man employed to look after cattle in America

**coy coyer, coyest**

ADJECTIVE If someone behaves in a **coy** way, they pretend to be shy and modest.

**crab crabs**

NOUN a crustacean with four pairs of legs, two claws, and a flat, round body covered by a shell

**ack** **cracks, cracking, cracked**

VERB **1** If something **cracks**, or if something **cracks** it, it becomes damaged, with lines appearing on its surface.

VERB **2** If you **crack** a joke, you tell it.

VERB **3** If you **crack** a problem or code, you solve it.

NOUN **4** one of the lines appearing on something when it cracks

NOUN **5** a narrow gap ● *My ring fell into a* ***crack*** *in the pavement.*

**acker** **crackers**

NOUN **1** a thin, crisp biscuit that is often eaten with cheese

NOUN **2** a paper-covered tube that pulls apart with a bang, and usually has a toy and paper hat inside

**ackle** **crackles, crackling, crackled**

VERB **1** If something **crackles**, it makes a series of short sharp sounds. ● *The bonfire started to* ***crackle*** *as the flames grew higher.*

NOUN **2** a short sharp sound

**adle** **cradles, cradling, cradled**

NOUN **1** a box-shaped bed for a baby

VERB **2** If you **cradle** something in your arms or hands, you hold it there carefully.

**aft** **crafts**

NOUN **1** an activity that needs skill with the hands, such as weaving, carving or pottery

NOUN **2** a boat, plane or spacecraft

**aftsman** **craftsmen**

NOUN a man who makes things skilfully with his hands

**aftswoman** **craftswomen**

NOUN a woman who makes things skilfully with her hands

**afty** **craftier, craftiest**

ADJECTIVE **Crafty** people get what they want by tricking other people in a clever way.

SYNONYMS: cunning, wily

**ag** **crags**

NOUN a steep, rugged rock or peak

**am** **crams, cramming, crammed**

VERB If you **cram** people or things into a place, you put more in than there is room for. ● *I* ***crammed*** *my dirty washing into the washing machine.*

**amp** **cramps**

NOUN pain caused when muscles contract

**cramped**

ADJECTIVE If a room or a building is **cramped**, it is not big enough for the people or things in it.

**crane** **cranes, craning, craned**

NOUN **1** a machine that moves heavy things by lifting them in the air

NOUN **2** a large bird with a long neck and long legs

VERB **3** If you **crane** your neck, you extend your head in a particular direction to see or hear something better.

**crash** **crashes, crashing, crashed**

NOUN **1** an accident in which a moving vehicle hits something and is damaged

NOUN **2** a sudden, loud noise

VERB **3** If a vehicle **crashes**, it hits something and is badly damaged.

**crate** **crates**

NOUN a large box used for transporting or storing things

**crater** **craters**

NOUN a wide hole in the ground caused by something hitting it or by an explosion ● *The surface of the moon has many* ***craters***.

WORD HISTORY

from Greek *krater* meaning mixing-bowl

**crave** **craves, craving, craved**

VERB If you **crave** something, you want it very much. ● *I* ***craved*** *a bar of chocolate.*

**craving** **cravings**

NOUN a feeling of wanting something very much

**crawl** **crawls, crawling, crawled**

VERB **1** When you **crawl**, you move forward on your hands and knees.

VERB **2** When an insect or vehicle **crawls** somewhere, it moves there very slowly.

**crayon** **crayons**

NOUN a coloured pencil or a stick of coloured wax

**craze** **crazes**

NOUN something that is very popular for a short time

**crazy** **crazier, craziest**

ADJECTIVE **1** (*informal*) very strange or foolish

ADJECTIVE **2** (*informal*) If you are **crazy** about something or someone, you like them very much.

**creak** creaks, creaking, creaked
VERB **1** If something **creaks**, it makes a harsh sound when it moves or when you stand on it.
NOUN **2** a harsh, squeaking noise

**creaky** creakier, creakiest
ADJECTIVE Something that is **creaky** makes a harsh sound when it moves or when you stand on it. • *creaky* floorboards

**cream** creams
NOUN **1** a thick, yellowish-white liquid taken from the top of milk
NOUN **2** a substance that you can rub into your skin to make it soft or protect it
ADJECTIVE **3** a yellowish-white colour

**crease** creases, creasing, creased
NOUN **1** an irregular line that appears on cloth or paper when it is crumpled
NOUN **2** a straight line on something that has been pressed or folded neatly • *Dad ironed a sharp* **crease** *in his best trousers.*
VERB **3** If you **crease** something, you make lines appear on it.

**create** creates, creating, created
VERB If someone **creates** something, they cause it to happen or exist.

**creation** creations
NOUN **1** **Creation** is when someone makes something happen or exist.
NOUN **2** something that has been made

**creative**
ADJECTIVE **Creative** people are good at inventing and developing new ideas.

**creature** creatures
NOUN any living thing that can make itself move

**crèche** crèches
NOUN a place where small children are looked after while their parents are working

WORD HISTORY
from old French *crèche* meaning crib or manger

**credit** credits
NOUN **1** a system where you pay for something in small amounts, regularly over a period of time
NOUN **2** praise given to you for good work
PLURAL NOUN **3** **Credits** are the list of people who helped make a film, record or television programme.
PHRASE **4** If your bank account is **in credit**, you have money in it.

**credit card** credit cards
NOUN a plastic card that allows someone to buy goods on credit rather than paying wi cash

**creek** creeks
NOUN a narrow inlet where the sea comes a long way into the land

**creep** creeps, creeping, crept
VERB If you **creep** somewhere, you move there quietly and slowly.

**creepy** creepier, creepiest
ADJECTIVE strange and frightening • *The film was* **creepy**.

SYNONYMS: eerie, spooky

**cremate** cremates, cremating, cremated
VERB If someone is **cremated** when they d their body is burned instead of buried.

**crematorium** crematoriums or crematoria
NOUN a building in which people are cremated

**crescent** crescents
NOUN a curved shape that is wider in the middle than at the ends, like a new moon

**cress**
NOUN a plant with small, strong-tasting leaves, used in salads

**crest** crests
NOUN **1** the highest part of a hill or wave
NOUN **2** a tuft of feathers on top of a bird's head
NOUN **3** a special sign of something, such a a school or other organisation

**crevice** crevices
NOUN a narrow crack or gap in rock

**crew** crews
NOUN The **crew** of a ship, aeroplane or spacecraft are the people who operate it.

**cricket** crickets
NOUN **1** an outdoor game played by two teams, who take turns at scoring runs by hitting a ball with a bat
NOUN **2** a small, jumping insect that produces sounds by rubbing its wings together

**ied**
VERB the past tense and past participle of **cry**

**ime crimes**
NOUN an action for which you can be punished by law

**iminal criminals**
NOUN **1** someone who has committed a crime
ADJECTIVE **2** involving or relating to crime

**imson**
NOUN **1** a dark, purplish-red colour
ADJECTIVE **2** having a dark, purplish-red colour

**inkle crinkles, crinkling, crinkled**
VERB **1** If something **crinkles**, it becomes slightly creased or folded.
NOUN **2** a small crease or fold

**ipple cripples, crippling, crippled**
VERB If someone is **crippled** by something, they are injured so severely that they can never move properly again.

**ippling**
ADJECTIVE causing so much pain that someone is not able to move properly

**isis crises**
NOUN a serious or dangerous situation
• The food **crisis** was caused by drought.

**isp crisper, crispest; crisps**
ADJECTIVE **1** pleasantly fresh and firm
• **crisp** lettuce leaves
NOUN **2** a thin slice of potato that has been fried until it is hard and crunchy

**itic critics**
NOUN **1** someone who writes reviews of books, films, plays or musical performances for newspapers or magazines
NOUN **2** a person who criticises someone or something publicly

**itical**
ADJECTIVE **1** A **critical** time or situation is a very important and serious one when things must be done correctly.
ADJECTIVE **2** If the state of a sick or injured person is **critical**, they are in danger of dying.
ADJECTIVE **3** Someone who is **critical** judges people and things very severely.

**iticise criticises, criticising, criticised;**
also spelt **criticize**
VERB If you **criticise** someone or something, you say what you think is wrong with them.

**iticism criticisms**
NOUN **1** spoken or written disapproval of someone or something

NOUN **2** A **criticism** of a book, film or play is an examination of its good and bad points.

**croak croaks, croaking, croaked**
VERB **1** When animals and birds **croak**, they make harsh, low sounds.
NOUN **2** a harsh, low sound

**croaky croakier, croakiest**
ADJECTIVE If your voice is **croaky**, it sounds low and harsh as if you have a sore throat.

**crochet crochets, crocheting, crocheted**
NOUN **1** a kind of knitting done with a hooked needle and cotton or wool
VERB **2** If you **crochet**, you use a hooked needle and wool or cotton to make lacy material for things such as clothes and shawls.

PRONUNCIATION TIP
This word is pronounced **kroh**-shay.

**crockery**
NOUN things you use for eating and drinking, such as plates, cups, bowls and saucers

**crocodile crocodiles**
NOUN a large, scaly, meat-eating reptile that lives in tropical rivers

WORD HISTORY
from Greek *krokodeilos* meaning lizard

**crocodile clip crocodile clips**
NOUN a small clip used for making electrical connections

**crocus crocuses**
NOUN **Crocuses** are yellow, purple or white flowers that grow in early spring.

**crook crooks**
NOUN **1** a criminal
NOUN **2** The **crook** of your arm or leg is the soft, inside part of your elbow or your knee.
NOUN **3** a long stick with a hooked end used by shepherds

**crooked**
ADJECTIVE **1** bent or twisted
ADJECTIVE **2** dishonest

**crop crops, cropping, cropped**
NOUN **1** plants such as wheat and potatoes that are grown for food
NOUN **2** the plants collected at harvest time
• They gather two **crops** of rice a year.
VERB **3** If you **crop** something such as your hair, you cut it very short.

a
b
c
d
e
f
g
h
i
j
k
l
m
n
o
p
q
r
s
t
u
v
w
x
y
z

**95**

**cross** crosses, crossing, crossed; crosser, crossest

VERB **1** If you **cross** something, such as a room or a road, you go to the other side of it.

VERB **2** Lines or roads that **cross** meet and go across each other.

VERB **3** If you **cross** your arms, legs or fingers, you put one on top of the other.

NOUN **4** a mark or a shape like + or ×

ADJECTIVE **5** Someone who is **cross** is rather angry.

**cross out**

VERB If you **cross out** words on a page, you draw a line through them.

**cross-country**

NOUN the sport of running across open countryside, rather than on roads or a track

**crossing** crossings

NOUN **1** a place where you can cross the road, a railway or a river

NOUN **2** a journey by ship to a place across the sea

**crossroads**

NOUN a place where two roads meet and cross each other

**cross-section** cross-sections

NOUN **1** the flat part of something that you see when you cut straight through it to see inside • *We looked at **cross-sections** of kiwi fruit and oranges.*

NOUN **2** a typical sample of people or things • *We interviewed a **cross-section** of teenagers.*

**crossword** crosswords

NOUN a word puzzle in which you work out answers to clues and write them in a grid

**crouch** crouches, crouching, crouched

VERB If you **crouch**, you lower your body with your knees bent.

**crow** crows, crowing, crowed

NOUN **1** a large black bird that makes a loud, harsh sound

VERB **2** When a cock **crows**, it makes a series of loud sounds, usually early in the morning.

**crowbar** crowbars

NOUN a heavy, iron bar used as a lever or for forcing things open

**crowd** crowds, crowding, crowded

NOUN **1** a large group of people gathered together

VERB **2** When people **crowd** around someone or something, they gather closely together around them.

**crown** crowns, crowning, crowned

NOUN **1** a circular ornament made of gold or jewels, which a king or queen wears on their head

VERB **2** When a king or queen is **crowned**, a crown is put on their head and they are officially made king or queen.

**crucial**

ADJECTIVE Something that is **crucial** is very important.

**crucifixion** crucifixions

NOUN **Crucifixion** is when a person is tied nailed to a cross and left there to die.

**crucify** crucifies, crucifying, crucified

VERB When a person is **crucified** they are tied or nailed to a cross and left there to d

**crude** cruder, crudest

ADJECTIVE **1** rough and simple • *a **crude** she made of old boxes*

ADJECTIVE **2** rude and vulgar

**cruel** crueller, cruellest

ADJECTIVE **Cruel** people deliberately cause pain or distress to other people or to animals.

SYNONYMS: brutal, unkind

**cruelly**

ADVERB in a way that deliberately causes p or distress to other people or to animals

**cruelty**

NOUN behaviour in which someone deliberately causes pain or distress to oth people or to animals

**cruise** cruises, cruising, cruised

NOUN **1** a holiday in which you travel on a ship and visit places

VERB **2** When a vehicle **cruises**, it moves a constant, moderate speed.

**crumb** crumbs

NOUN a very small piece of bread or cake

**crumble** crumbles, crumbling, crumbled

VERB When something **crumbles**, or whe you **crumble** it, it breaks into small piec

**crumple** crumples, crumpling, crumpled

VERB If you **crumple** paper or cloth, you squash it so that it is full of creases and folds.

**crunch crunches, crunching, crunched**
VERB If you **crunch** something, you crush it noisily, for example between your teeth or under your feet.

**crusade crusades**
NOUN **1** In the Middle Ages, the **Crusades** were a number of expeditions to Palestine by Christians who were attempting to recapture the Holy Land from Muslims.
NOUN **2** a long and determined attempt to achieve something

**WORD HISTORY**
From Spanish *cruzar* meaning to take up the cross

**crusader crusaders**
NOUN **1** In the Middle Ages, the **Crusaders** were Christians who made expeditions to Palestine to try to recapture the Holy Land from Muslims.
NOUN **2** someone who makes a long and determined attempt to achieve something

**crush crushes, crushing, crushed**
VERB **1** If you **crush** something, you squeeze it hard until its shape is destroyed. • *He crushed the empty can.*
VERB **2** If you **crush** against someone or something, you press hard against them. • *We crushed against each other in the crowded bus.*

**crust crusts**
NOUN **1** the hard outside part of a loaf
NOUN **2** a hard layer on top of something • *the Earth's crust*
→ Have a look at the illustration for **earth**

**crustacean crustaceans**
NOUN an animal with a hard outer shell and several pairs of legs, which usually lives in water • *Crabs, lobsters and shrimps are crustaceans.*

**PRONUNCIATION TIP**
This word is pronounced krus-**tay**-shun.

**crutch crutches**
NOUN a support like a long stick that you lean on if you have injured your leg or foot • *I was on crutches while my ankle healed.*

**cry cries, crying, cried**
VERB **1** When you **cry**, tears come from your eyes because you are unhappy or hurt.
VERB **2** If you **cry** something, you shout it or say it loudly.

NOUN **3** a shout or other loud sound made with your voice

**crypt crypts**
NOUN an underground room beneath a church, usually used as a burial place

**crystal crystals**
NOUN **1** a piece of a mineral that has formed naturally into a regular shape
NOUN **2** a type of transparent rock, used in jewellery
NOUN **3** a type of very high-quality glass

**cub cubs**
NOUN **1** the young of some wild animals • *a fox **cub*** • *a lion **cub***
NOUN **2** The **Cubs** is an organisation for young boys before they join the Scouts.

**cube cubes**
NOUN a solid shape with six square faces that are all the same size

**cubic**
ADJECTIVE **1** shaped like a cube
ADJECTIVE **2** used to describe volume when you measure height, width and depth • *a **cubic** metre*

**cubicle cubicles**
NOUN a small enclosed area in a place such as a sports centre or a shop, where you can dress and undress

**cuboid cuboids**
NOUN a rectangular, three-dimensional box shape. A **cuboid** has six faces, all of which are rectangles.

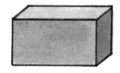

**cuckoo cuckoos**
NOUN a grey bird with a two-note call.
**Cuckoos** lay their eggs in other birds' nests.

**97**

**cucumber** cucumbers

NOUN a long, thin, green vegetable that is eaten raw

**cud**

NOUN food that has been chewed and digested more than once by cows, sheep or other animals that have more than one stomach

**cuddle** cuddles, cuddling, cuddled

VERB 1 If you **cuddle** someone, you hold them closely in your arms as a way of showing your affection.

NOUN 2 If you give someone a **cuddle**, you cuddle them.

**cuddly** cuddlier, cuddliest

ADJECTIVE 1 If a person or animal is **cuddly**, you want to cuddle them.

ADJECTIVE 2 A **cuddly** toy is soft and is intended for children to cuddle.

**cuff** cuffs

NOUN the end part of a sleeve, especially a shirt sleeve

**cul-de-sac** cul-de-sacs

NOUN a road that does not lead to any other roads because one end is blocked off

WORD HISTORY

from French *cul + de + sac* meaning bottom of the bag

**culprit** culprits

NOUN someone who has done something harmful or wrong

**cult** cults

NOUN 1 a small religious group, especially one that is considered strange

ADJECTIVE 2 very popular or fashionable among a particular group of people

• *It became a **cult** film.*

**cultivate** cultivates, cultivating, cultivated

VERB When someone **cultivates** land, they grow crops on it.

**cultivation**

NOUN **Cultivation** is when someone grows crops on land.

**culture** cultures

NOUN the ideas, customs and art of a particular society

**cunning**

ADJECTIVE A **cunning** person or plan achiev things in a clever way, often by deceiving people.

SYNONYMS: crafty, sly, wily

**cup** cups, cupping, cupped

NOUN 1 a small, round container with a handle, which you drink from

NOUN 2 a large metal container with two handles, which is given as a prize

VERB 3 If you **cup** your hands, you put ther together to make a shape like a cup.

**cupboard** cupboards

NOUN 1 a piece of furniture with doors and shelves

NOUN 2 a very small room for storing thing in • *The broom is in the **cupboard** under th stairs.*

**curator** curators

NOUN the person in a museum or art galler in charge of its contents

**curb** curbs, curbing, curbed

VERB If you **curb** something, you keep it within limits. • *You must **curb** your spendi on comics.*

**curdle** curdles, curdling, curdled

VERB When milk **curdles**, it turns sour.

**cure** cures, curing, cured

VERB 1 If a doctor **cures** someone of an illness, they help them get better.

NOUN 2 something that heals or helps someone to get better • *There is still no cu for a cold.*

VERB 3 If someone **cures** meat or fish, they smoke it to give it flavour and preserve it.

**curfew** curfews

NOUN a rule or a law stating that people must stay indoors between particular time at night

**curiosity** curiosities

NOUN 1 the desire to know something or about many things

NOUN 2 something unusual and interesting

**rious**

ADJECTIVE **1** Someone who is **curious** wants to know more about something.

SYNONYMS: inquisitive, nosy

ADJECTIVE **2** Something that is **curious** is unusual or difficult to understand.

SYNONYMS: strange, peculiar

**rl curls, curling, curled**

NOUN **1 Curls** are lengths of hair shaped in tight curves and circles.

NOUN **2** a curved or spiral shape ● *A curl of smoke rose from the chimney.*

VERB **3** If something **curls**, it moves in a curve or spiral. ● *Smoke curled up the chimney.*

**rly curlier, curliest**

ADJECTIVE **1 Curly** hair has tight curves and circles in it.

ADJECTIVE **2** curved in shape

**rrant currants**

NOUN a small, dried grape. **Currants** are often used in cakes and puddings.

**rrency currencies**

NOUN A country's **currency** is its coins and banknotes.

**rrent currents**

NOUN **1** a steady continuous flowing movement of water or air

NOUN **2** An electric **current** is a flow of electricity through a wire or circuit.

ADJECTIVE **3** Something that is **current** is happening now. ● *current fashion trends*

**rriculum curriculums or curricula**

NOUN the different courses taught at a school or university

**rry curries**

NOUN an Indian dish made with hot spices

**rse curses, cursing, cursed**

NOUN **1** an evil spell ● *She said the old house had a curse on it.*

VERB **2** If you **curse**, you swear because you are angry.

**rsor cursors**

NOUN a sign on a computer monitor that shows where the next letter or symbol is

**rtain curtains**

NOUN a hanging piece of material that can be pulled across a window

**rtsy curtsies, curtsying, curtsied**

NOUN **1** a little bobbing bow to show respect

● *I made a little curtsy to the Queen.*

VERB **2** the action of making a curtsy

**curve curves, curving, curved**

NOUN **1** a smooth, gradually bending line

VERB **2** When something **curves**, it moves in a curve or has the shape of a curve.

● *The lane curved to the right.*

**curved**

ADJECTIVE moving in a curve or having the shape of a curve

**cushion cushions, cushioning, cushioned**

NOUN **1** a soft object that you put on a seat to make it more comfortable

VERB **2** When something **cushions** something else, it reduces its effect. ● *The pile of leaves cushioned his fall.*

**custard**

NOUN a sweet, yellow sauce made from milk and eggs

**custody**

NOUN **1** If someone has **custody** of a child, they have the legal right to keep it and look after it.

PHRASE **2** Someone who is **in custody** is being kept in prison until they can be tried in a court.

WORD HISTORY

from Latin *custos* meaning a guard

**custom customs**

NOUN something that people usually do

● *the custom of decorating the house for Christmas*

**customary**

ADJECTIVE usual

**customer customers**

NOUN a person who buys things from a shop or company

**customs**

NOUN the place at a border, airport or harbour where you declare any goods that you are bringing into the country

**cut cuts, cutting, cut**

VERB **1** If you **cut** something, you use a pair of scissors, a knife or another sharp tool to mark it or remove parts of it.

VERB **2** If you **cut** yourself, you injure yourself with a sharp object.

NOUN **3** a mark made with a knife or a sharp tool

NOUN **4** a reduction in something ● *There were lots of price cuts during the sales.*

a
b
c
d
e
f
g
h
i
j
k
l
m
n
o
p
q
r
s
t
u
v
w
x
y
z

**cutlery**
NOUN knives, forks and spoons

**cyberattack cyberattacks**
NOUN an attempt to damage or break into a computer system, usually to get the information stored there • *The company claimed its website had been hit by a* **cyberattack**.

**cyberbullying**
NOUN sending nasty or threatening messages to someone on an electronic device like a phone, tablet or computer • *The girl was a victim of* **cyberbullying**.

**cycle cycles, cycling, cycled**
NOUN 1 a bicycle
NOUN 2 a series of events that is repeated again and again • *the* **cycle** *of the seasons*
VERB 3 When you **cycle**, you ride a bicycle.

**cyclist cyclists**
NOUN someone who rides a bicycle

**cyclone cyclones**
NOUN a violent wind that blows in a spiral like a corkscrew

**cygnet cygnets**
NOUN a young swan

**cylinder cylinders**
NOUN 1 a hollow or solid shape with straight sides and equal circular faces at each end
NOUN 2 the part of an engine that the piston moves in

**cylindrical**
ADJECTIVE Something that is **cylindrical** has a hollow or solid shape with straight sides and equal circular faces at each end.

**cymbal cymbals**
NOUN a circular brass plate used as a percussion instrument. **Cymbals** are clashed together or hit with a stick.

# Dd

**dab dabs, dabbing, dabbed**
VERB 1 f you **dab** something, you touch it several times using quick light movemen
• *He* **dabbed** *the stain with a tissue.*
VERB 2 If you **dab**, you do a dance move where you put one arm in front of your fa and the other out to the side.

**dabble dabbles, dabbling, dabbled**
VERB If you **dabble** in something, you wor or play at it without being seriously invol in it.

**dad** or **daddy dads** or **daddies**
NOUN (*informal*) Your **dad** or your **daddy** i your father.

**daffodil daffodils**
NOUN a plant with yellow, trumpet-shaped flowers that blooms in spring

**daft dafter, daftest**
ADJECTIVE silly and not very sensible

**dagger daggers**
NOUN a weapon like a short knife

**daily**
ADJECTIVE occurring every day

**dainty daintier, daintiest**
ADJECTIVE very delicate and pretty

**dairy dairies**
NOUN 1 a shop or company that supplies milk and milk products
NOUN 2 In New Zealand, a **dairy** is a small shop selling groceries.
ADJECTIVE 3 **Dairy** products are foods made from milk, such as butter, cheese, cream and yogurt.

**daisy daisies**
NOUN a small, wild flower with a yellow centre and small, white petals

**WORD HISTORY**
from Old English *deagesege* meaning day's eye, because the daisy opens in the dayti and closes at night

**lmatian Dalmatians**
ɔUN a large, smooth-haired white dog with
lack or brown spots

**m dams**
ɔUN a barrier built across a river to hold
ack water

**mage damages, damaging,
amaged**
ERB If you **damage** something, you harm
r spoil it.

**mp damper, dampest**
DJECTIVE slightly wet

**mson damsons**
ɔUN **1** a small, blue-black plum
ɔUN **2** the tree that damsons grow on

**nce dances, dancing, danced**
ERB **1** When you **dance**, you move around
ɳ time to music.
ɪOUN **2** a series of rhythmic movements that
ou do in time to music
ɪOUN **3** a social event where people dance
ɪith each other

**ndelion dandelions**
ɔUN a wild plant with yellow flowers that
ɔrm a ball of fluffy seeds

WORD HISTORY
rom Old French *dent de lion* meaning lion's
ɔoth, referring to the shape of the leaves

**ndruff**
ɔUN small, loose scales of dead skin in
omeone's hair

**nger dangers**
ɔUN the possibility that someone may be
ɑarmed or killed

SYNONYMS: peril, risk

**ngerous**
DJECTIVE If something is **dangerous**, it
ʂ likely to harm or kill someone. ● *It is*
***dangerous** to walk close to the edge of the cliff.*

SYNONYMS: unsafe, hazardous

**ngerously**
DVERB in a way that is likely to harm or kill
omeone ● *He was **dangerously** overweight.*

**ngle dangles, dangling, dangled**
ERB When something **dangles**, or when
ɾou **dangle** it, it swings or hangs loosely.
● *We sat by the pool and **dangled** our legs in
he water.*

**dappled**
ADJECTIVE marked with patches of a different
or darker shade ● *The lawn was **dappled***
*with the shadows of the leafy trees.*

**dare dares, daring, dared**
VERB **1** If you **dare** to do something, you
have the courage to do it. ● *She doesn't **dare***
*to tell them how she really feels.*
VERB **2** If you **dare** someone to do
something, you challenge them to do it.
● *I **dare** you to ask him his name.*

WORD HISTORY
from Old English *durran* meaning to venture
or to be bold

**daredevil daredevils**
NOUN a person who enjoys doing dangerous
things

**daring**
ADJECTIVE **1** bold and willing to take risks
● *Ben was probably more **daring** than I was.*
NOUN **2** the courage required to do things
that are dangerous

**dark darker, darkest**
ADJECTIVE **1** If it is **dark**, there is not enough
light to see properly.

ANTONYM: light

ADJECTIVE **2 Dark** colours have a lot of black,
grey or brown tones in them.

ANTONYM: light

NOUN **3** The **dark** is when there is no light.
● *Many children are scared of the **dark**.*

**darken darkens, darkening, darkened**
VERB If something **darkens**, it becomes
darker than it was before. ● *The sky*
***darkened** as the storm approached.*

**darkness**
NOUN the state of being dark ● *The house was
in complete **darkness**.*

**darling darlings**
NOUN You call someone **darling** if you love
them or like them very much.

**darn darns, darning, darned**
VERB When you **darn** a hole in a garment,
you mend it with crossing stitches.

a
b
c
d
e
f
g
h
i
j
k
l
m
n
o
p
q
r
s
t
u
v
w
x
y
z

**101**

**dart** darts, darting, darted
NOUN **1** a small, pointed arrow
NOUN **2 Darts** is a game in which the players throw **darts** at a round board divided into numbered sections.
VERB **3** If you **dart** somewhere, you move there quickly and suddenly.

**dash** dashes, dashing, dashed
VERB **1** If you **dash** somewhere, you rush there.
NOUN **2** the punctuation mark (–) which may be used to show a break in a sentence, or instead of brackets to separate extra information from the main text

**dashboard** dashboards
NOUN the instrument panel in a car

**data**
NOUN information, usually in the form of facts or statistics

---

**LANGUAGE TIP**
*Data* is really a plural word, but is usually used as a singular word: *Customer data is stored here.*

---

**database** databases
NOUN a collection of information stored in a computer

**date** dates
NOUN **1** a particular day or year that can be named • *What is your **date** of birth?*
NOUN **2** If you have a **date**, you have an appointment to meet someone.
NOUN **3** a small, brown, sticky fruit with a stone inside. **Dates** grow on palm trees.

**daughter** daughters
NOUN Someone's **daughter** is their female child.

**dawdle** dawdles, dawdling, dawdled
VERB If you **dawdle**, you are slow about doing something or going somewhere.
• *Don't **dawdle**, we have to be there in ten minutes.*

**dawn** dawns
NOUN the time in the morning when light first appears in the sky

**day** days
NOUN **1** the time taken between one midnight and the next. There are 24 hours in one **day**.
NOUN **2** the period of light between sunrise and sunset

**daydream** daydreams, daydreaming, daydreamed
NOUN **1** pleasant thoughts about things th you would like to happen
VERB **2** When you **daydream**, you drift of into a daydream.

**daylight**
NOUN the part of the day when it is light

**daytime**
NOUN the part of the day when it is light

**daze**
PHRASE If you are **in a daze**, you are confused and bewildered.

**dazzle** dazzles, dazzling, dazzled
VERB If a bright light **dazzles** you, it blind you for a moment.

**dazzling**
ADJECTIVE A **dazzling** light is so bright that blinds you for a moment.

**de-**
PREFIX added to some words to mean remo or reversal of something • *She **de**bugged computer program.* • *We had to **de**frost the windscreen before leaving.*

**dead**
ADJECTIVE **1** no longer living
ADJECTIVE **2** no longer functioning • *The pho went **dead**.*
ADVERB **3** precisely or exactly • *We arrived **dead** on eight o'clock.*

**deadly** deadlier, deadliest
ADJECTIVE **1** likely or able to cause death
• *a **deadly** disease*
ADVERB **2** used to emphasise how serious or unpleasant something is • ***deadly** dangerous* • ***deadly** serious*

**deaf** deafer, deafest
ADJECTIVE **Deaf** people are unable to hear anything or unable to hear well.

**deafening**
ADJECTIVE A **deafening** sound is so loud th you cannot hear anything else.

**deal** deals, dealing, dealt
NOUN **1** an agreement or arrangement, especially in business
VERB **2** When you **deal** cards, you give the out to the players.
PHRASE **3 A good deal** or **a great deal** of something is a lot of it.
**deal with**
VERB If you **deal with** something, you d what is necessary to sort it out.

**ar dearer, dearest**
NOUN **1** You call someone **dear** as a sign of affection.
ADJECTIVE **2** Something that is **dear** is very expensive.
ADJECTIVE **3** You use **dear** at the beginning of a letter, with the name of the person you are writing to. ● *Dear Sunita.*

**ath deaths**
NOUN the end of the life of a human being or other animal or plant

**bate debates, debating, debated**
NOUN **1** argument or discussion
NOUN **2** a formal discussion in which opposing views are expressed
VERB **3** When people **debate** something, they discuss it in a formal way.

**bit card debit cards**
NOUN a plastic card that allows someone to buy goods using the money in their bank account

**bris**
NOUN fragments or rubble left after something has been destroyed ● *After the eruption, volcanic debris was found scattered for miles.*

**bt debts**
NOUN a sum of money that someone owes

**but debuts**
NOUN a performer's first public appearance

**cade decades**
NOUN a period of ten years

**caffeinated**
ADJECTIVE **Decaffeinated** coffee or tea has had most of the caffeine removed.

**cagon decagons**
NOUN a flat shape with ten straight sides

**cathlon decathlons**
NOUN an athletic competition in which competitors take part in ten different events

**cay decays, decaying, decayed**
VERB When things **decay**, they rot or go bad.

**ceased**
ADJECTIVE (*formal*) A **deceased** person is someone who has recently died.

**ceit**
NOUN behaviour that makes people believe something to be true that is not true

**ceive deceives, deceiving, deceived**
VERB If you **deceive** someone, you make them believe something that is not true.

**decelerate decelerates, decelerating, decelerated**
VERB To **decelerate** is to slow down.

ANTONYM: accelerate

**December**
NOUN the twelfth month of the year. **December** has 31 days.

**decent**
ADJECTIVE honest and respectable

**deception deceptions**
NOUN **1** something that is intended to trick or deceive someone
NOUN **2** the act of deceiving someone

**deceptive**
ADJECTIVE likely to make people believe that something is true when it is not

**decibel decibels**
NOUN the unit used to measure how loud a sound is

**decide decides, deciding, decided**
VERB If you **decide** to do something, you choose to do it, usually after thinking about it carefully.

SYNONYM: make up one's mind

**deciduous**
ADJECTIVE **Deciduous** trees lose their leaves in the autumn every year.

**decimal decimals**
ADJECTIVE **1** A **decimal** system involves counting in units of ten.
NOUN **2** A **decimal**, or **decimal** fraction, is a fraction in which a dot, called a **decimal** point, separates the whole numbers on the left from tenths, hundredths and thousandths on the right. For example, 0.5 represents $\frac{5}{10}$ (or $\frac{1}{2}$); 0.05 represents $\frac{5}{100}$ (or $\frac{1}{20}$). The number of digits to the right of the decimal point are **decimal** places. ● *3.142 is pi given to three decimal places.*

**decision decisions**
NOUN a choice or judgement that you make about something

**decisive**
ADJECTIVE **1** A **decisive** person is able to make decisions quickly.
ADJECTIVE **2** having an important influence on the result of something ● *The first goal was a decisive moment in the match.*

a
b
c
d
e
f
g
h
i
j
k
l
m
n
o
p
q
r
s
t
u
v
w
x
y
z

## deck decks

NOUN a downstairs or upstairs area on a bus or ship

→ Have a look at the illustration for **ship**

## declare declares, declaring, declared

VERB **1** If you **declare** something, you say it firmly and forcefully.

SYNONYMS: announce, proclaim, state

VERB **2** (*formal*) If something is **declared**, it is announced publicly. • *War was **declared** in 1939.*

## decline declines, declining, declined

VERB **1** If something **declines**, it becomes smaller or weaker. • *The number of students has **declined** this year.*

VERB **2** If you **decline** something, you politely refuse to accept it or do it.

## decode decodes, decoding, decoded

VERB If you **decode** a coded message, you convert it into ordinary language.

## decompose decomposes, decomposing, decomposed

VERB If something **decomposes**, it rots after it dies.

## decorate decorates, decorating, decorated

VERB **1** If you **decorate** something, you make it more attractive by adding things to it.

VERB **2** If you **decorate** a room or building, you paint or wallpaper it.

## decoy decoys

NOUN something used to lead a person or animal into a trap

## decrease decreases, decreasing, decreased

VERB If something **decreases**, or if you **decrease** it, it becomes less. • *The number of children in the class **decreased** rapidly.*

ANTONYM: increase

## decree decrees, decreeing, decreed

NOUN **1** an official order by the government, church or the rulers of a country

VERB **2** If someone **decrees** something, they announce formally that it will happen.

## dedicate dedicates, dedicating, dedicated

VERB **1** If you **dedicate** yourself to something, you give your time and energy to it.

VERB **2** If you **dedicate** a book or piece of music to someone, you say that it is writt[en] for them.

## deduct deducts, deducting, deducted

VERB If you **deduct** an amount from a tot[al] you take away.

## deed deeds

NOUN **1** something that is done • *a good* **deed**

NOUN **2** an important piece of paper or document that an agreement is written o[n]

## deep deeper, deepest

ADJECTIVE **1** going a long way down from th[e] surface • *a **deep** hole*

ADJECTIVE **2** great or intense • ***deep** affectio[n]*

ADJECTIVE **3** a low sound • *a **deep** voice*

## deer

NOUN a large, fast-running, graceful mammal with hooves, that lives wild in parts of Britain and other countries. Male **deer** have antlers.

**LANGUAGE TIP**
The plural of *deer* is *deer* or *deers*.

## deface defaces, defacing, defaced

VERB If you **deface** something, you damag[e] its appearance in some way. • *The gang **defaced** the walls with spray paint.*

## defeat defeats, defeating, defeated

VERB **1** If you **defeat** someone or somethin[g] you win a victory over them, or cause ther[m] to fail.

NOUN **2** the state of being beaten or of faili[ng] • *The team was downhearted after its **defea**[t]*

## defect defects, defecting, defected

NOUN **1** a fault or flaw in something

VERB **2** If someone **defects**, they leave thei[r] own country or organisation and join an opposing one.

## defective

ADJECTIVE Something that is **defective** is no[t] perfect or has something wrong with it.

## defence defences

NOUN **1** something that protects you agains[t] attack • *The walls around the castle were a good defence against invaders.*

NOUN **2** A country's **defences** are its arme[d] forces and its weapons.

**fend defends, defending, defended**
VERB **1** If you **defend** someone or something, ou protect them from harm or danger.
VERB **2** If you **defend** a person or their ideas, ou argue in support of them.

**fendant defendants**
NOUN a person in a court of law who is ccused of a crime

**fer defers, deferring, deferred**
VERB If you **defer** something, you put off oing it until later.

**fiance**
NOUN behaviour that shows you are not /illing to obey someone

**fiant**
ADJECTIVE If you are **defiant**, you behave in a /ay that shows you are not willing to obey omeone.

**ficiency deficiencies**
NOUN A **deficiency** is when there is not nough of something.

**ficient**
ADJECTIVE lacking in something

**fine defines, defining, defined**
VERB If you **define** something, you say what : is or what it means.

**finite**
ADJECTIVE **1** clear and unlikely to be changed • We must arrange a **definite** date for the party.
ADJECTIVE **2** true rather than being someone's uess or opinion

LANGUAGE TIP
here is no a in *definite*.

**finitely**
ADVERB certainly; without doubt • I am **efinitely** going on holiday next week.

**finition definitions**
NOUN a statement explaining the meaning of word or an idea

**flate deflates, deflating, deflated**
VERB If you **deflate** something, such as a tyre r balloon, you let all the air or gas out of it.

ANTONYMS: inflate, blow up

**forestation**
NOUN the cutting down or the destruction of ll the trees in an area

**deformed**
ADJECTIVE disfigured or abnormally shaped

**defrost defrosts, defrosting, defrosted**
VERB **1** If you **defrost** frozen food, you let it thaw out.
VERB **2** If you **defrost** a freezer or refrigerator, you remove the ice from it.

**defuse defuses, defusing, defused**
VERB **1** If someone **defuses** a bomb, they remove its fuse or detonator so that it cannot explode.
VERB **2** If you **defuse** a dangerous or tense situation, you make it less dangerous or tense.

**defy defies, defying, defied**
VERB If you **defy** a person or a law, you openly refuse to obey.

**degree degrees**
NOUN **1** a unit of measurement for temperatures, angles, and longitude and latitude, written as ° after a number • The temperature was 20 °C. • A right angle is a ninety-**degree** angle.
NOUN **2** an amount of a feeling or quality • As captain you have a high **degree** of responsibility.
NOUN **3** a university qualification gained after completing a course of study there

**dehydrated**
ADJECTIVE If someone is **dehydrated**, they are weak or ill because they have lost too much water from their body.

**deity deities**
NOUN a god or goddess

PRONUNCIATION TIP
This word is pronounced **day**-i-ti.

**dejected**
ADJECTIVE If you are **dejected**, you are sad and gloomy.

**dejection**
NOUN a sad and gloomy feeling

**delay delays, delaying, delayed**
VERB **1** If you **delay** doing something, you put it off until later.

SYNONYM: postpone

VERB **2** If something **delays** you, it makes you late or slows you down.
NOUN **3** If there is a **delay**, something does not happen until later than planned or expected.

a
b
c
d
e
f
g
h
i
j
k
l
m
n
o
p
q
r
s
t
u
v
w
x
y
z

**105**

**delete** deletes, deleting, deleted
VERB If you **delete** something written, you cross it out or remove it.

**deliberate**
ADJECTIVE **1** done on purpose or planned in advance
ADJECTIVE **2** slow and careful in speech and action • **deliberate** movements

**deliberately**
ADVERB **1** on purpose or planned in advance • Police believe the fire was started **deliberately**.
ADVERB **2** in a slow and careful way • He spoke slowly and **deliberately**.

**delicate**
ADJECTIVE **1** light and attractive • a **delicate** perfume
ADJECTIVE **2** fragile and needing to be handled carefully • a **delicate** china cup
ADJECTIVE **3** precise or sensitive • **delicate** instruments

**delicatessen** delicatessens
NOUN a shop selling unusual or imported foods

**delicious**
ADJECTIVE **Delicious** food or drink has an extremely pleasant taste.

SYNONYMS: delectable, scrumptious

**delight** delights, delighting, delighted
NOUN **1** great pleasure or joy
VERB **2** If something **delights** you, or if you are **delighted** by it, it gives you a lot of pleasure.

**delighted**
ADJECTIVE very pleased and happy

**delinquent** delinquents
NOUN a young person who commits minor crimes

**delirious**
ADJECTIVE **1** unable to speak or act in a rational way because of illness or fever
ADJECTIVE **2** wildly excited and happy

**deliver** delivers, delivering, delivered
VERB **1** If you **deliver** something to someone, you take it and give it to them.
VERB **2** If someone **delivers** a baby, they help the woman who is giving birth.

**delta** deltas
NOUN a triangular piece of land at the mouth of a river where it divides into separate streams

**deluge** deluges
NOUN a sudden, heavy downpour of rain

**demand** demands, demanding, demanded
VERB **1** If you **demand** something, you as for it forcefully.
NOUN **2** If there is **demand** for something lot of people want to buy it or have it.

**democracy** democracies
NOUN a system of government in which th people choose their leaders by voting for them in elections

**democratic**
ADJECTIVE using a system of government in which the people choose their leaders by voting for them in elections

**demolish** demolishes, demolishing, demolished
VERB If someone **demolishes** a building, they knock it down.

**demolition**
NOUN **Demolition** is when a building is knocked down.

**demon** demons
NOUN a devil or an evil spirit

**demonstrate** demonstrates, demonstrating, demonstrated
VERB **1** If you **demonstrate** something to somebody, you show them how to do it o how it works.
VERB **2** If people **demonstrate**, they marc or gather together to show that they opp or support something.

**demonstration** demonstrations
NOUN **1** If someone gives a **demonstrati** they show how to do something or how something works.
NOUN **2** a march or a gathering of people to show publicly what they think about something

**den** dens
NOUN **1** a home or hiding place of a wild animal
NOUN **2** a special place where you can do what you want without being disturbed

**denial** denials
NOUN **1** A **denial** of something is a statement that it is untrue.
NOUN **2** The **denial** of a request is the refu to grant it.

**nim denims**
NOUN strong, cotton cloth used for making clothes, especially jeans

**WORD HISTORY**
From French *serge de Nîmes*, meaning serge (a type of cloth) from Nîmes

**nominator denominators**
NOUN In mathematics, the **denominator** is the bottom number of a fraction.

**nse denser, densest**
ADJECTIVE **1** Something that is **dense** contains a lot of things or people in a small area. *We cut our way through the **dense** forest.*
ADJECTIVE **2** difficult to see through • *The **dense** fog prevented us from enjoying the view over the hills.*

**nsity densities**
NOUN **1 Density** is how many people or things are contained in an area.
NOUN **2** In science, **density** is the amount of much space something occupies (its volume) in relation to the amount of matter in it (its mass).

**nt dents, denting, dented**
VERB **1** If you **dent** something, you damage its surface by hitting it.
NOUN **2** a hollow in the surface of something

**ntal**
ADJECTIVE to do with teeth

**ntist dentists**
NOUN a person who is qualified to treat people's teeth

**ntures**
PLURAL NOUN false teeth

**ny denies, denying, denied**
VERB **1** If you **deny** something, you say that it is not true.
VERB **2** If you are **denied** something, you are refused it.

**odorant deodorants**
NOUN a substance used to hide or prevent the smell of sweat on your body

**part departs, departing, departed**
VERB When you **depart**, you leave.

**partment departments**
NOUN one of the sections into which a large shop or an organisation is divided

**department store department stores**
NOUN a very large shop divided into departments, each selling different types of goods

**departure departures**
NOUN **Departure** is when you leave a place.

**depend depends, depending, depended**
VERB **1** If one thing **depends** on another, it is influenced by it. • *The cooking time **depends** on the size of the potato.*
VERB **2** If you **depend** on someone or something, you trust them and rely on them.

**dependable**
ADJECTIVE If someone is **dependable**, you can trust them to be helpful, sensible and reliable.

**depict depicts, depicting, depicted**
VERB If you **depict** someone or something, you paint, draw or describe them.

**deport deports, deporting, deported**
VERB If someone is **deported** from a country they are sent out of it, either because they have no right to be there, because they have done something wrong or because they did not ask permission to be there.

**deposit deposits, depositing, deposited**
VERB **1** If you **deposit** something, you put it down or leave it somewhere.
NOUN **2** a sum of money given in part payment for goods or services

**depot depots**
NOUN **1** a place where supplies of food or equipment are stored until they are needed
NOUN **2** a large building or yard where buses or railway engines are kept when they are not being used

**depressed**
ADJECTIVE sad and gloomy

**depression depressions**
NOUN **1** a state of mind in which someone feels unhappy and has no energy or enthusiasm for anything
NOUN **2** a hollow in the ground or on any other surface
NOUN **3** a time when there is a lot of unemployment and poverty

**deprive deprives, depriving, deprived**
VERB If you **deprive** someone of something, you take it away from them or prevent them from having it.

a
b
c
d
e
f
g
h
i
j
k
l
m
n
o
p
q
r
s
t
u
v
w
x
y
z

**107**

## depth depths

NOUN **1** the measurement or distance between the top and bottom of something, or the back and front of something • *The **depth** of the swimming pool at the deep end is 1.5 m.*

PHRASE **2 In depth** means thoroughly. • *We studied the poem **in depth**.*

## deputy deputies

NOUN a person who helps someone in their job and acts on their behalf when they are away

## derail derails, derailed, derailing

VERB If a train is **derailed**, it comes off the railway tracks.

## derivation derivations

NOUN The **derivation** of something is where it has come from.

## derive derives, deriving, derived

VERB **1** (*formal*) If you **derive** something from someone or something, you get it from them. • *He **derives** great pleasure from music.*

VERB **2** If something is **derived** from something else, it comes from that thing. • *His name is **derived** from a Greek word.*

## descant descants

NOUN **1** The **descant** to a tune is another tune played at the same time but at a higher pitch.

ADJECTIVE **2** A **descant** musical instrument plays the highest notes in a range of instruments. • *a **descant** recorder*

## descend descends, descending, descended

VERB If someone or something **descends**, they move downwards. • *We **descended** to the basement in the lift.*

ANTONYM: ascend

## descendant descendants

NOUN A person's **descendants** are all the people in later generations who are related to them.

## describe describes, describing, described

VERB If you **describe** someone or something, you say what they are like.

## desert deserts, deserting, deserted

NOUN **1** an area of land, usually in a hot region, that has almost no water, rain, tr or plants • *the Sahara **Desert***

VERB **2** If someone **deserts** you, they leave you and no longer help or support you.

PRONUNCIATION TIP
The noun is pronounced **dez**-ert. The ver pronounced de-**zert**.

## deserted

ADJECTIVE A **deserted** building or place is o that people have left and never come bac to.

## deserve deserves, deserving, deserve

VERB If you **deserve** something, you earn or have a right to it.

## design designs, designing, designed

VERB **1** If you **design** something new, you plan what it should be like.

NOUN **2** a drawing from which something can be built or made

NOUN **3** a decorative pattern of lines or shapes

## desire desires, desiring, desired

VERB **1** If you **desire** something, you want

NOUN **2** a strong feeling of wanting something

SYNONYMS: longing, want, wish

## desk desks

NOUN a piece of furniture with a flat or sloping top, which you sit at to write, rea or work

## desktop

ADJECTIVE small enough to be used at a des • *a **desktop** computer*

## desolate

ADJECTIVE **1** deserted and bleak • *a desolat mountain top*

ADJECTIVE **2** lonely, very sad, and without h

## desolation

NOUN **1 Desolation** is when a place is deserted and bleak.

NOUN **2** the feeling of being lonely, very sa and without hope

## despair despairs, despairing, despair

NOUN **1** a total loss of hope

VERB **2** If you **despair**, you lose hope completely.

**sperate**

ADJECTIVE **1** If you are **desperate**, you are n such a bad situation that you will try anything to change it.

ADJECTIVE **2** A **desperate** situation is extremely dangerous or serious.

**spicable**

ADJECTIVE Something that is **despicable** is nasty, cruel or evil.

**spise despises, despising, despised**

VERB If you **despise** someone or something, you have a very low opinion of them.

**spite**

PREPOSITION If you do something **despite** some difficulty, you manage to do it anyway.

**ssert desserts**

NOUN a sweet food that you eat at the end of a meal

**PRONUNCIATION TIP**

This word is pronounced de-**zert**.

**stination destinations**

NOUN the place you are going to

**stined**

ADJECTIVE meant to happen • *They were destined to meet.*

**stiny destinies**

NOUN Your **destiny** is your fate: the things that will happen to you in the future.

**stitute**

ADJECTIVE without money or possessions, and therefore in great need

**stroy destroys, destroying, destroyed**

VERB If you **destroy** something, you damage it so much that it is completely ruined.

SYNONYMS: demolish, ruin, wreck

**struction**

NOUN the process of damaging something so much that it is completely ruined.

**structive**

ADJECTIVE Something that is **destructive** can cause great damage, harm or injury.

SYNONYM: damaging

**tach detaches, detaching, detached**

VERB If you **detach** something, you remove or unfasten it.

**detachable**

ADJECTIVE able to be removed or unfastened from something • *a coat with a detachable hood*

**detached**

ADJECTIVE separate or standing apart • *It was a detached house, standing alone at the top of the hill.*

**detail details**

NOUN **1** an individual fact or feature of something • *I remember every detail of that film.*

PLURAL NOUN **2 Details** about something are information about it. For example, your **details** might be your name and address.

**detain detains, detaining, detained**

VERB If you **detain** someone, you keep them from going somewhere or doing something.

**detect detects, detecting, detected**

VERB If you **detect** something, you notice or find it. • *X-rays can detect broken bones.*

**detective detectives**

NOUN a person, usually a police officer, whose job is to investigate crimes

**detector detectors**

NOUN an instrument used to detect the presence of something • *a metal detector*

**detention**

NOUN **1** a form of punishment in which a pupil is made to stay in school for extra time when other children do not have to

NOUN **2** arrest or imprisonment

**deter deters, deterring, deterred**

VERB If you **deter** someone from doing something, you persuade them not to do it or try to stop them in some way.

**detergent detergents**

NOUN a chemical substance used for washing or cleaning things

**deteriorate deteriorates, deteriorating, deteriorated**

VERB If something **deteriorates**, it gets worse.

**determination**

NOUN great strength and will to do something

**determined**

ADJECTIVE having your mind firmly made up • *She was determined to pass her exams.*

a
b
c
d
e
f
g
h
i
j
k
l
m
n
o
p
q
r
s
t
u
v
w
x
y
z

A
B
C
D
E
F
G
H
I
J
K
L
M
N
O
P
Q
R
S
T
U
V
W
X
Y
Z

**deterrent deterrents**
NOUN something that prevents people from doing something, usually by making them afraid to do it ● *We have a car alarm as a **deterrent** to thieves.*

**detest detests, detesting, detested**
VERB If you **detest** someone or something, you dislike them intensely.

WORD HISTORY
from Latin *detestari* meaning to curse

**detonate detonates, detonating, detonated**
VERB If someone **detonates** a bomb or mine, they cause it to explode.

**detour detours**
NOUN If you make a **detour** on a journey, you go by a longer or less direct route.

**devastate devastates, devastating, devastated**
VERB A place that has been **devastated** has been severely damaged or destroyed.

**devastation**
NOUN extreme damage or destruction that affects a large area or a lot of people ● *The storm caused **devastation** across three states.*

**develop develops, developing, developed**
VERB 1 When something **develops**, it grows or becomes more advanced.
VERB 2 If you **develop** photographs or film, you produce a visible image from them.

**development developments**
NOUN gradual growth or progress ● *There have been great **developments** in technology over the past fifty years.*

**device devices**
NOUN a machine or tool that is used for a particular purpose

**devil devils**
NOUN an evil spirit

**devious**
ADJECTIVE **Devious** people behave in an underhand, nasty and secretive way.

**devise devises, devising, devised**
VERB If you **devise** something, you invent it or design it.

**devoted**
ADJECTIVE very loving and loyal

**devour devours, devouring, devoured**
VERB 1 If you **devour** food, you eat it quick and greedily.
VERB 2 If one creature **devours** another, it eats it.
VERB 3 If you **devour** a book, you read it ve quickly.

**devout**
ADJECTIVE very deeply religious

**dew**
NOUN drops of moisture that form on the ground and other cool surfaces at night

**diabetes**
NOUN a condition in which a person has too much sugar in their blood

**diabetic**
ADJECTIVE suffering from a condition in which you have too much sugar in your blood

**diagnose diagnoses, diagnosing, diagnosed**
VERB If someone **diagnoses** an illness or problem, they identify what is wrong.

**diagonal diagonals**
NOUN 1 a straight line that slopes from one corner of a shape to another
ADJECTIVE 2 in a slanting direction
● *a **diagonal** line*

WORD HISTORY
from Greek *diagonios* meaning from angle to angle

**diagram diagrams**
NOUN a drawing that shows or explains something, for example a Carroll diagram a Venn diagram

**dial dials, dialling, dialled**
NOUN 1 the part of a clock or meter where time or a measurement is shown
VERB 2 If you **dial** a phone number, you press the buttons to select the number yo want.

**dialect dialects**
NOUN the form of a language spoken in a particular area

**dialogue dialogues**
NOUN In a novel, play or film, **dialogue** is conversation.

**ameter diameters**

NOUN the length of a straight line drawn across a circle through its centre

**amond diamonds**

NOUN **1** a precious stone made of pure carbon

NOUN **2** a shape with four straight sides of equal length that are not at right angles to each other

**aphragm diaphragms**

NOUN a muscle between your lungs and your stomach that is used when you breathe

→ Have a look at the illustration for **respiratory system**

**arrhoea**

NOUN a condition that affects your bowels so that you can't stop going to the lavatory

**ary diaries**

NOUN a notebook with a separate space or page for each day of the year

**ce dices, dicing, diced**

NOUN **1** a small cube with dots on each of its six faces

VERB **2** If you **dice** food, you cut it into small cubes.

**LANGUAGE TIP**

*Dice* is really a plural word, but is usually used as a singular word: *The dice is on the table.*

**ctate dictates, dictating, dictated**

VERB **1** If you **dictate** something, you say it or read it aloud for someone else to write down.

VERB **2** If you **dictate** to someone, you give them orders in a bossy way.

**ctation dictations**

NOUN **Dictation** is when you say something or read something aloud for someone else to write down.

**dictionary dictionaries**

NOUN a book in which words are listed alphabetically and their meanings explained

**did**

VERB the past tense of **do**

**didgeridoo didgeridoos**

NOUN an Australian wind instrument made from a long, hollowed-out piece of wood

**didn't**

VERB a contraction of *did not*

**die dies, dying, died**

VERB **1** When humans, other animals or plants **die**, they stop living.

VERB **2** When something **dies**, **dies away** or **dies down**, it becomes less intense and disappears. • *The wind **died down**.*

**diesel diesels**

NOUN **1** a heavy fuel used in trains, buses and lorries

NOUN **2** a vehicle with a diesel engine

**diet diets**

NOUN **1** the food you usually eat

NOUN **2** If you are on a **diet**, you eat only certain foods for health reasons or to lose weight.

**difference differences**

NOUN **1** the way in which things are unlike each other

NOUN **2** the amount by which one number is less than another

NOUN **3** a change in someone or something

**different**

ADJECTIVE If one thing is **different** from another, it is not like it.

**LANGUAGE TIP**

There are two *es* in *different*.

**difficult**

ADJECTIVE **1** **Difficult** things are not easy to do, understand or solve.

ADJECTIVE **2** Someone who is **difficult** behaves in an unreasonable way.

**difficulty difficulties**

NOUN a problem

**dig digs, digging, dug**

VERB **1** If you **dig**, you make a hole in earth or sand, especially with a spade.

VERB **2** If you **dig** something, you poke it.

a
b
c
d
e
f
g
h
i
j
k
l
m
n
o
p
q
r
s
t
u
v
w
x
y
z

**111**

A
B
C
D
E
F
G
H
I
J
K
L
M
N
O
P
Q
R
S
T
U
V
W
X
Y
Z

**digest** digests, digesting, digested

VERB To **digest** food means to break it down in the gut so that it can be easily absorbed and used by the body.

**digestible**

ADJECTIVE Food that is **digestible** is easily digested.

**digestive system**

NOUN Your **digestive system** is the system in your body that digests the food you eat.

**digit** digits

NOUN **1** a written symbol for any of the numbers from zero (0) to nine (9). The number 46, for example, has two **digits**.
NOUN **2** a finger or toe

**digital**

ADJECTIVE **1** **Digital** computers and devices record or send information in the form of thousands of very small signals.
ADJECTIVE **2** **Digital** instruments, such as clocks or watches, have changing numbers instead of a dial with hands.

ANTONYM: analogue

**dignified**

ADJECTIVE **Dignified** people are calm, and behave in a way that other people admire and respect.

**dilemma** dilemmas

NOUN a situation where you have to choose between two alternatives that are equally difficult or unpleasant

**diligence**

NOUN **Diligence** is when you work hard and carefully.

**diligent**

ADJECTIVE hard-working and showing care

**dilute** dilutes, diluting, diluted

VERB If you **dilute** a liquid, you add water or another liquid to it to make it weaker.

**dim** dimmer, dimmest; dims, dimming, dimmed

ADJECTIVE **1** lacking in brightness and badly lit
VERB **2** If lights **dim**, or are **dimmed**, they become less bright.

**dimension** dimensions

NOUN The **dimensions** of something are its measurements or its size.

**diminish** diminishes, diminishing, diminished

VERB If something **diminishes**, or you **diminish** it, it reduces in size or importance.

**diminutive** diminutives

ADJECTIVE **1** very small
NOUN **2** **Diminutives** are suffixes that you add to words to show affection or that something is small. For example, -let or -e are **diminutives**. • notelet • statuette

**dimple** dimples

NOUN a small hollow in someone's cheek or chin

**din**

NOUN a very loud and unpleasant noise

**dine** dines, dining, dined

VERB (formal) When you **dine**, you eat dinner in the evening.

**dinghy** dinghies

NOUN a small boat that is rowed, sailed or powered by an outboard motor

**dingo** dingoes

NOUN an Australian wild dog

**dingy** dingier, dingiest

ADJECTIVE shabby and dirty to look at

PRONUNCIATION TIP
This word is pronounced **din**-ji.

**dinner** dinners

NOUN the main meal of the day, eaten either in the evening or in the middle of the day

**dinosaur** dinosaurs

NOUN a large reptile that lived in prehistoric times

WORD HISTORY
from Greek deinos + sauros meaning fearful lizard

**dip** dips, dipping, dipped

VERB **1** If you **dip** something into a liquid, you lower it in and take it out again quickly

VERB **2** If something **dips**, it slopes downwards or goes below a certain level.
• *The road **dipped** suddenly.*
NOUN **3** a downward slope or hollow
• *There was a **dip** in the road.*
NOUN **4** a quick swim
NOUN **5** a savoury mixture for eating, in which you dip crisps, crackers or vegetables

**diploma diplomas**
NOUN a certificate that is awarded to a student who has successfully completed a course of study

**diplomat diplomats**
NOUN an official who negotiates with another country on behalf of his or her own country

**diplomatic**
ADJECTIVE If you are **diplomatic**, you are tactful and say and do things without offending people.

**direct directs, directing, directed**
ADVERB **1** If you go **direct** to a place, you go straight there. • *This train goes **direct** to Paris.*
ADJECTIVE **2** If someone's speech or behaviour is **direct**, they are honest and say what they mean.

SYNONYMS: frank, open, straightforward

VERB **3** If you **direct** someone to a place, you show them how to get there.
VERB **4** Someone who **directs** a film or play decides the way it is made and performed.

**direction directions**
NOUN **1** the way that someone or something is moving or pointing
PLURAL NOUN **2** instructions that tell you how to do something or how to get somewhere

**direct message direct messages**
NOUN a message sent to someone privately on a social media website

**director directors**
NOUN **1** a senior manager of a company
NOUN **2** the person who decides how a film or play is made and performed

**directory directories**
NOUN **1** a book that gives lists of information, such as people's names, addresses and telephone numbers

NOUN **2** an area of a computer disk which contains one or more files or other directories

**dirt**
NOUN **1** any unclean substance such as mud, dust or stains
NOUN **2** earth or soil

**dirty dirtier, dirtiest**
ADJECTIVE **1** marked or covered with dirt

SYNONYMS: filthy, grubby, mucky

ADJECTIVE **2** unfair or dishonest

**dis-**
PREFIX added to some words to make them mean the opposite. For example, **dis**contented means not content.

**disability disabilities**
NOUN a condition or illness that limits the way in which someone can use their body or part of their body

**disabled**
ADJECTIVE A **disabled** person has a disability.

**disadvantage disadvantages**
NOUN something that makes things difficult

**disagree disagrees, disagreeing, disagreed**
VERB **1** If you **disagree** with someone, you have a different opinion or view from them.
VERB **2** If you **disagree** with an action or proposal, you believe it is wrong.

**disagreeable**
ADJECTIVE unpleasant or unhelpful and unfriendly • *The woman was very **disagreeable** and did not even offer to help.*

**disappear disappears, disappearing, disappeared**
VERB **1** If someone or something **disappears**, they go where they cannot be seen or found.
VERB **2** If something **disappears**, it stops existing or happening.

**disappoint disappoints, disappointing, disappointed**
VERB If someone or something **disappoints** you, they fail to live up to what you expected.

**disapproval**
NOUN **Disapproval** is thinking that something or someone is bad or wrong.

a
b
c
d
e
f
g
h
i
j
k
l
m
n
o
p
q
r
s
t
u
v
w
x
y
z

**113**

A
B
C
D
E
F
G
H
I
J
K
L
M
N
O
P
Q
R
S
T
U
V
W
X
Y
Z

**disapprove disapproves, disapproving, disapproved**
VERB If you **disapprove** of something or someone, you think they are bad or wrong.

**disapproving**
ADJECTIVE showing that you think something or someone is bad or wrong
• a **disapproving** look

**disaster disasters**
NOUN **1** a very damaging event or accident, such as an earthquake or a plane crash

SYNONYMS: calamity, catastrophe

NOUN **2** a complete failure • The party was a **disaster**.

**disastrous**
ADJECTIVE Something that is **disastrous** is a complete failure.

**disc discs**; also spelt **disk**
NOUN **1** anything with a flat, circular shape, such as a DVD
NOUN **2** a disc-shaped storage device used in computers • All my music is stored on the hard **disc**.

**discard discards, discarding, discarded**
VERB If you **discard** something, you throw it away because it is of no use to you anymore.

**discharge discharges, discharging, discharged**
VERB **1** If a doctor **discharges** someone from hospital, they allow them to leave.
VERB **2** If something **discharges** or is **discharged**, it is given or sent out. • Cars **discharge** exhaust fumes into the atmosphere.

**disciple disciples**
NOUN a follower of someone or something

WORD HISTORY
from Latin *discipulus* meaning pupil

**discipline disciplines, disciplining, disciplined**
NOUN **1** making people obey rules, by training them and by punishing them when they break the rules
NOUN **2** the ability to behave and work in a controlled way
VERB **3** If a parent or teacher **disciplines** a child, they punish them.

**disco discos**
NOUN a party or a club where people go to dance to pop music

**discomfort**
NOUN slight pain or worry

**disconnect disconnects, disconnecting, disconnected**
VERB If you **disconnect** something, you detach it from something else or break its connection.

**discontinue discontinues, discontinuing, discontinued**
VERB If you **discontinue** something, you stop doing it.

**discount discounts**
NOUN a reduction in the price of something

**discourage discourages, discouraging, discouraged**
VERB **1** If you **discourage** someone, you take away their enthusiasm for doing something.
VERB **2** If you **discourage** someone from doing something, you try to persuade them not to do it.

**discouragement**
NOUN a feeling of being less enthusiastic about something and less determined to continue doing it

**discouraging**
ADJECTIVE making you feel less enthusiastic and less determined to continue doing something

**discover discovers, discovering, discovered**
VERB If you **discover** something, you find it or learn about it for the first time.
• She **discovered** that they'd escaped.

**discreet**
ADJECTIVE If you are **discreet**, you keep private things to yourself and can be trusted with a secret.

**discretion**
NOUN the quality that you have if you are able to keep private things to yourself and can be trusted with a secret

**discriminate discriminates, discriminating, discriminated**
VERB **1** If you **discriminate** between people, you treat them differently, and often unfairly, because of their race, religion or gender.
VERB **2** If you are **discriminating**, you can recognise differences between things and use your judgement to make choices.

**scrimination**

NOUN **1 Discrimination** is when people are treated differently, and often unfairly, because of their race, religion or gender.
NOUN **2 Discrimination** is when you can recognise differences between things and use your judgement to make choices.

**scus discuses**

NOUN a flat, circular weight that athletes throw in a competition

**scuss discusses, discussing, discussed**

VERB When people **discuss** something, they talk about it in detail.

**scussion discussions**

NOUN **1** A **discussion** is a detailed conversation about something, especially something important. • *We had a discussion about what we were going to do.*
NOUN **2 Discussion** is when people talk about it in detail. • *There was a lot of discussion about the new school uniform.*

**sease diseases**

NOUN an illness that affects human beings, other animals or plants

**sgrace disgraces, disgracing, disgraced**

NOUN **1** something unacceptable • *Tidy your room – it's a disgrace.*
VERB **2** If you **disgrace** yourself, you do something that others disapprove of.

**sgruntled**

ADJECTIVE If you are **disgruntled**, you are cross and discontented about something.

**sguise disguises, disguising, disguised**

VERB **1** If you **disguise** yourself, you change your appearance so that people will not recognise you.
NOUN **2** something you wear or a change you make to your appearance so that people will not recognise you

**sgust disgusts, disgusting, disgusted**

NOUN **1** a very strong feeling of dislike and loathing
VERB **2** If you **disgust** someone, you make them feel a strong sense of dislike and disapproval.

**sgusting**

ADJECTIVE **1** extremely unpleasant • *The bin smells disgusting.*
ADJECTIVE **2** shocking or very wrong • *It's disgusting that people still have to sleep on the streets.*

**dish dishes**

NOUN **1** a shallow container for cooking or serving food
NOUN **2** a particular kind of food, or food cooked in a particular way • *a vegetarian dish*

**disheartened**

ADJECTIVE If you are **disheartened**, you feel disappointed.

**dishonest**

ADJECTIVE not truthful or fit to be trusted

**dishwasher dishwashers**

NOUN a machine that washes crockery, cutlery, pots and pans

**disinfectant disinfectants**

NOUN a chemical substance that kills germs

**disintegrate disintegrates, disintegrating, disintegrated**

VERB If an object **disintegrates**, it breaks into many pieces and so is destroyed.

**disintegration**

NOUN **Disintegration** is when something breaks apart into many small pieces.

**disk**

NOUN another spelling of **disc**

**dislike dislikes, disliking, disliked**

VERB If you **dislike** something or someone, you think they are unpleasant.

**dislocate dislocates, dislocating, dislocated**

VERB If you **dislocate** a bone in your body, you put it out of its usual position by accident.

**disloyal**

ADJECTIVE Someone who is **disloyal** to their friends or family does not support them or does things that could harm them.

**dismal**

ADJECTIVE depressing and bleak • *It was a dismal day, with rain pouring down and cold winds blowing.*

WORD HISTORY
from Latin *dies mali* meaning evil days

**dismantle dismantles, dismantling, dismantled**

VERB If you **dismantle** something, you take it apart.

**dismay dismays, dismaying, dismayed**

VERB **1** If something **dismays** you, it worries and alarms you.
NOUN **2** a feeling of fear and worry

A
B
C
D
E
F
G
H
I
J
K
L
M
N
O
P
Q
R
S
T
U
V
W
X
Y
Z

**dismiss** dismisses, dismissing, dismissed
VERB **1** If you **dismiss** something, you decide that it is not important enough for you to think about.
VERB **2** If someone is **dismissed**, they are told to leave a place or leave their job. • *She **dismissed** the class.*

**dismount** dismounts, dismounting, dismounted
VERB to get off a horse or a bicycle

**disobedience**
NOUN **Disobedience** is when a person breaks the rules or does not do what someone tells them to do.

**disobedient**
ADJECTIVE breaking the rules or not doing what someone tells you to do

**disobey** disobeys, disobeying, disobeyed
VERB If you **disobey** the rules, you break them. If you **disobey** a person, you refuse to do as they say.

**disorder** disorders
NOUN **1** a state of untidiness
NOUN **2** lack of organisation
NOUN **3** an illness • *a stomach **disorder***

**disorganised**; also spelt **disorganized**
ADJECTIVE Someone or something that is **disorganised** is muddled, confused or badly prepared.

**dispatch** dispatches, dispatching, dispatched
VERB **1** If you **dispatch** someone or something to a particular place, you send them there for a particular reason.
NOUN **2** an official message

**dispensary** dispensaries
NOUN a place where medicines are prepared and given out

**dispersal**
NOUN The **dispersal** of something is its spreading or scattering out in many directions.

**disperse** disperses, dispersing, dispersed
VERB If a group of people **disperses**, the people in it go away in different directions.

**display** displays, displaying, displayed
NOUN **1** an arrangement of things designed to attract people's attention • *a firework **display***
VERB **2** If you **display** something, you put it on show.
VERB **3** If you **display** an emotion, you behave in a way that shows how you feel.

**disposable**
ADJECTIVE **Disposable** things are designed to be thrown away after they have been used.

**dispose** disposes, disposing, disposed
VERB If you **dispose** of something, you get rid of it. • *We **disposed** of our litter carefully.*

**disprove** disproves, disproving, disproved
VERB If you **disprove** something, you show that it is not true.

**dispute** disputes, disputing, disputed
NOUN **1** an argument
VERB **2** If you **dispute** a fact or theory, you say that it is incorrect or untrue.

**disqualify** disqualifies, disqualifying, disqualified
VERB If someone **disqualifies** someone from a competition or activity, they officially stop them from taking part in it. • *The team was **disqualified** from the competition for cheating.*

**disregard** disregards, disregarding, disregarded
VERB **1** If you **disregard** someone or something, you take no notice of them.
NOUN **2** If you show **disregard** for something, you show that you do not care for it.

**disrespect**
NOUN contempt or lack of respect

**disrespectful**
ADJECTIVE showing that you do not respect someone

**disrupt** disrupts, disrupting, disrupted
VERB to cause problems and stop something continuing in its usual way • *Rain **disrupted** the school's sports day.*

WORD HISTORY
from Latin *dirumpere* meaning to smash to pieces

**disruptive**
ADJECTIVE causing problems and stopping something from continuing in its usual way

**dissatisfied**
ADJECTIVE not pleased or contented

**dissect** **dissects, dissecting, dissected**
VERB When you **dissect** a plant or part of the body of an animal, you cut it up carefully so that you can examine it closely.

**dissolve** **dissolves, dissolving, dissolved**
VERB If you **dissolve** something, or if something **dissolves** in a liquid, it mixes with the liquid and becomes part of it.

**distance** **distances**
NOUN **1** The **distance** between two points is the amount of space between them.
NOUN **2** the fact of being far away ● *My friend's house is a great **distance** from mine.*

**distant**
ADJECTIVE far away in space or time
● *a **distant** planet*

**distil** **distils, distilling, distilled**
VERB When you **distil** a liquid, you purify it by boiling it and condensing the vapour.

**distinct**
ADJECTIVE **1** If one thing is **distinct** from another, there is an important difference between them. ● *The word "chest" has two **distinct** meanings.*
ADJECTIVE **2** If something is **distinct**, you can hear, smell, see or sense it clearly.

**distinction** **distinctions**
NOUN **1** a difference between two things
NOUN **2** a quality of excellence and superiority ● *a woman of **distinction***
NOUN **3** the highest level of achievement in an examination

**distinctive**
ADJECTIVE If something is **distinctive**, it has a special quality that makes it recognisable. ● *Peppermint has a **distinctive** smell.*

**distinguish** **distinguishes, distinguishing, distinguished**
VERB **1** If you can **distinguish** one thing from another, you can see or understand the difference between them.
VERB **2** If you can **distinguish** something, you can see, hear or taste it. ● *I heard shouting but couldn't **distinguish** the words.*

**distort** **distorts, distorting, distorted**
VERB **1** If you **distort** something, you twist it out of shape.
VERB **2** If you **distort** an argument or the truth, you alter the facts to suit yourself.

**distract** **distracts, distracting, distracted**
VERB If you **distract** someone, you take their attention away from what they are doing.

**distraction** **distractions**
NOUN someone or something that takes your attention away from what you are doing

**distress** **distresses, distressing, distressed**
NOUN **1** **Distress** is suffering caused by pain or sorrow.
VERB **2** If something **distresses** you, it causes you to be upset or worried.
PHRASE **3** If someone or something is **in distress**, they are in danger and need help.

**distribute** **distributes, distributing, distributed**
VERB **1** If you **distribute** things, you hand them out or deliver them.
VERB **2** If you **distribute** something, you share it among a number of people.

**district** **districts**
NOUN an area of a town or country

**distrust** **distrusts, distrusting, distrusted**
VERB **1** If you **distrust** someone, you are suspicious of them because you are not sure whether they are honest.
NOUN **2** suspicion

**disturb** **disturbs, disturbing, disturbed**
VERB If you **disturb** someone, you interrupt their peace or privacy.

**disturbance** **disturbances**
NOUN **1** something that interrupts someone's peace or privacy
NOUN **2** a situation in which people behave in a noisy or violent way in the street or another public place

**disused**
ADJECTIVE If something is **disused**, it is neglected or no longer used.

**ditch** **ditches**
NOUN a channel cut into the ground at the side of a road or field

**dive** **dives, diving, dived**
VERB **1** If you **dive**, you plunge head first into deep water.
VERB **2** If something or someone **dives**, they move suddenly and quickly. ● *The birds **dived** to catch the insects.*

a
b
c
d
e
f
g
h
i
j
k
l
m
n
o
p
q
r
s
t
u
v
w
x
y
z

**117**

A
B
C
D
E
F
G
H
I
J
K
L
M
N
O
P
Q
R
S
T
U
V
W
X
Y
Z

**diver** divers
NOUN **1** a person who uses breathing apparatus to swim or work under water
NOUN **2** a person who takes part in diving competitions
NOUN **3** a bird that catches its food by diving into water

**diverse**
ADJECTIVE If things are **diverse**, they show a wide range of differences. • *There was a* ***diverse*** *collection of paintings in the gallery.*

**diversion** diversions
NOUN **1** an alternative road you can use if the main one is blocked
NOUN **2** something that takes your attention away from what you are doing

**divert** diverts, diverting, diverted
VERB **1** to make traffic use a different road because the main one is blocked
VERB **2** to take someone's attention away from something

**divide** divides, dividing, divided
VERB **1** When you **divide** something, or when it divides, it separates into two or more parts. • *We* ***divided*** *the cake into six equal slices.*

ANTONYM: multiply

VERB **2** If something **divides** two areas, it forms a barrier between them. • *A tall hedge* ***divided*** *the two gardens.*

ANTONYM: multiply

VERB **3** If you **divide** a larger number by a smaller number, or into a smaller number, you calculate how many times the larger number contains the smaller number. • *Thirty-five* ***divided*** *by five is seven (35 ÷ 5 = 7). Six* ***divided*** *into three is two.*

**divine**
ADJECTIVE having the qualities of a god or goddess

**divisible**
ADJECTIVE A number that is **divisible** can be divided by another number. • *8, 20, 46 and 166 are all* ***divisible*** *exactly by two.*

**division**
NOUN the process of dividing numbers or things

**divorce** divorces, divorcing, divorced
VERB When married couples **divorce**, they end their marriage legally.

**Diwali**
NOUN a Hindu festival of light, celebrated in the autumn

**DIY**
NOUN the activity of making or repairing things yourself. **DIY** is an abbreviation for *do-it-yourself.*

**dizzy** dizzier, dizziest
ADJECTIVE If you feel **dizzy**, you feel that you are losing your balance and are about to fall.

**DJ** DJs
NOUN someone who introduces and plays pop records on the radio or at a night club. **DJ** is an abbreviation for *disc jockey.*

**DM** DMs
NOUN an abbreviation for *direct message*

**DNA**
NOUN an acid in the chromosomes in the centre of the cells of living things. It is an abbreviation for *deoxyribonucleic acid.*

**do** does, doing, did, done
VERB **1** If you **do** something, you get on and finish it. • *I've* ***done*** *my homework.*
VERB **2** You can use **do** with other verbs. • ***Do*** *you like ice cream?*
VERB **3** If you ask people what they **do**, you want to know what their job is.

**docile**
ADJECTIVE A **docile** person or other animal is calm and unlikely to cause any trouble.

**dock** docks
NOUN an enclosed space in a harbour where ships go to be loaded, unloaded or repaired

**doctor** doctors
NOUN a person who is qualified in medicine and treats people who are ill

**document** documents, documenting, documented
NOUN **1** a piece of paper that provides an official record of something
NOUN **2** a piece of text or graphics that is stored as a file on a computer and can be edited
VERB **3** If you **document** something, you make a detailed record of it.

**documentary** documentaries
NOUN a radio or television programme, or a film, that gives information about real events

**dodecagon dodecagons**
NOUN a flat shape with twelve straight sides

**dodge dodges, dodging, dodged**
VERB If you **dodge** something, you move suddenly to avoid being seen, hit or caught.

**dodgy**
ADJECTIVE (*informal*) dangerous, risky or unreliable

**dodo dodos**
NOUN an extinct very large bird that was unable to fly

**doe does**
NOUN a female deer, rabbit or hare

**does**
VERB a present tense of **do**

**doesn't**
VERB a contraction of *does not*

**dog dogs**
NOUN a mammal that is often kept as a pet or used to guard or hunt things

**dole doles, doling, doled**
VERB If you **dole** something out, you give a certain amount of it to each individual in a group.

**doll dolls**
NOUN a toy that looks like a baby or a person

**dollar dollars**
NOUN a unit of money in the USA, Australia, Canada, New Zealand and some other countries. A **dollar** is worth 100 cents.

**dolphin dolphins**
NOUN a mammal that lives in the sea

**dome domes**
NOUN a rounded roof

**domestic**
ADJECTIVE involving or concerned with the home and family • *Dogs and cats are often kept as **domestic** pets.*

**dominant**
ADJECTIVE most powerful or important

**dominate dominates, dominating, dominated**
VERB 1 If someone or something **dominates** a situation or an event, they are the most powerful or important thing in it.
VERB 2 If one person **dominates** another, they have power and control over them.

**WORD HISTORY**
from Latin *dominari* meaning to be lord over

**domino dominoes**
NOUN a small, rectangular block marked with two groups of spots on one side, used for playing the game called **dominoes**

**donate donates, donating, donated**
VERB If you **donate** something, you give it, especially to a charity.

**done**
VERB the past participle of **do**

**donkey donkeys**
NOUN an animal like a horse, but smaller and with longer ears

**donor donors**
NOUN someone who donates something, such as a blood **donor** or someone who gives to charity

**don't**
VERB a contraction of *do not*

**doodle doodles, doodling, doodled**
NOUN 1 a drawing done when you are thinking about something else or when you are bored
VERB 2 When you **doodle**, you draw doodles.

**doomed**
ADJECTIVE If someone or something is **doomed** to an unhappy or unpleasant experience, they are certain to suffer it.

**door doors**
NOUN a swinging or sliding panel for opening or closing the entrance to something

**dormitory dormitories**
NOUN a large bedroom where several people sleep

**dormouse dormice**
NOUN a mammal, like a large mouse, with a furry tail

**dose doses**
NOUN a measured amount of a medicine or drug

**dot dots, dotting, dotted**
NOUN 1 a very small, round mark, such as a full stop or a decimal point
VERB 2 When things **dot** a place or an area they are scattered all over it. • *The hillside was **dotted** with trees.*
PHRASE 3 If you arrive somewhere **on the dot**, you arrive at exactly the right time.

a
b
c
d
e
f
g
h
i
j
k
l
m
n
o
p
q
r
s
t
u
v
w
x
y
z

**119**

## double doubles, doubling, doubled
ADJECTIVE **1** twice the usual size
ADJECTIVE **2** consisting of two parts
VERB **3** If something **doubles**, or if you **double** it, it becomes twice as large.
• *The number of pupils has **doubled** over the last year.*
NOUN **4** Your **double** is someone who looks exactly like you.

## double bass double basses
NOUN a very large stringed instrument • *My brother plays the **double bass** in a jazz band.*

## doubt doubts, doubting, doubted
VERB If you **doubt** something, you think that it is probably not true or possible. • *I **doubt** if I'll be allowed to go to the party.*

## doubtful
ADJECTIVE uncertain or unlikely

## doubtless
ADVERB certainly; without any doubt

## dough
NOUN a mixture of flour and water used to make bread, pastry or biscuits

## doughnut doughnuts
NOUN a ring of sweet dough cooked in hot fat

## dove doves
NOUN a bird of the pigeon family that makes a soft, cooing sound

## down
PREPOSITION **1** towards the ground, towards a lower level, or in a lower place • *A man came **down** the stairs to meet them.*
ADVERB **2** towards the ground, towards a lower level, or in a lower place • *Mum came **down** to the sitting room.*
ADVERB **3** If you put something **down**, you place it on a surface.
ADVERB **4** If an amount of something goes **down**, it decreases. • *The water level in the river has gone **down**.*
NOUN **5** the tiny, soft feathers on baby birds

## downcast
ADJECTIVE If you are **downcast**, you feel sad and without hope.

## downhill
ADVERB down a slope

## download downloads, downloading, downloaded
VERB When you **download** a program from a disk or from the internet, you move it into a file on your own computer.

## downpour downpours
NOUN a very heavy shower of rain

## downstairs
ADVERB **1** If you go **downstairs**, you go towards the ground floor.
ADJECTIVE **2** on a lower floor

## doze dozes, dozing, dozed
VERB When you **doze**, you sleep lightly for a short period.

## dozen dozens
NOUN **1** A **dozen** is twelve.
ADJECTIVE **2** A **dozen** things are twelve of them.

## Dr
NOUN an abbreviation for *Doctor*

## drab
ADJECTIVE plain, dull and unattractive

## draft drafts
NOUN an early plan for a story, a book, a letter or a speech that you are going to write

## drag drags, dragging, dragged
VERB If you **drag** a heavy object somewhere, you pull it there slowly and with difficulty.

## dragon dragons
NOUN In stories and legends, **dragons** are large, fire-breathing, lizard-like creatures with claws and leathery wings.

## dragonfly dragonflies
NOUN a colourful insect that is often found near water

## drain drains, draining, drained
NOUN **1** a pipe that carries water or sewage away from a place, or an opening in a surface that leads to the pipe
VERB **2** If you **drain** something, or if it **drains**, liquid flows out of it or off it.

## drake drakes
NOUN a male duck

## drama dramas
NOUN **1** a serious play for the theatre, television or radio
NOUN **2** You can refer to the exciting aspects of a situation as **drama**.

## dramatic
ADJECTIVE Something **dramatic** is very exciting, interesting and impressive.

## drank
VERB the past tense of **drink**

**rape drapes, draping, draped**
VERB If you **drape** a piece of material over something, you hang it loosely.

**rastic**
ADJECTIVE A **drastic** course of action is very severe and is usually taken urgently.

**raught draughts**
NOUN **1** a current of cold air
PLURAL NOUN **2 Draughts** is a game for two people, played on a chessboard with round pieces.

PRONUNCIATION TIP
This word is pronounced **draft**.

**aughty draughtier, draughtiest**
ADJECTIVE If a building or room is **draughty**, you can feel a current of cold air in it.

PRONUNCIATION TIP
This word is pronounced **drafty**.

**aw draws, drawing, drew, drawn**
VERB **1** When you **draw** something, you use a pen or pencil to make a picture of it.
VERB **2** If you **draw** the curtains, you pull them so that they cover or uncover the window.
NOUN **3** the result of a game or competition in which both sides have the same score, so nobody wins
PHRASE **4** If you **draw lots**, you decide who will do something by a method that depends on chance, such as taking names out of a hat.

**awback drawbacks**
NOUN a problem that upsets a plan • One **drawback** of eating too much chocolate is that you feel sick.

**awbridge drawbridges**
NOUN a bridge at the entrance to a castle that could be pulled up to prevent people from getting in
→ Have a look at the illustration for **castle**

**awer drawers**
NOUN part of a desk or other piece of furniture that is shaped like a box and slides in and out

**awing drawings**
NOUN a picture made with a pencil, pen or crayon

**awing pin drawing pins**
NOUN a short nail with a broad flat top. You pin papers to a board by pressing a drawing pin through them with your thumb.

**dread dreads, dreading, dreaded**
VERB If you **dread** something, you feel very worried and frightened about it.

**dreadful**
ADJECTIVE very bad or unpleasant • The weather has been **dreadful** this week.

SYNONYMS: atrocious, awful, terrible

**dreadlocks**
PLURAL NOUN a hairstyle where the hair is grown long and twisted into tightly curled strands

**dream dreams, dreaming, dreamed** or **dreamt**
NOUN **1** a series of events that you experience in your mind while asleep
NOUN **2** a hope or ambition that you often think about because you would very much like it to happen
VERB **3** When you **dream**, you see events in your mind while you are asleep.

LANGUAGE TIP
You can write either *dreamed* or *dreamt* as the past form of *dream*.

**dreary drearier, dreariest**
ADJECTIVE extremely dull and boring

**drenched**
ADJECTIVE soaking wet

**dress dresses, dressing, dressed**
NOUN **1** a piece of clothing worn by women and girls, made up of a top and skirt joined together
NOUN **2 Dress** is used to describe clothing or costumes in general, such as national **dress** or fancy **dress**.
VERB **3** When you **dress**, you put on your clothes.
VERB **4** When you **dress** a wound, you clean it and treat it.

**dress up**
VERB When you **dress up**, you put on clothes that make you look like something else. • Let's **dress up** as witches for the party.

**dressing dressings**
NOUN **1** a bandage or plaster to put on a wound
NOUN **2** a mixture of oils and spices that can be added to salads and other dishes to heighten the flavour

**dressing gown** **dressing gowns**
NOUN a long, warm garment, usually worn over night clothes

**drew**
VERB the past tense of **draw**

**dribble** **dribbles, dribbling, dribbled**
VERB 1 If a person or animal **dribbles**, saliva trickles from their mouth.
VERB 2 In sport, when you **dribble** a ball, you move it along by repeatedly tapping it with your foot, your hand or a stick.

**drift** **drifts, drifting, drifted**
VERB 1 When something **drifts**, it is carried along by the wind or by water.
VERB 2 When people **drift**, they move aimlessly from one place or one activity to another.
NOUN 3 snow or sand piled up by the wind
NOUN 4 (*informal*) the general meaning of something

**drill** **drills, drilling, drilled**
NOUN 1 a tool for making holes
NOUN 2 a routine exercise or routine training
VERB 3 If you **drill** a hole, you make a hole using a drill.

**drink** **drinks, drinking, drank, drunk**
VERB 1 When you **drink** a liquid, you take it into your mouth and swallow it.
NOUN 2 A **drink** is an amount of liquid for drinking.

**drip** **drips, dripping, dripped**
VERB 1 When liquid **drips**, it falls in small drops.
VERB 2 When an object **drips**, drops of liquid fall from it. • *Stop that tap* **dripping**.
NOUN 3 a drop of liquid that is falling

**drive** **drives, driving, drove, driven**
VERB 1 When someone **drives** a car, bus or other vehicle, they make it move, and control where it goes.
VERB 2 If something **drives** a machine, it supplies the power that makes it work.
NOUN 3 a journey in a vehicle
NOUN 4 a private road that leads from a public road to a person's house

**driver** **drivers**
NOUN the person who makes a car, bus or other vehicle move, and who controls whe it goes

**drizzle**
NOUN light rain

**drone** **drones, droning, droned**
VERB 1 If something **drones**, it makes a low continuous humming noise.
NOUN 2 a continuous, low, dull sound
NOUN 3 a male bee

**drool** **drools, drooling, drooled**
VERB If someone **drools**, saliva drips from their mouth continuously.

**droop** **droops, drooping, drooped**
VERB If something **droops**, it hangs or sag downwards with no strength or firmness.

**drop** **drops, dropping, dropped**
VERB 1 If you **drop** something, you let it fa
VERB 2 If something **drops**, it falls straight down.
VERB 3 If the level or the amount of something **drops**, it becomes less.
NOUN 4 a very small, round quantity of liqu
NOUN 5 the distance between the top and the bottom of something • *There was a fift metre* **drop** *to the river below.*

**drought** **droughts**
NOUN a long period during which there is r rain

**drove**
VERB the past tense of **drive**

**drown** **drowns, drowning, drowned**
VERB When someone **drowns**, or when the are **drowned**, they die because they have gone under water and cannot breathe.

**drowsy** **drowsier, drowsiest**
ADJECTIVE feeling sleepy

**drug** **drugs**
NOUN 1 a chemical used by the medical profession to treat people with illnesses o diseases
NOUN 2 a substance that some people sme smoke, inject or swallow because of its stimulating or calming effects. **Drugs** ca be harmful to health and may be illegal.

**drum** **drums**
NOUN 1 a musical instrument consisting o skin stretched tightly over a round frame
NOUN 2 an object or container shaped like **drum** • *an oil* **drum**

**runk drunker, drunkest**
VERB **1** the past participle of **drink**
ADJECTIVE **2** If someone is **drunk**, they have consumed too much alcohol.

**ry drier** or **dryer, driest; dries, drying, dried**
ADJECTIVE **1** Something that is **dry** is not wet, and contains no water or liquid.
VERB **2** When you **dry** something, or when it **dries**, liquid is removed from it.

**ual**
ADJECTIVE having two parts, functions or aspects ● *This is a **dual**-purpose room – it is both the office and the spare bedroom.*

**ual carriageway dual carriageways**
NOUN a road with several lanes in each direction

**ubious**
ADJECTIVE **1** not entirely honest, safe or reliable
ADJECTIVE **2** doubtful ● *I felt **dubious** about the idea.*

**uchess duchesses**
NOUN a woman who has the same rank as a duke, or who is a duke's wife or widow

**uck ducks, ducking, ducked**
NOUN **1** a bird that lives in water and has webbed feet and a large flat bill
VERB **2** If you **duck**, you move your head quickly downwards in order to avoid being hit by something.
VERB **3** If you **duck** someone, you push them under water for a very short time.

**uckling ducklings**
NOUN a young duck

**ue**
ADJECTIVE expected to happen or arrive
● *The train is **due** at eight o'clock.*

**uel duels**
NOUN a fight arranged between two people

**uet duets**
NOUN a piece of music sung or played by two people

**ug**
VERB the past tense of **dig**

**uke dukes**
NOUN a nobleman with a rank just below that of a prince

**dull duller, dullest**
ADJECTIVE **1** not interesting ● *I thought the story was rather **dull**.*
ADJECTIVE **2** not bright, sharp or clear ● *a **dull** day*

**dumb dumber, dumbest**
ADJECTIVE **1** unable to speak ● *She was so shocked that she was momentarily struck **dumb**.*
ADJECTIVE **2** (*informal*) stupid

**dumbfounded**
ADJECTIVE If you are **dumbfounded**, you are so shocked or surprised about something that you cannot speak.

**dummy dummies**
NOUN **1** a rubber or plastic teat given to a baby to suck to keep it happy
NOUN **2** an imitation or model of something that is used for display ● *I first saw the jacket on a **dummy** in a shop window.*

**dump dumps, dumping, dumped**
VERB **1** If you **dump** something somewhere, you put it there in a careless way.
NOUN **2** a place where rubbish is left
NOUN **3** (*informal*) You refer to a place as a **dump** when it is unattractive and unpleasant to live in.

**dune dunes**
NOUN a hill of sand near the sea or in the desert

**dung**
NOUN body waste excreted by large animals

**dungarees**
PLURAL NOUN trousers that have a bib covering the chest and straps over the shoulders

WORD HISTORY
named after *Dungri* in India, where dungaree material was first made

**dungeon dungeons**
NOUN an underground prison

**dunk dunks, dunking, dunked**
VERB If you **dunk** something, you dip it into water or some other liquid for a short time.

**duo duos**
NOUN any two people who do something together, especially a pair of musical performers

**duplicate** duplicates, duplicating, duplicated

VERB **1** If someone **duplicates** something, they make an exact copy of it.

NOUN **2** something that is identical to something else, or an exact copy

PRONUNCIATION TIP

The verb is pronounced **dyoo**-pli-kayt. The noun is pronounced **dyoo**-pli-kut.

**duplication**

NOUN **Duplication** is when you make an exact copy of something.

**durable**

ADJECTIVE Things that are **durable** are very strong and last a long time.

**duration**

NOUN the length of time during which something happens or exists

**during**

PREPOSITION happening throughout a particular time or while something else is going on • We had an ice cream **during** the interval.

**dusk**

NOUN the time just before nightfall when it is not completely dark

**dust** dusts, dusting, dusted

NOUN **1** dry, fine, powdery material such as particles of earth, dirt or pollen

VERB **2** When you **dust** furniture or other objects, you remove dust from them using a duster.

VERB **3** If you **dust** a surface with something powdery, you cover it lightly with that substance. • **Dust** the top of the cake with icing sugar.

**dustbin** dustbins

NOUN a large container for rubbish

**duster** dusters

NOUN a cloth for dusting things

**dusty** dustier, dustiest

ADJECTIVE covered with dust

**duty** duties

NOUN **1** Your **duty** is what you should do because it is part of your job or because it is expected of you.

PHRASE **2** When workers are **on duty**, they are at work.

**duvet** duvets

NOUN a large bed cover filled with feathers similar material, which you use instead of sheets and blankets

**DVD** DVDs

NOUN a type of compact disc that can store large amounts of video and sound information. **DVD** is an abbreviation for digital video or versatile disc.

**dwarf** dwarfs, dwarfing, dwarfed

NOUN **1** a person or thing that is smaller th average

VERB **2** If one thing **dwarfs** another, it is so much bigger that it makes it look very small. • The mountains **dwarfed** the village

**dwindle** dwindles, dwindling, dwindl

VERB If something **dwindles**, it becomes smaller or weaker. • Their supplies of firewood **dwindled**. • As it got later the ligh **dwindled**.

**dye** dyes, dyeing, dyed

VERB **1** If you **dye** something, you change i colour by soaking it in a special liquid.

NOUN **2** a substance used to change the colour of something such as cloth or hair

**dying**

VERB the present participle of **die**

**dyke** dykes; also spelt **dike**

NOUN a thick wall or barrier that prevents o river or the sea from flooding the land

**dynamic**

ADJECTIVE A **dynamic** person is full of energ ambition and new ideas.

**dynamite**

NOUN a powerful explosive

**dynamo** dynamos

NOUN a device that uses movement to produce electricity. A **dynamo** can be use for lighting bicycle lamps.

**dynasty** dynasties

NOUN a series of rulers of a country, all belonging to the same family

**dyslexia**

NOUN a certain type of difficulty with readi and spelling

**dyslexic**

ADJECTIVE having a condition that makes it difficult to read and spell

# Ee

**ch**

ADJECTIVE **1** every one of a group • *Each book* *is beautifully illustrated.*

PRONOUN **2** every one of a group • *We each* *have different needs and interests.*

**ger**

ADJECTIVE If you are **eager**, you are keen to do something. • *She was eager to hear all about* *my trip.*

SYNONYM: enthusiastic

**gle eagles**

NOUN a large bird of prey

**r ears**

NOUN Your **ears** are the parts of your body on either side of your head, with which you hear sounds.

**rache**

NOUN a pain in your ear • *I had really bad* *earache.*

**rdrum eardrums**

NOUN the thin skin inside your ear, which vibrates when sound waves reach it

**earlobe earlobes**

NOUN Your **earlobes** are the soft parts at the bottom of your ears.

**early earlier, earliest**

ADVERB **1** before the arranged or expected time • *She arrived early to get a place at the* *front.*

ADJECTIVE **2** near the beginning of something • *I like to go for a walk in the* *early morning.*

**earn earns, earning, earned**

VERB **1** If you **earn** money, you receive it in return for work that you do. • *He earned* *some money washing the car.*

VERB **2** If you **earn** something such as praise, you receive it because you deserve it.

**earnest**

ADJECTIVE If you are **earnest** about something, you are very serious about it.

**earnings**

PLURAL NOUN the money or payment that you receive for working

**earphone earphones**

NOUN a very small speaker worn in your ear so you can listen to your phone, a radio or an MP3 player

**earring earrings**

NOUN a piece of jewellery that you wear on your ear

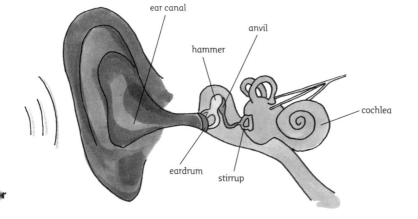

ear canal

anvil

hammer

cochlea

eardrum

stirrup

a
b
c
d
e
f
g
h
i
j
k
l
m
n
o
p
q
r
s
t
u
v
w
x
y
z

**125**

## earth

NOUN **1** The **Earth** is the planet we live on.

→ Have a look at the illustrations for **greenhouse effect** and **solar system**

NOUN **2** another word for **soil**

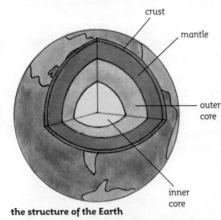

the structure of the Earth

## earthquake earthquakes

NOUN a violent shaking of the ground caused by movement of the Earth's crust

## earthworm earthworms

NOUN a worm that lives in the soil

## earwig earwigs

NOUN a small, brown insect with pincers at the tail end of its body

### WORD HISTORY

from Old English *earwicga* meaning ear insect, because it was once believed that earwigs would creep into people's ears

## ease eases, easing, eased

VERB **1** When something **eases**, it becomes less difficult or intense. • *The rain **eased** as the dark clouds were blown away.*

NOUN **2** a lack of difficulty or trouble • *She finished her homework with **ease**.*

VERB **3** If you **ease** something, you move it gently and slowly. • *He **eased** himself into the chair.*

## easel easels

NOUN an upright frame that supports a picture that someone is painting

## easily

ADVERB If you do something **easily**, you do without difficulty.

## east

NOUN one of the four main points of the compass. The sun rises in the **east**. The abbreviation for **east** is E.

→ Have a look at the illustration for **compass point**

## Easter

NOUN a Christian religious festival in sprin celebrating Christ's return to life after his death

### WORD HISTORY

from Old English *Eostre*, a goddess whose festival was at the spring equinox

## eastern

ADJECTIVE in or from the east

## easy easier, easiest

ADJECTIVE If something is **easy**, you can do without difficulty.

## eat eats, eating, ate, eaten

VERB When you **eat** food, you chew it and swallow it.

## ebb ebbs, ebbing, ebbed

VERB When the sea or the tide **ebbs**, it goes out.

## ebony

NOUN a hard, dark-coloured wood

## e-book e-books

NOUN a book for reading on an electronic device

## e-card e-cards

NOUN a digital card that you send over the internet • *I sent her an **e-card** on her birthday.*

## eccentric

ADJECTIVE Someone who is **eccentric** has habits or opinions that other people thin are odd or peculiar.

## echo echoes, echoing, echoed

NOUN **1** the repeat of a sound caused by th sound being reflected off a surface

VERB **2** When a sound **echoes**, it is reflected off a surface so that it can be heard again. • *Their cries **echoed** back from the mountain.*

**...ipse eclipses**
NOUN A solar **eclipse** happens when the
moon passes between the sun and the
earth and part or all of the sun is hidden
from view. A lunar **eclipse** happens when
the Earth is between the sun and the moon,
so that for a short time the shadow of the
earth makes the moon look red.

**solar eclipse**

**lunar eclipse**

**...ological**
ADJECTIVE involving the relationship between
living things and their environment

**...ologically**
ADVERB in a way that involves the
relationship between living things and their
environment

**...ologist ecologists**
NOUN someone who studies the relationship
between living things and their
environment

**...ology**
NOUN the relationship between living things
and their environment, or the study of this
relationship

**...nomical**
ADJECTIVE If you are **economical**, you are not
wasteful with money or things.

**...nomically**
ADVERB in a way that is not wasteful with
money or things

**...nomics**
NOUN the system of organising the money,
production and trade of a country, region
or group

**economist economists**
NOUN someone who studies the way in
which industries, banks and businesses are
organised to make money

**economy economies**
NOUN The **economy** of a country or region is
the way in which its industries, banks and
businesses are organised to make money.

**ecosystem ecosystems**
NOUN the relationship between plants and
animals and their environment

**ecstasy**
NOUN a feeling of extreme happiness

**ecstatic**
ADJECTIVE feeling extremely happy

**eczema**
NOUN a skin condition that makes the skin
rough and itchy

**edge edges**
NOUN the part along the side or end of
something

**edible**
ADJECTIVE Things that are **edible** are safe
to eat.

**edit edits, editing, edited**
VERB **1** If you **edit** a piece of writing, you
correct it.
VERB **2** If you **edit** a film or a television
programme, you select different parts of it
and arrange them in a particular order.

**edition editions**
NOUN An **edition** of a book or newspaper
is one or all of the copies printed at one
time.

**editor editors**
NOUN **1** someone who is responsible for the
contents of a newspaper or magazine
NOUN **2** someone who edits a piece of
writing, a film or a television programme

**editorial editorials**
NOUN an article in a newspaper or
magazine which expresses the opinion of
the editor

**educate educates, educating, educated**
VERB If you **educate** someone about
something, you teach them so that they
learn about it.

**education**
NOUN When you receive an **education**, you
get knowledge and understanding through
learning.

a
b
c
d
e
f
g
h
i
j
k
l
m
n
o
p
q
r
s
t
u
v
w
x
y
z

**127**

## educational

ADJECTIVE **1** relating to teaching and learning
• the English **educational** system
ADJECTIVE **2** Something that is **educational** teaches you something that you did not know before. • Some programmes can be very **educational**.

## eel eels

NOUN a long, thin fish shaped like a snake

## eerie eerier, eeriest

ADJECTIVE strange and frightening • There was an **eerie** silence after the thunderstorm.

## effect effects

NOUN **1** something that happens as a result of something else • The **effects** of global warming are now becoming clear.
NOUN **2** the impression something makes • The **effect** of the moonlight in the mist was eerie.

## effective

ADJECTIVE If something is **effective**, it works well and gives the results that were intended.

## efficient

ADJECTIVE capable of doing something well, without wasting time or energy

## effort efforts

NOUN the physical or mental energy needed to do something

## effortless

ADJECTIVE done easily and without much effort

## eg; also spelt e.g.

**eg** means for example.

## egg eggs

NOUN **1** a rounded object produced by female birds, reptiles, fish and insects. The young animal develops in the **egg** until it is ready to hatch.

→ Have a look at the illustration for **life cycle**

NOUN **2** a hen's **egg** used as food

## Eid

NOUN a religious Muslim festival

**PRONUNCIATION TIP**
This word is pronounced **eed**.

## eight

NOUN **Eight** is the number 8.

## eighteen

NOUN **Eighteen** is the number 18.

## eighteenth eighteenths

NOUN **1** one of eighteen equal parts of something
ADJECTIVE **2** The **eighteenth** item in a serie the one that you count as number eighte

## eighth eighths

NOUN **1** one of eight equal parts of something. It can be written as ⅛.
ADJECTIVE **2** The **eighth** item in a series is t one that you count as number eight. It c be written as 8th.

## eightieth

NOUN **1** one of eighty equal parts of something
ADJECTIVE **2** The **eightieth** item in a series is the one that you count as number eighty.

## eighty

NOUN **Eighty** is the number 80.

## either

PRONOUN **1** You use **either** to refer to one c two things or people. • She has two brothe and I don't like **either**.
ADJECTIVE **2** You use **either** to refer to one of two things or people. • You can choose **either** date to come.
ADJECTIVE **3** You also use **either** to refer to both of two things. • There were fields on **either** side of the road.
CONJUNCTION **4** You use **either** to refer to each of two possible alternatives. • You c **either** come with me or stay here.

## eject ejects, ejecting, ejected

VERB If you **eject** someone or something, you push or send them out of something
• There is a small button to **eject** DVDs.

## elaborate

ADJECTIVE having many different parts, ofte very detailed or complicated

## elastic

NOUN rubber material that stretches when you pull it, and returns to its original sha when you let it go

## elated

ADJECTIVE very happy or excited

## elbow elbows

NOUN the joint where your arm bends in t middle

**...er**

ADJECTIVE Your **elder** brother or sister is older than you.

**...erly**

ADJECTIVE Someone who is **elderly** is old.

**...est**

ADJECTIVE If you are the **eldest** person in a family, you are the oldest.

**...ct** **elects, electing, elected**

VERB If you **elect** someone, you choose them as your representative by voting for them.

**...ction** **elections**

NOUN When there is an **election**, people choose someone to represent them by voting for them.

WORD HISTORY

from Latin *eligere* meaning to select

**...ctric**

ADJECTIVE powered or produced by electricity

**...ctrical**

ADJECTIVE powered by or involving electricity
• The fire was caused by an **electrical** fault.
• **electrical** goods

**...ctrician** **electricians**

NOUN a person whose job it is to install and repair electrical equipment

**...ctricity**

NOUN a form of energy that provides power for heating, lighting and machines

WORD HISTORY

from Greek *elektron* meaning amber. In early experiments, scientists rubbed amber in order to get an electrical charge.

**...ctrocute** **electrocutes, electrocuting, electrocuted**

VERB If someone **electrocutes** themselves, they accidentally kill themselves or injure themselves badly by touching a strong electric current.

**...ctrocution**

NOUN **Electrocution** is when someone is killed or injured because a strong electric current passes through their body.

**...ctron** **electrons**

NOUN a particle with a negative electrical charge

➔ Have a look at the illustration for **atom**

**electronic**

ADJECTIVE An **electronic** device contains transistors or silicon chips that control an electric current. Computers and televisions are examples of **electronic** devices. • They sell laptops and other **electronic** devices.

**electronically**

ADVERB in a way that involves electronic equipment • **electronically** controlled gates

**elegance**

NOUN the quality someone or something has when they are attractive and graceful

**elegant**

ADJECTIVE attractive and graceful

**element** **elements**

NOUN **1** a part of something that combines with others to make a whole
NOUN **2** In chemistry, an **element** is a substance that is made up of only one atom.
NOUN **3** The **elements** are the weather, especially when it is bad.

**elephant** **elephants**

NOUN a very large mammal with a long trunk, large ears, thick skin and ivory tusks

**eleven**

NOUN **Eleven** is the number 11.

**eleventh** **elevenths**

NOUN **1** one of eleven equal parts of something. It can be written as $\frac{1}{11}$.
ADJECTIVE **2** The **eleventh** item in a series is the one that you count as number eleven. It can be written as $11^{th}$.

**elf** **elves**

NOUN a small, mischievous creature in fairy stories

**eligible**

ADJECTIVE If you are **eligible** for something, you are suitable or have the right qualifications for it. • You are **eligible** to enter the under-twelves competition.

**eliminate** **eliminates, eliminating, eliminated**

VERB If you **eliminate** something or someone, you get rid of them.

**ellipse** **ellipses**

NOUN a regular oval shape

a
b
c
d
e
f
g
h
i
j
k
l
m
n
o
p
q
r
s
t
u
v
w
x
y
z

## ellipsis
NOUN a sequence of three dots (...) which shows that some text has been missed out in a piece of writing, or suggests that it is not finished • *Two red eyes appeared in the cave ...*

## elm elms
NOUN a tall tree with broad leaves

## else
ADJECTIVE **1** besides or as well as • *What **else** do you see?*
PHRASE **2 Or else** means otherwise. • *You'd better hurry, **or else** you'll miss the bus.*

## elsewhere
ADVERB If you do something **elsewhere**, you do it in another place.

## email emails, emailing, emailed; also spelt e-mail
NOUN **1 Email** is a system of sending messages from one computer to another. It is short for *electronic mail*.
NOUN **2** When you send an **email**, you send a message from one computer to another.
VERB **3** If you **email** someone, you send an email to them.

## embark embarks, embarking, embarked
VERB **1** When you **embark**, you go on to a ship at the start of your journey.
VERB **2** When you **embark** on a project, you start it.

## embarrass embarrasses, embarrassing, embarrassed
VERB If you **embarrass** someone, you make them feel ashamed or awkward.

**LANGUAGE TIP**
There are two *r*s and two *ss* in *embarrass*, *embarrassed*, *embarrassing* and *embarrassment*.

## embarrassed
ADJECTIVE feeling ashamed or awkward

## embarrassing
ADJECTIVE making you feel ashamed or awkward

## embarrassment
NOUN the feeling you have when you feel ashamed or awkward

## embassy embassies
NOUN the building in which an ambassador and his or her staff work

## emblem emblems
NOUN an object or a design representing an organisation or a country

## embrace embraces, embracing, embraced
VERB If you **embrace** someone, you put your arms round them to show your affection for them.

## embroider embroiders, embroidering, embroidered
VERB If you **embroider** fabric, you sew a decorative design on to it.

## embroidery
NOUN **Embroidery** is when you sew a decorative design on to fabric, or the design that you sew.

## embryo embryos
NOUN an unborn animal, such as a human being, in the very early stages of development

## emerald emeralds
NOUN **1** a bright-green precious stone
NOUN **2** a bright green colour
ADJECTIVE **3** having a bright-green colour

## emerge emerges, emerging, emerged
VERB If you **emerge** from somewhere, you come out from it.

## emergence
NOUN **Emergence** is when something starts to be known about or noticed.

## emergency emergencies
NOUN an unexpected and serious situation that must be dealt with quickly

## emigrate emigrates, emigrating, emigrated
VERB If you **emigrate**, you leave your native country and go to live permanently in another one.

ANTONYM: immigrate

## emigration
NOUN **Emigration** is when you leave your native country and go to live permanently in another one.

ANTONYM: immigrate

## eminent
ADJECTIVE If someone is **eminent**, they are well known and respected for what they do.

**emission emissions**

NOUN **1 Emission** is when something lets out light, sound, heat or smell.
NOUN **2 Emissions** are gases or other substances that a vehicle or factory lets out into the air.

**emit emits, emitting, emitted**

VERB If something **emits** light, sound, heat or smell, it produces it or lets it out.

**emoji emojis**

NOUN a digital image that you use to express a feeling or an idea in a text or a post on a social media website ● *He added a "wink" emoji to his message to show that he was joking.*

**emotion emotions**

NOUN a strong feeling, such as love or fear

**emotional**

ADJECTIVE **1** having strong feelings that you show to other people, especially by crying ● *He got very emotional when it was time to say goodbye.*
ADJECTIVE **2** involving your feelings and how you control them ● *emotional problems*

**emperor emperors**

NOUN a male ruler of an empire

**emphasis emphases**

NOUN the special importance or stress put on something ● *When you read out the poem, you must put emphasis on the important words.*

**emphasise emphasises, emphasising, emphasised**; also spelt **emphasize**

VERB If you **emphasise** something, you make it look or sound more important than the things around it. ● *He emphasised the word by underlining it.*

**empire empires**

NOUN a group of countries controlled by one ruler ● *The Roman Empire covered many lands.*

**WORD HISTORY**
from Latin *imperium* meaning rule

**employ employs, employing, employed**

VERB If you **employ** someone, you pay them to work for you.

**employee employees**

NOUN someone who works for someone else

**employer employers**

NOUN the person or company that someone works for

**employment**

NOUN the state of having a paid job

**empress empresses**

NOUN **1** a female ruler of an empire
NOUN **2** the wife or widow of an emperor

**emptiness**

NOUN **Emptiness** is when there is nothing or nobody in a place.

**empty emptier, emptiest; empties, emptying, emptied**

ADJECTIVE **1** having nothing or nobody inside

ANTONYM: full

VERB **2** If you **empty** something, you remove the contents.

**emu emus**

NOUN a large Australian bird that can run fast but cannot fly

**enable enables, enabling, enabled**

VERB If you **enable** something to happen, you make it possible. ● *The ramp enables people in wheelchairs to access the library.*

**enchanted**

ADJECTIVE If you are **enchanted** by something or someone, you are fascinated or charmed by them. ● *The audience were enchanted by her dancing.*

**encircle encircles, encircling, encircled**

VERB If you **encircle** someone or something, you surround them completely.

**enclose encloses, enclosing, enclosed**

VERB **1** If you **enclose** something with a letter, you put it in the same envelope.
VERB **2** If you **enclose** an object or area, you surround it with something solid. ● *They enclosed the garden with a strong fence.*

**encore encores**

NOUN an extra item at the end of a performance, when the audience asks for more

**WORD HISTORY**
from French *encore* meaning again

**encounter encounters, encountering, encountered**

VERB **1** If you **encounter** someone or something, you meet them or are faced with them. ● *Did you encounter any problems?*
NOUN **2** a meeting, especially when it is difficult or unexpected

A
B
C
D
E
F
G
H
I
J
K
L
M
N
O
P
Q
R
S
T
U
V
W
X
Y
Z

**encourage encourages, encouraging, encouraged**
VERB If you **encourage** someone, you give them the confidence to do something.

**encouragement**
NOUN support and praise that you give to someone so that they have the confidence to do something

**encouraging**
ADJECTIVE giving someone the confidence to do something

**encyclopedia encyclopedias**; also spelt **encyclopaedia**
NOUN a book or set of books that gives information about a number of different subjects

**end ends, ending, ended**
NOUN 1 The **end** of something is the furthest point of it.
NOUN 2 The **end** of an event is the last part of it.
VERB 3 When something **ends**, it finishes.

**endanger endangers, endangering, endangered**
VERB If someone **endangers** something, they cause it to be in a dangerous or harmful situation.

**endangered**
ADJECTIVE An **endangered** animal or plant may soon not exist because there are not many of them.

**endeavour endeavours, endeavouring, endeavoured**
VERB If you **endeavour** to do something, you try very hard to do it.

**ending endings**
NOUN The **ending** of something is when it finishes.

**endless**
ADJECTIVE Something that is **endless** has, or seems to have, no end. • His **endless** chatter was very boring.

**endure endures, enduring, endured**
VERB 1 If you **endure** someone or something unpleasant, you put up with them.
VERB 2 If something **endures**, it continues or lasts.

**enduring**
ADJECTIVE continuing for a very long time

**enemy enemies**
NOUN Your **enemy** is someone who is very much against you and may wish to harm you.

**energetic**
ADJECTIVE full of energy

SYNONYMS: active, lively

**energy energies**
NOUN 1 the physical strength needed to do active things • He is saving his **energy** for next week's race.
NOUN 2 the power that makes things move, light up, make a sound or get hotter
• electrical **energy** • nuclear **energy**

**engage engages, engaging, engaged**
VERB 1 If you **engage** in an activity, you take part in it.
VERB 2 If you **engage** someone to do something, you pay them to do it.

**engaged**
ADJECTIVE 1 If two people are **engaged**, they have agreed to marry each other.
ADJECTIVE 2 If a phone number is **engaged**, it is busy. • Every time I tried to phone you, your number was **engaged**.

**engine engines**
NOUN 1 the part of a vehicle that produces the power to make it move

→ Have a look at the illustration for **aeroplane**

NOUN 2 the large vehicle that pulls a railway train

**engineer engineers**
NOUN a person trained in designing and building machinery and electrical devices or roads and bridges

**engineering**
NOUN the job of designing and building machinery and electrical devices

**engrave engraves, engraving, engraved**
VERB If you **engrave** a hard surface, you cut letters or designs into it with a tool.
• He **engraved** the stone with an unusual design.

**engraving engravings**
NOUN 1 the work or skill of cutting letters or designs into a hard surface with a tool
NOUN 2 a design that has been cut into a hard surface with a tool

**joy enjoys, enjoying, enjoyed**
VERB **1** If you **enjoy** something, it gives you pleasure.
VERB **2** If you **enjoy** yourself, you are happy and have fun.

**joyable**
ADJECTIVE Something that is **enjoyable** gives you pleasure.

**joyment**
NOUN a feeling of pleasure that you get from having or doing something

**large enlarges, enlarging, enlarged**
VERB When you **enlarge** something, you make it bigger.

**ormous**
ADJECTIVE very large in size or amount

SYNONYMS: vast, huge, massive

**ough**
ADJECTIVE **1** as much or as many as is necessary • Do you have **enough** money to buy that?
ADVERB **2** as much or as many as is necessary • John is old **enough** to work and earn money.

**quire enquires, enquiring, enquired**
VERB If you **enquire** about something or someone, you ask for information about them.

**rol enrols, enrolling, enrolled**
VERB If you **enrol** for something, such as a course or a society, you register to join or become a member of it.

**sure ensures, ensuring, ensured**
VERB If you **ensure** that something happens, you make certain that it happens. • I will **ensure** that I arrive on time.

**ter enters, entering, entered**
VERB **1** To **enter** a place means to go into it.
VERB **2** If you **enter** a competition, you take part in it.
VERB **3** If you **enter** something in a diary or a list, you write it down.

**terprise enterprises**
NOUN **1** something new and exciting that you try to do
NOUN **2** a large business or company

**terprising**
ADJECTIVE able to think of new ideas and ways of doing things

**entertain entertains, entertaining, entertained**
VERB If you **entertain** someone, you do something to amuse them.

**enthusiasm**
NOUN If you show **enthusiasm** for something, you show much interest and excitement about it.

**enthusiastic**
ADJECTIVE If you are **enthusiastic** about something, you are very keen on it and talk or behave in a way that shows how much you like it.

**enthusiastically**
ADVERB in a way that shows you are very keen on something

**entire**
ADJECTIVE whole or complete • The **entire** class went on the trip.

**entirely**
ADVERB wholly and completely • My sister and I are **entirely** different.

**entrance entrances**
NOUN the doorway or gate to a building or area

ANTONYM: exit

**entry entries**
NOUN **1** the act of entering a place • No **entry** after 11 p.m.
NOUN **2** something you write in order to take part in a competition • Send your **entry** to the address below.
NOUN **3** something written in a diary or list • the **entry** for March 23 in her diary

**envelope envelopes**
NOUN the paper cover in which you put a letter

**envious**
ADJECTIVE If you are **envious**, you wish you could have what someone else has.

**environment environments**
NOUN **1** Your **environment** is your surroundings, especially the conditions in which you live or work.
NOUN **2** the natural world around us • Many people are keen to preserve the **environment**.

LANGUAGE TIP
There is an *n* before the *m* in *environment*.

**envy envies, envying, envied**
VERB If you **envy** someone, you wish that you had what they have.

a
b
c
d
e
f
g
h
i
j
k
l
m
n
o
p
q
r
s
t
u
v
w
x
y
z

133

### epicentre epicentres

NOUN The **epicentre** of an earthquake is the place where it is felt most strongly as it is where the earthquake started.

### epidemic epidemics

NOUN an outbreak of a disease that takes place in one area, spreading quickly and affecting many people

### epilepsy

NOUN a condition of the brain that causes seizures and periods of unconsciousness

### epileptic

ADJECTIVE caused by a brain condition that makes someone have seizures and periods of unconsciousness • an **epileptic** seizure

### epilogue epilogues

NOUN a passage or speech which is added to the end of a book or play as a conclusion

### episode episodes

NOUN **1** one of the programmes in a serial on television or radio
NOUN **2** an event or period of time, especially one that is important or unusual

### epitaph epitaphs

NOUN words about a person who has died, usually found on their gravestone

### equal equals, equalling, equalled

ADJECTIVE **1** being the same in size, number amount
VERB **2** If something **equals** another thing is the same in quality, amount or value.
VERB **3** In mathematics, the symbol (=) stands for **equals**. The numbers before i equal the numbers after it. For example, $3 + 3 = 6$.

### equally

ADVERB to the same extent or in the same amounts • We shared the sweets **equally** between the three of us.

### equation equations

NOUN a mathematical number sentence stating that two amounts or values are t same. $3 + 6 = 9$ is an **equation** because what is on the left equals what is on the right.

### equator

NOUN an imaginary line drawn round the middle of the Earth, lying halfway betwee the North and South Poles

→ Have a look at the illustration

### equatorial

ADJECTIVE at or near the equator

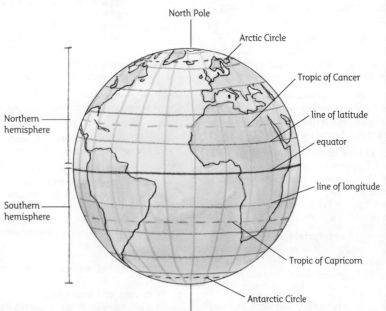

North Pole
Arctic Circle
Tropic of Cancer
line of latitude
Northern hemisphere
equator
line of longitude
Southern hemisphere
Tropic of Capricorn
Antarctic Circle
South Pole

**uilateral**

DJECTIVE An **equilateral** triangle has sides hat are all the same length, and angles hat are all the same size.

**uinox equinoxes**

OUN one of the two days in the year when he day and night are of equal length. The pring **equinox** occurs in March and the utumn **equinox** in September.

**WORD HISTORY**

rom Latin *aequinoctium* meaning equal ight

**uip equips, equipping, equipped**

ERB If you **equip** yourself, you collect ogether everything that you need to do a articular thing.

**uipment**

OUN all the things that are needed or used or a particular job or activity • *camping equipment*

**uivalent equivalents**

DJECTIVE **1** equal in use, size, value or effect

DJECTIVE **2** In mathematics, **equivalent** means of equal value. Fractions can be **equivalent** if they are of equal value, for xample ¾ = ½. Different forms can be **equivalent**, for example 0.5 = ½ = 50%.

OUN **3** something that has the same use, ize, value or effect as something else • *One mile is the equivalent of 1.6 kilometres.*

**ase erases, erasing, erased**

ERB If you **erase** writing, you rub it out.

**ect erects, erecting, erected**

ERB If you **erect** something, you put it up or construct it. • *They erected the tent in the garden.*

**osion**

OUN the gradual wearing away of rock or oil by the weather, the sea or a river • *soil erosion*

**errand errands**

NOUN If you run an **errand** for someone, you go a short distance to do a job for them, such as taking a message or fetching something.

**erratic**

ADJECTIVE not following a regular pattern • *His attendance at school was erratic.*

**erratically**

ADVERB in a way that does not follow a regular pattern

**error errors**

NOUN a mistake, or something that is wrong

**erupt erupts, erupting, erupted**

VERB **1** When a volcano **erupts**, it throws out a lot of hot lava and ash.

VERB **2** When a situation **erupts**, it begins suddenly and violently. • *A family row erupted.*

**escalator escalators**

NOUN a mechanical moving staircase

**escape escapes, escaping, escaped**

VERB **1** If you **escape** from someone or something, you succeed in getting away from them.

VERB **2** If you **escape** something unpleasant or difficult, you succeed in avoiding it. • *She was lucky to escape serious injury.*

NOUN **3** If you make an **escape** from somewhere, you manage to get away.

**escort escorts, escorting, escorted**

NOUN **1** a person or vehicle that travels with another in order to protect or guide them

VERB **2** If you **escort** someone, you go with them somewhere, especially in order to protect or guide them. • *I will escort you round the new buildings.*

**Eskimo Eskimos**

NOUN a name that used to be used for a member of a group of people who live in North America, Greenland and eastern Siberia. This name is not used now because it is rude. Those people in this group who come from North America and Greenland are called Inuits.

**especially**

ADVERB You say **especially** to show that something applies more to one thing, person or situation than to others. • *It is always cold at the top of the mountain, especially when the wind is blowing.*

## espionage
NOUN the act of spying to get secret information, especially to find out military or political secrets

**WORD HISTORY**
from French *espionner* meaning to spy

## essay essays
NOUN a short piece of writing on a particular subject, especially one written as an exercise by a student

## essential essentials
ADJECTIVE **1** Something that is **essential** is absolutely necessary.
NOUN **2** something that is very important or necessary

## establish establishes, establishing, established
VERB **1** If you **establish** something, you set it up and keep it going.
VERB **2** If you **establish** a fact, you confirm that it is definitely correct.

## estate estates
NOUN **1** a large area of land in the country, owned by one person or organisation
NOUN **2** an area of land that has been developed for housing or industry
• *a housing **estate***

## estate agent estate agents
NOUN a person who works for a company that sells houses and land

## estimate estimates, estimating, estimated
VERB **1** If you **estimate** an amount or quantity, you calculate it approximately.
• *They **estimated** that the trip would take around three hours.*
NOUN **2** an approximate calculation of an amount or quantity • *The final cost was twice the original **estimate**.*

**PRONUNCIATION TIP**
The verb is pronounced **ess**-ti-mayt. The noun is pronounced **ess**-ti-mit.

## estuary estuaries
NOUN the wide part of a river near where it joins the sea, and where fresh water mixes with salt water

## etc.
a written abbreviation for *et cetera*

## et cetera
**Et cetera** means *and so on* or *and similar things*.

**WORD HISTORY**
from a Latin phrase that means the other things

## eternal
ADJECTIVE lasting forever, or seeming to last forever

SYNONYMS: endless, everlasting, perpetual

## ethnic
ADJECTIVE connected with a particular racial group of people • *There were many different **ethnic** groups in the school.*

**WORD HISTORY**
from Greek *ethnos* meaning race

## etymology etymologies
NOUN the study of the history and origin of words

## EU
NOUN an abbreviation for *European Union*

## euro euros
NOUN the unit of currency used in many countries in Europe, including Germany, France, Italy, Ireland, Spain and the Netherlands

## euthanasia
NOUN the act of helping someone to die painlessly, so that they do not suffer during an incurable illness

**WORD HISTORY**
from Greek *eu* meaning well and *thanatos* meaning death

## evacuate evacuates, evacuating, evacuated
VERB If people **evacuate**, or are **evacuated**, they move from somewhere dangerous to a place of safety. • *The police **evacuated** shoppers from a store after a bomb scare.*

## evacuee evacuees
NOUN someone who is sent away from a dangerous place, for example because there is a war there

## evaluate evaluates, evaluating, evaluated
VERB If you **evaluate** something, you assess how good and useful it is.

**aluation evaluations**
NOUN a judgement of how good or useful omething is

**aporate evaporates, evaporating, vaporated**
ERB When a liquid **evaporates**, it gradually hanges from a liquid into a gas or vapour.

**WORD HISTORY**
rom Latin *vapor* meaning steam

**aporation**
OUN the process of a liquid gradually hanging into a gas or vapour • *This slowed he* **evaporation** *of water from the soil.*

➔ Have a look at the illustration for **water ycle**

**en**
DJECTIVE **1** An **even** number is one that can e divided by two , such as 2, 4 and 6.

ANTONYM: odd

DJECTIVE **2** An **even** surface is level, smooth nd flat.
DJECTIVE **3** An **even** measurement or rate tays at about the same level. • *Keep the ooker at an* **even** *temperature.*
DVERB **4 Even** is used to say that something s greater in degree than something else. • *He was speaking* **even** *more slowly than sual.*
HRASE **5 Even if** or **even though** are used o introduce something that is surprising in elation to the rest of the sentence. • *She did ot say anything,* **even though** *she had been eft out again.*

**ening evenings**
NOUN the part of the day between the end of he afternoon and the time you go to bed

**ent events**
NOUN **1** something that happens, especially vhen it is unusual or important

SYNONYMS: happening, incident, occurrence

NOUN **2** an organised activity, such as a ports match or a concert

**entually**
DVERB in the end • *It was a long way, but we got there* **eventually**.

**er**
DVERB at any time in the past or future • *That's the biggest dog I've* **ever** *seen.*

**evergreen evergreens**
NOUN An **evergreen** is a plant that does not lose its leaves in the winter.

**every**
ADJECTIVE **1 Every** is used to refer to all the members of a group or all the parts of something. • *Every shop in the town was closed.*
ADJECTIVE **2 Every** is also used to indicate that something happens at regular intervals. • *The clock strikes* **every** *hour.*
PHRASE **3** If something happens **every other** day or week, it happens on alternate days or weeks. • *Practice sessions are held* **every other** *week.*

**everybody**
PRONOUN every person

**everyone**
PRONOUN all the people in a group

**everything**
PRONOUN all or the whole of something

**everywhere**
ADVERB in many or most places

**evict evicts, evicting, evicted**
VERB To **evict** someone means to officially force them to leave a place they are occupying.

**evidence**
NOUN **1** anything that causes you to believe that something is true or exists
NOUN **2** the information used in a court of law to try to prove something

**evident**
ADJECTIVE If something is **evident**, it is clear and obvious.

**evil**
NOUN **1 Evil** is used to refer to all the wicked or bad things that happen in the world.
ADJECTIVE **2** Someone or something **evil** is very bad and causes harm to people.

**evolution**
NOUN a process that takes place over many generations. During this time, living things slowly change as they adapt to different environments.

**evolutionary**
ADJECTIVE to do with or involving the process of evolution

**137**

a b c d e f g h i j k l m n o p q r s t u v w x y z

A
B
C
D
E
F
G
H
I
J
K
L
M
N
O
P
Q
R
S
T
U
V
W
X
Y
Z

**evolve** evolves, evolving, evolved

VERB When living things **evolve**, they slowly change as they adapt to different environments. • *Many people believe that man **evolved** from apes.*

**ewe** ewes

NOUN a female sheep

**ex-**

PREFIX former • *the **ex**-prime minister*

**exact**

ADJECTIVE If something is **exact**, it is accurately measured or made.

**exactly**

ADVERB 1 You use **exactly** to say that something is accurate. • *These predictions are not always **exactly** right.*
ADVERB 2 You use **exactly** to show that you agree with someone. • *"You think he stole your bike?" "**Exactly**."*

**exaggerate** exaggerates, exaggerating, exaggerated

VERB If you **exaggerate**, you make something seem better, worse, bigger or more important than it really is.

**LANGUAGE TIP**
There are two gs but only one r in *exaggerate* and *exaggeration*.

**exaggeration** exaggerations

NOUN 1 **Exaggeration** is when you make something seem better, worse, bigger or more important than it really is.
NOUN 2 a statement that makes something seem better, worse, bigger or more important than it really is • *He said he had fifty followers, but that's an **exaggeration**.*

**exam** exams

NOUN an official test that aims to find out your knowledge in a subject • *a science* **exam**

**examination** examinations

NOUN 1 the full word for **exam**
NOUN 2 If someone makes an **examination** of something, they look at it very carefully.

**examine** examines, examining, examined

VERB 1 If you **examine** something, you inspect it carefully.
VERB 2 If a doctor **examines** you, he or she checks your body to find out how healthy you are.

**example** examples

NOUN 1 something that is typical of a particular group of things

SYNONYMS: sample, specimen

NOUN 2 Someone who is an **example** to others is worth imitating.
PHRASE 3 You use **for example** to give an example of something you are talking about. • *large mammals, **for example** wh*

**WORD HISTORY**
from Latin *exemplum* meaning pattern

**exasperate** exasperates, exasperatin exasperated

VERB If someone or something **exasperat** you, they annoy and frustrate you.

**exasperating**

ADJECTIVE annoying and frustrating

**exasperation**

NOUN the feeling you have when you are annoyed and frustrated

**excavate** excavates, excavating, excavated

VERB 1 When someone **excavates**, they remove earth from the ground by digging
VERB 2 When archaeologists **excavate** objects, they carefully uncover remains in the ground to discover information about the past. • *They found some interesting Roman artefacts while they were **excavatin***

**excavation** excavations

NOUN 1 the process of digging a large hole the ground
NOUN 2 the process of digging in the ground to find very old objects in order to discove information about the past

**excavator** excavators

NOUN 1 a machine that digs holes in the ground and moves earth
NOUN 2 a person who digs in the ground to find very old objects in order to discover information about the past

**exceed** exceeds, exceeding, exceeded

VERB If something **exceeds** a particular amount, it is greater than that amount.

**excel** excels, excelling, excelled

VERB If someone **excels** in or at something they are very good at doing it.

**excellence**

NOUN the quality that something has when is extremely good

**cellent**
ADJECTIVE very good indeed

SYNONYMS: first-rate, outstanding, superb

**cept**
PREPOSITION apart from or not including someone or something • *Everyone laughed except Ben.*

**ception exceptions**
NOUN somebody or something that is not included in a general rule • *All my family are musicians, with the exception of my father.*

**ceptional**
ADJECTIVE If someone or something is **exceptional**, they are unusual or remarkable in some way. For example, they may be very clever or have special talents.

**cerpt excerpts**
NOUN a short piece of writing, music or film that is taken from a longer piece

**cess excesses**
NOUN too much of something

**cessive**
ADJECTIVE more than is needed or allowed

**change exchanges, exchanging, exchanged**
VERB If you **exchange** something for something else, you replace it with that thing. • *I took the shoes back to the shop and exchanged them for another pair.*

**change rate exchange rates**
NOUN The **exchange rate** of a country's unit of currency is the amount of a different currency that you get when you change from one currency into the other.

**cite excites, exciting, excited**
VERB If something **excites** you, it makes you feel very happy and enthusiastic.

**cited**
ADJECTIVE feeling very happy because something good has happened or will happen • *I'm really excited about the party.*

**citedly**
ADVERB in a happy way because something good has happened or will happen

**citement**
NOUN a very happy feeling because something good has happened or will happen

**citing**
ADJECTIVE making you feel excited

**exclaim exclaims, exclaiming, exclaimed**
VERB When you **exclaim**, you cry out suddenly or loudly because you are excited or shocked.

**exclamation exclamations**
NOUN something that you say suddenly or loudly because you are excited or shocked

**exclamation mark exclamation marks**
NOUN a punctuation mark (!) used in writing to show a strong feeling

**exclude excludes, excluding, excluded**
VERB If you **exclude** someone from a place or activity, you prevent them from entering or taking part.

ANTONYM: include

**exclusion**
NOUN **Exclusion** is when you prevent someone from entering a place or taking part in an activity.

ANTONYM: inclusion

**exclusive**
ADJECTIVE **1** available to a small group of rich or privileged people
ADJECTIVE **2** belonging to a particular person or group only • *Our group will have exclusive use of the pool.*

**excruciating**
ADJECTIVE extremely painful

**excursion excursions**
NOUN a short journey or outing

**excuse excuses, excusing, excused**
NOUN **1** a reason you give to explain why something has been done, has not been done or will not be done
VERB **2** If you **excuse** someone's behaviour, you give reasons for why they behaved in that way.
PHRASE **3** You say **excuse me** to try to catch somebody's attention or to apologise for an interruption.

PRONUNCIATION TIP
The noun is pronounced ex-**kyooss**. The verb is pronounced ex-**kyooz**.

**execute executes, executing, executed**
VERB To **execute** somebody means to kill them as a punishment for a crime.

a
b
c
d
e
f
g
h
i
j
k
l
m
n
o
p
q
r
s
t
u
v
w
x
y
z

A
B
C
D
E
F
G
H
I
J
K
L
M
N
O
P
Q
R
S
T
U
V
W
X
Y
Z

**execution executions**
NOUN An **execution** is when somebody is killed as a punishment for a crime.

**executive executives**
NOUN a person who works at a senior level in a company

**exercise exercises, exercising, exercised**
NOUN **1** any activity that you do in order to get fit or stay healthy
NOUN **2** a piece of work that you do for practice
VERB **3** When you **exercise**, you do activities that help you to get fit and stay healthy.

**exert exerts, exerting, exerted**
VERB If you **exert** yourself, you make a great deal of effort to do something.

**exhale exhales, exhaling, exhaled**
VERB When you **exhale**, you breathe out.

ANTONYM: inhale

**exhaust exhausts, exhausting, exhausted**
VERB **1** If something **exhausts** you, it makes you very tired.
VERB **2** If something has been **exhausted**, it has been used up. ● *Logging companies have largely **exhausted** the country's forests.*
NOUN **3** the pipe that carries the gas or steam out of the engine of a vehicle

**exhausted**
ADJECTIVE If you are **exhausted**, you are very tired.

**exhibit exhibits, exhibiting, exhibited**
VERB **1** If someone **exhibits** something, they put it on show for others to see, especially in a gallery or museum.
NOUN **2** something that is put on show for others to see, especially in a gallery or museum

**exhibition exhibitions**
NOUN a public display of works of art, products or skills

**exile exiles, exiling, exiled**
NOUN **1** a person who is not allowed to live in their own country
VERB **2** If someone is **exiled**, they are sent away from their own country, usually as a punishment.

**exist exists, existing, existed**
VERB If something **exists**, it is in the world as a real thing.

**existence**
NOUN the fact that something is a real thing or situation ● *We can understand the **existence** of stars and planets.*

**exit exits, exiting, exited**
NOUN **1** a doorway through which you can leave a public place

ANTONYM: entrance

NOUN **2** If you make an **exit**, you leave a place.

ANTONYM: entrance

VERB **3** If you **exit** a place, you leave it.

**exotic**
ADJECTIVE If something is **exotic**, it is unusual and interesting, usually because it comes from another country.

**expand expands, expanding, expanded**
VERB If something **expands**, or if you **expand** it, it becomes larger.

ANTONYM: contract

**expanse expanses**
NOUN a large area of something such as the sky or land

**expansion**
NOUN **Expansion** is when something becomes larger.

ANTONYM: contraction

**expect expects, expecting, expected**
VERB **1** If you **expect** something to happen, you believe that it will happen.
VERB **2** If you are **expecting** someone, you are waiting for them to arrive.
VERB **3** If you **expect** something, you believe that you ought to get it or have it.
● *I'm **expecting** you to help me.*

**expectation expectations**
NOUN **1** An **expectation** is what you believe will happen.
NOUN **2** Your **expectations** are how you think a situation should be or how you think somebody should behave.

**expedition expeditions**
NOUN **1** an organised journey made for a special purpose, often to explore
NOUN **2** the party of people who go on an expedition ● *The **expedition** set out through the rainforest.*

**pel expels, expelling, expelled**
VERB **1** If someone **expels** a person from a school or club, they tell them officially to leave because they have behaved badly.
VERB **2** If a gas or liquid is **expelled** from a place, it is forced out of it.

**pense expenses**
NOUN the amount of money it costs to do something or buy something • *They could not afford the **expense** of the school trip.*

**pensive**
ADJECTIVE If something is **expensive**, it costs a lot of money.

**perience experiences, experiencing, experienced**
NOUN **1** all the things that you have done or that have happened to you • *No previous **experience** is necessary for this job.*
NOUN **2** something that you do or something that happens to you, especially something new or unusual • *What has been your most enjoyable **experience**?*
VERB **3** If you **experience** something, it happens to you or you are affected by it. • *We had never **experienced** this kind of holiday before.*

**periment experiments, experimenting, experimented**
NOUN **1** a scientific test that aims to prove or discover something
VERB **2** If you **experiment** with something or on something, you do a scientific test to prove or discover something about it.

**perimental**
ADJECTIVE done to prove or discover something

**pert experts**
NOUN a person who is very skilled at something or who knows a lot about a particular subject

SYNONYMS: authority, specialist

**pire expires, expiring, expired**
VERB If something **expires**, it comes to an end and you can no longer use it.

**plain explains, explaining, explained**
VERB If you **explain** something, you give information about it or reasons for it so that it can be understood.

SYNONYMS: clarify, make clear

**explanation explanations**
NOUN An **explanation** explains something.

**explanatory**
ADJECTIVE Something that is **explanatory** gives information about something or reasons for it so that you can understand it.

**explode explodes, exploding, exploded**
VERB If something such as a bomb **explodes**, it bursts with great force.

**exploit exploits, exploiting, exploited**
VERB **1** If somebody **exploits** a person or a situation, they take advantage of them for their own ends.
NOUN **2** something daring or interesting that somebody has done

PRONUNCIATION TIP
The verb is pronounced ex-**ploit**. The noun is pronounced **ex**-ploit.

**exploration**
NOUN **Exploration** is when you travel around a place to discover what it is like.

**explore explores, exploring, explored**
VERB If you **explore** a place, you travel around it to discover what it is like.

**explorer explorers**
NOUN someone who travels to a place that people do not know much about, in order to discover what it is like • *space **explorers***

**explosion explosions**
NOUN An **explosion** is when something such as a bomb bursts with great force.

**explosive explosives**
ADJECTIVE **1** If something is **explosive**, it is likely to explode.
NOUN **2** something that can cause an explosion

**export exports, exporting, exported**
VERB **1** If someone **exports** goods, they sell them to another country.

ANTONYM: import

NOUN **2 Exports** are goods that are sold to another country.

PRONUNCIATION TIP
The verb is pronounced ex-**port**. The noun is pronounced **ex**-port.

a
b
c
d
e
f
g
h
i
j
k
l
m
n
o
p
q
r
s
t
u
v
w
x
y
z

A
B
C
D
E
F
G
H
I
J
K
L
M
N
O
P
Q
R
S
T
U
V
W
X
Y
Z

**expose** exposes, exposing, exposed
VERB **1** If you **expose** something, you uncover it so that it can be seen.
VERB **2** If a person is **exposed** to something dangerous, they are put in a situation in which that thing might harm them. • *The patients were isolated so that no one else would be **exposed** to the disease.*

**exposure**
NOUN the harmful effect of the weather on the body if a person is outside too long without any protection

**express** expresses, expressing, expressed
VERB **1** When you **express** an idea or feeling, you show what you think or feel by saying or doing something. • *She **expressed** her gratitude by giving me a hug.*
ADJECTIVE **2** very fast • *an **express** train*

**expression** expressions
NOUN **1** Your **expression** is the look on your face that shows what you are thinking or feeling.
NOUN **2** The **expression** of ideas or feelings is the act of showing them through words, actions or art.
NOUN **3** An **expression** is a phrase with a special meaning, such as *nosy parker*.

**expressive**
ADJECTIVE showing what someone thinks or feels • *He has a very **expressive** face.*

**expulsion**
NOUN **1** **Expulsion** is when someone is officially told to leave a school or club because they have behaved badly.
NOUN **2** **Expulsion** is when a gas or liquid is forced out of a place.

**exquisite**
ADJECTIVE Something that is **exquisite** is extremely beautiful and pleasing.

**extend** extends, extending, extended
VERB If you **extend** something, you make it longer or bigger.

**extension** extensions
NOUN **1** a room or building that is added on to an existing building
NOUN **2** an additional telephone connected to the same landline as another telephone

**extensive**
ADJECTIVE **1** covering a large area • *The gardens are **extensive**.*
ADJECTIVE **2** very great in effect • *After the storm the house required **extensive** repairs.*

**extent** extents
NOUN The **extent** of something is its length or the area it covers.

**exterior** exteriors
NOUN the outside of something

**exterminate** exterminates, exterminating, exterminated
VERB To **exterminate** people or animals means to kill a lot of them deliberately.

**extermination**
NOUN **Extermination** is when a lot of people or animals are deliberately killed.

**external**
ADJECTIVE existing or happening on the outside of something • *The **external** walls the house need painting.*

**extinct**
ADJECTIVE **1** An **extinct** species of animal or plant does not exist anymore.
ADJECTIVE **2** An **extinct** volcano is no longer likely to erupt.

**extinction**
NOUN **Extinction** is when a species of animal or plant does not exist anymore.

**extinguish** extinguishes, extinguishing, extinguished
VERB If you **extinguish** a light or fire, you put it out.

**extra**
ADJECTIVE more than is usual, necessary or expected • *He used the **extra** time to check his work.*

SYNONYMS: added, additional, further

**extract** extracts, extracting, extracted
VERB **1** If you **extract** something from a place you get it out, often by force. • *The dentist had to **extract** my wisdom tooth.*
NOUN **2** a small section taken from a book or a piece of music

PRONUNCIATION TIP
The verb is pronounced ex-**trakt**. The noun is pronounced **ex**-trakt.

**extraordinary**
ADJECTIVE very unusual or surprising

SYNONYMS: exceptional, remarkable

**xtraterrestrial**

ADJECTIVE If something is **extraterrestrial**, it happens or exists beyond the Earth's atmosphere.

**xtravagance**

NOUN **Extravagance** is when you spend a lot of money, especially more than you should do.

**xtravagant**

ADJECTIVE spending or costing more money than is reasonable or affordable

**xtreme extremes**

ADJECTIVE **1** very great in degree or intensity • **extreme** cold

NOUN **2** the furthest point or edge of something

NOUN **3** the highest or furthest degree of something • You experience **extremes** of temperature in the desert, where it is very cold at night and very hot during the day.

**xtremely**

ADVERB very • The illness is **extremely** rare.

**e eyes, eyeing** or **eying, eyed**

NOUN **1** the parts of a human or other animal's body with which they see

→ Have a look at the illustrations for **insect**, **spider** and **whale**

VERB **2** To **eye** something means to look at it. • They **eyed** each other's new shoes with interest.

**eyebrow eyebrows**

NOUN Your **eyebrows** are the lines of hair that grow on the ridges of bone above your eyes. • She raised her **eyebrows** in surprise when she saw her dad's new hat.

**eyelash eyelashes**

NOUN Your **eyelashes** are the hairs that grow on the edges of your eyelids.

**eyelid eyelids**

NOUN Your **eyelids** are the folds of skin that cover your eyes when they are closed. • I was so tired that my **eyelids** started to droop.

**eyesight**

NOUN the ability to see • His **eyesight** is not very good, so he wears glasses.

**eyewitness eyewitnesses**

NOUN someone who has seen something happen and can describe it, especially an accident or a crime • The police appealed for any **eyewitnesses** to the crash to come forward.

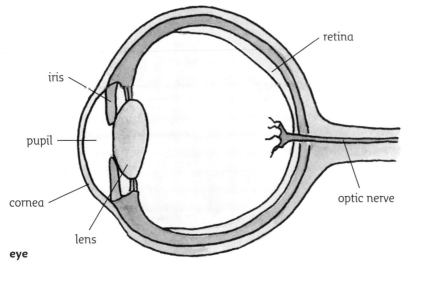

iris

pupil

cornea

lens

eye

retina

optic nerve

A
B
C
D
E
F
G
H
I
J
K
L
M
N
O
P
Q
R
S
T
U
V
W
X
Y
Z

## fable fables
NOUN a story intended to teach a moral lesson • the well-known **fable** of the tortoise and the hare

## fabric fabrics
NOUN cloth • Silk is a delicate **fabric**.

## fabulous
ADJECTIVE **1** wonderful or very impressive
ADJECTIVE **2 Fabulous** creatures are only found in legends or fairytales.

## face faces, facing, faced
NOUN **1** the front part of your head, from your chin to your forehead
NOUN **2** a surface or side of something • We could see the north **face** of the mountain.
VERB **3** If you **face** something or someone, you are opposite them and look in their direction.
VERB **4** If you **face** in a certain direction, you look there.

## Facetime Facetimes, Facetiming, Facetimed
VERB (trademark) If you **Facetime** someone, you call them using a video connection.

## facility facilities
NOUN a piece of equipment or a service that is provided for a particular purpose • The school has excellent sports **facilities**.

## fact facts
NOUN **1** a piece of information that is true, or something that has actually happened
PHRASE **2 In fact** and **as a matter of fact** mean *actually* or *really* and are used for emphasis. • **As a matter of fact**, I do like the idea.

## factor factors
NOUN **1** something that affects an event or situation • One of the main **factors** in our success was our strong team.

SYNONYMS: element, part

NOUN **2** The **factors** of a number are the whole numbers that will divide exactly into it. • Two and five are **factors** of 10: 2 × 5 = 10, 10 ÷ 5 = 2, 10 ÷ 2 = 5.

## factory factories
NOUN a building or group of buildings where goods are made in large quantities

## factual
ADJECTIVE If something is **factual**, it has actually happened.

## fade fades, fading, faded
VERB When something **fades**, it slowly becomes less bright or less loud. • The colour has **faded** from my favourite T-shirt.

## Fahrenheit
NOUN the temperature scale that has the freezing point for water at 32 °F and the boiling point at 212 °F

PRONUNCIATION TIP
This word is pronounced **fa**-ren-hite.

## fail fails, failing, failed
VERB **1** If you **fail** to do something, you do not succeed in doing it.

ANTONYM: succeed

VERB **2** If you **fail** an exam, your marks are too low and you do not pass.
VERB **3** If someone or something **fails** to do something that they should have done, they do not do it. • The bomb **failed** to explode.
PHRASE **4 Without fail** means definitely or regularly. • He plays football every Sunday **without fail**.

## failure failures
NOUN **1** a lack of success in doing something • Her attempt to win the race ended in **failure**.
NOUN **2** an unsuccessful person, thing or action

## faint fainter, faintest; faints, fainting, fainted
ADJECTIVE **1** A sound, colour or feeling that is **faint** is not strong or intense. • Their voice grew **fainter** as they moved away.
ADJECTIVE **2** If you feel **faint**, you feel dizzy or unsteady. • I was feeling **faint**, so I sat down.
VERB **3** If you **faint**, you lose consciousness for a short time.

**fair** **fairer, fairest**; **fairs**

ADJECTIVE **1** Something that is **fair** seems reasonable to most people.

ADJECTIVE **2** If the weather is **fair** it is fine.

ADJECTIVE **3** quite good or moderate • *I think I have a **fair** chance of passing my exams.*

ADJECTIVE **4** People who are **fair** have light-coloured hair.

NOUN **5** a form of entertainment that takes place outside, with stalls, games and rides

**fairground** **fairgrounds**

NOUN an open piece of ground where fairs are held

**fairly**

ADVERB **1** quite or rather • *My room's **fairly** small.*

ADVERB **2** in a way that seems reasonable to most people • *Everyone should be treated **fairly**.*

**fairness**

NOUN **Fairness** is when something seems reasonable to most people.

**fairy** **fairies**

NOUN In stories, **fairies** are small, supernatural creatures with magical powers.

**fairy tale** **fairy tales**

NOUN a story of magical events

**faith** **faiths**

NOUN **1** If you have **faith** in someone, you trust them.

NOUN **2** a religious belief

**faithful**

ADJECTIVE If you are **faithful** to someone or something, you are loyal and continue to support them. • *He is one of my most **faithful** friends.*

**fake** **fakes, faking, faked**

NOUN **1** an imitation of something, made to trick people into thinking that it is genuine

ADJECTIVE **2** imitation and not genuine • *The coat was made of **fake** fur.*

VERB **3** If you **fake** a feeling, you pretend that you are experiencing it. • *I **faked** illness to avoid the games lesson.*

**fall** **falls, falling, fell, fallen**

VERB **1** If someone or something **falls**, or **falls** over, or **falls** down, they drop towards the ground. • *The snow **fell** all day, covering the fields and trees.*

VERB **2** to become lower or less • *The temperature usually **falls** at night.*

VERB **3** If you **fall ill**, you become ill.

VERB **4** If you **fall asleep**, you begin to sleep.

VERB **5** If you **fall in love**, you begin to love someone.

NOUN **6** If you have a **fall**, you fall over.

**fall out**

VERB If you **fall out** with someone, you disagree and quarrel with them.

**false**

ADJECTIVE **1** untrue or incorrect

ADJECTIVE **2** not real or genuine, but intended to seem real • *Grandad has **false** teeth.*

**fame**

NOUN the state of being very well known

**familiar**

ADJECTIVE **1** well-known or easy to recognise • *The room was full of **familiar** faces.*

ANTONYM: unfamiliar

ADJECTIVE **2** If you are **familiar with** something, you know it or understand it well. • *He was very **familiar with** the local area.*

ANTONYM: unfamiliar

**family** **families**

NOUN a group of people who are related to each other, especially parents and their children

**family tree** **family trees**

NOUN a diagram that shows how different members of a family are related to each other

**famine** **famines**

NOUN a serious shortage of food that may cause many deaths

WORD HISTORY

from Latin *fames* meaning hunger

**famished**

ADJECTIVE very hungry

**famous**

ADJECTIVE very well-known

**fan** **fans, fanning, fanned**

NOUN **1** If you are a **fan** of something or someone famous, you like them very much.

NOUN **2** a hand-held or mechanical device that moves air to make it cooler

VERB **3** If you **fan** yourself, you cool the air around you with a fan.

a b c d e f g h i j k l m n o p q r s t u v w x y z

**145**

## fancy fancies, fancying, fancied; fancier, fanciest
VERB **1** If you **fancy** something, you want to have it.
ADJECTIVE **2** highly decorated and special

## fancy dress
NOUN clothing worn for a party at which people dress up to look like a particular character or animal

## fang fangs
NOUN a long, sharp tooth

## fantastic
ADJECTIVE **1** wonderful and very pleasing

SYNONYM: marvellous

ADJECTIVE **2** strange or unusual, like a fantasy

WORD HISTORY
from Greek *phantasia* meaning imagination

## fantasy fantasies
NOUN an imaginative story that is unlikely to happen in real life

## far farther or further, farthest or furthest
ADVERB **1** a long distance away

ANTONYMS: near, close

ADJECTIVE **2** You can use **far** to ask questions about distance. • *How far is the nearest supermarket?*

ANTONYMS: near, close

## fare fares
NOUN the amount that you pay to travel on a bus, train or plane

## farewell
INTERJECTION goodbye

## far-fetched
ADJECTIVE unlikely to be true

## farm farms, farming, farmed
NOUN **1** an area of land and buildings, used for growing crops or raising animals
VERB **2** If someone **farms** land, they plant crops or keep animals there.

## farmer farmers
NOUN someone who looks after a farm

## farming
NOUN the work of planting crops or keeping animals on a farm

## fascinate fascinates, fascinating, fascinated
VERB If something **fascinates** you, it interests and attracts you.

## fascinating
ADJECTIVE very interesting

## fashion fashions
NOUN a style of dress or way of behaving that is popular at a particular time

## fashionable
ADJECTIVE popular at a particular time
• *fashionable clothes*

## fashionably
ADVERB in a way that is popular at a particular time

## fast faster, fastest; fasts, fasting, fasted
ADJECTIVE **1** If something is **fast**, it moves quickly. • *Our car is very fast.*
ADJECTIVE **2** If a clock is **fast**, it shows a time that is ahead of the real time.
ADVERB **3** If something happens **fast**, it happens quickly or with great speed.
• *Can you run fast?*
ADVERB **4** If a clock goes **fast**, it keeps showing a time that is ahead of the real time.
PHRASE **5** If you are **fast asleep**, you are in deep sleep.
VERB **6** If you **fast**, you eat no food for a period of time, usually for religious reasons

## fasten fastens, fastening, fastened
VERB If you **fasten** something, you close it attach it firmly to something else.

## fastener fasteners
NOUN something that is used to join two parts of something together, especially on a piece of clothing, for example a button on a coat

## fastening fastenings
NOUN something that is used to join two parts of something together

## fat fatter, fattest
ADJECTIVE **1** having a lot of flesh on the body
NOUN **2** the greasy, white substance that animals and humans have under their skin It is used to store energy and helps to keep them warm.
NOUN **3** the greasy or oily substance from animals and plants that is used in cooking

## fatal
ADJECTIVE A **fatal** accident or illness causes someone's death.

**tally**
ADVERB in a way that causes someone's death • He was **fatally** injured.

**te fates**
NOUN **1** a power that some people believe controls events
NOUN **2** Someone's **fate** is what becomes of them.

**ther fathers**
NOUN a male parent

**ther-in-law fathers-in-law**
NOUN the father of someone's husband or wife

**tigue**
NOUN extreme tiredness

**ult faults, faulting, faulted**
NOUN **1** a mistake or something wrong with the way something is made
NOUN **2** If something bad is your **fault**, you are to blame for it.
VERB **3** If you **fault** someone or something, you find something wrong with them. • You can't **fault** his piano playing.

**ultless**
ADJECTIVE without any mistakes or anything wrong

**ulty**
ADJECTIVE If something is **faulty**, there is something wrong with it.

**una**
NOUN animals, especially those that are found in a particular area • the flora and **fauna** of the African jungle

**vour favours, favouring, favoured**
NOUN **1** If you do someone a **favour**, you do something to help them.
VERB **2** If you **favour** someone or something, you prefer them to others.

**vourite favourites**
ADJECTIVE **1** Your **favourite** person or thing is the one you like best. • Peaches are my **favourite** fruit.
NOUN **2** Someone's **favourite** is the person or thing they like best. • I like all sports, but soccer is my **favourite**.

**wn fawns**
NOUN **1** a young deer
NOUN **2** a light-brown colour
ADJECTIVE **3** having a light-brown colour

**fax faxes**
NOUN an exact copy of a document sent electronically along a phone line using a special machine

**fear fears, fearing, feared**
NOUN **1** the feeling of worry you have when you think that you are in danger or that something bad might happen
VERB **2** If you **fear** someone or something, you are afraid of them.

**fearful**
ADJECTIVE If you are **fearful** of someone or something, you are afraid of them.

**fearless**
ADJECTIVE If you are **fearless**, you are brave and have no fear.

**fearsome**
ADJECTIVE frightening or terrible

**feast feasts**
NOUN a large and special meal for many people

**feat feats**
NOUN a difficult and impressive achievement

**feather feathers**
NOUN A bird's **feathers** are the light, soft growths covering its body.

**feature features**
NOUN **1** a particular part or characteristic of something that is interesting or important
PLURAL NOUN **2** Your **features** are your eyes, nose, mouth and other parts of your face.
• Your **features** are similar to your mother's.

**February**
NOUN the second month of the year. **February** usually has 28 days, but has 29 days in a leap year.

LANGUAGE TIP
There is an r after the b in February.

**fed**
VERB the past participle of **feed**

**fed up**
ADJECTIVE (informal) unhappy or bored
• I'm **fed up** with this rainy weather.

**fee fees**
NOUN a charge or payment for a job, service or activity

**feeble feebler, feeblest**
ADJECTIVE weak, with no strength or power

a
b
c
d
e
f
g
h
i
j
k
l
m
n
o
p
q
r
s
t
u
v
w
x
y
z

**147**

## feed feeds, feeding, fed

VERB **1** If you **feed** a person or animal, you give them food. • *She feeds the pigeons every day.*

VERB **2** When an animal or baby **feeds**, it eats. • *These insects feed on wood.*

VERB **3** If you **feed** something into a machine, you put it in there. • *They fed the information into a computer.*

## feel feels, feeling, felt

VERB **1** If you **feel** an emotion or sensation, you experience it. • *I felt very happy on my birthday.*

VERB **2** If you **feel** something, you touch it. • *The doctor felt my forehead.*

PHRASE **3** If you **feel like** doing something, you want to do it.

## feeler feelers

NOUN **Feelers** are long, thin antennae on the heads of some insects, used to sense things around them.

## feeling feelings

NOUN **1** an emotion • *Finishing my homework gave me a feeling of satisfaction.*

NOUN **2** a physical sensation • *I had a feeling of pins and needles in my foot.*

NOUN **3** Your **feelings** about something are your general attitudes or thoughts about it.

## feet

PLURAL NOUN the plural of **foot**

## feline

ADJECTIVE relating to the cat family, or like a cat • *The dancer moved with feline grace.*

## felt

VERB **1** the past tense and past participle of **feel**

NOUN **2** a thick cloth made by pressing short threads together

## female females

NOUN **1** a person or animal that can have babies or lay eggs

ANTONYM: male

ADJECTIVE **2** concerning or relating to females

ANTONYM: male

## feminine

ADJECTIVE relating to women or considered to be typical of women

ANTONYM: masculine

WORD HISTORY
from Latin *femina* meaning woman

## fence fences

NOUN a wooden or wire barrier between tw areas of land

## ferment ferments, fermenting, fermented

VERB When beer, wine or fruit **ferments**, a chemical change takes place and alcohol often produced.

## fern ferns

NOUN a plant with long, feathery leaves an no flowers

## ferocious

ADJECTIVE violent and fierce

## ferret ferrets

NOUN a small mammal that can be trained to hunt rabbits or rats

WORD HISTORY
from Old French *furet* meaning little thief

## ferry ferries, ferrying, ferried

NOUN **1** a boat that carries people and vehicles across short stretches of water • *We took the ferry across to France.*

VERB **2** If someone **ferries** people or goods somewhere, they transport them there, usually on a short, regular journey. • *A fle of buses ferried people to the concert.*

## fertile

ADJECTIVE **1** If soil is **fertile** it can produce strong, healthy plants.

ADJECTIVE **2** If a human or other animal is **fertile**, they are able to have babies or young.

## fertilise fertilises, fertilising, fertilise also spelt fertilize

VERB **1** When an egg is **fertilised**, the process of reproduction has begun. • *Poll fertilises the female part of a plant.*

VERB **2** When you **fertilise** land, you put manure or chemicals on to it to help the growth of plants.

## fertiliser; also spelt fertilizer

NOUN a substance such as manure or chemicals added to the soil to improve plant growth

**festival festivals**
NOUN **1** an organised series of events and performances • *The film **festival** at Cannes in France is very famous.*
NOUN **2** a time when something special is celebrated • *Harvest **festival** is in the autumn.*

**fetch fetches, fetching, fetched**
VERB If you **fetch** something, you go to where it is and bring it back. • *She **fetched** a towel from the bathroom.*

**fête fêtes**; also spelt **fete**
NOUN an outdoor event with games, displays and goods for sale • *The school **fête** was a big success.*

PRONUNCIATION TIP
This word is pronounced **fayt**.

WORD HISTORY
from the French *feste* meaning feast

**feud feuds, feuding, feuded**
NOUN **1** a long-running and bitter quarrel, especially between families
VERB **2** When people **feud**, they quarrel over a long period of time.

PRONUNCIATION TIP
This word is pronounced **fyood**.

**fever fevers**
NOUN If you have a **fever**, your temperature is higher than usual because you are ill.

**feverish**
ADJECTIVE If you are **feverish**, you have a higher body temperature than usual.

**few fewer, fewest**
ADJECTIVE **1** not many • *I saw him a **few** moments ago.*
PRONOUN **2** a small number of things or people • ***Few** of the houses still had lights on.*

LANGUAGE TIP
Use *fewer* to talk about things that can be counted and *less* for things that can't be counted: *fewer apples; less time.*

**fiancé fiancés**
NOUN Someone's **fiancé** is the man to whom they are engaged to be married.

PRONUNCIATION TIP
This word is pronounced fee-**on**-say.

WORD HISTORY
the words *fiancé* and *fiancée* are from Old French *fiancer* meaning to promise or betroth

**fiancée fiancées**
NOUN Someone's **fiancée** is the woman to whom they are engaged to be married.

PRONUNCIATION TIP
This word is pronounced fee-**on**-say.

**fiasco fiascos**
NOUN When something is a **fiasco**, it fails completely, especially in a ridiculous or disorganised way.

PRONUNCIATION TIP
This word is pronounced fee-**ass**-koh.

**fib fibs, fibbing, fibbed**
VERB **1** If you **fib** about something, you tell a small lie about it.
NOUN **2** a small lie

**fibber fibbers**
NOUN someone who tells fibs

**fibre fibres**
NOUN **1** a thin thread of a substance used to make cloth • *Many fabrics today are made from artificial **fibres**.*
NOUN **2** a part of plants that can be eaten but not digested by your body • ***Fibre** is good for your digestive system.*

**fickle**
ADJECTIVE If you are **fickle**, you keep changing your mind about what you want.

**fiction**
NOUN stories about imaginary people and events

ANTONYM: non-fiction

**fictional**
ADJECTIVE from a book or story about imaginary people and events • *Harry Potter is a **fictional** character.*

**fiddle fiddles, fiddling, fiddled**
VERB **1** If you **fiddle** with something, you keep touching it and playing with it in a restless way.
NOUN **2** another word for **violin**

a
b
c
d
e
f
g
h
i
j
k
l
m
n
o
p
q
r
s
t
u
v
w
x
y
z

**fidget** fidgets, fidgeting, fidgeted
VERB If you **fidget**, you keep changing your position or making small restless movements because you are nervous or bored.

**field** fields
NOUN **1** an area of land where crops are grown or animals are kept
NOUN **2** an area of land where sports are played • a football **field**
NOUN **3** a particular subject or area of interest

**fiend** fiends
NOUN **1** a devil or evil spirit
NOUN **2** a very wicked or cruel person

PRONUNCIATION TIP
This word is pronounced **feend**.

**fierce** fiercer, fiercest
ADJECTIVE very aggressive or intense • a **fierce** dog • **fierce** competition

**fiery** fierier, fieriest
ADJECTIVE If you are **fiery**, you show great anger, energy or passion in what you do.

**fifteen**
NOUN **Fifteen** is the number 15.

**fifteenth** fifteenths
NOUN **1** one of fifteen equal parts of something
ADJECTIVE **2** The **fifteenth** item in a series is the one that you count as number fifteen.

**fifth**
NOUN **1** one of five equal parts of something. It can be written as ⅕.
ADJECTIVE **2** The **fifth** item in a series is the one that you count as number five. It can be written as 5$^{th}$.

**fiftieth** fiftieths
NOUN **1** one of fifty equal parts of something
ADJECTIVE **2** The **fiftieth** item in a series is the one that you count as number fifty.

**fifty**
NOUN **Fifty** is the number 50.

**fig** figs
NOUN a very sweet fruit that is full of seeds and can be eaten dried

**fight** fights, fighting, fought
VERB **1** When people **fight**, they take part in a battle, a boxing match, or in some other attempt to hurt or kill someone.
VERB **2** If you **fight** something, or if you fight against it, you try in a determined way to

stop it happening. • I've **fought** all my life against cruelty to animals.
NOUN **3** a situation in which people hit or t to hurt each other

SYNONYMS: battle, conflict

**figurative**
ADJECTIVE If you use a word or expression in **figurative** sense, you use it for effect, wit a more abstract or imaginative meaning than its usual one. For example, you could write about a person as if he or she was a bird. • He flew down the stairs. • She perche on a chair.

**figure** figures
NOUN **1** a written number • He wrote the **figures** down and then added them up.
NOUN **2** Your **figure** is the shape of your body.
NOUN **3** a diagram or table in a book or a magazine

**figure of speech** figures of speech
NOUN an expression, such as a metaphor o simile, where the words should not be tak literally. She was as cold as ice (simile). The road was a ribbon of moonlight (metaphor).

**file** files, filing, filed
NOUN **1** a box or folder in which papers are kept
NOUN **2** In computing, a **file** is a set of related data with its own name. • He copie the **file** onto his memory stick.
NOUN **3** a tool with rough surfaces, used for smoothing and shaping hard materials
VERB **4** When someone **files** something, the put it in its correct place with others that are similar. • They **filed** the students' papers alphabetically.
VERB **5** When a group of people **file** somewhere, they walk one behind the othe in a line. • The children **filed** out of the scho
PHRASE **6** If people walk **in single file**, they walk one behind the other.

**fill** fills, filling, filled
VERB **1** If you **fill** something, or if it **fills** up, it becomes full. • The arena soon began to **fill** up.
VERB **2** If something **fills** a space, there is very little room left. • The water **filled** the ju
**fill in**
VERB If you **fill in** a form, you write information in the spaces on it.

**ling fillings**

NOUN **1** the mixture inside a sandwich, cake or pie

NOUN **2** a small amount of metal or plastic that a dentist puts into a hole in a tooth

**m films, filming, filmed**

NOUN **1** a series of moving pictures that can be shown in a cinema or on television

NOUN **2** a strip of thin plastic that is used in some types of camera to take photographs

NOUN **3** a very thin layer of powder or liquid • *A film of dust covered every surface.*

VERB **4** If you **film** someone or something, you use a camera to take moving pictures of them.

**ter filters, filtering, filtered**

NOUN **1** a device that allows some substances, lights or sounds to pass through it, but not others • *The suntan cream acted as a filter against the harmful rays of the sun.*

NOUN **2** something you can choose on some apps that allows you to change your photographs in some way

VERB **3** If you **filter** something, you pass it through a filter to remove tiny particles from it.

**thy filthier, filthiest**

ADJECTIVE very dirty

**tration**

NOUN the process of passing a liquid through a filter to remove tiny particles from it

**n fins**

NOUN a flat object on the body of a fish that helps it to swim and keep its balance

→ Have a look at the illustrations for **fish** and **whale**

**nal finals**

ADJECTIVE **1** The **final** thing in a series is the last one, or the one that happens at the end. • *the final chapter of a book*

ADJECTIVE **2** A decision that is **final** cannot be changed or questioned. • *The judges' decision is final.*

NOUN **3** The **final** is the last game or contest in a series, that decides the overall winner.

**nalist finalists**

NOUN someone who takes part in the final of a competition

**finally**

ADVERB **1** If something **finally** happens, it happens after a long delay. • *Finally*, he answered the phone.

SYNONYMS: at last, eventually

ADVERB **2** You use **finally** to introduce the last point or topic. • *Finally*, I would like to thank everyone for coming.

SYNONYMS: in conclusion, lastly

**finance finances, financing, financed**

NOUN **1 Finance** describes affairs to do with money.

VERB **2** If someone **finances** something, they provide the money for it.

**find finds, finding, found**

VERB **1** If you **find** someone or something, you see them or discover where they are. • *He eventually found the book under his bed.*

VERB **2** If you **find** something, you know it from experience. • *I find that air travel tires me.*

**find out**

VERB If you **find out** something, you learn or discover something. • *He wants to find out what really happened.*

**fine finer, finest; fines**

ADJECTIVE **1** Something that is **fine** is very good or very beautiful.

ADJECTIVE **2** If something is **fine** it is satisfactory or suitable. • *That outfit is fine for the party.*

ADJECTIVE **3** If you are **fine**, you are well and happy.

ADJECTIVE **4 Fine** sand or powder is made up of very small particles.

ADJECTIVE **5** When the weather is **fine**, it is bright and sunny.

NOUN **6** a sum of money that must be paid as a punishment

**finger fingers**

NOUN one of the four long structures at the end of your hands that you use to feel and hold things

**fingernail fingernails**

NOUN the hard coverings at the ends of your fingers

**fingerprint fingerprints**

NOUN the unique marks made by the tip of your fingers when you touch something

a
b
c
d
e
f
g
h
i
j
k
l
m
n
o
p
q
r
s
t
u
v
w
x
y
z

A
B
C
D
E
F
G
H
I
J
K
L
M
N
O
P
Q
R
S
T
U
V
W
X
Y
Z

**finish** finishes, finishing, finished
VERB **1** When you **finish** something, you do the last part of it and complete it.
VERB **2** When something **finishes**, it ends. • The film **finished** at eight o'clock.
NOUN **3** The **finish** of something is the last part of it. • There was a very exciting **finish** to the match.

SYNONYMS: close, conclusion, end

**fir** firs
NOUN an evergreen tree with thin, needle-like leaves and cones

**fire** fires, firing, fired
NOUN **1** the flames produced when something burns
NOUN **2** a mass of burning material • We lit a **fire** on the beach.
NOUN **3** a device that uses electricity, coal, gas or wood to heat a room
VERB **4** If someone **fires** a gun, they shoot a bullet. • He **fired** the gun into the air.
VERB **5** (informal) If an employer **fires** someone, that person loses their job.
PHRASE **6** If something is **on fire**, it is burning.

**fire brigade** fire brigades
NOUN the organisation that has the job of putting out fires

**fire engine** fire engines
NOUN a vehicle used by firefighters to help them put out fires

**fire escape** fire escapes
NOUN an emergency exit or staircase for use if there is a fire

**fire extinguisher** fire extinguishers
NOUN a device that contains water or foam that is sprayed on to fires to put them out

**firefighter** firefighters
NOUN a person whose job is to put out fires

**fireplace** fireplaces
NOUN the opening beneath a chimney where a fire can be lit

**fireproof**
ADJECTIVE If something is **fireproof**, it is resistant to fire.

**firework** fireworks
NOUN a small object that produces coloured sparks or smoke when lit

**firm** firmer, firmest; firms
ADJECTIVE **1** Something that is **firm** is fairly hard and does not change shape very much

when it is pressed. • I like sleeping on a **firm** mattress.
ADJECTIVE **2** A **firm** grasp or push is strong c controlled. • His handshake was **firm** and confident.
ADJECTIVE **3** Someone who is **firm** behaves i a fairly strict way and will not change the mind.
NOUN **4** a business that sells or produces something • an engineering **firm**

**first** firsts
ADJECTIVE **1** happening, coming or done bef all the others • January is the **first** month o the year.
ADJECTIVE **2** the most important • Her painti won **first** prize.
NOUN **3** the person or thing that happens c comes before all the others • I was the **firs** to arrive.
ADVERB **4** happening, coming or done befor all the others • Andrea came **first** in the 10 metres race.
ADVERB **5** the time before any others • They **first** met in 1995.
PHRASE **6** You use **at first** to refer to what happens to start with, or what happens a the beginning of something.

**first aid**
NOUN simple treatment given as soon as possible to a person who is injured or who suddenly becomes ill

**first class**
ADJECTIVE Something that is **first class** is of the highest quality or standard.

**first person**
NOUN In grammar, the **first person** refers yourself when you are speaking or writing It is expressed as I or me. • William wrote h story in the **first person**.

**fish** fishes, fishing, fished
NOUN **1** an animal with a tail and fins that lives in water
VERB **2** If you **fish**, you try to catch fish.

→ Have a look at the illustration

LANGUAGE TIP
The plural of the noun fish can be either fi or fishes, but fish is more common.

**fisherman** fishermen
NOUN someone who catches fish for a living or as a sport

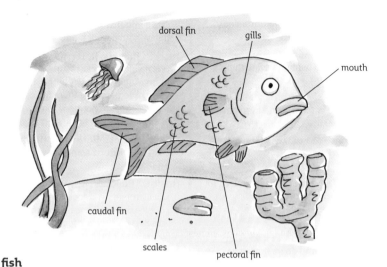

dorsal fin

gills

mouth

caudal fin

scales

pectoral fin

**fish**

**...hing**

NOUN the activity or job of trying to catch fish

**...t fists**

NOUN a hand with the fingers curled tightly ...owards the palm

**...fits, fitting, fitted; fitter, fittest**

VERB **1** If something **fits**, it is the right shape or size for a particular person or position. ● *a computer that **fits** into your pocket*

VERB **2** If you **fit** something, you put it ...ecurely in place. ● *We need to **fit** a new pane ...f glass in the broken window.*

VERB **3** If something **fits** a particular ...ituation, person or thing, it is suitable or ...ppropriate.

NOUN **4** A **fit** of laughter, coughing, rage or ...anic is a sudden, uncontrolled outburst of ...t. ● *They collapsed in a **fit** of laughter.*

NOUN **5** If someone has a **fit**, they lose ...onsciousness and their body makes ...ncontrollable movements.

ADJECTIVE **6** Someone who is **fit** is healthy and ...hysically strong.

**...ness**

NOUN Someone's **fitness** is how healthy ...nd physically strong they are. ● *exercises to ...mprove **fitness***

**...e**

NOUN **Five** is the number 5.

**fix fixes, fixing, fixed**

VERB **1** If you **fix** something somewhere, you attach it there securely. ● *He **fixed** the clock to the wall.*

VERB **2** If you **fix** something that is broken, you repair it.

SYNONYM: mend

**fixture fixtures**

NOUN **1** a sports event that takes place on a particular date

NOUN **2** an object such as a cupboard or a bath that is fixed in position in a building

**fizz fizzes, fizzing, fizzed**

VERB When something **fizzes** it makes a hissing or bubbling sound.

**fizzy fizzier, fizziest**

ADJECTIVE A **fizzy** drink has a gas called carbon dioxide in it to make it bubbly.

**flag flags**

NOUN a piece of cloth that has a particular colour or design, and is used as the symbol of a country or as a signal

**flake flakes, flaking, flaked**

NOUN **1** a small, thin piece of something ● *Flakes of rust came off the old bicycle.*

VERB **2** When something such as paint **flakes**, small, thin pieces of it come off.

**flaky flakier, flakiest**

ADJECTIVE breaking easily into small, thin pieces

**flame flames**
NOUN a hot, bright stream of burning gas
• The **flames** of the fire flickered.

**flamingo flamingos** or **flamingoes**
NOUN a long-legged wading bird with pink feathers and a long neck

**flammable**
ADJECTIVE likely to catch fire and burn easily

**flan flans**
NOUN a flat, open tart that can be sweet or savoury

**flannel flannels**
NOUN 1 a small square of towelling, used for washing yourself
NOUN 2 a lightweight woollen fabric

**flap flaps, flapping, flapped**
VERB 1 If something **flaps**, or if you **flap** it, it moves quickly up and down or from side to side. • The flag was **flapping** in the wind.
NOUN 2 a loose piece of something, such as cloth or plastic, that is attached at one edge
• a cat **flap**

**flare flares, flaring, flared**
NOUN 1 a device that produces a brightly coloured flame, used especially as an emergency signal
VERB 2 If a fire **flares**, it suddenly burns much more vigorously.

**flash flashes, flashing, flashed**
NOUN 1 a sudden, short burst of light • There was a **flash** of lightning in the middle of the storm.
VERB 2 If a light **flashes**, or if you **flash** it, it shines suddenly and briefly. • The light from the lighthouse **flashed** in the night.
VERB 3 If something **flashes**, it moves or happens very quickly. • A car **flashed** past the window.

**flask flasks**
NOUN a special bottle used for keeping drinks hot or cold, and for carrying around with you. It is an abbreviation for vacuum flask or Thermos flask.

**flat flats; flatter, flattest**
NOUN 1 a set of rooms for living in. A **flat** is part of a larger building. • We live in a block of **flats**.
ADJECTIVE 2 Something that is **flat** is level and smooth.
ADJECTIVE 3 A **flat** tyre or ball has not got enough air in it.
ADJECTIVE 4 A **flat** battery has lost its electrical charge.

**flatten flattens, flattening, flattened**
VERB If you **flatten** something, you make it flat or flatter.

**flatter flatters, flattering, flattered**
VERB If you **flatter** someone, you praise them in an exaggerated way, either to please them or to persuade them to do something
• When she **flatters** me I know she wants me to do something for her.

**flaunt flaunts, flaunting, flaunted**
VERB If you **flaunt** something, you show it off to others.

**flavour flavours, flavouring, flavoured**
NOUN 1 the taste of food and drink • This cheese has a very strong **flavour**.
VERB 2 If you **flavour** food, you add something to it to give it a particular taste
• You can **flavour** the pasta sauce with herbs

**flaw flaws**
NOUN a fault or weakness in something

**flax**
NOUN a plant that is used for making rope and cloth

**flea fleas**
NOUN a small, wingless, jumping insect that feeds on blood

**fleece fleeces**
NOUN A sheep's **fleece** is its coat of wool.

**fleet fleets**
NOUN a group of ships or vehicles owned by the same organisation, or travelling together

**flesh**
NOUN the soft part of your body between the bones and the skin

**flew**
VERB the past tense of **fly**

**flex flexes, flexing, flexed**
NOUN 1 a length of wire covered in plastic, that carries electricity to an appliance
VERB 2 If you **flex** your muscles, you bend and stretch them.

**flexibility**
NOUN **Flexibility** is the quality that something has when it can be bent easily without breaking.

**flexible**
ADJECTIVE Something that is **flexible** can be bent easily without breaking.

**ck flicks, flicking, flicked**
VERB **1** If you **flick** something, you move it sharply with your finger. • *He flicked through the pages of the book to find where he was up to.*
NOUN **2** a sudden, quick movement or sharp touch with the finger • *The cat gave a sudden flick of its tail.*

**cker flickers, flickering, flickered**
VERB If a light or a flame **flickers**, its brightness comes and goes.

**es**
PLURAL NOUN the plural of **fly**

**ght flights**
NOUN **1** a journey made by aeroplane
NOUN **2** the action of flying or the ability to fly
NOUN **3** A **flight** of stairs or steps is a row of them.
NOUN **4** the action of running away • *The girl took flight when she saw the big dog.*

**ght attendant flight attendants**
NOUN a person who looks after the passengers on an aeroplane

**msy flimsier, flimsiest**
ADJECTIVE made of something very thin and easily damaged • *The shelter they made in the garden was very flimsy.*

**nch flinches, flinching, flinched**
VERB If you **flinch**, you make a sudden, small movement in fear or pain. • *She flinched when the dentist's drill started.*

SYNONYMS: cringe, wince

**ng flings, flinging, flung**
VERB If you **fling** something somewhere, you throw it there using a lot of force. • *He flung his shoes into the corner.*

**nt flints**
NOUN a very hard, grey-black stone used for building

**p flips, flipping, flipped**
VERB If you **flip** something, you turn it over quickly. • *He flipped open the book to start his homework.*

**pper flippers**
NOUN one of the flat limbs of an animal like a penguin or seal that they use for swimming

**oat floats, floating, floated**
VERB **1** Something that **floats** is supported by liquid. • *A branch floated down the river.*
VERB **2** If something **floats** in the air, it hangs in the air or moves slowly through it. • *A leaf floated on the breeze.*

NOUN **3** an object attached to a fishing line to keep the hook floating in the water
NOUN **4** an amount of money that a shop or stall keeps for change

**flock flocks, flocking, flocked**
NOUN **1** a group of birds, sheep or goats
VERB **2** If people **flock** somewhere, they go there in large numbers.

**flood floods, flooding, flooded**
NOUN **1** If there is a **flood**, a large amount of water covers an area that is usually dry.
NOUN **2** A **flood** of something is a large amount of it occurring suddenly. • *There was a flood of emails after the programme.*
VERB **3** If water **floods** an area that is usually dry, or if the area **floods**, it becomes covered with water. • *He left the tap running and flooded the kitchen.*

**floodlight floodlights**
NOUN a very powerful outdoor light that is used to illuminate buildings and sports fields

**floor floors**
NOUN **1** the part of a room that you walk on
NOUN **2** one of the levels in a building • *Our flat is on the fifth floor of the building.*

**flop flops, flopping, flopped**
VERB **1** If someone or something **flops**, they fall loosely and heavily. • *He flopped down on to the sofa when he got home.*
VERB **2** (*informal*) If something **flops**, it fails. • *The play flopped after some bad reviews.*

**flora**
NOUN plants, especially those that grow in a particular area • *the flora and fauna of the African jungle*

**florist florists**
NOUN a person or shop selling flowers

**flour**
NOUN a white or brown powder made by grinding grain. It is used for making bread, cakes and pastry.

**flourish flourishes, flourishing, flourished**
VERB Something that **flourishes** develops or grows successfully or healthily.

**WORD HISTORY**
from Latin *florere* meaning to flower

a
b
c
d
e
f
g
h
i
j
k
l
m
n
o
p
q
r
s
t
u
v
w
x
y
z

A
B
C
D
E
**F**
G
H
I
J
K
L
M
N
O
P
Q
R
S
T
U
V
W
X
Y
Z

## flow flows, flowing, flowed

VERB **1** If something **flows** somewhere, it moves there in a steady and continuous manner. • *The river **flows** south from the town.*
NOUN **2** A **flow** of something is a steady, continuous movement of it. • *There is a constant **flow** of traffic down the main road.*

## flow chart flow charts

NOUN a diagram that shows the sequence of steps and choices that lead to various results and courses of action

## flower flowers, flowering, flowered

NOUN **1** the part of a plant that grows at the end of a stem. It carries the reproductive parts of the plant from which the fruit and seeds develop.

→ Have a look at the illustration for **plant**

VERB **2** When a plant **flowers**, its flowers open.

## flown

VERB the past participle of **fly**

## flu

NOUN an abbreviation of *influenza*. **Flu** is an illness similar to a bad cold, but more serious.

## fluent

ADJECTIVE Someone who is **fluent** in a foreign language can speak it correctly and without hesitation.

## fluently

ADVERB Someone who speaks a foreign language **fluently** can speak it correctly and without hesitation.

## fluff

NOUN soft, light, woolly threads or fibres bunched together

## fluffy fluffier, fluffiest

ADJECTIVE soft and woolly • *The kitten was small, grey and very **fluffy**.*

## fluid fluids

NOUN a liquid • *Drink plenty of **fluids** in hot weather.*

## fluke flukes

NOUN an accidental success • *It must be a **fluke** that I did so well in my exams.*

## fluorescent

ADJECTIVE **1** When something is **fluorescent** it gives out its own light when another light is shone on it.
ADJECTIVE **2** A **fluorescent** light is in the form a tube that shines with a harsh, bright light

## fluoride

NOUN a chemical mixture that is often added to drinking water and to toothpaste because it is thought to prevent tooth decay

leaf

petal

pollen

roots

stem

stigma

stamen

**sh flushes, flushing, flushed**
VERB **1** If you **flush**, your face goes red.
VERB **2** If you **flush** a toilet or something such as a pipe, you force water through it to clean it.

**te flutes**
NOUN a musical wind instrument in the shape of a long tube with holes along it. You play it by blowing over a hole near one end while holding it sideways to your mouth.

**tter flutters, fluttering, fluttered**
VERB If something **flutters**, it flaps or waves with small, quick movements. • I felt the bird **flutter** in my hands.

**flies, flying, flew, flown**
NOUN **1** an insect with two pairs of wings
VERB **2** When a bird, insect or aircraft **flies**, it moves through the air. • The bird **flew** away.
VERB **3** If you **fly** somewhere, you travel there in an aircraft.

**er flyers**
NOUN a piece of paper that advertises something

**ing**
NOUN **1** the activity of travelling in a plane
ADJECTIVE **2** moving through the air

**over flyovers**
NOUN a bridge that takes one road over the top of another one

**al foals**
NOUN a young horse

**am foams, foaming, foamed**
NOUN **1** a mass of tiny bubbles • The bubble bath produced a lot of **foam**.
VERB **2** When something **foams**, it forms a mass of small bubbles. • The powder **foamed** in the washing machine.

**cus focuses, focusing, focused or focusses, focussing, focussed**
VERB **1** If you **focus** your eyes or a camera on something, you adjust your eyes or the camera so that the image is clear. • She **focused** her eyes on the ball.
VERB **2** If you **focus** on a particular topic, you concentrate on it.
PHRASE **3** If an image is **in focus**, the edges of the image are clear and sharp. If it is **out of focus**, the edges are blurred.

**WORD HISTORY**
from Latin focus meaning hearth, which was seen as the centre of a Roman home

**LANGUAGE TIP**
You can spell the inflections of focus with one s or two ss in the middle but the spellings with one s are much more common: focuses, focusing, focused.

**fodder**
NOUN food given to horses and cattle

**foe foes**
NOUN If someone is your **foe**, they are your enemy.

**foetus foetuses; also spelt fetus**
NOUN A **foetus** is an unborn child or other animal in the womb.

**fog**
NOUN a thick mist caused by tiny drops of water in the air

**foil foils, foiling, foiled**
VERB **1** If you **foil** someone's attempt at something, you prevent it from succeeding. • The police officer **foiled** the robbery.
NOUN **2** thin, paper-like sheets of metal used to wrap food

**fold folds, folding, folded**
VERB **1** If you **fold** something, you bend it so that one part lies over another. • He **folded** the letter and put it back in the envelope.
NOUN **2** a crease or bend in paper or cloth

**folder folders**
NOUN **1** a thin piece of folded cardboard used for keeping papers together
NOUN **2** a group of files that are stored together on a computer

**foliage**
NOUN the leaves of plants

**folk**
PLURAL NOUN **1** people • These are the **folk** I was telling you about.
ADJECTIVE **2** **Folk** music and art are traditional or typical of the people of a particular area. • My dad likes Irish **folk** music.

**folklore**
NOUN the traditional stories and beliefs of a community

**157**

## follow **follows, following, followed**

VERB **1** If you **follow** someone or something, you move along behind them. • We **followed** him up the steps.

VERB **2** If you **follow** a path or a sign, you go somewhere using the path or sign to direct you. • I **followed** the signs to the dining room.

VERB **3** If you **follow** instructions or advice, you do what you are told.

VERB **4** If you **follow** an explanation or the plot of a story, you understand each stage of it.

VERB **5** If you **follow** someone on a social media website, you choose to look at the messages and pictures that they post.

## follower **followers**

NOUN someone who chooses to look at the messages and pictures that someone else posts on a social media website

## fond **fonder, fondest**

ADJECTIVE If you are **fond** of someone or something, you like them.

## font **fonts**

NOUN **1** a large, stone bowl in a church that holds the water for baptisms

NOUN **2** a style of printed writing. There are many **fonts** to choose from, for example, Helvetica, Times, Courier or Frutiger.

## food **foods**

NOUN what people and other animals eat

## food chain **food chains**

NOUN a series of living things that are linked together because each one feeds on another in the chain

→ Have a look at the illustration

## fool **fools, fooling, fooled**

NOUN **1** someone who is silly and is not sensible

VERB **2** If you **fool** someone, you deceive or trick them. • Don't be **fooled** by his appearance.

## foolish

ADJECTIVE stupid or silly

## foolproof

ADJECTIVE If something is **foolproof**, it cannot fail.

## foot **feet**

NOUN **1** the part of a human or other animal's body at the end of their leg

→ Have a look at the illustration for **bird**

NOUN **2** the part of something that is farth from the top • The hotel was at the **foot** of mountain.

NOUN **3** a unit of length equal to 12 inches about 30.5 centimetres

## football **footballs**

NOUN **1** a game such as soccer and Americ **football**, in which the ball can be kicked and two teams try to score goals

NOUN **2** a ball used in these games

## footballer **footballers**

NOUN someone who plays soccer or Ameri football, especially as their job

## foothold **footholds**

NOUN a place where you can put your foot when climbing

## footpath **footpaths**

NOUN a path for people to walk on, especi in the countryside

## footprint **footprints**

NOUN **1** the mark made by a foot on the ground

NOUN **2** You can call the impact that something has on the environment its **footprint**. • Many countries are working h to reduce their carbon **footprint**.

## footstep **footsteps**

NOUN the sound made by someone's feet when they are walking • They heard **footsteps** in the corridor.

## for

PREPOSITION **1** to be used by or given to a particular person • I bought a present **for** brother.

PREPOSITION **2** **For** is used when explaining the reason, cause or purpose of somethin • I'm going shopping **for** a pair of shoes.

PREPOSITION **3** You use **for** to show a distanc time or quantity. • I have been waiting here **for** ages.

PREPOSITION **4** If you are **for** something, you support it. • My parents are all **for** the new school.

ANTONYM: against

## forbid **forbids, forbidding, forbade, forbidden**

VERB If someone **forbids** you to do something, they order you not to do it.

## forbidden

ADJECTIVE not allowed

# FOOD CHAIN

a
b
c
d
e
f
g
h
i
j
k
l
m
n
o
p
q
r
s
t
u
v
w
x
y
z

**force** forces, forcing, forced
VERB **1** If you **force** someone to do something, you make them do it.
NOUN **2** violence or great strength • *He used a lot of force to pull the wall down.*
NOUN **3** an organised group of people, especially soldiers or police • *The police force helped to maintain order at the football match.*
NOUN **4** a push or pull. **Forces** are measured in newtons.

**forceful**
ADJECTIVE **1** giving your opinions very strongly, and good at persuading people • *He has a very forceful personality.*
ADJECTIVE **2** A **forceful** argument or reason is clear and likely to persuade people
ADJECTIVE **3** using a lot of physical force

**forcefully**
ADVERB **1** in a way that is likely to persuade people
ADVERB **2** with a lot of physical force

**forecast** forecasts, forecasting, forecast or forecasted
NOUN **1** A **forecast** says what is likely to happen. • *the weather forecast*
VERB **2** If you **forecast** an event, you say what is likely to happen. • *We forecast that we would win the game.*

**foreground** foregrounds
NOUN In a picture, the **foreground** is the part that seems nearest to you.

**forehead** foreheads
NOUN the area at the front of your head, above your eyebrows and below your hair

**foreign**
ADJECTIVE belonging to or involving a country that is not your own • *It is useful to learn a foreign language.*

**foreigner**
NOUN someone who comes from a country that is not your own

**forest** forests
NOUN a large area of trees growing close together

**forever**
ADVERB permanently or continually

**forfeit** forfeits, forfeiting, forfeited
VERB If you **forfeit** something, you have to give it up as a penalty.

**forgave**
VERB the past tense of **forgive**

**forge** forges, forging, forged
NOUN **1** a place where a blacksmith works making metal goods by hand
VERB **2** If someone **forges** metal, they hammer and bend it into shape while it is hot.
VERB **3** Someone who **forges** money, documents or paintings makes illegal copies of them.

**forgery** forgeries
NOUN **1** the crime of making false copies of something
NOUN **2** an illegal false copy of something

**forget** forgets, forgetting, forgot, forgotten
VERB If you **forget** something, you do not remember it.

**forgetful**
ADJECTIVE Someone who is **forgetful** often forgets things.

**forgive** forgives, forgiving, forgave, forgiven
VERB If you **forgive** someone who has done something wrong, you stop being angry with them.

**fork** forks
NOUN **1** an instrument with prongs on the end of a handle, used for eating food or for digging earth
NOUN **2** If there is a **fork** in a road or river, it divides into two or more parts.

**forlorn**
ADJECTIVE If you are **forlorn**, you are unhappy and lonely.

**form** forms, forming, formed
NOUN **1** a particular type or kind of something • *Running is a form of exercise.*
NOUN **2** the shape or pattern of something • *Cut out your paper in the form of a star.*
NOUN **3** a class in school
NOUN **4** a piece of paper with questions and spaces where you fill in your answers
VERB **5** If you **form** something, you make it or give it a particular shape. • *Please all stand up and form a circle.*
VERB **6** If something **forms**, it develops or comes into existence. • *The puddles formed on the pavement after the rain.*

**mal**

ADJECTIVE **1 Formal** speech, writing or behaviour is correct and serious, rather than relaxed and friendly. ● *At the prizegiving everyone wore **formal** clothes.*

ANTONYM: informal

ADJECTIVE **2** A **formal** action or event is an official one that follows accepted rules.

ANTONYM: informal

**mat formats**

NOUN the way something is arranged and presented ● *The **format** of the book is easy to follow.*

**mation formations**

NOUN **1** the start or creation of something

NOUN **2** the pattern or shape of something

**mer**

ADJECTIVE **1** happening or existing before now, or in the past ● *The **former** tennis champion presented the trophy to the new champion.*

NOUN **2 Former** refers to the first of two things mentioned. ● *Exams and coursework are both important, but the **former** must take priority this term.*

**merly**

ADVERB before now, or in the past ● *The hotel was **formerly** a farmhouse.*

**mula formulae** or **formulas**

NOUN a group of letters, numbers or symbols that stand for a mathematical or scientific rule

**t forts**

NOUN a strong, fortified building built for defence

**tieth fortieths**

NOUN **1** one of forty equal parts of something

ADJECTIVE **2** The **fortieth** item in a series is the one that you count as number forty.

**tify fortifies, fortifying, fortified**

VERB If someone **fortifies** a building, they make it stronger against attack.

**tnight fortnights**

NOUN a period of two weeks

**tress fortresses**

NOUN a very strong and well-protected castle or town

**tunate**

ADJECTIVE lucky

**fortunately**

ADVERB You use **fortunately** to say that it is lucky that something has happened. ● ***Fortunately**, no one was hurt in the accident.*

**fortune fortunes**

NOUN **1** luck

NOUN **2** a lot of money

**forty**

NOUN **Forty** is the number 40.

**forward forwards**

ADVERB **1** If you move something **forward** or **forwards**, you move it towards the front.

NOUN **2** In a game like hockey or football, a **forward** is someone in an attacking position.

**fossil fossils**

NOUN the remains or impression of an animal or plant from a previous age, which has been preserved in rock

**fossil fuel fossil fuels**

NOUN fuel such as coal or oil that is formed from the rotting of plants or animals from millions of years ago

**fossilise fossilises, fossilising, fossilised**; also spelt fossilize

VERB to become a fossil by being preserved in rock

**foster fosters, fostering, fostered**

VERB If someone **fosters** a child, they look after the child for a period in their home, but do not become his or her legal parent.

**foster child foster children**

NOUN a child who lives with you for a period of time because their own parents cannot look after them

a
b
c
d
e
f
g
h
i
j
k
l
m
n
o
p
q
r
s
t
u
v
w
x
y
z

**161**

**foster home** **foster homes**
NOUN a home where a child goes to live for a period of time when their own parents cannot look after them

**foster parent** **foster parents**
NOUN someone who looks after a child for a period of time, but who does not become the child's legal parent

**fought**
VERB the past tense of **fight**

**foul** **fouler, foulest; fouls**
ADJECTIVE **1** dirty and very unpleasant • *There was a foul smell coming from the drains.*
NOUN **2** In sport, a **foul** is an action that breaks the rules.

**found** **founds, founding, founded**
VERB **1** the past tense and past participle of **find**
VERB **2** If someone **founds** an organisation or company, they create it. • *He founded the charity ten years ago.*

**foundation** **foundations**
NOUN **1** the basic ideas on which something is based • *A good education is the foundation for a successful life.*
PLURAL NOUN **2** The **foundations** of a building are the layer of concrete or bricks below the ground on which it is built.
NOUN **3** the founding of something

**fountain** **fountains**
NOUN an ornamental structure in which a jet of water is forced into the air by a pump

**fountain pen** **fountain pens**
NOUN a pen that has a nib which is supplied with ink from a container inside the pen

**four**
NOUN **Four** is the number 4.

**fourteen**
NOUN **Fourteen** is the number 14.

**fourteenth** **fourteenths**
NOUN **1** one of fourteen equal parts of something
ADJECTIVE **2** The **fourteenth** item in a series is the one that you count as number fourteen.

**fourth**
ADJECTIVE The **fourth** item in a series is the one that you count as number four. It can be written as 4$^{th}$.

**fowl** **fowls**
NOUN a bird, such as chicken or duck, that is kept or hunted for its meat or eggs

**fox** **foxes**
NOUN a wild mammal that looks like a do and has reddish-brown fur and a thick te

**foyer** **foyers**
NOUN a large entrance hall just inside the main doors of a cinema, hotel or public building

PRONUNCIATION TIP
This word is pronounced **foy**-ay.

**fracking**
NOUN a method of getting oil or gas from rock by forcing liquid and sand into the r

**fraction** **fractions**
NOUN **1** In mathematics, a **fraction** is a p of a whole number.
NOUN **2** a tiny proportion or amount of something

**fracture** **fractures, fracturing, fractu**
NOUN **1** a crack or break in something, especially a bone
VERB **2** If something **fractures**, or if you **fracture** it, it breaks. • *She fractured he arm while playing netball.*

**fragile**
ADJECTIVE easily broken or damaged

**fragility**
NOUN the quality that something has whe is easily broken or damaged.

**fragment** **fragments**
NOUN a small piece or part of something • *There were fragments of glass on the flo after I dropped the vase.*

**fragrant**
ADJECTIVE Something that is **fragrant** sme sweet or pleasant.

**frail** **frailer, frailest**
ADJECTIVE weak or fragile

**frame** **frames, framing, framed**
NOUN **1** the structure surrounding a door, window or picture
VERB **2** If you **frame** a picture, you make a frame for it.

**framework** **frameworks**
NOUN a structure that forms a support or frame for something • *wooden shelves on steel framework*

**frantic**
ADJECTIVE If you are **frantic**, you behave in a wild, desperate way because you are anxious or frightened.

**ntically**
ɔVERB in a wild and desperate way

**ud frauds**
ɔUN the crime of getting money by deceit

**ught**
ɔJECTIVE **1** If a situation is **fraught**, it is full
f potential problems or difficulties.
ɔJECTIVE **2** If someone is **fraught**, they are
ɔnse and upset.

**yed**
ɔJECTIVE If material is **frayed**, the edges are
ɔorn and ragged.

**ɔak freaks**
ɔUN **1** A **freak** is someone whose
ɔppearance or behaviour is very unusual.
ɔJECTIVE **2** A **freak** event is very unusual.
 *We had a **freak** storm in the middle of the
ɔmmer.*

**ɔkle freckles**
ɔUN a small, light-brown spot on
ɔomeone's skin, especially their face

**ɔkled**
ɔJECTIVE having small, light-brown spots on
ɔur skin, especially your face

**ɔ freer, freest; frees, freeing, freed**
ɔJECTIVE **1** If something is **free**, you can have
 without paying for it.
ɔJECTIVE **2** Someone who is **free** is no longer
 prisoner.
ɔJECTIVE **3** If someone is **free**, they are not
ɔusy. • *Are you **free** on Saturday afternoon?*
ɛRB **4** If you **free** someone or something
ɔhat is trapped, you release them.

**ɔedom**
ɔUN If you have the **freedom** to do
ɔomething, you are free to do it.

**ɔe verse**
ɔUN poetry that does not use patterns of
ɔhyme or rhythm

**ɔeway freeways**
ɔUN In Australia, South Africa and the USA,
 **freeway** is a road for fast-moving traffic.

**ɔeze freezes, freezing, froze, frozen**
ɛRB **1** When a liquid **freezes**, or when
ɔomething **freezes** it, it becomes solid
ɔecause it is very cold.
ɛRB **2** If you **freeze** food, you make it very
ɔold to preserve it.
ɛRB **3** If you **freeze**, you suddenly stop
ɔoving because there is danger.
ɔJECTIVE **4** You say you are **freezing** when
ɔou are very cold.

**freezer freezers**
NOUN a refrigerator in which you can store
food for a long time at very low temperatures

**freezing**
ADJECTIVE You say you are **freezing** when you
are very cold.

**freezing point**
NOUN the temperature at which a liquid
starts to change into a solid

**freight**
NOUN goods moved by lorries, ships or other
transport

**frenzied**
ADJECTIVE done by someone who is behaving
in a wild and uncontrolled way • *a **frenzied**
attack*

**frenzy frenzies**
NOUN If someone is in a **frenzy**, their
behaviour is wild and uncontrolled.

**frequency frequencies**
NOUN **1** The **frequency** of an event is how
often it happens.
NOUN **2** The **frequency** of a sound or radio
wave is the rate at which it vibrates.

**frequency table frequency tables**
NOUN a chart where you write down how
often something happens

**frequent**
ADJECTIVE If something happens at **frequent**
intervals, it happens often.

**frequently**
ADVERB happening often or a lot of the time
• *He was **frequently** unhappy.*

**fresh fresher, freshest**
ADJECTIVE **1** not old or used • *We put **fresh**
towels out for the guests.*
ADJECTIVE **2** **Fresh** food has been made or
picked recently, and is not tinned or frozen.
ADJECTIVE **3** **Fresh** water is water that is not
salty. • *The water in a river or lake is **fresh**
water.*

**freshwater**
ADJECTIVE A **freshwater** animal lives in a
river, lake or pool and not in the sea.

**fret frets, fretting, fretted**
VERB **1** If you **fret** about something, you
worry about it.
NOUN **2** The **frets** on a stringed instrument,
such as a guitar, are the metal ridges across
its neck.

a
b
c
d
e
f
g
h
i
j
k
l
m
n
o
p
q
r
s
t
u
v
w
x
y
z

**163**

**friction**
NOUN **1** the force that slows things down and can stop them from moving
NOUN **2 Friction** between people is disagreement and quarrels. • *There was a lot of friction between the two families.*

**Friday Fridays**
NOUN the sixth day of the week, coming between Thursday and Saturday

WORD HISTORY
from Old English *Frigedæg* meaning Freya's day. Freya was the Norse goddess of love.

**fridge fridges**
NOUN a short form of *refrigerator*

**friend friends, friending, friended**
NOUN **1** someone you know well and like, but who is not related to you
VERB **2** If you **friend** someone, you ask them to be your friend on a social media website.

**friendly friendlier, friendliest**
ADJECTIVE A **friendly** person is kind and pleasant to others.

**friendship friendships**
NOUN the state of being friends with someone • *Her friendship means a lot to me.*

**frieze friezes**
NOUN a decorative band, often around the top of a wall. It can be a carving, or a long strip of paper with a picture or pattern on it.

**fright**
NOUN a sudden feeling of fear

**frighten frightens, frightening, frightened**
VERB If something or someone **frightens** you, they make you afraid.

**frightened**
ADJECTIVE afraid or scared

**frightening**
ADJECTIVE making you feel afraid or scared

**frill frills**
NOUN a strip of material with a lot of folds in it, attached to something as decoration

**fringe fringes**
NOUN **1** the hair that hangs over a person's forehead • *She had a long fringe that almost covered her eyes.*
NOUN **2** a decoration on clothes and other objects, consisting of a row of hanging threads • *There is a fringe along the bottom of the curtains.*

**frivolous**
ADJECTIVE Someone who is **frivolous** beha[ves] in a silly or light-hearted way, especially when they should be serious or sensible.

**frizzy frizzier, frizziest**
ADJECTIVE **Frizzy** hair has tight, wiry curls.

**frog frogs**
NOUN a small, amphibious animal with lo[ng] back legs

→ Have a look at the illustration

**frogspawn**
NOUN a jelly-like substance containing th[e] eggs of frogs

→ Have a look at the illustration for **frog**

**frolic frolics, frolicking, frolicked**
VERB When children and other young animals **frolic**, they run around and pla[y] a lively way. • *In the spring, the lambs fro[lic] in the fields.*

**from**
PREPOSITION **1 From** tells you where someo[ne] or something started. • *The river flows fr[om] the north.*
PREPOSITION **2** If you take something **from** [an] amount, you reduce the amount by that much. • *If you take 5 from 20 you are left with 15.*
PREPOSITION **3** You use **from** to state the ra[nge] of something. • *Lunchtime is from 12 o'cl[ock] to 1 o'clock.*

**front fronts**
NOUN **1** the part of something that faces forward • *a jacket with buttons down the front*
ADJECTIVE **2** The **front** part of something is [the] part that is furthest forward. • *I like to sit [in] the front seats of the cinema.*
NOUN **3** In a war, the **front** is the place wh[ere] two armies are fighting.
NOUN **4** At the seaside, the **front** is the roc[k] or promenade that runs alongside the beach.
NOUN **5** When talking about the weather, [a] **front** is a line where cold air meets warm air.

→ Have a look at the illustration for **weather**

**frontier frontiers**
NOUN a border between two countries • *Th[eir] passports were checked at the frontier.*

**st frosts**
NUN powdery, white ice that forms on the ground when the temperature outside falls below freezing

**sty frostier, frostiest**
 JECTIVE When it is **frosty**, the temperature outside falls below freezing and powdery, white ice forms on the ground.

**th froths, frothing, frothed**
NUN **1** a mass of small bubbles on the surface of a liquid
RB **2** If a liquid **froths**, small bubbles appear on its surface.

**thy frothier, frothiest**
JECTIVE If a liquid is **frothy**, there are a lot small bubbles on its surface.

**wn frowns, frowning, frowned**
RB **1** If you **frown**, you move your eyebrows closer together and wrinkle your forehead, usually because you are annoyed, worried or puzzled.
NUN **2** an expression on the face of someone who is frowning

**ze**
RB the past tense of **freeze**

**frozen**
VERB **1** the past participle of **freeze**
ADJECTIVE **2** If you say you are **frozen**, you mean you have become very cold. ● *My fingers were absolutely frozen.*

**fruit fruits**
NOUN the part of a plant that develops after the flower has been fertilised, that contains the seeds. Apples, oranges and bananas are all **fruit**.
→ Have a look at the illustration for **plant**

---

WORD HISTORY
from Latin *fructus* meaning produce or benefit

---

**frustrate frustrates, frustrating, frustrated**
VERB **1** If something **frustrates** you, it prevents you doing what you want and makes you upset.
VERB **2** If you **frustrate** something, such as a plan, you prevent it. ● *They deliberately frustrated my attempts to do my homework.*

a
b
c
d
e
f
g
h
i
j
k
l
m
n
o
p
q
r
s
t
u
v
w
x
y
z

frog

frogspawn

**cycle of a frog**   froglet          tadpole

A B C D E **F** G H I J K L M N O P Q R S T U V W X Y Z

**frustrated**
ADJECTIVE upset or annoyed because you cannot do or achieve what you want

**frustrating**
VERB making you feel frustrated

**frustration**
NOUN the feeling of being frustrated

**fry fries, frying, fried**
VERB When you **fry** food, you cook it in a pan containing hot fat.

**fudge**
NOUN a soft, brown sweet made from butter, milk and sugar

**fuel fuels**
NOUN a substance such as coal, gas, oil or wood that is burned to provide heat or power

**fugitive fugitives**
NOUN someone who is running away or hiding, especially from the police

**fulcrum fulcrums or fulcra**
NOUN the point at which something is balancing or turning

**fulfil fulfils, fulfilling, fulfilled**
VERB 1 If you **fulfil** a promise, you keep it.
VERB 2 If something **fulfils** you, it gives you satisfaction.

**fulfilling**
ADJECTIVE making you feel satisifed because you are doing something good • a **fulfilling** life

**fulfilment**
NOUN the feeling you have when you are satisifed because you are doing something good

**full fuller, fullest**
ADJECTIVE 1 Something that is **full** contains as much as it is possible to hold. • The bus was **full** so we had to wait for the next one.

ANTONYM: empty

ADJECTIVE 2 to the greatest possible extent • The radio was playing at **full** volume.
ADJECTIVE 3 complete or whole • I will tell you the **full** story later.
ADVERB 4 completely or wholly • Turn the taps **full** on.

**fullness**
NOUN **Fullness** is when something conto as much as it is possible to hold.

ANTONYM: emptiness

**full stop full stops**
NOUN the punctuation mark (.) used at th end of a sentence and after an abbrevio or initial

**full-time**
ADJECTIVE If you have a **full-time** job, you work for the whole of each normal work week.

**fully**
ADVERB completely • Are you **fully** recover from your illness?

**fumble fumbles, fumbling, fumbled**
VERB If you **fumble**, you feel or handle something clumsily. • I **fumbled** with th door handle because it was so dark.

**fume fumes, fuming, fumed**
PLURAL NOUN 1 **Fumes** are unpleasant-smelling gases and smoke that are sometimes poisonous, and are produced burning and by some chemicals.
VERB 2 If something **fumes**, it produces smoke or gas.
VERB 3 If you **fume**, you are very angry.

**fun**
NOUN 1 pleasant, enjoyable and light-hearted activity • Let's have some **fun**!
ADJECTIVE 2 If someone or something is **fu** you enjoy being with them or you enjoy doing it. • She is always **fun** to be with.
PHRASE 3 If you **make fun** of someone or something, you tease them or make joke about them.

**function functions, functioning, functioned**
VERB 1 If a thing **functions**, it works as it should.
NOUN 2 The **function** of someone or something is their purpose or the work t are supposed to do.

**functional**
ADJECTIVE 1 If a thing **functional**, it works it should.
ADJECTIVE 2 designed to be useful, not just look attractive

**fund funds**
NOUN an amount of money that is collecte for a particular purpose

**...damental**

...JECTIVE If something is **fundamental**, it is ...sic and necessary. • *You must understand ...e **fundamental** rules of the game before you ...n progress.*

**...eral funerals**

...OUN a ceremony for the burial or cremation ...f someone who has died

**...gal**

...JECTIVE involving or caused by a fungus • *a ...ungal infection*

**...gus fungi** or **funguses**

...OUN an organism, such as a mushroom or ...ould, that does not have flowers or leaves

**...nel funnels**

...OUN **1** an open cone that narrows to a ...ube, and is used to pour substances into ...ontainers

...OUN **2** a metal chimney on a ship or steam ...ngine

➤ Have a look at the illustration for **ship**

**...ny funnier, funniest**

...JECTIVE **1** causing amusement or laughter • *He told us a **funny** story.*

SYNONYMS: amusing, comical, humorous

...JECTIVE **2** strange or puzzling • *We could ...ear a **funny** noise.*

SYNONYMS: odd, peculiar

**...r**

...OUN the thick hair that grows on the bodies ...f many animals • *Polar bears have thick **fur**.*

**...rious**

...JECTIVE extremely angry

**...rnace furnaces**

...OUN a very large, hot oven used for heating ...lass and melting metal

**...rnish furnishes, furnishing, ...urnished**

...ERB If you **furnish** a house or a room, you ...ut furniture into it.

**...rniture**

...OUN movable objects such as tables, chairs ...nd wardrobes that you need inside a ...uilding • *bedroom **furniture***

**...rrow furrows**

...OUN a shallow, straight channel dug into ...he earth by a plough

**...rry furrier, furriest**

...JECTIVE covered with fur • *furry animals*

**further furthest**

ADVERB or ADJECTIVE another word for *farther*

**furtive**

ADJECTIVE secretive, sly and cautious

**fury**

NOUN violent or extreme anger

WORD HISTORY
from Latin *furia* meaning madness

**fuse fuses, fusing, fused**

NOUN **1** a safety device in an electrical plug or appliance, consisting of a piece of wire that melts to stop the electric current if a fault occurs

VERB **2** When an electrical appliance **fuses**, it stops working because the fuse has melted to protect it.

**fuss fusses, fussing, fussed**

NOUN **1** unnecessarily anxious or excited behaviour

VERB **2** If someone **fusses**, they behave with unnecessary anxiety and concern for unimportant things.

**fussy fussier, fussiest**

ADJECTIVE If you are **fussy**, you worry too much about unnecessary details.

**future futures**

NOUN **1** the period of time after the present • *He is already making plans for his **future**.*
ADJECTIVE **2** relating to or occurring at a time after the present
PHRASE **3 In future** means from now on. • *Be more careful **in future**.*

**fuzzy fuzzier, fuzziest**

ADJECTIVE **1** soft and fluffy
ADJECTIVE **2** If a picture is **fuzzy**, it is not clear.

a
b
c
d
e
f
g
h
i
j
k
l
m
n
o
p
q
r
s
t
u
v
w
x
y
z

**167**

# Gg

**g**

an abbreviation for *gram*

**gadget** **gadgets**

NOUN a small mechanical device or tool

**gain** **gains, gaining, gained**

VERB **1** If you **gain** something, you get more of it or get something you didn't have before. ● *She was pleased when she began to* **gain** *better marks.*

VERB **2** If a clock or watch **gains** time, it starts telling a later time than it is. ● *I think my watch has* **gained** *five minutes. It says five past one and the clock says one o'clock.*

**gala** **galas**

NOUN a special, public celebration or performance ● *a swimming* **gala**

**galaxy** **galaxies**

NOUN a huge group of stars that extends over millions of kilometres

**gale** **gales**

NOUN an extremely strong wind

**gallant**

ADJECTIVE brave and honourable

**gall bladder** **gall bladders**

NOUN the part of your body beside your liver that helps to break down fat cells

→ Have a look at the illustration for **stomach**

**galleon** **galleons**

NOUN a large Spanish sailing ship in the sixteenth and seventeenth centuries

**gallery** **galleries**

NOUN a building where paintings and oth works of art are shown

**gallon** **gallons**

NOUN a measure of liquid that is equal to eight pints or 4.55 litres

**gallop** **gallops, galloping, galloped**

VERB When a horse **gallops**, it runs very f so that during each stride all four feet ar off the ground at the same time.

**gallows**

NOUN a framework on which criminals use to be hanged

**gamble** **gambles, gambling, gamble**

VERB When someone **gambles**, they bet money on the result of a contest or race.

**game** **games, gaming, gamed**

NOUN **1** an activity with a set of rules that played by individuals or teams against ea other

NOUN **2** a term for wild birds and animals that are hunted for food or sport, such as pheasant or boar

VERB **3** If you **game**, you play video games

**gamer** **gamers**

NOUN someone who plays video games

**gaming**

NOUN **Gaming** is playing video games.

**gammon**

NOUN cured meat from a pig, similar to bac but usually in thicker and larger slices

**gander** **ganders**

NOUN a male goose

**gang** **gangs, ganging, ganged**

NOUN **1** a group of people who join together some purpose, for example to commit a cri

VERB **2** (*informal*) If people **gang up** on you, they join together to oppose you.

● *Sometimes male chimps gang up on anoth group member.*

**gangster** **gangsters**

NOUN a violent criminal who is a member o a gang

**gangway** **gangways**

NOUN **1** a space left between rows of seats, for example in a train or cinema, for peop to walk through

NOUN **2** a movable passenger bridge betwe a ship and the shore

**ol**
NOUN or VERB another spelling of **jail**

**p gaps**
NOUN a space between two things or a hole in something solid • *He was just able to squeeze through the **gap** in the hedge.*

**pe gapes, gaping, gaped**
VERB **1** If you **gape**, you stare with your mouth wide open.
VERB **2** If something **gapes**, it is wide open.

**rage garages**
NOUN **1** a building in which you can keep a car
NOUN **2** a place where cars are repaired or where petrol is sold

**rbage**
NOUN In American English, **garbage** is rubbish, especially waste from a kitchen.

**rden gardens**
NOUN an area of land next to a house, with plants, trees and grass

**rdener gardeners**
NOUN a person who looks after a garden as a job or as a hobby

**rgle gargles, gargling, gargled**
VERB When you **gargle**, you rinse the back of your throat by putting some liquid in your mouth and making a bubbling sound without swallowing the liquid.

**rgoyle gargoyles**
NOUN a stone carving below the roof of an old building, in the shape of an ugly person or animal

**rlic**
NOUN the small, white bulb of an onion-like plant that has a strong taste and smell and is used in cooking

**rment garments**
NOUN an item of clothing

**s gases**
NOUN a substance that is not a liquid or a solid. The particles in a **gas** are far apart and can move around quickly. Air is a mixture of **gases**. The bubbles in fizzy lemonade contain a **gas** called carbon dioxide.

→ Have a look at the illustration for **state of matter**

**gasp gasps, gasping, gasped**
VERB If you **gasp**, you quickly draw in your breath through your mouth because you are surprised or in pain.

**gate gates**
NOUN a barrier that can be opened or shut and is used to close off the entrance to a field, garden or path

**gateau gateaux**
NOUN a rich, layered cake with cream in it

WORD HISTORY
from French *gâteau* meaning cake

**gather gathers, gathering, gathered**
VERB **1** If you **gather** things, you collect or pick them. • *I **gathered** some flowers from the garden.*
VERB **2** When people **gather**, they come together in a group. • *We **gathered** at my house before we went to the party.*
VERB **3** If you **gather** information, you learn it, often from hearing or reading about it. • *I **gather** you passed your exams.*

**gathering gatherings**
NOUN a meeting of people who gather together for a particular purpose

**gauge gauges, gauging, gauged**
VERB **1** If you **gauge** something, you estimate or work out how much of it there is or how much is required.
NOUN **2** an instrument used for measuring • *The fuel **gauge** shows that we need more petrol.*

→ Have a look at the illustration for **car**

**gauze**
NOUN a thin, cotton cloth, often used for bandages

**gave**
VERB the past tense of **give**

**gaze gazes, gazing, gazed**
VERB If you **gaze** at something, you look steadily at it for a long time. • *We **gazed** up at the stars.*

**gazelle gazelles**
NOUN a small antelope found in Africa and Asia

a
b
c
d
e
f
g
h
i
j
k
l
m
n
o
p
q
r
s
t
u
v
w
x
y
z

## gear gears

NOUN **1** The **gears** in a car or on a bicycle are a set of cogs that work together to send power to the wheels.

→ Have a look at the illustration for **bicycle**

NOUN **2** the clothes or equipment that you need for an activity • *climbing* **gear**

## geese

PLURAL NOUN the plural of **goose**

## gel gels

NOUN a smooth, soft, jelly-like substance • *hair* **gel**

## gem gems

NOUN a jewel or precious stone

## gender genders

NOUN The **gender** of a person or animal is whether they are male or female.

## gene genes

NOUN one of the parts of the chromosomes found inside the cells of an organism. Offspring inherit **genes** from their parents.

**PRONUNCIATION TIP**
This word is pronounced **jeen**.

## general generals

ADJECTIVE **1** relating to the whole of something or to most things in a group • *There has been a* **general** *improvement in your work.*

ADJECTIVE **2** including or involving a range of different things • *There was a* **general** *knowledge quiz at the end of term.*

NOUN **3** an army officer of very high rank

PHRASE **4 In general** is used to indicate that a statement is true in most cases, or that it applies to most people or things.
• *In general, people take their holidays over the summer.*

## general election general elections

NOUN an election in which people vote for who they want to represent them in the national parliament

## generally

ADVERB You use **generally** to say what usually happens or what is usually true. • *I* **generally** *get home from school about 4 o'clock.*

## generate generates, generating, generated

VERB If someone or something **generates** something else, they produce or create it.
• *They built a new power station to* **generate** *more electricity.*

## generation generations

NOUN **1** all the people of a similar age
• *the younger* **generation**

NOUN **2** the length of time that it takes for children to grow up and have children of their own • *The next* **generation** *will see more changes.*

## generator generators

NOUN a machine that produces electricity from another form of energy, such as wi or water power

## generous

ADJECTIVE A **generous** person gives or shar what they have, especially time or money

## genetic

ADJECTIVE involving or caused by a gene
• *genetic* diseases

## genetically

ADVERB in a way that involves a gene or ge

## genetically modified

ADJECTIVE **Genetically modified** plants and animals have had one or more genes changed, for example so that they resist pests and diseases better.

## genie genies

NOUN a magical being that obeys the wishe of the person who controls it • *Aladdin rubbed his magic lamp and the* **genie** *appea*

**WORD HISTORY**
from Arabic *jinni* meaning demon

## genitals

PLURAL NOUN The **genitals** are the reproductive organs. The technical name **genitalia**.

## genius geniuses

NOUN a highly intelligent, creative or talen person • *a mathematical* **genius**

## genre genres

NOUN a particular type of literature, painti music or film

## gentle gentler, gentlest

ADJECTIVE Someone or something that is **gentle** is mild and calm. • *A* **gentle** *bree blew across the field.*

ANTONYMS: violent, rough

## gentleman gentlemen

NOUN **1** a man who is polite and well-educated

NOUN **2** a polite way of referring to any ma

**...uine**
ADJECTIVE real and exactly what it appears to
... ● *It's a **genuine** diamond.*

**...graphical**
ADJECTIVE relating to the study of the physical
...atures of the Earth, its countries, climate
...nd people

**...graphy**
NOUN the study of the physical features of
...e Earth, its countries, climate and people

**...logist geologists**
NOUN someone who studies the Earth's
...tructure, especially the layers of rock and
...oil that make up the surface of the Earth

**...logy**
NOUN the study of the Earth's structure,
...specially the layers of rock and soil that
...ake up the surface of the Earth

**...ometry**
NOUN that part of mathematics that deals
...ith lines, angles, curves and shapes

**...ranium geraniums**
NOUN a plant with bright red, pink or white
...owers

**...rbil gerbils**
NOUN a small rodent with long back legs that
...s often kept as a pet

**...rm germs**
NOUN a very small organism that can cause
...isease

**...rminate germinates, germinating,
germinated**
VERB When a seed **germinates**, it starts to
...row.

**...rmination**
NOUN the process of a seed starting to
...row ● *Dry weather in May affected the
**germination** of our carrots this year.*

➜ Have a look at the illustration for **plant**

**...station**
NOUN the period during which babies grow
...nside their mother's body before they are
...orn

**...sture gestures, gesturing, gestured**
NOUN 1 a movement of your hands or head
...hat suggests a message or feeling ● *She
made an angry **gesture** with her fist.*
VERB 2 If you **gesture**, you move your hands
...r head in order to communicate a message
...r feeling. ● *She **gestured** to me to come over.*

**get gets, getting, got**
VERB 1 If you **get** something, you fetch it or
receive it. ● *He **got** his report on the last day
of term.*
VERB 2 If you **get** a bus, you travel on it.
VERB 3 If you **get** a meal ready, you prepare
it.
VERB 4 If you **get** someone to do something
for you, you persuade them to do it.
VERB 5 If you **get** a joke, you understand it.
VERB 6 If you **get** ill, you become ill.
VERB 7 If you **get** to a place, you arrive there.

**geyser geysers**
NOUN a natural spring out of which hot water
and steam gush in spurts. There are many
geysers in Iceland and New Zealand.

---

**WORD HISTORY**
from Old Norse *geysa* meaning to gush

---

**ghastly ghastlier, ghastliest**
ADJECTIVE extremely horrible and unpleasant

**ghost ghosts**
NOUN the spirit of a dead person that
appears to someone who is still alive ● *She
believes she saw a **ghost** in the old house.*

**giant giants**
NOUN 1 a huge person in a myth or legend
ADJECTIVE 2 much larger than other similar
things ● *There was a **giant** Christmas tree in
the town centre.*

**giddiness**
NOUN the feeling you have if you feel unsteady and unable to balance properly, usually because you are ill

**giddy giddier, giddiest**
ADJECTIVE If you feel **giddy**, you feel unsteady on your feet, usually because you are ill.

**gift gifts**
NOUN **1** something that you give someone as a present
NOUN **2** a natural skill or ability • *He has a* **gift** *for acting.*

**gifted**
ADJECTIVE If you are **gifted**, you have special talents. • *She is a* **gifted** *musician.*

**gigabyte gigabytes**
NOUN a unit of storage in a computer, equal to 1024 megabytes

**gigantic**
ADJECTIVE extremely large • *She was keen to ride on the* **gigantic** *big wheel.*

SYNONYMS: huge, massive, enormous

**giggle giggles, giggling, giggled**
VERB If you **giggle**, you laugh in a nervous, quiet way.

**gill gills**
NOUN the organs on the sides of a fish that it uses for breathing

→ Have a look at the illustration for **fish**

**gimmick gimmicks**
NOUN something that is not really necessary, but is unusual and used to attract interest
• *The new shop needed a* **gimmick** *to attract customers.*

**gin**
NOUN a strong, colourless alcoholic drink made from grain and juniper berries

**ginger**
NOUN **1** a plant root with a hot, spicy flavour, used in cooking
ADJECTIVE **2** bright orangey-brown

**Gipsy**
NOUN another spelling of **Gypsy**

**giraffe giraffes**
NOUN a large African mammal with a very long neck, long legs and yellowish skin with dark patches

**girder girders**
NOUN a strong metal or concrete beam us in building

**girl girls**
NOUN a female child

**girlfriend girlfriends**
NOUN Someone's **girlfriend** is the woma girl with whom they are having a roman relationship.

**give gives, giving, gave, given**
VERB **1** If you **give** something to someone you hand it to them or provide it for them
• *Please would you* **give** *me back the book lent to you?*
VERB **2** If you **give** a party, you host it.
VERB **3** **Give** can be used to express an action. • **give** *a speech* • **give** *the door a p*
PHRASE **4** If something **gives way**, it collapses.

**glacier glaciers**
NOUN a huge, frozen river of slow-moving
→ Have a look at the illustration

**glad gladder, gladdest**
ADJECTIVE happy or pleased

**gladiator gladiators**
NOUN In ancient Rome, **gladiators** were slaves trained to fight in arenas to provid entertainment.

**glance glances, glancing, glanced**
VERB **1** If you **glance** at something, you lo at it quickly. • *He* **glanced** *at his watch.*
NOUN **2** a quick look

**gland glands**
NOUN an organ in your body which produc and releases special chemicals. Some **glands** help to get rid of waste products from your body. Sweat **glands** are small **glands** in your skin that produce sweat.

**glare glares, glaring, glared**
VERB **1** If you **glare** at someone, you look c them angrily.
NOUN **2** a hard, angry look

**glass glasses**
NOUN **1** the hard, transparent substance th windows and bottles are made of
NOUN **2** a container made of glass, from which you can drink • *a* **glass** *of water*

**glasses**
PLURAL NOUN two lenses in a frame, that sor people wear over their eyes to improve the eyesight

peak
arête
corrie
side glacier
moraine
main glacier
crevasse
** glacier**

**glaze glazes, glazing, glazed**
NOUN **1** a smooth, shiny surface on pottery or food
VERB **2** If you **glaze** pottery or food, you cover it with a glaze.
VERB **3** If someone **glazes** a window, they fit a sheet of glass into the window frame.

**gleam gleams, gleaming, gleamed**
VERB **1** If something **gleams**, it shines and reflects light. ● *He polished the silver teapot until it gleamed.*
NOUN **2** a pale, shining light ● *There was a gleam of light at the end of the dark tunnel.*

**glide glides, gliding, glided**
VERB **1** If you **glide**, you move smoothly. ● *The skater glided across the ice.*
VERB **2** When birds or aeroplanes **glide**, they float on air currents.

**glider gliders**
NOUN an aeroplane without an engine, that flies by floating on air currents

**glimmer glimmers, glimmering, glimmered**
NOUN **1** a faint, unsteady light ● *There was a glimmer of light ahead.*
VERB **2** If something **glimmers**, it produces a faint, unsteady light.

**glimpse glimpses, glimpsing, glimpsed**
NOUN **1** a brief sight of something
VERB **2** If you **glimpse** something, you see it briefly. ● *They glimpsed a rare bird through the trees.*

**glisten glistens, glistening, glistened**
VERB If something **glistens**, it shines or sparkles. ● *The frost glistened in the moonlight.*

**glitter glitters, glittering, glittered**
VERB **1** If something **glitters**, it shines in a sparkling way. ● *The diamond glittered in the sunlight.*
NOUN **2** sparkling light

**gloat gloats, gloating, gloated**
VERB If you **gloat**, you cruelly show how pleased you are about your own success or someone else's failure.

**global**
ADJECTIVE to do with the whole world ● *Pollution of the atmosphere is a global concern.*

**global warming**
NOUN an increase in the world's overall temperature, believed to be caused by a thinning of the ozone layer

**globe globes**
NOUN **1** the Earth, the planet you live on
NOUN **2** a sphere fixed to a stand, with a map of the world on it

**gloom**
NOUN **1** darkness or dimness ● *I could not see in the gloom of the forest.*
NOUN **2** a feeling of unhappiness or despair

**gloomily**
ADVERB **1** in a way that shows you are unhappy
ADVERB **2** in a way that is depressing

**173**

A
B
C
D
E
F
G
H
I
J
K
L
M
N
O
P
Q
R
S
T
U
V
W
X
Y
Z

### gloomy gloomier, gloomiest
ADJECTIVE **1** Something that is **gloomy** is dull and dark, and sometimes depressing.
• It was a **gloomy** winter day.
ADJECTIVE **2** If you are **gloomy**, you are unhappy.

### glorious
ADJECTIVE beautiful and splendid • We were lucky to have **glorious** weather while we were on holiday.

### glory glories
NOUN something considered splendid or admirable • They enjoyed the **glory** of their son's success.

### gloss
NOUN a bright shine on a smooth surface

### glossary glossaries
NOUN a list of explanations of specialist words, usually found at the back of a book

### glossy glossier, glossiest
ADJECTIVE smooth and shiny • This new shampoo makes my hair **glossy**.

### glove gloves
NOUN **Gloves** cover your hands and keep them warm or give them protection.

### glow glows, glowing, glowed
VERB **1** If something **glows**, it shines with a dull, steady light.
NOUN **2** a dull, steady light
NOUN **3** a strong feeling of pleasure or happiness

### glucose
NOUN a natural sugar found in plants and produced in the bodies of animals, including humans, to give them energy

### glue glues, gluing or glueing, glued
NOUN **1** a substance used for sticking things together
VERB **2** If you **glue** one object to another, you stick them together using glue.

### glutton gluttons
NOUN a person who eats too much

### GMT
NOUN an abbreviation for Greenwich Mean Time

### gnarled
ADJECTIVE If something is **gnarled** it is old, twisted and rough. • There is a big, **gnarled** tree in the churchyard.

### gnash gnashes, gnashing, gnashed
VERB If you **gnash** your teeth, you make a noise with them by grinding them togeth because you are angry or upset.

### gnat gnats
NOUN a tiny flying insect that bites

### gnaw gnaws, gnawing, gnawed
VERB If someone or something **gnaws** at something, they chew and bite at it repeatedly. • The hamster **gnawed** at the bars of its cage.

### gnome gnomes
NOUN a tiny old man in fairy stories, who usually lives underground

### go goes, going, went, gone
VERB **1** If you **go** somewhere, you walk, mo or travel there.
VERB **2** If something **goes** well, it is a success.
VERB **3** If you **go**, you start to move. • Wher you hear the whistle, **go** as fast as you can.
VERB **4** If something **goes** somewhere, it leads there. • This road **goes** to the centre o town.
VERB **5** If something **goes**, it works properl • My watch doesn't **go** any more.
VERB **6** become • This fruit has **gone** bad.
NOUN **7** an attempt or a turn at doing something
VERB **8** disappear • The mist has **gone**.
VERB **9** If you are **going** to do something, y will do it.

### go down
VERB **1** If you **go down** with an illness, y catch it.
VERB **2** If something **goes down** well, people like it. If it **goes down** badly, th do not like it.

### go off
VERB **1** If you **go off** someone or something, you stop liking them.
VERB **2** If a bomb **goes off**, it explodes.

### go on
VERB **1** If you **go on** doing something, yo continue to do it.
VERB **2** If you **go on** about something, yo keep talking about it in a rather boring way.
VERB **3** If something is **going on**, it is happening.

### go through
VERB If you **go through** an unpleasant event, you experience it.

**al goals**

NOUN **1** In games like football and hockey, the **goal** is the space into which the players try to get the ball to score a point.

NOUN **2** In games like football and hockey, if a player scores a **goal**, they get the ball into the **goal**.

NOUN **3** something that you hope to achieve • *Our **goal** is to raise as much money as possible for charity.*

**at goats**

NOUN an animal similar to a sheep, with shaggy hair, a beard and horns

**bble gobbles, gobbling, gobbled**

VERB **1** If you **gobble** food, you eat it very quickly.

VERB **2** When a turkey **gobbles**, it makes a loud gurgling sound.

**blet goblets**

NOUN a kind of drinking cup or glass

**blin goblins**

NOUN a small, ugly and mischievous creature found in fairy stories

**d gods**

PROPER NOUN **1 God** is the being worshipped by Christians and Jews as the creator and ruler of the world.

NOUN **2** any of the beings that are believed in many religions to have power over an aspect of the world • *Mars was the Roman **god** of war.*

**ddess goddesses**

NOUN a female god

**dparent godparents**

NOUN someone who agrees, at a child's christening, to be responsible for their religious upbringing

**ggles**

PLURAL NOUN special glasses that fit closely round your eyes to protect them • *I usually wear **goggles** when I go swimming.*

**-kart go-karts**

NOUN a small motorised vehicle that can be raced

**old**

NOUN **1** a valuable, yellow-coloured metal, used for making jewellery and as an international currency

ADJECTIVE **2** made of gold • *a solid **gold** necklace*

**olden**

ADJECTIVE gold in colour or made of gold • *a beach of **golden** sand*

**goldfish**

NOUN a small, orange fish, often kept as a pet in a bowl or pond

**LANGUAGE TIP**

The plural of *goldfish* can be either *goldfish* or *goldfishes*, but *goldfish* is more common.

**golf**

NOUN a game in which players use special clubs to hit a ball into holes that are spread out over a large area of grassy land

**gondola gondolas**

NOUN a long, narrow boat used on the canals in Venice. **Gondolas** are propelled by using a long pole.

**gone**

VERB the past participle of **go**

**gong gongs**

NOUN a flat, circular piece of metal that is hit with a hammer to make a loud sound, often as a signal for something • *They sounded the **gong** for dinner.*

**good better, best**

ADJECTIVE **1** pleasant or enjoyable • *The weather turned out to be **good**.*

ADJECTIVE **2** of a high quality • *The food was very **good**.*

ADJECTIVE **3** sensible or valid • *The rain gives me a **good** reason for staying at home.*

ADJECTIVE **4** well-behaved • *Have the children been **good**?*

PHRASE **5 For good** means forever. • *He decided to leave **for good**.*

**goodbye**

GREETING You say **goodbye** when you are leaving someone or ending a phone conversation.

**goodness**

NOUN the quality of being good and kind

**good night**

GREETING You say **good night** to someone when you are leaving them at night.

**goods**

PLURAL NOUN things that are bought and sold in a shop or warehouse • *The shop sold household **goods**.*

**google googles, googling, googled**

VERB If you **google** a person or thing, you search the internet for information about them.

**175**

**goose** geese
NOUN a fairly large bird, with webbed feet and a long neck

**gooseberry** gooseberries
NOUN a round, green berry that grows on a bush and has a sharp taste

**gore** gores, goring, gored
NOUN **1** the blood from a wound
VERB **2** If an animal **gores** someone, it wounds them by sticking a horn or tusk into them.

**gorge** gorges, gorging, gorged
NOUN **1** a deep, narrow valley
VERB **2** If you **gorge** yourself, you eat a lot of food greedily.

**gorgeous**
ADJECTIVE extremely pleasant or attractive
• *a gorgeous dress*

**gorilla** gorillas
NOUN a very strong, large ape, that lives in family groups

**gory** gorier, goriest
ADJECTIVE involving a lot of blood and violence
• *a gory film*

**gosling** goslings
NOUN a young goose

**gospel** gospels
NOUN one of the four books in the New Testament that describe the life and teachings of Jesus Christ

**gossip** gossips, gossiping, gossiped
NOUN **1** informal conversation, often about people's private affairs
VERB **2** If you **gossip**, you talk informally with someone, especially about other people.

**got**
VERB the past tense of **get**

**gouge** gouges, gouging, gouged
VERB If you **gouge** something out, you scoop it out forcefully with a pointed object. • *She gouged a hole in the apple with a knife.*

**govern** governs, governing, governed
VERB When someone **governs** something, they rule or control it, especially a country or state.

**government** governments
NOUN The **government** is the group of people who officially control a country.

**LANGUAGE TIP**
There is an *n* before the *m* in *government*.

**governor** governors
NOUN **1** someone who controls or helps to run a state or organisation
NOUN **2** In Australia, New Zealand and oth[er] commonwealth countries the **Governor** represents the British King or Queen.

**GP** GPs
NOUN an abbreviation of *general practitione[r]* A **GP** is a doctor who treats all kinds of illnesses, and sends people to a specialist necessary.

**grab** grabs, grabbing, grabbed
VERB If you **grab** something, you take it or pick it up quickly and roughly.
• *He grabbed a sandwich before running f[or] the bus.*

**grace** graces
NOUN **1** an elegant and attractive way of moving
NOUN **2** a short prayer before or after a mea[l]
NOUN **3** a pleasant and kind way of behavi[ng]

**graceful**
ADJECTIVE If you are **graceful**, you move in [a] smooth and elegant way.

**gracious**
ADJECTIVE kind, polite and pleasant
• *He always acts in a gracious and though[tful] manner.*

**grade** grades, grading, graded
VERB **1** If someone **grades** things, they jud[ge] them according to their quality.
NOUN **2** the mark that you get in an exam

**gradient** gradients
NOUN a slope or the steepness of a slope
• *The gradient of this hill means it will be difficult to climb.*

**gradual**
ADJECTIVE happening or changing slowly ove[r] a long period of time • *Her spelling showed gradual improvement.*

**gradually**
ADVERB slowly over a long period of time
• *Prices have gradually increased.*

**graduate** graduates
NOUN someone who has a degree from a university or college

**graffiti**
NOUN slogans or drawings scribbled on wal[ls]

**grain grains**
NOUN **1** a cereal plant, such as wheat, that is grown and harvested for food
NOUN **2** a seed from a cereal plant such as wheat or rice
NOUN **3** a tiny, hard particle of something • *I have got grains of sand in my shoes from walking on the beach.*
NOUN **4** the natural pattern of lines in a piece of wood, made by the fibres in it

**gram grams**
NOUN a unit of mass and weight (g). There are one thousand **grams** in a kilogram (kg).

**grammar**
NOUN the rules of a language that state how words can be combined to form sentences

**grand grander, grandest**
ADJECTIVE splendid or impressive

**grandad grandads**
NOUN (*informal*) grandfather

**grandchild grandchildren**
NOUN Someone's **grandchildren** are the children of their son or daughter.

**granddaughter granddaughters**
NOUN Someone's **granddaughter** is the daughter of their son or daughter.

**grandfather grandfathers**
NOUN Your **grandfather** is your father's father or your mother's father.

**grandmother grandmothers**
NOUN Your **grandmother** is your father's mother or your mother's mother.

**grandparent grandparents**
NOUN Your **grandparents** are the parents of your father or mother.

**grandson grandsons**
NOUN Someone's **grandson** is the son of their son or daughter.

**granite**
NOUN a very strong, hard rock often used in building

**granny grannies**
NOUN (*informal*) grandmother

**grant grants, granting, granted**
NOUN **1** an amount of money that an official body gives to someone for a particular purpose • *He was given a grant to go to university.*
VERB **2** If you **grant** something to someone, you allow them to have it. • *I will grant you a wish.*

**grape grapes**
NOUN a small, green or purple fruit that grows in bunches on vines. **Grapes** are eaten raw or used to make wine.

**grapefruit grapefruits**
NOUN a large, round, yellow citrus fruit

**graph graphs**
NOUN a diagram that gives information about how two sets of numbers and measurements are related

**graphic graphics**
ADJECTIVE **1** A **graphic** description is very detailed and clear.
PLURAL NOUN **2 Graphics** are drawings, designs and diagrams. • *computer graphics*

**graphics**
NOUN the activity of drawing or making pictures, especially in publishing or computing

**grasp grasps, grasping, grasped**
VERB **1** If you **grasp** something, you hold it firmly. • *He grasped both my hands.*
VERB **2** If you **grasp** an idea, you understand it. • *She finally grasped the answer.*

**grass grasses**
NOUN the common green plant that grows on lawns and in parks

**grasshopper grasshoppers**
NOUN an insect with long back legs that it uses for jumping and making a high-pitched sound

**grate grates, grating, grated**
VERB **1** If you **grate** food, you shred it into small pieces by rubbing it against a tool called a grater.
NOUN **2** a framework of metal bars in a fireplace for holding coal or wood • *A wood fire burned in the grate.*

**grateful**
ADJECTIVE If you are **grateful** for something, you feel thankful for it. • *I'm grateful to you for your help.*

SYNONYM: appreciative

**gratitude**
NOUN If you show **gratitude** to someone for something, you are thankful.

SYNONYMS: thankfulness, appreciation

a
b
c
d
e
f
g
h
i
j
k
l
m
n
o
p
q
r
s
t
u
v
w
x
y
z

**177**

A B C D E F G H I J K L M N O P Q R S T U V W X Y Z

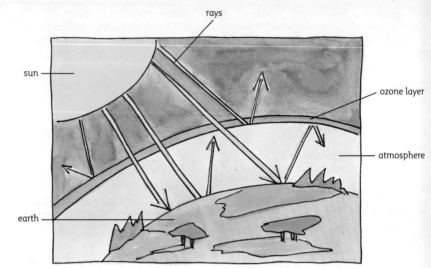

rays

sun

ozone layer

atmosphere

earth

**greenhouse effect**

**grave** graves; graver, gravest
NOUN **1** a place where a dead person is buried
ADJECTIVE **2** (*formal*) very serious • *We are in* **grave** *danger.*

**gravel**
NOUN small stones used for making roads and paths

**graveyard** graveyards
NOUN a place where people are buried, usually in a churchyard

**gravity**
NOUN the force that pulls things down towards the Earth

**gravy**
NOUN a brown sauce made from meat juices

**graze** grazes, grazing, grazed
VERB **1** When animals **graze**, they eat grass that is growing. • *The cows* **grazed** *in the field.*
VERB **2** If something **grazes** a part of your body, it scrapes against it, injuring you slightly.
NOUN **3** a slight injury caused by something scraping against your skin

**grease** greases, greasing, greased
NOUN **1** a substance used for oiling machines
NOUN **2** animal fat used in cooking
VERB **3** If you **grease** something, you put grease on it. • *Lightly* **grease** *a baking tray.*

**great** greater, greatest
ADJECTIVE **1** very large in size, amount or degree • *She had* **great** *difficulty in staying awake.*
ADJECTIVE **2** very important • *a* **great** *artist*
ADJECTIVE **3** very good • *That's a* **great** *idea.*

**greedily**
ADVERB in a greedy way

**greedy** greedier, greediest
ADJECTIVE Someone who is **greedy** wants more of something than is necessary or fa

**green** greener, greenest; greens
NOUN **1** a colour between yellow and blue o the spectrum. Grass and leaves are usuall **green**.
NOUN **2** a smooth, flat area of grass • *We played cricket on the village* **green**.
ADJECTIVE **3** having a colour between yellow and blue

**green belt** green belts
NOUN an area of land with fields or parks around a town or city, where people are no allowed to build houses or factories by law

**greengrocer** greengrocers
NOUN a shopkeeper who sells fruit and vegetables

**greenhouse** greenhouses
NOUN a glass building in which people grow plants that need to be kept warm

**greenhouse effect**
NOUN the gradual increase in the temperature of the Earth's atmosphere because the heat absorbed from the sun is not able to escape

→ Have a look at the illustration

**Greenwich Mean Time**
NOUN **Greenwich Mean Time** is the standard time in Great Britain which is used to work out the time in the rest of the world.

**greet** greets, greeting, greeted
VERB If you **greet** someone, you say something friendly and welcoming to them when you meet them.

**greeting** greetings
NOUN the words or actions that you use when you meet someone

**grenade** grenades
NOUN a small bomb that can be thrown by hand

WORD HISTORY
from Spanish *granada* meaning pomegranate, which is a similar shape to a grenade

**grew**
VERB the past tense of **grow**

**grey** greyer, greyest
NOUN **1** the colour of ashes or of clouds on a rainy day
ADJECTIVE **2** having the colour of ashes or of clouds on a rainy day

**grid** grids
NOUN a pattern of lines crossing each other to form squares

→ Have a look at the illustration for **map**

**grief**
NOUN extreme sadness

**grieve** grieves, grieving, grieved
VERB If you **grieve** you are very sad, especially because someone has died.

**grill** grills, grilling, grilled
NOUN **1** the part of a cooker where food is cooked by heat from above • *Place the fish under a hot grill.*
VERB **2** If you **grill** food, you cook it under or over direct heat. • *We grilled the chicken on the barbecue.*

**grim** grimmer, grimmest
ADJECTIVE If a situation or piece of news is **grim**, it is very unpleasant and worrying.

**grimace** grimaces
NOUN a twisted facial expression that shows disgust or pain

**grime**
NOUN thick dirt that gathers on the surface of something

**grimy**
ADJECTIVE covered in dirt • *grimy windows*

**grin** grins, grinning, grinned
VERB **1** If you **grin**, you have a broad smile.
NOUN **2** a broad smile

**grind** grinds, grinding, ground
VERB **1** If you **grind** something, you crush it into a fine powder. • *He ground the mud into the carpet.*
VERB **2** If you **grind** your teeth, you rub your upper and lower teeth together.
PHRASE **3** If something **grinds to a halt**, it slows down and stops.

**grip** grips, gripping, gripped
VERB **1** If you **grip** something, you hold it firmly. • *He gripped his mother's hand tightly.*
NOUN **2** a handle on a bat or racket • *The grip on his tennis racket needed repairing.*

**gristle**
NOUN the tough, rubbery part of meat that is difficult to eat

**groan** groans, groaning, groaned
VERB **1** If you **groan**, you make a long, low sound of pain, unhappiness or disapproval.
NOUN **2** the sound you make when you groan

**grocer** grocers
NOUN a person who runs a shop that sells all kinds of food and household supplies

**groceries**
PLURAL NOUN the goods that you buy in a grocer's shop

**groove** grooves
NOUN a deep line cut into a surface

**grope** gropes, groping, groped
VERB If you **grope** for something, you feel for it with your hands because you cannot see it.

a
b
c
d
e
f
g
h
i
j
k
l
m
n
o
p
q
r
s
t
u
v
w
x
y
z

A
B
C
D
E
F
G
H
I
J
K
L
M
N
O
P
Q
R
S
T
U
V
W
X
Y
Z

**gross grosser, grossest**

ADJECTIVE **1** extremely bad • *I made a **gross** error on my exam paper.*

ADJECTIVE **2 Gross** language or behaviour is very rude.

ADJECTIVE **3** The **gross** amount of something is its total, without anything taken away. For example, the **gross** weight of something is its total weight, including the weight of its container.

ADJECTIVE **4** unpleasantly fat or ugly

**grotesque**

ADJECTIVE **1** exaggerated and absurd

ADJECTIVE **2** very strange and ugly

**grotto grottoes** or **grottos**

NOUN a small cave that people visit because it is attractive

**ground grounds**

NOUN **1** the surface of the land • *They sat on the **ground**.*

NOUN **2** an area of land, especially land that is used for a particular purpose • *a football **ground***

PLURAL NOUN **3** The **grounds** of a large building are the garden or area of land that surrounds it. • *We camped in the **grounds** of the stately home.*

PLURAL NOUN **4** (*formal*) The **grounds** for something are the reason for it. • *I had **grounds** to believe that he was telling the truth.*

VERB **5** the past tense and past participle of *grind*

**group groups, grouping, grouped**

NOUN **1** a number of things or people that are linked in some way • *a small **group** of friends*

VERB **2** When things or people **group** together, they are linked in some way. • *We **grouped** together for the school photograph.*

**group chat group chats**

NOUN a chat on a social media website involving a number of people

**grovel grovels, grovelling, grovelled**

VERB If you **grovel**, you behave in an unpleasantly humble way towards someone you think is important.

**WORD HISTORY**

from Middle English *on grufe* meaning lying on your belly

**grow grows, growing, grew, grown**

VERB **1** When someone or something **grows** it gets bigger or increases. • *Children grow at different rates.*

VERB **2** When people **grow** plants, they plant them and look after them.

VERB **3** You use **grow** to say that someone or something gradually changes into a different state. • *He's **growing** old.*

**grow up**

VERB When a child **grows up**, they become an adult.

**growl growls, growling, growled**

VERB **1** When an animal **growls**, it makes a l rumbling sound, usually because it is angry

NOUN **2** the sound an animal makes when growls

**grown-up grown-ups**

NOUN an adult

**growth**

NOUN The process by which something develops to its full size.

**grub grubs**

NOUN **1** a worm-like creature that is the young of some insects, after it has hatche but before it becomes an adult

NOUN **2** (*informal*) food

**grubby grubbier, grubbiest**

ADJECTIVE rather dirty • *That shirt looks a bit **grubby**.*

**grudge grudges**

NOUN If you have a **grudge** against someone, you resent them because they have harmed or upset you in the past.

**gruelling**

ADJECTIVE difficult and exhausting • *It was a long and **gruelling** race.*

**gruesome**

ADJECTIVE shocking and horrible • *The film u unsuitable for the children because it was so **gruesome**.*

**gruff gruffer, gruffest**

ADJECTIVE If someone's voice is **gruff**, it sounds rough and unfriendly.

**grumble grumbles, grumbling, grumbled**

VERB **1** If you **grumble**, you complain in a bad-tempered way.

NOUN **2** a bad-tempered complaint

**grumpily**

ADVERB in a bad-tempered way

**grumpy grumpier, grumpiest**
ADJECTIVE bad-tempered and fed-up • *She is often **grumpy** in the morning.*

**grunt grunts, grunting, grunted**
VERB **1** If a person or a pig **grunts**, they make a short, low, gruff sound.
NOUN **2** the sound a person or a pig makes when they grunt

**guarantee guarantees, guaranteeing, guaranteed**
NOUN **1** a promise by a company to do something, especially to replace or repair a product free of charge within a given time period if it develops a fault • *This television has a five-year **guarantee**.*
VERB **2** If something or someone **guarantees** something, they promise that it will happen. • *I **guarantee** that after all your hard work the day will be a success.*

**guard guards, guarding, guarded**
VERB **1** If you **guard** a person or object, you watch them carefully, either to protect them or to stop them from escaping.
NOUN **2** a person whose job is to guard a person, object or place

**guardian guardians**
NOUN someone who has been legally appointed to look after a child, but is not the child's parent

**guerrilla guerrillas**; also spelt **guerilla**
NOUN a member of a small, unofficial army fighting an official army

**guess guesses, guessing, guessed**
VERB **1** If you **guess** something, you form an opinion about it without knowing all the relevant facts. • *She **guessed** that he was probably older than her.*
NOUN **2** an attempt to give an answer or opinion about something without knowing all the relevant facts • *If you don't know the answer, have a **guess**.*

**guest guests**
NOUN someone who has been invited to stay at your home or attend an event

**guide guides, guiding, guided**
NOUN **1** someone who shows you round places, or leads the way through difficult country
VERB **2** If you **guide** someone somewhere, you lead them there.

**guidebook guidebooks**
NOUN a book that gives information about a place

**guillotine guillotines**
NOUN a piece of equipment with a long, sharp blade, used for cutting paper

**WORD HISTORY**
named after Joseph-Ignace *Guillotin*, who first recommended the guillotine as a way of executing people

**guilt**
NOUN **1** the unhappy feeling of having done something wrong
NOUN **2** Someone's **guilt** is the fact that they have done something wrong. • *After hearing the evidence, the jury felt that his **guilt** was clear.*

**guiltily**
ADVERB in a way that shows you know you have done something wrong

**guilty guiltier, guiltiest**
ADJECTIVE **1** If you are **guilty** of doing something wrong, you did it.

ANTONYM: innocent

ADJECTIVE **2** feeling unhappy and ashamed because you think you have done something wrong or not done something that you should have done • *I felt **guilty** about lying to my mum.*

**guinea pig guinea pigs**
NOUN **1** a small, furry mammal without a tail, often kept as a pet
NOUN **2** a person used to try something out • *You will be a **guinea pig** in this experiment.*

**guitar guitars**
NOUN a musical instrument with six strings and a long neck

**gulf gulfs**
NOUN a very large bay

**gull gulls**
NOUN a sea bird with long wings, white and grey or black feathers, and webbed feet

**gullible**
ADJECTIVE If someone is **gullible**, they are easily tricked.

**gulp gulps, gulping, gulped**
VERB **1** If you **gulp** food or drink, you swallow large quantities of it quickly and noisily.
NOUN **2** a large quantity of food or drink swallowed quickly and noisily

a
b
c
d
e
f
g
h
i
j
k
l
m
n
o
p
q
r
s
t
u
v
w
x
y
z

**181**

A
B
C
D
E
F
G
H
I
J
K
L
M
N
O
P
Q
R
S
T
U
V
W
X
Y
Z

**gum gums**
NOUN **1** Your **gums** are the firm flesh in which your teeth are set.
NOUN **2** a soft, flavoured substance that people chew but do not swallow
NOUN **3** glue

**gumboot gumboots**
NOUN a wellington boot

**gumtree gumtrees**
NOUN a eucalyptus or other tree that produces gum

**gun guns**
NOUN a weapon that fires bullets or shells

**gunpowder**
NOUN a powder that explodes when it is lit. It is used for making things such as fireworks.

**gurdwara gurdwaras**
NOUN a Sikh place of worship

**gust gusts**
NOUN a sudden rush of wind • *A **gust** of wind blew his hat off.*

**gutter gutters**
NOUN the edge of a road next to the pavement, where rain collects and flows away

**gym gyms**
NOUN a hall or room for sports and exercise. It is short for *gymnasium*.

**gymkhana gymkhanas**
NOUN a competition in which people take part in horse-riding contests

**gymnasium gymnasiums**
NOUN a room with special equipment for physical exercises

**gymnastics**
NOUN physical exercises, especially ones using equipment such as bars and ropes

**Gypsy Gypsies**; also spelt **Gipsy**
NOUN a member of an ethnic group scattered across most countries of Europe, the Middle East and the Americas. Many members of this group still have a nomadic lifestyle, although some are settled on sites and in houses. Some Gypsies dislike this name, and prefer to be called Romany.

**WORD HISTORY**
from *Egyptian* because in the 16th century they were thought to have come from Egypt

**habit habits**
NOUN something that you do often or regularly

**habitat habitats**
NOUN the natural home of a plant or animc

**hack hacks, hacking, hacked**
VERB **1** If you **hack** at something, you cut it using rough strokes.
VERB **2** If someone **hacks** into a computer system, they break into the system, usuall to get the information stored there. • *He is charged with **hacking** into the firm's compu system.*

**had**
VERB the past participle of **have**

**haddock**
NOUN an edible sea fish

**LANGUAGE TIP**
The plural of *haddock* can be either *haddoc* or *haddocks*, but *haddock* is more common.

**hadn't**
VERB a contraction of *had not*

**haggard**
ADJECTIVE A person who is **haggard** looks ve tired and ill.

**haggis haggises**
NOUN a Scottish dish made of the minced internal organs of a sheep, boiled together with oatmeal and spices in a skin

**haggle haggles, haggling, haggled**
VERB If you **haggle** with someone, you argu with them about the price of something.

**haiku haiku**
NOUN a short, Japanese verse form in 17 syllables

**hail hails, hailing, hailed**
NOUN **1** frozen rain
VERB **2** When it is **hailing**, frozen rain is falling.

**hailstone hailstones**
NOUN a drop of frozen rain

**hair hairs**
NOUN one of the large number of fine threads that grow on your head and body. **Hair** grows on the bodies of some other animals.

**haircut haircuts**
NOUN the cutting of someone's hair and the style into which it is cut

**hairdresser hairdressers**
NOUN a person who is trained to cut and style hair

**hairstyle hairstyles**
NOUN the way in which your hair is arranged or cut

**hairy hairier, hairiest**
ADJECTIVE covered in a lot of hair

**hajj**
NOUN the pilgrimage to Mecca that every Muslim must make at least once in their life, if they are healthy and wealthy enough to do so

WORD HISTORY
from Arabic *hajj* meaning pilgrimage

**halal**; also spelt **hallal**
NOUN meat from animals that have been killed according to Muslim law

**half halves**
NOUN **1** one of two equal parts that make up a whole. It can be written as ½. • *the second half of the match*
ADJECTIVE **2** with one of two equal parts that make up a whole • *My cup is only half full.*
ADVERB **3** You can use **half** to say that something is only partly true. • *I half expected to see the teacher walk in.*
PHRASE **4 Half past** refers to a time that is thirty minutes after a particular hour. • *half past twelve*

**halfway**
ADVERB If something is **halfway** between two points or two times, it is at the middle point between them.

**hall halls**
NOUN **1** the room just inside the front entrance of a house that leads into the other rooms
NOUN **2** a large room or building for public events • *a school hall*

**hallo**
GREETING another spelling of **hello**

**Halloween**
NOUN **Halloween** is October 31st. In the past people thought that ghosts and witches would be about on this night, and it is now celebrated by children dressing up, often as ghosts and witches.

**hallucinate hallucinates, hallucinating, hallucinated**
VERB If someone **hallucinates**, they imagine that they see strange things, for example because they are ill.

**halo haloes** or **halos**
NOUN a circle of light around something, especially the head of a holy person in a picture

**halt halts, halting, halted**
VERB **1** When someone or something **halts**, they stop. • *They halted a short distance from the house.*
PHRASE **2** When something **comes to a halt**, it stops.

**halter halters**
NOUN a strap fastened round a horse's head so that it can be led easily

**halve halves, halving, halved**
VERB If you **halve** something, you divide it into two equal parts.

**ham**
NOUN meat from the hind leg of a pig

**hamburger hamburgers**
NOUN a flat disc of minced meat, fried and eaten in a bread roll

WORD HISTORY
named after *Hamburg* in Germany, the city where they were first made

**hammer hammers, hammering, hammered**
NOUN **1** a tool consisting of a heavy piece of metal at the end of a handle, used for hitting nails into things
VERB **2** If you **hammer** something, you hit it repeatedly with a hammer.

**hammock hammocks**
NOUN a piece of net or canvas hung between two supports and used as a bed

a
b
c
d
e
f
g
h
i
j
k
l
m
n
o
p
q
r
s
t
u
v
w
x
y
z

**183**

## hamper hampers, hampering, hampered

NOUN 1 a large basket with a lid, used for carrying food

VERB 2 If something **hampers** you, it makes it difficult for you to do what you are trying to do. • *The bad weather **hampered** their expedition.*

## hamster hamsters

NOUN a small, furry rodent, often kept as a pet

## hand hands, handing, handed

NOUN 1 the part of your body at the end of your arm, below the wrist

NOUN 2 The **hands** of a clock or watch are the pointers that indicate what time it is.

NOUN 3 In a game of cards, a **hand** is the set of cards dealt to each player.

VERB 4 If you **hand** something to someone, you pass it to them.

PHRASE 5 If you **give a hand**, you help someone to do something.

PHRASE 6 If you do something **by hand**, you do it using your hands rather than a machine.

PHRASE 7 If something gets **out of hand**, it becomes beyond your control.

## handbag handbags

NOUN a small bag, usually carried by a woman

## handcuffs

PLURAL NOUN two strong metal rings joined by chains that are locked round a prisoner's wrists

## handful handfuls

NOUN 1 A **handful** of something is the amount of it you can hold in your hand.

NOUN 2 a small number or quantity of something • *Only a **handful** of people were invited to the party.*

## handicap handicaps

NOUN a disadvantage, or anything that makes it more difficult to do something

## handicraft handicrafts

NOUN an activity that involves making things with your hands, such as pottery or knitting

## handkerchief handkerchiefs

NOUN a small square of fabric used for blowing your nose

## handle handles, handling, handled

NOUN 1 the part of a tool, bag, cup or other object that you hold in order to pick it up or use it • *door **handle***

VERB 2 If you **handle** an object, you hold it or touch it with your hands.

VERB 3 If you **handle** something, you deal with it successfully. • *She **handled** the str of the examination very well.*

## handlebars

PLURAL NOUN the bars with handles that are used to steer a bicycle

→ Have a look at the illustration for **bicyc**

## handset handsets

NOUN The **handset** of a telephone connect to a landline is the part that you speak in and listen with.

## handsome

ADJECTIVE very attractive in appearance

## handstand handstands

NOUN the act of balancing upside down on your hands, with your feet in the air

## handwriting

NOUN Someone's **handwriting** is their sty of writing with a pen or pencil.

## handy handier, handiest

ADJECTIVE If something is **handy**, it is useful or conveniently near.

## hang hangs, hanging, hung or hanged

VERB 1 If you **hang** something on a hook, nail or line, or if it **hangs** there, it is attached so that it does not touch the ground. • *His jacket **hung** from a hook on t door.*

VERB 2 To **hang** someone means to kill the by suspending them by a rope around the neck.

**LANGUAGE TIP**

When *hang* means to kill someone by suspending them by a rope, the past tense and past participle are *hanged*.

## hang about or hang around

VERB (*informal*) If you **hang about** or **hang around** somewhere, you stay or wait there. • *Although he had left, he still **hung around** outside his old school.*

## hang on

VERB 1 If you **hang on** to something, you hold it tightly or keep it.

VERB 2 (*informal*) If you **hang on**, you wa

**hang up**

VERB If you **hang up** when you are speaking on the phone, you press a key or put down the receiver and end the call.

**hangar hangars**

NOUN a large building where aircraft are kept

**hanger hangers**

NOUN a piece of shaped wood, plastic or wire for hanging up clothes

**hang-glider hang-gliders**

NOUN a glider that is made for one or two people who hang below the frame in a harness

**Hanukkah** or **Chanukah**

NOUN an eight-day Jewish festival of lights

**haphazard**

ADJECTIVE not organised or planned • He piled the books up in a **haphazard** way.

**happen happens, happening, happened**

VERB 1 When something **happens**, it occurs or takes place.

VERB 2 If you **happen** to do something, you do it by chance. • I **happened** to notice he'd dropped his glove.

**happily**

ADVERB 1 in a happy way • The children were playing **happily**.

ANTONYM: miserably

ADVERB 2 You say **happily** to show that you are willing to do something. • I would **happily** share a room with my brother.

ANTONYM: reluctantly

**happiness**

NOUN a feeling of great contentment or pleasure

**happy happier, happiest**

ADJECTIVE 1 full of contentment or joy

ANTONYMS: miserable, sad

ADJECTIVE 2 If you are **happy** with something, you are satisfied with it.

ANTONYM: dissatisfied

ADJECTIVE 3 If you are **happy** to do something, you are willing to do it.

ANTONYM: reluctant

**harass harasses, harassing, harassed**

VERB If someone **harasses** you, they annoy or trouble you continually.

**harbour harbours**

NOUN a protected area of deep water where boats can be moored

**hard harder, hardest**

ADVERB 1 with a lot of effort • If I work **hard**, I'll pass my tests.

ADVERB 2 with a lot of force • I kicked the ball very **hard**.

ADJECTIVE 3 requiring a lot of effort • The sponsored walk was **hard** work.

ADJECTIVE 4 difficult • **hard** sums

ADJECTIVE 5 not easy to bend or break

**hard disk hard disks**

NOUN a part of a computer that holds a large amount of information

**harden hardens, hardening, hardened**

VERB If something **hardens** it becomes hard or gets harder. • The glue took a long time to **harden**.

**hardly**

ADVERB only just • I could **hardly** believe it.

**hardship**

NOUN a time or situation of suffering and difficulty

**hardware**

NOUN 1 tools and equipment for use in the home and garden

NOUN 2 computer machinery rather than computer programs

**hardy hardier, hardiest**

ADJECTIVE tough and able to bear cold and difficult conditions

**hare hares**

NOUN an animal like a large rabbit, but with longer ears and legs

**harm harms, harming, harmed**

VERB 1 If someone **harms** someone or something, they injure or damage them.

SYNONYM: hurt

NOUN 2 injury or damage

SYNONYM: hurt

**harmful**

ADJECTIVE having a bad effect on something • Too much sun can be **harmful** to your skin.

**harmless**

ADJECTIVE safe to use or be near

a
b
c
d
e
f
g
h
i
j
k
l
m
n
o
p
q
r
s
t
u
v
w
x
y
z

**harmonica** harmonicas
NOUN a small musical instrument played by moving it across the lips and blowing and sucking air through it. Also called a mouth organ.

**harmony** harmonies
NOUN 1 a state of peaceful agreement and cooperation ● *The neighbours lived in* **harmony**.
NOUN 2 In music, **harmony** is the pleasant combination of two or more notes played at the same time.

**harness** harnesses, harnessing, harnessed
NOUN 1 a set of straps fastened round an animal to control it or attach it to something, such as a horse to a cart
VERB 2 If you **harness** an animal, you put a harness on it.
VERB 3 If someone **harnesses** something, they control it so that they can use it.
● *The windmills* **harnessed** *the power of the wind.*

**harp** harps
NOUN a musical instrument consisting of a triangular frame with vertical strings that you pluck with your fingers

**harpist** harpists
NOUN someone who plays a harp

**harpoon** harpoons
NOUN a barbed spear attached to a rope, thrown or fired from a gun and used for catching whales or large fish

**harsh** harsher, harshest
ADJECTIVE 1 **Harsh** living conditions or climates are rough and unpleasant.

SYNONYMS: hard, severe, tough

ADJECTIVE 2 **Harsh** actions or remarks are unkind and show no sympathy.

**harshly**
ADVERB in a way that is unkind and shows no sympathy

**harshness**
NOUN 1 **Harshness** is when living conditions or climates are rough and unpleasant.
NOUN 2 **Harshness** is when someone's actions or remarks are unkind and show no sympathy.

**harvest** harvests
NOUN the act of gathering a crop, or the time when this is done

WORD HISTORY
from Old German *herbist* meaning autumn

**has**
VERB part of the verb *have*

**hashtag** hashtags
NOUN a word or phrase with a hash sign (#) in front of it, to show that it is the topic of message on a social media website
● *All my friends posted tweets using the* **hashtag** *#silent.*

**hasn't**
VERB a contraction of *has not*

**hassle** hassles, hassling, hassled
NOUN 1 (*informal*) Something that is a **hassle** is difficult or causes trouble. ● *Organising the school trip is always a* **hassle**.
VERB 2 If you **hassle** someone, you annoy them by repeatedly asking them to do something.

**hasty** hastier, hastiest
ADJECTIVE done quickly and without preparation ● *Do not give a* **hasty** *answer.*

**hat** hats
NOUN a covering for the head

**hatch** hatches, hatching, hatched
VERB 1 When an egg **hatches**, or when a bird or a reptile **hatches** from an egg, the shell breaks open and the young bird or reptile comes out.
NOUN 2 an opening in a wall where food can be passed through

**hatchback** hatchbacks
NOUN a car with a door at the back that opens upwards

**hatchet** hatchets
NOUN a small axe

**hate** hates, hating, hated
VERB If you **hate** someone or something, you dislike them very much.

**hateful**
ADJECTIVE very nasty and unpleasant

**hatred**
NOUN an extremely strong feeling of dislike

**haul** hauls, hauling, hauled
VERB If you **haul** something somewhere, you pull it with great effort.

**haunt** haunts, haunting, haunted
VERB If a ghost **haunts** a place, it is seen or heard there regularly.

**aunted**

ADJECTIVE Somewhere that is **haunted** is visited often by a ghost. • *People believe that the house on the hill is* **haunted**.

**ave has, having, had**

VERB **1** If you **have** something, it belongs to you or you possess it.

VERB **2** If you **have** something such as a cold or an accident, you feel or experience it.

VERB **3** If you **have** something such as lunch or a letter, you take or get it.

VERB **4** If you **have** something such as a haircut, you cause it to be done.

PHRASE **5** If you **have to** do something, you must do it. • *I* **have to** *clean my room before I go out.*

VERB **6** **Have** can be used with other verbs to form the past tense. • *I* **have** *already read that book.*

**aven't**

VERB a contraction of *have not*

**avoc**

NOUN disorder and confusion • *The bad weather played* **havoc** *with our plans.*

**awk hawks**

NOUN a bird of prey with short, rounded wings and a long tail

**ay**

NOUN grass that has been cut and dried and is used to feed animals

**ay fever**

NOUN an allergy to pollen and grass, causing sneezing and watering eyes

**aystack haystacks**

NOUN a large, firmly-built pile of hay, usually covered and left out in the open

**azard hazards**

NOUN something that could be dangerous to you • *The pollution in the city centre is a health* **hazard**.

**WORD HISTORY**

from the Arabic *al zahr* meaning the dice, because games using dice involved risk

**aze**

NOUN If there is a **haze**, it is difficult to see clearly because there is moisture or smoke in the air.

**azel hazels**

NOUN **1** a small tree with edible nuts

ADJECTIVE **2** a green-brown colour • *He has* **hazel** *eyes.*

**hazelnut hazelnuts**

NOUN the nut of the hazel tree. It has a hard, smooth, light-brown shell.

**hazy hazier, haziest**

ADJECTIVE dim or vague • **hazy** *sunshine* • *a* **hazy** *memory*

**he**

PRONOUN **He** is used to refer to a man, boy or male animal that has already been mentioned.

**head heads, heading, headed**

NOUN **1** the part of a human or other animal's body that has their eyes, brain and mouth in it

→ Have a look at the illustration for **insect**

NOUN **2** the top or front of something, or the most important end of it • *We went to the* **head** *of the queue.*

NOUN **3** When you toss a coin, the side called **heads** is the one with the **head** on it.

NOUN **4** In an organisation or group of people, the **head** is the main person in charge.

VERB **5** If you **head** something, you lead it. • *She* **headed** *the expedition to the North Pole.*

VERB **6** If you **head** somewhere, you go in that direction or towards something. • *We* **headed** *to the canteen for lunch.*

VERB **7** If you **head** a ball, you hit it with your head. • *He* **headed** *the ball into the goal.*

**headache headaches**

NOUN a pain in your head

**heading headings**

NOUN a piece of writing that is written or printed at the top of a page

**headlight headlights**

NOUN the large, powerful lights on the front of a motor vehicle

→ Have a look at the illustration for **car**

**headline headlines**

NOUN The **headline** of a newspaper is the heading printed in big, bold letters on the front page at the top of an article.

**headphones**

NOUN a pair of small speakers that you wear over your ears to listen to a radio, a television or a stereo without other people hearing

**headquarters**

NOUN the main place from which an organisation is run

a
b
c
d
e
f
g
h
i
j
k
l
m
n
o
p
q
r
s
t
u
v
w
x
y
z

**187**

**head teacher head teachers**
NOUN the teacher who is in charge of a school

**heal heals, healing, healed**
VERB If a cut or a wound **heals**, it gets better.
• *The cut on my leg **healed** quickly.*

**health**
NOUN the condition of someone's body and mind • *I felt in very good **health** after our holiday.*

**healthy healthier, healthiest**
ADJECTIVE **1** Someone who is **healthy** is fit and well, and is not suffering from any illness. • *She goes to the gym to stay **healthy**.*
ADJECTIVE **2** Something that is **healthy** is good for you. • *You should try and eat a **healthy** diet.*

**heap heaps, heaping, heaped**
NOUN **1** an untidy pile of things
VERB **2** If you **heap** things, you pile them up.

**hear hears, hearing, heard**
VERB **1** When you **hear** sounds, you are aware of them because they reach your ears.
• *We could **hear** the waves crashing on the beach.*
VERB **2** When you **hear** from someone, they write to you or phone you.

**heard**
VERB the past tense and past participle of **hear**

**hearing**
NOUN **1** the ability to hear
NOUN **2** If someone gives you a **hearing**, they let you give your point of view and listen to you.

**hearse hearses**
NOUN a large car that carries the coffin at a funeral

**heart hearts**
NOUN **1** the organ in your chest that pumps the blood around your body

→ Have a look at the illustration for **organ**

NOUN **2** Your **heart** is also thought of as the centre of your emotions and feelings.
• *When his hamster died it broke his **heart**.*
NOUN **3** the most central or important part of something • *It is always busy in the **heart** of the city.*
NOUN **4** courage
NOUN **5** a curved shape like this ♥, or a playing card with this shape on it

PHRASE **6** If you learn something **by heart**, you learn it so that you know it from memory.

right atrium
aorta
left atri
right ventricle
left ventric

**heart attack heart attacks**
NOUN a serious medical condition in which someone's heart suddenly beats irregular or stops completely

**hearth hearths**
NOUN the floor of a fireplace

PRONUNCIATION TIP
This word is pronounced **harth**.

**heat heats, heating, heated**
NOUN **1** warmth or the quality of being hot
• *the fierce **heat** of the sun*
NOUN **2** a contest or race in a competition that decides who will compete in the final
VERB **3** When you **heat** something, you war it.

**heater heaters**
NOUN a device used to produce heat in orde to warm a place, such as a room or a car

**heath**
NOUN a large open area of land covered in rough grass or heather, with very few trees

**heather**
NOUN a plant with small purple or white flowers that grows wild on hills and moorlar

**heave heaves, heaving, heaved**
VERB If you **heave** something, you lift, push or throw it with a lot of effort.

**heaven**
NOUN In some religions, **heaven** is the plac where God lives and where good people gc when they die.

**avy heavier, heaviest**

ADJECTIVE **1** Something that is **heavy** weighs a lot.

ANTONYM: light

ADJECTIVE **2** You use **heavy** to talk about how much something weighs. • How **heavy** is the baby?

**brew**

NOUN an ancient language that is now spoken in Israel by the Jewish people

**ctare hectares**

NOUN a unit for measuring an area of land, equal to 10,000 square metres or about .471 acres

**ctic**

ADJECTIVE involving a lot of rushed activity • She leads a very **hectic** life.

**'d**

a contraction of he had or he would

**dge hedges**

NOUN a row of bushes along the edge of a garden, field or road

**dgehog hedgehogs**

NOUN a small, brown mammal with sharp spikes covering its back

**el heels**

NOUN **1** the back part of your foot, below your ankle

NOUN **2** the part on the bottom at the back of a shoe or sock

**ifer heifers**

NOUN a young cow that has not yet had calves

**ight heights**

NOUN **1** a measurement from the bottom to the top of someone or something

NOUN **2** a high position or place • He's afraid of **heights**.

NOUN **3** the highest or most important part of something • He's at the **height** of his success.

**ir heirs**

NOUN the person who is entitled to inherit someone's property or title • the **heir** to the throne

PRONUNCIATION TIP

This word is pronounced **air**.

**ld**

VERB the past tense of **hold**

**helicopter helicopters**

NOUN an aircraft with rotating blades instead of wings, that enable it to take off vertically

**helium**

NOUN a gas that is lighter than air. It is sometimes used to fill party balloons.

**he'll**

a contraction of he will or he shall

**hell**

NOUN **1** In some religions, **hell** is the place where the Devil lives and where wicked people are sent to be punished when they die.

NOUN **2** (informal) If you say that something is **hell**, you mean that it is very unpleasant.

**hello**

GREETING You say **hello** when you meet someone or answer the phone.

**helmet helmets**

NOUN a hard hat that you wear to protect your head

**help helps, helping, helped**

VERB **1** If you **help** someone, you make something easier or better for them.

NOUN **2** assistance • Thanks for your **help**.

**helpful**

ADJECTIVE If you are **helpful**, you cooperate with others and support them.

**helping helpings**

NOUN a portion of food at a meal

**helpless**

ADJECTIVE If you are **helpless**, you are unable to protect yourself or do anything useful.

**hem hems, hemming, hemmed**

NOUN **1** The **hem** of a garment is the edge of it that has been folded up and stitched in place.

VERB **2** If you **hem** a garment, you make a hem on it.

**hemisphere hemispheres**

NOUN one half of the Earth or a sphere

→ Have a look at the illustration for **equator**

a
b
c
d
e
f
g
h
i
j
k
l
m
n
o
p
q
r
s
t
u
v
w
x
y
z

**189**

**hen hens**
NOUN **1** a female chicken
NOUN **2** any female bird

**heptagon heptagons**
NOUN a flat shape with seven straight sides

**her**
PRONOUN **1** refers to a woman, girl or female animal that has already been mentioned
● *I like Amy. I often play with **her**.*
ADJECTIVE **2** shows that something belongs to a woman, girl or female animal that has already been mentioned ● *Mum is going to wear **her** blue jumper.*

**heraldry**
NOUN the study of coats of arms

**herb herbs**
NOUN a plant whose leaves are used as a medicine or to flavour food

**herbivore herbivores**
NOUN an animal that eats only plants

**herbivorous**
ADJECTIVE eating only plants

**herd herds, herding, herded**
NOUN **1** a large group of animals grazing together ● *a **herd** of cattle*
VERB **2** If you **herd** animals or people, you make them move together as a group. ● *The teachers **herded** the children on to the bus.*

**here**
ADVERB at, to or in the place where you are

**hereditary**
ADJECTIVE passed on to a child from a parent

**heritage**
NOUN The **heritage** of a country is all its traditions, customs and art that have been passed from one generation to another.

**hermit hermits**
NOUN someone who prefers to live a simple life alone and far from other people, often for religious reasons

**hero heroes**
NOUN **1** the main male character in a book, film or play
NOUN **2** a person who is admired because they have done something brave or good

**heroine heroines**
NOUN the main female character in a book, play or film

**heron herons**
NOUN a wading bird with very long legs and a long beak and neck

**herring herrings**
NOUN a silvery fish that lives in large shoals in northern seas

**hers**
PRONOUN refers to something that belongs or relates to a woman, girl or other female animal

**herself**
PRONOUN refers to the same woman, girl or female animal who does an action and is affected by it ● *She pulled **herself** up.*

**he's**
a contraction of *he is* or *he has*

**hesitate hesitates, hesitating, hesitate**
VERB If you **hesitate**, you pause or show uncertainty.

**hexagon hexagons**
NOUN a flat shape with six straight sides

**hexagonal**
ADJECTIVE having six straight sides

**hibernate hibernates, hibernating, hibernated**
VERB Animals that **hibernate** spend the winter in a state like a deep sleep.

**hibernation**
NOUN **Hibernation** is when an animal spends the winter in a state like a deep sleep.

**hiccup hiccups, hiccupping, hiccupped**
also spelt **hiccough**
NOUN **1** a short, uncontrolled sound in your throat
VERB **2** When you **hiccup**, you make short, uncontrolled sounds in your throat.

**hide hides, hiding, hid, hidden**
VERB **1** If you **hide** something, you put it where it cannot be seen, or prevent it from being discovered. ● *He **hid** his disappointment*
VERB **2** If you **hide**, you go somewhere where you cannot be seen or found easily.

**...eous**

...JECTIVE extremely ugly or unpleasant

**...roglyphics**

...URAL NOUN ancient Egyptian writing that ...ses pictures instead of words. It involves ...ver 700 picture signs.

**...RONUNCIATION TIP**

...his word is pronounced hy-ro-**gliff**-iks.

**...h higher, highest**

...JECTIVE **1 High** refers to how much ...omething measures from the bottom to the ...op. • *The statue was three metres **high**.*

...JECTIVE **2** great in degree, quantity or ...ntensity • *My aunt bought a house, despite ...e **high** price.*

ANTONYM: low

...DVERB **3** a long way above the ground ...*He jumped **high** into the air.*

ANTONYM: low

**...hlight highlights, highlighting, ...ighlighted**

...OUN **1** the most interesting part of ...omething • *The **highlight** of the week was ...ur trip to the cinema.*

...ERB **2** If you **highlight** a point or a problem, ...ou emphasise it.

**...jh-rise**

...JECTIVE **High-rise** buildings are very tall.

**...jhway highways**

...OUN a main road

**hijab hijabs**; also spelt hejab

NOUN a veil worn by some Muslim women in public, covering the hair and the chest

**PRONUNCIATION TIP**

This word is pronounced hi-**jab**.

**hijack hijacks, hijacking, hijacked**

VERB If someone **hijacks** a vehicle, they take control of it unlawfully and by force.

**hike hikes, hiking, hiked**

VERB **1** If you **hike**, you go for a long walk across country.

NOUN **2** a long and demanding walk

**hilarious**

ADJECTIVE very funny

**hill hills**

NOUN a high, rounded piece of ground

**hilt hilts**

NOUN the handle of a knife or sword

**him**

PRONOUN refers to a man, boy or male animal that has already been mentioned • *Let's invite Ben. I really like **him**.*

**himself**

PRONOUN refers to the same man, boy or male animal that does an action and is affected by it • *He pushed **himself** to the front of the crowd.*

**hind hinds**

NOUN **1** a female deer

ADJECTIVE **2** The **hind** legs of an animal are its back legs.

a
b
c
d
e
f
g
h
i
j
k
l
m
n
o
p
q
r
s
t
u
v
w
x
y
z

**hieroglyphics**

## hinder hinders, hindering, hindered
VERB If you **hinder** someone or something, you get in their way and make it difficult for them to do what they want to do.

## hindrance
NOUN someone or something that causes difficulties or is an obstruction

## Hindu Hindus
NOUN a person who believes in Hinduism, an Indian religion that has many gods and involves the belief that people have another life on Earth after death

## hinge hinges
NOUN the movable joint that attaches a door or window to its frame

## hint hints, hinting, hinted
NOUN 1 an indirect suggestion ● *He dropped* **hints** *about his birthday present.*
NOUN 2 a helpful piece of advice
VERB 3 If you **hint** that something is true, you suggest it indirectly. ● *The teacher* **hinted** *that they had all done well in the tests.*

## hip hips
NOUN Your **hips** are the joints and the bony parts at the top of your thigh and below your waist.

## hippopotamus hippopotamuses or hippopotami
NOUN a large, African mammal with thick, wrinkled skin and short legs, that lives near rivers

### WORD HISTORY
from Greek *hippos* + *potamos* meaning river horse

## hire hires, hiring, hired
VERB 1 If you **hire** something, you pay money to use it for a period of time.
PHRASE 2 Something that is **for hire** is available for people to hire. ● *There are bicycles* **for hire** *down by the beach.*

## his
ADJECTIVE shows that something belongs to a man, boy or other male animal that has already been mentioned ● *He took off* **his** *coat.*

## hiss hisses, hissing, hissed
VERB If someone or something **hisses**, they make a long s sound.

## historic
ADJECTIVE important in the past, or likely to be seen as important in the future

## historical
ADJECTIVE occurring in the past, or relating the study of the past

## history histories
NOUN 1 the study of the past
NOUN 2 the set of facts that are known ab. a place or subject ● *There was a leaflet on* **history** *of the stately home.*

### WORD HISTORY
from Greek *historein* meaning to narrate story

## hit hits, hitting, hit
VERB 1 If you **hit** someone or something, y strike or knock them with force.
VERB 2 If something **hits** you, it affects you suddenly and forcefully. ● *The answer suddenly* **hit** *me.*
NOUN 3 If someone or something is a big they are a great success.
NOUN 4 the action of hitting something

## hitch hitches, hitching, hitched
VERB 1 If you **hitch** something, you tie it u using a loop.
VERB 2 (*informal*) If you **hitch** somewhere, you travel by getting lifts from passing vehicles.
NOUN 3 a slight problem of difficulty ● *The plans went ahead without a* **hitch**.

## hitchhike hitchhikes, hitchhiking, hitchhiked
VERB to travel by getting lifts from passing vehicles

## hitchhiker hitchhikers
NOUN a person who travels by hitchhiking

## hive hives
NOUN 1 a beehive
NOUN 2 A place that is a **hive** of activity is very busy.

## hoard hoards, hoarding, hoarded
VERB 1 If you **hoard** things, you save them even though they may no longer be usefu
NOUN 2 a store of things that has been sav or hidden

## hoarse hoarser, hoarsest
ADJECTIVE A **hoarse** voice sounds rough and unclear.

**ax hoaxes**
NOUN a trick or an attempt to deceive someone • *It turned out to be a hoax.*

**bby hobbies**
NOUN something that you do for enjoyment in your spare time

**ckey**
NOUN a game in which two teams use long sticks with curved ends to try to hit a small ball into the other team's goal

**e hoes**
NOUN a long-handled gardening tool with a small, square blade, used to remove weeds and break up the soil

**gmanay**
NOUN New Year's Eve and its celebrations in Scotland

**ist hoists, hoisting, hoisted**
VERB If someone **hoists** something, they lift it, especially using ropes and pulleys, a crane or other machinery.

**ld holds, holding, held**
VERB 1 If you **hold** something, you carry it or keep it in place, usually with your hands or arms.
VERB 2 If you **hold** a meeting or a party, you arrange it and cause it to happen.
VERB 3 If you **hold** someone responsible for something, you decide that they did it.
VERB 4 If something **holds** a certain amount, it can contain that amount. • *This jug holds a litre of water.*
VERB 5 If you **hold** something, you possess it. • *She holds the world long jump record.*
NOUN 6 the part of a ship or aircraft where cargo or luggage is stored
NOUN 7 If someone has a **hold** over you, they have power over you.
NOUN 8 If you keep a **hold** on something, you hold it securely.

**le holes**
NOUN an opening or hollow space in something

**oli**
NOUN a Hindu festival celebrated in spring

**oliday holidays**
NOUN 1 a period of time spent away from home for enjoyment
NOUN 2 a day when people do not go to work or school because of a national festival • *In Britain, Christmas Day is always a holiday.*

**hollow hollows, hollowing, hollowed**
ADJECTIVE 1 Something that is **hollow** has a hole or space inside it.

ANTONYM: solid

NOUN 2 a small valley or sunken place
VERB 3 If you **hollow** something out, you make it hollow. • *We hollowed out the pumpkin to make a lantern for Halloween.*

**holly**
NOUN an evergreen tree or shrub with spiky leaves. It often has red berries in winter.

**hologram holograms**
NOUN a three-dimensional picture made by laser beams

**holster holsters**
NOUN a holder for a hand gun, worn at the side of the body or under the arm

**holy holier, holiest**
ADJECTIVE Something that is **holy** relates to God or to a particular religion.

**home homes**
NOUN 1 the building or place in which you live
NOUN 2 A nursing **home** is a building in which elderly or ill people live and are looked after.
NOUN 3 the place where you feel you belong

**homeless**
ADJECTIVE Someone who is **homeless** has nowhere to live.

**homelessness**
NOUN the situation when someone has nowhere to live

**home page home pages**
NOUN the first page you see on a website, which tells you about the site and has links to the information or services provided

**homesick**
ADJECTIVE If you are **homesick**, you are unhappy because you are away from your home and family. • *I enjoyed my exchange trip to Germany, but I did feel homesick sometimes.*

**homework**
NOUN school work given to pupils to be done at home

**homograph homographs**
NOUN one of a group of words spelt in the same way but with different meanings, such as *saw* (meaning a tool for cutting) and *saw* (the past tense of *see*)

193

**homonym** homonyms

NOUN one of a group of words that are pronounced or spelt in the same way but have different meanings; for example *eight* and *ate*, or *bank* (meaning a slope) and *bank* (meaning a place where you keep your money)

**homophone** homophones

NOUN one of a group of words with different meanings that are pronounced in the same way but spelt differently. *Write* and *right* are **homophones**.

**honest**

NOUN If you are **honest**, you can be trusted to tell the truth.

SYNONYMS: trustworthy, truthful

**honestly**

ADVERB You use **honestly** to emphasise that what you are saying is true. • *I didn't do it.* **Honestly**! • *I can* **honestly** *say that she is the best teacher I've ever had.*

**honey**

NOUN a sweet, edible, sticky substance made by bees

**honeycomb** honeycombs

NOUN a wax structure made with six-sided cells by bees for storing honey

**honeymoon** honeymoons

NOUN a holiday for a newly married couple after their wedding

**honour** honours, honouring, honoured

NOUN 1 An **honour** is an award given to someone for something they have done.
NOUN 2 If you feel that it is an **honour** to do something, you feel proud or privileged to do it.
VERB 3 If you **honour** someone, you give them special praise or attention, or an award.

**hood** hoods

NOUN 1 a loose covering for the head, usually part of a coat or jacket
NOUN 2 In American English, the **hood** of a car is the cover over the engine at the front.

**hoodie** hoodies

NOUN a piece of clothing made of thick cotton with a hood, which covers your upper body • *She wore jeans and a red* **hoodie**.

**hoof** hooves or hoofs

NOUN the hard, bony part of the feet of horses, cattle and deer

**hook** hooks, hooking, hooked

NOUN 1 a curved piece of metal or plastic that is used for catching things or for holding things up
VERB 2 If you **hook** one thing on to another you attach it there using a hook. • *He* **hooked** *the caravan to the car.*

**hooligan** hooligans

NOUN a destructive and violent person

**hooliganism**

NOUN noisy and violent behaviour

**hoop** hoops

NOUN a large wooden, metal or plastic ring

**hoot** hoots, hooting, hooted

VERB 1 If a car horn **hoots**, it makes a loud honking noise.
VERB 2 If someone **hoots**, they make a long *oo* sound like an owl or a car horn. • *We* **hooted** *with laughter at his joke.*

**hop** hops, hopping, hopped

VERB 1 If you **hop**, you jump on one foot.
VERB 2 When animals such as kangaroos, birds or insects **hop**, they jump with two more feet together.

**hope** hopes, hoping, hoped

VERB 1 If you **hope** that something will happen, you want or expect it to happen.
NOUN 2 the wish or expectation that things will go well in the future

**hopeful**

ADJECTIVE If you are **hopeful** about something, you hope it will turn out well.

**hopefully**

ADVERB 1 You use **hopefully** to say what you hope will happen. • **Hopefully**, *your mum will let you come to the park with us.*
ADVERB 2 in a way that shows you are hopeful • *She looked at him* **hopefully**.

**hopeless**

ADJECTIVE 1 You say something is **hopeless** when it is very bad and you do not feel it can get any better.
ADJECTIVE 2 unable to do something well • *I'm* **hopeless** *at art.*

**hopelessly**

ADVERB 1 You use **hopelessly** to emphasise that a situation is very bad and you do not feel it can get any better. • *Everything was* **hopelessly** *disorganised.*
ADVERB 2 in a way that shows you have no hope • *He stared* **hopelessly** *out of the window.*

**rde hordes**
NOUN a large group or number of people or other animals

**rizon horizons**
NOUN the distant line where the sky seems to touch the land or sea

**rizontal**
ADJECTIVE flat and level with, or parallel to the ground

**rn horns**
NOUN 1 a warning device on a vehicle that makes a loud noise
NOUN 2 one of the hard, pointed things that grow from the head of a cow or goat

**rnet hornets**
NOUN 1 a type of very large wasp
PHRASE 2 A situation described as **a hornet's nest** is very difficult to deal with and likely to cause trouble.

**roscope horoscopes**
NOUN a prediction about what is going to happen to someone, based on the position of the stars when they were born

**rrible**
ADJECTIVE disagreeable and unpleasant

**rrific**
ADJECTIVE If something is **horrific**, it horrifies people.

**rrify horrifies, horrifying, horrified**
VERB If someone or something **horrifies** you, they make you feel disgusted and shocked.

**rror**
NOUN a strong feeling of alarm caused by something very unpleasant

**rse horses**
NOUN a large mammal with a mane and tail, that people can ride

**rse chestnut horse chestnuts**
NOUN a large tree with flowers and shiny, brown nuts known as conkers

**rsepower**
NOUN a unit used for measuring how powerful an engine is

**rseshoe horseshoes**
NOUN a U-shaped piece of iron that is nailed to the bottom of a horse's hoof to protect it

**ose hoses**
NOUN a long, flexible tube through which liquid or gas can be passed • *a garden hose*

**hospitable**
ADJECTIVE If you are **hospitable**, you are friendly, welcoming and generous to others.

**hospital hospitals**
NOUN a place where sick people are looked after by doctors and nurses

**host hosts, hosting, hosted**
NOUN 1 the person who gives a party or organises an event, and who welcomes and looks after the guests
NOUN 2 a large number of things • *There was a **host** of things to do at the fair.*
VERB 3 If you **host** an event, you organise it and act as the host.

**hostage hostages**
NOUN a person who is illegally held prisoner and threatened with injury or death unless certain demands are met by other people

**hostel hostels**
NOUN a large house where people can stay cheaply for a short time • *a youth **hostel***

**hostile**
ADJECTIVE If someone is **hostile** to you, they behave in an unfriendly aggressive way towards you.

**hot hotter, hottest**
ADJECTIVE 1 having a high temperature
ADJECTIVE 2 having a burning taste caused by spices

**hotel hotels**
NOUN a building where people stay, paying for their room and meals

**hound hounds**
NOUN a dog, especially one used for hunting or racing

**hour hours**
NOUN a period of 60 minutes

WORD HISTORY
from Greek *hora* meaning season or time of day

**house houses**
NOUN a building where people live

**household households**
NOUN 1 all the people who live as a group in a house or flat
PHRASE 2 Someone who is **a household name** is very well known.

a
b
c
d
e
f
g
h
i
j
k
l
m
n
o
p
q
r
s
t
u
v
w
x
y
z

**housewife housewives**
NOUN a married woman who does not have a paid job, but instead looks after her home and children

**housework**
NOUN all the work done in the home, like the cleaning and cooking

**hover hovers, hovering, hovered**
VERB When a bird, insect or aircraft **hovers**, it stays in the same place in the air.

**hovercraft hovercraft** or **hovercrafts**
NOUN a vehicle that can travel over water or land supported by a cushion of air

**how**
ADVERB used to ask about, explain or refer to the way something is done ● **How** did you get so dirty?

**however**
ADVERB **1** You use **however** when you are adding a comment that contrasts with what has just been said. ● He is very chatty and seems confident. **However**, he is quite shy.
ADVERB **2** You use **however** to say that something makes no difference to a situation. ● **However** hard she tried, nothing seemed to work.

**howl howls, howling, howled**
VERB **1** If someone or something **howls**, they make a long, loud wailing noise such as that made by a dog or a baby when it is upset.
NOUN **2** a long, loud wailing noise

**hub hubs**
NOUN **1** the centre part of a wheel
→ Have a look at the illustration for **turbine**
NOUN **2** the most important or active part of a place or organisation

**huddle huddles, huddling, huddled**
VERB **1** If you **huddle** up, or are **huddled**, you are curled up with your arms and legs close to your body.
VERB **2** When people or animals **huddle** together, they sit or stand close to each other, often for warmth.

**hug hugs, hugging, hugged**
VERB If you **hug** someone, you put your arms round them and hold them close to you, usually to comfort them or to show affection.

**huge**
ADJECTIVE extremely large in amount, size or degree ● The party was a **huge** success.

SYNONYMS: enormous, gigantic, vast

**hull hulls**
NOUN The **hull** of a ship is the main part of its body that sits in the water.

**hum hums, humming, hummed**
VERB **1** If something **hums**, it makes a continuous, low noise.
VERB **2** If you **hum**, you sing with your lips closed.
NOUN **3** a continuous, low noise

**human humans**
ADJECTIVE **1** relating to or concerning people ● We are all part of the **human** race.
NOUN **2** a person

**WORD HISTORY**
from Latin *homo* meaning man

**human being human beings**
NOUN a person

**humane**
ADJECTIVE showing kindness and sympathy towards others

**humanity**
NOUN **1** the human race
NOUN **2** Someone who shows **humanity** is kind and sympathetic.

**humble humbler, humblest**
ADJECTIVE A **humble** person is modest and thinks that they are not very important.

**humbly**
ADVERB in a modest way that shows you that you are not very important

**humid**
ADJECTIVE If the weather is **humid**, the air feels damp, heavy and warm.

**humidity**
NOUN **1 Humidity** is when the air feels damp, heavy and warm.
NOUN **2 Humidity** is the amount of moisture in the air.

**humiliate humiliates, humiliating, humiliated**
VERB If you **humiliate** someone, you make them feel ashamed or appear stupid to other people.

**miliation**

NOUN the feeling of being ashamed or embarrassed because you have been made to look stupid

**nour humours, humouring, umoured**

NOUN **1** the quality of being funny

NOUN **2** the ability to be amused by certain things • *She's got a peculiar sense of umour*.

VERB **3** If you **humour** someone, you try to please them, so that they will not become upset.

**mp humps**

NOUN a small, rounded lump or mound • *a camel's hump*

**nch hunches, hunching, hunched**

VERB **1** If you **hunch** your shoulders, you raise them and push them forward, bending forward slightly.

VERB **2** If you have a **hunch** about something, you have an idea that something will happen.

**ndred hundreds**

NOUN A **hundred** is the number 100.

**ndredth hundredths**

NOUN **1** one of a hundred equal parts of something. It can be written as 1/100.

ADJECTIVE **2** The **hundredth** item in a series is the one that you count as number one hundred. It can be written as 100th.

**ng**

VERB a past tense and past participle of **ang**

**nger**

NOUN the need or desire to eat

**ngrily**

ADVERB in a way that shows you are hungry

**ngry hungrier, hungriest**

ADJECTIVE If you are **hungry**, you need or want food.

**nt hunts, hunting, hunted**

VERB **1** If you **hunt** for something, you search for it.

VERB **2** When people **hunt**, they chase and kill wild animals for food or sport.

NOUN **3** the act of searching for something • *The neighbours joined in the hunt for the missing cat.*

**rdle hurdles**

NOUN **1** one of the frames or barriers that you jump over in an athletics race called

**hurdles** • *She knocked over the last hurdle, but still managed to win the race.*

NOUN **2** a problem or difficulty • *Several hurdles had to be overcome before the school play could go ahead.*

**hurl hurls, hurling, hurled**

VERB If you **hurl** something, you throw it with great force.

**hurricane hurricanes**

NOUN a very violent storm with strong winds

**hurry hurries, hurrying, hurried**

VERB **1** If you **hurry** somewhere, you go there quickly.

VERB **2** If you **hurry** someone or something, you try to make something happen more quickly.

PHRASE **3** If you are **in a hurry** to do something, you want to do it quickly. If you do something **in a hurry**, you do it quickly.

**hurry up**

VERB If you tell someone to **hurry up**, you try to get them to do something more quickly.

**hurt hurts, hurting, hurt**

VERB **1** If you **hurt** yourself or someone else, you injure or cause physical pain to yourself or someone else.

VERB **2** If a part of your body **hurts**, you feel pain there.

VERB **3** If you **hurt** someone, or **hurt** their feelings, you upset them by being unkind towards them.

ADJECTIVE **4** If you are **hurt**, you are injured.

ADJECTIVE **5** If you feel **hurt**, you are upset because of someone's unkindness towards you. • *She was hurt that they did not invite her to the party.*

**WORD HISTORY**

from Old French *hurter* meaning to knock against

**hurtle hurtles, hurtling, hurtled**

VERB If someone or something **hurtles**, they move along very fast in an uncontrolled way. • *The car hurtled along the bumpy road.*

**husband husbands**

NOUN Someone's **husband** is the man they are married to.

**hustle hustles, hustling, hustled**

VERB **1** If you **hustle** someone, you make them move by pushing and jostling them.

VERB **2** If you **hustle**, you go somewhere or do something in a hurry.

a
b
c
d
e
f
g
h
i
j
k
l
m
n
o
p
q
r
s
t
u
v
w
x
y
z

**197**

**hut huts**
NOUN a small house or shelter

**hutch hutches**
NOUN a wooden box with wire mesh at one side, in which small pets can be kept

**hydrant hydrants**
NOUN a pipe connected to the main water supply of a town and used for emergencies

**hydraulic**
ADJECTIVE operated by water or other fluid that is under pressure

**hydroelectric**
ADJECTIVE **Hydroelectric** power is electricity produced from the energy of moving water.

**hydrogen**
NOUN a colourless gas that is the lightest and most common element in the world. **Hydrogen**-filled balloons may explode because this gas is very flammable.

**hyena hyenas**; also spelt **hyaena**
NOUN a wild, dog-like animal found in Africa and Asia, that hunts in packs

WORD HISTORY
from Greek *huaina* meaning hog

**hygiene**
NOUN the state of being clean and free of germs

**hymn hymns**
NOUN a Christian song in praise of God

**hyphen hyphens**
NOUN a punctuation mark (-) used to join together words or parts of words, as in *left-handed*

**hypocrisy**
NOUN behaviour that shows that someone does not really believe what they say they do

**hypocrite hypocrites**
NOUN someone who pretends to have certain views and beliefs that are different from their actual views and beliefs

**hypocritical**
ADJECTIVE behaving in a way that shows you do not really have the beliefs that you say you do

**hypothermia**
NOUN a condition in which a person is very ill because their body has been extremely cold for a long time ● *After spending the night stuck on the mountain, the climbers had* **hypothermia**.

**I**
PRONOUN A speaker or writer uses **I** to refe themselves.

**ice**
NOUN water that has frozen solid

**iceberg icebergs**
NOUN a large mass of ice floating in the s

WORD HISTORY
from Dutch *ijsberg* meaning ice mounta

**ice cream ice creams**
NOUN a very cold, sweet, creamy food

**ice skate ice skates, ice skating, ice skated**; also spelt **ice-skate**
NOUN **1** a boot with a metal blade on the bottom, that you wear to move around ice
VERB **2** When you **ice-skate**, you move a on the ice wearing ice skates.

**icicle icicles**
NOUN a piece of ice shaped like a pointed stick, that hangs down from a surface

**icing**
NOUN a sweet covering for a cake or biscu

**n icons**

NOUN **1** a picture on a computer screen representing a program that can be activated by moving the cursor over it

NOUN **2** a holy picture of Christ, the Virgin Mary or a saint

NOUN an abbreviation of *Information and Communication Technology*. **ICT** is the use of computers, telephones, television and radio to store, organise and give out information.

**icier, iciest**

ADJECTIVE **1** Something that is **icy** is very cold. *We tried to shelter from the icy wind.*

ADJECTIVE **2** An **icy** road has ice on it.

contraction of *I had* or *I would*

**a ideas**

NOUN **1** a plan or possible course of action

NOUN **2** an opinion or belief

NOUN **3** If you have an **idea** of something, you have a general but not a detailed knowledge of it. • *Could you give me an idea of the cost?*

**al**

ADJECTIVE The **ideal** person or thing for a particular purpose is the best possible one.

**ntical**

ADJECTIVE exactly the same • *They are identical twins.*

**ntifiable**

ADJECTIVE possible to recognise and name

**ntification**

NOUN a document, such as a driving licence or passport, that states who you are

**ntify identifies, identifying, identified**

VERB If you **identify** someone or something, you recognise and name them.

**ntity identities**

NOUN the things that make you who you are

**om idioms**

NOUN a group of words that, when used together, mean something different from when the words are used individually. For example, *it rained cats and dogs.*

**ot idiots**

NOUN someone who is stupid or foolish

**otic**

ADJECTIVE very stupid

**idle idler, idlest**

ADJECTIVE **1** If you are **idle**, you are doing nothing.

ADJECTIVE **2** Machines or factories that are **idle** are not being used.

ADJECTIVE **3** lazy

**idleness**

NOUN **1** **Idleness** is when a person or machine is doing nothing.

NOUN **2** laziness

**idly**

ADVERB **1** without any particular purpose • *He was playing idly with his pen.*

ADVERB **2** without doing anything

**idol idols**

NOUN a famous person who is loved and admired by fans

**i.e.**

**i.e.** means *that is.* • *Please meet me in three days' time, i.e. on Sunday.*

WORD HISTORY

from Latin *id est* meaning that is

**if**

CONJUNCTION **1** on condition that • *You can watch TV if you do your homework first.*

CONJUNCTION **2** whether • *I asked him if he could come to the party.*

**igloo igloos**

NOUN a dome-shaped house built out of blocks of snow by Inuit people

WORD HISTORY

from *igdlu*, an Inuit word meaning house

**ignite ignites, igniting, ignited**

VERB If you **ignite** something, or it **ignites**, you set it on fire or it catches fire.

WORD HISTORY

from Latin *ignis* meaning fire

**ignorant**

ADJECTIVE If you are **ignorant** of something, you do not know about it.

**ignore ignores, ignoring, ignored**

VERB If you **ignore** someone or something, you do not take any notice of them.

**iguana iguanas**

NOUN a large, tropical lizard

a
b
c
d
e
f
g
h
i
j
k
l
m
n
o
p
q
r
s
t
u
v
w
x
y
z

**199**

## il-

PREFIX You add **il-** to the beginning of a word to mean that it is not something. For example, **il**legal means not legal, and **il**legible means not legible.

## I'll

a contraction of *I will* or *I shall*

## ill

ADJECTIVE unhealthy or sick

SYNONYM: unwell

WORD HISTORY
from Norse *illr* meaning bad

## illegal

ADJECTIVE If something is **illegal** it is forbidden by the law.

SYNONYMS: criminal, unlawful

## illegible

ADJECTIVE Writing that is **illegible** is unclear and very difficult to read.

ANTONYM: legible

## illegibly

ADVERB in a way that is unclear and very difficult to read

ANTONYM: legibly

## illegitimate

ADJECTIVE If something is **illegitimate** it is not allowed by law, or is not accepted as fair by most people.

## illiterate

ADJECTIVE unable to read or write

ANTONYM: literate

## illness illnesses

NOUN **1** the state or experience of being ill
NOUN **2** a particular disease • *Flu is a common **illness** during the winter months.*

## illogical

ADJECTIVE An **illogical** feeling or action is not reasonable or sensible.

ANTONYM: logical

## illuminate illuminates, illuminating, illuminated

VERB If you **illuminate** something, you shine light on to it so that it is easier to see, or you decorate it with lights.

## illumination illuminations

NOUN one of the coloured lights put up to decorate a town, especially at Christmas

## illusion illusions

NOUN **1** an idea that you think is true, but not • *We were under the **illusion** that this going to be an easy project.*
NOUN **2** something that seems to be there but does not really exist

## illustrate illustrates, illustrating, illustrated

VERB **1** If you **illustrate** a book, you help explain its meaning by putting in picture and diagrams.
VERB **2** If you **illustrate** a point when you are speaking, you make its meaning clea often by giving examples.

## illustration illustrations

NOUN a picture or a diagram that helps to explain something

## illustrator illustrators

NOUN someone who creates the pictures t go into books

## I'm

a contraction of *I am*

## im-

PREFIX You add **im-** to the beginning of a word to mean not something. For examp something that is **im**movable cannot be moved, and something that is **im**perfect not perfect.

## image images

NOUN a picture or photograph • *There are some beautiful **images** in the book.*

## imagery

NOUN The **imagery** of a poem or book is t words that are used to produce a picture the mind of the reader.

## imaginary

ADJECTIVE Something that is **imaginary** ex only in your mind, not in real life.

ANTONYM: real

## imagination imaginations

NOUN If you show **imagination**, you have the ability to form ideas and pictures in your mind.

**aginative**

ADJECTIVE If you are **imaginative**, you find
easy to create new and exciting ideas in
our mind.

ANTONYM: unimaginative

**agine imagines, imagining,
magined**

VERB If you **imagine** something or someone,
ou create a picture of them in
our mind.

**am**

NOUN a person who leads a group in prayer
n a mosque

**itate imitates, imitating, imitated**

VERB If you **imitate** someone or something,
ou copy them.

SYNONYM: mimic

**itation imitations**

NOUN a copy of something else

**mature**

ADJECTIVE **1** Something that is **immature** is
not fully grown or developed.

ANTONYM: mature

ADJECTIVE **2** An **immature** person does not
behave in a sensible way.

ANTONYM: mature

**mediate**

ADJECTIVE Something that is **immediate**
happens or is done without delay.

**mediately**

ADVERB If something happens **immediately**,
it happens at once.

**mense**

ADJECTIVE very large

SYNONYMS: huge, vast

**merse immerses, immersing,
immersed**

VERB **1** If you **immerse** something, you cover
it completely with liquid.

VERB **2** If you **immerse** yourself in an activity,
you become completely occupied with it.

**mersion**

NOUN **1** **Immersion** is when you cover
something completely with liquid.

NOUN **2** **Immersion** is when you become
completely involved in an activity.

**immigrant immigrants**

NOUN someone who has come to live in a
country from another country

**immigrate immigrates, immigrating,
immigrated**

VERB If someone **immigrates**, they come
to live permanently in a country that is not
their own.

ANTONYM: emigrate

**immobile**

ADJECTIVE If something or someone is
**immobile**, they are not moving.

**immoral**

ADJECTIVE If someone is **immoral**, they do
not follow most people's standards of
acceptable behaviour.

**immortal**

ADJECTIVE **1** Someone or something that
is **immortal** is famous and will be
remembered for a long time.

ADJECTIVE **2** Something that is **immortal** will
last forever.

**immune**

ADJECTIVE If you are **immune** to a particular
disease, you cannot catch it.

**immunisation**; also spelt
**immunization**

NOUN **Immunisation** is when a doctor or
nurse gives you an injection so that you are
protected from catching a disease.

**immunise immunises, immunising,
immunised**; also spelt **immunize**

VERB If a doctor or nurse **immunises** you
against a disease, they give you an injection
so that you are protected from the disease.

**immunity**

NOUN If you have **immunity** to a particular
disease, you cannot catch it.

**impact impacts**

NOUN **1** The **impact** of one object on another
is the force with which it hits it.

NOUN **2** If something has an **impact** on a
situation or person, it has a strong effect
on them.

WORD HISTORY
from Latin *impactus* meaning pushed
against

a
b
c
d
e
f
g
h
i
j
k
l
m
n
o
p
q
r
s
t
u
v
w
x
y
z

**201**

**impartial**

ADJECTIVE If you are **impartial** about something, you are fair and unbiased.

ANTONYM: partial

**impatience**

NOUN a feeling of being annoyed because you do not want to wait for someone or something

ANTONYM: patience

**impatient**

ADJECTIVE If you are **impatient**, you become annoyed easily because you do not want to wait for someone or something.

ANTONYM: patient

**impatiently**

ADVERB in a way that shows you are annoyed because you do not want to wait for someone or something

ANTONYM: patiently

**imperfect**

ADJECTIVE Something that is **imperfect** has faults.

**imperial**

ADJECTIVE 1 relating to an empire, emperor or empress

ADJECTIVE 2 The **imperial** system of measurement is a system that uses inches, feet and yards, ounces and pounds, and pints and gallons.

**impersonal**

ADJECTIVE Something that is **impersonal** makes you feel that individuals and their feelings do not matter.

**impersonate** impersonates, impersonating, impersonated

VERB If you **impersonate** someone, you pretend to be that person.

**impertinent**

ADJECTIVE If you are **impertinent**, you are disrespectful and rude to someone.

**imply** implies, implying, implied

VERB If you **imply** that something is the case, you suggest it but do not say it directly.

• Are you **implying** that I lied?

**import** imports, importing, imported

VERB 1 If someone **imports** something, they buy it or bring it in from another country.

ANTONYM: export

NOUN 2 **Imports** are goods brought into a country from another country.

ANTONYM: export

PRONUNCIATION TIP

The verb is pronounced im-**port**. The noun is pronounced **im**-port.

**important**

ADJECTIVE 1 Something that is **important** is very valuable, necessary or significant. • It is **important** not to tell lies.

ADJECTIVE 2 An **important** person has a lot of influence or power.

**impose** imposes, imposing, imposed

VERB If someone **imposes** something on someone, they force it on them.

**imposing**

ADJECTIVE If someone or something is **imposing**, they look impressive and important.

**impossibility** impossibilities

NOUN something that cannot happen or cannot be done

**impossible**

ADJECTIVE Something that is **impossible** cannot happen or cannot be done. • It is **impossible** to see in the dark.

**impossibly**

ADVERB in a way that does not seem possible

**imposter** imposters

NOUN An **imposter** is someone who pretends to be someone else, usually as part of a trick or a crime.

**impractical**

ADJECTIVE If someone or something is **impractical**, they are not sensible or realistic. • It is **impractical** to camp in this wet weather.

ANTONYM: practical

**ress impresses, impressing, npressed**

RB **1** If you **impress** someone, you cause em to admire or respect you.
RB **2** If you **impress** something on meone, you make sure that they nderstand it and remember it.

**pression impressions**

UN **1** An **impression** of someone or mething is a vague idea or feeling at you have about them. ● *I have the npression that I've met you before.*
UN **2** a mark made by pressing ● *You leave n impression when you press a coin into utty then take it away.*
UN **3** an imitation of a person, animal or ing

**pressive**

DJECTIVE If someone or something is mpressive, it causes you to admire or espect it.

**prison imprisons, imprisoning, nprisoned**

RB If someone **imprisons** another person, hey put them in prison or lock them up omewhere.

**prisonment**

OUN **Imprisonment** is when someone is ept in prison or is locked up somewhere.

**probable**

DJECTIVE not probable or likely to happen

ANTONYM: probable

**proper fraction improper ractions**

OUN In mathematics, an **improper fraction** is a fraction where the numerator s bigger than the denominator.

**prove improves, improving, improved**

VERB If something **improves**, or if you **improve** it, it gets better.

**provement improvements**

NOUN a change that shows something or someone is getting better

**provise improvises, improvising, improvised**

VERB **1** If you **improvise** something, you make or do something without planning it in advance, and with whatever materials are available. ● *In order to save money the children **improvised** their costumes for the school play.*

VERB **2** When musicians or actors **improvise**, they make up the music or words as they go along.

**impudent**

ADJECTIVE If you are **impudent**, you are rude and disrespectful.

**impulse impulses**

NOUN If you have an **impulse** to do something, you have a strong urge to do it immediately.

**impulsive**

ADJECTIVE Someone who is **impulsive** does things immediately without thinking about the possible risks or problems.

**in**

PREPOSITION **1** at or inside ● *The cow was **in** the field.*
PREPOSITION **2** during ● *It snows **in** winter.*
ADVERB **3** towards the inside of a place or thing ● *I knocked on the door, and went **in**.*
ADVERB **4** at home ● *Is Jake **in**?*

**in-**

PREFIX You add **in-** to the beginning of a word to mean not something. For example, **in**accurate means not accurate, and **in**accessible means not accessible.

**inability inabilities**

NOUN If you have an **inability** to do something, you cannot do it.

ANTONYM: ability

**inaccessible**

ADJECTIVE If something is **inaccessible**, it is very difficult or impossible to reach.

ANTONYM: accessible

**inaccurate**

ADJECTIVE If something is **inaccurate**, it is incorrect.

ANTONYM: accurate

**inadequate**

ADJECTIVE If something is **inadequate**, there is not enough of it, or it is not good enough for a particular purpose.

ANTONYM: adequate

**inanimate**

ADJECTIVE not alive. For example, rocks and furniture are **inanimate**.

a
b
c
d
e
f
g
h
i
j
k
l
m
n
o
p
q
r
s
t
u
v
w
x
y
z

## inaudible

ADJECTIVE If something is **inaudible**, it cannot be heard.

ANTONYM: audible

## incapable

ADJECTIVE Someone who is **incapable** of doing something is not able to do it.

ANTONYM: capable

## incendiary

ADJECTIVE An **incendiary** device is designed to set fire to things.

## incense

NOUN a spicy substance that gives off a sweet smell when it is burned

## incessant

ADJECTIVE If something is **incessant**, it continues without stopping. • *The sound of the rain on the windows was **incessant**.*

## inch inches

NOUN a unit of length equal to about 2.54 centimetres

WORD HISTORY
from Latin *uncia* meaning twelfth part; there are twelve inches in a foot

## incident incidents

NOUN an event or occurrence, especially an unusual one

## incidentally

ADVERB If something happens **incidentally**, it happens along with something else, as a minor part of it.

## incinerate incinerates, incinerating, incinerated

VERB If you **incinerate** something, you burn it until only ashes are left.

## incineration

NOUN the process of burning something until only ashes are left

## incisor incisors

NOUN Your **incisors** are the sharp teeth at the front of your mouth, used for biting and cutting food.

→ Have a look at the illustration for **teeth**

## inclination inclinations

NOUN If you have an **inclination** to do something, you want to do it.

## incline inclines, inclining, inclined

VERB **1** If you are **inclined** to do something, you often do it or you would like to do it.
NOUN **2** a slope

PRONUNCIATION TIP
The verb is pronounced in-**klyn**. The noun is pronounced **in**-klyn.

## include includes, including, included

VERB If one thing **includes** another, the second thing is part of the first thing.
• *Meals are **included** in the price at this hotel.*

ANTONYM: exclude

## inclusive

ADJECTIVE When something is **inclusive**, it includes everything and nothing is left out. • *The price for the meal was **inclusive**, so Gran had nothing extra to pay for our milkshakes.*

## incognito

ADVERB If someone is **incognito**, they are in disguise.

WORD HISTORY
from Latin *in* + *cognitus* meaning not known

## income incomes

NOUN the money a person earns

## incomplete

ADJECTIVE Something that is **incomplete** is not complete or finished.

ANTONYM: complete

## incongruous

ADJECTIVE If something is **incongruous** in a particular place or situation, it seems unsuitable and out of place.

## inconsiderate

ADJECTIVE If you are **inconsiderate**, you do not consider the needs or feelings of others. • *What an **inconsiderate** thing to do!*

ANTONYM: considerate

## inconspicuous

ADJECTIVE If someone or something is **inconspicuous**, they are not noticeable or obvious, and cannot easily be seen.

ANTONYM: conspicuous

## inconvenient

ADJECTIVE If something is **inconvenient**, it is awkward and causes difficulties.
● an **inconvenient** time to call

ANTONYM: convenient

## incorporate incorporates, incorporating, incorporated

VERB If someone **incorporates** one thing into another thing, they include the first thing so that it becomes part of the second.

## incorrect

ADJECTIVE Something that is **incorrect** is wrong or untrue.

ANTONYM: correct

## increase increases, increasing, increased

VERB 1 If something **increases**, or if you **increase** it, it becomes larger in number, level or amount. ● Her dad **increased** her pocket money.

ANTONYM: decrease

NOUN 2 a rise in the number, level or amount of something ● There has been an **increase** in the number of children walking to school.

ANTONYM: decrease

## incredible

ADJECTIVE totally amazing or impossible to believe

SYNONYM: unbelievable

## incubate incubates, incubating, incubated

VERB When eggs **incubate**, or a bird **incubates** them, they are kept warm until they hatch.

## incubator incubators

NOUN a piece of hospital equipment in which sick or weak newborn babies are kept warm and safe

## incurable

ADJECTIVE If someone has an **incurable** disease, they cannot be cured.

ANTONYM: curable

## indebted

ADJECTIVE If you are **indebted** to someone, you are very grateful to them.

## indecent

ADJECTIVE Something that is **indecent** is shocking or rude.

ANTONYM: decent

## indecisive

ADJECTIVE If someone is **indecisive**, they find it difficult to make up their mind.

ANTONYM: decisive

## indeed

ADVERB 1 You use **indeed** to emphasise a point that you are making. ● The cake was very good **indeed**.
ADVERB 2 You use **indeed** to show that you agree with something. ● "Are you going to the party?" "**Indeed** I am."

## indefinite

ADJECTIVE If something is **indefinite**, it is vague and unclear.

ANTONYM: definite

## indefinitely

ADVERB If something goes on **indefinitely**, there is no clear time when it will finish and it can go on for an unlimited time.

## indent indents, indenting, indented

VERB If you **indent** a paragraph when you write, you start the first line further to the right, away from the margin.

## independence

NOUN 1 the ability to do things yourself without help from other people
NOUN 2 the freedom to make your own decisions and not be controlled by anyone else

## independent

ADJECTIVE 1 If you are **independent**, you are able to do things yourself and do not need help from other people.
ADJECTIVE 2 free and not controlled by anyone

## independently

ADVERB without help from other people

**205**

## indestructible
ADJECTIVE If something is **indestructible**, it cannot be destroyed.

## index indexes
NOUN an alphabetical list at the back of a book which tells you where to find information in the book

## indicate indicates, indicating, indicated
VERB 1 If you **indicate** something to someone, you point it out or show it to them.

VERB 2 If the driver of a vehicle **indicates**, they give a signal to show which way they are going to move or turn. • *The cyclist **indicated** that he was turning right.*

## indicator indicators
NOUN 1 something that tells you what something is like or what is happening

NOUN 2 A car's **indicators** are the lights at the front and back that are used to show when it is turning left or right.

→ Have a look at the illustration for **car**

## indifferent
ADJECTIVE If you are **indifferent** to something, you have no interest in it.

## indigestion
NOUN a pain you get when you have difficulty digesting food

## indignant
ADJECTIVE If you are **indignant** about something, you are angry about it because you think it is unfair.

## indigo
ADJECTIVE deep blue or violet

## indirect
ADJECTIVE If something happens in an **indirect** way, it does not happen in a straightforward way.

ANTONYM: direct

## indispensable
ADJECTIVE absolutely necessary; essential

## indistinct
ADJECTIVE not clear

ANTONYM: distinct

## individual individuals
ADJECTIVE 1 relating to one particular person or thing • *Each child in the class gets **individual** attention.*

ADJECTIVE 2 single or separate • *Each sweet i the packet comes in an **individual** wrapper.*

NOUN 3 a person, different from any other person • *We should treat people as **individuals**.*

## indoor
ADJECTIVE happening inside a building • *The hotel has an **indoor** swimming pool.*

## indoors
ADVERB If something happens **indoors**, it takes place inside a building.

## indulge indulges, indulging, indulged
VERB 1 If you **indulge** in something, you allow yourself to do it because you enjoy i

VERB 2 If you **indulge** someone, you allow them to have or do what they want.

## indulgence indulgences
NOUN 1 something that you allow yourself have or do because you like it

NOUN 2 **Indulgence** is when you allow someone to have or do what they want.

## industrial
ADJECTIVE to do with the work and processes involved in making things in factories

## industrious
ADJECTIVE If you are **industrious**, you work hard.

## industry industries
NOUN 1 the work involved in making things in factories

NOUN 2 all the people and processes involve in manufacturing a particular thing • *My dad works in the computer **industry**.*

WORD HISTORY
from Latin *industria* meaning diligence or hard work

## inedible
ADJECTIVE If something is **inedible**, it is too unpleasant or poisonous to eat.

## inefficient
ADJECTIVE badly organised, wasteful and slow

## inevitable
ADJECTIVE certain to happen

## inexpensive
ADJECTIVE not costing much

## inexplicable
ADJECTIVE If something is **inexplicable**, you cannot explain it.

**explicably**

ADVERB in a way that cannot be explained

**famous**

ADJECTIVE Someone or something that is **infamous** is well known for their bad qualities.

SYNONYM: notorious

PRONUNCIATION TIP
This word is pronounced **in**-fum-uss.

**fant infants**

NOUN a baby or very young child

WORD HISTORY
from Latin *infans* meaning unable to speak

**fantry**

NOUN In an army, the **infantry** are soldiers who fight on foot rather than in tanks or on horses.

**fatuated**

ADJECTIVE If you are **infatuated** with someone, you are so much in love with them that you cannot think reasonably about them.

**fect infects, infecting, infected**

VERB If someone or something **infects** another person or animal, they pass a disease on to them.

**fection infections**

NOUN an illness caused by germs

**fectious**

ADJECTIVE Something that is **infectious** spreads from one person to another.
• *Measles is an **infectious** disease.*

**fer infers, inferring, inferred**

VERB If you **infer** that something is happening or is correct, you work it out from the details you already have.

**ference inferences**

NOUN something that you think must be true, based on the details that you already have

**ferior**

ADJECTIVE Something that is **inferior** is not as good as something else of a similar kind.
• *The trainers were of **inferior** quality.*

**feriority**

NOUN **Inferiority** is a lower quality or level of importance than something else.

**inferno infernos**

NOUN a huge and fierce fire

**infertile**

ADJECTIVE **1 Infertile** soil is of poor quality and plants cannot grow well in it.
ADJECTIVE **2** A person, animal or plant that is **infertile** is unable to reproduce.

**infested**

ADJECTIVE If something is **infested**, it is full of pests, like insects, rats or fleas.

**infinite**

ADJECTIVE If something is **infinite**, it is endless and without limits.

**infinitely**

ADVERB very much • *I think good health is **infinitely** more important than having lots of money.*

**infinitive infinitives**

NOUN the base form of a verb. An **infinitive** often has "to" in front of it, for example *to be* or *to see*.

**infinity**

NOUN a number that is larger than any other number and cannot be given an exact value

**infirm**

ADJECTIVE If someone is **infirm**, they are weak because they are ill or old.

**infirmary infirmaries**

NOUN a hospital

**inflammable**

ADJECTIVE An **inflammable** material burns easily.

**inflammation**

NOUN painful redness or swelling of a part of the body

**inflatable**

ADJECTIVE An **inflatable** object must be filled with air before you use it.

**inflate inflates, inflating, inflated**

VERB If you **inflate** something, you put air or a gas such as helium into it to make it swell.

ANTONYM: deflate

**inflation**

NOUN a general increase in the price of goods and services in a country

**inflexible**

ADJECTIVE If someone or something is **inflexible**, they cannot be bent or altered.

a
b
c
d
e
f
g
h
i
j
k
l
m
n
o
p
q
r
s
t
u
v
w
x
y
z

**207**

A
B
C
D
E
F
G
H
I
J
K
L
M
N
O
P
Q
R
S
T
U
V
W
X
Y
Z

**inflict** inflicts, inflicting, inflicted
VERB If you **inflict** something unpleasant on someone, you make them suffer it.

**influence** influences, influencing, influenced
VERB If you **influence** someone or something, you have an effect on what they do or what happens.

**influential**
ADJECTIVE Someone who is **influential** is important and can influence people or events.

WORD HISTORY
from Latin *influentia* meaning power flowing from the stars

**influenza**
NOUN (*formal*) flu

**inform** informs, informing, informed
VERB If you **inform** somebody about something, you let them know about it.

**informal**
ADJECTIVE relaxed and casual

**informally**
ADVERB in a relaxed and casual way • *She was* **informally** *dressed in jeans and a T-shirt.*

**information**
NOUN knowledge about something • *He used the encyclopedia to find more* **information**.

**information technology**
NOUN the storage and communication of information using computers

**informative**
ADJECTIVE Something that is **informative** gives you information.

**infrastructure** infrastructures
NOUN the basic facilities such as transport, communications, power supplies and buildings, which enable a country to function properly

**infuriate** infuriates, infuriating, infuriated
VERB If someone or something **infuriates** you, they make you very angry.

**infuriating**
ADJECTIVE making you very angry

**ingenious**
ADJECTIVE Something that is **ingenious** is clever and involves new ideas.

**ingratitude**
NOUN If you show **ingratitude**, you show lack of care or thanks for something that has been done for you.
ANTONYM: gratitude

**ingredient** ingredients
NOUN **Ingredients** are the things that something is made from, especially in cookery.

**inhabit** inhabits, inhabiting, inhabite
VERB If you **inhabit** a place, you live there.

**inhabitant** inhabitants
NOUN If you are an **inhabitant** of a place, you live there.

**inhalation**
NOUN **Inhalation** is breathing in.

**inhale** inhales, inhaling, inhaled
VERB When you **inhale** something, you breathe it in.
ANTONYM: exhale

**inherit** inherits, inheriting, inherited
VERB 1 If you **inherit** money or property, yc receive it from someone who has died.
VERB 2 If you **inherit** a feature or quality fro a parent or ancestor, you are born with it.
• *Her children have* **inherited** *her love of spo*

**inheritance**
NOUN 1 Your **inheritance** is the money or property you get from someone who has died.
NOUN 2 the physical or mental qualities tho you get from your parents

**inhospitable**
ADJECTIVE 1 If you are **inhospitable**, you are unwelcoming to people who visit you.
ADJECTIVE 2 An **inhospitable** place is an unpleasant and difficult place to live in.

**inhuman**
ADJECTIVE 1 not human or not behaving like human
ADJECTIVE 2 extremely cruel

**initial** initials
NOUN 1 one of the capital letters that begin each word of a name
ADJECTIVE 2 first or at the beginning

**initiative**
NOUN If you show **initiative**, you have the ability to see what needs to be done and d it, without relying on others.

**ect injects, injecting, injected**
VERB If a doctor or nurse **injects** you, they use a needle and syringe to put medicine into your body.

**WORD HISTORY**
From Latin in + jacere meaning to throw into

**ure injures, injuring, injured**
VERB If you **injure** someone, you hurt or harm them in some way.

**ury injuries**
NOUN damage to part of a person's or animal's body

**ustice**
NOUN If someone suffers **injustice**, they are treated unfairly.

**k**
NOUN the coloured liquid used for writing or printing

**land**
ADJECTIVE 1 If a place is **inland**, it is away from the coast. • **inland** lakes
ADVERB 2 away from the coast • Most of the population lives **inland**.

**let inlets**
NOUN a narrow bay or channel of water that goes inland from the sea, a lake or a river

**mate inmates**
NOUN someone who lives in an institution, such as a prison

**n inns**
NOUN a small, old country pub or hotel

**ner**
ADJECTIVE contained inside a place or object • The **inner** tube of my front tyre has a puncture.

**nings**
NOUN In cricket, an **innings** is a period of time when a particular team is batting.

**nocence**
NOUN **Innocence** is when someone is not guilty of a crime or of doing something wrong.

ANTONYM: guilt

**nocent**
ADJECTIVE not guilty of a crime or of doing something wrong

ANTONYM: guilty

**innocently**
ADVERB 1 without intending to harm or offend anyone • The argument began **innocently** enough.
ADVERB 2 in a way that shows you do not have much experience of bad things that can happen • "What's the problem?" Carl asked **innocently**.

**innovation innovations**
NOUN a completely new idea, product or way of doing things

**inoculate inoculates, inoculating, inoculated**
VERB If a doctor or nurse **inoculates** you, they give you an injection to protect you from catching a particular disease.

**inoculation**
NOUN **Inoculation** is the process of giving people injections to protect them from catching particular diseases.

**input inputs, inputting, input**
NOUN 1 Your **input** is your contribution and what you put into something. • The class project requires **input** from everyone.
NOUN 2 In computing, **input** is information that is fed into a computer.
VERB 3 To **input** information into a computer means to feed it in.

**inquest inquests**
NOUN an official inquiry to find out what caused a person's death

**inquire inquires, inquired, inquiring;** also spelt **enquire**
VERB If you **inquire** about something, you ask for information about it.

**inquiry inquiries**
NOUN 1 an official investigation
NOUN 2 a question or a request for information

**inquisitive**
ADJECTIVE Someone who is **inquisitive** is keen to find out about things.

**insane**
ADJECTIVE Someone or something **insane** is mad.

**inscription inscriptions**
NOUN the words that are carved or engraved on something such as a monument, gravestone or coin, or written in the front of a book

a
b
c
d
e
f
g
h
i
j
k
l
m
n
o
p
q
r
s
t
u
v
w
x
y
z

**209**

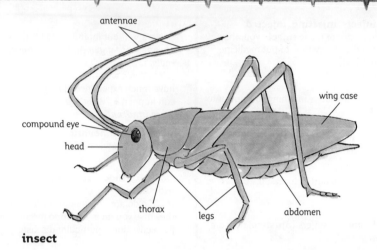

antennae

wing case

compound eye

head

thorax

legs

abdomen

insect

## insect insects
NOUN a small animal with six legs and no backbone, with its skeleton on the outside. **Insects** often have wings, for example beetles, butterflies and grasshoppers.

WORD HISTORY

from Latin *insectum* meaning animal that has been cut into, because the bodies of many insects are divided into parts

## insecticide insecticides
NOUN a poisonous chemical used to kill insects

## insecure
ADJECTIVE **1** If you feel **insecure**, you lack confidence and feel worried.
ADJECTIVE **2** If something is **insecure**, it is not fixed properly.

## insecurity insecurities
NOUN the feeling you have when you are not confident about yourself because you think that you are not good enough

## inseparable
ADJECTIVE **1** If people are **inseparable**, they are always together. ● *The three of them are such good friends, they're **inseparable**.*
ADJECTIVE **2** If things are **inseparable**, they cannot be parted.

## insert inserts, inserting, inserted
VERB If you **insert** an object into something, you put it inside. ● *He **inserted** the key into the lock.*

## inside insides
PREPOSITION **1 Inside** means in something. ● *I waited **inside** the house.*

ANTONYM: outside

ADJECTIVE **2** describes something that is in something else ● *an **inside** pocket*

ANTONYM: outside

ADVERB **3** into a building ● *We chatted for a while before going **inside**.*

ANTONYM: outside

NOUN **4** The **inside** of something is the part that is surrounded by the main part, and is often hidden. ● *I painted the **inside** of the she*

ANTONYM: outside

PHRASE **5 Inside out** means with the inside part facing outwards. ● *Her umbrella blew **inside out**.*

PLURAL NOUN **6** Your **insides** are the parts within your body that cannot be seen.

LANGUAGE TIP

Do not use *of* after *inside* when it is a preposition. It is correct to say *I waited insi the shop*, not *I waited inside of the shop.*

## insight insights
NOUN If you show **insight** into a problem, you show a deep and accurate understanding of it.

## insignificance
NOUN the quality that something has when is small and unimportant

**significant**
ADJECTIVE small and unimportant

**insist insists, insisting, insisted**
VERB If you **insist** on something, you demand it forcefully. • *As it was already dark, she **insisted** on giving us a lift home.*

**insistent**
ADJECTIVE If you are **insistent**, you insist on having or doing something.

**insolence**
NOUN very rude behaviour that shows no respect

**insolent**
ADJECTIVE very rude and showing no respect

**insolently**
ADVERB in a very rude way that shows no respect

**insoluble**
ADJECTIVE **1** impossible to solve
ADJECTIVE **2** unable to dissolve

**insomnia**
NOUN difficulty in sleeping

**inspect inspects, inspecting, inspected**
VERB If you **inspect** something, you examine or check it carefully.

**inspector inspectors**
NOUN **1** someone in authority whose job it is to inspect things
NOUN **2** a rank of police officer

**inspiration**
NOUN someone or something that gives you new ideas for something • *Her experiences in China were the **inspiration** for this book.*

**inspire inspires, inspiring, inspired**
VERB If someone or something **inspires** you, they give you new ideas, confidence and enthusiasm.

**install installs, installing, installed**
VERB If you **install** something, you put it in place so that it is ready to be used.

**installation**
NOUN the process of putting something in place so that it is ready to be used

**instalment instalments**
NOUN **1** If you pay for something in **instalments**, you pay small amounts of money regularly over a period of time.
NOUN **2** one of the parts of a story or television series

**instance instances**
NOUN **1** a particular example or occurrence of something
PHRASE **2** You use **for instance** to give an example of something you are talking about. • *In some countries, **for instance** in Spain, many shops are closed at lunchtime.*

**instant instants**
NOUN **1** a moment or short period of time
ADJECTIVE **2** immediate and without delay
• *The book was an **instant** success.*

**instantly**
ADVERB immediately • *His booming voice was **instantly** recognizable.*

**instead**
ADVERB If you do one thing **instead** of another, you do the first thing and not the second thing. • *They took the stairs **instead** of the lift.*

**instinct instincts**
NOUN a natural tendency to do something in a particular way • *Her **instincts** told her to run away as quickly as possible.*

**institute institutes**
NOUN an organisation set up for a purpose, such as teaching or research

**institution institutions**
NOUN a large, important organisation, such as a university or bank

**instruct instructs, instructing, instructed**
VERB **1** If you **instruct** someone to do something, you tell them to do it.
VERB **2** If someone **instructs** you in a subject or skill, they teach you about it.

**instruction instructions**
NOUN If you follow an **instruction**, you do what someone tells you to do.

**instructor instructors**
NOUN someone who teaches you how to do something • *a ski **instructor***

**instrument instruments**
NOUN **1** a tool that is used to do a particular job
NOUN **2** an object, such as a piano or guitar, that you play to make music

**instrumental**
ADJECTIVE **Instrumental** music is performed by instruments and not by voices.

A
B
C
D
E
F
G
H
I
J
K
L
M
N
O
P
Q
R
S
T
U
V
W
X
Y
Z

### insufficient
ADJECTIVE not enough for a particular purpose • *There is **insufficient** flour to make two cakes.*

### insulate **insulates, insulating, insulated**
VERB If you **insulate** something, you cover it with materials such as foam or plastic to stop heat or electricity passing out of it.

### insulation
NOUN a thick layer of a substance that keeps something warm, especially a building

### insulator **insulators**
NOUN a material that insulates something

### insulin
NOUN a substance that controls the level of sugar in your blood

### insult **insults, insulting, insulted**
VERB 1 If you **insult** someone, you offend them by being rude to them.
NOUN 2 a rude remark that offends someone

---

**PRONUNCIATION TIP**
The verb is pronounced in-**sult**. The noun is pronounced **in**-sult.

---

### insurance
NOUN an amount of money paid on a regular basis to a company that, in return, will pay you money if you have an accident or need medical treatment

### intact
ADJECTIVE If something is **intact**, it is complete and undamaged.

### integer **integers**
NOUN a whole number. For example, 2 is an **integer** but 2½ is not.

### integrate **integrates, integrating, integrated**
VERB If a person **integrates** into a group, they become a part of it.

### integrity
NOUN the quality of being honest and trustworthy

### intellectual
ADJECTIVE involving thought, ideas and understanding • *an **intellectual** exercise, like learning French*

### intelligence
NOUN Your **intelligence** is your ability to understand and learn things.

### intelligent
ADJECTIVE clever and able to understand things easily

### intend **intends, intending, intended**
VERB If you **intend** to do something, you decide or plan to do it.

### intense
ADJECTIVE very great in strength or amount • *intense heat*

### intensity
NOUN the strength of something such as a feeling, colour or temperature

### intensive
ADJECTIVE If something is **intensive**, it involves a lot of energy or effort over a sh◆ time.

### intention **intentions**
NOUN an idea or a plan of what you mean do • *He had every **intention** of working ha. that day.*

### intentional
ADJECTIVE If something is **intentional**, it is done on purpose.

### intentionally
ADVERB deliberately • *I would never **intentionally** hurt anyone.*

### inter-
PREFIX You add **inter-** to a word to mean between or among two or more people or things. • ***inter**-school competitions* • ***inter**national travel*

### interactive
ADJECTIVE If a computer is **interactive**, it allows two-way communication between itself and the person using it, so that information can pass in both directions.

### intercept **intercepts, intercepting, intercepted**
VERB If you **intercept** someone or somethi◆ as they move from one place to another, you stop them reaching their destination.

### intercom **intercoms**
NOUN a device that people use to communicate with each other if they are i◆ different rooms

**terest interests, interesting, interested**
NOUN **1** a thing you enjoy doing
NOUN **2** **Interest** is an extra payment that you receive if you have invested money, or an extra payment that you make if you have borrowed money.
VERB **3** If something **interests** you, you want to know more about it.

**terface interfaces**
NOUN The **interface** of a particular piece of computing software is how it looks on screen and how easy it is to use.

**terfere interferes, interfering, interfered**
VERB **1** If you **interfere** in a situation, you try to influence it, although it does not concern you.
VERB **2** If you **interfere** with a plan, you get in the way of it.

**terior interiors**
NOUN **1** the inside part of something • the **interior** of the building
ADJECTIVE **2** inside • the **interior** walls

**terjection interjections**
NOUN a word or phrase spoken suddenly to expresses an emotion, such as surprise, excitement or anger. For example, *Help!* is an **interjection**.

**termediate**
ADJECTIVE An **intermediate** stage occurs in the middle, between two others. • *This dance class is for beginners. The next one is at intermediate level.*

**ternal**
ADJECTIVE happening on, or part of, the inside of something • *Your lungs are **internal** organs.*

**ternational**
ADJECTIVE involving different countries • *This is an important **international** match.*

**ternet**; also spelt **Internet**
NOUN a worldwide system where people communicate using computers

**terpret interprets, interpreting, interpreted**
VERB **1** If you **interpret** something, you decide what it means. • *I tried to interpret his painting.*
VERB **2** If you **interpret** what someone is saying, you immediately translate it into another language.

**interpretation interpretations**
NOUN Your **interpretation** of something is what you think it means.

**interpreter interpreters**
NOUN someone who translates what another person is saying into a different language

**interrogate interrogates, interrogating, interrogated**
VERB If you **interrogate** someone, you ask them a lot of questions in order to get information from them.

**interrogation interrogations**
NOUN the process of asking someone a lot of questions in order to get information from them

**interrogator interrogators**
NOUN someone who asks another person a lot of questions in order to get information from them

**interrupt interrupts, interrupting, interrupted**
VERB If you **interrupt** someone, you start talking while they are talking.

**intersect intersects, intersecting, intersected**
VERB When two roads **intersect**, they cross each other.

**intersection intersections**
NOUN **1** a point where two roads cross over each other
NOUN **2** the point where lines, arcs or sets cross each other

**interval intervals**
NOUN a short break during a play, concert or performance

**intervene intervenes, intervening, intervened**
VERB If you **intervene** in a situation, you step in, usually to sort out an argument or fight.

**intervention**
NOUN **Intervention** is when you do something to help stop an argument or fight.

**interview interviews, interviewing, interviewed**
NOUN **1** a formal meeting where someone is asked questions
VERB **2** When someone **interviews** you, they ask you questions, usually in order to find out if you are suitable for something in particular.

**intestinal**

ADJECTIVE involving the long tube in your body that carries food from your stomach

**intestine** **intestines**

NOUN the part of your digestive system that carries food from your stomach. Your **intestines** are long tubes folded up inside your abdomen.

→ Have a look at the illustrations for **organ** and **stomach**

**intimate**

ADJECTIVE **1** If you are **intimate** with someone, you are very friendly with them.
ADJECTIVE **2** **Intimate** details or thoughts are personal or private.

**intimidate** **intimidates, intimidating, intimidated**

VERB If you **intimidate** someone, you frighten them in a threatening way.

**WORD HISTORY**
from Latin *timidus* meaning fearful

**intimidating**

ADJECTIVE making you feel frightened

**into**

PREPOSITION **1** If you go **into** something, you go inside it. ● *Come into the house.*
PREPOSITION **2** If you bump or crash **into** something, you bump or crash against it.

**intrepid**

ADJECTIVE brave and fearless

**intricate**

ADJECTIVE detailed and complicated

**intrigue** **intrigues, intriguing, intrigued**

VERB If something **intrigues** you, you are fascinated by it and curious about it.

**introduce** **introduces, introducing, introduced**

VERB **1** If you **introduce** one person to another, you tell them each other's name so that they can get to know each other.
VERB **2** If you **introduce** someone to something, they learn about it for the first time from you. ● *My friend **introduced** me to water-skiing on holiday.*

**introduction** **introductions**

NOUN a piece of writing at the beginning of a book, that tells you what the book is about

**introductory**

ADJECTIVE giving information that tells you what a book or speech is about

**intrude** **intrudes, intruding, intruded**

VERB If you **intrude** on someone or something, you disturb them.

**intruder** **intruders**

NOUN a person who forces their way into someone else's property without their consent ● *The security guard caught an **intruder** last night.*

**intrusion** **intrusions**

NOUN someone or something that disturbs y

**intrusive**

ADJECTIVE disturbing someone

**intuition** **intuitions**

NOUN the ability to know about something without thinking about it or being able to explain it

**intuitive**

ADJECTIVE based on a feeling rather than on facts or knowledge ● *She has an **intuitive** understanding of human nature.*

**intuitively**

ADVERB in a way that is based on a feeling rather than on facts or knowledge

**Inuit** **Inuits**

NOUN a member of a group of people who live in North America or Greenland, and who lived there before European settlers arrived

**invade** **invades, invading, invaded**

VERB If an army **invades** a country, it enter it by force.

**invalid** **invalids**

NOUN **1** someone who is so ill that they nee to be looked after by someone else
ADJECTIVE **2** If something is **invalid**, it canno be accepted because there is something wrong with it. ● *Your ticket is **invalid** for th train service.*

**PRONUNCIATION TIP**
The noun is pronounced **in**-va-lid. The adjective is pronounced in-**val**-id.

**invaluable**

ADJECTIVE extremely useful

**invasion** **invasions**

NOUN the forceful entering or attacking of a place ● *At the end of the match, there was an **invasion** of the pitch by fans.*

**vent invents, inventing, invented**
VERB **1** If you **invent** something, you are the first person to think of it or make it.
VERB **2** If you **invent** a story or an excuse, you make it up.

**vention inventions**
NOUN **1** something that has been designed and made for the first time
NOUN **2 Invention** the process of designing and making something for the first time.
NOUN **3** an excuse or explanation that is not true

**ventive**
ADJECTIVE good at thinking of new and interesting ideas

**ventiveness**
NOUN **Inventiveness** is the ability to think of new and different ideas.

**ventor inventors**
NOUN someone who is the first person to think of or make something

**verse**
NOUN (formal) In mathematics, if you turn something upside down or back to front, you have its **inverse**. • The **inverse** of 23 is 32.

**vert inverts, inverting, inverted**
VERB **1** If you **invert** something, you turn it upside down.
VERB **2** If you **invert** a fraction, the top number changes places with the bottom number.

**vertebrate invertebrates**
NOUN an animal without a backbone

**verted commas**
NOUN punctuation marks (" ") are used to show where speech begins and ends
• "Good morning!" she cried.

**vest invests, investing, invested**
VERB If you **invest** money in something, you try to increase its value, for example by putting it into a bank or building society so that it will gain interest.

**vestigate investigates, investigating, investigated**
VERB If someone **investigates** something, they try to find out all the facts about it.
• Police are still **investigating** the accident.

SYNONYMS: examine, look into, study

**investigation investigations**
NOUN If you conduct an **investigation** into something, you examine it carefully and try to find out the facts about it.
• The police have begun an **investigation** into the accident.

**investigator investigators**
NOUN someone who tries to find out all the facts about something

**investment investments**
NOUN **1 Investment** is the process of putting money into a bank or business in order to make some money.
NOUN **2** an amount of money that you put into a bank or business in order to make some money
NOUN **3** something you buy that will be very useful • The city travel card is a good **investment**.

**investor investors**
NOUN someone who puts money into a bank or business in order to make some money

**invincible**
ADJECTIVE If something is **invincible**, it cannot be defeated.

**invisibility**
NOUN the quality that something has when you cannot see it

**invisible**
ADJECTIVE If something is **invisible**, you cannot see it.

**invitation invitations**
NOUN a request for someone to come to something, such as a party

**invite invites, inviting, invited**
VERB If you **invite** someone to an event, you ask them to come to it.

**involve involves, involving, involved**
VERB **1** If a situation or activity **involves** something, that thing is a necessary part of it. • Being president **involves** a lot of responsibility.
VERB **2** If you **involve** yourself in something, you take part in it. • I'm **involved** in the production of the school play.

**ir-**
PREFIX a variation of in-, meaning not. For example, **ir**relevant means not relevant, and **ir**replaceable means not replaceable.

**irate**
ADJECTIVE very angry

a
b
c
d
e
f
g
h
i
j
k
l
m
n
o
p
q
r
s
t
u
v
w
x
y
z

**215**

A
B
C
D
E
F
G
H
I
J
K
L
M
N
O
P
Q
R
S
T
U
V
W
X
Y
Z

**iris irises**

NOUN the coloured part of your eye

→ Have a look at the illustration for **eye**

**WORD HISTORY**

from Greek *iris* meaning rainbow or coloured circle

**iron irons, ironing, ironed**

NOUN **1** a hard, dark metal used to make steel

NOUN **2** an appliance you heat up and press on clothes to remove creases

VERB **3** If you **iron** clothes, you use a hot iron to remove creases from them.

**ironic**

ADJECTIVE using words, often in a humorous way, to say the opposite of what you really mean

**ironing**

NOUN the work of using a hot iron to remove creases from clothes

**irony**

NOUN When you use **irony**, you use words, often in a humorous way, to say the opposite of what you really mean.

**irrational**

ADJECTIVE If you act in an **irrational** way, you show no reason or logic in what you do.

**irregular**

ADJECTIVE **1** Something that is **irregular** is not smooth or straight, or does not make a regular pattern.

ADJECTIVE **2 Irregular** verbs do not follow the usual rules.

**irrelevance**

NOUN something that has nothing to do with what is being said or discussed

**irrelevant**

ADJECTIVE If something is **irrelevant**, it has nothing to do with what is being said or discussed.

**irresistible**

ADJECTIVE **1** If something is **irresistible**, it cannot be controlled. • *I had an **irresistible** urge to laugh.*

ADJECTIVE **2** If someone is **irresistible**, they are very attractive.

**irresponsible**

ADJECTIVE If you do something in an **irresponsible** way, you act thoughtlessl and carelessly.

SYNONYMS: careless, thoughtless

**irreversible**

ADJECTIVE If something is **irreversible**, it cannot be reversed or changed back to th way it was before.

**irrigate irrigates, irrigating, irrigated**

VERB To **irrigate** land is to supply it with water brought through pipes or ditches.

• *In hot, dry countries the land is **irrigated**.*

**WORD HISTORY**

from Latin *rigare* meaning to moisten

**irrigation**

NOUN the process of supplying land with water through pipes or ditches

**irritable**

ADJECTIVE If you are **irritable**, you are easily annoyed.

**irritate irritates, irritating, irritated**

VERB If something **irritates** you, it annoys you.

**irritation**

NOUN the feeling of being annoyed

**is**

VERB a present tense of **be**

**Islam**

NOUN the Muslim religion, which teaches that there is only one God, Allah, and Mohammed is his prophet

**island islands**

NOUN a piece of land surrounded by water

**isle isles**

NOUN a literary word for an island

**isn't**

VERB a contraction of *is not*

**isolate isolates, isolating, isolated**

VERB **1** If you **isolate** yourself, you separate yourself from other people. • *I isolated myself in my room.*

VERB **2** To **isolate** a sick person or animal means to keep them away from others so that the disease does not spread.

**ꞃsceles**

DJECTIVE An **isosceles** triangle has two sides ꝍf the same length and two equal angles.

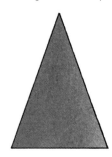

**ꝸ ISPs**

NOUN a business that provides access to the ꞁnternet. **ISP** is an abbreviation for *internet service provider*.

**ꞅue issues**

NOUN **1** an important subject that people are ꞇalking about • The **issue** of homeless people ꞌs important to many people.

NOUN **2** a particular newspaper or magazine • this week's **issue** of the local paper

PRONOUN **1** used to refer to something that ꞁas already been mentioned. **It** can also ꞃefer to babies or other animals whose gender is not known. • *I like that dog.* **It** *is very friendly.*

PRONOUN **2** You use **it** to talk about the weather, ꞇime or date. • **It**'s *been raining all day.*

NOUN an abbreviation of *Information Technology*

**ꞁlics**

PLURAL NOUN letters printed in a particular sloping way. They are often used for emphasis. • *This writing is in* **italics**.

**ꞇh itches, itching, itched**

VERB **1** When a part of your body **itches**, you have an unpleasant feeling that makes you want to scratch it.

NOUN **2** an unpleasant feeling on your skin that makes you want to scratch it

**ꞁm items**

NOUN one of a collection or list of objects • *Milk is the most important* **item** *on my shopping list.*

**ꞁnerary itineraries**

NOUN The **itinerary** of a journey is a detailed plan of where to go and what to see along the route.

**it's**

a contraction of *it is* or *it has*

---

**LANGUAGE TIP**
Do not confuse *it's* with *its*.

---

**its**

ADJECTIVE **Its** is used to refer to something belonging to things, children or animals that have already been mentioned. • *The cat won't eat.* **Its** *bowl needs cleaning.*

---

**LANGUAGE TIP**
Do not confuse *its* with *it's*.

---

**I've**

a contraction of *I have*

**ivory**

NOUN **1** the valuable, creamy-white bone that forms the tusk of an elephant. It is used to make ornaments.

NOUN **2** a creamy-white colour

ADJECTIVE **3** having a creamy-white colour

**ivy**

NOUN an evergreen plant that creeps along the ground and up walls

a
b
c
d
e
f
g
h
i
j
k
l
m
n
o
p
q
r
s
t
u
v
w
x
y
z

### jab jabs, jabbing, jabbed

VERB **1** If you **jab** something, you poke at it roughly.

NOUN **2** a sharp, sudden poke • *a jab in the ribs*

NOUN **3** (*informal*) an injection • *a measles jab*

### jack jacks

NOUN **1** a piece of equipment for lifting heavy objects, especially for lifting a car when changing a wheel

NOUN **2** In a pack of cards, a **jack** is a card whose value is between a ten and a queen.

### jackal jackals

NOUN a wild animal related to the dog

### jacket jackets

NOUN **1** a short coat

NOUN **2** the paper cover of a book

### jackpot jackpots

NOUN the top prize in a gambling game • *He was excited to hear he had won the jackpot in the lottery.*

### jagged

ADJECTIVE A **jagged** rock has a rough, uneven shape with sharp edges.

### jail jails, jailing, jailed; also spelt gaol

NOUN **1** a building where people convicted of a crime are locked up

VERB **2** To **jail** someone means to lock them up in a jail.

### jam jams, jamming, jammed

NOUN **1** a food made by boiling fruit with sugar

NOUN **2** a situation where there are so many people or things that it is difficult to move • *There is often a traffic jam at that junction.*

VERB **3** If you **jam** something into a place, you squeeze it in. • *He jammed his clothes into the suitcase.*

VERB **4** If you **jam** something, or if it **jams**, it becomes stuck. • *The coin was jammed in the slot.*

### January

NOUN the first month of the year. **January** has 31 days.

### jar jars, jarring, jarred

NOUN **1** a glass container used for storing food

VERB **2** If something **jars**, you find it unpleasant or annoying.

### jargon

NOUN language containing lots of technical words, used by particular groups of people • *Our doctor often uses jargon.*

### jaundice

NOUN an illness of the liver, where the skin and the whites of the eyes become yellow

### javelin javelins

NOUN a long spear that is thrown in sports competitions

### jaw jaws

NOUN **1** the bone in which teeth are set

NOUN **2** the mouth and teeth of a person or animal

### jazz

NOUN a style of popular music with a strong rhythm

### jealous

ADJECTIVE If you are **jealous**, you feel envious of others, wanting to have what they have or wanting to be like them.

### jealously

ADVERB in a way that shows you feel envious of someone else and want to have what they have or want to be like them

### jealousy

NOUN the feeling of being unhappy because you want to have what someone else has or because you want to be like them

### jeans

PLURAL NOUN cotton trousers, often made of denim

### Jeep Jeeps

NOUN (trademark) a four-wheeled motor vehicle designed for driving over rough ground

### jeer jeers, jeering, jeered

VERB **1** If you **jeer** at someone, you insult them in a loud, unpleasant way.

NOUN **2** Jeers are rude and insulting remarks.

**ly jellies**
NOUN **1** a clear, sweet food eaten as a dessert
NOUN **2** a type of clear, set jam ● *I like mint jelly with lamb.*

**llyfish jellyfishes**
NOUN a sea animal with a clear, soft body and tentacles that may sting

**rk jerks, jerking, jerked**
VERB **1** If you **jerk** something, you give it a sudden, sharp pull.
VERB **2** If something **jerks**, it moves suddenly and sharply.

**rsey jerseys**
NOUN a knitted garment for the upper half of the body

**t jets**
NOUN **1** an aeroplane that can fly very fast
NOUN **2** a rush of air, steam or liquid that is forced out under pressure

**tty jetties**
NOUN a wide stone wall or wooden platform at the edge of the sea or a river, where boats can be moored

**w Jews**
NOUN a person who practises the religion of Judaism or who is of Hebrew descent

**wel jewels**
NOUN a precious stone, often used to decorate valuable items such as rings or necklaces

**welled**
ADJECTIVE decorated with precious stones

**weller jewellers**
NOUN a person who makes or sells jewellery

**wellery**
NOUN the ornaments that people wear, like rings and necklaces

**wish**
ADJECTIVE to do with the religion of Judaism or Hebrew people ● the **Jewish** festival of Hanukah

**gsaw jigsaws**
NOUN a puzzle that is made up of odd-shaped pieces that must be fitted together to make a picture

**ngle jingles**
NOUN **1** a short, catchy phrase or rhyme with music, used to advertise something on radio or television
NOUN **2** a gentle ringing sound

**job jobs**
NOUN **1** the work that someone does to earn money
NOUN **2** anything that has to be done

**jockey jockeys**
NOUN someone who rides a horse in a race

**joey joeys**
NOUN a young kangaroo

**jog jogs, jogging, jogged**
VERB **1** If you **jog**, you run slowly, often for exercise.
VERB **2** If you **jog** something, you knock it slightly so that it shakes or moves. ● *My pen slipped when he jogged my arm.*

**jogger joggers**
NOUN someone who runs slowly for exercise

**jogging**
NOUN the activity of running slowly

**join joins, joining, joined**
VERB **1** If you **join** a club, you become a member of it.
VERB **2** When two things **join**, or when one thing **joins** another, they come together. ● *The two streams join and form a river.*

SYNONYMS: connect, link

**join in**
VERB If you **join in** an activity, you take part in it.

**joiner joiners**
NOUN a person who makes wooden window frames, doors and furniture

**joint joints**
ADJECTIVE **1** shared by or belonging to two or more people ● *The project was a joint effort.*
NOUN **2** a part of your body, such as your elbow or knee, where two bones meet and are able to move together

**joke jokes, joking, joked**
NOUN **1** something that you say to make people laugh
VERB **2** If you **joke**, you say something amusing or tell a funny story.

**jolly jollier, jolliest**
ADJECTIVE If you are **jolly**, you are happy and cheerful.

a b c d e f g h i j k l m n o p q r s t u v w x y z

**219**

A B C D E F G H I J K L M N O P Q R S T U V W X Y Z

**jolt jolts, jolting, jolted**
VERB **1** If something **jolts**, it moves or shakes roughly and violently. • *The bus jolted along the bumpy road.*
VERB **2** If something or someone **jolts** you, they bump into you clumsily.
NOUN **3** a sudden, jerky movement
NOUN **4** an unpleasant shock or surprise

**jostle jostles, jostling, jostled**
VERB If people or animals **jostle**, they push and bump into each other roughly, usually because they are in a crowd.

**jot jots, jotting, jotted**
VERB If you **jot** something down, you write a quick, brief note.

**journal journals**
NOUN **1** a magazine that deals with a particular interest
NOUN **2** a diary where you write what happens each day

**journalist journalists**
NOUN a person whose job is to gather news and write about it for a newspaper or magazine, or present it on television or radio

**journey journeys**
NOUN the act of travelling from one place to another

**joy joys**
NOUN **1** a feeling of great happiness or pleasure
NOUN **2** something that makes you happy or gives you pleasure • *It was a joy to see my friend again.*

**joystick joysticks**
NOUN **1** a lever in a plane that the pilot uses to control height and direction
NOUN **2** a lever that controls the cursor on a computer screen, especially in computer games

**jubilee jubilees**
NOUN a special anniversary of an event such as a coronation • *Queen Elizabeth's Golden Jubilee was in 2002.*

**WORD HISTORY**
from Hebrew *yobhel* meaning ram's horn, blown during festivals and celebrations to mark the freedom of Hebrew slaves each 50th year, known as the jubilee

**Judaic**
ADJECTIVE to do with the religion of the Jewish people

**Judaism**
NOUN the religion of the Jewish people. It is based on a belief in one God, and draws its laws from the Old Testament.

**judge judges, judging, judged**
NOUN **1** the person in a law court who decides how criminals should be punished according to the law
NOUN **2** the person who chooses the winner of a competition
VERB **3** If a person **judges** someone or something, they act as a judge.
VERB **4** If you **judge** someone or something, you decide what they are like.

**judgment judgments**; also spelt **judgement**
NOUN an opinion that you have after thinking carefully about something

**judo**
NOUN a sport in which two people try to force each other to the ground using special throwing techniques. It originated in Japan as a form of self-defence.

**WORD HISTORY**
from Japanese *ju do* meaning gentleness or

**jug jugs**
NOUN a container with a handle and a lip, used for holding and pouring liquids

**juggernaut juggernauts**
NOUN a large, heavy lorry

**WORD HISTORY**
from Hindi *Jagannath*, the name of a huge idol of the god Krishna, which is wheeled through the streets of Puri in India every year

**juggle juggles, juggling, juggled**
VERB When someone **juggles** they throw different objects into the air, keeping more than one object in the air at the same time without dropping them.

**juice juices**
NOUN the liquid that can be obtained from fruit, vegetables and other food
• *orange juice*

**cy juicier, juiciest**
ADJECTIVE having a great deal of juice ● *The orange was very **juicy**.*

**y**
NOUN the seventh month of the year. **July** has 31 days.

**nble jumbles, jumbling, jumbled**
NOUN **1** an untidy muddle of things
NOUN **2** articles for a **jumble** sale
VERB **3** If you **jumble** things, you mix them up untidily.

**nble sale jumble sales**
NOUN an event where second-hand items are sold to raise money cheaply, often for charity

**np jumps, jumping, jumped**
VERB **1** When you **jump**, you spring off the ground using the muscles in your legs.
VERB **2** If someone **jumps**, they make a sudden, sharp movement because they are surprised.

**nper jumpers**
NOUN a warm piece of clothing that covers the top part of your body

**ction junctions**
NOUN a place where roads or railway lines meet or cross

**ne**
NOUN the sixth month of the year. **June** has 30 days.

**ngle jungles**
NOUN a dense, tropical forest where many trees and other plants grow close together

**WORD HISTORY**
From Hindi *jangal* meaning wasteland

**nior**
ADJECTIVE **1** A **junior** official or employee holds a lower position in an organisation. ● *She will be a **junior** doctor after finishing her training.*
ADJECTIVE **2** younger ● *He is the **junior** of the two brothers.*

**nk junks**
NOUN **1** old, unwanted or worthless things that are sold cheaply or thrown away
NOUN **2** a Chinese sailing boat that has a flat bottom and wide sails

**nk food**
NOUN food that is easy and quick to prepare, or bought ready to eat, but is not always very good for you

**jury juries**
NOUN a group of people in a court of law who are chosen to listen to the facts about a crime and then decide whether the accused person is guilty or not

**just**
ADJECTIVE **1** Someone who is **just** is fair.
ADVERB **2** If something has **just** happened, it happened a very short time ago.
ADVERB **3** If you **just** do something, you almost don't do it. ● *He **just** managed to climb the fence.*
ADVERB **4** If something is **just** what you want, it is exactly what you want.

**justice**
NOUN **1** fairness in the way that people are treated
NOUN **2** the system of laws created by a community

**justifiable**
ADJECTIVE acceptable and done for good reasons

**justification justifications**
NOUN a good reason for doing something ● *There can be no **justification** for this level of violence.*

**justify justifies, justifying, justified**
VERB **1** If you **justify** what you are doing or saying, you prove or explain why it is reasonable or necessary.
VERB **2** If you **justify** a piece of text, you change the spaces between the words so that each line of text is exactly the same length.

**jut juts, jutting, jutted**
VERB If something **juts** out, it sticks out beyond a surface or an edge. ● *The pier **jutted** out into the sea.*

**juvenile juveniles**
ADJECTIVE **1** suitable for or to do with young people
ADJECTIVE **2** childish and rather silly
NOUN **3** a young person not old enough to be considered an adult

a b c d e f g h i j k l m n o p q r s t u v w x y z

**221**

# Kk

### kaleidoscope **kaleidoscopes**
NOUN a toy made of a tube with a hole at one end. When you look through the hole and twist the other end of the tube, you can see a changing pattern of colours.

### kangaroo **kangaroos**
NOUN a large, Australian marsupial with very strong back legs that it uses for jumping

### karate
NOUN a sport in which people fight each other using only their hands, elbows, feet and legs

**WORD HISTORY**
from Japanese *kara* + *te* meaning empty hand

### kayak **kayaks**
NOUN a covered canoe with a small opening for the person sitting in it, originally used by Inuit people

### kebab **kebabs**
NOUN pieces of meat or vegetable grilled on a stick

**WORD HISTORY**
from Arabic *kabab* meaning roast meat

### keel **keels**
NOUN a long piece of wood or steel along the bottom of a boat

→ Have a look at the illustration for **ship**

### keen **keener, keenest**
ADJECTIVE **1** If you are **keen** to do something, or for something to happen, you want very much to do it or for it to happen. • *I was* **keen** *to meet my cousins from Australia.*
ADJECTIVE **2** If you are **keen** on something or someone, you are fond of them or attracted to them.
ADJECTIVE **3** If your senses are **keen**, you are able to see, hear, taste and smell things very clearly or strongly.

### keep **keeps, keeping, kept**
VERB **1** If you **keep** something, you have i and don't give it away. • *I will* **keep** *this book forever.*
VERB **2** If you **keep** an animal, you look a it. • *He* **keeps** *rabbits.*
VERB **3** If you **keep** something somewher you store it there. • *I* **keep** *my bicycle in i garage.*
VERB **4** If you **keep** doing something, you it again and again.
VERB **5** If something **keeps** you a certain way, you stay that way because of it.
• *The duvet* **keeps** *me warm.*
VERB **6** If you **keep** a promise, you do wh you have said you will do.
VERB **7** If you **keep** a secret, you do not te to anyone else.
NOUN **8** the main tower inside the walls o castle

→ Have a look at the illustration for **cas**

### keeper **keepers**
NOUN **1** a person whose job is to look afte the animals in a zoo
NOUN **2** a goalkeeper in soccer or hockey
• *The* **keeper** *managed to stop the ball anc save the penalty.*

### kennel **kennels**
NOUN **1** a small hut for a dog to sleep in
NOUN **2** A **kennels** is a place where dogs bred, trained or looked after .

### kept
VERB the past tense and past participle of **keep**

### kerb **kerbs**
NOUN the raised edge of a pavement, that separates it from the road • *You must loo both ways for traffic before stepping off the* **kerb**.

### kernel **kernels**
NOUN the part of a nut that is inside the s

### kestrel **kestrels**
NOUN a type of small hawk

### ketchup
NOUN a cold sauce, usually made from tomatoes

### kettle **kettles**
NOUN a covered container with a spout, in which you boil water

**keys**

NOUN **1** a specially shaped piece of metal that fits in a lock, and is turned in order to open the lock

NOUN **2** The **keys** on a piano or a computer are the buttons that you press in order to operate it.

ADJECTIVE **3** Key words or sentences are the important ones in a piece of text.

NOUN **4** information arranged in a way that can be used to identify animals, plants and materials. You can use a **key** to help you name an unknown animal, plant or material.

**keyboard keyboards**

NOUN a set of keys on a phone, computer or piano

→ Have a look at the illustration for **computer**

**keyhole keyholes**

NOUN the hole in a lock where you put a key

**kg** abbreviation for *kilogram*

**khaki**

NOUN **1** a yellowish-brown colour

ADJECTIVE **2** having a yellowish-brown colour. Soldiers' uniforms are often made of **khaki** material.

WORD HISTORY

from Urdu *kaki* meaning dusty

**kick kicks, kicking, kicked**

VERB **1** If you **kick** someone or something, you hit them with your foot.

NOUN **2** If you give something a **kick**, you hit it with your foot.

NOUN **3** (*informal*) If you get a **kick** out of something, you enjoy it very much.

**kick off**

VERB When a soccer or rugby team **kicks off**, they begin playing.

**kid kids, kidding, kidded**

NOUN **1** (*informal*) a child

NOUN **2** a young goat

VERB **3** If you **kid** someone, you tease them and try to make them believe something that isn't true.

SYNONYM: tease

**kidnap kidnaps, kidnapping, kidnapped**

VERB If someone **kidnaps** someone else, they take them away by force and demand something in exchange for returning them.

WORD HISTORY

from *kid* + *nap* meaning child stealing; in the 17th century children were kidnapped to work on American plantations

**kidney kidneys**

NOUN one of the two organs in your body that remove waste products from your blood

→ Have a look at the illustration for **organ**

**kill kills, killing, killed**

VERB If someone **kills** a person, animal or plant, they make them die.

**kiln kilns**

NOUN an oven for baking china or pottery until it becomes hard and dry

**kilo kilos**

NOUN a kilogram

**kilogram kilograms**

NOUN a unit of mass and weight (kg) equal to 1000 grams

**kilohertz**

NOUN a unit of measurement of radio waves (kHz) equal to 1000 hertz

**kilometre kilometres**

NOUN a unit of distance (km) equal to 1000 metres

**kilowatt kilowatts**

NOUN a unit of power (kW) equal to 1000 watts

**kilt kilts**

NOUN a tartan skirt worn by men as part of Scottish Highland dress

**kimono kimonos**

NOUN a long, loose garment with wide sleeves and a sash, worn in Japan

**kin**

PLURAL NOUN Your **kin** are your relatives.

**kind kinder, kindest; kinds**

ADJECTIVE **1** Someone who is **kind** behaves in a caring and helpful way towards other people.

SYNONYM: considerate

NOUN **2** a particular thing of the same type as other things • *I do not like this **kind** of bread.*

SYNONYMS: sort, class

**223**

## kindly

ADVERB **1** in a way that shows you are kind • *Danny has **kindly** offered to help.*

ADJECTIVE **2** a word that means **kind**, used in stories • *a **kindly** old lady*

## kindness

NOUN the quality that someone has when they are kind

## king **kings**

NOUN a man who is the head of state in a country, and who inherited his position from his parents

## kingdom **kingdoms**

NOUN a country that is governed by a king or queen

## kingfisher **kingfishers**

NOUN a brightly-coloured bird that lives near water and feeds on fish

## kiosk **kiosks**

NOUN a small shop or hut where you can buy newspapers, snacks, and sweets

## kipper **kippers**

NOUN a herring that has been dried in smoke to preserve it and give it a special taste

## kiss **kisses, kissing, kissed**

VERB **1** When you **kiss** someone, you touch them with your lips in order to show your affection.

NOUN **2** When you give someone a **kiss**, you kiss them.

## kit **kits**

NOUN **1** a collection of equipment and clothing that you use for a sport or other activity • *football **kit***

NOUN **2** a set of parts that you fit together to make something • *I got a model aeroplane **kit** for my birthday.*

## kitchen **kitchens**

NOUN a room used for cooking and preparing food

## kite **kites**

NOUN **1** a light frame covered with paper or cloth, that you fly in the air at the end of a long string

NOUN **2** a plane shape like a diamond, wi two pairs of equal sides and no right an

## kitten **kittens**

NOUN a very young cat

## kiwi **kiwi** or **kiwis**

NOUN **1** a type of bird found in New Zeala **Kiwis** cannot fly.

NOUN **2** (*informal*) Someone who comes fr New Zealand is called a **kiwi**.

**WORD HISTORY**

A Maori word

## kiwi fruit **kiwi fruits**

NOUN a fruit with a brown, hairy skin and green flesh

## km

an abbreviation for *kilometre*

## knack

NOUN an ability to do something easily

## knead **kneads, kneading, kneaded**

VERB If you **knead** dough, you press it an squeeze it with your hands before baking

## knee **knees**

NOUN the joint in your leg between your ankle and your hip

## kneel **kneels, kneeling, knelt**

VERB When you **kneel**, or **kneel down**, y bend your legs and lower your body so th one or both knees are touching the grou

## knew

VERB the past tense of **know**

## knickers

PLURAL NOUN underpants worn by women girls

**ife knives**
NOUN a sharp, metal tool used for cutting things

**ight knights, knighting, knighted**
NOUN 1 In medieval times, a **knight** was a nobleman who served his king or lord in battle. ● *King Arthur and the **Knights** of the Round Table*
VERB 2 If a king or queen **knights** a man, they give him the title *Sir* before his name.

WORD HISTORY
from Old English *cniht* meaning servant

**it knits, knitting, knitted**
VERB If you **knit** a piece of clothing, you make it from wool, using knitting needles or a knitting machine.

**ob knobs**
NOUN a round handle or switch on doors, furniture and machinery

**ock knocks, knocking, knocked**
VERB 1 If you **knock** on something, you hit it hard with your hand to make a noise. ● *I knocked on the door when I arrived.*
VERB 2 If you **knock** against something, you bump into it.

**ocker knockers**
NOUN a metal lever attached to a door, that you use to knock on the door

**ot knots, knotting, knotted**
NOUN 1 a fastening made by passing one end of a piece of string or fabric through a loop and pulling it tight ● *The **knot** in my laces was so tight that I could not undo it.*
NOUN 2 a hard, round spot on a piece of wood, where a branch grew on the tree
NOUN 3 a unit for measuring the speed of ships and aircraft
VERB 4 If you **knot** a piece of string, you tie a knot in it.

**ow knows, knowing, knew, known**
VERB 1 If you **know** something, you have it clearly in your mind and you do not need to learn it. ● *I **know** how to swim.*
VERB 2 If you **know** a person, place or thing, you are familiar with them. ● *I've **known** him for five years.*

**owledge**
NOUN all the information and facts that you know ● *general **knowledge***

**uckle knuckles**
NOUN one of the joints in your fingers

**koala koalas**
NOUN an Australian marsupial with grey fur and small, tufted ears. **Koalas** live in trees and eat eucalyptus leaves.

**Koran** or **Qur'an**
NOUN the holy book of Islam

WORD HISTORY
from Arabic *kara'a* meaning to read

**kosher**
ADJECTIVE **Kosher** food has been specially prepared to be eaten according to Jewish law.

a
b
c
d
e
f
g
h
i
j
k
l
m
n
o
p
q
r
s
t
u
v
w
x
y
z

## Ll

**l**

an abbreviation for *litre*

### label labels, labelling, labelled
NOUN **1** a piece of paper or plastic attached to something and giving information about it • The **label** on the bottle told him when to have his medicine.
VERB **2** If you **label** something, you put a label on it.

### laboratory laboratories
NOUN a place where scientific experiments are carried out

### labour
NOUN **1** hard work
NOUN **2** In Britain, **Labour,** or the **Labour** Party, is one of the main political parties.

### Labrador Labradors
NOUN a large dog with short black, golden or chocolate brown hair

### labyrinth labyrinths
NOUN a complicated series of paths or passages that are difficult to find your way around

### lace laces, lacing, laced
NOUN **1** a fine, decorated cloth, with a pattern of many holes in it
NOUN **2** one of the thin pieces of material that are used to fasten shoes
VERB **3** When you **lace** up your shoes, you fasten them by tying their laces.

### lack lacks, lacking, lacked
NOUN **1** If there is a **lack** of something, there is not enough of it or there is none of it.
• Despite his **lack** of training, he won the race.
VERB **2** If someone or something **lacks** something, they do not have it.

### lacquer lacquers
NOUN thin, clear paint that you put on wood to protect it and make it shiny

### lactic acid
NOUN a type of acid that is found in sour and is also produced by your muscles w you have been exercising a lot

### lactose
NOUN a type of sugar which is found in m and which is sometimes added to food

### ladder ladders
NOUN a wooden or metal frame consistin two long poles with short bars in betwee **Ladders** are used for climbing up and down things.

### ladle ladles
NOUN a long-handled spoon with a deep, round bowl, which you use to serve soup

### lady ladies
NOUN **1** a polite word for woman
NOUN **2** In Britain, **Lady** is the title of the of a knight or a lord.

### ladybird ladybirds
NOUN a small, flying beetle with a round body, usually red, patterned with black spots

### lag lags, lagging, lagged
VERB **1** If a person or a thing **lags** behind, they make slower progress than other people or other things and do not keep u
• Don't **lag** behind, or you'll get lost!
VERB **2** If you **lag** pipes or water tanks, yo cover them with insulating material to st heat escaping and prevent freezing.

### lager lagers
NOUN a kind of light beer

### lagoon lagoons
NOUN an area of water separated from the sea by reefs or sand

### laid
VERB the past tense of **lay**

### lain
VERB the past participle of some meanings lie • It must have **lain** there for days.

### lair lairs
NOUN a place where a wild animal lives

### lake lakes
NOUN a large area of fresh water surround by land

### lamb lambs
NOUN **1** a young sheep
NOUN **2** the meat from a lamb

**...e**

ADJECTIVE **1** Someone who is **lame** has an ...jured leg and cannot walk easily.
...JECTIVE **2** A **lame** excuse is unconvincing.

**...ely**

...VERB in a way that does not seem ...nthusiastic or convincing

**...eness**

...UN **Lameness** is when a person or animal ...as an injured leg and cannot walk easily.

**...p lamps**

...UN a device that produces light • *Please ...rn on the table* **lamp** *now that it is getting ...rk.*

**...ppost lampposts**

...UN a tall column in a street, with a lamp ... the top

**...ce lances**

...UN a long spear that was used in the past ...y soldiers on horseback

**...d lands, landing, landed**

...UN **1** an area of ground • *We camped on ...e* **land** *surrounding the castle.*
...UN **2** the parts of the Earth's surface that ...re not covered by water
...RB **3** When someone or something **lands** ...omewhere, they reach the ground after ...oving through the air.
...RB **4** When you **land** somewhere on a ...lane or a ship, you arrive there.

**...ding landings**

...UN the flat area at the top of a flight of ...tairs in a building

**...dlady landladies**

...UN a woman who owns a house or small ...otel and who lets rooms to people

**...dline landlines**

...UN A **landline** is the telephone connection ...hat comes into a building using cables, ...ather than a mobile phone connection.

**...dlord landlords**

...UN **1** a man who owns a house or small ...otel and who lets rooms to people
...UN **2** a person who looks after a public ...ouse
...UN **3** someone who owns a large amount ...f land or houses and lets some of it out in ...eturn for rent

**...dmark landmarks**

...UN a noticeable feature in a landscape, ...hat you can use to check your position
• *The tower on the hill is a local* **landmark**.

**landscape landscapes**

NOUN everything you can see when you look across an area of land

**lane lanes**

NOUN **1** a narrow road, especially in the country
NOUN **2** one of the parallel strips into which a road, a race track or a swimming pool is divided

**language languages**

NOUN a system of words used by a particular group of people to communicate with each other

**lantern lanterns**

NOUN a lamp in a metal frame with glass sides

**lap laps, lapping, lapped**

NOUN **1** the flat area formed by your thighs when you are sitting down
NOUN **2** one circuit of a running track or racecourse
VERB **3** When water **laps** against something, it gently moves against it in little waves.
VERB **4** When an animal **laps** a drink, it uses its tongue to flick the liquid into its mouth.

**lapel lapels**

NOUN the part of a collar that folds back over the front of a jacket or coat

**lapse lapses, lapsing, lapsed**

NOUN **1** a moment of bad behaviour by someone who usually behaves well
NOUN **2** a period of time that has passed
VERB **3** If you **lapse** into a different way of behaving, you start behaving that way.
• *The class* **lapsed** *into silence.*
VERB **4** If something such as a promise or an agreement **lapses**, it is no longer valid.

**laptop laptops**

NOUN a portable computer small enough to fit on your lap, which is especially useful if you are travelling

**lard**

NOUN fat from a pig, used in cooking

**larder larders**

NOUN a room for storing food, often next to a kitchen

**large larger, largest**

ADJECTIVE bigger than usual

**largely**

ADVERB to a great extent • *It was* **largely** *a party for his birthday, but we celebrated his sister's exam results too.*

a
b
c
d
e
f
g
h
i
j
k
l
m
n
o
p
q
r
s
t
u
v
w
x
y
z

**227**

## lark larks, larking, larked

NOUN **1** a small, brown bird with a very pleasant song

NOUN **2** If you do something for a **lark**, you do it in a high-spirited or mischievous way for fun.

VERB **3** If you **lark** about, you enjoy yourself in a high-spirited way.

## larva larvae

NOUN an insect after it has hatched from its egg, and before it becomes an adult. A caterpillar is the **larva** of a butterfly.

## lasagne

NOUN an Italian dish made with wide, flat sheets of pasta, meat or vegetables and cheese sauce

**WORD HISTORY**
from Latin *lasanum* meaning cooking pot

## laser lasers

NOUN **1** a narrow beam of concentrated light produced by a special machine. It is used to cut very hard materials and in some kinds of surgery.

NOUN **2** the machine that produces the beam of light

**WORD HISTORY**
from the first letters of *Light Amplification by Stimulated Emission of Radiation*

## lash lashes, lashing, lashed

NOUN **1** Your **lashes** are the hairs growing on the edge of your eyelids.

VERB **2** If rain **lashes** down, it beats down strongly.

VERB **3** If you **lash** things together, you tie them together firmly.

### lash out

VERB If you **lash out** at someone you speak to them or strike them harshly.

## lasso lassoes or lassos, lassoing, lassoed

NOUN **1** a length of rope looped at one end with a slip-knot, used by cowboys to catch cattle and horses

VERB **2** If you **lasso** an animal, you catch it by throwing the loop of a lasso around its neck.

## last lasts, lasting, lasted

ADJECTIVE **1** The **last** person or thing is the one that comes after all the others of the same kind. • *I was the last person to arrive.*

ADJECTIVE **2** The **last** one of a group of things is the only one that remains after all the others have gone. • *No one wanted the la piece of pizza.*

ADJECTIVE **3** The **last** thing or event is the recent one. • *The last time we went to the beach it rained.*

VERB **4** If something **lasts**, it continues to exist or happen. • *The sunny weather see to have lasted for ages.*

VERB **5** If something **lasts** for a particular time, it remains in good condition for th time.

PHRASE **6 At last** means after a long time • *The bus arrived at last.*

## late later, latest

ADJECTIVE **1** If something or someone is lat they arrive after the time that was arran or expected.

ADJECTIVE **2** If something is **late**, it happen near the end of something. • *The visiting team scored a late goal.*

ADVERB **3** If something happens **late**, it happens after the time that was arrange expected. • *She always arrives late at sch*

ADVERB **4** If something happens **late**, it happens near the end of something. • *In the summer it doesn't get dark until la the evening.*

## lately

ADVERB If something happened **lately**, it happened recently. • *We've had a lot of homework lately.*

## lather

NOUN the frothy foam that you get when y rub soap in water

## Latin

NOUN **1** the language of ancient Rome

ADJECTIVE **2 Latin** peoples and cultures are those of countries such as France, Italy, Spain and Portugal, whose languages developed from Latin.

## latitude latitudes

NOUN The **latitude** of a place is its distan north or south of the equator measured i degrees.

→ Have a look at the illustration for **equator**

## latter

NOUN **1** You use **latter** to refer to the seco of two things you have just mentioned. • *They were eating sandwiches and cakes (th latter bought from Mrs Paul's bakery).*

ADJECTIVE **2** The **latter** part of something is the second or later part of it. • *the latter stages of the race*

**gh laughs, laughing, laughed**
ʀʙ **1** When you **laugh**, you make a noise
at shows that you are amused or happy.
ᴜɴ **2** the sound you make when you laugh

**ghter**
ᴜɴ laughing or the sound of people laughing

**nch launches, launching, launched**
ʀʙ **1** When someone **launches** a ship,
ey put it into water for the first time.
ʀʙ **2** When someone **launches** a rocket,
ey send it into space.

**ndry laundries**
ᴜɴ **1** dirty clothes and sheets that are
ɪng washed or waiting to be washed
ᴜɴ **2** a business that washes and irons
othes and sheets

**a**
ᴜɴ the very hot, liquid rock that shoots out
a volcano when it erupts, and becomes
lid as it cools

ᴐ Have a look at the illustration for
**olcano**

**atory lavatories**
ᴜɴ a toilet

**ender**
ᴜɴ a small bush with blue flowers that
ave a strong, pleasant scent

**ish**
ᴅᴊᴇᴄᴛɪᴠᴇ If you are **lavish**, you are very
enerous with your time, money or gifts.

**v laws**
ᴜɴ **1** the system of rules developed by the
overnment of a country, that tells people
hat they are allowed to do
ᴜɴ **2** one of the rules established by a
overnment, that tells people what they are
llowed to do

**vn lawns**
ᴏᴜɴ a piece of well-kept grass, usually in a
ark or garden

**wnmower lawnmowers**
ᴏᴜɴ a machine for cutting grass

**wyer lawyers**
ᴏᴜɴ someone who is trained in the law and
vho speaks for people in court

**y lays, laying, laid**
ᴇʀʙ **1** When you **lay** something somewhere,
ou place it there.
ᴇʀʙ **2** If you **lay** the table, you put things
uch as knives and forks on the table ready
or a meal.

VERB **3** When a bird **lays** an egg, an egg
comes out of its body.

**layer layers**
NOUN a single thickness of something
underneath or above something else • *There
was a thin **layer** of snow on the ground.*

**layout layouts**
NOUN the pattern in which something is
arranged • *The clear **layout** of this book
makes it a lot easier to use.*

**laziness**
NOUN **Laziness** is the habit of being idle and
unwilling to work.

**lazy lazier, laziest**
ADJECTIVE If you are **lazy**, you are idle and are
unwilling to work.

**lb**
an abbreviation for *pound*

**lead leads, leading, led**
VERB **1** If you **lead** someone somewhere, you
go in front of them in order to show them
the way.
VERB **2** If a road or door **leads** somewhere,
you can get to that place by following the
road or going through the door.
VERB **3** If you **lead** in a race or competition,
you are at the front.
VERB **4** Someone who **leads** a group of
people is in charge of them.
NOUN **5** If you take the **lead** in a race or
competition, or if you are in the **lead**, you
are winning.
NOUN **6** a length of leather or chain attached
to an animal's collar, used for controlling
the animal
NOUN **7** an electric cable for connecting
an electrical appliance to a battery or the
mains
NOUN **8** a soft, grey, heavy metal
NOUN **9** The **lead** in a pencil is the part that
makes marks on paper.

PRONUNCIATION TIP
Meanings 1-7 are pronounced **leed**.
Meanings 8 and 9 are pronounced **led**.

**leader leaders**
NOUN **1** If you are the **leader** of a group, you
are in charge of it.
NOUN **2** If you are the **leader** in a race or a
competition, you are winning.

**229**

**leaf leaves**

NOUN **1** a flat structure growing from the stem of a plant. Most plants have green **leaves**.

→ Have a look at the illustrations for **flower** and **photosynthesis**

NOUN **2** one of the sheets of paper in a book

**leaflet leaflets**

NOUN a piece of paper or thin booklet with information or advertisements

**leafy leafier, leafiest**

ADJECTIVE **1** having a lot of leaves • *green leafy vegetables*

ADJECTIVE **2** A place that is **leafy** has a lot of trees. • *He grew up in a leafy suburb of London.*

**league leagues**

NOUN a group of people, clubs or countries that have joined together for a particular purpose or because they share a common interest

**leak leaks, leaking, leaked**

VERB **1** If a container or other object **leaks**, it has a hole through which gas or liquid escapes.

NOUN **2** If a container or other object has a **leak**, it has a hole through which gas or liquid escapes.

**lean leans, leaning, leant or leaned; leaner, leanest**

VERB **1** When you **lean** in a particular direction, you bend your body in that direction. • *She leant out of the window.*

VERB **2** When you **lean** on something, you rest your body against it for support. • *He was leaning on the railing.*

VERB **3** If you **lean** something somewhere, you place it there so that its weight is supported. • *He leaned his bike against the wall.*

ADJECTIVE **4** If meat is **lean**, it does not have much fat.

---

**LANGUAGE TIP**

You can write either *leant* or *leaned* as the past form of *lean*.

---

**leap leaps, leaping, leapt or leaped**

VERB **1** If you **leap** somewhere, you jump a long distance or high in the air.

NOUN **2** a jump over a long distance or high in the air

**leap year leap years**

NOUN A **leap year** has 366 days instead 365, with an extra day in February. It oc every four years.

**learn learns, learning, learnt or lear**

VERB When you **learn** something, you g knowledge or a skill by practice or by be taught. • *He's learning to play the pianc*

---

**LANGUAGE TIP**

You can write either *learnt* or *learned* as past form of *learn*.

---

**lease leases**

NOUN A **lease** is an agreement that lets someone use a house or a flat in return rent.

**least**

ADJECTIVE **1** a smaller amount than anyone anything else • *He ate the least amount c food because he felt ill.*

ADVERB **2** a smaller amount than anyone anything else • *He is one of the least frier people I have ever met.*

NOUN **3** the smallest possible amount of something

PHRASE **4** You use **at least** to show that yo are referring to the minimum amount of something, and that the true amount m be greater. • *There were at least 500 peop at the concert.*

**leather**

NOUN animal skin that has been specially treated so that it can be used to make shoes, clothes, bags and other things

**leave leaves, leaving, left**

VERB **1** When you **leave** a place or person you go away from them.

VERB **2** If you **leave** something somewhere you let it stay there, or put it there before you go away. • *I left my bags in the car.*

VERB **3** If you **leave** a job or a school, you stop being a part of it.

VERB **4** In arithmetic, when you take one number from another, it **leaves** a third number. For example, if you take 2 from it **leaves** 10.

NOUN **5** holiday time • *I'm going to use my leave to go abroad this year.*

**lecture lectures**

NOUN a formal talk intended to teach peop about a particular subject

**led**

VERB the past tense of **lead**

**ge ledges**
UN a narrow shelf on the side of a cliff or
ck face, or on the outside of a building,
rectly under a window

**k leeks**
UN a long vegetable of the onion family,
at is white at one end and has green
aves at the other

RB **1** the past tense of **leave**
OUN **2** one of the two opposite directions,
des or positions. The **left** is the side of a
age that you begin reading on in English.

ANTONYM: right

JECTIVE **3** on the **left** of something • *a cut*
*er his **left** eye*

ANTONYM: right

JECTIVE **4** If a certain amount of something
left or **left over**, it remains when the rest
as gone. • *They have two games **left** to play.*
DVERB **5** on or towards the **left** of something
*Turn **left** at the corner.*

ANTONYM: right

**tovers**
URAL NOUN the bits of uneaten food that are
eft at the end of a meal

**legs**
OUN **1** one of the long parts of a human or
ther animal's body that they stand on and
valk with

→ Have a look at the illustrations for **bird**,
**nsect** and **spider**

OUN **2** The **legs** of a pair of trousers are the
parts that cover your legs.
OUN **3** The **legs** of a table or chair are the
parts that rest on the floor and support it.
NOUN **4** A **leg** of a journey or a sports match
s one part of it. • *The first **leg** of the race was
very hard work.*

**gacy legacies**
NOUN property or money that is given to
someone in the will of a person who has
died

**gal**
ADJECTIVE relating to the law

**gend legends**
NOUN a very old and popular story

**legible**
ADJECTIVE Writing that is **legible** is clear
enough to be read.

ANTONYM: illegible

**legislation**
NOUN a law or group of laws made by a
government

**legitimate**
ADJECTIVE If something is **legitimate** it is
allowed by law, or is accepted as fair by
most people.

**leisure**
NOUN time when you do not have to work
and can do things that you enjoy

**lemon lemons**
NOUN a yellow citrus fruit with a sour taste

**lemonade**
NOUN a sweet drink made from lemons,
water and sugar. **Lemonade** is often fizzy.

**lend lends, lending, lent**
VERB **1** If you **lend** something to someone,
you let them have it for a period of time.
VERB **2** If a person or bank **lends** you money,
they give you money and you agree to pay it
back later, usually with interest.

**length lengths**
NOUN **1** The **length** of something is the
distance from one end to the other.
• *We walked the **length** of the street.*
NOUN **2** The **length** of an event or activity is
the amount of time it continues. • *The film
is over two hours in **length**.*

**lengthen lengthens, lengthening,
lengthened**
VERB If you **lengthen** something, you make
it longer.

ANTONYM: shorten

**lengthy lengthier, lengthiest**
ADJECTIVE Something that is **lengthy** lasts for
a long time. • *The speech was rather **lengthy**.*

**lens lenses**
NOUN **1** a thin, curved piece of glass, plastic or
other transparent material that makes things
appear larger or clearer • *a camera **lens***
NOUN **2** the part of the eye behind the pupil
that focuses light and helps you to see clearly

→ Have a look at the illustration for **eye**

**lent**
VERB the past tense and past participle of **lend**

231

### Lent

NOUN the forty-day period before Easter when some Christians fast or give up something that they enjoy

### lentil lentils

NOUN **Lentils** are small, dried, red or brown seeds that are cooked and eaten in soups, stews and curries.

### leopard leopards

NOUN a large wild cat, with yellow fur and black or brown spots, found in Africa and Asia

### leotard leotards

NOUN a tight-fitting garment that covers the body rather like a swimming costume, which is worn for dancing or exercise

### less

ADJECTIVE **1** a smaller amount of something • It is **less** than three weeks until we go back to school.

ANTONYM: more

PRONOUN **2** a smaller amount • Dad says I should spend **less**.

ANTONYM: more

ADVERB **3** You use **less** in front of some adjectives and adverbs to form comparatives. • I am **less** worried about the test than I was last time.

ANTONYM: more

PREPOSITION **4** You use **less** to show that one number or amount is to be subtracted from another. • You can have your pocket money, **less** the money you borrowed last week.

LANGUAGE TIP
Use less to talk about things that can't be counted and fewer for things that can be counted: less time; fewer apples.

### lesson lessons

NOUN **1** a fixed period of time during which people are taught something by a teacher
NOUN **2** an experience that makes you understand something important

### let lets, letting, let

VERB **1** If you **let** someone do something, you allow them to do it.
VERB **2** If someone **lets** a house or flat that they own, they allow others to use it in return for payment.

### lethal

ADJECTIVE Something that is **lethal** can kill you. • A gun is a **lethal** weapon.

WORD HISTORY
from Latin letum meaning death

### let's

VERB a contraction of let us

### letter letters

NOUN **1** a message written on paper and s to someone, usually through the post
NOUN **2** one of the written symbols that go together to make words

### letter box letter boxes; also spelt lette box

NOUN **1** an oblong gap in a front door, through which letters are delivered
NOUN **2** a large, metal container in the str or at a post office, for posting letters

### lettering

NOUN You use **lettering** to describe writin that is done in a certain way. • The poster had large black **lettering**.

### lettuce lettuces

NOUN a vegetable with large, green leaves that you eat in salads

### leukaemia; also spelt leukemia

NOUN a serious illness that affects the bloc

WORD HISTORY
from Greek leukos meaning white and hai meaning blood

### level levels, levelling, levelled

NOUN **1** the height, position or amount of something • This is the lowest **level** of rain for years.
NOUN **2** a standard or grade of achievemen • Now that I have passed this piano exam, I will move on to the next **level**.

SYNONYMS: grade, stage

ADJECTIVE **3** A surface that is **level** is completely flat.
ADJECTIVE **4** If one thing is **level** with anothe it is at the same height or position.
VERB **5** If you **level** something, you make it flat.

### level crossing level crossings

NOUN a place where traffic is allowed to dri across a railway track

**er levels**

NOUN **1** a handle on a machine that you pull in order to make the machine work
NOUN **2** a bar that you wedge underneath a heavy object and press down on to make the object move

**bility liabilities**

NOUN If you say that someone is a **liability**, you mean that they cause problems or embarrassment.

**ble**

ADJECTIVE **1** Something that is **liable** to happen will probably happen. • *Britain is liable to be cold in January.*
ADJECTIVE **2** If someone is **liable** for something such as a crime or a debt, they are legally responsible for it.

**liars**

NOUN a person who tells lies

**eral**

ADJECTIVE **1** If someone is **liberal**, they are tolerant of other people's behaviour and opinions.
ADJECTIVE **2** If you are **liberal** with something, you are generous with it.

**erty**

NOUN the freedom to do what you want to do and go where you want to go

**rarian librarians**

NOUN a person who works in, or is in charge of, a library

**rary libraries**

NOUN a building in which books are kept, especially a public building from which people can borrow books

LANGUAGE TIP
There is an *r* after the *b* in *library*.

**ence licences**

NOUN an official document that gives you permission to do, use or own something • *You have to pass a test before you receive a full driving licence.*

LANGUAGE TIP
The noun *licence* ends in *ce*.

**ense licenses, licensing, licensed**

VERB If someone **licenses** an activity, they give official permission for it to be carried out.

LANGUAGE TIP
The verb *license* ends in *se*.

**lichen lichens**

NOUN a green or greeny-grey mossy growth, found on rocks, trees and walls

PRONUNCIATION TIP
This word is pronounced **lie**-kun.

**lick licks, licking, licked**

VERB If you **lick** something, you move your tongue over it. • *I licked the stamp and stuck it to the envelope.*

**lid lids**

NOUN a cover for a box, jar or other container

**lie lies, lying, lay, lain**

VERB **1** If someone or something **lies** somewhere, they rest there in a flat position.
VERB **2** You use **lie** to say where something is or what its position is. • *The village lies to the east of the river.*

LANGUAGE TIP
The past tense of this verb *lie* is *lay*. Do not confuse it with the verb *lay* meaning 'put'.

**lie lies, lying, lied**

VERB **1** If you **lie**, you say something that you know is not true. • *He lied about his age.*
NOUN **2** something you say that you know is not true

**lieutenant lieutenants**

NOUN a junior officer in the army or navy

PRONUNCIATION TIP
This word is pronounced lef-**ten**-ant.

**life lives**

NOUN **1** the state of being alive that makes people, animals and plants different from objects • *A baby's first few minutes of life are important.*
NOUN **2** your existence from the time you are born until the time you die • *For the first time in his life he was sorry.*

**lifeboat lifeboats**

NOUN a boat used for rescuing people who are in danger at sea

**233**

## life cycle life cycles

NOUN the series of changes and developments in the life of a living thing • *There are several stages in the **life cycle** of a butterfly.*

→ Have a look at the illustration

## lifeguard lifeguards

NOUN a person whose job is to rescue people who are in difficulty in the sea or in a swimming pool

## life jacket life jackets

NOUN a sleeveless, inflatable jacket that keeps you afloat in water

## lifelike

ADJECTIVE A picture or a sculpture that is **lifelike** looks very real, almost as if it is alive.

SYNONYM: realistic

## lifeline lifelines

NOUN something that helps you to survive or helps an activity to continue • *His help was a real **lifeline** to me after I had so many difficulties.*

## lifetime lifetimes

NOUN the period of time during which you are alive

## lift lifts, lifting, lifted

VERB 1 If you **lift** something, you move it to a higher position.
NOUN 2 a device that carries people or goods from one floor to another in a building

## light lights, lighting, lighted or lit; lighter, lightest

NOUN 1 the brightness from the sun, moon, fire or lamps, that lets you see things

NOUN 2 a lamp or other device that gives brightness
ADJECTIVE 3 If it is **light**, there is enough li from the sun to see things.

ANTONYM: dark

ADJECTIVE 4 A **light** colour is pale.

ANTONYM: dark

ADJECTIVE 5 A **light** object does not weigh much.

ANTONYM: heavy

VERB 6 If you **light** a fire, you make it sta burning.

## lighten lightens, lightening, lighten•

VERB 1 When something **lightens**, it becomes brighter and less dark. • *After t storm the sky **lightened**.*
VERB 2 If you **lighten** a load, you make it less heavy. • *My case was too heavy, so I **lightened** it by taking out three books.*

## lighter lighters

NOUN a device for lighting something, su as a fire or a cigarette

## lighthouse lighthouses

NOUN a tower by the sea, that shines a powerful light to guide ships and warn them of danger

## lighting

NOUN The **lighting** in a room or building the way it is lit.

## lightning

NOUN very bright flashes of light you see i the sky, usually during a thunderstorm. **Lightning** is caused by electrical activit the atmosphere.

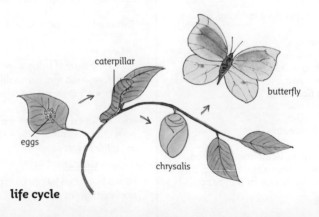

caterpillar

butterfly

eggs

chrysalis

life cycle

**t year light years**
UN the distance that light travels in a year, hich is about 6 million miles or 9.5 million ometres

**likes, liking, liked**
RB **1** If you **like** someone or something, u find them pleasing.
UN **2** a symbol on a social media website at you click to show that you like mething that someone has posted • *The video got over 200 **likes**.*
EPOSITION **3** If one thing is **like** another, they e similar.

**able**; also spelt **likable**
JECTIVE A **likeable** person is pleasant and endly.

**ly likelier, likeliest**
JECTIVE If something is **likely**, it will obably happen or is probably true.

**c lilacs**
UN **1** a small tree with sweet-smelling usters of mauve, pink or white flowers
UN **2** a pale mauve colour

**lilies**
UN a plant with trumpet-shaped flowers of rious colours

**b limbs**
UN Your **limbs** are your arms and legs.

**e limes**
UN **1** a small, green citrus fruit, rather like lemon
UN **2** a bright green colour
UN **3** a chemical substance used in ment or as a fertiliser

**erick limericks**
UN an amusing nonsense poem of five lines

**it limits, limiting, limited**
UN **1** the largest or smallest amount of mething that is possible or allowed
*The speed **limit** on this road is 30 mph.*
RB **2** If you **limit** something, you restrict to a certain amount or number. • *The ildren were **limited** to two biscuits each.*

**ousine limousines**
UN a large, luxurious car, usually driven by chauffeur

**p limps, limping, limped; limper, mpest**
RB **1** If you **limp**, you walk in an uneven ay because you have hurt your leg or foot.
UN **2** an uneven way of walking • *While her g was in plaster she walked with a **limp**.*

ADJECTIVE **3** Something that is **limp** is soft or weak.

**limpet limpets**
NOUN a small shellfish with a pointed shell, that attaches itself very firmly to rocks

**line lines, lining, lined**
NOUN **1** a long, thin mark
NOUN **2** a number of people or things that are arranged in a row
NOUN **3** a long piece of string or wire
• *a washing **line***
NOUN **4** a number of words together, for example the **lines** in a play are the words that an actor has to speak • *This is my favourite **line** in the poem.*
NOUN **5** a railway or railway track
VERB **6** If people or things **line** something, they make a border or edge along it.
• *Crowds **lined** the streets to see the Queen.*

**line graph line graphs**
NOUN a kind of graph where the information is shown by using straight lines to join points

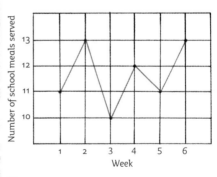

**linen**
NOUN **1** a type of cloth made from a plant called flax
NOUN **2** household goods made of cloth, such as sheets and tablecloths

**liner liners**
NOUN a large passenger ship that makes long sea journeys

**linesman linesmen**
NOUN an official at a sports match who watches the lines of the field or court and decides if the ball has gone outside them

a
b
c
d
e
f
g
h
i
j
k
l
m
n
o
p
q
r
s
t
u
v
w
x
y
z

**235**

**linger** lingers, lingering, lingered
VERB If someone or something **lingers**, they stay for a long time. • *The smell **lingered** in the kitchen.*

**linguist** linguists
NOUN someone who studies languages and can speak them well

**lining** linings
NOUN any material that is used to line the inside of something • *There is a fleece **lining** in this jacket.*

**link** links, linking, linked
NOUN **1** one of the rings in a chain
NOUN **2** a relationship or connection between two things • *There is a **link** between the weather and the clothes we wear.*
NOUN **3** a physical connection between two things or places • *There is a rail **link** between the two cities.*
VERB **4** If someone or something **links** people, places, or things, they join them together. • *They want to **link** the village to the town with a better road.*

**lion** lions
NOUN a large member of the cat family that is found in Africa. Male **lions** have long hair on their head and neck, called a mane.

**lioness** lionesses
NOUN a female lion

**lip** lips
NOUN Your **lips** are the two outer edges of your mouth.

**lipstick** lipsticks
NOUN a cosmetic for colouring the lips, usually in the form of a small stick

**liquid** liquids
NOUN a substance such as water, which is neither a gas nor a solid and which can be poured. The particles in a **liquid** are close together but can move around. A **liquid** always takes the shape of the container it is in.

→ Have a look at the illustration for **state of matter**

**liquidiser** liquidisers; also spelt **liquidizer**
NOUN an electric machine used for making food into liquid • *Dad put strawberries, bananas and milk in the **liquidiser** and mixed us a delicious milkshake.*

**liquorice**; also spelt **licorice**
NOUN **1** a root used to flavour sweets
NOUN **2** sweets flavoured with liquorice

**lisp** lisps, lisping, lisped
NOUN **1** Someone who has a **lisp** pronoun the sounds s and z like th.
VERB **2** If someone **lisps**, they speak with lisp.

**list** lists, listing, listed
NOUN **1** a set of words or items written on after the other • *a shopping **list***
VERB **2** If you **list** a number of things, you write them or say them one after anothe

**listen** listens, listening, listened
VERB **1** If you **listen** to someone, you pay attention to what they are saying.
VERB **2** If you **listen** to something, you pa attention to its sound. • *She enjoys **listen** to music.*

**lit**
VERB the past tense and past participle of **light**

**literacy**
NOUN the ability to read and write

**literal**
ADJECTIVE according to the most basic an obvious meaning of a word or text, rathe than a figurative meaning

**literally**
ADVERB You use **literally** to emphasise th what you are saying is actually true, eve though it seems unlikely. • *We **literally** almost died of thirst.*

**literary**
ADJECTIVE connected with or knowledgeabl about literature

**literate**
ADJECTIVE If you are **literate**, you are able read and write.

**literature**
NOUN Novels, plays and poetry are referre as **literature**.

**WORD HISTORY**
from Latin *litteratura* meaning writing

**litre** litres
NOUN a unit for measuring liquid (l) equal 1000 millilitres or about 1.76 pints

**er litters, littering, littered**

NOUN **1** rubbish in the street and other public places

NOUN **2** baby animals born at the same time to the same mother

VERB **3** If things **litter** a place, they are scattered all over it. • *Paper littered the pavement.*

**le less, lesser, least**

ADJECTIVE **1** small in size or amount • *Stay a little longer.*

ANTONYMS: big, large

ADJECTIVE **2** not much • *I had very little money.*

PRONOUN **3** not much • *He ate little at the meal.*

NOUN **4** A **little** is a small amount or degree of something. • *He showed me a little of his work.*

**e lives, living, lived**

VERB **1** If someone or something **lives**, they are alive.

VERB **2** If you **live** in a place, that is where your home is. • *He lives with his parents.*

VERB **3** The way someone **lives** is the kind of life they have. • *We live quite simply.*

ADJECTIVE **4** **Live** television or radio is broadcast while the event is taking place.

ADJECTIVE **5** **Live** animals or plants are alive, rather than dead or artificial.

**PRONUNCIATION TIP**

The verb rhymes with "give". The adjective rhymes with "five".

**ely livelier, liveliest**

ADJECTIVE full of energy and enthusiasm

**er livers**

NOUN a large organ in your body that cleans your blood and stores substances such as vitamins and minerals

➤ Have a look at the illustrations for **organ** and **stomach**

**estream livestreams, livestreaming, livestreamed**

VERB If you **livestream** something as it is happening, you play it directly from the internet. • *The game will be livestreamed on the website.*

**ing**

ADJECTIVE **1** If someone or something is **living**, they are alive.

NOUN **2** Someone who works for a **living**, works to earn the money needed in order to live. • *He makes a living by selling cars.*

**living room living rooms**

NOUN a room in a house where you sit and relax, doing such things as watching television and reading

**lizard lizards**

NOUN a reptile with short legs and a tail

**llama llamas**

NOUN a South American animal that looks rather like a small camel with thick hair and no hump

**load loads, loading, loaded**

VERB **1** If you **load** a vehicle or container, you put things into it.

VERB **2** When you **load** a camera, you put film into it.

NOUN **3** something large or heavy that is being carried • *a tractor with a big load of hay*

NOUN **4** (informal) A **load** of something, or **loads** of something, means a lot of it. • *He's got loads of CDs.*

**loaf loaves**

NOUN a large piece of bread in a shape that can be cut into slices

**loan loans, loaning, loaned**

NOUN **1** a sum of money that you borrow

VERB **2** If you **loan** something to someone, you lend it to them.

**loathe loathes, loathing, loathed**

VERB If you **loathe** someone or something, you feel a very strong dislike for them.

**lobster lobsters**

NOUN an edible shellfish with two front claws and eight legs

**local locals**

ADJECTIVE **1** existing in or belonging to the area where you live • *the local newspaper*

NOUN **2** someone who lives in and comes from a particular area

**locality localities**

NOUN a small area of a country or a city • *Golden eagles can be seen in certain localities in Scotland.*

**locate locates, locating, located**

VERB **1** If you **locate** someone or something, you find out where they are.

VERB **2** If something is **located** in a place, it is in that place.

**location** locations

NOUN the place where something is found or where something happens • *She couldn't remember the exact* **location** *of the church.*

**loch** lochs

NOUN In Scottish English, a **loch** is a lake. • *They say there is a monster in* **Loch** *Ness.*

**lock** locks, locking, locked

VERB **1** If you **lock** something, you fasten it with a key.

VERB **2** If you **lock** something in a place, you put it there and fasten the lock. • *They* **locked** *the money in the safe.*

NOUN **3** a device that prevents something from being opened except with a key • *He heard a key in the* **lock***.*

**locker** lockers

NOUN a small cupboard for someone's personal belongings, for example in a changing room

**locket** lockets

NOUN a small piece of jewellery worn on a chain around the neck, which opens so that you can put a small photograph inside

**locomotive** locomotives

NOUN a railway engine

**locust** locusts

NOUN an insect like a large grasshopper, that travels in huge swarms and eats crops

**loft** lofts

NOUN the space immediately under the roof of a house, often used for storing things

**log** logs

NOUN **1** a thick piece of wood from a branch or trunk of a tree, that has fallen or been cut off

NOUN **2** an official written account of what happens each day • *The captain wrote each day's events in the ship's* **log***.*

**logic**

NOUN a way of reasoning that makes sense

**logical**

ADJECTIVE Something that is **logical** is sensible and reasonable. • *a* **logical** *explanation*

**logically**

ADVERB in a way that makes sense

**logo** logos

NOUN the special design that is put on all the products of an organisation

**loiter** loiters, loitering, loitered

VERB If you **loiter** in a place, you stand around without going very far or doing v much. • *After school they* **loitered** *round the shops.*

**lollipop** lollipops

NOUN a hard sweet on the end of a stick

---

WORD HISTORY

from Romani *lolli* meaning red and *pobb* meaning apple

---

**lolly** lollies

NOUN **1** a lollipop

NOUN **2** a flavoured ice or ice cream on a stick

**lonely** lonelier, loneliest

ADJECTIVE **1** If you are **lonely**, you are unhappy because you are alone.

ADJECTIVE **2** A **lonely** place is one that very few people visit.

**long** longer, longest; longs, longing, longed

ADJECTIVE **1** continuing for a great amount time • *There had been no rain for a* **long** *ti*

ADVERB **2** You use **long** to talk about amounts of time. • *How* **long** *is the film?*

ADJECTIVE **3** great in length or distance • *It'* **long** *way home.*

ADJECTIVE **4** You use **long** to talk about the distance that something measures from end to the other.

PHRASE **5** If something **no longer** happens used to happen but does not happen now

VERB **6** If you **long** to do something, you want to do it very much.

**long for**

VERB If you **long for** something to happ you want it to happen very much.

**long division** long divisions

NOUN a method of dividing one large num by another one, where you write out all th stages instead of doing them in your hea or on a calculator

**longitude** longitudes

NOUN a position measured in degrees east west of an imaginary line passing throug Greenwich in London

→ Have a look at the illustration for **equator**

**ok looks, looking, looked**

VERB **1** If you **look** at something, you turn your eyes towards it so that you can see it.

VERB **2** If you **look** for someone or something, you try to find them.

VERB **3** If you describe the way that something **looks**, you are describing its appearance. • *He looked a bit pale.*

NOUN **4** If you take a **look** at something, you look at it. • *Lucy took a last look in the mirror.*

SYNONYM: glance

NOUN **5** The **look** on your face is the expression on it.

**ook after**

VERB If you **look after** someone or something, you take care of them.

**ook forward**

VERB If you **look forward** to something, you want it to happen because you think you will enjoy it.

**ook out**

VERB You say **look out** to warn someone of danger. • *Look out! There's a car coming.*

**okout lookouts**

NOUN **1** someone who is watching for danger, or a place where someone watches for danger

PHRASE **2** If you are **on the lookout** for something, you are watching or waiting for it to happen.

**om looms, looming, loomed**

NOUN **1** a machine for weaving cloth

VERB **2** If something **looms** in front of you, it suddenly appears as a tall, unclear and sometimes frightening shape. • *A monster loomed out of the darkness.*

VERB **3** If a situation or event is **looming**, it is likely to happen soon and is rather worrying. • *A storm is looming on the horizon.*

**op loops, looping, looped**

NOUN **1** a curved or circular shape in something such as a piece of string or wire

VERB **2** If you **loop** rope or string around an object, you place it in a loop around the object. • *He looped the rope over the horse's neck.*

**ose looser, loosest**

ADJECTIVE **1** not firmly held or fixed in place • *a loose tooth*

ADJECTIVE **2** not tight • *a loose jacket*

ADVERB **3** If people or animals break **loose**, or are set **loose**, they are released after they have been held back or tied up.

PRONUNCIATION TIP
This word is pronounced **looss**.

LANGUAGE TIP
Do not confuse *loose* with *lose*.

**loot loots, looting, looted**

VERB **1** If someone **loots** shops and houses, they steal goods from them, especially during a riot or war.

NOUN **2** stolen money or goods

**lopsided**

ADJECTIVE Something that is **lopsided** is uneven because one side is different from the other, for example one side is heavier or larger.

**lord lords**

NOUN In Britain, **Lord** is a title used in front of the names of some men.

**lorry lorries**

NOUN a large vehicle for transporting goods by road

**lose loses, losing, lost**

VERB **1** If you **lose** something, you cannot find it, or you no longer have it because it has been taken from you. • *He lost his place in the team.*

VERB **2** If you **lose** a fight or an argument, you are beaten.

PRONUNCIATION TIP
This word is pronounced **looz**.

LANGUAGE TIP
Do not confuse *lose* with *loose*.

**loss losses**

NOUN The **loss** of something is the fact of having lost it or of having less of it.

**lost**

VERB **1** the past tense and past participle of **lose**

ADJECTIVE **2** If you are **lost**, you do not know where you are.

ADJECTIVE **3** If something is **lost**, you cannot find it.

## lot lots
NOUN **1** a large amount of something • a **lot** of children
NOUN **2** very much or very often • I miss him a **lot**.
NOUN **3** the whole of something • He had a whole packet of biscuits and ate the **lot**.

## lotion lotions
NOUN a liquid that you put on your skin to protect or soften it • suntan **lotion**

## lottery lotteries
NOUN a way of raising money by selling tickets and giving prizes to people who have winning tickets, which are selected at random

## loud louder, loudest
ADJECTIVE A **loud** noise produces a lot of sound.

## loudly
ADVERB in a way that produces a lot of sound

## loudspeaker loudspeakers
NOUN a piece of electrical equipment that produces the sound in things such as radios, phones and CD players

## lounge lounges, lounging, lounged
NOUN **1** a room in a house, hotel or airport where people can sit and relax
VERB **2** If you **lounge** around, you lean against something or lie around in a lazy way.

## louse lice
NOUN a small insect that lives on people's bodies

## love loves, loving, loved
VERB **1** If you **love** someone or something, you have strong feelings of affection for them.
VERB **2** If you would **love** to do something, you want very much to do it.
NOUN **3** a strong feeling of affection for someone or something
PHRASE **4** If you are **in love** with someone, you feel strongly attracted to them romantically.

## lovely lovelier, loveliest
ADJECTIVE very beautiful, attractive, pleasant or enjoyable • We had a **lovely** day out.

## low lower, lowest
ADJECTIVE **1** Something that is **low** is close the ground.

ANTONYM: high

ADJECTIVE **2** below average in value or amo • The temperature was **low** for the time of y

ANTONYM: high

ADVERB **3** close to the ground • An aeropla flew **low** over the beach.

ANTONYM: high

## lower lowers, lowering, lowered
VERB **1** If you **lower** something, you move downwards. • She **lowered** the bucket int the well.
ADJECTIVE **2** The **lower** of two things is the bottom one. • the **lower** deck of the bus

## lower-case
ADJECTIVE **Lower-case** letters are small letters, not capital letters.

## loyal
ADJECTIVE If you are **loyal**, you are firm in your friendship or support for someone o something.

## lozenge lozenges
NOUN **1** a small sweet with medicine in it, that you can suck if you have a sore thro or a cough
NOUN **2** a diamond shape, like a rhombus

## lubricant lubricants
NOUN an oily substance that you put on something such a machine so that it mov smoothly

## lubricate lubricates, lubricating, lubricated
VERB If someone **lubricates** something, t put oil or grease on to it so that it moves smoothly.

WORD HISTORY
from Latin lubricus meaning slippery

## lubrication
NOUN the process of putting oil or grease o something such as a machine so that it moves smoothly

## luck
NOUN **1** something that happens by chanc • We had good **luck** with the weather. • It u bad **luck** that I lost the game of Monopoly.
PHRASE **2** You say **good luck** to someone when you are wishing them success.

**ckily**

ADVERB You use **luckily** to say that is lucky that something happened. • *Luckily, the cup didn't break when I dropped it.*

**cky luckier, luckiest**

ADJECTIVE Someone who is **lucky** has a lot of good luck.

ANTONYM: unlucky

**ggage**

NOUN Your **luggage** is the bags and suitcases that you take with you when you travel.

**kewarm**

ADJECTIVE slightly warm

**ll lulls, lulling, lulled**

NOUN **1** a pause in something, or a short time when it is quiet and calm
VERB **2** If you **lull** someone, you calm them and make them feel safe.

**llaby lullabies**

NOUN a song used for sending a baby or child to sleep

**mber lumbers, lumbering, lumbered**

NOUN **1** wood that has been roughly cut up
VERB **2** If you **lumber** around, you move heavily and clumsily.

**minous**

ADJECTIVE Something that is **luminous** glows in the dark without being hot.

**mp lumps**

NOUN a solid piece of something

**nar**

ADJECTIVE relating to the moon • *The lunar module landed safely on the moon*

WORD HISTORY
from Latin *luna* meaning moon

**nch lunches**

NOUN a meal eaten in the middle of the day

**ng lungs**

NOUN Your **lungs** are the two organs inside your chest that you breathe with.

→ Have a look at the illustration for **organ**

**rch lurches, lurching, lurched**

VERB **1** If someone or something **lurches**, they make a sudden, jerky movement.
PHRASE **2** If someone leaves you **in the lurch**, they leave you in a difficult or dangerous situation, instead of helping you.

**lure lures, luring, lured**

VERB If you **lure** someone or something, you tempt them into going somewhere or doing something. • *He lured the cat back into the house with some milk.*

**lurk lurks, lurking, lurked**

VERB If someone **lurks** somewhere, they hide there and wait.

**lush lusher, lushest**

ADJECTIVE In a **lush** field or garden, the grass or plants are healthy and growing thickly.

**lute lutes**

NOUN an old-fashioned, stringed musical instrument that is plucked like a guitar

**luxury luxuries**

NOUN **1** great comfort, especially among expensive and beautiful surroundings
NOUN **2** A **luxury** is something that you would like to have but do not need, and is usually expensive.

**lying**

VERB the present participle of **lie**

**lyrics**

PLURAL NOUN The **lyrics** of a song are the words.

# Mm

**m**
an abbreviation for *metre*

**macaroni**
NOUN short, hollow tubes of pasta

---

**WORD HISTORY**
an Italian word; from Greek *makaria*
meaning food made from barley

---

**machine machines**
NOUN a piece of equipment designed to do
a particular job. It is usually powered by
an engine or by electricity. • *a washing*
***machine***

**machine gun machine guns**
NOUN a gun that works automatically, firing
a continuous stream of bullets very quickly

**machinery**
NOUN machines in general • *farm **machinery***
• *factory **machinery***

**mackintosh mackintoshes**
NOUN a raincoat made from waterproof cloth

**mad madder, maddest**
ADJECTIVE **1** Someone who is **mad** has a
severe mental illness that causes them to
behave in strange ways.
ADJECTIVE **2** If you describe someone as **mad**,
you mean that they are very foolish.
ADJECTIVE **3** (*informal*) Someone who is **mad**
is angry.
PHRASE **4** If you are **mad about** someone or
something, you like them very much. • *She
had always been **mad about** football.*

**made**
VERB the past tense and past participle of
**make**

**magazine magazines**
NOUN a weekly or monthly publication
containing articles and photographs

**maggot maggots**
NOUN the larva of some kinds of fly.
**Maggots** look like small, fat worms.

**magic**
NOUN **1** In fairy stories, **magic** is a special
power that can make impossible things
happen.
NOUN **2** the art of performing tricks to
entertain people

**magical**
ADJECTIVE **1** using a special power to make
impossible things happen • ***magical** pow*
ADJECTIVE **2** exciting, beautiful and special
• *The island is tiny but truly **magical**.*

**magician magicians**
NOUN **1** a person who performs tricks that
seem like magic to entertain people
NOUN **2** In fairy stories, a **magician** is a m
with magic powers.

**magistrate magistrates**
NOUN an official who acts as a judge in a la
court that deals with less serious crimes

**magma**
NOUN molten rock that is formed in very hot
conditions inside the Earth

→ Have a look at the illustration for
**volcano**

**magnet magnets**
NOUN a piece of iron or steel that attracts
other objects made of iron or steel towards
it. **Magnets** can also push away, or repel,
other **magnets**.

**magnetic**
ADJECTIVE Something that is **magnetic** is
attracted towards a magnet. Only iron,
steel, nickel and cobalt are **magnetic**.

**magnification**
NOUN **Magnification** is the process of
making something look bigger than it real
is, for example by using a microscope.

**magnificent**
ADJECTIVE extremely beautiful or impressive

SYNONYMS: imposing, splendid

---

**WORD HISTORY**
from Latin *magnificus* meaning great in
deeds

---

**magnify magnifies, magnifying,
magnified**
VERB When a microscope or lens **magnifies**
something, it makes it look bigger than it
actually is.

**agnifying glass** **magnifying glasses**
NOUN a glass lens that magnifies things, making them appear bigger than they really are

**agpie** **magpies**
NOUN a large, black-and-white bird with a long tail

**ahogany**
NOUN a hard, reddish-brown wood used for making furniture

**aid** **maids**
NOUN a female servant

**aiden name** **maiden names**
NOUN the surname a woman had before she married

**ail** **mails, mailing, mailed**
NOUN 1 the letters and parcels delivered to you by the post office
NOUN 2 same as **email**
VERB 3 If you **mail** a letter, you send it by post.
VERB 4 If you **mail** someone, you send them an email.

**WORD HISTORY**
from Old French *male* meaning bag

**aim** **maims, maiming, maimed**
VERB To **maim** someone is to injure them very badly for life.

**ain** **mains**
ADJECTIVE 1 most important or largest • *My main interest is music.*

SYNONYMS: chief, major, principal

NOUN 2 The **mains** are the large pipes or cables that carry gas, water or electricity to a building.

**ainland**
NOUN the main part of a country or continent, not including the islands around it

**ainly**
ADVERB mostly, chiefly or usually • *We eat mainly vegetarian food.*

**aintain** **maintains, maintaining, maintained**
VERB 1 If you **maintain** something, you keep it going at a particular rate or level. • *You will need to maintain this level of fitness if you want to take part in the finals.*
VERB 2 If you **maintain** a machine or a building, you keep it in good condition.
VERB 3 If you **maintain** a belief or an opinion, you have it and state it clearly.

**maize**
NOUN a tall plant that produces sweet corn

**majestic**
ADJECTIVE big, beautiful and impressive • *majestic mountains*

**majesty** **majesties**
NOUN 1 You say **His Majesty** when you are talking about a king, and **Her Majesty** when you are talking about a queen.
NOUN 2 the quality of being dignified and impressive

**major** **majors**
ADJECTIVE 1 more important or more serious than other things • *She has a major role in the school play.*

ANTONYM: minor

NOUN 2 an army officer of the rank immediately above captain

**majority** **majorities**
NOUN more than half of a group • *The majority of the passengers became ill.*

**make** **makes, making, made**
VERB 1 If you **make** something, you create or produce it. • *This is the cake I made yesterday.*
VERB 2 If you **make** someone or something do something, you force them to do it or cause it to happen. • *Her mother made her do her homework every night.*
VERB 3 If you **make** a promise to do something, you say you will definitely do it.
VERB 4 Two amounts added together **make** a sum. • *3 and 5 make 8.*
VERB 5 If you **make** a phone call, you use a phone to speak to someone.
NOUN 6 the name of the product of a particular manufacturer • *What make is your bicycle?*

**make-believe**
NOUN a fantasy of pretend or imaginary things

**make-up**
NOUN coloured creams and powders that women and actors put on their faces

**malaria**
NOUN a serious tropical disease, caught from mosquitoes, that causes fever and shivering

**WORD HISTORY**
from Italian *mal* + *aria* meaning bad air, because people used to think that the bad air coming from the swamps around Rome caused the fever

a
b
c
d
e
f
g
h
i
j
k
l
m
n
o
p
q
r
s
t
u
v
w
x
y
z

**243**

A
B
C
D
E
F
G
H
I
J
K
L
**M**
N
O
P
Q
R
S
T
U
V
W
X
Y
Z

## male **males**

NOUN **1** a person or animal that cannot have babies or lay eggs

ANTONYM: female

ADJECTIVE **2** concerning or relating to males

ANTONYM: female

## malevolent

ADJECTIVE **1** **Malevolent** people want to cause harm or do evil things.

ADJECTIVE **2** A **malevolent** act is cruel and spiteful.

PRONUNCIATION TIP
This word is pronounced ma-**lev**-oh-lent.

## malfunction **malfunctions, malfunctioning, malfunctioned**

VERB If a machine **malfunctions**, it fails to work properly.

## malicious

ADJECTIVE **Malicious** talk or behaviour is intended to harm someone.

## mall **malls**

NOUN a sheltered place with cafés, shops and restaurants • *a shopping* **mall**

## mallet **mallets**

NOUN a wooden hammer with a square head

## malnutrition

NOUN a condition resulting from not eating enough healthy food or not having enough to eat

## mammal **mammals**

NOUN an animal that gives birth to live babies and feeds its young with milk from the mother's body. Human beings, dogs and whales are all **mammals**.

WORD HISTORY
from Latin *mamma* meaning breast

## mammoth **mammoths**

ADJECTIVE **1** very large indeed
NOUN **2** a huge animal that looked like a hairy elephant with long tusks. **Mammoths** became extinct a long time ago.

## man **men; mans, manning, manned**

NOUN **1** an adult, male human being

ANTONYM: woman

NOUN **2** Human beings, both male and female, are sometimes referred to as **man** • *Primitive* **man** *lived in caves.*
VERB **3** If you **man** something, you are in charge of it or you operate it. • *Can you* **man** *the bookstall?*

## manage **manages, managing, managed**

VERB **1** If you **manage** to do something, you succeed in doing it even if it is difficult • *We* **managed** *to find somewhere to sit.*
VERB **2** If someone **manages** an organisation or business, they are responsible for controlling it.

## management

NOUN **1** the controlling and organising of a business
NOUN **2** the people who control an organisation

## manager **managers**

NOUN a man or woman who is responsible for running a business or organisation

## mane **manes**

NOUN long hair growing from the neck of a lion or a horse

## manger **mangers**

NOUN a feeding box in a barn or stable

## mangle **mangles, mangling, mangled**

VERB **1** If you **mangle** something, you crush or twist it out of shape.
NOUN **2** an old-fashioned piece of equipment consisting of two large rollers, for squeezing water out of wet clothes

## mango **mangoes** or **mangos**

NOUN a sweet yellow fruit that grows in tropical climates

## mankind

NOUN used to refer to all human beings • *Pollution is a threat to* **mankind**.

## manner **manners**

NOUN **1** the way you do something or behave
PLURAL NOUN **2** If you have good **manners**, you behave very politely.

**manoeuvre manoeuvres, manoeuvring, manoeuvred**
VERB **1** If you **manoeuvre** something into place, you move it there skilfully. • *Mum* **manoeuvred** *the car into the small parking space.*
NOUN **2** A **manoeuvre** is a clever thing that you do or say in order to make something happen the way you want it to.

PRONUNCIATION TIP
This word is pronounced ma-**noo**-ver.

**manor manors**
NOUN a large country house with land, especially one that was built in the Middle Ages

**mansion mansions**
NOUN a very large house

**manslaughter**
NOUN the accidental killing of a person

**mantelpiece mantelpieces**
NOUN a shelf over a fireplace

**mantle mantles**
NOUN the part of the Earth between the crust and the core
→ Have a look at the illustration for **earth**

**manual manuals**
ADJECTIVE **1 Manual** work involves physical strength or skill with your hands, rather than mental skill.
ADJECTIVE **2 Manual** equipment is operated by hand rather than being automatic or operated by electricity or a motor. • *a* **manual** *whisk*
NOUN **3** a book that tells you how to use a machine • *an instruction* **manual**

WORD HISTORY
from Latin *manus* meaning hand

**manufacture manufactures, manufacturing, manufactured**
VERB **1** If someone **manufactures** goods, they make them in a factory.
NOUN **2** The **manufacture** of goods is the making of them in a factory.

**manure**
NOUN animal dung used to improve the soil

**manuscript manuscripts**
NOUN a handwritten or typed copy of a book, play or piece of music before it is printed

WORD HISTORY
from Latin *manus* meaning hand and *scribere* meaning to write

**many**
ADJECTIVE **1** If there are **many** people or things, there are a large number of them.
ADJECTIVE **2** You use **many** to talk about how great a number or quantity is. • *How* **many** *tickets do you need?*
PRONOUN **3** You use **many** to talk about how great a number or quantity is. • *He made a list of his friends. There weren't* **many**.

**map maps**
NOUN a detailed drawing of an area of land, showing its shape and features as it would appear if you saw it from above • *You can see the park beside the river on this* **map**.

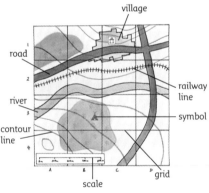

**maple maples**
NOUN a tree that has large leaves with five points

**marathon marathons**
NOUN a race in which people run 26 miles along roads • *My dad is training for the London* **Marathon**.

WORD HISTORY
named after *Marathon*, a place from which a messenger ran more than 20 miles to Athens, bringing news of a victory in 490 BC

**marble**
NOUN a very hard, cold stone that is often polished to show the coloured patterns in it

**march** marches, marching, marched
NOUN **1** an organised protest in which a large group of people walk somewhere together
VERB **2** When soldiers **march**, they walk with quick regular steps as a group.
NOUN **3** music with a strong beat for marching to

**March**
NOUN the third month of the year. **March** has 31 days.

WORD HISTORY
from Latin *Martius* month of Mars, the Roman god of war

**mare** mares
NOUN an adult female horse

**margarine**
NOUN a soft substance made from vegetable oil and animal fats, and used like butter

**margin** margins
NOUN **1** the blank space at the top and bottom and on each side of a written or printed page
NOUN **2** If you win a race or a competition by a large or small **margin**, you win it by a large or small amount.

**marina** marinas
NOUN a harbour for pleasure boats and yachts

**marine** marines
NOUN **1** a soldier who is trained for duties at sea
ADJECTIVE **2** relating to or involving the sea, and the animals and plants that live in the sea

**mark** marks, marking, marked
NOUN **1** a small stain or damaged area on a surface
NOUN **2** a score given to a student for homework or for an exam
NOUN **3** a written or printed symbol
VERB **4** If something **marks** a surface, it stains or damages it in some way.
VERB **5** When a teacher **marks** a student's work, they decide how good it is and give it a mark.
VERB **6** If you **mark** the opposing player in a team game such as hockey or netball, you stay close to them and prevent them from getting the ball.

**market** markets, marketing, marketed
NOUN **1** a place where goods are bought and sold, usually outdoors
VERB **2** If someone **markets** a product, they sell it in an organised way.

**marketing**
NOUN the part of a business that has to do with how goods or services are sold to customers

**marmalade**
NOUN a type of jam made from oranges or lemons

**maroon**
NOUN **1** a dark reddish-purple colour
ADJECTIVE **2** having a dark reddish-purple colour

**marquee** marquees
NOUN a very large tent used at a fair, a wedding or other outdoor events

WORD HISTORY
from French, meaning awning

**marriage** marriages
NOUN **1** the relationship between two people who are married
NOUN **2** a wedding ceremony

**married**
VERB **1** the past tense and past participle of **marry**
ADJECTIVE **2** If someone is **married**, they have a husband or a wife.

**marrow** marrows
NOUN a long, thick, green vegetable with cream-coloured flesh

**marry** marries, marrying, married
VERB When two people **marry**, they legally become partners in a special ceremony.

**marsh** marshes
NOUN an area of land that is permanently wet

**marshmallow** marshmallows
NOUN a soft, spongy sweet, usually pink or white

**marsupial** marsupials
NOUN an animal that carries its young in a pouch. Koalas, kangaroos and wallabies are **marsupials**.

WORD HISTORY
from Greek *marsupion* meaning purse

**martial**
ADJECTIVE **Martial** describes anything to do with military matters, war and soldiers.

**martial arts**
PLURAL NOUN The **martial arts** are techniques of self-defence, such as judo and karate, that come from the Far East.

**martyr martyrs**
NOUN someone who suffers or is killed for their beliefs

**marvel marvels, marvelling, marvelled**
VERB 1 If you **marvel** at something, you are filled with amazement and admiration for it. ● *We **marvelled** at the sight of people swimming with the dolphins.*
NOUN 2 something that fills you with surprise and admiration

**marvellous**
ADJECTIVE wonderful or excellent

**marzipan**
NOUN a paste made of almonds, sugar and egg. It is put on top of cakes or used to make small sweets.

**mascot mascots**
NOUN a person, animal or toy that is thought to bring good luck

**masculine**
ADJECTIVE typical of men, rather than women
ANTONYM: feminine

**mask masks, masking, masked**
NOUN 1 something you wear over your face for protection or as a disguise
VERB 2 If you **mask** something, you cover it so that it is protected or disguised.

**mass masses**
NOUN 1 a large amount or heap of something
NOUN 2 In science, **mass** is the amount of matter in an object. **Mass** is measured in grams (g).
NOUN 3 A **Mass** is a communion service in a Roman Catholic church.
ADJECTIVE 4 involving or affecting a large number of people

**massacre massacres, massacring, massacred**
NOUN 1 the killing of a very large number of people in a violent and cruel way
VERB 2 To **massacre** a group of people means to kill them in large numbers in a violent and cruel way.

**massage massages, massaging, massaged**
VERB 1 If you **massage** someone, you rub parts of their body in order to help them relax or to relieve pain.
NOUN 2 treatment that involves rubbing parts of the body

**massive**
ADJECTIVE extremely large
SYNONYMS: huge, vast, enormous

**mast masts**
NOUN the tall, upright pole that supports the sails of a boat

**master masters, mastering, mastered**
VERB 1 If you **master** a skill, you learn how to do it well.
NOUN 2 someone who is very skilled at something ● a **master** of disguise
NOUN 3 a male teacher

**masterpiece masterpieces**
NOUN an excellent painting, novel, film or other work of art that has been made with great skill ● *The 'Mona Lisa' is considered a **masterpiece**.*

**mat mats**
NOUN 1 a small piece of carpet or other material that is put on floors for protection or decoration
NOUN 2 a small piece of cloth or other material that is put on a table or other surface to protect it

**match matches, matching, matched**
NOUN 1 an organised game of football, cricket or some other sport
NOUN 2 a small, thin wooden stick tipped with a chemical that produces a flame when you strike it against a rough surface. **Matches** are used to light things.
VERB 3 If colours **match**, they go well together. ● *My dress **matched** my shoes.*
VERB 4 If you **match** one thing with another, you find the connection between them.

**mate mates, mating, mated**
NOUN 1 (*informal*) Your **mates** are your friends.
NOUN 2 The first **mate** on a ship is second in importance after the captain.
VERB 3 When a pair of animals **mate**, they come together in order to breed.

**material materials**
NOUN 1 cloth
NOUN 2 anything from which something else can be made ● *artists' **materials***

**maternal**

ADJECTIVE **1** used to describe things relating to a mother • *My maternal grandfather was Welsh.*
ADJECTIVE **2** A woman who is **maternal** has strong motherly feelings.

**maternity**

ADJECTIVE relating to or involving pregnant women and childbirth • *The baby was born in the maternity wing of the hospital.*

**mathematical**

ADJECTIVE involving numbers, quantities and shapes

**mathematically**

ADVERB in a way that involves numbers, quantities and shapes

**mathematician mathematicians**

NOUN someone who studies numbers, quantities and shapes

**mathematics**

NOUN the study of numbers, quantities and shapes

**maths**

NOUN an abbreviation of *mathematics*

**matinee matinees**

NOUN an afternoon performance at a theatre or cinema

**PRONUNCIATION TIP**

This word is pronounced **mat**-i-nay.

**matrix matrices**

NOUN In mathematics, a **matrix** is a set of numbers or letters set out in rows and columns.

**PRONUNCIATION TIP**

This word is pronounced **may**-trix. The plural is pronounced **may**-tri-sees.

**matt**

ADJECTIVE dull rather than shiny • *Mum painted the front door matt green.*

**matter matters, mattering, mattered**

NOUN **1** a task or situation that you have to attend to • *We will have to discuss the matter with the head teacher.*

SYNONYMS: affair, business, subject

NOUN **2** any substance • *The scientists explored how matter behaves at high temperatures.*
VERB **3** If something **matters**, it is important.
PHRASE **4** If you ask **What's the matter?**, you want to know what is wrong.

**mattress mattresses**

NOUN a large, flat, spongy pad that is put on a bed to make it comfortable to sleep on

**mature matures, maturing, matured**

VERB **1** When a child or other young animal **matures**, it becomes an adult.
ADJECTIVE **2** fully grown or developed

**maturely**

ADVERB If someone behaves **maturely**, they behave in a sensible way like you would expect an adult to behave.

**maturity**

NOUN **Maturity** is when a person or animal is fully grown or developed.

**maul mauls, mauling, mauled**

VERB If an animal **mauls** someone, they savagely attack and badly injure them.

**mauve**

NOUN **1** a light purple colour
ADJECTIVE **2** having a light purple colour

**PRONUNCIATION TIP**

This word rhymes with "stove".

**maximum**

ADJECTIVE **1** The **maximum** amount is the most that is possible or allowed. • *The maximum score for this question is five mark*

ANTONYM: minimum

NOUN **2** the most that is possible or allowed • *Pupils are allowed a maximum of two pounds to spend on the school trip.*

ANTONYM: minimum

**may**

VERB **1** If something **may** happen, it is possible that it will happen.
VERB **2** If you **may** do something, you are allowed to do it.

**May**

NOUN the fifth month of the year. **May** has 31 days.

**WORD HISTORY**

probably from the Roman goddess *Maia*

**maybe**

ADVERB If you think there is a possibility that something will happen, but you are not sure, you use **maybe**. • *Maybe we will be allowed to go to the cinema tonight.*

**ayonnaise**
NOUN a thick salad dressing made with egg yolks and oil

**ayor mayors**
NOUN someone who has been elected to represent the people of a town at official functions

**aze mazes**
NOUN a system of complicated passages which it is difficult to find your way through

**e**
PRONOUN A speaker or writer uses **me** to refer to himself or herself.

**eadow meadows**
NOUN a field of grass

**eagre**
ADJECTIVE very small and poor • **meagre** portions

**eal meals**
NOUN 1 an occasion when people eat
NOUN 2 the food people eat at meal times

**ean means, meaning, meant; meaner, meanest**
VERB 1 If you ask someone what something **means**, you want them to explain it to you.
VERB 2 If you **mean** to do something, you intend to do it.

SYNONYMS: aim, plan

VERB 3 If something **means** a lot to you, it is important to you.
ADJECTIVE 4 unkind
ADJECTIVE 5 Someone who is **mean** is unwilling to share with others.
NOUN 6 In mathematics, the **mean** is the average of a set of numbers.

**eander meanders, meandering, meandered**
VERB If a road or river **meanders**, it has a lot of bends in it.

PRONUNCIATION TIP
This word is pronounced mee-**an**-der.

WORD HISTORY
from *Maiandros*, the name of a Greek river

**eaning meanings**
NOUN The **meaning** of a word, expression or gesture is what it refers to or expresses. • Do you know the **meaning** of the proverb "more haste, less speed"?

**meanwhile**
ADVERB If something happens, and **meanwhile** something else is happening, the two things are happening at the same time.

**measles**
NOUN an infectious illness that causes a high temperature and red spots on the skin • an outbreak of **measles**

WORD HISTORY
from Germanic *masele* meaning spot on the skin

**measure measures, measuring, measured**
VERB 1 If you **measure** something, you find out the size or amount of it. • First **measure** the length of the table.
NOUN 2 a unit used to measure something
NOUN 3 a container or an instrument, such as a ruler or a measuring jug, that you use to measure something
NOUN 4 an action that you take to achieve something

**measurement measurements**
NOUN the result you obtain when you measure something

**meat meats**
NOUN the flesh of animals that people cook and eat • As a vegetarian, I don't eat **meat** or fish.

**mechanic mechanics**
NOUN someone whose job is to repair and maintain machines and engines

**mechanical**
ADJECTIVE 1 to do with machinery. Anything **mechanical** is worked by machinery.
ADJECTIVE 2 If you do something in a **mechanical** way, you do it without thinking about it.

**medal medals**
NOUN a small piece of decorative metal, often shaped like a large coin and attached to a ribbon, given as an award for bravery or as a prize in sport

**meddle meddles, meddling, meddled**
VERB If you **meddle**, you interfere and try to change things without being asked.

# media

**PLURAL NOUN** You can refer to the television, radio and newspapers as the **media**.

**LANGUAGE TIP**
*Media* is the plural of *medium* but it is becoming more common for it to be used as a singular noun: *The media is obsessed with celebrities.*

## median medians

**NOUN** In mathematics, the **median** of a set of numbers is the middle number once the numbers have been arranged in order of size. • *The **median** of 4, 0, 1, 2, 3 is 2, as 2 is in the middle once they are organised in order.*

## medical

**ADJECTIVE** to do with the treatment of people who are ill

## medication medications

**NOUN** a substance that is used to treat illness

## medicine medicines

**NOUN 1** a substance that you take to help cure an illness
**NOUN 2** the care and treatment of people who are ill

## medieval; also spelt mediaeval

**ADJECTIVE** relating to the period between about 1100–1500 AD, especially in Europe

## mediocre

**ADJECTIVE** Something that is **mediocre** is of average or poor quality or standard. • *The film was **mediocre**.*

**PRONUNCIATION TIP**
This word is pronounced mee-dee-**oh**-ker.

## Mediterranean

**NOUN 1** the large sea between southern Europe and northern Africa
**ADJECTIVE 2** relating to the **Mediterranean** or the countries adjoining it

## medium mediums or media

**ADJECTIVE 1** If something is of **medium** size, it is neither large nor small.
**NOUN 2** a means of communicating or expressing something

## meek meeker, meekest

**ADJECTIVE** A **meek** person is timid and does what other people say.

## meet meets, meeting, met

**VERB 1** If you **meet** someone, you make an arrangement to go to the same place at the same time as they do. • *Let's **meet** at my house.*
**VERB 2** If you **meet** someone, you come face to-face with them or are introduced to them for the first time. • *We **met** on our first day at school.*

## meeting meetings

**NOUN 1** an event at which people discuss things or make decisions
**NOUN 2** an occasion when you meet someone by arrangement

## megabyte megabytes

**NOUN** a unit of storage in a computer, equal to 1,048,576 bytes

## melancholy

**ADJECTIVE** If you feel **melancholy**, you feel very sad.

## melodramatic

**ADJECTIVE** behaving in an exaggerated, emotional way

## melody melodies

**NOUN** a tune

**WORD HISTORY**
from Greek *meloidia* meaning singing

## melon melons

**NOUN** a large, juicy fruit with a green or yellow skin and many seeds inside

## melt melts, melting, melted

**VERB** When something **melts**, or when you **melt** it, it changes from a solid to a liquid because it has been heated.

## melting point

**NOUN** the temperature at which a solid starts to change into a liquid

## member members

**NOUN** one of the people or things belonging to a group

## membrane membranes

**NOUN** a very thin skin

## memoir memoirs

**NOUN** a book or article that you write about your own life or about the life of someone who you have known well

## memorable

**ADJECTIVE** **Memorable** things or people are likely to be remembered because they are special or unusual.

## memorial memorials

**NOUN** a structure built to remind people of a famous person or event • *a war **memorial***

**emorise memorises, memorising, memorised**; also spelt **memorize**
VERB If you **memorise** something, you learn it so well that you remember it and can repeat it exactly. • *She **memorised** all the times tables from 2 to 12 in one week.*

**emory memories**
NOUN **1** your ability to remember things
NOUN **2** A computer's **memory** is its capacity to store information.

**emory card memory cards**
NOUN a small card containing computer memory that is used in digital cameras and other devices

**emory stick memory sticks**
NOUN a small device that connects to a computer and allows you to store and copy information

**en**
PLURAL NOUN the plural of **man**

**enace menaces, menacing, menaced**
NOUN **1** someone or something that is likely to cause harm • *That dog is a **menace**.*
VERB **2** If someone or something **menaces** you, they threaten to harm you.

**enacing**
ADJECTIVE threatening and making you think something bad is going to happen to you

**enacingly**
ADVERB in a threatening way that makes you think something bad is going to happen to you

**end mends, mending, mended**
VERB If you **mend** something that is broken, you repair or fix it.

**enstruate menstruates, menstruating, menstruated**
VERB When a woman **menstruates**, blood comes from her womb. This normally happens once a month.

**ental**
ADJECTIVE relating to the mind and the process of thinking • ***mental** arithmetic*

**ention mentions, mentioning, mentioned**
VERB **1** If you **mention** something, you speak or write briefly about it.
NOUN **2** a brief comment about someone or something

**menu menus**
NOUN **1** a list of the food and drink you can buy in a restaurant or café
NOUN **2** a list of options shown on a computer screen, which the user must choose from

**mercenary mercenaries**
ADJECTIVE **1** Someone who is **mercenary** is mainly interested in getting money.
NOUN **2** a soldier who is paid to fight for a foreign country

**merchandise**
NOUN goods for buying and selling • *The market stalls were full of all kinds of **merchandise**.*

**merchant merchants**
NOUN a trader who imports and exports goods

**mercury**
NOUN a silver-coloured metallic element that is liquid at room temperature. **Mercury** is used in some thermometers.

**mercy mercies**
NOUN If you show **mercy**, you are kind and forgiving instead of punishing someone.

**merge merges, merging, merged**
VERB When two things **merge**, they combine or join together to make one thing. • *The two roads **merged** at the junction.*

**meridian meridians**
NOUN one of the lines on maps or globes, drawn from the North Pole to the South Pole, that help to describe the position of a place

**merit merits, meriting, merited**
NOUN **1** If something has **merit**, it is good or worthwhile.
NOUN **2** The **merits** of something are its advantages or good qualities. • *I can see now the **merits** of working hard.*
VERB **3** If something or someone **merits** a particular treatment, they deserve that treatment. • *He **merits** a place in the team.*

**mermaid mermaids**
NOUN a creature in stories, with a woman's body and a fish's tail instead of legs

**merry merrier, merriest**
ADJECTIVE happy and cheerful

**mesh**
NOUN threads of wire, plastic or other material twisted together like a net

a
b
c
d
e
f
g
h
i
j
k
l
m
n
o
p
q
r
s
t
u
v
w
x
y
z

**251**

A
B
C
D
E
F
G
H
I
J
K
L
M
N
O
P
Q
R
S
T
U
V
W
X
Y
Z

**mess** messes, messing, messed
NOUN **1** something dirty or untidy
NOUN **2** something full of problems
**mess about** or **mess around**
VERB If you **mess about** or **mess around**, you spend time doing silly or casual things. • *Stop messing about and get on with your work.*
**mess up**
VERB If you **mess up** something, you make it untidy, spoil it or do it badly. • *He'd already messed up one piece of paper.*

**message** messages, messaging, messaged
NOUN **1** a piece of information or a request from one person to another
VERB **2** If you **message** someone, you write to them on a social media website. • *I'll message you with my address.*

**messenger** messengers
NOUN someone who takes a message

**messy** messier, messiest
ADJECTIVE **1** dirty or untidy
ADJECTIVE **2** complicated or confused • *He's got himself into a messy situation.*

**met**
VERB the past tense and past participle of **meet**

**metal** metals
NOUN a hard substance such as iron, steel, copper or lead. **Metals** are good conductors of heat and electricity.

**metallic**
ADJECTIVE made of metal or like metal

**metaphor** metaphors
NOUN an imaginative way of describing one thing as another thing. For example, if a person is shy and timid, you could describe them as a mouse.

**meteor** meteors
NOUN a piece of rock or metal moving rapidly through space, that burns very briefly and brightly when it enters the Earth's atmosphere

**meteorite** meteorites
NOUN a piece of rock from space that has landed on Earth

**meteorologist** meteorologists
NOUN someone who studies the weather

**meteorology**
NOUN the study of the weather

**meter** meters
NOUN a device that measures and records something, such as a gas **meter** that records how much gas a household has used

**method** methods
NOUN a particular way of doing something • *Use the method I showed you to work out the sum.*

**methodical**
ADJECTIVE **Methodical** people do things in a careful and organised way.

**metre** metres
NOUN a unit of length (m) equal to 100 centimetres

**metric**
ADJECTIVE The **metric** system of measurement is a system that uses metres, grams and litres.

**mew** mews, mewing, mewed
VERB When a cat **mews**, it makes a short, high-pitched noise.

**miaow** miaows, miaowing, miaowed
NOUN **1** the noise a cat makes
VERB **2** When a cat **miaows**, it makes a crying sound.

**mice**
PLURAL NOUN the plural of **mouse**

**micro-**
PREFIX added to some words to mean very small. For example, a **micro**computer is a very small computer.

**microbe** microbes
NOUN a very small, living thing that can only be seen through a microscope. **Microbes** can feed, grow and reproduce.

**microchip** microchips
NOUN a small piece of silicon that has electronic circuits printed on it, and is used in computers and electronic equipment

**microhabitat** microhabitats
NOUN a very small habitat

**micro-organism** micro-organisms
NOUN a very small organism that can only be seen under a powerful microscope. Some **micro-organisms** are harmful and cause disease. Others, such as yeast, are helpful. Microbes, germs and viruses are sometimes called **micro-organisms**.

**crophone microphones**
NOUN a device that is used to record sounds or make them louder

**croscope microscopes**
NOUN a piece of equipment that magnifies very small objects so that you can study them ● *When the class looked at a leaf through the microscope, they could see the small veins that they had not been able to see before.*

**croscopic**
ADJECTIVE too small to be seen without using a microscope

**crowave microwaves**
NOUN a type of oven that cooks food very quickly by radiation

**id-**
PREFIX used to form words that refer to the middle part of a place or a period of time ● *We had a break midmorning.*

**idday**
NOUN twelve o'clock in the middle of the day

**iddle middles**
NOUN 1 The **middle** of something is the part furthest from the edges, ends or surface. ● *He stood in the middle of the room.*
NOUN 2 The **middle** of an event is the part that comes after the first part and before the last part. ● *There was an interval in the middle of the play.*
ADJECTIVE 3 The **middle** thing in a series is the one with an equal number of things on each side. ● *M and N are the middle letters in the alphabet.*

**iddle Ages**
NOUN In European history, the **Middle Ages** were the period between about 1100 AD and 1500 AD.

**idnight**
NOUN twelve o'clock at night

**idwife midwives**
NOUN a nurse who is trained to help women during pregnancy and at the birth of their baby

**ight**
VERB 1 You use **might** to say that something will possibly happen or is possibly true. ● *I might not be back until tomorrow.*
NOUN 2 If you do something with all your **might**, you do it with all your strength and energy.

**migraine migraines**
NOUN a severe headache that makes you feel very ill

**migrant migrants**
NOUN 1 A **migrant** or a **migrant** worker is a person who moves from one place to another, usually to find work ● *Migrants arrived for the fruit-picking season.*
NOUN 2 a bird, fish or animal that migrates from one part of the world to another ● *The spotted flycatcher, a migrant from Africa, arrives in Britain in May.*

**migrate migrates, migrating, migrated**
VERB 1 If people **migrate**, they move from one place to another, especially to find work.
VERB 2 When birds or animals **migrate**, they move to a different place at a particular season, usually to breed or to find food.

**migration**
NOUN 1 **Migration** is when people move from one place to another, especially to find work.
NOUN 2 **Migration** is when birds or animals move to a different place at a particular season, usually to breed or to find food.

**migratory**
ADJECTIVE **Migratory** birds or animals move to a different place at a particular season, usually to breed or to find food.

**mild milder, mildest**
ADJECTIVE Something that is **mild** is gentle, and not very strong or severe. ● *mild weather*

**mildew**
NOUN a soft, white fungus that grows on things when they are warm and damp

**mile miles**
NOUN a unit of distance equal to about 1.6 kilometres

WORD HISTORY
from Latin *milia passuum* meaning a thousand paces

**mileage mileages**
NOUN the distance you have travelled, measured in miles ● *The mileage from home to the hotel was 120 miles.*

**military**
ADJECTIVE to do with the armed forces of a country

a
b
c
d
e
f
g
h
i
j
k
l
m
n
o
p
q
r
s
t
u
v
w
x
y
z

**253**

A
B
C
D
E
F
G
H
I
J
K
L
**M**
N
O
P
Q
R
S
T
U
V
W
X
Y
Z

**milk** milks, milking, milked
NOUN **1** the white liquid produced by mammals to feed their young. People drink cows' and goats' **milk** and make it into butter, cheese and yogurt.
VERB **2** When someone **milks** a cow or other animal, they get milk from it by pulling its udders.

**milkman** milkmen
NOUN a man who delivers milk to your house

**mill** mills
NOUN **1** a building where grain is crushed to make flour
NOUN **2** a factory for making materials such as steel, wool or cotton • *a cotton* **mill**
NOUN **3** a small device for grinding something. For example, a pepper **mill** grinds peppercorns.

**millennium** millennia or millenniums
NOUN a period of 1000 years

**milligram** milligrams
NOUN a unit of weight (mg). There are 1000 **milligrams** in a gram.

**millilitre** millilitres
NOUN a unit for measuring liquid (ml). There are 1000 **millilitres** in a litre.

**millimetre** millimetres
NOUN a unit of length (mm). There are 10 **millimetres** in a centimetre.

**million** millions
NOUN A **million** is the number 1,000,000.

**millionaire** millionaires
NOUN someone who has money or property worth at least a million pounds or dollars

**millionth** millionths
NOUN **1** one of a million equal parts of something
ADJECTIVE **2** The **millionth** item in a series is the one that you count as number million. It can be written as 1000000$^{th}$.

**mime** mimes, miming, mimed
NOUN **1** the use of movements and gestures to express something or to tell a story without using speech
VERB **2** If you **mime** something, you describe or express it using mime.

**mimic** mimics, mimicking, mimicked
VERB **1** If you **mimic** someone's actions or voice, you imitate them in an amusing way.
NOUN **2** a person who can imitate other people

**minaret** minarets
NOUN a tall, thin tower on a mosque

**mince** minces, mincing, minced
NOUN **1** meat that has been ground into ve small pieces
VERB **2** If you **mince** meat, you grind it int very small pieces.

**mincemeat**
NOUN a sweet mixture of dried fruits used, example, in mince pies

**mind** minds, minding, minded
NOUN **1** Your **mind** is your ability to think, together with your memory and all the thoughts you have. • *He could still see her face in his* **mind**.
PHRASE **2** If you **change your mind**, you change a decision that you have made or an opinion that you have.
VERB **3** If you do not **mind** what happens what something is like, you do not have a strong preference about it. • *I don't* **mind** *where we go*.
VERB **4** If you tell someone to **mind** something, you are warning them to be careful. • **Mind** *that plate, it's hot.*
VERB **5** If you **mind** something for someone you look after it for a while.

**mindless**
ADJECTIVE **1** **Mindless** behaviour is stupid a destructive.
ADJECTIVE **2** A **mindless** job or activity is so simple, or repeated so often, that you do need to think about it at all.

SYNONYM: repetitive

**mine** mines
PRONOUN **1** something belonging or relating to the person who is speaking or writing • *He's a good friend of* **mine**.
NOUN **2** a place where deep holes or tunne are dug under the ground in order to extr minerals • *a coal* **mine**
NOUN **3** a bomb hidden in the ground or underwater, that explodes when people o things touch it

**minefield** minefields
NOUN an area of land or water where explosive mines have been laid

**miner** miners
NOUN a person who works underground in mines to find and dig out coal, diamonds, gold and other minerals • *a coal* **miner**

**neral minerals**
NOUN small particles that make up different rocks. For example, quartz and diamonds are **minerals**.

**neral water**
NOUN water that comes from a natural spring

**ngle mingles, mingling, mingled**
VERB If things **mingle**, they become mixed together.

**ni-**
PREFIX used with another word to describe something shorter or smaller than the usual size • a **mini**skirt

**niature**
ADJECTIVE a tiny copy of something much larger • I bought a **miniature** version of the iffel Tower as a souvenir.

**nibus minibuses**
NOUN a van with seats in the back, that is used as a small bus

**nimum**
ADJECTIVE **1** A **minimum** amount of something is the smallest amount that is possible, allowed or needed.

ANTONYM: maximum

NOUN **2** the smallest amount of something that is possible, allowed or needed

ANTONYM: maximum

**nister ministers**
NOUN **1** a person who is in charge of a particular government department
NOUN **2** a member of the clergy, especially in a Protestant church

**WORD HISTORY**
from Latin minister meaning servant

**nistry ministries**
NOUN a government department that deals with a particular area of work • the **Ministry** of Education

**nk minks**
NOUN an expensive fur used to make coats and hats

**nnow minnows**
NOUN a very small, freshwater fish

**minor**
ADJECTIVE less important or serious than other things • He had a **minor** part in the play.

ANTONYM: major

**minority minorities**
NOUN less than half of a group of people or things

**minstrel minstrels**
NOUN a singer and entertainer in medieval times

**mint mints**
NOUN **1** a plant with strong-smelling leaves used as flavouring in cooking
NOUN **2** a sweet flavoured with these leaves
NOUN **3** the place where the official coins of a country are made
ADJECTIVE **4** If something is in **mint** condition, it is like new.

**minus**
PREPOSITION **1** You use **minus** (−) to show that one number is being subtracted from another. • Ten **minus** six equals four (10 − 6 = 4).
ADJECTIVE **2** **Minus** before a number means that the number is less than zero. • There are sometimes temperatures of **minus** 65 °C (−65 °C) in the Arctic.

**minute minutes**
NOUN **1** a unit of time equal to sixty seconds
NOUN **2** a short period of time • See you in a **minute**.
ADJECTIVE **3** extremely small • A **minute** amount of milk is needed.

**PRONUNCIATION TIP**
The noun is pronounced **min**-it. The adjective is pronounced my-**nyoot**.

**miracle miracles**
NOUN a surprising and wonderful event, especially one believed to have been caused by God

**WORD HISTORY**
from Latin mirari meaning to wonder at

**mirage mirages**
NOUN an image that you can see in the distance in very hot weather, but that does not actually exist

**PRONUNCIATION TIP**
This word is pronounced mi-**rarzh**.

255

**mirror mirrors**
NOUN an object made of glass in which you can see your reflection

**mis-**
PREFIX added to some words to mean badly or wrongly. For example, **mis**behave means to behave badly, and **mis**calculate means to calculate wrongly.

**misbehave misbehaves, misbehaving, misbehaved**
VERB If someone **misbehaves**, they are naughty or behave badly.

**misbehaviour**
NOUN naughty or bad behaviour

**miscarriage miscarriages**
NOUN **1** If a woman has a **miscarriage**, she gives birth to a baby too early, before it is able to survive in the outside world.
NOUN **2** A **miscarriage** of justice is a wrong decision made by a court, which results in an innocent person being punished.

**miscellaneous**
ADJECTIVE A **miscellaneous** group is made up of a mixture of people or things that are different from each other.

PRONUNCIATION TIP
This word is pronounced miss-uh-**lay**-nee-uss.

**mischief**
NOUN naughty behaviour, teasing people or playing tricks

**mischievous**
ADJECTIVE If you are **mischievous**, you enjoy being naughty by teasing or playing tricks on people.

**miser misers**
NOUN a mean person who enjoys hoarding money, but hates spending it

**miserable**
ADJECTIVE If you are **miserable**, you are very unhappy.

**miserly**
ADJECTIVE Someone who is **miserly** is mean and hates spending money.

**misery miseries**
NOUN great unhappiness
SYNONYM: grief

**misfire misfires, misfiring, misfired**
VERB If a plan **misfires**, it goes wrong.

**misfit misfits**
NOUN a person who cannot get on with ot people or fit into a group

**misfortune misfortunes**
NOUN an unpleasant occurrence that is regarded as bad luck • I had the **misfortu** to fall off my bike.

**mishap mishaps**
NOUN an accidental or unfortunate happening that is not very serious
• Grandma had a small **mishap** when her blew away.

**misjudge misjudges, misjudging, misjudged**
VERB If you **misjudge** someone or something, you form a wrong or unfair opinion of them.

**mislay mislays, mislaying, mislaid**
VERB If you **mislay** something, you canno remember where you put it.

**mislead misleads, misleading, misle**
VERB If you **mislead** someone, you make them believe something that is not true.

**misprint misprints**
NOUN a mistake such as a spelling mistak something that has been printed

**miss misses, missing, missed**
VERB **1** If you **miss** someone or something you feel sad because they are no longer with you.
VERB **2** If you **miss** a bus, plane or train, yo arrive too late to catch it.
VERB **3** If you **miss** an event or activity, yo fail to attend it. • I had to **miss** my piano lesson.
VERB **4** If you **miss** something that you are aiming at, you fail to hit it. • The arrow **missed** the target.
NOUN **5 Miss** is used before the name of a girl or unmarried woman. • My teacher th year is **Miss** Weston.

**missile missiles**
NOUN **1** a weapon that moves long distanc through the air and explodes when it reaches its target • nuclear **missiles**
NOUN **2** any object thrown to harm someo or something

**missing**
ADJECTIVE Something that is **missing** is los or not in its usual place. • One of my shoe is **missing**.

**ssion missions**

ᴏᴜɴ **1** a journey made by a military
ᴇroplane or space rocket to carry out a task
ᴏᴜɴ **2** an important task that has to be
ᴏne

**ssionary missionaries**

ᴏᴜɴ a Christian who has been sent to a
ᴏreign country to work for the Church

**sspell misspells, misspelling,
ᴀisspelt or misspelled**

ᴇʀʙ If you **misspell** a word, you spell it
ᴡrongly.

**st mists**

ᴏᴜɴ many tiny drops of water in the air that
ᴀake it hard to see clearly

**stake mistakes, mistaking, mistook,
ᴀistaken**

ᴏᴜɴ **1** If you make a **mistake**, you do
ᴏmething wrong without intending to.
There are some spelling **mistakes** in your
ᴏmework.
ᴇʀʙ **2** If you **mistake** someone or
ᴏmething for another person or thing, you
ᴡrongly think that they are the other person
ᴏr thing. • I **mistook** him for his brother.

**stletoe**

ᴏᴜɴ a plant that grows on trees and has
ᴡhite berries on it

**stook**

ᴇʀʙ the past tense of **mistake**

**streat mistreats, mistreating,
ᴀistreated**

ᴇʀʙ If you **mistreat** a person or an animal,
ᴏu treat them badly and make them suffer.

**stress mistresses**

ᴏᴜɴ **1** a woman schoolteacher • There is a
ᴀew French **mistress**.
ᴏᴜɴ **2** a woman who is in charge of
ᴏmething or someone

**strust mistrusts, mistrusting,
ᴀistrusted**

ᴠᴇʀʙ **1** If you **mistrust** someone, you feel
ᴛhat that they are not to be trusted.

ᴀɴᴛᴏɴʏᴍ: trust

ɴᴏᴜɴ **2** the feeling of not being able to trust
ᴏmeone or something

ᴀɴᴛᴏɴʏᴍ: trust

**misunderstand misunderstands,
misunderstanding, misunderstood**

ᴠᴇʀʙ If you **misunderstand** someone, you
do not properly understand what they say or
do. • He **misunderstood** the instructions and
took the wrong turning.

**misunderstanding
misunderstandings**

ɴᴏᴜɴ If people have a **misunderstanding**,
they have a disagreement or a slight quarrel
about something.

**misuse misuses, misusing, misused**

ɴᴏᴜɴ **1** The **misuse** of something is the
incorrect or dishonest use of it.
ᴠᴇʀʙ **2** If you **misuse** something, you use it
wrongly or dishonestly.

**mix mixes, mixing, mixed**

ᴠᴇʀʙ **1** If you **mix** things, you combine them.
ᴠᴇʀʙ **2** A **mixed** number is made up of a
whole number and a fraction.

**mix up**

ᴠᴇʀʙ If you **mix up** things, you get
confused.

**mixed up**

ᴀᴅᴊᴇᴄᴛɪᴠᴇ confused • I got **mixed up** and went
to the wrong place.

**mixture mixtures**

ɴᴏᴜɴ **1** two or more things mixed together
• They felt a **mixture** of fear and excitement as
they climbed the wall.
ɴᴏᴜɴ **2** a substance consisting of two or
more other substances that have been
mixed together

**ml**

an abbreviation for millilitre

**mm**

an abbreviation for millimetre

**mnemonic mnemonics**

ɴᴏᴜɴ a word, short poem, or sentence that
can help you remember things such as
spelling rules • Never Eat Slimy Worms is a
**mnemonic** for the points of the compass.

**moan moans, moaning, moaned**

ᴠᴇʀʙ **1** If you **moan**, you make a low,
miserable sound because you are in pain or
unhappy.
ᴠᴇʀʙ **2** If you **moan** about something, you
complain about it.
ɴᴏᴜɴ **3** a low cry of pain or unhappiness

a b c d e f g h i j k l m n o p q r s t u v w x y z

257

**moat moats**

NOUN a wide, deep ditch around a castle, usually filled with water, to help defend the building

→ Have a look at the illustration for **castle**

**mob mobs, mobbing, mobbed**

NOUN **1** a large, disorganised crowd of people

VERB **2** If a group **mobs** someone, they gather closely around them in a disorderly way. • *The fans mobbed the band.*

**mobile mobiles**

ADJECTIVE **1** able to move or be moved easily • *He's much more mobile since getting his new wheelchair.*

NOUN **2** short for **mobile phone**

NOUN **3** an ornament made up of several parts that hang from threads and move in the breeze

**mobile phone mobile phones**

NOUN a small phone that you can carry around with you

**mock mocks, mocking, mocked**

VERB **1** If you **mock** someone, you tease them or try to make them look foolish.

SYNONYMS: laugh at, make fun of

ADJECTIVE **2** not genuine • *The ring is made of mock diamonds.*

**mode modes**

NOUN **1** a particular way of behaving or of doing something

NOUN **2** In mathematics, the mode is the most popular or most frequently occurring value. • *Of the following numbers – 5, 5, 6, 7, 7, 7, 8 – 7 is the mode.*

**model models**

NOUN **1** a smaller copy of something that shows what it looks like or how it works in real life • *a model of how the building will look*

NOUN **2** a type or version of a product • *Which model of computer did you choose?*

NOUN **3** a person who wears clothes that are being displayed to possible buyers, or who poses for a photographer or artist

ADJECTIVE **4** a smaller copy of something that shows what it looks like or how it works in real life • *Mark has a model railway in his bedroom.*

ADJECTIVE **5** A **model** student is an excellent example of a student.

**modem modems**

NOUN a piece of equipment that links a computer to the telephone system so that data can be sent from one computer to another

**moderate moderates, moderating, moderated**

ADJECTIVE **1** A **moderate** amount of something is not too much or too little o

ADJECTIVE **2** Moderate ideas and opinions not extreme.

VERB **3** If something **moderates** or is **moderated**, it becomes less extreme. • *He should moderate his temper.*

PRONUNCIATION TIP

The adjective is pronounced **mod**-er-ut. verb is pronounced **mod**-er-ayt.

**modern**

ADJECTIVE new and involving the latest idea or equipment

WORD HISTORY

from Latin *modo* meaning just recently

**modest**

ADJECTIVE **1** quite small in size or amount • *He inherited a modest amount of money.*

ADJECTIVE **2** Modest people do not boast about how clever or how rich they are.

ANTONYM: boastful

**modesty**

NOUN the quality that someone has when they do not boast about how clever or ho rich they are

**modify modifies, modifying, modified**

VERB If you **modify** something, you chang it slightly to improve it. • *When he had modified his bike, it went much faster.*

**module modules**

NOUN **1** one of the parts which, when put together, form a whole unit or object

NOUN **2** a part of a spacecraft that can do certain things away from the main body • *the lunar module*

**moist moister, moistest**

ADJECTIVE slightly wet, damp

**moisten moistens, moistening, moistened**

VERB If you **moisten** something, you make slightly wet.

**moisture**

NOUN tiny drops of water in the air or on th ground

**lar molars**
NOUN Your **molars** are the large teeth at the back of your mouth.
▸ Have a look at the illustration for **teeth**

**le moles**
NOUN **1** a small animal with black fur. **Moles** ve in tunnels underground.
NOUN **2** a dark, slightly-raised spot on your kin

**lecular**
DJECTIVE to do with molecules

**lecule molecules**
NOUN A **molecule** is made up of two or more toms held together.

**llusc molluscs**
NOUN an animal with a soft body and no ackbone. Snails, slugs, clams and mussels re all **molluscs**.

**lten**
DJECTIVE **Molten** rock or metal has been eated to a very high temperature and has nelted to become a thick liquid. • *When the olcano erupted, **molten** lava flowed down the mountainside.*

**ment moments**
NOUN **1** a very short period of time • *I paused for a **moment**.*

SYNONYMS: instant, second

NOUN **2** the point at which something happens • *At that **moment**, the doorbell rang.*
PHRASE **3** If something is happening **at the moment**, it is happening now.

**mentum**
NOUN the ability that an object has to continue moving as a result of its mass and the speed at which it is already moving

**onarchy monarchies**
NOUN a system in which a queen or king reigns in a country

**onastery monasteries**
NOUN a place where monks live and work

WORD HISTORY
from Latin *monasterium* meaning to live alone

**onastic**
ADJECTIVE to do with monks or life in a monastery

**Monday Mondays**
NOUN the second day of the week, coming between Sunday and Tuesday

WORD HISTORY
from Old English *Monandæg* meaning moon's day

**money**
NOUN the coins and banknotes that you use to buy things

**mongrel mongrels**
NOUN a dog with parents of different breeds

**monitor monitors, monitoring, monitored**
VERB **1** If you **monitor** something, you regularly check its condition and progress.
NOUN **2** a machine used to check or record things
NOUN **3** the visual display unit of some computers
NOUN **4** a school pupil chosen to do special duties by the teacher

**monk monks**
NOUN a member of a male religious community

**monkey monkeys**
NOUN an agile animal that has a long tail and climbs trees

**mono-**
PREFIX having one of something, for example a **mono**rail is a single rail, and a sound that is **mono**tone has only one tone

**monologue monologues**
NOUN a long speech by one person during a play or conversation

**monotonous**
ADJECTIVE always the same in way that is very dull and boring • *a **monotonous** voice*

**monotony**
NOUN the quality that something has when it is always the same in a way that is dull and boring

**monsoon monsoons**
NOUN the season of very heavy rain in Southeast Asia

**monster monsters**
NOUN **1** a large, imaginary creature that looks very frightening
NOUN **2** a cruel and frightening person
ADJECTIVE **3** extremely large • *She gave him a **monster** TV set for his birthday.*

a
b
c
d
e
f
g
h
i
j
k
l
m
n
o
p
q
r
s
t
u
v
w
x
y
z

**259**

A
B
C
D
E
F
G
H
I
J
K
L
**M**
N
O
P
Q
R
S
T
U
V
W
X
Y
Z

**WORD HISTORY**

from Latin *monstrum* meaning omen or warning

### month months

NOUN one of the twelve periods that a year is divided into

### monthly

ADJECTIVE **1** happening or appearing once every month • *There is a **monthly** fee to pay for the club.*

ADVERB **2** once every month • *The magazine is published **monthly**.*

### monument monuments

NOUN a large structure built to remind people of a famous person or event

**WORD HISTORY**

from Latin *monere* meaning to remind

### moo moos, mooing, mooed

VERB **1** When cows **moo**, they make a long, deep sound.

NOUN **2** the long, deep sound that cows make

### mood moods

NOUN the way you are feeling at a particular time

### moodily

ADVERB in a way that shows you are annoyed or unhappy

### moody moodier, moodiest

ADJECTIVE **1** **Moody** people change their mood often and very quickly, seemingly for no reason.

ADJECTIVE **2** depressed and miserable

### moon moons

NOUN an object that moves round the Earth once every four weeks. You see the **moon** as a shining circle or crescent in the sky at night. Some other planets have **moons**.

### moonlight

NOUN the light that comes from the moon at night

### moor moors, mooring, moored

NOUN **1** a high area of open land • *The farmer had flocks of sheep grazing on the **moors**.*

VERB **2** If you **moor** a boat, you attach it to the land with a rope.

### moose

NOUN a North American deer or elk, with large, flat antlers

**LANGUAGE TIP**

The plural of *moose* is *moose*.

### mop mops, mopping, mopped

NOUN **1** a tool for washing floors. It has a string or a sponge head at the end of a l[ ] handle.

VERB **2** If you **mop** something, you wipe it clean it up with a mop or a cloth.

### mope mopes, moping, moped

VERB If you **mope**, you feel miserable and sorry for yourself • *Don't sit around and **mope** – go out and do something you enjoy*

### moral morals

PLURAL NOUN **1** **Morals** are values based on beliefs that are acceptable to a particular society.

ADJECTIVE **2** relating to beliefs about what is right and wrong • *moral values*

NOUN **3** the lesson taught by a story, that usually tells you that good behaviour is best

### morale

NOUN Your **morale** is the amount of confidence and optimism you feel.

• *The **morale** of the school was high.*

### morality

NOUN **1** society's beliefs about what is good or bad behaviour

NOUN **2** The **morality** of an action or way behaving is whether people think it is right or wrong. • *People argue about the **morality** of hunting animals.*

### morally

ADVERB to do with beliefs about what is right and wrong • *Stealing is **morally** wrong.*

### morbid

ADJECTIVE If you are **morbid**, you have a great interest in unpleasant things, especially death and illness.

**WORD HISTORY**

from Latin *morbus* meaning illness

**e**

ECTIVE **1** a greater number or extent than
mething else • *More than 1500 schools
»k part in the event.*

NTONYMS: fewer, less

ECTIVE **2** an additional thing or amount of
mething • *I would like some more orange
ce.*

ONOUN **3** an additional thing or amount
something • *We should do more to help
ople.*

VERB **4 More** means to a greater degree or
tent. • *We can talk more later.*

VERB **5** You use **more** to show that
mething is repeated. • *Repeat the exercise
»ce more.*

VERB **6** You use **more** in front of
me adjectives and adverbs to form
mparatives. • *He did it more carefully the
cond time.*

**ning mornings**

JUN **1** the early part of the day, before noon
JUN **2** the part of the day between midnight
d midday

**rse code**

JUN a code for sending messages by radio
gnals. Each letter is represented by a
ries of dots (short sounds) and dashes
»nger sounds).

**rsel morsels**

JUN a small piece of food

**rtal mortals**

JECTIVE **1** a **mortal** wound causes death
JECTIVE **2** unable to live forever and certain
» die
JUN **3** an ordinary person

**rtar mortars**

JUN **1** a mixture of sand, water and cement
sed to hold bricks firmly together
JUN **2** a short cannon that fires missiles
gh into the air

**rtgage mortgages**

JUN a loan that people get from a bank or
uilding society in order to buy a house

**rtuary mortuaries**

JUN a special room in a hospital where
ead bodies are kept before being buried or
remated

**saic mosaics**

JUN a design made of small, coloured
tones, tiles or pieces of coloured glass set
to concrete or plaster

**mosque mosques**

NOUN a building where Muslims go to worship

**WORD HISTORY**
from Arabic *masjid* meaning temple

**mosquito mosquitoes** or **mosquitos**

NOUN a small, flying insect that bites people
and animals in order to suck their blood

**moss mosses**

NOUN a soft, small, green plant that grows
on damp soil or stone

**most**

ADJECTIVE **1 Most** of a group of things or
people means nearly all of them. • *Most
people prefer sunny weather.*
ADJECTIVE **2** a larger amount than anyone or
anything else • *She has the most points.*
ADVERB **3** You use **most** in front of adjectives
or adverbs to form superlatives. • *the most
breathtaking scenery in the world*

**motel motels**

NOUN a hotel for people who are travelling by
car, with parking spaces close to the rooms

**moth moths**

NOUN an insect like a butterfly that usually
flies at night

**mother mothers**

NOUN Your **mother** is your female parent.

**mother-in-law mothers-in-law**

NOUN the mother of someone's husband or
wife

**motion motions**

NOUN movement

**motionless**

ADJECTIVE If someone or something is
**motionless**, they are not moving at all.

**motivate motivates, motivating,
motivated**

VERB If you **motivate** someone, you
make them determined to do or achieve
something.

**motivated**

ADJECTIVE **1** determined to do or achieve
something
ADJECTIVE **2** done for a particular reason
• *The decision was politically motivated.*

**motivation**

NOUN **1** determination to do or achieve
something
NOUN **2** the reason why someone does
something

**261**

**motive** **motives**
NOUN a reason or purpose for doing something

**motor** **motors**
NOUN a part of a vehicle or machine. The **motor** uses fuel to make the vehicle or machine work

SYNONYM: engine

**motorbike** **motorbikes**
NOUN a heavy two-wheeled vehicle that is driven by an engine

**motorcycle** **motorcycles**
NOUN another word for **motorbike**

**motorist** **motorists**
NOUN a person who drives a car or rides a motorbike

**motorway** **motorways**
NOUN a wide road built for fast travel over long distances

**motto** **mottoes** or **mottos**
NOUN a short sentence or phrase that is a rule for good or sensible behaviour. For example, *everything in moderation*.

**mould** **moulds, moulding, moulded**
VERB 1 If you **mould** a substance, you make it into a particular shape. • **Mould** the *dough into balls*.
NOUN 2 a container used to make something into a particular shape • *a jelly* **mould**
NOUN 3 a soft, grey or green growth that forms on old food or damp walls

**mouldy** **mouldier, mouldiest**
ADJECTIVE Something that is **mouldy** is covered with mould. • *This old bread had gone* **mouldy**.

**moult** **moults, moulting, moulted**
VERB When an animal or bird **moults**, it loses its hair or feathers so that new ones can grow.

**mound** **mounds**
NOUN 1 a small, man-made hill
NOUN 2 a large, untidy pile

**mount** **mounts, mounting, mounted**
VERB 1 If you **mount** a horse or bicycle, you climb onto it.
VERB 2 If something **mounts**, it increases in amount. • *The contributions for the tombola were* **mounting**.
VERB 3 If you **mount** a picture or a photograph, you put it in a frame or an album to display it.

NOUN 4 a mountain, especially as part of the name • **Mount** *Everest is the highest mountain in the world.*

**mountain** **mountains**
NOUN a very high piece of land with steep sides • *Ben Nevis is the highest* **mountain** *Scotland.*

**mountaineer** **mountaineer**
NOUN a person who climbs mountains

**mourn** **mourns, mourning, mourne**
VERB If you **mourn** for someone who has you feel sad and think about them a lot.

**mouse** **mice**
NOUN 1 a small, furry rodent with a long
NOUN 2 a computer device that you move hand to control the position of a cursor the screen

→ Have a look at the illustration for **computer**

**moustache** **moustaches**
NOUN the hair that grows on a man's upp lip

**mouth** **mouths**
NOUN 1 the lips of a human or animal, or space behind them where the tongue ar teeth are

→ Have a look at the illustrations for **fis** and **respiratory system**

NOUN 2 the entrance to a cave or a hole
NOUN 3 the place where a river flows into the sea

**mouthful** **mouthfuls**
NOUN the amount of food you put in your mouth • *Don't take such huge* **mouthfuls**

**movable**
ADJECTIVE Something that is **movable** can moved from one place to another.

**move** **moves, moving, moved**
VERB 1 When you **move** something, or wh it **moves**, its position changes. • *The tra began to* **move** *out of the station.*
VERB 2 If you **move** or **move house**, you to live in a different place.
VERB 3 If something **moves** you, it causes you to feel a deep emotion. • *The film* **moved** *us to tears.*
NOUN 4 a change from one place or positi to another, especially in a game • *It's yo* **move**.

**movement movements**
NOUN **1** the action of changing position or moving from one place to another
NOUN **2** a group of people who act together to try and make something happen • *the animal rights movement*
NOUN **3** one of the main parts of a piece of classical music

**movie movies**
NOUN another name for **film**

**moving**
ADJECTIVE Something that is **moving** makes you feel deep sadness or emotion. • *a moving story*

**mow mows, mowing, mowed, mown**
VERB If you **mow** grass, you cut it with a lawnmower.

**MP MPs**
NOUN someone who has been elected by the people of an area to represent them in Parliament. **MP** is an abbreviation for *Member of Parliament*.

**MP3 player MP3 players**
NOUN a device that plays audio and video files, used for listening to music

**Mr**
NOUN **Mr** is used before a man's name when you are speaking to him or talking about him. • *My teacher is called Mr Jones.*

**Mrs**
NOUN **Mrs** is used before the name of a married woman when you are speaking or referring to her. • *"Good morning, Mrs Green."*

**Ms**
NOUN **Ms** is used before a woman's name when you are speaking or referring to her. **Ms** does not show whether the woman is married or not.

**much**
ADVERB **1** You use **much** to indicate the great size, extent or intensity of something. • *He's much taller than you.*
ADVERB **2** If something does not happen **much**, it does not happen often. • *He doesn't talk much.*
PRONOUN **3** a large amount of something • *There isn't much left.*
ADJECTIVE **4** You use **much** to talk about the size or amount of something. • *I've eaten too much food.*

**mud**
NOUN wet, sticky earth

**muddle muddles, muddling, muddled**
NOUN **1** a state of disorder or untidiness
VERB **2** If you **muddle** things, you mix them up.

**WORD HISTORY**
from Dutch *moddelen* meaning to make muddy

**muddy**
ADJECTIVE covered in or full of wet, sticky earth • *muddy boots*

**muesli**
NOUN a mixture of cereal flakes, chopped nuts and dried fruit that you can eat with milk for breakfast

**muffled**
ADJECTIVE A sound that is **muffled** is low or difficult to hear.

**mug mugs, mugging, mugged**
NOUN **1** a large, deep cup
VERB **2** (*informal*) If someone **mugs** you, they attack you in the street in order to steal your money.

**mule mules**
NOUN the offspring of a female horse and a male donkey

**multimedia**
NOUN You use **multimedia** when you are talking about computer programs and products which involve sound, pictures, and film, as well as text.

**multiple multiples**
ADJECTIVE **1** consisting of many parts or having many uses
NOUN **2** a number that can be divided exactly by another number • *2, 4, 6, 8, 10 and 12 are all multiples of 2.*

**multiplication**
NOUN the process of multiplying one number by another

**multiply multiplies, multiplying, multiplied**
VERB **1** When you **multiply** one number by another, you calculate the total you would get if you added the first number to itself the number of times shown by the second number. • *Six multiplied by three is 18 ($6 \times 3 = 18$), because $6 + 6 + 6 = 18$.*
VERB **2** When something **multiplies**, it increases greatly in number or amount.

a b c d e f g h i j k l m n o p q r s t u v w x y z

A
B
C
D
E
F
G
H
I
J
K
L
M
N
O
P
Q
R
S
T
U
V
W
X
Y
Z

**multitude multitudes**
NOUN (*formal*) a very large number of people or things

**mum mums**
NOUN (*informal*) mother

**mumble mumbles, mumbling, mumbled**
VERB If you **mumble**, you speak very quietly and indistinctly.

**mummy mummies**
NOUN **1** (*informal*) Your **mummy** is your mother.
NOUN **2** a dead body that was preserved long ago by being rubbed with special oils and wrapped in cloth • *Mummies have been found in tombs in Egypt.*

WORD HISTORY
(sense 2) from Persian *mum* meaning wax

**mumps**
NOUN a disease that causes painful swelling in the neck

**munch munches, munching, munched**
VERB If you **munch** something, you chew it steadily and thoroughly.

**mural murals**
NOUN a picture painted on a wall

**murder murders, murdering, murdered**
NOUN **1** the deliberate killing of a person
VERB **2** To **murder** someone means to kill them deliberately.

**murderer murderers**
NOUN someone who deliberately kills someone else

**murk**
NOUN darkness or dirt that is difficult to see through

WORD HISTORY
from Old Norse *myrkr* meaning darkness

**murky murkier, murkiest**
ADJECTIVE dark or dirty and hard to see through • *murky water*

WORD HISTORY
from Old Norse *myrkr* meaning darkness

**murmur murmurs, murmuring, murmured**
VERB **1** If you **murmur** something, you s⟨ ⟩ very quietly.
NOUN **2** something someone says that can hardly be heard • *They spoke in low murmurs*.

**muscle muscles**
NOUN Your **muscles** are the bundles of fi⟨ ⟩ connected to your bones, that enable yo⟨ ⟩ to move.

WORD HISTORY
from Latin *musculus* meaning little mous⟨ ⟩ because muscles were thought to look li⟨ ⟩ mice

**muscular**
ADJECTIVE **1 Muscular** people have strong, well-developed muscles.
ADJECTIVE **2** involving or affecting your muscles • *muscular pain*

**museum museums**
NOUN a public building where interesting valuable objects are kept and displayed

**mushroom mushrooms**
NOUN a fungus with a short stem and a round top. Some types of **mushroom** ar⟨ ⟩ edible.

**music**
NOUN **1** the pattern of sounds performed b⟨ ⟩ people singing or playing instruments
NOUN **2** the written symbols that represent musical sounds

**musical musicals**
ADJECTIVE **1** relating to playing or studying music • *She has considerable musical tale⟨ ⟩*
NOUN **2** a play or a film that uses songs an⟨ ⟩ dance to tell the story

**musician musicians**
NOUN a person who plays a musical instrument well

**Muslim Muslims**
NOUN **1** a person who believes in the Islam⟨ ⟩ religion and lives according to its rules
ADJECTIVE **2** relating to Islam

**mussel mussels**
NOUN a small, edible shellfish with a black shell

**st**

VERB **1** If you tell someone that they **must** do something, you make them feel that they ought to do it. ● *You **must** try this pudding – is delicious.*

VERB **2** If something **must** happen, it is very important or necessary that it happens. ● *You **must** be over 15 to see a film with a 15 certificate.*

VERB **3** If you think something is very likely, you think it **must** be so. ● *You **must** be Tom's brother.*

**stard**

NOUN a spicy-tasting yellow or brown paste made from seeds

**te**

ADJECTIVE If you are **mute**, you do not make any sounds. ● *I would have screamed, but I was **mute** with fear.*

**tilate mutilates, mutilating, mutilated**

VERB **1** If you **mutilate** something, you damage or spoil it.

VERB **2** If someone is **mutilated**, they have been very badly cut and injured.

**tineer mutineers**

NOUN a soldier or sailor who is part of a group of soldiers or sailors who rebel against their officers

**tiny mutinies, mutinying, mutinied**

VERB **1** If a group of sailors or soldiers **mutiny**, they rebel against their officers.

NOUN **2** a rebellion against someone in authority

**tter mutters, muttering, muttered**

VERB If you **mutter**, or if you **mutter** something, you speak very quietly so that it is difficult for people to hear you.

**tton**

NOUN the meat of an adult sheep

**tual**

ADJECTIVE **Mutual** is used to describe something that two or more people give to each other or share. ● *My dad and my brother have a **mutual** love of football.*

**uzzle muzzles, muzzling, muzzled**

NOUN **1** the nose and mouth of an animal

NOUN **2** a cover or a strap for a dog's nose and mouth to prevent it from biting

NOUN **3** the open end of a gun where the bullets come out

VERB **4** If you **muzzle** a dog, you put a muzzle on it.

**my**

ADJECTIVE **My** refers to something belonging to the person who is speaking or writing. ● *I ride **my** bicycle to school every day.*

**myself**

PRONOUN You use **myself** when you are speaking about yourself. ● *I was cross with **myself** for being so mean.*

**mysterious**

ADJECTIVE **1** strange and puzzling ● *They heard **mysterious** noises in the night.*

ADJECTIVE **2** If someone is being **mysterious**, they are being secretive about something. ● *Mum is being very **mysterious** about my birthday present.*

**mystery mysteries**

NOUN something that is not understood or known about ● *The identity of the burglar remains a **mystery**.*

**mystify mystifies, mystifying, mystified**

VERB If something **mystifies** you, you find it impossible to understand. ● *I am **mystified** by the disappearance of my sweater.*

**myth myths**

NOUN a story that was made up long ago to explain natural events and people's religious beliefs

# Nn

**nag** nags, nagging, nagged
VERB If you **nag** someone, you keep complaining to them or asking them to do something.

**nail** nails, nailing, nailed
NOUN **1** Your **nails** are the thin, hard areas covering the ends of your fingers and toes.
NOUN **2** a small piece of metal with a sharp point at one end, that you hammer into objects to hold them together
VERB **3** If you **nail** something somewhere, you fix it there using a nail.

**naïve**
ADJECTIVE If you are **naïve**, you believe that things are easier or less complicated than they really are, usually because of your lack of experience.

PRONUNCIATION TIP
This word is pronounced ny-**eeve**.

**naked**
ADJECTIVE not wearing any clothes

**name** names, naming, named
NOUN **1** a word that you use to identify a person, animal, place or thing
VERB **2** When you **name** someone or something, you give them a name.

**nameless**
ADJECTIVE not having a name or not identified
• a **nameless** terror

**nanny** nannies
NOUN a person whose job is to look after young children

**nap** naps, napping, napped
NOUN **1** a short sleep
VERB **2** When you **nap**, you have a short sleep.

**napkin** napkins
NOUN a small piece of cloth or paper used to wipe your hands and mouth after eating

**nappy** nappies
NOUN a piece of towelling or paper paddi worn round a baby's bottom

**narrate** narrates, narrating, narrate
VERB If you **narrate** a story, you tell it.

**narration**
NOUN **Narration** is telling a story.

**narrative** narratives
NOUN a story or an account of events

**narrator** narrators
NOUN the person in a book or a film or in radio or television broadcast, who tells t story or explains what is happening

**narrow** narrower, narrowest; narrow narrowing, narrowed
ADJECTIVE **1** Something that is **narrow** measures a small distance from one side to the other. • We walked down a **narrow** passageway.
VERB **2** If something **narrows**, it becomes less wide. • The track **narrowed** ahead.

**nasty** nastier, nastiest
ADJECTIVE very unpleasant

SYNONYMS: unkind, rude, disgusting

**nation** nations
NOUN a country and all the people who liv there

**national**
ADJECTIVE relating to a country or the whole country • He was dressed in the **national** costume.

**national anthem** national anthem:
NOUN the official song of a country

**nationality** nationalities
NOUN the fact of being a citizen of a particular nation • I'm not sure of her **nationality**, but I think she's Canadian.

**native** natives
ADJECTIVE **1** Your **native** country is the cour where you were born.
ADJECTIVE **2** Your **native** language is the language that you first learned to speak.
NOUN **3** A **native** of a place is someone wh was born there.

**Nativity**
NOUN In Christianity, the **Nativity** is the b of Christ, or the festival celebrating this.

**ural**

ADJECTIVE **1** normal and to be expected
*It's **natural** to want to do well.*

ADJECTIVE **2** existing or happening in nature,
rather than caused or made by people
*Wool is a **natural** material.*

ADJECTIVE **3** If you have a **natural** ability, you
are born with it. ● *She has a **natural** flair for
mathematics.*

**ural history**

NOUN the study of animals and plants

**urally**

ADVERB **1** You use **naturally** to say that
something is normal and to be expected.
● ***Naturally**, she was a bit nervous about her
first day at a new school.*

ADVERB **2** in a way that is caused by nature,
rather than caused or made by people ● *She
doesn't dye her hair. It's **naturally** red.*

ADVERB **3** You use **naturally** to say 'yes'
or 'of course'. ● *"Can I come with you?"
"**Naturally**".*

ADVERB **4** in a relaxed way without trying too
hard ● *Try to act **naturally**.*

**ture natures**

NOUN **1** animals, plants and all the other
things in the world that are not made by
people

NOUN **2** the basic quality or character of
a person or thing ● *They liked his warm,
generous **nature**.*

**ughtiness**

NOUN a child's bad behaviour

**ughty naughtier, naughtiest**

ADJECTIVE A child who is **naughty** behaves
badly.

**usea**

NOUN a feeling that you are going to be sick

**useous**

ADJECTIVE feeling that you are going to be sick

**utical**

ADJECTIVE relating to ships or navigation

**val**

ADJECTIVE relating to a navy

**vel navels**

NOUN the small hollow on the front of your
body, just below your waist

**navigate navigates, navigating,
navigated**

VERB When someone **navigates**, they work
out the direction in which a ship, plane or
car should go, using maps and sometimes
instruments.

**navigation**

NOUN **Navigation** is the process of working
out the direction in which a ship, plane or
car should go, using maps and sometimes
instruments.

**navigator navigators**

NOUN someone who works out the direction
in which a ship, plane or car should go,
using maps and sometimes instruments

**navy navies**

NOUN the part of a country's armed forces
that fights at sea

**near nearer, nearest; nears, nearing,
neared**

PREPOSITION **1** If something is **near** a place, it
is a short distance from it. ● *They live in a
cottage **near** the river.*

ADVERB **2** If you come **near** a place, you come
a short distance from it. ● *As we drew **near**, I
saw that the boot lid was up.*

VERB **3** When you are **nearing** a particular
place or time, you are approaching it and
will soon reach it. ● *I closed the curtains as
the visitor **neared** the door.*

**nearby**

ADJECTIVE **1** Something that is **nearby** is a
short distance away. ● *a **nearby** street*

ADVERB **2** a short distance away ● *He lives
**nearby**.*

**nearly**

ADVERB not completely, but almost
● *I've **nearly** finished my homework.*

**neat neater, neatest**

ADJECTIVE tidy and smart

**neatly**

ADVERB in a way that is tidy and smart

**necessary**

ADJECTIVE Something that is **necessary**
is needed or must be done. ● *It might be
**necessary** to leave quickly.*

LANGUAGE TIP
*Necessary* has one *c* and two *s*s.

a
b
c
d
e
f
g
h
i
j
k
l
m
n
o
p
q
r
s
t
u
v
w
x
y
z

A
B
C
D
E
F
G
H
I
J
K
L
M
N
O
P
Q
R
S
T
U
V
W
X
Y
Z

**necessity necessities**
NOUN **1** the need to do something
NOUN **2** something that is needed • *Water is a basic **necessity** of life.*

**neck necks**
NOUN **1** the part of your body that joins your head to the rest of your body
NOUN **2** the long, narrow part at one end of a bottle or guitar

**necklace necklaces**
NOUN a piece of jewellery that a person wears around their neck

**nectar**
NOUN a sweet liquid produced by flowers and collected by insects

**nectarine nectarines**
NOUN a soft, round fruit with a smooth yellow and red skin

**need needs, needing, needed**
VERB **1** If you **need** something, you cannot achieve what you want without having it or doing it. • *I **need** some help with my homework.*
PLURAL NOUN **2** Your **needs** are the things that you need to have.

SYNONYMS: necessities, requirements

**needle needles**
NOUN **1** a small, thin piece of metal with a hole at one end and a sharp point at the other, used for sewing
NOUN **2** **Needles** are long, thin pieces of steel or plastic, used for knitting.
NOUN **3** the sharp part of a syringe that goes into your skin when you have an injection
NOUN **4** the thin pointer on a dial or compass that moves to show a measurement or bearing
NOUN **5** Pine **needles** are the sharp, pointed leaves of a pine tree.

**needlework**
NOUN sewing or embroidery that is done by hand

**negative negatives**
ADJECTIVE **1** A **negative** answer means no.

ANTONYM: positive

ADJECTIVE **2** A **negative** number is less than zero.

ANTONYM: positive

NOUN **3** the image that is first produced when you take a photograph

**neglect neglects, neglecting, neglec**
VERB **1** If you **neglect** someone or something, you do not look after them properly. • *Ben **neglected** his hamster.*
NOUN **2** failure to look after someone or something properly • *Most of her plants c from **neglect**.*

**negotiate negotiates, negotiating, negotiated**
VERB When people **negotiate**, they talk about a situation in order to reach an agreement about it.

**neigh neighs, neighing, neighed**
NOUN A **neigh** is a loud, high-pitched sou made by a horse.

PRONUNCIATION TIP
This word is pronounced **nay**.

**neighbour neighbours**
NOUN someone who lives next door to you near you

**neighbourhood neighbourhoods**
NOUN Your **neighbourhood** is the area where you live.

**neither**
ADJECTIVE **1** You use **neither** to refer to not one or the other of two people or things. • *At first, **neither** child could speak.*
CONJUNCTION **2** You use **neither** in front of alternatives to mean not one and not the other. • *He spoke **neither** English nor Gern*

**neon**
NOUN a gas used in glass tubes to make lights and signs

**nephew nephews**
NOUN Someone's **nephew** is the son of th sister or brother.

**nerve nerves**
NOUN **1** long, thin fibres that send messag between your brain and other parts of yo body
NOUN **2** courage and calm in a difficult situation
NOUN **3** (*informal*) rudeness or cheek • *She had the **nerve** to answer back to the head teacher.*

**nervous**
ADJECTIVE easily worried and agitated

**nervously**
ADVERB in a way that shows you are worrie and anxious

**st nests**

NOUN a structure that birds, insects and other animals make, in which to lay eggs or rear their young

**stle nestles, nestling, nestled**

VERB If you **nestle** somewhere, you settle there comfortably, often very close to someone or something else. ● *My kitten loves to **nestle** in my lap.*

---

**PRONUNCIATION TIP**

This word is pronounced ness-**sl**.

---

**t nets**

NOUN **1** short for **internet**

NOUN **2** material made from threads woven together with small spaces in between

NOUN **3** a piece of this material used for a particular purpose, for example a fishing **net**

**tball**

NOUN a game in which two teams of seven players each try to score goals by throwing a ball through a net at the top of a pole

**ttle nettles**

NOUN a wild plant covered with little hairs that sting

**twork networks**

NOUN **1** a large number of lines or roads that cross each other at many points

NOUN **2** a group of computers connected to each other

**eutral**

ADJECTIVE **1** People who are **neutral** do not support either side in a disagreement or war.

ADJECTIVE **2** very pale or with very little colour ● *The carpet was a **neutral** cream colour.*

ADJECTIVE **3** neither acid nor alkali

**eutron neutrons**

NOUN a particle with no electrical charge

→ Have a look at the illustration for **atom**

**ever**

ADVERB at no time in the past, present or future ● *I've **never** met such a lovely person.*

**evertheless**

ADVERB in spite of what has just been said

**ew newer, newest**

ADJECTIVE **1** recently made, created or discovered ● *She's got a **new** film out.*

ADJECTIVE **2** different ● *We've got a **new** maths teacher.*

**ews**

NOUN up-to-date information about things that have happened

**newsagent newsagents**

NOUN a person or shop that sells newspapers and magazines

**newspaper newspapers**

NOUN a publication, on large sheets of folded paper, that is produced regularly and contains news and articles

**newt newts**

NOUN a small, amphibious creature with a moist skin, short legs and a long tail

**newton newtons**

NOUN a unit for measuring force (N)

---

**WORD HISTORY**

named after Sir Isaac *Newton*

---

**New Year**

NOUN the time when people celebrate the start of a year

**next**

ADJECTIVE **1** The **next** thing, person or event is the one that comes immediately after the present one. ● *We'll catch the **next** train.*

ADJECTIVE **2** The **next** place or person is the one nearest to you. ● *She lives in the **next** street.*

ADVERB **3** You use **next** to refer to an action that follows immediately after the present one. ● *What shall we do **next**?*

PHRASE **4** If one thing is **next to** another, it is at the side of it. ● *She sat down **next to** him.*

**nib nibs**

NOUN the pointed end of a pen, where the ink comes out

**nibble nibbles, nibbling, nibbled**

VERB **1** When you **nibble** something, you take small bites of it.

NOUN **2** a small bite of something

**nice nicer, nicest**

ADJECTIVE pleasant or kind

**nicely**

ADVERB **1** in a pleasant or kind way ● *If you ask Dad **nicely**, he might take you to the zoo.*

ADVERB **2** well ● *The jeans fit **nicely**.*

**nickname nicknames**

NOUN an informal name for someone or something

---

**WORD HISTORY**

from Middle English *an ekename* meaning an additional name

---

a
b
c
d
e
f
g
h
i
j
k
l
m
n
o
p
q
r
s
t
u
v
w
x
y
z

**nicotine**
NOUN an addictive substance found in tobacco

WORD HISTORY
named after Jacques *Nicot*, who first brought tobacco to France

**niece** **nieces**
NOUN Someone's **niece** is the daughter of their sister or brother. • *He bought a present for his* **niece**.

**night** **nights**
NOUN the time between sunset and sunrise, when it is dark

**nightdress** **nightdresses**
NOUN a loose dress that a woman or girl wears to sleep in

**nightfall**
NOUN the time of day when it starts to get dark • *By the time they got home it was* **nightfall**.

**nightingale** **nightingales**
NOUN a small, brown European bird, the male of which sings very beautifully, especially at night

**nightmare** **nightmares**
NOUN **1** a frightening dream • *She had a* **nightmare** *last night*.
NOUN **2** an unpleasant or frightening situation • *The whole journey was a* **nightmare**.

WORD HISTORY
from *night* + Old English *mare* meaning evil spirit

**nil**
NOUN zero or nothing, especially in sports scores • *Unfortunately, at half-time the score was still* **nil-nil**.

**nimble** **nimbler, nimblest**
ADJECTIVE able to move quickly and easily

**nine**
NOUN **Nine** is the number 9.

**nineteen**
NOUN **Nineteen** is the number 19.

**nineteenth**
NOUN **1** one of nineteen equal parts of something
ADJECTIVE **2** The **nineteenth** item in a series is the one that you count as number nineteen.

**ninetieth**
NOUN **1** one of ninety equal parts of something
NOUN **2** The **ninetieth** item in a series is t one that you count as number ninety.

**ninety**
NOUN **Ninety** is the number 90.

**ninth** **ninths**
NOUN **1** one of nine equal parts of somethi It can be written as ⅑.
ADJECTIVE **2** The **ninth** item in a series is the one that you count as number nine. It ca be written as 9th.

**nip** **nips, nipping, nipped**
VERB **1** If you **nip** someone or something, y give them a slight pinch or bite.
VERB **2** If you **nip** somewhere, you go there quickly. • *I have to* **nip** *to the shop for some m*
NOUN **3** A **nip** is small bite or pinch.

**niqab** **niqabs**
NOUN a veil worn by some Muslim women public, covering all the face except the eye

PRONUNCIATION TIP
This word is pronounced ni-**kab**.

**nitrogen**
NOUN a chemical element, usually found a: a colourless gas. **Nitrogen** makes up abc 78% of the Earth's atmosphere.

**no**
INTERJECTION **1** You say **no** when you do not want something or do not agree.

ANTONYM: yes

ADJECTIVE **2** none at all or not at all • *He has* **no** *excuse for his behaviour*.

**noble** **nobler, noblest**
ADJECTIVE If someone is **noble**, they are honest and brave, and deserve admiration

**nobody**
PRONOUN not a single person • *For a long tim* **nobody** *spoke*.

**nocturnal**
ADJECTIVE happening or active at night • *The hedgehog is a* **nocturnal** *animal*.

**nod** **nods, nodding, nodded**
VERB When you **nod** your head, you move it up and down, usually to say yes.

**noise** **noises**
NOUN a sound, especially one that is loud o unpleasant

**isy noisier, noisiest**

ADJECTIVE making a lot of noise, or full of noise

**mad nomads**

NOUN a person who travels from place to place rather than staying in just one • *The Bedouin people in Arabia are **nomads**.*

---

WORD HISTORY

from Latin *nomas* meaning wandering shepherd

---

**minate nominates, nominating, nominated**

VERB If a person **nominates** someone for a job or position, they formally suggest that they have it.

**n-**

PREFIX not, for example something that is **non**-existent does not exist

**nagon nonagons**

NOUN a flat shape with nine straight sides

**one**

PRONOUN not a single thing or person, or not even a small amount of something • *They asked me for my ideas, but I had **none**.*

**n-existent**

ADJECTIVE If you describe something as **non-existent**, it does not exist but you think that it should • *Good shops are virtually **non-existent** in the village.*

**n-fiction**

NOUN writing dealing with facts and events rather than imaginative storytelling

ANTONYM: fiction

**nsense**

NOUN foolish or meaningless words or behaviour

**nsmoking**

ADJECTIVE A **nonsmoking** area is a place where smoking is forbidden.

**nstop**

ADJECTIVE continuing without any pauses or breaks

SYNONYM: continuous

**oodle noodles**

NOUN a kind of pasta shaped into long, thin pieces

**oon**

NOUN midday

**no one**; also spelt **no-one**

PRONOUN not a single person • ***No one** goes to that play park any more.*

SYNONYM: nobody

**noose nooses**

NOUN a loop at the end of a piece of rope, with a knot that tightens when the rope is pulled

**nor**

CONJUNCTION used after *neither*, or to add emphasis • *Neither you **nor** I know the answer.* • *I couldn't afford to go to the fair, and **nor** could my friends.*

**normal**

ADJECTIVE usual and ordinary

**north**

NOUN one of the four main points of the compass. If you face the point where the sun rises, **north** is on your left. The abbreviation for **north** is N.

→ Have a look at the illustration for **compass point**

**north-east**

NOUN a point halfway between north and east. The abbreviation for **north-east** is NE.

→ Have a look at the illustration for **compass point**

**northern**

ADJECTIVE in or from the north • *The mountains of **northern** Spain are very beautiful.*

**north-west**

NOUN a point halfway between north and west. The abbreviation for **north-west** is NW.

→ Have a look at the illustration for **compass point**

**nose noses**

NOUN the part of your face above your mouth, that you use for smelling and breathing

→ Have a look at the illustration for **respiratory system**

**nostalgia**

NOUN a feeling of affection for the past, and sadness that things have changed

**nostalgic**

ADJECTIVE feeling affectionate about the past, and sad that things have changed

a
b
c
d
e
f
g
h
i
j
k
l
m
n
o
p
q
r
s
t
u
v
w
x
y
z

**nostril** nostrils

NOUN Your **nostrils** are the two openings in your nose that you breathe through.

**nosy** nosier, nosiest; also spelt nosey

ADJECTIVE **Nosy** people always want to know about other people's business, and like to interfere where they are not wanted.

**not**

ADVERB used to make a sentence mean the opposite • I am **not** very happy.

**note** notes

NOUN **1** a short letter

NOUN **2** You take **notes** to help you remember what has been said.

NOUN **3** In music, a **note** is a musical sound of a particular pitch, or a written symbol that represents this sound.

NOUN **4** a piece of paper money • a ten-pound **note**

**notebook** notebooks

NOUN a small book for writing notes in

**nothing**

PRONOUN not a single thing, or not a single part of something

**notice** notices, noticing, noticed

VERB **1** If you **notice** something, you become aware of it. • She **noticed** a bird sitting on the fence.

NOUN **2** a written announcement

PHRASE **3** If you **take notice of** something, you pay attention to it.

**noticeable**

ADJECTIVE obvious and easy to see

**notification** notifications

NOUN **1** an official statement telling someone about something

NOUN **2** a sound or symbol on your phone or computer telling you that someone has sent you a message or posted something on a social media website • When he switched on his phone, he had six new **notifications**.

**notify** notifies, notifying, notified

VERB If you **notify** someone of something, you officially inform them of it. • You must **notify** us of any change of address.

**notorious**

ADJECTIVE well known for something bad • a **notorious** criminal

**nought** noughts

NOUN the number 0, zero

**noun** nouns

NOUN a word that refers to a person, thing or idea. Examples of **nouns** are table, happiness and John.

**nourish** nourishes, nourishing, nourished

VERB If you **nourish** people or animals, you give them plenty of food.

**nourishing**

ADJECTIVE If food is **nourishing**, it is good for you and makes you strong and healthy.

**nourishment**

NOUN the food that your body needs to grow and stay healthy, including vitamins and minerals • "Eat your vegetables, they're full of **nourishment**."

**novel** novels

NOUN **1** a book that tells a long story about imaginary people and events

ADJECTIVE **2** new and interesting • This whole trip has been a **novel** experience.

**novelty** novelties

NOUN **1** the quality of being new and interesting

NOUN **2** something new and interesting

NOUN **3** a small object sold as a gift or souvenir

**November**

NOUN the eleventh month of the year. **November** has 30 days.

WORD HISTORY

from Latin November meaning the ninth month

**novice** novices

NOUN someone who is not yet experienced at something • Most of the group are **novices** at horse riding.

**now**

ADVERB **1** at the present time or moment

CONJUNCTION **2** as a result or consequence of a particular fact • Your writing will improve **now** you have a new pen.

**nowhere**

ADVERB not anywhere • There was **nowhere** to hide.

**nozzle** nozzles

NOUN a spout fitted onto the end of a pipe or hose to control the flow of liquid or gas

**nuclear**

ADJECTIVE relating to the energy produced when atoms are split • *We live near a nuclear power station.*

**nucleus nuclei**

NOUN **1** the central part of an atom or a cell

→ Have a look at the illustration for **atom**

NOUN **2** the important or central part of something • *We still have the nucleus of the team.*

**nude nudes**

ADJECTIVE **1** If someone is **nude**, they are naked.

NOUN **2** A **nude** is a picture or statue of a naked person.

**nudge nudges, nudging, nudged**

VERB **1** If you **nudge** someone, you push them gently with your elbow to get their attention or to make them move.

NOUN **2** a gentle push with your elbow

**nugget nuggets**

NOUN a small rough lump of something, especially gold

**nuisance nuisances**

NOUN someone or something that is annoying or causing problems

**numb**

ADJECTIVE unable to feel anything • *I was so cold my hands and feet felt numb.*

**number numbers, numbering, numbered**

NOUN **1** a word or symbol used for counting or calculating

NOUN **2** the series of numbers that you dial when you phone someone

VERB **3** If you **number** something, you give it a number, usually in a sequence. • *Please number each page you write on.*

**number bond number bonds**

NOUN any pair of numbers that add together to make up another number

**numeracy**

NOUN the ability to do arithmetic

**numeral numerals**

NOUN a symbol that is used to represent a number

**numerator numerators**

NOUN the top number of a fraction. It tells you the number of pieces or parts you are dealing with.

**numerical**

ADJECTIVE expressed in numbers or relating to numbers • *Please put these pages in numerical order.*

**numerous**

ADJECTIVE Things that are **numerous** exist or happen in large numbers. • *There are numerous things to do in a large city.*

**nun nuns**

NOUN a woman who has taken religious vows and is a member of a religious community

**nurse nurses, nursing, nursed**

NOUN **1** a person whose job is to look after people who are ill

VERB **2** If you **nurse** someone, you look after them when they are ill. • *I helped dad to nurse mum when she had flu.*

**nursery nurseries**

NOUN **1** a place where young children are looked after when their parents are working

NOUN **2** a place where plants are grown and sold

**nursery rhyme nursery rhymes**

NOUN a short poem or song for young children, such as *Little Miss Muffet* and *Jack and Jill*

**nursery school nursery schools**

NOUN a school for children aged three to five years old

**nut nuts**

NOUN **1** a fruit with a hard shell that grows on certain trees and bushes

NOUN **2** a piece of metal with a hole in the middle that a bolt screws into

**nutrient nutrients**

NOUN one of the substances that help plants and animals to grow • *Very heavy rainfall washes valuable nutrients from the soil.*

**nutrition**

NOUN the food that you eat that helps you to grow and keeps you healthy • *Good nutrition is vital for healthy development.*

a
b
c
d
e
f
g
h
i
j
k
l
m
n
o
p
q
r
s
t
u
v
w
x
y
z

**273**

### nutritious
ADJECTIVE If food is **nutritious** it helps you to grow and remain healthy. ● *Spinach is a very **nutritious** vegetable.*

### nylon
NOUN a type of strong, artificial fibre used for making, for example, clothes, ropes and brushes ● *The rock climbers used brightly coloured ropes made of **nylon** to abseil down the rock face.*

### oak oaks
NOUN a large tree that produces acorns. Th **oak** has a hard wood that is often used t make furniture.

### oar oars
NOUN a pole with a flat end used to row a boat through water

### oasis oases
NOUN a small area in a desert where water and plants are found

### oath oaths
NOUN a formal promise, especially a promi to tell the truth in a court of law

### oats
PLURAL NOUN a type of grain

### obedience
NOUN **Obedience** is when you do what someone tells you to do.

ANTONYM: disobedience

### obedient
ADJECTIVE If you are **obedient**, you do as yo are told.

ANTONYM: disobedient

### obey obeys, obeying, obeyed
VERB If you **obey** a person or an order, you what you are told to do.

### obituary obituaries
NOUN a piece of writing about the life and achievements of someone who has just di

### object objects, objecting, objected
NOUN **1** anything solid that you can touch see, and that is not alive ● *This painting is **object** of beauty.*
NOUN **2** an aim or purpose ● *The **object** of t marathon is to raise money.*
VERB **3** If you **object** to something, you dislike it, disagree with it or disapprove of

PRONUNCIATION TIP
The noun is pronounced **ob**-jekt. The verb pronounced ob-**jekt**.

**jection objections**

NOUN If you have an **objection** to something, you dislike it or disagree with it.

**lige obliges, obliging, obliged**

VERB **1** If you are **obliged** to do something, you have to do it.

VERB **2** If you **oblige** someone, you help them. • *He **obliged** us by showing the way.*

VERB **3** If you are **obliged** to someone, you are grateful to them. • *I would be much **obliged** if you could show me where this street is.*

**liging**

ADJECTIVE willing to help someone

**lique**

ADJECTIVE An **oblique** line slopes at an angle.

**long oblongs**

NOUN **1** a four-sided plane shape with four right angles, similar to a square but with two sides longer than the other two

ADJECTIVE **2** shaped like an oblong

**noxious**

ADJECTIVE extremely unpleasant

SYNONYMS: hateful, odious

**oe oboes**

NOUN a woodwind instrument that makes a high-pitched sound

WORD HISTORY
from French *haut bois* meaning literally high wood, a reference to the instrument's pitch

**oist oboists**

NOUN someone who plays the oboe

**scene**

ADJECTIVE very rude and likely to upset people

**scure obscures, obscuring, obscured**

ADJECTIVE **1** Something **obscure** is difficult to see or to understand.

ANTONYMS: obvious, clear

VERB **2** If something **obscures** something else, it makes it difficult to see or understand. • *The moon **obscured** the sun during the eclipse.*

**observant**

ADJECTIVE An **observant** person notices things that are not usually noticed.

**observation observations**

NOUN the act of watching something closely • *You will need to make careful **observations** of the experiment before you do the writing.*

WORD HISTORY
from Latin *observare* meaning to watch

**observe observes, observing, observed**

VERB If you **observe** someone or something, you watch them carefully.

**obsessed**

ADJECTIVE If you are **obsessed** with someone or something, you cannot stop thinking about them.

**obsession obsessions**

NOUN If someone has an **obsession** about something or someone, they cannot stop thinking about them.

**obsessive**

ADJECTIVE unable to stop thinking about someone or something

**obsolete**

ADJECTIVE out of date and no longer used

**obstacle obstacles**

NOUN something that is in your way and makes it difficult for you to do something

**obstinate**

ADJECTIVE Someone who is **obstinate** is stubborn and unwilling to change their mind.

**obstruct obstructs, obstructing, obstructed**

VERB If something **obstructs** a road or path, it blocks it.

**obtain obtains, obtaining, obtained**

VERB If you **obtain** something, you get it.

**obtuse**

ADJECTIVE In mathematics, an **obtuse** angle is an angle between 90° and 180°.

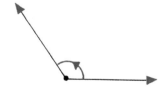

a
b
c
d
e
f
g
h
i
j
k
l
m
n
o
p
q
r
s
t
u
v
w
x
y
z

**275**

## obvious

ADJECTIVE easy to see or understand • *It was* **obvious** *that he didn't know the answer.*

## obviously

ADVERB You use **obviously** to show that something is easy to see or understand.
• **Obviously**, *you need to do your homework or you'll get into trouble.*

## occasion occasions

NOUN a time when something happens
• *I met her on several* **occasions**.

---

**LANGUAGE TIP**

There are two *c*s but only one *s* in *occasion*.

---

## occasional

ADJECTIVE happening sometimes, but not often
• *We go for an* **occasional** *walk in the woods.*

## occasionally

ADVERB sometimes, rather than always or never • *He misbehaves* **occasionally**.

## occupant occupants

NOUN the people who live or work in a building

## occupation occupations

NOUN a job or profession

## occupy occupies, occupying, occupied

VERB **1** The people who **occupy** a building are the people who live or work there.
VERB **2** If something **occupies** you, you spend your time doing it or thinking about it.

## occur occurs, occurring, occurred

VERB If something **occurs**, it happens.

### occur to

VERB If something **occurs to** you, you suddenly think of it or realise it.

## occurrence occurrences

NOUN something that happens • *Accidents in the factory were a frequent* **occurrence**.

## ocean oceans

NOUN one of the five very large areas of sea in the world

## o'clock

ADVERB You use **o'clock** after the number of the hour to say what the time is. • *We have to be at school by eight* **o'clock**.

## octagon octagons

NOUN a flat shape with eight straight sides

## octagonal

ADJECTIVE having eight straight sides

## octahedron octahedrons

NOUN a solid figure with eight identical flat surfaces

## octave octaves

NOUN the difference in pitch between the first note and the eighth note of a musical scale

## October

NOUN the tenth month of the year. **October** has 31 days.

---

**WORD HISTORY**

from Latin *October* meaning the eighth month, as it was the eighth month in the Roman calendar

---

## octopus octopuses

NOUN a sea creature with eight long tentacles that it uses to catch food

## odd odder, oddest

ADJECTIVE **1** strange or unusual
ADJECTIVE **2** **Odd** things do not match each other. • *She always ended up with* **odd** *socks.*
ADJECTIVE **3** **Odd** numbers cannot be divided exactly by two. 3 and 7 are examples of odd numbers.

ANTONYM: even

## odour odours

NOUN (*formal*) a strong smell

## oesophagus oesophagi

NOUN the passage between the mouth and the stomach

## of

PREPOSITION **1** consisting of or containing
• *a cup* **of** *tea*
PREPOSITION **2** used when talking about things that are characteristic of something
• *a woman* **of** *great importance*
PREPOSITION **3** belonging to or connected with
• *a friend* **of** *Eve*

# ff

PREPOSITION **1** away from or out of a place
• *They got **off** the bus.*

PREPOSITION **2** used to show separation or distance from a place • *There are several islands **off** the coast of Britain.*

ADVERB **3** used to show movement away from or out of a place • *At the next station, the man got **off**.*

ADVERB **4** not at school or work • *He took a day **off**.*

ADVERB **5** not switched on • *The television was **off**.*

ADJECTIVE **6** cancelled or postponed • *The match is **off**.*

ADJECTIVE **7** Food that is **off** is no longer fresh enough to eat, usually tastes unpleasant, and may make you ill.

**LANGUAGE TIP**
Do not use *of* after *off*. It is correct to say *I got off the bus*, not *I got off of the bus*.

## ffence **offences**

NOUN **1** a crime • *Burglary is a serious **offence**.*

PHRASE **2** If you **cause offence**, you embarrass or upset someone.

PHRASE **3** If you **take offence**, you feel that someone has been rude or hurtful to you.

## ffend **offends, offending, offended**

VERB **1** If you **offend** someone, you upset them.

VERB **2** If someone **offends**, they break the law.

## ffensive

ADJECTIVE If something is **offensive**, it is rude and upsetting.

## ffer **offers, offering, offered**

VERB **1** If you **offer** something to someone, you ask them if they would like it, or say that you are willing to do it. • *I **offered** to wash the car.*

NOUN **2** something that someone says they will give or do for you

## ffice **offices**

NOUN **1** a room where people work at desks

NOUN **2** a place where people can go for information, tickets or other services

## fficer **officers**

NOUN a person with a position of authority in the armed forces, the police or a government organisation

## official

ADJECTIVE approved by the government or by someone in authority

## offline

ADJECTIVE **1** If a computer is **offline**, it is not connected to the internet.

ADVERB **2** If you do something **offline**, you do it while not connected to the internet.

## offspring

NOUN (*formal*) You can refer to a person's children or to an animal's young as their **offspring**.

## often

ADVERB happening many times or a lot of the time • *He **often** goes swimming on Sunday.*

## ogre **ogres**

NOUN a cruel, frightening giant in fairy stories

## oil **oils, oiling, oiled**

NOUN **1** a thick, sticky liquid found underground that is used for fuel, lubrication and for making plastics and chemicals

NOUN **2** a thick, greasy liquid made from plants or animal fat • *cooking **oil***

VERB **3** If you **oil** something, you put oil in it or on it to make it work better. • *This squeaky hinge needs to be **oiled**.*

## oily **oilier, oiliest**

ADJECTIVE Something that is **oily** is covered with or contains oil.

## ointment **ointments**

NOUN a smooth, thick substance that you put on sore skin to heal it

## OK; also spelt **okay**

ADJECTIVE all right; fine • *She slipped on the ice but she was **OK**.*

## old **older, oldest**

ADJECTIVE **1** having lived or existed for a long time

ADJECTIVE **2** **Old** is used to give the age of someone or something. • *The baby is six months **old**.*

ADJECTIVE **3** You can use **old** to talk about something that is no longer used or has been replaced by something else. • *I bumped into my teacher from my **old** primary school.*

A
B
C
D
E
F
G
H
I
J
K
L
M
N
O
P
Q
R
S
T
U
V
W
X
Y
Z

## old-fashioned

ADJECTIVE **1** Something **old-fashioned** is out of date and no longer fashionable.

ANTONYM: fashionable

ADJECTIVE **2** If someone is **old-fashioned**, they believe in the values and standards of the past.

## olive olives

NOUN **1** a small green or black fruit containing a stone. **Olives** are usually pickled and eaten as a snack, or crushed to produce oil for cooking.

NOUN **2** a dark yellowish-green colour

ADJECTIVE **3** having a dark yellowish-green colour

## Olympic Games

NOUN (trademark) a series of international sporting contests held in a different country every four years

**WORD HISTORY**

The word *Olympic* comes from *Olympia* in Greece, where games were held in ancient times

## omelette omelettes

NOUN a dish made by beating eggs together and cooking them in a flat pan

## omit omits, omitting, omitted

VERB If you **omit** something, you do not include it. ● *She **omitted** to mention that her mother could not come.*

## omni-

PREFIX added to some words to mean all or everywhere, for example **omni**potent means all-powerful, and **omni**present means present everywhere

## omnibus omnibuses

NOUN **1** a book containing a collection of stories or articles by the same author or about the same subject

ADJECTIVE **2** An **omnibus** edition of a radio or television series contains two or more episodes that were originally shown separately.

## omnivore omnivores

NOUN an animal that eats all kinds of food, including meat and plants

## omnivorous

ADJECTIVE An **omnivorous** animal eats all kinds of food, including meat and plants.

## on

PREPOSITION **1** touching something or attache to it ● *We sat **on** the seat.*

PREPOSITION **2** If you are **on** a bus, a plane or train, you are inside it.

PREPOSITION **3** If something happens **on** a particular day, that is when it happens.

PREPOSITION **4** If something is done **on** an instrument or a machine, it is done using i

PREPOSITION **5** A book or a talk **on** a particula subject is about that subject.

ADVERB **6** If someone has a piece of clothing **on**, they are wearing it.

ADVERB **7** If your turn a machine or a switch **on**, you make it work. ● *"Please would you switch the radio **on**?"*

## once

ADVERB **1** If something happens **once**, it happens one time only. ● *I met her **once**, at a party.*

ADVERB **2** If something was **once** true, it was true in the past, but is no longer true. ● *The ground was **once** covered by trees.*

CONJUNCTION **3** If something happens **once** another thing has happened, it happens immediately afterwards. ● *I'll do my homework **once** I've finished my tea.*

PHRASE **4** If you do something **at once**, you do it immediately. ● *We must go home **at once**.*

PHRASE **5** If several things happen **at once**, they all happen at the same time. ● *He trie to hold three glasses **at once**.*

## one

NOUN **1** **One** is the number 1.

ADJECTIVE **2** When you refer to **one** person or **one** thing, you mean a single person or thing. ● *We have **one** main holiday a year.*

PRONOUN **3** **One** refers to a particular person or thing. ● *This book was the best **one** she ha read for ages.*

## onion onions

NOUN a small, round vegetable with a very strong taste

## online

ADJECTIVE **1** If a computer is **online**, it is connected to the internet.

ADVERB **2** If you do something **online**, you d it while connected to the internet.

**only**

ADVERB **1** You use **only** to show the one thing or person involved. ● *Only one girl was able to complete the race.*

ADVERB **2** You use **only** to make a condition that must happen before something else can happen. ● *You will be allowed in **only** if you have a ticket.*

ADVERB **3** You use **only** to emphasise that something is unimportant or small. ● *He's **only** very young.*

ADJECTIVE **4** If you talk about the **only** thing or person, you mean that there are no others. For example, if you are an **only** child, you have no brothers or sisters.

CONJUNCTION **5** You can use **only** to mean but or except. ● *He was very much like you, **only** with blond hair.*

**onomatopoeia**

NOUN the use of words that sound like the thing that they represent. *Hiss* and *buzz* are examples of **onomatopoeia**

---

**PRONUNCIATION TIP**

This word is pronounced on-uh-mat-uh-**pee**-a.

---

**onto**; also spelt **on to**

PREPOSITION If you put something **onto** an object, you put it on it. ● *He threw the pillow **onto** the bed.*

**ooze oozes, oozing, oozed**

VERB When a thick liquid **oozes**, it flows slowly. ● *The cold mud **oozed** over her toes.*

---

**WORD HISTORY**

from Old English *wos* meaning juice

---

**opaque**

ADJECTIVE If something is **opaque**, it does not let light through, so you cannot see through it. ● *opaque glass windows*

ANTONYM: clear

**open opens, opening, opened**

ADJECTIVE **1** Something that is **open** is not closed or fastened, allowing things to pass through. ● *A light breeze came through the **open** window.*

ADJECTIVE **2** not enclosed or covered ● *At last we were out in the **open** countryside.*

VERB **3** When you **open** something, or when it **opens**, it is moved so that it is no longer closed. ● *She **opened** the box of chocolates.*

VERB **4** When a shop or office **opens**, people are allowed to go in to do business.

VERB **5** If you **open** a book, you turn back the cover so that you can read it.

VERB **6** If something **opens**, it starts or begins.

ADJECTIVE **7** Someone who is **open** is honest and not secretive.

**opening openings**

NOUN **1** a hole or gap ● *There was a small **opening** in the fence.*

ADJECTIVE **2** coming first ● *He sang the **opening** song in the concert.*

NOUN **3** the first part of a book or film ● *I love the **opening** of that book.*

**openly**

ADVERB in a way that is honest and does not hide your feelings or any facts

**opera operas**

NOUN a play in which the words are sung rather than spoken

**operate operates, operating, operated**

VERB **1** When you **operate** a machine, you make it work. ● *I know how to **operate** the computer.*

VERB **2** When surgeons **operate**, they cut open a person's body to remove or repair a damaged part.

**operation operations**

NOUN **1** a form of medical treatment in which a surgeon cuts open a patient's body to remove or repair a damaged part

NOUN **2** a complex, planned event ● *Moving house is going to be quite a difficult **operation**.*

**opinion opinions**

NOUN a belief or view

**opponent opponents**

NOUN someone who is against you in an argument or a contest

**opportunity opportunities**

NOUN a chance to do something

**oppose opposes, opposing, opposed**

VERB If you **oppose** something or someone, you disagree with them and are against them.

**opposing**

ADJECTIVE **Opposing** means opposite or very different. ● *We managed to be friends even though we had **opposing** points of view.*

a
b
c
d
e
f
g
h
i
j
k
l
m
n
o
p
q
r
s
t
u
v
w
x
y
z

## opposite opposites

PREPOSITION **1** If one thing is **opposite** another, it is facing it. • *Our house is* ***opposite*** *the park.*
NOUN **2** If people or things are **opposites**, they are completely different from each other.

## opposition

NOUN **1** If there is **opposition** to something, there is resistance to it and people oppose it. • *There is a lot of* ***opposition*** *to the building of a new road.*
NOUN **2** In a games or sports event, the **opposition** is the person or team that you are competing against.

## opt opts, opting, opted

VERB **1** If you **opt** for something, you choose to do it. • *I* ***opted*** *to go to the Gym Club.*
VERB **2** If you **opt** out of something, you choose not to do it or be involved with it.
• *I* ***opted*** *out of football practice.*

## optical

ADJECTIVE concerned with vision, light or images

## optician opticians

NOUN someone who tests people's eyesight, and makes and sells glasses and contact lenses

## optimism

NOUN a hopeful feeling that everything will turn out well in the future

ANTONYM: pessimism

## optimist optimists

NOUN An **optimist** is a person who is always hopeful that everything will turn out well in the future.

ANTONYM: pessimist

## optimistic

ADJECTIVE believing that everything will turn out well in the future

ANTONYM: pessimistic

## option options

NOUN a choice between two or more things

## optional

ADJECTIVE If something is **optional**, you can choose whether to do it or not. • *Tennis is* ***optional*** *at our school.*

ANTONYM: compulsory

## or

CONJUNCTION used to link two alternatives or choices • *You need to decide whether to stay* ***or*** *leave.*

## oral

ADJECTIVE **1** spoken rather than written
• *Tomorrow we have our French* ***oral*** *examination.*
ADJECTIVE **2** to do with your mouth or using your mouth • ***Oral*** *hygiene is vital for healthy teeth.*

## orange oranges

NOUN **1** a round citrus fruit that is juicy and sweet and has a thick reddish-yellow skin
NOUN **2** a reddish-yellow colour
ADJECTIVE **3** having a reddish-yellow colour

**WORD HISTORY**
from Sanskrit *naranga* meaning orange

## orang-utan orang-utans; also spelt orang-utang

NOUN a large ape with reddish-brown hair

## orbit orbits, orbiting, orbited

NOUN **1** the curved path followed by an object going round a planet or the sun
VERB **2** If something **orbits** a planet or the sun, it goes round and round it. • *Our moon* ***orbits*** *the Earth.*

## orchard orchards

NOUN a piece of land where fruit trees are grown

## orchestra orchestras

NOUN a large group of musicians who play musical instruments together

## orchid orchids

NOUN a type of plant with beautiful and unusual flowers

## ordeal ordeals

NOUN a very difficult and unpleasant experience

## order orders, ordering, ordered

NOUN **1** a command given by someone in authority
NOUN **2** If things are arranged or done in a particular **order**, they are arranged or done in that sequence. • *alphabetical* ***order***
VERB **3** If you **order** someone to do something, you tell them firmly to do it.
VERB **4** When you **order** something, you ask for it to be brought or sent to you.

**ordinal**

ADJECTIVE An **ordinal** number a word like "first" and "tenth" that tells you where a particular thing occurs in order.

**ordinary**

ADJECTIVE not special or different in any way

**ore ores**

NOUN rock or earth from which metal can be obtained

**organ organs**

NOUN **1** Your **organs** are parts of your body that have a particular purpose, for example your lungs are the **organs** with which you breathe.

NOUN **2** a large musical instrument with a keyboard and windpipes through which air is forced to produce a sound

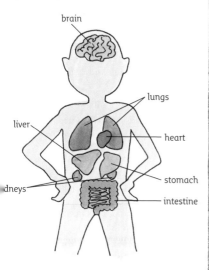

brain

lungs

liver

heart

kidneys

stomach

intestine

**organic**

ADJECTIVE **1 Organic** food is produced without the use of artificial fertilisers or pesticides.

ADJECTIVE **2** produced or found in living things

**organisation organisations**; also spelt **organization**

NOUN **1** any business or group of people working together for a purpose

NOUN **2** the act of planning and arranging something

**organise organises, organising, organised**; also spelt **organize**

VERB If you **organise** something, you plan and arrange it.

**organism organisms**

NOUN any living animal or plant

**oriental**

ADJECTIVE Something that is **oriental** comes from the Far East, which includes countries such as India, China and Japan. • *I like **oriental** food.*

**orienteering**

NOUN a sport in which people find their way from one place to another in the countryside, using a map and compass

**origin origins**

NOUN the beginning or cause of something • *The **origins** of man have been written about in many books.*

**original originals**

ADJECTIVE **1** the first or earliest • *The **original** owner of this house made lots of alterations.*

ADJECTIVE **2** imaginative and clever • *His paintings are highly **original**.*

NOUN **3** a work of art or a document that is the one that was produced first, and is not a copy

**originally**

ADVERB in the beginning or at first • *The house was **originally** a school.*

**ornament ornaments**

NOUN a small, attractive object that you display in your home or that you wear in order to look attractive

**ornithologist ornithologists**

NOUN someone who studies birds

**ornithology**

NOUN the study of birds

**orphan orphans**

NOUN a child whose parents are dead

**orphanage orphanages**

NOUN a place where orphans are looked after

**ostrich ostriches**

NOUN the largest bird in the world. **Ostriches** can run fast but cannot fly.

**other others**

PRONOUN **1** The **other** can mean the second of two things. • *One of the rooms is empty, but the **other** is not.*

ADJECTIVE **2 Other** people or things are different from those already mentioned.

ADJECTIVE **3** The **other** day means a few days ago.

281

A
B
C
D
E
F
G
H
I
J
K
L
M
N
O
P
Q
R
S
T
U
V
W
X
Y
Z

## otherwise

ADVERB **1** or else

ADVERB **2** apart from the thing mentioned
• The food was good, but **otherwise** the party was awful.

## otter otters

NOUN a small, furry animal with a long tail, that lives near water. **Otters** swim well and eat fish.

## ought

VERB **1** If you say that someone **ought** to do something, you mean they should do it.

VERB **2** If you say that something **ought** to be the case, you mean that you expect it to be the case. • He **ought** to be here by now.

## ounce ounces

NOUN a unit of weight equal to one-sixteenth of a pound or about 28.35 grams

## our

ADJECTIVE belonging to us • **Our** cat is black.

## ours

PRONOUN belonging to us • That cat is **ours**.

## ourselves

PRONOUN **Ourselves** is used when talking about a group of people that includes the speaker or writer. • We didn't hurt **ourselves** too badly.

## out

ADVERB **1** towards the outside of a place or thing • Take the ice cream **out** of the freezer.

ADVERB **2** not at home • I came to your door yesterday, but you were **out**.

## outbreak outbreaks

NOUN If there is an **outbreak** of something unpleasant, such as war, it suddenly occurs. • The **outbreak** of the disease made many people unwell.

## outburst outbursts

NOUN a sudden strong expression of emotion, especially anger or violent action • He apologised for his angry **outburst**.

## outcome outcomes

NOUN a result

## outdoor

ADJECTIVE happening or used outside

## outdoors

ADVERB If something happens **outdoors**, it takes place outside in the open air.

## outer

ADJECTIVE The **outer** parts of something are the parts furthest from the centre.
• the **outer** doors

## outer space

NOUN everything beyond the Earth's atmosphere

## outfit outfits

NOUN a set of clothes • I bought a new **outfit** for the party.

## outgoing

ADJECTIVE Someone who is **outgoing** is friendly and not shy. • She is always fun to be with as she has such an **outgoing** personality.

## outgrow outgrows, outgrowing, outgrew, outgrown

VERB **1** If you **outgrow** a piece of clothing, you grow too big to wear it. • I've already **outgrown** my best jeans.

VERB **2** If you **outgrow** a way of behaving, you stop behaving that way because you are older and more mature.

## outing outings

NOUN a trip made for pleasure

## outlaw outlaws, outlawing, outlawed

VERB **1** If someone **outlaws** something, the ban it.

NOUN **2** In the past, an **outlaw** was a crimin

## outlet outlets

NOUN **1** a hole or pipe through which water or air can flow away

NOUN **2** a shop that sells goods made by a particular manufacturer

## outline outlines, outlining, outlined

NOUN **1** The **outline** of something is its shape.

VERB **2** If you **outline** a plan or idea, you gi brief details of it.

## outlook outlooks

NOUN **1** Your **outlook** is your general attitude towards life. • His **outlook** on life always positive.

NOUN **2** The **outlook** of a situation is the way it is likely to develop. • The **outlook** fc the weather over the next few days is not very good.

## outnumber outnumbers, outnumbering, outnumbered

VERB If there is more of one group than of another, the first group **outnumbers** the second. • Boys **outnumber** girls in our clas.

**outpatient outpatients**
NOUN someone who receives treatment in hospital without staying overnight

**output outputs**
NOUN **1** the amount of something produced by a person or organisation
NOUN **2** The **output** of a computer is the information that it produces.

**outrage outrages, outraging, outraged**
VERB **1** If something **outrages** you, it angers and shocks you.
NOUN **2** a feeling of anger and shock
NOUN **3** something very shocking or violent

**outrageous**
ADJECTIVE making you feel angry and shocked

**outright**
ADJECTIVE **1** total and complete • *She made an* **outright** *refusal to come with us.*
ADVERB **2** completely, totally • *Smoking in the building has been banned* **outright***.*

**outside**
PREPOSITION **1** not inside • *The teacher found him* **outside** *the classroom.*
ADJECTIVE **2** describes something that is not inside a building • *The* **outside** *wall is painted white.*
ADVERB **3** out of a building • *She went* **outside** *to look for Sam.*
NOUN **4** The **outside** of something is the part that surrounds or encloses the rest of it. • *We wandered around the* **outside** *of the house.*

ANTONYM: inside

NOUN **5** not included in something • *The building will be closed* **outside** *school hours.*

LANGUAGE TIP
Do not use *of* after *outside* when it is a preposition. It is correct to say *I met her outside the school*, not *I met her outside of the school*.

**outskirts**
PLURAL NOUN the parts around the edge of a city or town • *Our home is on the* **outskirts** *of a large town.*

**outspoken**
ADJECTIVE **Outspoken** people give their opinions openly, even if they shock other people.

**outstanding**
ADJECTIVE extremely good

**outwit outwits, outwitting, outwitted**
VERB If you **outwit** someone, you use your intelligence or a clever trick to defeat them or get the better of them.

**oval ovals**
NOUN **1** a shape similar to a circle, but wider in one direction than the other
ADJECTIVE **2** shaped like an oval

WORD HISTORY
from Latin *ovalis* meaning egg-shaped

**oven ovens**
NOUN the part of a cooker that you use for baking or roasting food

**over overs**
PREPOSITION **1** directly above something or covering it • *She hung the picture* **over** *the fireplace.* • *He put his hands* **over** *his eyes.*
PREPOSITION **2** A view **over** an area is a view across it. • *I love the view* **over** *the lake to the mountains.*
PREPOSITION **3** If something happens **over** a period of time, it happens during that period. • *I went to New Zealand* **over** *Christmas.*
ADVERB **4** If an amount of something is left **over**, that amount remains.
ADVERB **5** If you lean **over**, you bend your body in a particular direction. • *He leant* **over** *to open the door of the car.*
ADVERB **6** If something rolls or turns **over**, it moves so that its other side is facing upwards.
ADJECTIVE **7** Something that is **over** is completely finished.
NOUN **8** In cricket, an **over** is a series of six balls bowled by one bowler.

**over-**
PREFIX too much, or to too great an extent. For example, if fruit is **over**ripe, it is too ripe, and if someone **over**eats, they eat too much.

**283**

## overall

ADVERB **1** taking into account all the parts or aspects of something • **Overall**, the project has been a success.

ADJECTIVE **2** describing something that takes into account all the parts or aspects of something • the **overall** cost of the school's new computers

## overalls

PLURAL NOUN a piece of clothing that you wear to protect your other clothes when you are working

## overboard

ADVERB If you fall **overboard**, you fall over the side of a ship into the water.

## overcast

ADJECTIVE When the sky is **overcast**, it is covered by thick cloud.

## overcoat overcoats

NOUN a thick, warm coat

## overcome overcomes, overcoming, overcame, overcome

VERB **1** If you **overcome** a problem or a feeling, you manage to deal with it or control it.

VERB **2** If you are **overcome**, you are affected by strong emotions. • They were **overcome** with happiness.

VERB **3** If you are **overcome** by fumes, gas or smoke, for example, you are made unconscious by them.

## overcrowded

ADJECTIVE If a place is **overcrowded**, there are too many things or people in it.

## overdue

ADJECTIVE If someone or something is **overdue**, they are late. • The train is now **overdue**.

## overflow overflows, overflowing, overflowed

VERB If a liquid **overflows**, it spills over the edge of its container. If a river **overflows**, it flows over its banks.

## overgrown

ADJECTIVE If a place is **overgrown**, it is thickly covered with plants and weeds.

## overhaul overhauls, overhauling, overhauled

VERB **1** If you **overhaul** something, you examine and check it carefully, and repair any faults.

NOUN **2** An **overhaul** is a careful and detailed examination of something in order to repair its faults.

## overhead

ADVERB **1** above your head, or in the sky • Seagulls flew **overhead**. • The **overhead** wires were being repaired.

ADJECTIVE **2** describing something that is above your head • The **overhead** wires were being repaired.

## overhear overhears, overhearing, overheard

VERB If you **overhear** someone's conversation, you hear what they are saying to someone else.

## overlap overlaps, overlapping, overlapped

VERB If one thing **overlaps** another, it covers part of the other thing.

## overload overloads, overloading, overloaded

VERB If you **overload** someone or something, you give them too much to do or to carry.

## overlook overlooks, overlooking, overlooked

VERB **1** If a building or window **overlooks** a place, it has a view of it from above.

VERB **2** If you **overlook** something, you ignore it or do not notice it.

## overnight

ADJECTIVE **1** during the night • We took an **overnight** flight.

ADVERB **2** describing something that happens during the night • We flew **overnight** to Canada.

ADVERB **3** sudden or suddenly • He seemed to become such a good player **overnight**.

## overseas

ADJECTIVE **1** describing things or people that are in or that come from foreign countries • We have some **overseas** students visiting the school.

ADVERB **2** abroad • My brother is going **overseas** for a year.

## oversleep oversleeps, oversleeping, overslept

VERB If you **oversleep**, you sleep on past the time you intended to wake up.

## overtake overtakes, overtaking, overtook, overtaken

VERB If you **overtake** someone or something, you pass them because you are moving faster than they are.

**ertime**

NOUN time that someone works in addition to their normal working hours

**erture overtures**

NOUN the opening piece of music at a concert, show or ballet

**erweight**

ADJECTIVE People or animals that are **overweight** are too heavy for their size.

**erwhelm overwhelms, overwhelming, overwhelmed**

VERB **1** If something **overwhelms** you, it affects you very strongly.

VERB **2** If one group of people **overwhelms** another, they completely defeat them.

VERB **3** If you **overwhelm** someone with something, you load them with too much of it. • *He was **overwhelmed** with work.*

**ve owes, owing, owed**

VERB **1** If you **owe** someone money, they have lent it to you and you have not yet paid it back.

VERB **2** If you **owe** a quality or skill to someone, you only have it because of them. • *He **owes** his success as a tennis player to his coach.*

**vl owls**

NOUN a bird of prey that hunts at night. **Owls** have large eyes and short, hooked beaks.

**vn owns, owning, owned**

ADJECTIVE **1** If something is your **own**, it belongs to you or is associated with you. • *She now has her **own** bedroom.*

PRONOUN **2** If something is your **own**, it belongs to you or is associated with you. • *His desk is a few centimetres from my **own**.*

VERB **3** If you **own** something, it belongs to you.

PHRASE **4 On your own** means alone.

**vner owners**

NOUN the person to whom something belongs

**oxen**

NOUN **Oxen** are cattle used for carrying or pulling things.

**ygen**

NOUN a colourless gas that makes up about 21% of the Earth's atmosphere. All animals and plants need **oxygen** to live, and fires need it to burn.

**oyster oysters**

NOUN a large, flat shellfish. Some **oysters** can be eaten, and others produce pearls.

**oz**

an abbreviation for *ounce*

**ozone**

NOUN a form of oxygen that is poisonous and has a strong smell

WORD HISTORY
from Greek *ozein* meaning smell

**ozone layer**

NOUN a layer of the Earth's atmosphere that protects living things from the harmful radiation of the sun

→ Have a look at the illustration for **greenhouse effect**

a
b
c
d
e
f
g
h
i
j
k
l
m
n
o
p
q
r
s
t
u
v
w
x
y
z

# P p

## pace paces, pacing, paced

NOUN **1** the distance you move when you take one step

NOUN **2** Your **pace** is the speed at which you are walking or running.

VERB **3** If you **pace**, you walk up and down, usually because you are anxious or impatient.

## Pacific

NOUN the ocean separating North and South America from Asia and Australia

## pacifism

NOUN the belief that all violence and war is wrong

## pacifist pacifists

NOUN someone who is opposed to all violence and war

## pacify pacifies, pacifying, pacified

VERB If you **pacify** someone who is angry, you calm them.

## pack packs, packing, packed

VERB **1** If you **pack** things, you put them neatly into a container, bag or box.

NOUN **2** a complete set of playing cards

NOUN **3** a group of wolves or dogs

## package packages

NOUN a small parcel

## packaging

NOUN the wrapping or container in which an item is sold or sent • *Make sure you recycle all of the **packaging**.*

## packet packets

NOUN a small box or bag in which something is sold

## pact pacts

NOUN a formal agreement or treaty

## pad pads

NOUN **1** a set of sheets of paper glued together at one end

NOUN **2** a thick, soft piece of material

NOUN **3** one of the soft parts under an animal's paws

## paddle paddles, paddling, paddled

NOUN **1** a short pole with a broad blade at one or both ends, used to move a small b or a canoe

VERB **2** If someone **paddles** a boat, they move it using a paddle.

VERB **3** If you **paddle**, you walk in shallow water with bare feet.

## paddock paddocks

NOUN a small field where horses are kept

## padlock padlocks, padlocking, padlocked

NOUN **1** a special kind of metal lock used t fasten two things together

VERB **2** If you **padlock** something, you loc with a padlock.

## pagan pagans

NOUN **1** someone who does not believe in of the main religions of the world

ADJECTIVE **2** involving beliefs and worship outside the main religions of the world • *pagan myths and cults*

## page pages

NOUN **1** one side of a sheet of paper in a bc or magazine • *Turn to **page** four.*

NOUN **2** a single sheet of paper

## pagoda pagodas

NOUN a tall, elaborately decorated Buddhis or Hindu temple

## paid

VERB past tense and past participle of **pay**

## pail pails

NOUN a bucket

## pain pains

NOUN **1** a feeling of discomfort and hurt in your body, caused by an illness or injury

PHRASE **2** If you are **in pain** you are hurting

### WORD HISTORY

from Latin *poena* meaning punishment

## painful

ADJECTIVE causing emotional or physical pa

## painkiller painkillers

NOUN a drug that reduces or stops pain

## painless

ADJECTIVE Something that is **painless** caus no pain.

**int paints, painting, painted**
NOUN **1** a coloured liquid used to decorate buildings and make pictures
VERB **2** If you **paint** a picture of something, you make a picture of it using paint.
VERB **3** If you **paint** something such as a wall, you cover it with paint.

**inting paintings**
NOUN **1** a picture that someone has created using paints
NOUN **2** the activity of painting pictures

**ir pairs**
NOUN **1** two things of the same type that are meant to be used together • a **pair** of socks
NOUN **2** objects that have two main parts of the same size and shape • a **pair** of scissors

**LANGUAGE TIP**
Do not confuse *pair* with *pear*.

**l pals**
NOUN (*informal*) a friend

**WORD HISTORY**
from the Romani for brother

**lace palaces**
NOUN a large, grand house, especially the home of a king or queen

**laeontology**
NOUN the scientific study of fossils

**le paler, palest**
ADJECTIVE not strong or bright in colour

**lette palettes**
NOUN a board on which an artist mixes colours

**lindrome palindromes**
NOUN a word or a phrase that is the same whether you read it backwards or forwards, for example "refer"

**lm palms**
NOUN **1** a tropical tree with no branches and broad, long leaves at the top of its trunk. **Palm** trees often produce fruit, such as coconuts or dates.
NOUN **2** the flat area on the inside of your hand

**mper pampers, pampering, pampered**
VERB If you **pamper** someone, you give them a lot of kindness and comfort.

**pamphlet pamphlets**
NOUN a very thin book in paper covers, giving information about something

**pan pans**
NOUN a round metal container with a long handle, used for cooking things

**pancake pancakes**
NOUN a thin, flat piece of fried batter that can be served with savoury or sweet fillings

**panda pandas**
NOUN a large animal, rather like a bear, that lives in China. A giant **panda** has black fur with large patches of white.

**pane panes**
NOUN a sheet of glass in a window or door

**panel panels**
NOUN **1** a group of people who are chosen to discuss or decide something
NOUN **2** a flat piece of wood, metal or other material that is part of a larger object, such as a door or a wall

**panic panics, panicking, panicked**
NOUN **1** a sudden strong feeling of fear or anxiety
VERB **2** If you **panic**, you become so afraid or anxious that you cannot act sensibly.

**panorama panoramas**
NOUN an extensive view over a wide area of land

**panoramic**
ADJECTIVE giving a view over a wide area of land • The restaurant had **panoramic** views.

**pansy pansies**
NOUN a small brightly coloured garden flower with large round petals

**pant pants, panting, panted**
VERB If you **pant**, you take short, quick breaths through your mouth.

**panther panthers**
NOUN a large wild animal belonging to the cat family, especially the black leopard

**pantomime pantomimes**
NOUN a funny musical play, usually based on a fairy story and performed at Christmas

**pants**
PLURAL NOUN **1** underpants or knickers
PLURAL NOUN **2** another word for **trousers**

a b c d e f g h i j k l m n o p q r s t u v w x y z

287

## paper papers

NOUN **1** a material that you write on or wrap things with
NOUN **2** a newspaper

**WORD HISTORY**
from *papyrus*, the plant from which paper was made in ancient Egypt, Greece and Rome

## paperback paperbacks

NOUN a book with a thin cardboard cover

## papier-mâché

NOUN a mixture of mashed wet paper and glue that can be moulded into shapes, then dried and decorated to make bowls, ornaments and other objects

**PRONUNCIATION TIP**
This word is pronounced pap-yey **mash**-ay.

**WORD HISTORY**
from French, meaning chewed paper

## parable parables

NOUN a short story that makes a moral or religious point

## parachute parachutes

NOUN a large umbrella-like piece of fabric attached by lines to a person or package so that it can fall safely to the ground from an aircraft

## parade parades, parading, paraded

NOUN **1** a line of people or vehicles moving together through a public place in order to celebrate something
VERB **2** When people **parade**, they walk together in a group, usually in front of spectators.
VERB **3** When soldiers **parade**, they gather together for inspection.

## paradise

NOUN **1** According to some religions, **paradise** is a wonderful place where good people go when they die.
NOUN **2** Somewhere very beautiful and wonderful in real life can be called **paradise**. • *Some of the beaches we went to on holiday were **paradise**.*

## paraffin

NOUN a strong-smelling liquid used as a fuel

## paragraph paragraphs

NOUN a section of a piece of writing. **Paragraphs** begin on a new line.

## parallel

ADJECTIVE If two lines or objects are **parall**, they are the same distance apart along t whole of their length.

## parallelogram parallelograms

NOUN a four-sided shape, each side of wh is parallel to the opposite side

## paralyse paralyses, paralysing, paralysed

VERB If something such as an accident **paralyses** you, it makes you unable to move part of your body.

## paralysed

ADJECTIVE If a part of your body is **paralyse** you cannot move it. • *Since the accident m uncle has been **paralysed** from the waist do*

## paralysis

NOUN **Paralysis** is when you cannot move part of your body, for example because of an accident.

## paramedic paramedics

NOUN a person who does some types of medical work, for example for the ambulance service

## parasite parasites

NOUN a small animal or plant that lives or inside a larger animal or plant

**WORD HISTORY**
from Greek *parasitos* meaning someone v eats at someone else's table

## parasitic

ADJECTIVE A **parasitic** animal or plant lives or inside a larger animal or plant.

## paratroops or paratroopers

PLURAL NOUN soldiers trained to be dropped from aircraft by parachute

## parcel parcels

NOUN something wrapped up in paper

## parched

ADJECTIVE **1** very dry and in need of water
• *The earth was **parched** during the drough*
ADJECTIVE **2** very thirsty • *I was **parched** afte the race.*

## pardon pardons, pardoning, pardone

PHRASE **1** You say **pardon** or **I beg your pardon** when you want someone to repe something they have said.
VERB **2** If you **pardon** someone, you forgiv or excuse them for something they have done wrong.

**ent parents**

ₒUN Your **parents** are your father and ₒther.

**enthesis parentheses**

ₒUN **Parentheses** are brackets that you ₚt around words or numbers to indicate ₐat they are separate or less important.

**ish parishes**

ₒUN an area with its own church and priest ₐvicar

**k parks, parking, parked**

ₑRB **1** When someone **parks** a vehicle, they ₐive it into a position where it can be left.
ₒUN **2** a public area with grass and trees

**liament parliaments**

ₒUN the group of people who make or ₐange the laws of a country

**ₐole**

ₒUN When prisoners are given **parole**, they ₐre released early on condition that they ₑhave well.

**ₐrot parrots**

ₒUN a brightly coloured tropical bird with a ₐurved beak

**ₐsley**

ₒUN a herb with curly leaves used for ₐavouring in cooking

**ₐsnip parsnips**

ₒUN a long, pointed, cream-coloured root ₑegetable

**ₐt parts, parting, parted**

ₒUN **1** a piece of something, and not all of it
ₒUN **2** If you have a **part** in a play, you have ₐ role in it.
ₑRB **3** If you **part** people or things, you ₑeparate them.

**ₐrtial**

ₐDJECTIVE **1** not complete or whole
ₚHRASE **2** If you are **partial to** someone or ₑomething, you like them.

**ₐrticipate participates, participating, participated**

ₑERB If you **participate** in an activity, you ₐtake part in it or join in with other people.

**ₐrticiple participles**

ₒUN a word that is formed from a verb ₐand used as part of the verb or as an ₐadjective. For example, *eating* is the present **participle** of *eat*, and *loaded* is the past **participle** of *load*.

**particle particles**

NOUN **1** a very small piece of something
● There were **particles** of dust floating in the air.
NOUN **2** a piece of a substance that is even smaller than an atom, for example a proton or an electron

**particular**

ADJECTIVE **1** to do with only one person or thing ● That **particular** recipe is very easy to make.
ADJECTIVE **2** If you are **particular**, you are fussy and pay attention to detail.

**particularly**

ADVERB You say **particularly** to show that something applies more to one thing, person or situation than to others. ● A good diet is **particularly** important for pregnant women.

**partition partitions**

NOUN a screen separating one part of a room or vehicle from another

**partly**

ADVERB to some extent, but not completely
● It's **partly** my fault.

**partner partners**

NOUN **1** Someone's **partner** is the person they are married to or living with.
NOUN **2** one of two people who do something together, such as dancing or running a business

**part of speech parts of speech**

NOUN one of the groups that words are divided into in grammar, such as a noun or an adjective

**partridge partridges**

NOUN a brown game bird with a round body and a short tail

**part-time**

ADJECTIVE If you have a **part-time** job, you work for only a part of each normal working day or week.

**party parties**

NOUN **1** a social occasion when people meet to enjoy themselves, often in order to celebrate something
NOUN **2** a group of people who are doing something together ● A **party** of school children visited the museum.

a
b
c
d
e
f
g
h
i
j
k
l
m
n
o
p
q
r
s
t
u
v
w
x
y
z

**289**

**pass** passes, passing, passed
VERB **1** If you **pass** someone or something, you go past them without stopping.
VERB **2** If you **pass** something to someone, you give it to them.
VERB **3** If you **pass** an examination, you are successful in it.

**passage** passages
NOUN **1** a long, narrow corridor or space that connects two places • *There was a passage from the front garden through to the back garden.*
NOUN **2** a section of a book or piece of music

**passenger** passengers
NOUN a person travelling in a vehicle, aircraft or ship

**passion** passions
NOUN a very strong feeling

**passive**
ADJECTIVE **1** Someone who is **passive** does not take action or react strongly to things.
NOUN **2** In grammar, the **passive**, or **passive** voice, is the form of the verb in which the person or thing to which an action is being done is the subject of the sentence. For example, the sentence *The burglar was seen by the police* is in the **passive**. For the active, or active voice, the subject of the sentence is the person or thing doing the activity: *The police saw the burglar.*

ANTONYM: active

**Passover**
NOUN an eight-day Jewish festival held in spring

**passport** passports
NOUN an official document showing your identity and nationality, that you need to show when you enter or leave a country

**password** passwords
NOUN **1** a secret word known to only a few people. It allows people on the same side to recognise a friend.
NOUN **2** a word you need to know to get into some computer files

**past**
NOUN **1** the period of time before the present
ADJECTIVE **2 Past** events are ones that happened or existed before the present.
PREPOSITION **3** You use **past** to tell the time when it is thirty minutes or less after a particular hour. • *It's ten past eleven.*
PREPOSITION **4** If you go **past** something, you move towards it and continue until you are

on the other side. • *She walked right pas~~t~~ Anita.*
ADVERB **5** Something that goes **past** mov~~es~~ towards you and continues until you ar~~e~~ the other side. • *An ambulance drove pa~~st~~.*
PREPOSITION **6** Something that is **past** a pl~~ace~~ is situated on the other side of it. • *The ~~place~~ is just past the next village.*

**pasta**
NOUN a dried mixture of flour, eggs and water, formed into different shapes

WORD HISTORY
an Italian word meaning flour mixture

**paste** pastes, pasting, pasted
NOUN **1** a soft, sticky mixture that can be spread easily
VERB **2** If you **paste** something somewhe~~re~~ you stick it there with glue.

**pasteurised**; also spelt **pasteurize~~d~~**
ADJECTIVE **Pasteurised** milk has been hea~~ted~~ by a special process to kill bacteria.

WORD HISTORY
after the French chemist Louis *Pasteur* w~~ho~~ invented the process

**pastime** pastimes
NOUN something that you enjoy doing in your spare time

**pastry** pastries
NOUN **1** a mixture of flour, fat and water th~~at~~ is used for making pies
NOUN **2** a small cake • *There is a selection o~~f~~ pastries for tea.*

**pasture** pastures
NOUN an area of grass where cows, horses and sheep can graze

**pasty** pasties; pastier, pastiest
NOUN **1** a small pie containing meat and vegetables
ADJECTIVE **2** Someone who is **pasty** looks po~~or~~ and unhealthy.

PRONUNCIATION TIP
The noun rhymes with "nasty". The adjective rhymes with "tasty".

**pat** pats, patting, patted
VERB If you **pat** someone or something, yo~~u~~ tap them lightly with an open hand.

**ch patches, patching, patched**
NOUN **1** a piece of material used to cover a hole in something ● *She put a **patch** over the hole in her jeans.*
NOUN **2** an area of a surface that is different in appearance from the rest ● *We want to grow vegetables on that **patch** of ground.*
VERB **3** If you **patch** something that has a hole in it, you mend it by fixing something over the hole.

**chy patchier, patchiest**
ADJECTIVE uneven in quantity, quality or both ● *We drove through **patchy** fog.*

**é pâtés**
NOUN a paste made from meat, fish or vegetables, and spread on toast or biscuits

---

**PRONUNCIATION TIP**
This word is pronounced pa-**tay**.

---

**WORD HISTORY**
from the French word for paste

---

**tent patents**
NOUN the official right given to someone to make something they have invented. It stops others from copying it.

**ternal**
ADJECTIVE relating to or like a father

---

**WORD HISTORY**
from Latin *pater* meaning father

---

**th paths**
NOUN **1** a strip of ground for people to walk or ride along
NOUN **2** the direction in which something travels ● *The trail of smoke showed the **path** of the plane.*

**thetic**
ADJECTIVE **1** If something is **pathetic**, it makes you feel pity.
ADJECTIVE **2** very poor or unsuccessful ● *He made a **pathetic** attempt to swim.*

---

**WORD HISTORY**
from Greek *pathetikos* meaning sensitive

---

**tience**
NOUN the ability to stay calm in a difficult or irritating situation

**tient patients**
ADJECTIVE **1** If you are **patient**, you stay calm in a difficult or irritating situation.

NOUN **2** a person receiving treatment from a doctor

**patiently**
ADVERB calmly even though you are in a difficult or annoying situation

**patio patios**
NOUN a paved area close to a house

**patriot patriots**
NOUN someone who loves their own country and is very loyal to it

**patriotic**
ADJECTIVE showing that you love your country and are very loyal to it

**patriotism**
NOUN behaviour or beliefs that show you love your country and are very loyal to it

**patrol patrols, patrolling, patrolled**
VERB **1** When soldiers, police or guards **patrol** an area, they walk or drive around it to make sure there is no trouble.
NOUN **2** a group of people patrolling an area

**patter patters, pattering, pattered**
VERB **1** If something **patters** on a surface, it makes quick, light, tapping sounds.
● *The rain **pattered** against the window.*
NOUN **2** a series of light, tapping sounds
● *We could hear the **patter** of light rain.*

**pattern patterns**
NOUN **1** a design of shapes repeated at regular intervals
NOUN **2** a drawing that can be copied to make something else, such as clothes

**pause pauses, pausing, paused**
VERB **1** If you **pause**, you stop speaking or doing something for a short time.
NOUN **2** a period when something stops for a short time before continuing

**pavement pavements**
NOUN a raised pathway with a hard surface along the side of a road

---

**WORD HISTORY**
from Latin *pavimentum* meaning hard floor

---

**pavilion pavilions**
NOUN a building at a sports ground, especially a cricket pitch, where players can change

**paw paws**
NOUN the foot of an animal that has claws and pads

a
b
c
d
e
f
g
h
i
j
k
l
m
n
o
p
q
r
s
t
u
v
w
x
y
z

**291**

**pawn** pawns, pawning, pawned
VERB **1** If you **pawn** something, you leave it with someone called a pawnbroker who lends you money. When you repay the money, the pawnbroker will give back the item you **pawned**.
NOUN **2** the smallest and least valuable piece in the game of chess

**pay** pays, paying, paid
VERB **1** If you **pay** someone, you give them money in exchange for something.
PHRASE **2** If you **pay attention**, you listen carefully to what is being said.

**payment** payments
NOUN If you make a **payment** for something, you give someone money in exchange for goods or a service.

**PC** PCs
NOUN **1** the abbreviation of *personal computer*
NOUN **2** In Britain, **PC** is also the abbreviation of *police constable*.

**PE**
NOUN an abbreviation of *physical education*, which is the sports that you do at school

**pea** peas
NOUN a small, round green seed that is eaten as a vegetable

**peace**
NOUN **1** a state of undisturbed calm and quiet
NOUN **2** If a country is at **peace**, it is not at war.

LANGUAGE TIP
Do not confuse *peace* with *piece*.

**peaceful**
ADJECTIVE quiet and calm

**peach** peaches
NOUN a soft, round fruit with yellow flesh and a yellow and red skin

**peacock** peacocks
NOUN a large male bird with very long green and blue tail feathers that it can spread out in a fan. The female is called a peahen.

**peak** peaks
NOUN **1** the highest point of a mountain
→ Have a look at the illustration for **glacier**
NOUN **2** The **peak** of an activity or process is the point at which it is strongest or most successful.
NOUN **3** the part of a cap that sticks out over your eyes

**peal** peals
NOUN the loud musical sound made by b ringing one after another

**peanut** peanuts
NOUN a small nut that grows under the ground

**pear** pears
NOUN a green or yellow fruit that is narro the top and wider at the bottom

LANGUAGE TIP
Do not confuse *pear* with *pair*.

**pearl** pearls
NOUN a hard, round, creamy-white ball us in jewellery. **Pearls** grow inside the shel an oyster.

**peasant** peasants
NOUN a person who works on the land, earning little money

**peat**
NOUN dark-brown decaying plant materia found in cool, wet regions. Dried **peat** ca be used as fuel or fertiliser.

**pebble** pebbles
NOUN a smooth, round stone often found the beach

**peck** pecks, pecking, pecked
VERB If a bird **pecks** something, it bites at quickly with its beak. ● *The birds pecked the seeds on the ground.*

**peculiar**
ADJECTIVE strange and unusual ● *She thougl the food tasted **peculiar**.*

**peculiarity**
NOUN the quality that something or someo has when they are strange and unusual

**peculiarly**
ADVERB in a way that is strange and unusu ● *She thought the food tasted **peculiar**.*

**pedal** pedals, pedalling, pedalled
VERB **1** When you **pedal** a bicycle, you push the pedals around with your feet to make it move.
NOUN **2** a control lever that you press with your foot to make a machine or vehicle wo
→ Have a look at the illustration for **bicyc**

**pedestrian** pedestrians
NOUN someone who is walking ● *Only **pedestrians** are allowed down this street.*

**igree pedigrees**
ECTIVE **1** A **pedigree** animal is bred from
single breed and its ancestors are known
d recorded.
UN **2** a list of a person's or an animal's
cestors

**k peeks, peeking, peeked**
RB **1** If you **peek** at something, you have a
ick look at it.
UN **2** a quick look at something

**l peels, peeling, peeled**
UN **1** the skin of a fruit or vegetable
RB **2** When you **peel** fruit or vegetables,
u remove the skin.
RB **3** If a layer of something **peels**, it
mes off a surface. ● *Paint was* **peeling** *off*
e walls.

**ep peeps, peeping, peeped**
ERB **1** If you **peep** at something, you have
quick, secretive look at it, or you look at it
hrough a small opening.
OUN **2** a quick look at something

**er peers, peering, peered**
ERB **1** If you **peer** at something, you look at
t very hard. ● *He* **peered** *into the dark room.*
OUN **2** Your **peers** are your equals in age,
nterests and background.

**g pegs**
OUN **1** a plastic or wooden clip for attaching
lothes to a washing line
OUN **2** a hook where you can hang things

**lican pelicans**
NOUN a large water bird with a pouch
beneath its beak in which it stores fish

**llet pellets**
NOUN a small ball of food, paper, lead or
other material

**lt pelts, pelting, pelted**
NOUN **1** the skin and fur of an animal,
especially when it is used for making
clothes
VERB **2** If you **pelt** someone with something,
you throw it at them very hard.
VERB **3** If rain **pelts** down, it rains very hard.

**lvis pelvises**
NOUN the group of bones near the bottom of
your spine to which your legs are attached
→ Have a look at the illustration for
**skeleton**

**en pens**
NOUN **1** an instrument with a pointed end
used for writing with ink

NOUN **2** a small, fenced area where farm
animals are kept ● *a sheep* **pen**

**penalty penalties**
NOUN **1** a punishment
NOUN **2** In sport, a **penalty** is an advantage
or point given to one team when their
opponents break the rules.

**pence**
NOUN a plural form of **penny**

**pencil pencils**
NOUN a small stick of wood with a type of
soft mineral called graphite in the centre,
used for drawing or writing

WORD HISTORY
from Latin *pencillus* meaning painter's
brush

**pendant pendants**
NOUN a piece of jewellery attached to a chain
and worn round the neck

**penetrate penetrates, penetrating,
penetrated**
VERB If someone or something **penetrates**
an object or area, they succeed in getting
into or through it. ● *Eventually they*
**penetrated** *the forest and found the cabin.*

**pen friend pen friends**
NOUN someone living in a different place
or country whom you write to regularly,
although you may never have met each
other

**penguin penguins**
NOUN a black and white bird with webbed
feet and small wings like flippers.
**Penguins** are found mainly in the
Antarctic.

**penicillin**
NOUN a powerful antibiotic obtained from
fungus and used to treat infections

**peninsula peninsulas**
NOUN an area of land almost surrounded by
water

WORD HISTORY
from Latin *paene + insula* meaning almost
an island

**penis penises**
NOUN A man's **penis** is the part of the body
he uses when urinating.

**penknife penknives**
NOUN a small folding knife

a
b
c
d
e
f
g
h
i
j
k
l
m
n
o
p
q
r
s
t
u
v
w
x
y
z

**293**

## penny pennies or pence

NOUN a unit of currency in Britain and some other countries. In Britain, there are 100 **pence** in a pound.

## pension pensions

NOUN a regular sum of money paid to a retired or widowed person or to someone with a disability

## pentagon pentagons

NOUN a flat shape with five straight sides

## pentagonal

ADJECTIVE having five straight sides

## pentathlon pentathlons

NOUN a sports contest in which athletes compete in five different events

**WORD HISTORY**
from Greek *pente* meaning five and *athlon* meaning contest

## people

PLURAL NOUN human beings – men, women and children

## pepper peppers

NOUN **1** a hot-tasting powdered spice used for flavouring in cooking
NOUN **2** a hollow green, red or yellow vegetable, with sweet-flavoured flesh

## peppermint peppermints

NOUN **1** a plant with a strong taste. It is used for making sweets and in medicine.
NOUN **2** a sweet flavoured with peppermint

## per

PREPOSITION **Per** means *for each* and is used when speaking about prices, measurements, rates and ratios
• *60 kilometres **per** hour* • *three times **per** year* • *90p **per** kilo*

## perceive perceives, perceiving, perceived

VERB If you **perceive** something, you see, notice or understand it.

## per cent

PHRASE You use **per cent** to show amount out of a hundred. The symbol for per cent %. • *She got 98 **per cent** (98%) for her ma test.*

**WORD HISTORY**
from Latin *per* meaning each and *centum* meaning hundred

## percentage percentages

NOUN an amount or rate expressed as a number of hundredths

## perceptive

ADJECTIVE Someone who is **perceptive** not and understands things more quickly tha other people.

SYNONYMS: observant, sharp

## perch perches, perching, perched

VERB **1** If you **perch** on something, you sit the edge of it.
VERB **2** When a bird **perches** on somethin it stands on it.
NOUN **3** a short rod for a bird to stand on
NOUN **4** an edible freshwater fish

## percussion

ADJECTIVE **Percussion** instruments are musical instruments that you hit or shake to produce sounds, such as drums and tambourines

## percussionist percussionists

NOUN someone who plays musical instruments that you hit or shake, such as drums and tambourines

## perennial

ADJECTIVE occurring or lasting for many year

## perfect perfects, perfecting, perfected

ADJECTIVE **1** Something that is **perfect** is as good as it possibly can be.
VERB **2** If you **perfect** something, you make as good as it possibly can be.

**PRONUNCIATION TIP**
The adjective is pronounced **pur**-fikt. The verb is pronounced pur-**fekt**.

## perform performs, performing, performed

VERB **1** If you **perform** a play or piece of music, you do a show of it in front of an audience.
VERB **2** If you **perform** a task or action, you do it.

A B C D E F G H I J K L M N O P Q R S T U V W X Y Z

**rformance performances**
NOUN an entertainment provided for an
udience • *The orchestra gave an excellent
performance*.

**rformer performers**
NOUN someone who does something in front
of an audience, such as acting, dancing or
playing a piece of music

**rfume perfumes**
NOUN **1** a pleasant-smelling liquid that
people put on their skin
NOUN **2** a pleasant smell • *These roses have a
lovely* **perfume**.

**rhaps**
ADVERB You use **perhaps** when you are
not sure if something is true or possible.
• **Perhaps** we could see you tomorrow?

**ril perils**
NOUN (*formal*) great danger

**rilous**
ADJECTIVE (*formal*) very dangerous

**rimeter perimeters**
NOUN **1** the distance all the way round the
edge of an area
NOUN **2** the edge or boundary of something

**riod periods**
NOUN **1** a particular length of time • *We will
be away for a* **period** *of a few months*.
NOUN **2** A woman's **period** is the monthly
bleeding from her womb.
NOUN **3** In American English, a **period** is a
full stop.

**riodical periodicals**
NOUN a magazine that is published regularly

**riodic table**
NOUN a table showing the chemical elements
arranged in a particular order

**riscope periscopes**
NOUN a tube with mirrors placed in it so that
you can see things that are otherwise out of
sight. **Periscopes** are used for seeing out of
submarines.

**rish perishes, perishing, perished**
VERB **1** If fruit, rubber or fabric **perishes**, it
rots.
VERB **2** (*formal*) If someone or something
**perishes**, they die or are destroyed.

**rishable**
ADJECTIVE If food or a material is **perishable**,
it can rot.

**perm perms**
NOUN If someone has a **perm**, their hair is
curled and treated with chemicals to keep
the curls for several months.

**permanent**
ADJECTIVE lasting forever or present all the
time

**permission**
NOUN If you have **permission** to do
something, you are allowed to do it.

**permit permits, permitting, permitted**
VERB **1** If someone or something **permits**
you to do something, they allow it or make
it possible. • *We* **permit** *children to ride
bicycles to school*.

SYNONYM: give permission

NOUN **2** an official document that says that
you are allowed to do something

**PRONUNCIATION TIP**
The verb is pronounced pur-**mit**. The noun
is pronounced **pur**-mit.

**perpendicular**
ADJECTIVE A line that is **perpendicular** to
another one meets it at a right angle (90°).

**perpetual**
ADJECTIVE never ending

**perplexed**
ADJECTIVE If you are **perplexed**, you are
puzzled and do not know what to do.

SYNONYM: confused

**persecute persecutes, persecuting,
persecuted**
VERB If someone **persecutes** another
person, they continually treat them with
cruelty and unfairness, often because of
their religious beliefs.

**persecution**
NOUN **Persecution** is when someone
continually treats another person in a cruel
and unfair way, especially because of their
religious beliefs.

**persecutor persecutors**
NOUN someone who continually treats
another person in a cruel and unfair way,
especially because of their religious beliefs

**perseverance**
NOUN the quality someone has when they
keep trying to do something and do not
give up

a
b
c
d
e
f
g
h
i
j
k
l
m
n
o
p
q
r
s
t
u
v
w
x
y
z

**295**

**persevere** perseveres, persevering, persevered

VERB If you **persevere**, you keep trying to do something and do not give up.

**persist** persists, persisting, persisted

VERB 1 If something **persists**, it continues and will not stop. ● *The rain* **persisted** *all day.*

VERB 2 If you **persist** in doing something, you continue with it in spite of difficulties or opposition.

**person** people or persons

NOUN 1 a man, woman or child

SYNONYMS: human being, individual

NOUN 2 In grammar, the first **person** is the speaker (I), the second **person** is the person being spoken to (you), and the third **person** is anyone else being referred to (he, she, they).

PHRASE 3 If you do something **in person**, you do it yourself rather than letting someone else do it for you.

WORD HISTORY
from Latin *persona* meaning actor's mask

LANGUAGE TIP
The usual plural of *person* is *people*. *Persons* is much less common, and is used only in formal English.

**personal**

ADJECTIVE 1 belonging or relating to a particular person

SYNONYMS: individual, own

ADJECTIVE 2 **Personal** matters are personal things that you may not wish to discuss with other people. ● *I cannot tell you for* **personal** *reasons.*

**personality** personalities

NOUN Your **personality** is your character and nature. ● *She's got a very lively* **personality**.

**personally**

ADVERB 1 in person ● *He came to school to thank us* **personally** *for the money we raised for the charity.*

ADVERB 2 You use **personally** to express your own opinion of something. ● **Personally**, *I don't mind where we go.*

**personnel**

PLURAL NOUN the people who work for an organisation

**perspective** perspectives

NOUN 1 the impression of distance and de in a picture or a drawing

NOUN 2 a particular way of thinking about something or looking at something ● *Wh is your* **perspective** *on discipline?*

**perspiration**

NOUN sweat or the process of sweating

**perspire** perspires, perspiring, perspired

VERB When people **perspire**, they sweat.

**persuade** persuades, persuading, persuaded

VERB If you **persuade** someone to do something, or **persuade** them that something is true, you make them do it o believe it by giving them good reasons.

**persuasion**

NOUN the process of trying to make someo do something or believe something by giving them good reasons

**persuasive**

ADJECTIVE able to make someone do something or believe something by using good reasons ● *a* **persuasive** *argument*

**pessimism**

NOUN the feeling that bad things will alway happen

**pessimist** pessimists

NOUN If you are a **pessimist**, you think tha bad things will always happen.

ANTONYM: optimist

**pessimistic**

ADJECTIVE believing that bad things will always happen

ANTONYM: optimistic

**pest** pests

NOUN 1 an insect or other small animal that damages plants or food supplies

NOUN 2 someone who keeps bothering or annoying you

**pester** pesters, pestering, pestered

VERB If you **pester** someone, you keep bothering them or asking them to do something.

sticide **pesticides**

OUN a chemical sprayed onto plants to kill
nsects and grubs

**pets**

OUN **1** a tame animal kept at home

OUN **2** a person who is treated as a
favourite

**al petals**

OUN one of the coloured outer parts of a
ower that attract insects. Some **petals** are
erfumed.

→ Have a look at the illustration for **flower**

**ition petitions**

OUN a written document, signed by a lot of
eople, requesting official action be taken
n something

**rified**

DJECTIVE If you are **petrified**, you are very
ightened.

SYNONYM: terrified

**trol**

OUN a liquid that is used as a fuel for motor
ehicles

**ty pettier, pettiest**

DJECTIVE trivial and unimportant ● *We should
ot argue over **petty** things.*

**w pews**

OUN a long wooden seat with a back, that
eople sit on in church

OUN The **pH** of a solution or of the soil is a
easurement of how acid or alkaline it is.
ubstances with a **pH** above 7 are alkaline
nd substances with a **pH** below 7 are acid.

**antom phantoms**

OUN **1** a ghost

DJECTIVE **2** imagined or unreal

**armacy pharmacies**

OUN a shop where medicines are sold

**ase phases**

OUN a particular stage in the development
f something

**easant pheasants**

OUN a large, long-tailed game bird

**enomenal**

DJECTIVE unusually great or good ● *The show
as a **phenomenal** success.*

**enomenally**

DVERB in a way that is unusually good

**phenomenon phenomena**

NOUN something that happens or exists,
especially something extraordinary or
remarkable ● *The eclipse was a fascinating
**phenomenon**.*

**philosophy philosophies**

NOUN **1** the study or creation of ideas about
humans, their relationship to the universe
and beliefs

NOUN **2** a set of beliefs a person has

**phobia phobias**

NOUN a deep fear or dislike of something

**phobic**

ADJECTIVE having a deep fear or dislike of
something ● *I'm **phobic** about spiders.*

**phoenix phoenixes**

NOUN an imaginary bird that, according to
myth, sets fire to itself every five hundred
years, and rises from the ashes

PRONUNCIATION TIP
This word is pronounced **fee**-niks.

**phone phones, phoning, phoned**

NOUN **1** a piece of electrical or electronic
equipment for talking directly to someone
who is in a different place

VERB **2** If you **phone** someone, you speak to
them using a phone.

WORD HISTORY
short for *telephone*

**phonetics**

NOUN the study of the sounds made in
speech

**phoney phonier, phoniest**; also spelt
**phony**

ADJECTIVE false, not genuine, and meant to
trick ● *He had a **phoney** passport.*

ANTONYM: genuine

**photo photos**

NOUN an abbreviation of **photograph**

**photocopier photocopiers**

NOUN a machine that makes instant copies
of documents

**photocopy photocopies, photocopying,
photocopied**

VERB **1** If you **photocopy** a document, you
make a copy of it using a photocopier.

NOUN **2** a copy of a document made using a
photocopier

a
b
c
d
e
f
g
h
i
j
k
l
m
n
o
p
q
r
s
t
u
v
w
x
y
z

**297**

## photograph photographs, photographing, photographed

NOUN **1** a picture taken with a camera and then printed on special paper • *She took lots of photographs of her friends.*

VERB **2** If you **photograph** someone or something, you use a camera to take a picture of them.

## photographer photographers

NOUN someone whose job is to take photographs

## photography

NOUN the job or hobby of taking photographs

## photosynthesis

NOUN the process by which green plants make their own food from carbon dioxide and water in the presence of sunlight

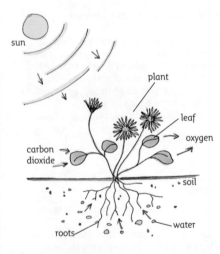

sun

plant

leaf

oxygen

carbon dioxide

soil

water

roots

## phrase phrases

NOUN a short group of words or musical notes

## physical

ADJECTIVE concerning the body rather than the mind

**WORD HISTORY**
from Greek *phusis* meaning nature

## physical education

NOUN physical exercise and sports that you do at school

## physics

NOUN the scientific study of the forces and properties of matter, such as heat, light, sound and electricity

## pi

NOUN a number, approximately 3.142, which is equal to the circumference a circle divided by its diameter and usually represented by the Greek letter π

## pianist pianists

NOUN someone who plays the piano

## piano pianos

NOUN a large musical instrument with a r of black and white keys. When the keys a pressed, little hammers hit wires to prod different notes.

## piccolo piccolos

NOUN a high-pitched wind instrument like small flute

## pick picks, picking, picked

VERB **1** If you **pick** someone or something, you choose them. • *I picked Hannah for r partner.*

VERB **2** If you **pick** a flower or a fruit, you break it off from where it is growing.

VERB **3** If someone **picks** a lock, they open with a piece of wire instead of a key.

### pick on

VERB If you **pick on** someone, you treat them unkindly and unfairly.

### pick up

VERB **1** If you **pick up** someone or something, you lift them.

VERB **2** If you **pick up** someone or something from a place, you collect th from there. • *What time will you pick me up?*

## picket pickets, picketing, picketed

VERB **1** When a group of people **picket** a place of work during a strike, they stand outside and try to persuade other workers not to go in to work.

NOUN **2** a group of people who picket a pla

## pickle pickles

NOUN **Pickles** are vegetables or fruit preserved in vinegar or salt water.

**kpocket pickpockets**
ᴐᴜɴ a thief who steals things from pockets
ɪr bags

**ɴic picnics, picnicking, picnicked**
ᴐᴜɴ **1** a meal eaten out of doors
ᴐᴜɴ **2** to have a picnic

**ﬞtogram pictograms**
ᴐᴜɴ a type of graph that uses small
ɪctures to show information

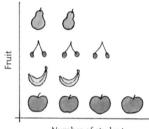

Fruit

Number of students
who prefer it

**ﬞtorial**
ᴐᴊᴇᴄᴛɪᴠᴇ relating to or using pictures • *The*
*ook is a **pictorial** history of air travel.*

**ﬞture pictures**
ᴐᴜɴ a drawing, painting, photograph or
ɪlevision image of someone or something

**ﬞturesque**
ᴐᴊᴇᴄᴛɪᴠᴇ A place that is **picturesque** is very
ﬞttractive and unspoiled.

**WORD HISTORY**
ﬞrom Italian *pittoresco* meaning in the style
ﬞf a painter

**ﬞ pies**
ᴊᴏᴜɴ a dish of meat, vegetables or fruit
ﬞovered with pastry

**ﬞce pieces**
ᴊᴏᴜɴ **1** a portion or part of something • *a*
*ake divided into six **pieces***
ᴊᴏᴜɴ **2** an individual thing of a particular
ﬞind • *This is a good **piece** of work.*
ᴊᴏᴜɴ **3** a coin • *a 50 pence **piece***

**LANGUAGE TIP**
ﬞo not confuse *piece* with *peace*.

**pie chart pie charts**
ɴᴏᴜɴ a circular diagram that is divided into
segments to show how a quantity or an
amount of something is shared

Favourite sports

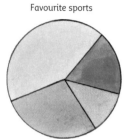

 Football    Cricket

Athletics    Tennis

**pier piers**
ɴᴏᴜɴ a large structure at the seaside, with
a platform built from the shore out into the
sea, that people can walk along

**pierce pierces, piercing, pierced**
ᴠᴇʀʙ If a sharp object **pierces** something, it
goes through it, making a hole.

**piercing**
ᴀᴅᴊᴇᴄᴛɪᴠᴇ **1** a **piercing** sound is high pitched
and sharp, and it hurts your ears

SYNONYM: shrill

ᴀᴅᴊᴇᴄᴛɪᴠᴇ **2** Someone with **piercing** eyes
seems to stare at you intensely.

**pig pigs**
ɴᴏᴜɴ a farm animal with pink or black skin,
a curly tail and a snout, that is kept for its
meat. Pork, ham and bacon all come from
**pigs**.

**pigeon pigeons**
ɴᴏᴜɴ a grey bird with a small head and large
chest, often found in towns and cities

**piglet piglets**
ɴᴏᴜɴ a young pig

**pigsty pigsties**
ɴᴏᴜɴ **1** a small shelter with an enclosed area
where pigs are kept
ɴᴏᴜɴ **2** If you say a place is like a **pigsty**,
you mean that it is very dirty and untidy.

a
b
c
d
e
f
g
h
i
j
k
l
m
n
o
p
q
r
s
t
u
v
w
x
y
z

**299**

**pigtail pigtails**
NOUN a plait of hair ● *She wore her hair in* **pigtails**.

**pike pikes**
NOUN 1 a large freshwater fish with strong, sharp teeth
NOUN 2 a weapon used in medieval times. A **pike** was a long pole with a spike on the end.

**pile piles, piling, piled**
NOUN 1 a quantity of things lying on top of one another
VERB 2 If you **pile** things somewhere, you put them on top of one another.

**pilgrim pilgrims**
NOUN a person who goes on a journey to a holy place for religious reasons

**pilgrimage pilgrimages**
NOUN a journey to a holy place for religious reasons

**pill pills**
NOUN a small, round tablet of medicine that you swallow

**pillar pillars**
NOUN a tall, solid structure like a large post, often made of stone and usually supporting part of a building

**pillow pillows**
NOUN a large cushion that you rest your head on when you are in bed

**pilot pilots**
NOUN 1 a person who is trained to fly an aircraft
NOUN 2 the person who guides a ship into port

**pimple pimples**
NOUN a small spot on the skin

**pin pins, pinning, pinned**
NOUN 1 a thin, pointed piece of metal, used to fasten things like paper or cloth together
VERB 2 If you **pin** something, you attach it with a pin.

**pincers**
PLURAL NOUN 1 The **pincers** of a crab or a lobster are its large front claws.
PLURAL NOUN 2 a tool consisting of two pieces of metal hinged in the middle, used for gripping and pulling things

**pinch pinches, pinching, pinched**
VERB 1 If you **pinch** something, you squeeze it between your thumb and first finger.
VERB 2 (*informal*) If someone **pinches** something, they steal it.
NOUN 3 A **pinch** of something is the amount that you can hold between your thumb and first finger. ● *Add a **pinch** of salt to the soup.*

**pine pines, pining, pined**
NOUN 1 an evergreen tree with very thin leaves called needles
VERB 2 If you **pine** for something or someone, you feel sad because they are there.

**pineapple pineapples**
NOUN a large, oval tropical fruit with sweet yellow flesh and thick, woody skin

**pink pinker, pinkest**
ADJECTIVE pale reddish-white

**pint pints**
NOUN a unit of measurement for liquids equal to about 0.568 litres

**pioneer pioneers**
NOUN one of the first people to go to a place or to do something new

**pip pips**
NOUN 1 the hard seeds in a fruit
NOUN 2 a short, high-pitched sound

**pipe pipes, piping, piped**
NOUN 1 a long, hollow tube through which liquid or gas can flow
NOUN 2 an object that is used for smoking tobacco, consisting of a small hollow bowl attached to a thin tube
NOUN 3 a tube-shaped musical instrument
VERB 4 If liquid or gas is **piped** somewhere, is transferred there through a pipe.

**pipeline pipelines**
NOUN 1 a large underground pipe that carries oil or gas over a long distance
PHRASE 2 If something is **in the pipeline**, is already planned or has begun.

**pirate pirates**
NOUN a sailor who attacks and robs other ships

**pistol pistols**
NOUN a small gun held in the hand

**pit pits**
NOUN 1 a large hole in the ground
NOUN 2 a coal mine

A B C D E F G H I J K L M N O P Q R S T U V W X Y Z

**ch pitches, pitching, pitched**

NOUN **1** an area of ground marked out for
playing a game such as football or cricket

NOUN **2** The **pitch** of a sound is how high or
ow it is.

NOUN **3** a black substance painted onto roofs
nd boat bottoms to make them waterproof

VERB **4** If you **pitch** something somewhere,
ou throw it there with a lot of force.

VERB **5** If you **pitch** a tent, you put it up.

**cher pitchers**

NOUN a large jug

**chfork pitchforks**

NOUN a long-handled fork with two large
rongs, used for lifting and moving hay

**fall pitfalls**

NOUN one of the difficulties or dangers of a
ituation

**ta pittas**

NOUN a flat disc of bread with a hollow
nside, that can be filled with food

---

**WORD HISTORY**

om Greek, meaning a cake

---

**y pities, pitying, pitied**

VERB **1** If you **pity** someone, you feel sorry
or them.

NOUN **2** a feeling of sadness and concern for
omeone

NOUN **3** If you say that something is a **pity**,
ou mean it is disappointing. ● *It's a pity*
*e couldn't play tennis.*

**rot pivots, pivoting, pivoted**

VERB **1** If something **pivots**, it balances or
urns on a central point.

NOUN **2** the central point on which
omething balances or turns

**rotal**

ADJECTIVE very important and affecting how
omething develops

**zza pizzas**

NOUN a flat piece of dough usually covered
vith cheese, tomato and other savoury food
nd baked in an oven

---

**WORD HISTORY**

n Italian word

---

**acard placards**

NOUN a large notice carried at a
lemonstration or displayed in a public
lace ● *The man carried a placard*
*dvertising the furniture sale.*

---

**place places, placing, placed**

NOUN **1** a particular point, position, building
or area ● *They found a good place to camp.*

NOUN **2** a particular position in a race,
competition, or series ● *Last year she finished*
*in third place.*

NOUN **3** If you have a **place** in a team or on a
course, you are allowed to join the team or
course. ● *I eventually got a place at the new*
*school.*

VERB **4** If you **place** something somewhere,
you put it there. ● *She placed her hand*
*gently on my shoulder.*

PHRASE **5** When something **takes place**, it
happens. ● *The competition will take place*
*next month.*

**placid**

ADJECTIVE calm and not easily excited or upset

SYNONYMS: even-tempered, unexcitable

**plague plagues, plaguing, plagued**

NOUN **1** a very infectious disease that kills
large numbers of people

NOUN **2** A **plague** of unpleasant things is a
large number of them occurring at the same
time.

VERB **3** If you **plague** someone, you keep
pestering them.

VERB **4** If problems **plague** you, they keep
causing you trouble.

---

**PRONUNCIATION TIP**

This word is pronounced **playg**.

---

**plaice**

NOUN an edible European flat fish

---

**LANGUAGE TIP**

The plural of *plaice* is *plaice*.

---

**plaid plaids**

NOUN woven material with a tartan design

---

**PRONUNCIATION TIP**

This word is pronounced **plad**.

---

**plain plainer, plainest; plains**

ADJECTIVE **1** very simple in style, with no
pattern or decoration

ADJECTIVE **2** obvious or easy to understand

NOUN **3** a large, flat area of land with very
few trees

**plait** **plaits, plaiting, plaited**
VERB **1** If you **plait** hair or rope, you twist three lengths together in turn to make one thick length.
NOUN **2** a length of hair that has been plaited

PRONUNCIATION TIP
This word is pronounced **plat**.

**plan** **plans, planning, planned**
NOUN **1** a method of achieving something that has been worked out beforehand
VERB **2** If you **plan** something, you decide in detail what you are going to do.
VERB **3** If you **plan** to do something, you intend to do it.

**plane** **planes**
NOUN **1** an abbreviation of *aeroplane*
NOUN **2** a tool for smoothing wood
ADJECTIVE **3** A **plane** shape has a flat, level surface. A **plane** mirror is flat and not curved.

**planet** **planets**
NOUN a large sphere in space that orbits a sun. The Earth and Mars are both **planets** that revolve around our sun.

**plank** **planks**
NOUN a long rectangular piece of wood

**plankton**
NOUN a layer of tiny plants and animals that live just below the surface of a sea or lake

**plant** **plants, planting, planted**
NOUN **1** a living thing that grows in the earth and has a stem, leaves and roots.

→ Have a look at the illustration for **photosynthesis**

VERB **2** If you **plant** things such as flowers or trees, you put them in the ground so that they will grow.

**plantation** **plantations**
NOUN **1** a large area of land where crops such as tea, cotton or sugar are grown
NOUN **2** a large number of trees planted together

**plaque** **plaques**
NOUN **1** a flat piece of metal or porcelain, fixed to a wall, with an inscription on it in memory of a famous person or event
NOUN **2** a substance that forms around your teeth. It is made up of bacteria, saliva and food.

PRONUNCIATION TIP
This word is pronounced **plak**.

**plaster** **plasters**
NOUN **1** a paste made of sand, lime and water, that is used to form a smooth surface for inside walls and ceilings
NOUN **2** a strip of sticky material with a small pad, used for covering cuts on your body
● *The bleeding stopped once I had put a* ***plaster*** *on.*
NOUN **3 Plaster** of Paris is a white powder mixed with water, that becomes hard when it dries. It is used for making moulds and for holding broken bones in place while they heal

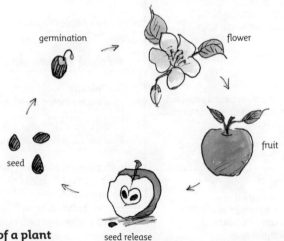

germination

flower

fruit

seed

seed release

**life cycle of a plant**

**...sterer plasterers**
NOUN someone whose job is to cover the walls and ceiling of a room with a paste made of sand, lime and water to form a smooth surface for painting

**...stic plastics**
NOUN 1 a light synthetic material made from oil by a chemical process. **Plastics** can be moulded into different shapes for many different uses.
ADJECTIVE 2 made of plastic

**...sticine**
NOUN (trademark) a soft, coloured material like clay, used for making models

**...te plates**
NOUN 1 a flat dish used to hold food
NOUN 2 a flat piece of hard material such as glass or metal

**...teau plateaus or plateaux**
NOUN a large area of high and fairly flat land

**WORD HISTORY**
from Old French *platel* meaning a flat piece of metal

**...tform platforms**
NOUN 1 a raised structure on which someone or something can stand
NOUN 2 the raised area in a railway station where passengers get on and off trains

**...tinum**
NOUN a valuable silver-coloured metal

**...typus platypuses**
NOUN an Australian mammal that lives in rivers. It has brown fur, webbed feet and a beak like a duck.

**WORD HISTORY**
from Greek *platus* meaning flat and *pous* meaning foot

**...y plays, playing, played**
VERB 1 When children **play**, they take part in games or use toys for fun.
VERB 2 When you **play** a sport or game, you take part in it.
VERB 3 If an actor **plays** a character in a play or film, they perform that role.
VERB 4 If you **play** a musical instrument, you produce music from it.
NOUN 5 **Play** is the activity of playing a game or sport.
NOUN 6 a story acted out in the theatre, on the radio or on television

**player players**
NOUN 1 someone who takes part in a sport or game • football **players**
NOUN 2 someone who plays a musical instrument • a violin **player**

**playground playgrounds**
NOUN a special area for children to play in

**playgroup playgroups**
NOUN an informal group of very young children who play together, supervised by adults

**playtime playtimes**
NOUN the time in a school day when children go out to play

**playwright playwrights**
NOUN a person who writes plays

**plea pleas**
NOUN 1 If you make a **plea**, you make an urgent request or an appeal for something.
NOUN 2 In a law court, a **plea** is someone's statement that they are guilty or not guilty.

**plead pleads, pleading, pleaded**
VERB 1 If you **plead** with someone, you beg them for something. • She came to **plead** for help.
VERB 2 In a law court, when a person **pleads** guilty or not guilty, they state that they are guilty or not guilty.

**pleasant**
ADJECTIVE nice, pleasing, enjoyable or attractive in some way

**please pleases, pleasing, pleased**
1 You say **please** when you are asking someone politely to do something. • Can you help me, **please**?
VERB 2 If something **pleases** you, it makes you feel happy and satisfied.

**pleasure pleasures**
NOUN a feeling of happiness, satisfaction or enjoyment

**pleat pleats**
NOUN a permanent fold in fabric, made by folding one part over another

**pledge pledges, pledging, pledged**
NOUN 1 a solemn promise
VERB 2 If you **pledge** something, you promise that you will do it or give it.

**plenty**
NOUN If you have **plenty** of something, you have more than enough for your needs.
• We've got **plenty** of time.

## pliable

ADJECTIVE If something is **pliable**, you can bend it without breaking it. • *This **pliable** material will be easier to work with.*

SYNONYM: flexible

## pliers

PLURAL NOUN a small tool with metal jaws for gripping small objects such as nails and bending wire

## plight plights

NOUN a difficult or dangerous situation
• the **plight** of the homeless

## plod plods, plodding, plodded

VERB If you **plod**, you walk slowly and heavily. • *We **plodded** home through the mud.*

## plop plops, plopping, plopped

NOUN **1** a gentle sound of something lightweight dropping into a liquid
VERB **2** If something **plops** into a liquid, it drops into it with a gentle sound.

## plot plots, plotting, plotted

NOUN **1** a secret plan made by a group of people
NOUN **2** The **plot** of a film, novel or play is the story.
VERB **3** If people **plot** to do something, they plan it secretly.

## plough ploughs, ploughing, ploughed

NOUN **1** a large farming tool that is pulled across a field to turn the soil over before planting seeds
VERB **2** When farmers **plough** land, they use a plough to turn over the soil.

## pluck plucks, plucking, plucked

VERB **1** If you **pluck** a fruit or flower, you remove it with a sharp pull.
VERB **2** If you **pluck** a dead bird, such as a chicken or a turkey, you pull the feathers off it before cooking it.
VERB **3** When you **pluck** a stringed instrument, you pull the strings and let them go.

## plug plugs, plugging, plugged

NOUN **1** a device that connects a piece of electrical equipment to an electric socket
NOUN **2** a thick circular piece of rubber or plastic that you use to block the hole in a sink or bath

### plug in

VERB If you **plug in** a piece of electrical equipment, you push its plug into an electric socket.

## plum plums

NOUN a small fruit with a smooth red or yellow skin and a stone in the middle

## plumage

NOUN a bird's feathers

## plumber plumbers

NOUN a person who connects and repairs water pipes

## plump plumper, plumpest

ADJECTIVE rounded, or slightly fat

## plunge plunges, plunging, plunged

VERB If you **plunge** somewhere, especially into water, you fall or rush there.

SYNONYMS: dive, drop, fall

## plural plurals

NOUN the form of a word that is used when referring to more than one person or thing
• *The usual **plural** of person is people.*

ANTONYM: singular

## plus

PREPOSITION **1** You use **plus** to show that one number is being added to another.
• *Two **plus** two equals four.*
PREPOSITION **2** You can use **plus** when you mention an additional item. • *She gave us our coats, **plus** a blanket.*

## plywood

NOUN wooden board made from several thin sheets of wood glued together under pressure

## p.m.

used to show times between 12 noon and 12 midnight • *I go to bed at 8 **p.m.** on schooldays and 9 **p.m.** at weekends.*

WORD HISTORY
from Latin *post meridiem* meaning after noon

## PM PMs

NOUN **1** an abbreviation for *prime minister*
NOUN **2** an abbreviation for *private message*

## pneumatic

ADJECTIVE operated by or filled with compressed air • *a **pneumatic** drill*

## pneumonia

NOUN a serious disease that affects a person's lungs and makes breathing difficult

**poach poaches, poaching, poached**
VERB **1** If someone **poaches** animals, they hunt them illegally on someone else's land.
VERB **2** When you **poach** food, especially fish, or an egg taken out of its shell, you cook it gently in hot liquid.

**poacher poachers**
NOUN someone who illegally hunts animals on someone else's land

**pocket pockets**
NOUN a small pouch for keeping things in, that forms part of a piece of clothing

**pocket money**
NOUN an amount of money given regularly to children by their parents

**pod pods**
NOUN a long, narrow seed container that grows on plants such as peas or beans

**podcast podcasts**
NOUN a file similar to a radio broadcast that can be downloaded for listening to on a computer or MP3 player

**poem poems**
NOUN a piece of writing, usually arranged in short rhythmic lines, with words chosen for their sound or impact

**poet poets**
NOUN a person who writes poems

**poetry**
NOUN poems, considered a form of literature

**point points, pointing, pointed**
VERB **1** If you **point** at or to something, you hold out your finger towards it to show where it is.
NOUN **2** the thin, sharp end of something such as a needle or knife
NOUN **3** a particular place or time ● *At some point during the night, the storm began.*
NOUN **4** a single mark in a competition ● *They won by 21 points to 18.*
NOUN **5** the purpose or the most important part of something ● *What do you think is the point of this exercise?*
NOUN **6** an opinion or fact expressed by someone ● *That's a very good point.*
NOUN **7** In mathematics, the decimal **point** in a number is marked by a dot, as in 5.2.
NOUN **8** one of the 32 marks on the circumference of a compass to show direction

**pointed**
ADJECTIVE A **pointed** object has a thin, sharp end.

**pointless**
ADJECTIVE Something that is **pointless** has no purpose.

**point of view points of view**
NOUN Your **point of view** is your opinion about something or your attitude towards it.

**poised**
ADJECTIVE If you are **poised** to do something, you are ready to do it at any moment.

**poison poisons, poisoning, poisoned**
NOUN **1** a substance that harms or kills you if you swallow it or absorb it
VERB **2** To **poison** someone means to harm them by giving them poison.

**poke pokes, poking, poked**
VERB If you **poke** someone or something, you give them a push with your finger or a sharp object.

**poke out**
VERB If something **pokes out** from behind or from underneath another thing, it shows. ● *The label poked out from the back of his anorak.*

**polar**
ADJECTIVE relating to the area around the North Pole or the South Pole ● *the polar regions*

**polar bear polar bears**
NOUN a large white bear that lives in the area around the North Pole

**pole poles**
NOUN **1** a long, slender, rounded piece of wood or metal
NOUN **2** The Earth has two **poles** at the opposite ends of its imaginary axis, called the North Pole and the South Pole.

→ Have a look at the illustration for **equator**

NOUN **3** either of the opposite ends of a magnet or electric cell

**pole vault**
NOUN an athletics event in which contestants jump over a high bar using a long, flexible pole to lift themselves into the air

**police**
PLURAL NOUN the official organisation responsible for making sure that people obey the law

**police officer police officers**
NOUN a member of the police force

a
b
c
d
e
f
g
h
i
j
k
l
m
n
o
p
q
r
s
t
u
v
w
x
y
z

**305**

**policy** policies

NOUN a set of plans and ideas, especially in politics or business • *What is their **policy** on education?*

**polish** polishes, polishing, polished

NOUN **1** a substance that you put on an object to clean it and make it shine
VERB **2** If you **polish** something, you put polish on it or rub it with a cloth to make it shine.

**polite**

ADJECTIVE Someone who is **polite** has good manners and is not rude to other people.

SYNONYM: courteous

**political**

ADJECTIVE to do with politics and politicians

**politician** politicians

NOUN a person who is involved in the government of a country

**politics**

NOUN the activity of governing a country

**poll** polls

NOUN a survey in which people are asked their opinions about something

**pollen**

NOUN a fine yellow or orange powder produced by the male part of a flowering plant

→ Have a look at the illustration for **flower**

**pollinate** pollinates, pollinating, pollinated

VERB A plant is **pollinated** when pollen from the male part of another plant lands on its female part. This leads to fertilisation and the formation of seeds.

**pollination**

NOUN the process by which plants are fertilised with pollen

**pollute** pollutes, polluting, polluted

VERB If water, air or land is **polluted**, it is dirty and dangerous to use or live in.

**pollution**

NOUN dirty or dangerous substances that pollute the water, air or land • *Recycling helps to control environmental **pollution**.*

**polo**

NOUN a game played between two teams of players on horseback. The players use wooden hammers with long handles to hit a ball.

**poltergeist** poltergeists

NOUN a noisy, mischievous ghost that moves or throws things around in a house

**poly-**

PREFIX added to some words to mean many, for example **poly**gons and **poly**hedrons are many-sided shapes

**polyester**

NOUN a man-made fibre, especially used to make clothes

**polygon** polygons

NOUN any two-dimensional shape whose sides are all straight

**polyhedron** polyhedra

NOUN a solid shape with many faces

**polystyrene**

NOUN a very light plastic, especially used as insulating material or to make containers

**polythene**

NOUN a type of plastic that is used to make thin sheets or bags

**pomposity**

NOUN the quality someone has when they think they are important and they show this by behaving in a way that is too serious and formal

**pompous**

ADJECTIVE Someone who is **pompous** thinks they are very important and behaves in a way that is too serious and formal.

**pond** ponds

NOUN a small area of water enclosed by land

**ponder** ponders, pondering, pondered

VERB If you **ponder**, you think carefully and seriously about something.

**pony** ponies

NOUN a small horse

**ponytail** ponytails

NOUN a hairstyle in which long hair is scooped up and tied at the back of the head so that it hangs down like a tail

**pool** pools

NOUN **1** a small area of still water, such as a pond or a puddle
NOUN **2** an abbreviation of *swimming pool*

**oor poorer, poorest**
ADJECTIVE **1** having very little money
ADJECTIVE **2** of a low quality or standard

**oorly**
ADJECTIVE **1** If you are **poorly**, you feel ill.
ADVERB **2** If something is done **poorly**, it is not done well.

**op pops, popping, popped**
NOUN **1** modern music, played and enjoyed especially by young people
NOUN **2** a short, sharp, explosive sound
NOUN **3** a fizzy, non-alcoholic drink
VERB **4** If you **pop** somewhere, you go there quickly for a short while. ● *I will **pop** in to see you before tea.*

**opcorn**
NOUN a snack food made from grains of maize that are heated until they puff up and burst

**ope Popes**
NOUN the head of the Roman Catholic Church

**oplar poplars**
NOUN a type of tall, narrow tree

**oppadom poppadoms**
NOUN thin, round, crisp bread, fried or roasted and served with Indian food

WORD HISTORY
from Tamil *pappadam* meaning lentil cake

**oppy poppies**
NOUN a plant with a large red flower on a hairy stem, that often grows in cornfields and meadows

**popular**
ADJECTIVE liked or approved of by a lot of people

**populated**
ADJECTIVE If a place is **populated**, people or animals live there.

**population populations**
NOUN **1** the people who live in a place
NOUN **2** the number of people living in a place

**porch porches**
NOUN a covered area at the entrance to a building

**porcupine porcupines**
NOUN a large rodent with long spines covering its body

WORD HISTORY
from Old French *porc d'espins* meaning pig with spines

**pore pores, poring, pored**
NOUN **1** The **pores** in your skin or on the surface of a plant are very small holes that allow moisture to pass through.
VERB **2** If you **pore** over a piece of writing or a diagram, you study it carefully.

**pork**
NOUN meat from a pig

**porous**
ADJECTIVE If something is **porous**, it lets water through.

**porpoise porpoises**
NOUN a sea mammal related to the dolphin

WORD HISTORY
from Latin *porcus* meaning pig and *piscis* meaning fish

**porridge**
NOUN a thick, sticky food made from oats cooked in water or milk

**port ports**
NOUN **1** a town or area that has a harbour or docks
NOUN **2** a place on a computer where you can attach another piece of equipment

→ Have a look at the illustration for **computer**

ADJECTIVE **3** The **port** side of a ship is the left side when you are facing the front.

**portable**
ADJECTIVE designed to be easily carried
● *a **portable** tripod*

**portcullis portcullises**
NOUN a strong gate above an entrance to a castle, that could be lowered to keep out enemies

→ Have a look at the illustration for **castle**

**porter porters**
NOUN **1** a person employed to carry luggage and other goods at a railway station or in a hotel
NOUN **2** a person employed to move patients from place to place in a hospital

a
b
c
d
e
f
g
h
i
j
k
l
m
n
o
p
q
r
s
t
u
v
w
x
y
z

A
B
C
D
E
F
G
H
I
J
K
L
M
N
O
**P**
Q
R
S
T
U
V
W
X
Y
Z

**porthole** **portholes**

NOUN a small window in the side of a ship or aircraft

→ Have a look at the illustration for **ship**

**portion** **portions**

NOUN **1** a part of something

SYNONYMS: bit, piece

NOUN **2** an amount of food sufficient for one person

**portrait** **portraits**

NOUN a picture or photograph of someone, often of only their head and shoulders

**pose** **poses, posing, posed**

NOUN **1** a way of standing, sitting or lying for a photograph to be taken, or a drawing or painting to be made of you • *Try to hold this **pose** while the others draw it.*

VERB **2** If you **pose** for a photograph or painting, you stay in a particular position so that someone can photograph or paint you.

VERB **3** If you **pose** as someone or something, you pretend to be someone or something you are not.

VERB **4** If something **poses** a problem or danger, it causes it. • *This polluted water could **pose** a threat to their health.*

**position** **positions, positioning, positioned**

NOUN **1** When someone or something is in a particular **position**, they are sitting or lying in that way. • *I raised myself to a sitting **position**.*

NOUN **2** The **position** that you are in is the situation that you are in. • *Your request puts me in a difficult **position**.*

PHRASE **3** If you are **in position** at the beginning of a race, you are ready to start.

VERB **4** If you **position** something, you put it in place.

**positive**

ADJECTIVE **1** If something is **positive**, it is certain.

ADJECTIVE **2** If someone is **positive**, they are confident and hopeful.

ADJECTIVE **3** A **positive** number is greater than zero.

ANTONYM: negative

**possess** **possesses, possessing, possessed**

VERB If you **possess** something, you own it.

**possession** **possessions**

NOUN a thing that you own, or that you have with you

**possessive**

ADJECTIVE **1** A **possessive** person wants to keep things for themselves.

NOUN **2** In grammar, the **possessive** is the form of a noun or pronoun used to show possession, for example, *my, his, theirs, Harry's.*

**possibility** **possibilities**

NOUN something that might happen

**possible**

ADJECTIVE If something is **possible**, it can be done or can happen.

**possibly**

ADVERB used to say that something may be true or may happen but you are not certain

**possum** **possums**

NOUN a nocturnal marsupial with thick fur and a long tail that lives in trees

**post** **posts, posting, posted**

NOUN **1** the system by which letters and parcels are collected and delivered

NOUN **2** letters and parcels that are delivered to you

NOUN **3** a piece of information, message or picture that you put on a website for other people to see

NOUN **4** an upright pole fixed into the ground

VERB **5** If you **post** a letter, you send it to someone through the post.

VERB **6** If you **post** a piece of information, message or picture on a website, you put it there so that other people can see it.

• *She **posted** the cat picture on Facebook to get more likes.*

**postage**

NOUN the money that you pay to send letters and parcels by post • *You will need to send extra money for **postage** and packing.*

**post box** **post boxes**

NOUN a box into which you put letters that are to be sent by post

**postcard** **postcards**

NOUN a card, often with a picture on one side, that you write on and send to someone without an envelope

**postcode** **postcodes**

NOUN a short sequence of letters and numbers at the end of an address

**oster posters**
NOUN a large notice, picture or advertisement that you stick on a wall

**ostman postmen**
NOUN a man who collects and delivers parcels and letters

**ost office post offices**
NOUN a building where you can buy stamps and post letters and parcels

**ostpone postpones, postponing, postponed**
VERB If you **postpone** an event, you arrange for it to take place at a later time than was originally planned.

**ostwoman postwomen**
NOUN a woman who collects and delivers parcels and letters

**otato potatoes**
NOUN a round, white root vegetable that has a brown or red skin and grows beneath the ground

**otential**
ADJECTIVE **1** capable of happening or of becoming a particular kind of person or thing ● *He's a **potential** world champion.*
NOUN **2** If someone or something has **potential**, they are capable of being successful or useful in the future.

**othole potholes**
NOUN **1** a hole in the surface of a road caused by bad weather or traffic
NOUN **2** a deep, natural hole in the ground that often leads to an underground cavern

**otion potions**
NOUN a drink containing medicine, poison or supposed magical powers

**WORD HISTORY**
from Latin *potio* meaning a drink

**otter potters, pottering, pottered**
NOUN **1** a person who makes pottery
VERB **2** If you **potter** about, you pass the time doing pleasant, unimportant things.

**ottery**
NOUN **1** pots, dishes and other items made from clay and fired in a kiln
NOUN **2** the craft of making pottery

**ouch pouches**
NOUN **1** a small, soft container with a fold-over top, like a bag or a pocket

NOUN **2** a pocket of skin in which marsupials carry their young

**poultry**
NOUN chicken, turkeys and other birds that are kept for their meat or eggs

**pounce pounces, pouncing, pounced**
VERB If a person or other animal **pounces** on something, they jump on it suddenly.

**pound pounds, pounding, pounded**
NOUN **1** the main unit of currency in Britain
NOUN **2** a unit of weight equal to 16 ounces, or about 0.454 kilograms
VERB **3** If you **pound** something, or **pound** on it, you hit it repeatedly or crush it.
VERB **4** If your heart **pounds**, it beats very fast and strongly.
VERB **5** If you **pound** somewhere, you run there with loud, heavy footsteps.

**pour pours, pouring, poured**
VERB **1** If you **pour** liquid out of a container, you tip the container until the liquid flows out.
VERB **2** If something **pours** somewhere, it flows there quickly and in large quantities.
VERB **3** If it is **pouring** with rain, it is raining very heavily.

**pout pouts, pouting, pouted**
VERB If you **pout**, you stick out your lips, or your bottom lip, because you are cross or annoyed.

**poverty**
NOUN the state of being very poor

**powder powders**
NOUN many tiny particles of a solid, dry substance, such as flour

**power powers**
NOUN **1** control over people and events
NOUN **2** physical strength
NOUN **3** the rate at which energy is changed from one form to another, such as electrical energy changed into light or heat

**powerful**
ADJECTIVE **Powerful** people or organisations have a great deal of power or influence.

**powerless**
ADJECTIVE If you are **powerless**, you are unable to control or influence events.

**power station power stations**
NOUN a building where electricity is produced

a
b
c
d
e
f
g
h
i
j
k
l
m
n
o
p
q
r
s
t
u
v
w
x
y
z

## practical

ADJECTIVE **1** Someone who is **practical** is efficient and sensible, and good at getting things done.
ADJECTIVE **2** Something that is **practical** is sensible and useful.
ADJECTIVE **3** involving real situations and doing things, rather than ideas or theories • *We will do some **practical** experiments in Science today.*

**WORD HISTORY**
from Greek *praktikos* meaning concerned with action

## practical joke practical jokes

NOUN a trick you play on someone

## practice practices

NOUN **1** regular training or exercise that you do to improve your skill at something
NOUN **2** A doctor's or lawyer's **practice** is their business.

**LANGUAGE TIP**
The noun *practice* ends in *ce*.

## practise practises, practising, practised

VERB **1** If you **practise** something, you do it regularly in order to do it better. • *She **practises** every day on the piano.*
VERB **2** When people **practise** a religion, custom or craft, they regularly take part in the activities associated with it. • *a custom still **practised** in some areas*
VERB **3** If you **practise** medicine or law, you work as a doctor or lawyer.

**LANGUAGE TIP**
The verb *practise* ends in *se*.

## prairie prairies

NOUN a large area of flat, grassy land in North America

## praise praises, praising, praised

VERB **1** If you **praise** someone or something, you say good things about them, or tell them they have done well.
NOUN **2** what you say or write when you praise someone or something

## pram prams

NOUN a small carriage, like a baby's cot on wheels, for pushing a baby around in

## prank pranks

NOUN a childish trick

## prawn prawns

NOUN a small, edible shellfish with a long t

## pray prays, praying, prayed

VERB When someone **prays**, they speak to God, to give thanks or to ask for help.

## prayer prayers

NOUN the activity of praying or the words said when someone prays

## pre-

PREFIX added to some words to mean before a particular time or event, for example **pre**school, **pre**war, **pre**history

## preach preaches, preaching, preached

VERB When someone **preaches**, they give a short talk on a religious or moral subject.

## preacher preachers

NOUN someone who gives a talk about a religious subject in a church or other religious place

## precarious

ADJECTIVE **1** Someone or something in a **precarious** position is not very safe or secure, and they may fall or fail at any time • *Her position was **precarious** because she needed only one point to win.*
ADJECTIVE **2** Something that is **precarious** is likely to fall because it is not well balanced or secured.

## precaution precautions

NOUN an action that is intended to prevent something unwanted or unpleasant from happening

## precede precedes, preceding, preceded

VERB **1** If one event **precedes** another, it happens before it. • *A short film **preceded** the talk about elephants.*
VERB **2** If you **precede** someone, you go in front of them.

## precinct precincts

NOUN a pedestrian shopping area

## precious

ADJECTIVE Something that is **precious** is valuable or important and should be looked after or used carefully.

**WORD HISTORY**
from Latin *pretiosus* meaning valuable

## precipice precipices

NOUN a very steep rock face or cliff

**ecipitation**
NOUN rain, snow, sleet or hail
→ Have a look at the illustration for **water cycle**

**ecise**
ADJECTIVE very accurate • *We will never know the **precise** details of what happened.*

SYNONYM: exact

**edator predators**
NOUN an animal that kills and eats other animals

**edatory**
ADJECTIVE A **predatory** animal kills and eats other animals.

**edecessor predecessors**
NOUN Someone's **predecessor** is the person who used to do their job before them.

**edicament predicaments**
NOUN a difficult or awkward situation

**edict predicts, predicting, predicted**
VERB If you **predict** something, you say what you think will happen in the future.

**een preens, preening, preened**
VERB When a bird **preens**, it cleans and tidies its feathers using its beak.

**eface prefaces**
NOUN an introduction at the beginning of a book, explaining what it is about or why it was written

**efect prefects**
NOUN a pupil who has special duties at a school

WORD HISTORY
from Latin *praefectus* meaning someone put in charge

**efer prefers, preferring, preferred**
VERB If you **prefer** one thing to another, you like it better than the other thing.

**eferable**
ADJECTIVE Something that is **preferable** to something else, is more suitable or you like it better than the other thing. • *We thought that going to the cinema was **preferable** to watching TV.*

**efix prefixes**
NOUN a letter or group of letters added to the beginning of a word to make a new word, for example *dis-*, *pre-* and *un-*

**pregnant**
ADJECTIVE A woman or other female animal who is **pregnant** has a baby developing in their womb.

**prehistoric**
ADJECTIVE existing at a time in the past before anything was written down

**prejudice prejudices**
NOUN an unreasonable and unfair dislike of or preference for a particular person or thing

**prejudiced**
ADJECTIVE having an unreasonable and unfair dislike of someone or something

**preliminary**
ADJECTIVE **Preliminary** activities take place before something starts and in preparation for it. • *They lost in the **preliminary** rounds of the competition.*

**prelude preludes**
NOUN 1 something that happens before an event and prepares you for it
NOUN 2 a short piece of music

**premature**
ADJECTIVE happening too early, or earlier than expected • *The **premature** baby had to spend time in hospital to gain weight.*

**premier premiers**
NOUN 1 The leader of a government is sometimes referred to as the **premier**.
NOUN 2 In Australia, the leader of a State government is called the **Premier**.
ADJECTIVE 3 considered to be the best or most important • *the **premier** department store*

PRONUNCIATION TIP
This word is pronounced **prem**-mee-uh.

WORD HISTORY
from Latin *primarius* meaning principal

**premiere premieres**
NOUN the first public performance of a new play or film • *The **premiere** of the new film is in London next week.*

PRONUNCIATION TIP
This word is pronounced **prem**-mee-er.

WORD HISTORY
from French *premier* meaning first

311

### premises
PLURAL NOUN buildings and land belonging to an organisation

### premium premiums
NOUN 1 an extra sum of money that has to be paid for something
NOUN 2 money paid regularly to an insurance company

### premonition premonitions
NOUN a feeling that something unpleasant is going to happen

### preoccupied
ADJECTIVE If you are **preoccupied**, you are deep in thought or totally involved with something, and you do not notice anything else. • *It is difficult to talk to him as he seems so **preoccupied**.*

### preparation preparations
NOUN 1 **Preparation** is the act of getting things ready.
NOUN 2 **Preparations** are all the things you do and the arrangements you make before an event can happen. • *We started making **preparations** for the party by buying some decorations.*

### prepare prepares, preparing, prepared
VERB If you **prepare** something, or **prepare** for something, you get it ready or get ready for it.

### preposition prepositions
NOUN a word that is used before a noun or pronoun to show how it is connected to other words. For example, in the sentence *I put the book on the table*, the word *on* is the **preposition**.

### prescribe prescribes, prescribing, prescribed
VERB If a doctor **prescribes** a medicine for a patient, he or she tells the patient what medicine they need and gives them a prescription.

### prescription prescriptions
NOUN a written instruction from a doctor to a chemist, to provide a person with a particular medicine

### presence
NOUN the **presence** of a person in a place is the fact that they are there

### present presents, presenting, presented
ADJECTIVE 1 If someone is **present** at a place or an event, they are there.

ADJECTIVE 2 happening now

SYNONYMS: contemporary, current

ANTONYM: absent

NOUN 3 the period of time that is taking place now
NOUN 4 something that you give to someone for them to keep, especially on their birthday or at Christmas, or on some other special occasion

SYNONYM: gift

VERB 5 If you **present** someone with something, or if you **present** it to them, you formally give it to them.

PRONUNCIATION TIP
Meanings 1, 2, 3 and 4 are pronounced **prez**-ent. Meaning 5 is pronounced pri-**zent**.

### presentation presentations
NOUN 1 a talk or a lecture showing or describing something
NOUN 2 a ceremony where awards or prizes are given
NOUN 3 The **presentation** of something is the way it looks. • *My teacher was pleased with the **presentation** of my project.*

### presently
ADVERB If something will happen **presently**, it will happen soon. • *I'll finish the job presently*.

### preservative preservatives
NOUN a substance or a chemical that stops things such as food from going bad

### preserve preserves, preserving, preserved
VERB If you **preserve** something, you make sure that it stays as it is and does not change or end.

### president presidents
NOUN The **president** of a country that has no king or queen is the leader of the country. • *the **President** of the United States*

### press presses, pressing, pressed
VERB 1 If you **press** something, you push it or hold it firmly against something else.
VERB 2 If you **press** clothes, you iron them.
VERB 3 If you **press** someone to do something, you try to make them do it.
NOUN 4 a machine for printing
NOUN 5 The **press** is a term used for all the newspapers and the journalists who work for them.

**essure pressures**

NOUN **1** the amount of force that is pushing on a particular area

NOUN **2** If there is **pressure** on you to do something, someone is trying to persuade or force you do it.

NOUN **3** If someone does something because of peer **pressure**, they do it because other people in their social group do it.

**esume presumes, presuming, presumed**

VERB If you **presume** something, you think that it is probably true without knowing for certain.

SYNONYMS: believe, suppose

**esumption presumptions**

NOUN something that you think is probably true without knowing for certain

**etend pretends, pretending, pretended**

VERB If you **pretend** that something is the case, you try to make people believe that it is true when it is not.

**etty prettier, prettiest**

ADJECTIVE **1** attractive and pleasant

ADVERB **2** (informal) quite or rather ● He spoke **pretty** good English.

**event prevents, preventing, prevented**

VERB If you **prevent** something, you stop it happening.

**eview previews**

NOUN **1** a showing of something like a film, play or exhibition before it is shown to the general public

NOUN **2** a version of a computer document or page that is shown before it is produced in its final form

**evious**

ADJECTIVE A **previous** time or thing is one that occurred before the present one.

● I'm happier in this class than I was in the **previous** one.

**eviously**

ADVERB before now

**ey preys, preying, preyed**

NOUN **1** an animal that is hunted and eaten by another animal

VERB **2** An animal that **preys** on another animal lives by hunting and eating it.

**price prices**

NOUN the amount of money that you pay to buy something ● The **price** of bread has increased significantly.

**priceless**

ADJECTIVE Something that is **priceless** is so valuable that it is difficult to work out how much it is worth.

**prick pricks, pricking, pricked**

VERB If you **prick** something, you stick a sharp object into it.

**prickle prickles, prickling, prickled**

NOUN **1** a small sharp point or thorn growing on a plant

VERB **2** If your skin **prickles**, it feels as if a lot of sharp points are being stuck into it.

**prickly pricklier, prickliest**

ADJECTIVE **1** A **prickly** plant has small sharp points or thorns on it.

ADJECTIVE **2** If your skin feels **prickly**, it feels as if a lot of sharp points are being stuck into it.

**pride prides**

NOUN **1** a feeling of satisfaction and pleasure you have when you, or people close to you, have done something well

NOUN **2** a feeling of dignity and self-respect

NOUN **3** a group of lions that live together

**priest priests**

NOUN **1** a member of the clergy in some Christian Churches

NOUN **2** someone who performs religious ceremonies in non-Christian religions

**prim primmer, primmest**

ADJECTIVE Someone who is **prim** always behaves very correctly and is easily shocked by anything rude.

**primary**

ADJECTIVE extremely important or most important

**primary colour primary colours**

NOUN The **primary colours** are red, yellow and blue. From these all the other colours can be made.

**primary school primary schools**

NOUN a school for children between the ages of 5 and 11

313

## prime

ADJECTIVE **1** main or most important
ADJECTIVE **2** of the best quality
ADJECTIVE **3** A **prime** number is a whole number which can only be divided by itself and 1 without leaving a remainder.

**WORD HISTORY**
from Latin *primus* meaning first

## prime minister **prime ministers**

NOUN the leader of the government

## primitive

ADJECTIVE **1** connected with a society in which people live very simply
ADJECTIVE **2** very simple, basic or old-fashioned • *Their accommodation was **primitive**, but they still enjoyed their trip.*

## primrose **primroses**

NOUN a small plant that has pale yellow flowers in spring

**WORD HISTORY**
from Latin *prima rosa* meaning first rose

## prince **princes**

NOUN a male member of a royal family, especially the son of a king or queen

## princess **princesses**

NOUN a female member of a royal family, especially the daughter of a king or queen, or the wife of a prince

## principal **principals**

ADJECTIVE **1** main or most important • *He had the **principal** role in the play.*
NOUN **2** the person in charge of a school or college

**LANGUAGE TIP**
Do not confuse *principal* with *principle*.

## principle **principles**

NOUN **1** a general rule or law about how something works
NOUN **2** a belief that you have about the way you should behave • *I try to help others as a matter of **principle**.*

**LANGUAGE TIP**
Do not confuse *principle* with *principal*.

## print **prints, printing, printed**

VERB **1** When words or pictures are **printed**, they are put onto paper in large numbers by a printing machine, for example to ma books or newspapers.
VERB **2** If you **print** your name, or some ot writing, you write letters that are not join up.
NOUN **3** The letters and numbers on the pages of a book or newspaper are referre to as the **print**. • *The columns of tiny prin were difficult to read.*

## printer **printers**

NOUN **1** a person who prints books and newspapers
NOUN **2** a machine that prints the data fro a computer onto paper

## print-out **print-outs**

NOUN a printed copy of information from c computer

## priority **priorities**

NOUN something that needs to be dealt wi first because it is more urgent or importo than other things • *He needed to make his homework a **priority**.*

## prism **prisms**

NOUN **1** In mathematics, a **prism** is any three-dimensional shape that has the sa size and shape of face at each end. A pri is the same size and shape along its leng
NOUN **2** a solid piece of clear glass or plas with flat sides, that can be used to separ light passing through it into the colours the rainbow

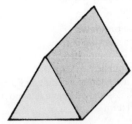

## prison **prisons**

NOUN a building where people who have broken the law are locked up as a punishment

## prisoner **prisoners**

NOUN someone who is kept in prison or he in captivity

## privacy

NOUN If you have **privacy**, you have somewhere private where you can be alo without being disturbed.

**ivate** privates

ADJECTIVE **1** for the use of only one person or group of people, rather than for the general public • *The hotel had a **private** beach.*
ADJECTIVE **2** meant to be kept secret
NOUN **3** a soldier of the lowest rank

**ivate message** private messages

NOUN a message sent to someone privately on a social media website

**ivilege** privileges

NOUN a special right or advantage that is given to a person or group

**ize** prizes

NOUN a reward given to the winner of a competition or game

**o-**

PREFIX supporting or being in favour of • *a **pro**-animal rights march*

ANTONYM: anti-

**obability**

NOUN the measure of how likely an event is

**obable**

ADJECTIVE likely to happen or likely to be true

**obably**

ADVERB likely but not certainly • *I am **probably** having a party for my birthday.*

**obation**

NOUN **1** a period of time during which a person convicted of a crime is supervised by a social worker called a **probation** officer, instead of being sent to prison
NOUN **2** a period of time when someone is tried out to see if they are suitable for a particular job

**obe** probes, probing, probed

VERB **1** If you **probe**, you investigate something, often by asking a lot of questions to discover the facts about it.
VERB **2** If you **probe** something, you gently push a long, thin instrument into it, usually to find something.
NOUN **3** a long, thin instrument used to look closely at something

**WORD HISTORY**

from Latin *probare* meaning to test

**problem** problems

NOUN **1** an unsatisfactory situation that causes difficulties

SYNONYMS: difficulty, predicament

NOUN **2** a puzzle or question that you solve using logical thought or mathematics

**procedure** procedures

NOUN a way of doing something, especially the correct or usual way • *The entire **procedure** takes about 15 minutes.*

**proceed** proceeds, proceeding, proceeded

VERB **1** If you **proceed** to do something, you do it after doing something else. • *He then **proceeded** to tell us the story.*
VERB **2** If you **proceed**, you move in a particular direction. • *We **proceeded** along the corridor.*
PLURAL NOUN **3** The **proceeds** of an event are the money that is obtained from it. • *The **proceeds** from the concert will go towards famine relief.*

**PRONUNCIATION TIP**

Meanings 1 and 2 are pronounced pro-**seed**. Meaning 3 is pronounced **pro**-seedz.

**WORD HISTORY**

from Latin *pro* + *cedere* meaning to go onward

**process** processes, processing, processed

NOUN **1** a series of actions or events that have a particular result
PHRASE **2** If you are **in the process** of doing something, you have started doing it but have not yet finished.
VERB **3** You **process** something when you put it through a series of actions in order to have a particular result. For example, you **process** milk to pasteurise it.

**procession** processions

NOUN a group of people or vehicles moving together in a line, often as part of a ceremony • *There was a **procession** of musicians along the high street on Sunday.*

**proclaim** proclaims, proclaiming, proclaimed

VERB If someone **proclaims** something, they announce it or make it known publicly.

**proclamation** proclamations

NOUN an important announcement that someone makes publicly

**prod** prods, prodding, prodded
VERB If you **prod** something or somebody, you give them a poke with your finger.

**produce** produces, producing, produced
VERB 1 If someone or something **produces** something, they make it or cause it to happen.
VERB 2 If you **produce** something from somewhere, you bring it out so that it can be seen. • The magician **produced** a rabbit out of the hat.
VERB 3 If you **produce** a film, play or other form of entertainment, you are in charge of organising it.
NOUN 4 food that is grown to be sold

PRONUNCIATION TIP
The verb is pronounced pro-**dewss**. The noun is pronounced **prod**-yooss.

**producer** producers
NOUN The **producer** of a record, film, play or programme is the person in charge of making it or putting it on. • a television **producer**

**product** products
NOUN 1 something that is made or produced to be sold
NOUN 2 The **product** is the answer to a multiplication sum. • The **product** of 4 and 6 is 24.

**production** productions
NOUN 1 the process of manufacturing or growing something in large quantities
NOUN 2 a version of something such as a play or a film

**profession** professions
NOUN a job for which you need special training and education • the medical **profession** • the teaching **profession**

**professional** professionals
ADJECTIVE 1 **Professional** is used to describe activities that are done to earn money rather than as a hobby. • He earns a lot of money as a **professional** footballer.
ADJECTIVE 2 You can use **professional** to describe work that is of a very high standard.
NOUN 3 someone who does a particular type of work to earn money

**professor** professors
NOUN the most senior teacher in a department of a British university, or a teacher at an American college or university

**proficient**
ADJECTIVE If you are **proficient** at somethin you can do it well. • I am pleased to see ho **proficient** you are in reading.

**profile** profiles
NOUN 1 the outline of a face seen from the side
NOUN 2 Your **profile** on a social media website is where you post your name, picture and other personal information.

WORD HISTORY
from Italian *profilare* meaning to sketch lightly

**profit** profits, profiting, profited
NOUN 1 an amount of money that you gain when you are paid more for something th it cost to buy or make
VERB 2 If you **profit** from something, you gain or benefit from it. • I think you will **profit** from some extra lessons.

**profound**
ADJECTIVE 1 very deep or intense • discoverie. that have a **profound** effect on life today
ADJECTIVE 2 showing or needing deep thoug or understanding • He asked a **profound** question for someone of his age.

**program** programs, programming, programmed
NOUN 1 a set of instructions that a comput follows in order to perform particular task
VERB 2 When someone **programs** a computer, they prepare a program and pu it into the computer.

**programme** programmes
NOUN 1 something that is broadcast on television or radio
NOUN 2 a planned series of events
NOUN 3 a booklet giving information about play, concert or show

**progress** progresses, progressing, progressed
NOUN 1 the process of gradually improving getting near to achieving something
VERB 2 If you **progress**, you become more advanced or skilful at something.
VERB 3 to continue or move forward • As th trip **progressed**, I began to feel sick.

PRONUNCIATION TIP
The noun is pronounced **proh**-gress. The verb is pronounced pro-**gress**.

**prohibit** prohibits, prohibiting, prohibited

VERB If someone **prohibits** something, they forbid it or make it illegal. • *Visitors are* **prohibited** *from smoking.*

**project** projects, projecting, projected

NOUN **1** a carefully planned task that requires a lot of time or effort

VERB **2** If you **project** an image onto a screen, you make it appear there using a projector.

VERB **3** If something **projects**, it sticks out.

PRONUNCIATION TIP

The noun is pronounced **proj**-ekt. The verb is pronounced pro-**jekt**.

**projector** projectors

NOUN a piece of equipment that produces a large image on a screen by shining light through a photographic slide or film strip

**prologue** prologues

NOUN a short piece of writing at the beginning of a book, or a speech that introduces a play

**prolong** prolongs, prolonging, prolonged

VERB If you **prolong** something, you make it last longer. • *We* **prolonged** *the holiday.*

**promenade** promenades

NOUN a path or road by the sea for walking along

PRONUNCIATION TIP

This word is pronounced prom-un-**ahd**.

**prominent**

ADJECTIVE **1** A **prominent** person is important or well known.

ADJECTIVE **2** very noticeable • *The church is a* **prominent** *landmark.*

WORD HISTORY

from Latin *prominere* meaning to stick out

**promise** promises, promising, promised

VERB **1** If you **promise** to do something, you say that you will definitely do it.

NOUN **2** a statement made by someone that they will definitely do something

NOUN **3** Someone or something that shows **promise** seems likely to be successful in the future.

**promising**

ADJECTIVE likely to be successful or good

**promote** promotes, promoting, promoted

VERB **1** If someone **promotes** something, they try to make it happen, or become more popular or successful.

VERB **2** If someone is **promoted**, they are given a more important job at work.

**prompt** prompts, prompting, prompted

VERB **1** If something or someone **prompts** you to do something, they encourage you or make you decide to do it.

VERB **2** If you **prompt** an actor, you remind them of their lines in a play if they forget them.

ADJECTIVE **3** A **prompt** action is done immediately, without any delay.

**prone**

ADJECTIVE **1** If you are **prone** to something, you have a tendency to be affected by it or to do it. • *I am* **prone** *to catching colds in the winter.*

ADJECTIVE **2** If you are **prone**, you are lying flat and face downwards.

**prong** prongs

NOUN The **prongs** of a fork are the long pointed parts.

**pronoun** pronouns

NOUN a word that is used to replace a noun. **Pronouns** are used instead of naming a person or a thing. *He, she* and *them* are all examples of **pronouns**.

**pronounce** pronounces, pronouncing, pronounced

VERB **1** When you **pronounce** a word, you say it.

VERB **2** When someone **pronounces** something, they state or announce it formally.

**pronunciation** pronunciations

NOUN the way a word is usually said

**proof**

NOUN If you have **proof** of something, you have evidence which shows that it is true or exists.

SYNONYM: confirmation

**prop** props, propping, propped

VERB **1** If you **prop** an object somewhere, you lean it against something for support.

NOUN **2** an object, such as a piece of wood or metal, used to support something

NOUN **3** an object or piece of furniture used on stage in the theatre, or on a film set

A
B
C
D
E
F
G
H
I
J
K
L
M
N
O
P
Q
R
S
T
U
V
W
X
Y
Z

## propaganda
NOUN information, sometimes untrue and often exaggerated, that is used by political groups to influence people

## propel propels, propelling, propelled
VERB To **propel** something is to push it forward.

## propeller propellers
NOUN a device on a boat or aircraft with rotating blades, that makes the boat or aircraft move

→ Have a look at the illustration for **aeroplane**

## proper
ADJECTIVE **1** If you do something in the **proper** way, you do it correctly.
ADJECTIVE **2** In mathematics, a **proper fraction** is a fraction where the denominator is bigger than the numerator.

## properly
ADVERB If something is done **properly**, it is done correctly and to the right standard.

## proper noun proper nouns
NOUN A proper noun is the name of a person, place or institution, and usually starts with a capital letter. For example, *Mary*, *London* and the *Statue of Liberty* are all **proper nouns**.

## property properties
NOUN **1** A person's **property** is something, or all the things, that belong to them.
NOUN **2** A **property** is a building and the land around it.
NOUN **3** a characteristic that something has • *A **property** of mint is its strong smell.*

WORD HISTORY
from Latin *proprietas* meaning something personal

## prophet prophets
NOUN a person who predicts what will happen in the future

## proportion proportions
NOUN **1** part of an amount or group
NOUN **2** The **proportion** of one amount to another is its size in relation to the whole amount, usually expressed as a fraction or percentage. • *The **proportion** of boys in the school is 58%.*

## propose proposes, proposing, propose
VERB **1** If you **propose** a plan or idea, you suggest it.
VERB **2** If you **propose** to someone, you ask them to marry you.

## proprietor proprietors
NOUN the owner of a shop or business

## prose
NOUN ordinary written language, rather tha poetry

## prosecute prosecutes, prosecuting, prosecuted
VERB If someone is **prosecuted**, they are charged with a crime and put on trial.

## prospect prospects, prospecting, prospected
NOUN **1** something that may happen in the future
NOUN **2** Your **prospects** are your chances o being successful in the future. • *If she wor. hard at school, her **prospects** are good.*
VERB **3** When people **prospect** for gold, oil other minerals, they search for them.

## prosper prospers, prospering, prospered
VERB When people or businesses **prosper**, they are successful and make money.

## prosperity
NOUN **Prosperity** is when people or businesses are successful and make mone

## prosperous
ADJECTIVE successful and rich

## protect protects, protecting, protected
VERB If you **protect** someone or something you prevent them from being harmed.

## protein proteins
NOUN a substance that is found in meat, eggs and milk. It is needed by your body te make you grow and keep you healthy.

## protest protests, protesting, protested
VERB **1** If you **protest**, you say or do something to show that you strongly disapprove of something.
NOUN **2** a demonstration or statement to show that you strongly disapprove of something

PRONUNCIATION TIP
The verb is pronounced pro-**test**. The nour is pronounced **pro**-test.

**rotestant Protestants**
NOUN someone who belongs to the branch of the Christian Church that separated from the Catholic Church in the sixteenth century

**roton protons**
NOUN a particle with a positive electrical charge
→ Have a look at the illustration for **atom**

**rototype prototypes**
NOUN a new type of machine or device which is still to be made in large numbers and sold

**otractor protractors**
NOUN a flat, semicircular instrument used for measuring angles

**otrude protrudes, protruding, protruded**
VERB (formal) If something **protrudes** from a surface or edge, it sticks out. • The handle of his racket **protruded** from his sports bag.

**otrusion protrusions**
NOUN (formal) something that sticks out from something else

**oud prouder, proudest**
ADJECTIVE 1 If you are **proud** of something, you feel satisfaction and pleasure because of something you own or have achieved.
ADJECTIVE 2 Someone who is **proud** has a lot of dignity and self-respect.

**ove proves, proving, proved or proven**
VERB If you **prove** that something is true, you show by means of argument or evidence that it is definitely true.

SYNONYMS: confirm, verify

**overb proverbs**
NOUN a short, well-known saying that gives advice or makes a comment about life. For example, A stitch in time saves nine.

**overbial**
ADJECTIVE well-known because of being part of a saying • Looking for his tooth in the long grass was like looking for the **proverbial** needle in a haystack.

**ovide provides, providing, provided**
VERB If you **provide** something for someone, you give it to them or make it available to them.

**ovince provinces**
NOUN one of the areas into which some large countries are divided • Each **province** has its own administration.

**provision provisions**
NOUN the act of supplying or making something available to people

**provisional**
ADJECTIVE A **provisional** arrangement is one that has been agreed on for the time being, but has not yet been made definite.

**provisions**
PLURAL NOUN supplies of food and drink

**provocation**
NOUN **Provocation** is when you deliberately try to make someone angry.

**provoke provokes, provoking, provoked**
VERB 1 If you **provoke** someone, you deliberately try to make them angry.
VERB 2 If something **provokes** a reaction or feeling, it causes it.

**prow prows**
NOUN the front part of a boat or ship

**prowl prowls, prowling, prowled**
VERB If a person or animal **prowls** around, they move around quietly and secretly, as if hunting.

**proximity**
NOUN (formal) nearness to someone or something • I lost my bag in the **proximity** of the swimming pool.

**prune prunes, pruning, pruned**
NOUN 1 a dried plum
VERB 2 When someone **prunes** a tree or shrub, they cut back some of the branches to make it grow well.

**pry pries, prying, pried**
VERB If someone **pries**, they try to find out about something secret or private.

**PS**
**PS** is written at the end of a letter to give an extra message. It is an abbreviation of postscript.

WORD HISTORY
from Latin postscribere meaning to write (scribere) after (post)

**psalm psalms**
NOUN one of the 150 songs, poems and prayers that form the Book of **Psalms** in the Bible

WORD HISTORY
from Greek psalmos meaning song accompanied on the harp

a
b
c
d
e
f
g
h
i
j
k
l
m
n
o
p
q
r
s
t
u
v
w
x
y
z

## pseudonym pseudonyms

NOUN a false name an author uses rather than using their real name

## psychiatric

ADJECTIVE to do with the study and treatment of mental illness • a **psychiatric** hospital

## psychiatrist

NOUN a doctor who treats mental illness

**PRONUNCIATION TIP**

This word is pronounced sy-**ky**-a-trist.

## psychiatry

NOUN the branch of medicine concerned with mental illness

**PRONUNCIATION TIP**

This word is pronounced sy-**ky**-a-tree.

**WORD HISTORY**

from Greek psukhe meaning mind and iatros meaning healer

## psychic

ADJECTIVE having unusual mental powers, such as the ability to read people's minds or predict the future

## psychology

NOUN the scientific study of the mind and of the reasons for people's behaviour

## PTO

an abbreviation of please turn over. **PTO** is written at the bottom of a page to show that there is more writing on the other side.

## pub pubs

NOUN a place where people go to buy and drink alcoholic and other drinks, and to talk to their friends. **Pub** is an abbreviation of public house.

## puberty

NOUN the stage when a person's body changes from that of a child into that of an adult

## public

NOUN 1 You can refer to people in general as the **public**. • The castle is open to the **public** on Sundays.
ADJECTIVE 2 relating to people in general • **public** opinion
ADJECTIVE 3 provided for everyone to use • We try to use **public** transport whenever possible.

## publication publications

NOUN 1 The **publication** of a book is the ⟨ of printing it and making it available.
NOUN 2 a book, newspaper or magazine

## publicity

NOUN information or advertisements abou⟨ an item or event to attract attention to it

## public school public schools

NOUN 1 In England and Wales, a **public school** is a private secondary school that charges fees.
NOUN 2 In Scotland and America, a **public school** is a state school.

## publish publishes, publishing, publish⟨

VERB 1 When a company **publishes** a boo⟨ newspaper or magazine, they print copies it and distribute it.
VERB 2 When a newspaper or magazine **publishes** an article or photograph, they print it.

## publisher publishers

NOUN a person or company that publishes books, newspapers or magazines

## pudding puddings

NOUN 1 a cooked sweet food, often made with flour and eggs, and usually served h⟨
NOUN 2 You can refer to the sweet course ⟨ meal as the **pudding**.

## puddle puddles

NOUN a small shallow pool of rain water or other liquid

## puff puffs, puffing, puffed

VERB 1 If you are **puffing**, you are breathir⟨ loudly and quickly with your mouth open.
VERB 2 If something **puffs out** or **puffs up** it swells and becomes larger and rounder
NOUN 3 a small blast of air, smoke or steam⟨

## pull pulls, pulling, pulled

VERB 1 If you **pull** something, you get hold it and move it towards you with force.
VERB 2 If a vehicle or an animal **pulls** something, they move it along behind the⟨
VERB 3 When you **pull** the curtains, you move them across a window.
VERB 4 If you **pull** a muscle, you damage it temporarily by stretching it too much.

### pull down

VERB If someone **pulls down** a building⟨ they demolish it.

### pull out

VERB If you **pull out** of an activity, you decide not to do it.

**ley pulleys**
NOUN a piece of machinery with a wheel and chain or rope over it, used for lifting heavy things

**lover pullovers**
NOUN a knitted piece of clothing, put on over your head, that covers the top part of your body

**lpit pulpits**
NOUN the small raised platform in a church or cathedral where a member of the clergy stands to preach

**lse pulses**
NOUN the regular beating of your heart as it pumps blood through your body. You can feel your **pulse** at your wrists and some other places on your body. Your **pulse** rate is a measure of how fast your heart is beating.

**mp pumps, pumping, pumped**
NOUN 1 a machine that is used to force a liquid or gas to move in a particular direction
VERB 2 If someone or something **pumps** a liquid or gas somewhere, they force it to flow in that direction, using a pump.

**mpkin pumpkins**
NOUN a very large, round, orange vegetable

**n puns**
NOUN a clever and amusing use of words so that what you say has two different meanings

**nch punches, punching, punched**
VERB 1 If you **punch** someone or something, you hit them hard with your fist.
NOUN 2 a hard hit with the fist

**nchline punchlines**
NOUN The **punchline** of a joke or a story is the last part, that makes it funny.

**nctual**
ADJECTIVE arriving at the correct time

SYNONYMS: on time, prompt

**nctuality**
NOUN arrival at the correct time

**nctuation**
NOUN the marks in writing that make it easier to understand, such as full stops, question marks and commas

**ncture punctures**
NOUN a small hole in a car or bicycle tyre, made by a sharp object

**pungency**
NOUN the quality something has when it has a strong, unpleasant smell or taste

**pungent**
ADJECTIVE having a strong, unpleasant smell or taste

**punish punishes, punishing, punished**
VERB To **punish** someone means to make them suffer for doing wrong.

**punishment punishments**
NOUN something unpleasant that is done to someone because they have done something wrong

**puny punier, puniest**
ADJECTIVE very small and weak

**pupa pupae**
NOUN an insect at the stage of development between a larva and a fully grown adult

SYNONYM: chrysalis

**pupil pupils**
NOUN 1 The **pupils** at a school are the children who attend it.
NOUN 2 Your **pupils** are the small, round, black holes in the centre of your eyes.

→ Have a look at the illustration for **eye**

**puppet puppets**
NOUN a doll that can be moved by pulling strings or by putting your hand inside its body

**puppy puppies**
NOUN a young dog

**purchase purchases, purchasing, purchased**
VERB 1 When you **purchase** something, you buy it.
NOUN 2 something that you have bought

**pure purer, purest**
ADJECTIVE 1 Something that is **pure** is not mixed with anything else.
ADJECTIVE 2 clean and free from harmful substances

**purification**
NOUN the process of removing dirty or harmful substances from something

**purify purifies, purifying, purified**
VERB If someone **purifies** something, they remove all dirty or harmful substances from it.

a
b
c
d
e
f
g
h
i
j
k
l
m
n
o
p
q
r
s
t
u
v
w
x
y
z

**321**

A
B
C
D
E
F
G
H
I
J
K
L
M
N
O
P
Q
R
S
T
U
V
W
X
Y
Z

**purple**
NOUN **1** a reddish-blue colour
ADJECTIVE **2** having a reddish-blue colour

**purpose purposes**
NOUN **1** the reason for something
NOUN **2** the thing that you want to achieve
PHRASE **3** If you do something **on purpose**, you do it deliberately.

**purr purrs, purring, purred**
VERB When a cat **purrs**, it makes a low vibrating sound because it is contented.

**purse purses**
NOUN **1** a container, usually made of leather, plastic or fabric and like a very small bag, for carrying money and credit cards
NOUN **2** In American English, a **purse** is a handbag.

**pursue pursues, pursuing, pursued**
VERB **1** If you **pursue** someone, you follow them in order to catch them.
VERB **2** If you **pursue** an activity or plan, you try to achieve it.

**pus**
NOUN a thick yellowish liquid that forms in an infected wound or a boil

**push pushes, pushing, pushed**
VERB If you **push** someone or something, you use force to move them away from you.

**pushchair pushchairs**
NOUN a small folding chair on wheels in which a baby or a toddler can be pushed along

**put puts, putting, put**
VERB **1** If you **put** something somewhere, you move it into that position.
VERB **2** If you **put** an idea in a particular way, you express it.
  **put off**
  VERB If you **put off** doing something, you delay it.
  **put out**
  VERB If you **put out** the light, you switch it off.
  **put up**
  VERB If you **put up** with something, you let it happen without complaining.

**putt putts**
NOUN In golf, a **putt** is a gentle stroke made when the ball is near the hole.

**putty**
NOUN a paste used to fix panes of glass into window frames

**puzzle puzzles, puzzling, puzzled**
VERB **1** If something **puzzles** you, it confu you and you do not understand it.
NOUN **2** a game or question that requires lot of thought to complete or solve

**PVC**
NOUN a plastic material used for making various things, including clothing, drainpipes and tiles. **PVC** is an abbrevia of *polyvinyl chloride*.

**pyjamas**
PLURAL NOUN loose trousers and a loose jac that you wear in bed

---

**WORD HISTORY**
from Persian *pay jama* meaning leg cloth

---

**pylon pylons**
NOUN a tall metal structure that carries overhead electricity cables

**pyramid pyramids**
NOUN **1** a three-dimensional shape with a flat base and flat triangular sides sloping upwards to a point
NOUN **2** an ancient stone structure in this shape, built over the tombs of Egyptian kings and queens

**python pythons**
NOUN a large snake that kills other animal by squeezing them with its body

---

**WORD HISTORY**
from Greek *Python*, a huge mythical serpe

---

# Qq

**ack quacks, quacking, quacked**
VERB **1** When a duck **quacks**, it makes a
oud harsh sound.
OUN **2** A **quack** is the sound made by a
uck.

**adrangle quadrangles**
OUN **1** a courtyard with buildings all round it
OUN **2** In geometry, a **quadrangle** is a
our-sided shape.

**adrant quadrants**
OUN a quarter of a circle

**adrilateral quadrilaterals**
OUN a plane shape with four straight sides

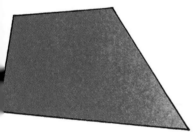

**adruple quadruples, quadrupling,
quadrupled**
VERB If you **quadruple** something, or if it
**quadruples**, it becomes four times greater
in number or size.

**adruplet quadruplets**
NOUN one of four children born at the same
time to the same mother

**ail quails**
NOUN a type of small game bird with a round
body and a short tail

**aint quainter, quaintest**
ADJECTIVE If something is **quaint**, it is
attractive and charming in an old-fashioned
or unusual way. ● *The quaint little village
was filled with thatched cottages.*

**quake quakes, quaking, quaked**
VERB **1** If you **quake**, you tremble because
you are very frightened.
VERB **2** If the ground **quakes**, it moves,
usually because of an earthquake.
NOUN **3** an abbreviation of *earthquake*

**Quaker Quakers**
NOUN a member of a Christian group called
the Society of Friends, that gathers together
for peaceful thought and prayer

**qualification qualifications**
NOUN Your **qualifications** are your skills and
achievements. You gain **qualifications** by
passing tests and examinations.

**qualify qualifies, qualifying, qualified**
VERB If you **qualify**, you pass examinations
and gain qualifications, often for a
particular job. ● *After many years of study
and training, she qualified as a doctor.*

**quality qualities**
NOUN **1** The **quality** of something is how
good it is.
NOUN **2** You can describe a particular
characteristic of a person or thing as a
**quality**. ● *His paintings have a childlike
quality.*

**quantity quantities**
NOUN an amount that you can measure or
count

**quarantine**
NOUN a period of time that a person or
animal has to spend apart from others to
prevent the possible spread of disease

**PRONUNCIATION TIP**
This word is pronounced **kwo**-ran-teen.

**WORD HISTORY**
from Italian *quarantina* meaning forty days

**quarrel quarrels, quarrelling,
quarrelled**
NOUN **1** an angry argument
VERB **2** If people **quarrel**, they have an angry
argument.

**quarry quarries**
NOUN a place where stone is removed from
the ground by digging or blasting

a
b
c
d
e
f
g
h
i
j
k
l
m
n
o
p
q
r
s
t
u
v
w
x
y
z

### quart quarts
NOUN a unit of liquid volume equal to two pints or about 1.136 litres

PRONUNCIATION TIP
This word is pronounced **kwort**.

### quarter quarters
NOUN **1** one of four equal parts of something. It can be written as ¼.
NOUN **2** When you are telling the time, **quarter** means fifteen minutes before or after the hour. ● *The programme starts at a **quarter** to six, and finishes at a **quarter** past.*
NOUN **3** an American or Canadian coin worth 25 cents, which is a **quarter** of a dollar

### quartet quartets
NOUN **1** a group of four musicians who sing or play together
NOUN **2** a piece of music written for four instruments or singers

### quartz
NOUN a type of hard, shiny crystal used in making very accurate watches and clocks

### quay quays
NOUN a place where boats are tied up and loaded or unloaded

### queasy queasier, queasiest
ADJECTIVE If you feel **queasy**, you feel slightly sick.

### queen queens
NOUN a female monarch or a woman married to a king

### queer queerer, queerest
ADJECTIVE very strange

### quench quenches, quenching, quenched
VERB If you **quench** your thirst, you have a drink so that you are no longer thirsty.

### query queries
NOUN a question ● *I cannot answer your **query**.*

### quest quests
NOUN a long search for something

### question questions, questioning, questioned
NOUN **1** a sentence that asks for information
VERB **2** If you **question** someone, you ask them questions.
PHRASE **3** If something is **out of the question**, it is impossible and not worth considering.

### question mark question marks
NOUN a punctuation mark (?) used at the of a question

### questionnaire questionnaires
NOUN a list of questions that people fill in part of a survey

### queue queues, queuing or queueing, queued
NOUN **1** a line of people or vehicles that a waiting for something
VERB **2** When people **queue**, or **queue u** they stand in a line waiting for somethin

LANGUAGE TIP
*Queuing* and *queueing* are both correct spellings.

### quibble quibbles, quibbling, quibble
VERB If you **quibble** about something, you argue about something that is not very important.

### quiche quiches
NOUN a tart with a savoury filling made of eggs

PRONUNCIATION TIP
This word is pronounced **keesh**.

### quick quicker, quickest
ADJECTIVE If you are **quick**, you move or do things with great speed.

### quicksand quicksands
NOUN an area of deep, wet sand that you sink into if you walk on it

### quid
NOUN (*informal*) In British English, a **quid** pound in money.

### quiet quieter, quietest
ADJECTIVE **1** If someone or something is **qui** they are not making much noise, or they not making any noise at all.
ADJECTIVE **2** A **quiet** place, time or situation calm and peaceful.
NOUN **3** silence

### quill quills
NOUN **1** a pen made from a feather
NOUN **2** A bird's **quills** are the large feathe on its wings and tail.
NOUN **3** A porcupine's **quills** are its spines.

### quilt quilts
NOUN a thick, soft, warm cover for a bed, usually padded

**quits, quitting, quit**
VERB If you **quit** something, you leave it or stop doing it.

**...ite**
ADVERB fairly but not very ● *She's **quite** old, but not as old as my grandma.*

**...iver quivers, quivering, quivered**
VERB **1** If something **quivers**, it trembles.
● *The leaves on the trees **quivered** in the breeze.*
NOUN **2** a container for carrying arrows

**...iz quizzes**
NOUN a game in which someone tests your knowledge by asking you questions

**...ota quotas**
NOUN a number or quantity of something that is allowed by the rules ● *We have already had our **quota** of class outings for this term.*

**...otation quotations**
NOUN a small part of a piece of writing taken from a book or speech

**...otation marks**
PLURAL NOUN the punctuation marks (" " ' ') that show where written speech or quotations begin and end

**...ote quotes, quoting, quoted**
VERB If you **quote** something that someone has written or said, you repeat their words.

**...otient quotients**
NOUN the number of times one number can be divided into another. For example, in 42 ÷ 6 = 7, 7 is the **quotient**.

**...ir'an**
NOUN another spelling of **Koran**

**rabbi rabbis**
NOUN a Jewish religious leader

**rabbit rabbits**
NOUN a small furry rodent with long ears

**rabies**
NOUN a disease that causes humans and some other animals, especially dogs, to go mad and die

**race races, racing, raced**
NOUN **1** a competition to see who is fastest at something
NOUN **2** a large group of people who look alike in some way. Different **races** have, for example, different skin colour or differently shaped eyes.
VERB **3** If you **race**, you take part in a race.
● *She has **raced** against some of the best in the world.*
VERB **4** If you **race** somewhere, you go there as quickly as possible. ● *He **raced** after the others.*

**racehorse racehorses**
NOUN a horse that is trained to run fast for races

**racial**
ADJECTIVE to do with the different races that people belong to

**racism**
NOUN **1** hostility shown by one race of people to another
NOUN **2** believing that one race of people is better than all others

**racist racists**
NOUN **1** someone who does not like people who belong to a different race from them, and treats them unfairly
ADJECTIVE **2** not liking people, or treating them unfairly because they belong to a different race from you

**rack racks**
NOUN a piece of equipment for holding things or hanging things on

A B C D E F G H I J K L M N O P Q R S T U V W X Y Z

## racket rackets

NOUN **1** a bat with an oval frame and strings across and down it, used in games like tennis

NOUN **2** If someone is making a **racket**, they are making a lot of noise.

## radar

NOUN a way of discovering the position or speed of objects, such as ships or aircraft, by using radio signals

**WORD HISTORY**
an abbreviation for *radio detecting and ranging*

## radiant

ADJECTIVE **1** shining or sparkling

ADJECTIVE **2** Someone who is **radiant** looks beautiful because they are so happy.

## radiate radiates, radiating, radiated

VERB **1** Things that **radiate** from something come out in lines from a central point, like the spokes of a wheel or the sun's rays.

VERB **2** When a fire or a light **radiates** heat or light, it gives them out.

## radiation

NOUN **1** very small particles given out by radioactive substances

NOUN **2** the heat and light energy given out from a source such as the sun

## radiator radiators

NOUN **1** a hollow metal device filled with hot water for heating a room

NOUN **2** the part of a car that is filled with water to cool the engine

## radio radios

NOUN **1** a system of sending sound over a distance by transmitting electrical signals

NOUN **2** the broadcasting of programmes for the public to listen to by radio

NOUN **3** a piece of equipment for listening to radio programmes • *They are in daily radio contact with the expedition.*

NOUN **4** a piece of equipment for sending and receiving **radio** messages • *A police officer raised the alarm on his radio.*

## radioactive

ADJECTIVE **Radioactive** substances give out energy in the form of powerful and harmful rays.

## radish radishes

NOUN a small salad vegetable with a red skin and white flesh, and with a hot taste

## radius radii

NOUN **1** a straight line going from the cen of a circle to the outside edge

NOUN **2** the length of a straight line going from the centre of a circle to the outside e

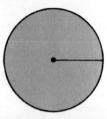

## raffle raffles, raffling, raffled

NOUN **1** a competition in which people bu numbered tickets and win a prize if their ticket is chosen

VERB **2** If you **raffle** something, you give i a prize in a raffle.

## raft rafts

NOUN a floating platform made from long pieces of wood tied together

## rafter rafters

NOUN the sloping pieces of wood that support a roof

## rag rags

NOUN **1** a piece of old cloth used to wipe o clean things

NOUN **2** If someone is dressed in **rags**, the are wearing very old, torn clothes.

## rage rages, raging, raged

NOUN **1** strong, uncontrollable anger

SYNONYMS: anger, fury, wrath

VERB **2** If something such as a storm or ba **rages**, it continues with great force or violence.

## ragged

ADJECTIVE torn or frayed, with rough edges

## raid raids, raiding, raided

VERB **1** When people **raid** a place, they ent it by force in order to attack it or to look fc something or someone.

NOUN **2** a sudden, surprise attack

## rail rails

NOUN **1** a fixed bar that you can hang things

NOUN **2** one of the heavy metal bars that trains run along

## railings

PLURAL NOUN a series of metal bars that ma up a fence

**ilway railways**
NOUN a route along which trains travel on metal tracks

→ Have a look at the illustration for **map**

**in rains, raining, rained**
NOUN **1** water falling from the clouds in small drops
VERB **2** When it **rains**, small drops of water fall from clouds in the sky.

**LANGUAGE TIP**
Do not confuse *rain* with *rein* or *reign*.

**inbow rainbows**
NOUN an arch of different colours that sometimes appears in the sky after it has been raining

**incoat raincoats**
NOUN a waterproof coat

**infall**
NOUN the amount of rain that falls in one place during a particular period of time

**inforest rainforests**
NOUN a dense forest of tall trees that grows in a tropical area where there is a lot of rain

→ Have a look at the illustration

**ise raises, raising, raised**
VERB **1** If you **raise** something, you make it higher. ● *He raised his hand.*
VERB **2** If you **raise** your voice, you speak more loudly.

VERB **3** If you **raise** money for something, you get people to give money towards it.

**raisin raisins**
NOUN a dried grape

**rake rakes**
NOUN a garden tool with a row of metal teeth and a long handle, for collecting together dead leaves or cut grass

**rally rallies**
NOUN **1** a competition in which vehicles race along public roads
NOUN **2** a large public meeting
NOUN **3** In tennis or squash, a **rally** is a continuous series of shots exchanged by the players.

**ram rams, ramming, rammed**
VERB **1** If you **ram** something somewhere, you push it there firmly. ● *She rammed her purse into her bag as she ran for the bus.*
VERB **2** If one vehicle **rams** another, it crashes into it.
NOUN **3** an adult male sheep

**Ramadan**
NOUN the ninth month of the Muslim year, during which Muslims eat and drink nothing during daylight

**WORD HISTORY**
from Arabic *Ramadan* meaning be hot, as the fasting takes place during a hot month

emergent layer

canopy

understorey

forest floor

## ramble rambles, rambling, rambled
NOUN **1** a long walk in the countryside
VERB **2** to go for a ramble
VERB **3** If you **ramble**, you talk in a confused way.

## rambler ramblers
NOUN someone who goes for a long walk in the countryside

## ramp ramps
NOUN a sloping surface linking two places that are at different levels

## rampage rampages, rampaging, rampaged
VERB If you **rampage**, you rush about wildly, causing damage.

## rampart ramparts
NOUN an earth bank, often with a wall on top, built to protect a castle or city

→ Have a look at the illustration for **castle**

## ramshackle
ADJECTIVE A **ramshackle** building is in very poor condition.

## ran
VERB the past tense of **run**

## ranch ranches
NOUN a large farm where cattle or horses are reared, especially in the USA

## random
ADJECTIVE **1** Something that is done in a **random** way is done by chance or without a definite plan. • We picked a **random** sample of twenty pupils.

SYNONYMS: chance, haphazard

NOUN **2** Something that is done at **random** is done by chance or without a definite plan. • We got ten replies and we picked one at **random**.

## rang
VERB the past tense of **ring**

## range ranges, ranging, ranged
NOUN **1** a selection or choice of different things of the same kind • This top is available in a wide **range** of colours.
NOUN **2** a set of values on a scale
NOUN **3** the maximum distance over which something can reach things or detect things
NOUN **4** a long line of hills or mountains
VERB **5** When a set of things **ranges** between two points, they vary within these points on a scale.

## ranger rangers
NOUN someone whose job is to look after a forest or park

## rank ranks
NOUN **1** a position or grade that someone holds in an organisation
NOUN **2** a row of people or things • We wen to the taxi **rank** outside the station to catch taxi home.

## ransack ransacks, ransacking, ransacked
VERB If you **ransack** a place, you disturb everything in order to search for or steal something, and leave it in a mess.

## ransom ransoms
NOUN money that is demanded by kidnappers to free someone they have tak prisoner

## rap raps, rapping, rapped
NOUN **1** a quick knock on something • There was a sharp **rap** on the door.
NOUN **2** a type of music in which the words are spoken in a rapid, rhythmic way
VERB **3** If you **rap** something, or **rap** on it, you hit it quickly several times.

## rapid
ADJECTIVE happening or moving very quickly

## rapier rapiers
NOUN a long thin sword with a sharp point

## rare rarer, rarest
ADJECTIVE **1** Something that is **rare** is not common or does not often happen.
ADJECTIVE **2** Meat that is **rare** is cooked very lightly.

## rascal rascals
NOUN someone who does naughty or mischievous things

## rash rashes
NOUN **1** an area of red spots that appear on your skin when you are ill or have an allerg
ADJECTIVE **2** If you are **rash**, you do somethin without thinking properly about it.

## rasher rashers
NOUN a thin slice of bacon

## raspberry raspberries
NOUN a small soft red fruit that grows on a bush

## rat rats
NOUN a rodent with a long tail, that looks li a large mouse

A
B
C
D
E
F
G
H
I
J
K
L
M
N
O
P
Q
R
S
T
U
V
W
X
Y
Z

**e rates**
OUN how quickly or slowly, or how often omething happens

**:her**
OVERB **1** fairly, or to a certain extent • **rather** *arge*
OVERB **2** If you would **rather** do one thing han another, you would prefer to do it. • *I 'on't want to go out. I'd **rather** stay here.*

**:io ratios**
OUN The **ratio** between two things shows ow many times one is bigger than another. **ratio** is used to compare two or more quantities, for example, if a class has 15 oys and 10 girls, the **ratio** of boys to girls s 15 to 10.

**:ion rations, rationing, rationed**
OUN **1** the amount of something you are llowed to have
ERB **2** When something is **rationed**, you are nly allowed a limited amount of it because here is a shortage.

**:ional**
DJECTIVE well thought out, sensible and easonable • *It was a **rational** decision.*

ANTONYM: irrational

**:ioning**
OUN a system in which people are only llowed a limited amount of something because there is not enough of it, for xample during a war

**:ttle rattles, rattling, rattled**
VERB When something **rattles**, or when you **rattle** it, it makes short, regular knocking sounds, for example because it is shaking.

**:ttlesnake rattlesnakes**
OUN a poisonous American snake that can rattle its tail

**ve raves, raving, raved**
VERB **1** If someone **raves**, they talk in an excited and uncontrolled way.
VERB **2** (*informal*) If you **rave** about something, you talk about it very enthusiastically.
OUN **3** (*informal*) a large dance event with electronic music

**ven ravens**
OUN **1** a large black bird with a deep, harsh call
ADJECTIVE **2 Raven** hair is black and shiny.

**ravenous**
ADJECTIVE very hungry

**ravine ravines**
NOUN a deep, narrow valley with steep sides

**ravioli**
NOUN an Italian dish made of small squares of pasta filled with meat or vegetable paste and served with sauce

**raw**
ADJECTIVE **1 Raw** food is uncooked.
ADJECTIVE **2** If part of your body is **raw**, the skin has been rubbed or scraped away.
ADJECTIVE **3** A **raw** substance is in its natural state before being processed.

**raw material raw materials**
NOUN natural substances used to make things

**ray rays**
NOUN a beam of light • *the sun's **rays***

→ Have a look at the illustration for **greenhouse effect**

**razor razors**
NOUN an instrument that people use for shaving

**re-**
PREFIX used to form words that show something is being done again. For example, if you **re**use something you use it again, if you read something again you **re**read it, and if you marry for a second time you **re**marry.

**reach reaches, reaching, reached**
VERB **1** When you **reach** a place, you arrive there.
VERB **2** When you **reach** for something, you stretch out your arm to touch or get hold of it. • *I can't **reach** that shelf.*

**react reacts, reacting, reacted**
VERB **1** When you **react** to something, you behave in a particular way because of it.
VERB **2** When two chemicals **react**, they combine to form another substance.

**reaction reactions**
NOUN **1** Your **reaction** to something is what you say, do or feel because of it.
NOUN **2** the process in which two chemicals combine to form another substance

**reactor reactors**
NOUN a device used to produce nuclear energy

a
b
c
d
e
f
g
h
i
j
k
l
m
n
o
p
q
r
s
t
u
v
w
x
y
z

**329**

## read reads, reading, read

VERB When you **read** something that is written, you look at it and understand or say aloud the words that are there.

## reader readers

NOUN The **readers** of a newspaper or magazine are the people who read it regularly.

## readily

ADVERB **1** willingly or eagerly • They **readily** tidied their bedrooms.
ADVERB **2** easily or quickly • Help was **readily** available.

## reading readings

NOUN **1** the act of reading books, newspapers or magazines
NOUN **2** The **reading** on a meter, gauge or other measuring instrument is the amount it shows.

## ready

ADJECTIVE If someone or something is **ready**, they are prepared for doing something.
• Your glasses will be **ready** in a fortnight.

## real

ADJECTIVE **1** actually true and not imagined

ANTONYM: imaginary

ADJECTIVE **2** genuine and not artificial

## realise realises, realising, realised; also spelt realize

VERB If you **realise** something, you become aware of it or understand it.

## realistic

ADJECTIVE **1** A **realistic** painting, story or film shows things in a way that is like real life.
ADJECTIVE **2** If you are **realistic** about a situation, you recognise and accept that it is true.

## reality

NOUN **1** what is real, and not imagined or invented

SYNONYMS: fact, truth

NOUN **2** If something has become a **reality**, it has happened. • Her dream of being a dancer had become a **reality**.

## really

ADVERB **1** You use **really** to emphasise a point. • It is a **really** good film.
ADVERB **2** You use **really** when you are talking about the true facts about something. • What was **really** going on?

## reap reaps, reaping, reaped

VERB When someone **reaps** a crop, such as corn, they cut and gather it.

## reappear reappears, reappearing, reappeared

VERB When people or things **reappear**, th can be seen again after they have been of sight.

## rear rears, rearing, reared

NOUN **1** The **rear** of something is the part the back.
VERB **2** To **rear** children or other young animals means to bring them up until th are able to look after themselves.
VERB **3** When a horse **rears**, it raises the front part of its body, so that its front leg are in the air.

## rearrange rearranges, rearranging, rearranged

VERB If you **rearrange** something, you organise it or arrange it in a different wa

## reason reasons, reasoning, reasoned

NOUN **1** the fact that explains why someth happens
VERB **2** to think in a logical way and draw conclusions
VERB **3** If you **reason** with someone, you discuss something with them in a sensib way.

## reasonable

ADJECTIVE **1** fair and sensible
ADJECTIVE **2** A **reasonable** amount is a fair large amount.

## reassure reassures, reassuring, reassured

VERB If you **reassure** someone, you say or things to calm their fears or stop them fr worrying.

## rebel rebels, rebelling, rebelled

NOUN **1** someone who does not agree with rules, and behaves differently from other people
NOUN **2** one of a group of people who are fighting against their own country's army order to change how it is ruled
VERB **3** When someone **rebels**, they refuse obey rules, and they behave differently fr other people.

---

PRONUNCIATION TIP
The noun is pronounced **reb**-el. The verb pronounced rib-**el**.

**ellion rebellions**
NOUN an organised act of resistance by a group of people to authority

**ellious**
ADJECTIVE Someone who is **rebellious** breaks rules and refuses to obey orders.

**ound rebounds, rebounding, rebounded**
VERB If something **rebounds**, it bounces back after hitting something.

**uild rebuilds, rebuilding, rebuilt**
VERB When something is **rebuilt**, it is built again after being damaged or destroyed.

**uke rebukes, rebuking, rebuked**
VERB If you **rebuke** someone, you tell them off for something wrong that they have done.

**all recalls, recalling, recalled**
VERB When you **recall** something, you remember it.

**ede recedes, receding, receded**
VERB **1** When something **recedes**, it moves away into the distance. • We watched the ide **receding**.
VERB **2** When a man's hair **recedes**, he starts o go bald from the front of his head.

**eipt receipts**
NOUN a piece of paper given to you as proof that you have paid for something or delivered something

**ceive receives, receiving, received**
VERB When you **receive** something, you get t after someone has given or sent it to you.

**ceiver receivers**
NOUN the part of a telephone connected to a andline that you hold near to your ear and your mouth

**cent**
ADJECTIVE A **recent** event is something that happened a short time ago.

**ception receptions**
NOUN **1** the place near the entrance of a hotel or office where appointments and enquiries are dealt with
NOUN **2** a formal party

**ceptionist receptionists**
NOUN In a hotel or office, the **receptionist** s the person who receives and welcomes visitors as they arrive, answers the phone and arranges appointments.

**recipe recipes**
NOUN a list of ingredients and instructions for cooking or preparing a particular dish • My grandma gave me her **recipe** for Yorkshire pudding.

**recital recitals**
NOUN a performance of poetry or music, usually by one person

**recitation**
NOUN When someone does a **recitation**, they say something such as a poem aloud.

**recite recites, reciting, recited**
VERB If you **recite** something such as a poem, you say it aloud.

**reckless**
ADJECTIVE If you are **reckless**, you do not care about any danger or damage you cause.

**reckon reckons, reckoning, reckoned**
VERB **1** If you **reckon** an amount, you calculate it.
VERB **2** If you **reckon** something is true, you think it is true.

**reclaim reclaims, reclaiming, reclaimed**
VERB **1** When you **reclaim** something, you fetch it after losing it or leaving it somewhere.
VERB **2** If land is **reclaimed**, it is made useable again, for example by draining water from it.

**recline reclines, reclining, reclined**
VERB to lean or lie back • We **reclined** on deckchairs in the sun.

**recognise recognises, recognising, recognised**; also spelt recognize
VERB When you **recognise** someone or something, you realise you know who or what they are.

**recoil recoils, recoiling, recoiled**
VERB If you **recoil**, you suddenly back away from something, usually because it shocks or horrifies you. • I **recoiled** from the huge spider.

**recollect recollects, recollecting, recollected**
VERB If you **recollect** something, you remember it.

**recollection recollections**
NOUN If you have a **recollection** of something, you remember it. • I have no **recollection** of seeing him that night.

a
b
c
d
e
f
g
h
i
j
k
l
m
n
o
p
q
r
s
t
u
v
w
x
y
z

**331**

## recommend recommends, recommending, recommended
VERB If you **recommend** something to someone, you suggest that they try it because you think it is good.

## reconcile reconciles, reconciling, reconciled
VERB When people are **reconciled**, they become friendly again after a quarrel.

## reconciliation
NOUN **Reconciliation** is when people become friendly again after they have been arguing.

## reconstruct reconstructs, reconstructing, reconstructed
VERB To **reconstruct** something that has been damaged means to build it again.

## record records, recording, recorded
NOUN **1** a written account of something

NOUN **2** a round, flat piece of plastic on which music has been recorded

NOUN **3** an achievement that is the best of its type • *He holds the world **record** for the high jump.*

VERB **4** If you **record** information, you write it down so that it can be referred to later.

VERB **5** If you **record** sounds and pictures, you copy them onto a tape or disc, or onto your phone or computer, so that they can be listened to or watched again.

**PRONUNCIATION TIP**
The noun is pronounced **rek**-ord. The verb is pronounced ri-**kord**.

## recorder recorders
NOUN **1** a small woodwind instrument

NOUN **2** a machine for copying sounds and pictures, such as a tape **recorder** or a video **recorder**

## recount recounts, recounting, recounted
VERB **1** If you **recount** a story, you tell it.

VERB **2** If you **recount** something such as votes, you count them for a second time.

**PRONUNCIATION TIP**
Meaning 1 is pronounced ri-**count**.
Meaning 2 is pronounced **ree**-count.

## recover recovers, recovering, recovered
VERB **1** When you **recover**, you get better after being ill.

VERB **2** If you **recover** something that has been lost or stolen, you get it back.

## recreation recreations
NOUN the things you do for enjoyment in your spare time

## recruit recruits, recruiting, recruited
VERB **1** If you **recruit** people, you persuad them to join a group or help with something.

NOUN **2** someone who has joined the army some other organisation

## rectangle rectangles NOUN a four-sided plane shape with four right angles

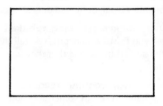

## rectangular
ADJECTIVE shaped like a rectangle

## recuperate recuperates, recuperatin recuperated
VERB When you **recuperate**, you graduall recover after being ill or injured.

## recur recurs, recurring, recurred
VERB If something **recurs**, it happens again.

## recycle recycles, recycling, recycled
VERB When you **recycle** something, you us it again for a different purpose.

## red redder, reddest; reds
NOUN **1** the colour of blood or of a ripe tome

ADJECTIVE **2** having the colour of blood or of ripe tomato

ADJECTIVE **3 Red** hair is between orange and brown in colour.

## redden reddens, reddening, reddened
VERB If something **reddens**, it becomes re• • *His face **reddened** with embarrassment.*

## red-handed
ADJECTIVE If you catch someone **red-hande•** you catch them while they are doing something wrong.

## redraft redrafts, redrafting, redrafted
VERB If you **redraft** a piece of writing, you rewrite it to improve or change it.

**duce reduces, reducing, reduced**
VERB If you **reduce** something, you make it smaller in size or amount.

SYNONYMS: cut, decrease

**duction reductions**
NOUN If there is a **reduction** in something, it becomes smaller or less. ● There are great **reductions** in prices during the sales.

**dundant**
ADJECTIVE **1** When people are made **redundant**, they lose their jobs because there is no more work for them.
ADJECTIVE **2** If something becomes **redundant**, it is no longer needed or useful.

**ed reeds**
NOUN **1** a hollow-stemmed plant that grows in shallow water or on wet ground
NOUN **2** a thin piece of cane or metal inside some wind instruments, that vibrates and makes a sound when air is blown over it

**ef reefs**
NOUN a long line of rocks or coral close to the surface of the sea

**ek reeks, reeking, reeked**
VERB **1** If something **reeks**, it has a strong, unpleasant smell.
NOUN **2** a strong, unpleasant smell

**el reels, reeling, reeled**
NOUN **1** a cylindrical object around which you wrap something such as a fishing line, a film or thread
NOUN **2** a fast Scottish dance
VERB **3** If you **reel**, you stagger and look as if you will fall.

**fer refers, referring, referred**
VERB **1** If you **refer** to someone or something, you mention them when you are speaking or writing.
VERB **2** If you **refer** to a book or other source of information, you look at it in order to find something out.
VERB **3** If someone **refers** a problem or a question to someone else, they pass it on to them to deal with.

**feree referees**
NOUN the official who controls a sports match and makes sure that the rules are not broken

**ference references**
NOUN **1** a mention of someone or something in a speech or a piece of writing
NOUN **2** a document written by someone who knows you, that describes your character and abilities, usually when you are applying for a job

**reference book reference books**
NOUN a book that you use to get information

**referendum referendums or referenda**
NOUN a vote in which all the people of voting age in a country are asked to say if they agree with a particular government policy or not

**refill refills, refilling, refilled**
VERB **1** If you **refill** something, you fill it again.
NOUN **2** a container of something to replace something that is used up ● I need a **refill** for my pen.

**refine refines, refining, refined**
VERB If substances such as oil or sugar are **refined**, all the impurities are taken out of them.

**refined**
ADJECTIVE Someone who is **refined** is very polite and well mannered.

**refinery refineries**
NOUN a factory where sugar or oil are refined

**reflect reflects, reflecting, reflected**
VERB **1** When rays of heat or light **reflect** off something, they bounce back from it.
VERB **2** When something smooth and shiny, such as a mirror, **reflects** something, it shows an image of it.
VERB **3** When you **reflect** on something, you think about it carefully.

**reflection reflections**
NOUN the image you see when you look in a mirror or in very clear, still water ● I looked closely at my **reflection** in the mirror.

**reflective**
ADJECTIVE If a surface or material is **reflective**, it bounces back rays of light or heat.

**reflex reflexes**
NOUN **1** a sudden uncontrollable movement that you make when a particular nerve is pressed or hit
NOUN **2** If you have good **reflexes**, you respond very quickly when something unexpected happens.

a
b
c
d
e
f
g
h
i
j
k
l
m
n
o
p
q
r
s
t
u
v
w
x
y
z

**333**

NOUN **3** In mathematics, a **reflex** angle is an angle between 180° and 360°.

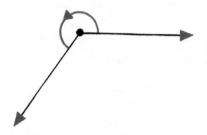

**reform** reforms, reforming, reformed
VERB **1** When organisations or laws are **reformed**, changes are made to them to improve them.
VERB **2** When people **reform**, they stop doing bad things such as committing crimes.

**refrain** refrains, refraining, refrained
VERB **1** (*formal*) If you **refrain** from doing something, you do not do it.
NOUN **2** a short, simple part of a song that is repeated

SYNONYM: chorus

**refresh** refreshes, refreshing, refreshed
VERB If something **refreshes** you, it makes you feel less tired or less thirsty.

**refreshing**
ADJECTIVE If something is **refreshing**, it makes you cool or less tired after you have been hot or busy. • *We went for a refreshing swim after walking along the beach.*

**refreshments**
PLURAL NOUN drinks and snacks

**refrigerator** refrigerators
NOUN an electrically cooled container for putting food in to keep it fresh

**refuel** refuels, refuelling, refuelled
VERB When an aircraft or vehicle is **refuelled**, it is filled with more fuel.

**refuge** refuges
NOUN a place where you go for safety and protection

SYNONYMS: haven, sanctuary, shelter

WORD HISTORY
from Latin *refugere* meaning to flee

**refugee** refugees
NOUN a person who has been forced to leav their country and live elsewhere, for exam because of war, famine or persecution

**refund** refunds, refunding, refunded
NOUN **1** a sum of money that is paid back t you, for example because you have return goods to a shop
VERB **2** If someone **refunds** your money, th pay it back to you.

**refuse** refuses, refusing, refused
VERB **1** If you **refuse** something, you say n to it, or decide firmly that you will not do or do not accept it.
NOUN **2** rubbish or waste

PRONUNCIATION TIP
The verb is pronounced ri-**fyooz**. The nou is pronounced **ref**-yooss.

**regal**
ADJECTIVE very grand and suitable for a king or queen

**regard** regards, regarding, regarded
VERB **1** To **regard** someone or something in a certain way is to think of them in tha way. • *We regarded him as a friend.*
VERB **2** to look closely at someone or something
NOUN **3** If you have a high **regard** for someo you have a very good opinion of them.

**regarding**
PREPOSITION on the subject of • *"I will now answer any questions regarding your homework," said the teacher.*

**regardless**
ADVERB If you do something **regardless** of something else or what may happen as a result, you do it anyway. • *The society helps anyone regardless of their age.*

**regards**
PLURAL NOUN kind wishes or friendly feelings for someone, usually sent in a message • *Give him my regards when you see him.*

**regatta** regattas
NOUN a race meeting for sailing or rowing boats

**reggae**
NOUN a type of music with a strong beat, originally from Jamaica

**regiment** regiments
NOUN a large group of soldiers commanded by a colonel

**gion regions**
NOUN a large area of a country or of the world

**gister registers, registering, registered**
NOUN **1** an official list that is used to keep a record of things that happen or people who attend an event
VERB **2** When something is **registered**, it is recorded on an official list.

**gret regrets, regretting, regretted**
VERB **1** If you **regret** something, you wish that it had not happened or you had not done it.
VERB **2** You can use **regret** to say you are sorry about something. ● *We **regret** any inconvenience caused to passengers by the delay.*

**grctful**
ADJECTIVE If you are **regretful**, you are sorry or sad about something.

**gular**
ADJECTIVE **1** **Regular** events happen at equal or frequent intervals.
ADJECTIVE **2** If you are a **regular** visitor somewhere, you go there often.

**gulate regulates, regulating, regulated**
VERB If someone or something **regulates** something, they control it. ● *My grandad takes tablets to **regulate** his blood pressure.*

**gulation regulations**
NOUN an official rule

**hearsal rehearsals**
NOUN a practice of a performance in preparation for the actual event

**hearse rehearses, rehearsing, rehearsed**
VERB When people **rehearse** a performance, they practise it in preparation for the actual event.

**ign reigns, reigning, reigned**
VERB **1** When a king or queen **reigns**, he or she is the leader of the country.
NOUN **2** The **reign** of a king or queen is the period when they reign.

LANGUAGE TIP
Do not confuse *reign* with *rain* or *rein*.

**ein reins**
NOUN one of the thin leather straps that you hold when you are riding a horse

LANGUAGE TIP
Do not confuse *rein* with *rain* or *reign*.

**reindeer**
NOUN a deer with large antlers, that lives in northern regions of the world

**reinforce reinforces, reinforcing, reinforced**
VERB If you **reinforce** something, you strengthen it.

**reject rejects, rejecting, rejected**
VERB If you **reject** something, you throw it away or refuse to accept it.

**rejoice rejoices, rejoicing, rejoiced**
VERB If you **rejoice**, you celebrate because you are very pleased about something.

**relate relates, relating, related**
VERB **1** If one thing **relates** to another, it is concerned or connected with it in some way, or can be compared with it.
VERB **2** If you **relate** a story, you tell it.

**related**
ADJECTIVE If people, animals or plants are **related**, they belong to the same family groups or species.

**relation relations**
NOUN **1** one of the people who are related to you, such as aunts, uncles and grandparents
NOUN **2** the way that one thing is connected or compared with another

**relationship relationships**
NOUN **1** The **relationship** between two people or groups is the way they feel and behave towards each other.
NOUN **2** a close friendship, especially one involving romantic feelings

**relative relatives**
ADJECTIVE **1** compared with other things or people of the same kind
NOUN **2** a member of your family

**relax relaxes, relaxing, relaxed**
VERB **1** When you **relax**, or when something **relaxes** you, you become calm and less worried or tense. ● *Massage is used to **relax** muscles.*
VERB **2** If you **relax**, you stop work and rest or enjoy your free time.

SYNONYMS: take it easy, unwind

a
b
c
d
e
f
g
h
i
j
k
l
m
n
o
p
q
r
s
t
u
v
w
x
y
z

A
B
C
D
E
F
G
H
I
J
K
L
M
N
O
P
Q
R
S
T
U
V
W
X
Y
Z

**relay** relays, relaying, relayed

VERB **1** If you **relay** something, such as a message, you pass it from one person to the next.

NOUN **2** a race between teams, in which each team member runs one part of the race

**release** releases, releasing, released

VERB If you **release** someone or something, you set them free or unfasten them.

**relent** relents, relenting, relented

VERB If someone **relents**, they give in and allow something that they refused to allow before.
• Dad **relented** and allowed us to stay up late.

**relevant**

ADJECTIVE connected with what is being discussed or dealt with

**reliable**

ADJECTIVE **Reliable** people and things can be trusted and depended upon.

**relic** relics

NOUN **1** an object or custom that has survived from an earlier time

NOUN **2** an object regarded as holy because it is thought to be connected with a saint

**relief**

NOUN If you feel **relief**, you feel glad because something unpleasant is over or has been avoided.

**relieve** relieves, relieving, relieved

VERB If something **relieves** an unpleasant feeling, it makes it less unpleasant.

**relieved**

ADJECTIVE If you are **relieved**, you are thankful that something worrying or unpleasant has stopped. • I was **relieved** when the exams were over.

**religion** religions

NOUN **1** belief in a god or gods

NOUN **2** a particular set of religious beliefs
• the Christian **religion**

**religious**

ADJECTIVE to do with religion

**relish** relishes, relishing, relished

VERB **1** If you **relish** something, you enjoy it very much. • He **relished** the thought of chocolate cake for tea.

NOUN **2** enjoyment • "I'm allowed to stay up as long as like," she said with **relish**.

NOUN **3** a savoury pickle

**reluctant**

ADJECTIVE If you are **reluctant** to do something, you do not want to do it.

**rely** relies, relying, relied

VERB If you **rely** on someone or something, you trust and depend on them. • I **relied** my friends to help me.

**remain** remains, remaining, remaine

VERB **1** If you **remain** in a particular place you stay there.

PLURAL NOUN **2** The **remains** of something the parts that are left after most of it has been destroyed or used.

**remainder**

NOUN **1** the part of something that is left

NOUN **2** In arithmetic, the **remainder** is th amount left over when one number cann be divided exactly by another.

**remark** remarks, remarking, remarke

VERB **1** If you **remark** on something, you mention it or comment on it.

NOUN **2** a comment you make or something you say

**remarkable**

ADJECTIVE impressive and noticeable
• Her tennis skills were **remarkable**.

**remedy** remedies, remedying, remedi

NOUN **1** a cure for something

NOUN **2** a way of dealing with a problem

VERB **3** If you **remedy** a problem, you put it right.

**remember** remembers, remembering remembered

VERB **1** If you **remember** someone or something from the past, you still have an idea of them and you are able to think about them.

VERB **2** If you **remember** to do something, you do it when you intended to.

VERB **3** If you **remember** something, it suddenly comes into your mind again.

**remind** reminds, reminding, remindee

VERB **1** If someone **reminds** you of something, they help you remember it.

VERB **2** If someone or something **reminds** you of another person or thing, they are similar to the other person or thing and make you think of them.

**remnant** remnants

NOUN a small part of something that is left after the rest has been used or destroyed

**morse**
NOUN (*formal*) a strong feeling of guilt and regret

**remote** remoter, remotest
ADJECTIVE **1** far away from where most people live
ADJECTIVE **2** far away in time

**remote control**
NOUN **1** a system of controlling a machine or vehicle from a distance, using radio or electronic signals
NOUN **2** a hand-held device for controlling a machine or vehicle from a distance
• *a TV remote control*

**removal** removals
NOUN **1** the act of taking something away
• *The house felt very bare after the removal of the furniture.*
ADJECTIVE **2** A **removal** company moves furniture from one building to another.

**remove** removes, removing, removed
VERB If you **remove** something, you take it away.

**rendezvous**
NOUN a meeting or meeting place

**renew** renews, renewing, renewed
VERB **1** If you **renew** something such as a piece of equipment, you replace it or parts of it with a new one or new parts.
VERB **2** If you **renew** an activity or relationship, you begin it again.

**renewable**
ADJECTIVE **1** able to be renewed • *a good source of renewable energy*
NOUN **2** a renewable form of energy, such as wind power or solar power • *Our energy mix needs more renewables.*

**renovate** renovates, renovating, renovated
VERB If you **renovate** something old, you repair it and restore it to good condition.

**renovation**
NOUN the process of repairing something old and restoring it to good condition

**renowned**
ADJECTIVE well known, especially for something good • *She's renowned for her kindness and compassion.*

**rent** rents, renting, rented
VERB **1** If you **rent** something, you pay the owner a regular sum of money to use it.
NOUN **2** the amount of money you pay regularly to use something that belongs to someone else

**rental** rentals
NOUN **1** the amount paid as rent
ADJECTIVE **2** to do with rent • *a small rental car*

**repair** repairs, repairing, repaired
NOUN **1** something that you do to mend something that is damaged
VERB **2** If you **repair** something that is damaged, you mend it.

**repay** repays, repaying, repaid
VERB **1** When you **repay** money, you give it back to the person who lent it to you.
VERB **2** If you **repay** a favour, you do something to help the person who helped you.

**repeat** repeats, repeating, repeated
VERB **1** If you **repeat** something, you say, write or do it again. • *Please can you repeat the question?*
NOUN **2** something that is done again or happens again

**repeatedly**
ADVERB again and again, several times
• *He knocked repeatedly on the door, but nobody answered.*

**repel** repels, repelling, repelled
VERB **1** If something **repels** you, it disgusts you.
VERB **2** If someone **repels** an attack, they defend themselves successfully against it.
VERB **3** If someone or something **repels** something, they push it away. • *True magnets can repel other magnets.*

**repetition**
NOUN If there is a **repetition** of something, it happens again or is repeated.

**repetitive**
ADJECTIVE Something that is **repetitive** is repeated over and over again, and can be extremely boring. • *Fruit picking is a repetitive job.*

a
b
c
d
e
f
g
h
i
j
k
l
m
n
o
p
q
r
s
t
u
v
w
x
y
z

**337**

A
B
C
D
E
F
G
H
I
J
K
L
M
N
O
P
Q
R
S
T
U
V
W
X
Y
Z

**replace** replaces, replacing, replaced
VERB **1** If you **replace** something, you put it back.
VERB **2** If you **replace** something old, broken or missing, you put another one or a new one in its place. ● *Ben replaced Tina in the team.*

**replay** replays, replaying, replayed
VERB **1** If you **replay** a tape or a film, you play it again.
NOUN **2** a sports match that is played for a second time

**replica** replicas
NOUN an accurate copy of something

**reply** replies, replying, replied
VERB **1** If you **reply** to something, you say or write something as an answer to it.
NOUN **2** what you say or write when you answer someone

**report** reports, reporting, reported
VERB **1** If you **report** that something has happened, you inform someone about it.
NOUN **2** an account of an event or situation

**reporter** reporters
NOUN someone who writes news articles or broadcasts news reports

**represent** represents, representing, represented
VERB If someone **represents** you, they act on your behalf.

**representative** representatives
NOUN a person who acts on behalf of another person or group of people

**reprieve** reprieves
NOUN a cancellation or postponement of a punishment, especially the death penalty

**reprimand** reprimands, reprimanding, reprimanded
VERB If you **reprimand** someone, you officially tell them that they should not have done something.

**reproach** reproaches, reproaching, reproached
VERB **1** If you **reproach** someone, you blame them for something, or criticise them.
NOUN **2** the act of reproaching someone

**reproduce** reproduces, reproducing, reproduced
VERB **1** If you **reproduce** something, you make a copy of it.
VERB **2** When living things **reproduce**, they produce more of their own kind. ● *Rats reproduce up to five times every year.*

**reproduction**
NOUN the process by which each living thing produces young

**reptile** reptiles
NOUN an animal such as a snake, turtle or lizard that has scales on its skin, lays eggs and is cold-blooded

**WORD HISTORY**
from Latin *reptilis* meaning creeping

**republic** republics
NOUN a country that has a president rather than a king or queen

**repulsion**
NOUN the force pushing two magnets away from each other

**repulsive**
ADJECTIVE horrible and disgusting

**reputation** reputations
NOUN the opinion that people have of someone or something

**request** requests, requesting, requested
VERB **1** If you **request** something, you ask for it politely or formally.
NOUN **2** If you make a **request** for something, you ask for it.

**require** requires, requiring, required
VERB **1** If you **require** something, you need it.
VERB **2** If you are **required** to do something, you have to do it. ● *You are required to report to the office at 9 a.m.*

**requirement** requirements
NOUN something you must have or must do

**rescue** rescues, rescuing, rescued
VERB **1** If you **rescue** someone, you save them from a dangerous or unpleasant situation.
NOUN **2** an attempt to save someone from a dangerous or unpleasant situation

**research** researches, researching, researched
NOUN **1** detailed study to discover facts about something
VERB **2** If you **research** something, you study it carefully to discover facts about it.

**resemble** resembles, resembling, resembled
VERB If one thing or person **resembles** another, they are similar to each other.

**resent** resents, resenting, resented
VERB If you **resent** something, you feel bitter and angry about it.

**serve reserves, reserving, reserved**
VERB **1** If you **reserve** something, you ask for
it to be kept aside or ordered for you, or you
keep it for a particular purpose. ● *We have*
*reserved this table for someone else.*
NOUN **2** an area of land where animals, birds
or plants are officially protected and can
safely breed
NOUN **3** If you are a **reserve** in a team, you
play if one of the other team members
cannot.

**served**
ADJECTIVE **1** kept for someone ● *All of these*
*tables are reserved.*
ADJECTIVE **2** People who are **reserved** are
quiet and shy.

**servoir reservoirs**
NOUN a lake, often artificial, used for storing
water before it is supplied to people

**PRONUNCIATION TIP**
This word is pronounced **rez**-uh-vwar.

**sidence residences**
NOUN (*formal*) Your **residence** is your home.

**sident residents**
NOUN A **resident** of a house or area is
someone who lives there.

**sign resigns, resigning, resigned**
VERB **1** If you **resign** from your job, you give
it up.
VERB **2** If you **resign** yourself to an
unpleasant situation, you accept it because
you know it cannot be changed.

**signation resignations**
NOUN **1** If you hand in your **resignation**, you
tell the company you work for that you have
decided to leave your job.
NOUN **2** the feeling you have when you
accept an unpleasant situation because you
know it cannot be changed

**sist resists, resisting, resisted**
VERB **1** If you **resist** something, you refuse to
accept it and try to stop it happening.
VERB **2** If you **resist** an attack, you fight
back.

**sistance**
NOUN **1** fighting or taking action against
something or someone ● *Her body's*
*resistance to disease helped her to get well.*
NOUN **2** Wind or air **resistance** is a force
which slows down a moving object or
vehicle. ● *The design of the bicycle has reduced*
*the effects of wind resistance.*

**resolute**
ADJECTIVE If you are **resolute**, you are
determined not to change your mind.

**resolution resolutions**
NOUN **1** determination
NOUN **2** If you make a **resolution**,
you promise yourself that you will do
something.

NOUN **3** a decision made at a meeting
● *The resolution to improve the play area was*
*agreed.*

**resolve resolves, resolving, resolved**
VERB **1** If you **resolve** a problem, you find a
way of sorting it out.
VERB **2** If you **resolve** to do something, you
make up your mind firmly to do it.
NOUN **3** determination to do something

**resort resorts, resorting, resorted**
NOUN **1** a place where a lot of people spend
their holidays, especially by the sea
VERB **2** If you **resort** to doing something, you
do it because everything else has failed and
you have no alternative.
PHRASE **3** If you do something **as a last**
**resort**, you do it because you can find no
other way of solving a problem.

**resource resources**
NOUN **1** The **resources** of a country,
organisation or person are the materials,
money or skills they have and can use.
NOUN **2** Natural **resources** are all the
land, forests, energy sources and minerals
existing naturally in a place that can be
used by people.

**resourceful**
ADJECTIVE A **resourceful** person is good at
solving problems and finding ways to do
things.

**respect respects, respecting, respected**
VERB **1** If you **respect** someone, you admire
and like them.
VERB **2** If you **respect** someone's feelings or
wishes, you treat them with consideration.
NOUN **3** a feeling of admiration for someone's
good qualities or achievements
NOUN **4** consideration for other people

**respectable**
ADJECTIVE Someone who is **respectable**
behaves in a way that is approved of in the
society where they live.

a b c d e f g h i j k l m n o p q r s t u v w x y z

**339**

## respiration

NOUN breathing • *His **respiration** was affected by his cold.*

## respiratory system **respiratory systems**

NOUN Your **respiratory system** is the system in your body that is to do with your breathing.

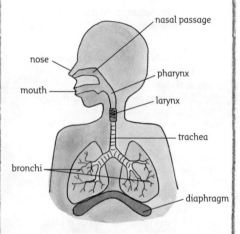

nasal passage

nose

pharynx

mouth

larynx

trachea

bronchi

diaphragm

## respond **responds, responding, responded**

VERB If you **respond** to someone or something, you react to them by doing or saying something.

## response **responses**

NOUN a reply or a reaction to something

## responsibility **responsibilities**

NOUN **1** If you have **responsibility** for someone or something, you are in charge of them. • *He has **responsibility** for organizing the school fair.*

NOUN **2** If you accept **responsibility** for something bad that has happened, you say that it is your fault. • *No one admitted **responsibility** for breaking the window*

NOUN **3** something that you have to do as part of your job

## responsible

ADJECTIVE **1** If you are **responsible** for something, you are in charge of it and must take the blame if it goes wrong. • *If we get a pet, you will be **responsible** for looking after it.*

ADJECTIVE **2** A **responsible** person is sensible, trustworthy and reliable.

ADJECTIVE **3** If you are **responsible** for something, you are the cause of it. • *She was **responsible** for the accident.*

## rest **rests, resting, rested**

VERB **1** If you **rest**, you take a break from what you are doing and relax for a while.

VERB **2** If you **rest** something against something else, you lean it there.

NOUN **3** The **rest** of something is all the par that are left or have not been mentioned.

NOUN **4** If you have a **rest**, you do not do anything active for a while.

NOUN **5** an object that supports something else, such as a headrest or a footrest

## restaurant **restaurants**

NOUN a place where you can buy and eat a meal • *an Italian **restaurant***

## restless

ADJECTIVE If you are **restless**, you find it hard to stay still or relaxed because you are bore or impatient.

## restore **restores, restoring, restored**

VERB If you **restore** something, you get it back to its original state.

## restrain **restrains, restraining, restrained**

VERB If you **restrain** someone or something you hold them back or stop them from doing what they want to.

## restrict **restricts, restricting, restricted**

VERB To **restrict** someone or something means to set limits on them. • *The police **restricted** parking outside the school.*

## result **results, resulting, resulted**

NOUN **1** The **result** of an action or situation is what happens because of it.

NOUN **2** The **result** of a contest, calculation or exam is the final score, figure or mark at the end of it.

VERB **3** If something **results** from a particular event, it is caused by that event.

## resume **resumes, resuming, resumed**

VERB If you **resume** something, you start doing it again after a break. • *After dinner, Dad **resumed** his work on the car.*

## retail

NOUN the activity of selling goods to the public, for example, in a shop

ANTONYM: wholesale

## retailer **retailers**

NOUN a business or person that sells things to people

**-tain retains, retaining, retained**
VERB If you **retain** something, you keep it.

**-taliate retaliates, retaliating, retaliated**
VERB If you **retaliate**, you do something to harm or upset someone because they have harmed or upset you.

**-tire retires, retiring, retired**
VERB 1 When older people **retire**, they leave their job and stop working.
VERB 2 If you **retire** from a race, you withdraw from it.

**-tort retorts, retorting, retorted**
VERB 1 If you **retort**, you reply angrily.
NOUN 2 a short, angry reply

**-trace retraces, retracing, retraced**
VERB If you **retrace** your steps, you go back exactly the same way you came.

**-treat retreats, retreating, retreated**
VERB If you **retreat** from someone or something unpleasant or dangerous, you move away from them.

**-trieve retrieves, retrieving, retrieved**
VERB If you **retrieve** something, you get it back or find it again.

**-turn returns, returning, returned**
VERB 1 If you **return** to a place, you go back there.
VERB 2 If you **return** something to someone, you give it back to them.
NOUN 3 the act of giving or putting something back
NOUN 4 a ticket for a journey to a place and back again

**-eunion reunions**
NOUN a meeting or a party at which people who have not seen each other for a long time get together

**-eunite reunites, reuniting, reunited**
VERB to bring people together again

**-ev revs, revving, revved**
VERB 1 When someone **revs** an engine, they press the accelerator to increase its speed.
NOUN 2 The speed of an engine is measured in **revs**, which is an abbreviation of *revolutions per minute*.

**-eveal reveals, revealing, revealed**
VERB 1 If you **reveal** something, you tell people about it.
VERB 2 If you **reveal** something that has been hidden, you uncover it.

**revenge**
NOUN the act of hurting someone who has hurt you

**revenue revenues**
NOUN money that a government, company or organisation receives

**Reverend**
NOUN a title used before the name of a member of the clergy

**reverse reverses, reversing, reversed**
VERB 1 If you **reverse** the order of things, you arrange them in the opposite order.
VERB 2 When someone **reverses** a car, they drive it backwards.

**reversible**
ADJECTIVE **Reversible** clothing can be worn with either side on the outside.

**review reviews, reviewing, reviewed**
NOUN 1 an article in a magazine or newspaper, or a talk on television or radio, giving an opinion of a new book, play or film
VERB 2 When someone **reviews** a book, play or film, they write an account or have a discussion expressing their opinion of it.

**revise revises, revising, revised**
VERB If you **revise** for an exam, you go over your work to make sure you know it properly.

**revive revives, reviving, revived**
VERB When you **revive** someone who has fainted, they become conscious again.

**revolt revolts, revolting, revolted**
NOUN 1 a violent uprising or rebellion against authority
VERB 2 When people **revolt**, they rebel against the system that governs them.
VERB 3 If something **revolts** you, it disgusts you.

**revolting**
ADJECTIVE horrible and disgusting

**revolution revolutions**
NOUN a violent attempt by a large number of people to change the way their country is run

**revolutionise revolutionises, revolutionising, revolutionised**; also spelt **revolutionize**
VERB If something is **revolutionised**, it is changed completely, usually for the better. ● *Science and technology have* **revolutionised** *the way we live.*

a
b
c
d
e
f
g
h
i
j
k
l
m
n
o
p
q
r
s
t
u
v
w
x
y
z

**341**

**revolve** **revolves, revolving, revolved**
VERB When something **revolves**, it turns in a circle around a central point.

**revolver** **revolvers**
NOUN a small gun held in the hand

**reward** **rewards, rewarding, rewarded**
NOUN **1** something you are given because you have done something good
VERB **2** If you **reward** someone, you give them a reward.

**rewarding**
ADJECTIVE Something that is **rewarding** gives you a lot of satisfaction. • *Nursing is a **rewarding** job.*

**rewind** **rewinds, rewinding, rewound**
VERB If you **rewind** a cassette or video tape, you wind it back to the beginning.

**rewrite** **rewrites, rewriting, rewrote, rewritten**
VERB If you **rewrite** something you have written, you write it again to make changes to it and improve it.

SYNONYM: redraft

**rhetorical**
ADJECTIVE A question that is **rhetorical** is asked in order to make a statement, rather than to get an answer. For example, *What's the world coming to?*

**rheumatism**
NOUN an illness that makes your joints and muscles stiff and painful

**rhinoceros** **rhinoceroses**
NOUN a large African or Asian mammal with one or two horns on its nose

WORD HISTORY
from Greek *rhin* meaning of the nose and *keras* meaning horn

**rhombus** **rhombuses** or **rhombi**
NOUN a plane shape like a diamond, with four equal sides and no right angles

**rhubarb**
NOUN a plant with long red stems that can be cooked with sugar and eaten

**rhyme** **rhymes, rhyming, rhymed**
VERB **1** If one word **rhymes** with another, both words have a very similar sound in their final syllable. For example, *Sally* rhymes with *valley*.
NOUN **2** a word that rhymes with another
• *He couldn't find a **rhyme** for "orange".*

LANGUAGE TIP
There is an *h* before the *y* in *rhyme* and *rhythm*.

**rhythm** **rhythms**
NOUN a regular series of sounds, movements or actions • *The poem was easy to learn because it had a strong **rhythm**.*

**rib** **ribs**
NOUN Your **ribs** are the curved bones that go from your spine to your chest.
→ Have a look at the illustration for **skeleton**

**ribbon** **ribbons**
NOUN a long, narrow piece of cloth used as a fastening or decoration

**rice**
NOUN white or brown grains taken from a cereal plant and used for food

**rich** **richer, richest; riches**
ADJECTIVE **1** Someone who is **rich** has a lot of money or possessions.
ADJECTIVE **2** Something that is **rich** in something contains a large amount of it.
• *Fruit is **rich** in vitamins.*
ADJECTIVE **3** **Rich** food contains a large amount of fat, oil or sugar.
PLURAL NOUN **4** **Riches** are valuable possessions or large amounts of money.

**rickshaw** **rickshaws**
NOUN a two-wheeled, hand-pulled cart used in Asia for carrying passengers

**ricochet** **ricochets, ricocheting** or **ricochetting, ricocheted** or **ricochetted**
VERB When an object **ricochets**, it hits a surface and then bounces away from it.

PRONUNCIATION TIP
This word is pronounced **rik**-oh-shay.

**d**

PHRASE When you **get rid of** something you do not want, you throw it away.

**ddle riddles**

NOUN an amusing or puzzling question, sometimes in rhyme, to which you must find an answer

**de rides, riding, rode, ridden**

VERB **1** When you **ride** a horse or a bicycle, you sit on it and control it as it moves along.

VERB **2** When you **ride** in a car, you travel in it.

NOUN **3** a journey on a horse or bicycle or in a vehicle

**dge ridges**

NOUN a long, narrow piece of high land

**dicule ridicules, ridiculing, ridiculed**

VERB **1** If you **ridicule** someone, you make fun of them in an unkind way.

NOUN **2** unkind laughter or teasing

**diculous**

ADJECTIVE very foolish

**fle rifles**

NOUN a gun with a long barrel

**g rigs, rigging, rigged**

NOUN **1** a large structure used for taking oil or gas from the ground or the sea bed ● *an oil rig*

VERB **2** When someone **rigs** a boat, they fit it with ropes and sails.

**ight rights**

NOUN **1** correct behaviour ● *At least he knew right from wrong.*

ANTONYM: wrong

NOUN **2** If you have a **right** to do something, you are allowed to do it.

NOUN **3** one of two opposite directions, sides or positions. If you are facing north and you turn to the **right**, you will be facing east.

ANTONYM: left

ADJECTIVE **4** If something is **right**, it is correct. ● *Jack was right about the result of the match.* ● *Is my answer right?*

ANTONYM: wrong

ADJECTIVE **5** on the **right** of something ● *He held out his right arm.*

ANTONYM: left

ADVERB **6** on or towards the **right** of something ● *Turn right at the corner.*

ANTONYM: left

**right angle right angles**

NOUN an angle of 90°

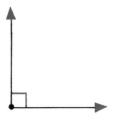

**right-angled**

ADJECTIVE A **right-angled** triangle has a right angle as one of its angles.

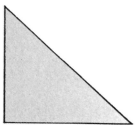

**rigid**

ADJECTIVE A **rigid** object is stiff and does not bend easily.

**rim rims**

NOUN the outer edge of something such as a bowl or wheel

→ Have a look at the illustration for **bicycle**

**rind rinds**

NOUN the skin on bacon, cheese and some fruits

**ring rings, ringing, rang, rung**

VERB **1** If you **ring** someone, you phone them.

VERB **2** When a phone or bell **rings**, it makes a clear, loud sound. ● *The school bell rings at nine o'clock.*

NOUN **3** a small circle of metal that you wear on your finger

A
B
C
D
E
F
G
H
I
J
K
L
M
N
O
P
Q
R
S
T
U
V
W
X
Y
Z

**ringleader** ringleaders
NOUN the leader of a group, who leads the others into mischief or crime

**rink** rinks
NOUN a large indoor area for ice skating or roller skating

**rinse** rinses, rinsing, rinsed
VERB When you **rinse** something, you wash it in clean water, without soap.

**riot** riots, rioting, rioted
NOUN 1 When there is a **riot**, a crowd of people behave violently in a public place.
VERB 2 When people **riot**, they behave violently in a public place.

**rip** rips, ripping, ripped
VERB If you **rip** something, you tear it.

**ripe** riper, ripest
ADJECTIVE **Ripe** fruit or grain is fully developed and ready to be eaten.

**ripple** ripples, rippling, rippled
NOUN 1 a little wave on the surface of calm water
NOUN 2 If there is a **ripple** of laughter or applause, people laugh or clap their hands gently for a short time.
VERB 3 When the surface of water **ripples**, little waves appear on it.

**rise** rises, rising, rose, risen
VERB 1 If something **rises**, it moves upwards.
• Wilson watched the smoke **rise** from the fire.
VERB 2 When the sun or moon **rises**, it appears from below the horizon.
NOUN 3 When something goes up, it is called a **rise**, for example a **rise** in the land or a **rise** in prices.
VERB 4 When you **rise**, you get out of bed.
VERB 5 If something such as a sound, or the level of a liquid or prices **rise**, they become higher.

**risk** risks, risking, risked
NOUN 1 If there is a **risk** of something unpleasant, it might happen.
NOUN 2 Someone or something that is a **risk** is likely to cause harm or have bad results.
VERB 3 If you **risk** something, you do something knowing that an unpleasant thing might happen as a result. • If he doesn't play, he **risks** losing his place in the team.

**ritual** rituals
NOUN 1 a traditional ceremony
ADJECTIVE 2 **Ritual** activities happen as part of a tradition or ritual.

**rival** rivals
NOUN Someone's **rival** is the person they a competing with.

**river** rivers
NOUN a large, continuous stretch of fresh water flowing in a channel across land, to larger **river**, a lake or the sea

→ Have a look at the illustration for **map**

**road** roads
NOUN a long stretch of hard ground built between two places so that people can travel along it easily

→ Have a look at the illustration for **map**

**roam** roams, roaming, roamed
VERB If you **roam** around, you wander around without any particular reason.

**roar** roars, roaring, roared
VERB 1 If something **roars**, it makes a very loud noise.
NOUN 2 a very loud noise

**roast** roasts, roasting, roasted
VERB 1 When you **roast** meat or other food, you cook it in an oven or over a fire.
ADJECTIVE 2 **Roast** meat or vegetables have been roasted.

**rob** robs, robbing, robbed
VERB If someone **robs** a person or place, the steal money or property from them.

**robe** robes
NOUN a long, loose piece of clothing that covers the body

**robin** robins
NOUN a small bird with a red breast

**robot** robots
NOUN a machine that moves and does thing automatically

WORD HISTORY
from Czech robota meaning work

**rock** rocks, rocking, rocked
NOUN 1 **Rock** is made up of small pieces of one or more minerals. The Earth's surface is made up of **rock**.
NOUN 2 A **rock** is a piece of rock.
NOUN 3 music with a strong beat, usually involving electric guitars and drums
NOUN 4 a hard sweet, usually brightly coloured and shaped like a long stick

VERB **5** When something **rocks**, or when you **rock** it, it moves regularly backwards and forwards or from side to side.

**rocket rockets**
NOUN **1** a space vehicle, usually shaped like a long pointed tube
NOUN **2** an explosive missile

**rod rods**
NOUN a long, thin pole or bar

**rode**
VERB the past tense of **ride**

**rodent rodents**
NOUN a small mammal with sharp front teeth that it uses for gnawing. Rabbits and mice are **rodents**.

WORD HISTORY
from Latin *rodere* meaning to gnaw

**rogue rogues**
NOUN a dishonest or mischievous person

**role roles**
NOUN An actor's **role** is the character that he or she plays in a play or film.

**roll rolls, rolling, rolled**
VERB **1** If something **rolls**, or if you **roll** it, it moves along a surface, turning over many times.
VERB **2** If you **roll** something, or **roll it up**, you wrap it around itself so that it has a rounded shape.
NOUN **3** A **roll** of paper or cloth is a long piece of it that has been rolled into a tube.
NOUN **4** a small, circular loaf of bread

**roller coaster roller coasters**
NOUN a pleasure ride at a fun fair, consisting of a small railway that goes up and down steep slopes and around bends

**roller skate roller skates**
NOUN **Roller skates** are shoes or boots with small wheels underneath.

**ROM**
NOUN a computer storage device that holds information that cannot be changed by the programmer. **ROM** is an abbreviation for *read only memory*.

**Roman Catholic Roman Catholics**
NOUN someone who belongs to the branch of the Christian Church that has the Pope in Rome as its leader

**romance romances**
NOUN **1** a love story
NOUN **2** If two people have a **romance**, they have a romantic relationship.

**Romani**; also spelt **Romany**
NOUN the language of Romany Gypsies

**Roman numerals**
PLURAL NOUN numbers written in the form of letters and used by ancient Romans. For example, I = 1, V = 5, X = 10, L = 50, C = 100, D = 500, M = 1000.

**romantic**
ADJECTIVE **1** to do with romance and love
ADJECTIVE **2** A **romantic** person is rather emotional and not very realistic about life and love.

**roof roofs**
NOUN the covering on top of a building or vehicle

**rook rooks**
NOUN **1** a large black bird
NOUN **2** a chess piece that can move any number of squares in a straight but not diagonal line. It is also called a castle.

**room rooms**
NOUN **1** a separate section in a building, divided from other **rooms** by walls
NOUN **2** If there is **room** for something, there is enough space for it.

**roost roosts, roosting, roosted**
NOUN **1** a place where birds rest or build their nests
VERB **2** When birds **roost**, they settle somewhere for the night.

**root roots**
NOUN **Roots** are the parts of a plant that usually grow underground. They anchor the plant and carry water from the soil.

→ Have a look at the illustrations for **flower** and **photosynthesis**

**root word root words**
NOUN a word that you can add a prefix or a suffix to in order to make other words. For example, in the words *unclear*, *clearly* and *cleared*, the **root word** is *clear*.

**rope ropes, roping, roped**
NOUN **1** a thick, strong cord made by twisting together several thinner cords
VERB **2** If you **rope** one thing to another, you tie them together with rope.

a
b
c
d
e
f
g
h
i
j
k
l
m
n
o
p
q
r
s
t
u
v
w
x
y
z

**345**

**rosary rosaries**

NOUN a string of beads that Catholics use for counting prayers

**rose roses**

NOUN **1** a flower that has a pleasant smell and grows on a bush with thorns
VERB **2** the past tense of **rise**

**rosette rosettes**

NOUN a large circular badge of coloured ribbons worn as a prize in a competition or to support a political party

**Rosh Hashanah**; also spelt **Rosh Hashana**

NOUN the festival celebrating the Jewish New Year

**rosy rosier, rosiest**

ADJECTIVE **1** reddish-pink • *Our cheeks were* ***rosy*** *after our walk on the windy beach.*
ADJECTIVE **2** hopeful and positive • *He always has a* ***rosy*** *outlook on life.*

**rot rots, rotting, rotted**

VERB When food, wood or other substances **rot**, or when something **rots** them, they decay and fall apart.

SYNONYM: decompose

**rotary**

ADJECTIVE moving or able to move in a circular direction around a fixed point

**rotate rotates, rotating, rotated**

VERB When something **rotates**, it turns with a circular movement, like a wheel.

**rotation rotations**

NOUN **1** a complete circular movement • *the* ***rotation*** *of a wheel* • *the* ***rotation*** *of the Earth*
NOUN **2** A shape that has **rotation** symmetry looks exactly the same when it is turned in a circular movement.
PHRASE **3** If you do things **in rotation**, you do them one after the other, and when you finish you start all over again.

**rotor rotors**

NOUN **1** the part of a machine that turns
NOUN **2** The **rotors**, or **rotor** blades, of a helicopter are the four long, flat pieces of metal on top of it, that rotate and lift it off the ground.

**rotten**

ADJECTIVE **1** Something that is **rotten** has decayed.
ADJECTIVE **2** (*informal*) bad, unpleasant or unfair • *I think it's a* ***rotten*** *idea.*

**rough rougher, roughest**

ADJECTIVE **1** uneven and not smooth • *His hands were hard and* ***rough***.

ANTONYM: smooth

ADJECTIVE **2** using too much force • *Don't be* ***rough*** *with that toy or you'll break it.*

ANTONYM: gentle

ADJECTIVE **3** approximate • *At a* ***rough*** *guess, is five o'clock.*

ANTONYMS: exact, precise

**roughly**

ADVERB **1** almost or approximately • *There a* ***roughly*** *100 marbles in that box.*
ADVERB **2** If you treat someone or something **roughly**, you treat them clumsily or violent

**round rounder, roundest; rounds**

ADJECTIVE **1** Something **round** is shaped like ball or a circle.
PREPOSITION **2** If something is **round** something else, it surrounds it.
PREPOSITION **3** If you go **round** something, yo go to the other side of it. • *Suddenly a car came* ***round*** *the corner.*
ADVERB **4** If something goes **round**, it move in a circle. • *The sails of the windmill went* ***round***.
ADVERB **5** If you turn or look **round**, you tur or look in a different direction.
ADVERB **6** If you move things **round**, you mo them so that they are in different places.
ADVERB **7** If you go **round** to someone's house, you visit them.
NOUN **8** one of a series of events, especially a competition
NOUN **9** a series of calls or deliveries • *Our house is the last one on the milkman's* ***round***
NOUN **10** a whole slice of bread, or a sandwich made of two slices
NOUN **11** a type of song in which people sin the same words but start at different times

**roundabout roundabouts**

NOUN **1** a meeting point of several roads wi a circle in the centre that vehicles have to travel around
NOUN **2** a circular platform that goes round and that children can ride on in a playgroun
NOUN **3** a large, circular platform with horse or cars on it, for children to ride on as it goes round and round

SYNONYM: merry-go-round

**rounded**

ADJECTIVE curved in shape

**⸱unders**
NOUN a team game in which players hit a ball with a bat and run round a circuit

**⸱use rouses, rousing, roused**
VERB **1** If you **rouse** someone, you wake them up.
VERB **2** If you **rouse** yourself, you make yourself get up and do something.
ADJECTIVE **3** Something that is **rousing**, such as a game, speech or song, makes you feel excited and emotional.

**⸱using**
ADJECTIVE Something that is **rousing**, such as a game, speech or song, makes you feel excited and emotional.

**⸱ute routes**
NOUN a way from one place to another • *the most direct **route** to the town centre*

**⸱utine routines**
ADJECTIVE **1 Routine** activities are done regularly.
NOUN **2** the usual way or order in which you do things

**⸱w rows, rowing, rowed**
VERB **1** When you **row** a boat, you use oars to make it move through the water.
NOUN **2** several objects or people in a line
NOUN **3** an argument
NOUN **4** a lot of noise

PRONUNCIATION TIP
Meanings 1 and 2 rhyme with "snow".
Meanings 3 and 4 rhyme with "cow".

**⸱wdily**
ADVERB in a noisy and rough way

**⸱wdy rowdier, rowdiest**
ADJECTIVE noisy and rough

**⸱yal**
ADJECTIVE belonging to or involving a queen, a king, or a member of their family

**SVP**
**RSVP** written at the end of a letter or an invitation means please reply.

WORD HISTORY
an abbreviation for the French expression *Répondez s'il vous plaît* meaning please reply

**⸱ub rubs, rubbing, rubbed**
VERB If you **rub** something, you move your hand, or a cloth, very firmly backwards and forwards over it.

**rubber rubbers**
NOUN **1** a strong, elastic substance used for making tyres, boots and other products
NOUN **2** a small piece of rubber or plastic that you use to remove mistakes when writing or drawing with a pencil

**rubbish**
NOUN **1** unwanted things or waste material

SYNONYMS: garbage, refuse, trash

NOUN **2** something foolish
NOUN **3** something of very poor quality

**rubble**
NOUN bits of old brick and stone

**ruby rubies**
NOUN a type of red jewel

**rucksack rucksacks**
NOUN a bag with shoulder straps for carrying things on your back

**rudder rudders**
NOUN a piece of wood or metal at the back of a boat or plane that is moved to make the boat or plane turn

→ Have a look at the illustrations for **aeroplane** and **ship**

**rude ruder, rudest**
ADJECTIVE **1** not polite
ADJECTIVE **2** embarrassing or offensive because of reference to body parts or bodily functions

**ruff ruffs**
NOUN a stiff circular collar with many pleats in it, popular in the 16th century.

**ruffle ruffles, ruffling, ruffled**
VERB **1** If you **ruffle** someone's hair, you move your hand quickly backwards and forwards over their head.
VERB **2** If something **ruffles** you, it makes you annoyed or upset.
NOUN **3 Ruffles** are small folds made in a piece of material for decoration.

**rug rugs**
NOUN **1** a small thick carpet
NOUN **2** a warm covering for your knees or for sitting on outdoors

**rugby**
NOUN a game played by two teams, who try to kick or throw an oval ball past a line at their opponents' end of the pitch

WORD HISTORY
named after *Rugby* School where it was first played

a b c d e f g h i j k l m n o p q r s t u v w x y z

## rugged

ADJECTIVE **1** Somewhere **rugged** is rocky, wild and unsheltered.

ADJECTIVE **2** Someone **rugged** is strong and tough.

## ruin ruins, ruining, ruined

VERB **1** If you **ruin** something, you destroy or spoil it completely.

NOUN **2** the part that is left after something has been severely damaged

## rule rules, ruling, ruled

NOUN **1 Rules** are instructions that tell you what you must do.

VERB **2** When someone **rules** a country or a group of people, they govern it and are in charge of its affairs.

## ruler rulers

NOUN **1** a person who rules a country

NOUN **2** a long, flat object with straight edges, marked with a scale, used for measuring things or drawing straight lines

## rum rums

NOUN a strong alcoholic drink made from sugar cane juice

## rumble rumbles, rumbling, rumbles

VERB **1** If something **rumbles**, it makes a continuous low sound. • *My stomach is rumbling because I am hungry.*

NOUN **2** a continuous deep sound • *There was a rumble of thunder.*

## rumour rumours

NOUN a piece of information or a story that people are talking about, but which may not be true

## run runs, running, ran

VERB **1** When you **run**, you move quickly, with both feet leaving the ground at each stride.

VERB **2** If you **run** water, you turn on the tap to let the water flow out.

VERB **3** If your nose is **running**, a lot of liquid is coming out of it.

VERB **4** If you **run** an activity or a place such as a school or shop, you are in charge of it.

VERB **5** If you **run away** from a place, you leave it suddenly and secretly.

### run out

VERB If you **run out** of something, you have no more left.

## rung rungs

NOUN one of the bars that form the steps of a ladder

## runner runners

NOUN **1** a person who runs as a sport, especially in competitions

NOUN **2** a person who takes messages or runs errands

NOUN **3** A **runner** on a plant such as a strawberry is a long shoot from which a new plant develops.

## runny runnier, runniest

ADJECTIVE flowing or moving like liquid

## runway runways

NOUN a long strip of ground used by aeroplanes for taking off and landing

## rural

ADJECTIVE to do with the countryside

## rush rushes, rushing, rushed

VERB **1** If you **rush** somewhere, or if you are **rushed** there, you go there quickly.

VERB **2** If you **rush** something, or if you are **rushed** into something, you do it too quickly.

NOUN **3** a type of plant that grows in or beside fresh water, such as rivers, ponds and lakes

## rust rusts, rusting, rusted

NOUN **1** a reddish-brown substance that forms on metal when it is exposed to water and the oxygen in the air

VERB **2** When metal **rusts**, it corrodes and a reddish-brown substance is formed. **Rusting** occurs when iron or steel is exposed to water and the oxygen in the air.

## rustle rustles, rustling, rustled

VERB If something **rustles**, it makes a soft, crisp sound as it moves, like the sound of dry leaves moving.

## rusty rustier, rustiest

ADJECTIVE **1** covered with rust • *The old bicycle was rusty.*

ADJECTIVE **2** not as good as it once was because of lack of practice • *Dad's maths is a bit rusty.*

## rut ruts

NOUN a deep, narrow groove in the ground made by the wheels of a vehicle

## ruthless

ADJECTIVE very harsh or cruel, and without any pity

## rye

NOUN a cereal crop that produces light-brown grain used to make flour

A B C D E F G H I J K L M N O P Q R S T U V W X Y Z

# Ss

**Sabbath** Sabbaths
NOUN the day of the week that some religious groups, such as Jews and Christians, use for rest and prayer

WORD HISTORY
from Hebrew *shabbath* meaning to rest

**sabotage** sabotages, sabotaging, sabotaged
NOUN 1 the deliberate damaging of machinery and equipment such as railway lines
VERB 2 If something is **sabotaged**, it is deliberately damaged.

**saboteur** saboteurs
NOUN someone who deliberately damages machinery and equipment such as railway lines

**sabre** sabres
NOUN 1 a heavy curved sword
NOUN 2 a light sword used in fencing

**sachet** sachets
NOUN a small packet containing something like sugar or shampoo

**sack** sacks
NOUN 1 a large bag made of rough material, for carrying such things as potatoes and grain • a *sack* of potatoes
PHRASE 2 (*informal*) If someone **gets the sack**, they are dismissed from their job by their employer.

**sacred**
ADJECTIVE holy, or connected with religion or religious ceremonies

**sacrifice** sacrifices, sacrificing, sacrificed
VERB If you **sacrifice** something valuable or important, you give it up.

**sad** sadder, saddest
ADJECTIVE If you are **sad**, you feel unhappy.

ANTONYM: happy

**sadden** saddens, saddening, saddened
VERB If something **saddens** you, it makes you feel sad.

**saddening**
ADJECTIVE making you feel sad

**saddle** saddles, saddling, saddled
NOUN 1 a leather seat strapped to an animal's back, for the rider to sit on
NOUN 2 the seat on a bicycle
VERB 3 If you **saddle** a horse, you put a saddle on it.

**safari** safaris
NOUN an expedition for hunting or observing wild animals

WORD HISTORY
from Swahili *safari* meaning journey

**safari park** safari parks
NOUN a large park where wild animals such as lions, giraffes and elephants are free to roam

**safe** safer, safest; safes
ADJECTIVE 1 If you are **safe**, you are not in any danger. • I feel very **safe** when I am inside the school.
ADJECTIVE 2 Something that is **safe** does not cause harm or danger. • We must try to make our roads **safer**.
NOUN 3 a strong metal box with special locks, in which you can keep valuable things

**safeguard** safeguards, safeguarding, safeguarded
VERB 1 If you **safeguard** something, you protect it.
NOUN 2 a law or a rule to help protect people or things from harm

**safety**
NOUN protection, being safe • child **safety** • Everyone believes that we should have **safety** in our homes.

**saga** sagas
NOUN a very long story, usually telling of many different adventures

**said**
VERB the past tense and past participle of **say**

## sail sails, sailing, sailed
VERB **1** When a ship **sails**, it moves across water.
VERB **2** If you **sail** somewhere, you go there by ship.
NOUN **3** one of the large pieces of material attached to a ship's mast. The wind blows against the **sail** and moves the ship.
NOUN **4** The arm of a windmill is called a **sail**.

## sailor sailors
NOUN **1** a member of a ship's crew
NOUN **2** someone who sails

## saint saints
NOUN a person who is given a special honour by a Christian Church, after they have died, because they lived a very holy life

## sake sakes
PHRASE If you do something for someone's **sake**, you do it to help or please them.

## salad salads
NOUN a mixture of foods eaten cold or warm, and often raw

## salami
NOUN a kind of spicy sausage

### WORD HISTORY
Italian plural of *salame*, from *salare* meaning to salt

## salary salaries
NOUN a payment made each month to an employee

## sale sales
NOUN **1** The **sale** of goods is the selling of them.
NOUN **2** an occasion when a shop sells things at reduced prices

## saliva
NOUN the watery liquid in your mouth that softens food, which helps you chew and digest it

## salmon
NOUN a large, edible, silver-coloured fish with pink flesh

### LANGUAGE TIP
The plural of *salmon* is *salmon*.

## salt
NOUN a white substance used to flavour and preserve food

## salute salutes, saluting, saluted
NOUN **1** a formal sign of respect. Soldiers g a **salute** by raising their right hand to th forehead.
VERB **2** If you **salute** someone, you give th a salute.

## salvage salvages, salvaging, salvaged
VERB If you **salvage** things, you save them from, for example, a wrecked ship or a destroyed building.

## same
ADJECTIVE **1** If two things are the **same**, they are like one another.
ADJECTIVE **2** just one thing and not two different ones • *They were born in the sam town.*

## sample samples, sampling, sampled
NOUN **1** a small amount of something that you can try or test, for example for quality to find out more about it
VERB **2** If you **sample** something, you try it • *I **sampled** his cooking.*

## sanctuary sanctuaries
NOUN **1** a place where you are safe from harm or danger
NOUN **2** a place where wildlife is protected

## sand sands
NOUN a substance consisting of tiny pieces stone. Beaches are made of **sand**.

## sandal sandals
NOUN **Sandals** are light shoes with straps, worn in warm weather.

## sandwich sandwiches
NOUN two slices of bread with a filling between them

### WORD HISTORY
named after the 4th Earl of Sandwich in the 18th century, who used to ask for beef served between two slices of bread when playing card games, so that he wouldn't get grease from his hands on the cards

**ndy sandier, sandiest**
ADJECTIVE **1** A **sandy** area is covered with
and. ● *We walked until we got to a long
andy beach.*
ADJECTIVE **2 Sandy** hair is a light orange-
brown colour.

**ne saner, sanest**
ADJECTIVE If someone is **sane**, they have a
healthy mind.

**ng**
VERB the past tense of **sing**

**nity**
NOUN A person's **sanity** is the health of their
mind.

**nk**
VERB the past tense of **sink**

**p saps, sapping, sapped**
NOUN **1** the juice found in the stems of plants
VERB **2** If something such as an illness **saps**
your energy or your strength, it gradually
weakens you.

**pling saplings**
NOUN a young tree

**pphire sapphires**
NOUN a blue precious stone

**rcastic**
ADJECTIVE If someone is **sarcastic**, they say
the opposite of what they really mean in
order to mock or insult someone.

**rdine sardines**
NOUN a small edible sea fish

**ri saris**
NOUN a piece of clothing consisting of a long
piece of material folded around the body,
worn especially by Indian women

WORD HISTORY
a Hindi word

**sh sashes**
NOUN a long piece of cloth worn round the
waist or over one shoulder

**it**
VERB the past tense and past participle of **sit**

**itchel satchels**
NOUN a leather or cloth bag with a long
strap, especially used for carrying books to
and from school

**satellite satellites**
NOUN **1** a spacecraft sent into space to orbit
the Earth, to collect information, or as part
of a communications system
NOUN **2** a natural object in space that moves
round another, larger object, such as a
planet or star

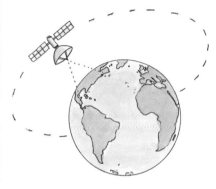

**satellite dish satellite dishes**
NOUN a dish-shaped aerial that receives
television signals sent by satellite

**satellite television**
NOUN television programmes received by
signals from artificial satellites

**satin satins**
NOUN a kind of smooth, shiny fabric often
made from silk

**satisfactorily**
ADVERB in an acceptable or adequate way

**satisfactory**
ADJECTIVE acceptable or adequate

**satisfy satisfies, satisfying, satisfied**
VERB If you **satisfy** someone, you do
something or give them something to make
them pleased or contented.

**saturated**
ADJECTIVE soaking wet

**Saturday Saturdays**
NOUN the seventh day of the week, coming
between Friday and Sunday

**sauce sauces**
NOUN a liquid eaten with food to add flavour
● *It's pasta with tomato **sauce** for dinner.*

**saucepan saucepans**
NOUN a deep metal pan with a handle and a
lid used for cooking

a
b
c
d
e
f
g
h
i
j
k
l
m
n
o
p
q
r
s
t
u
v
w
x
y
z

**351**

**saucer saucers**
NOUN a small curved plate for a cup to stand on

**sauna saunas**
NOUN If you have a **sauna**, you go into a very hot room in order to sweat, then have a cold bath or shower.

PRONUNCIATION TIP
This word is pronounced **saw**-nah.

WORD HISTORY
a Finnish word

**saunter saunters, sauntering, sauntered**
VERB If you **saunter** somewhere, you walk there slowly and casually.

**sausage sausages**
NOUN a mixture of minced meat and herbs formed into a tubular shape and served cooked

**savage savages, savaging, savaged**
ADJECTIVE **1** cruel and violent

SYNONYMS: brutal, vicious

VERB **2** If an animal **savages** you, it attacks you and bites you.

**savannah savannahs**
NOUN a grassy plain with few trees in a hot country

**save saves, saving, saved**
VERB **1** If you **save** someone, you rescue them or help to keep them safe.
VERB **2** If you **save** something, you keep it so that you can use it later.
VERB **3** If you **save** time, money or effort, you stop it from being wasted.

**savings**
PLURAL NOUN Your **savings** are money you have saved.

**saviour saviours**
NOUN **1** a person who saves others from danger or loss
PROPER NOUN **2** In Christianity, the **Saviour** is Jesus Christ.

**savoury**
ADJECTIVE salty or spicy • *Salt and vinegar crisps are my favourite* **savoury** *snack.*

**saw saws, sawing, sawed, sawn**
NOUN **1** a tool that has a blade with sharp teeth along one edge for cutting wood

VERB **2** If you **saw** something, you cut it wi a saw.
VERB **3** the past tense of **see**

**sawdust**
NOUN the fine powder produced when you saw wood

**saxophone saxophones**
NOUN a curved metal wind instrument ofte played in jazz bands

WORD HISTORY
named after Adolphe *Sax* (1814–1894), w invented the instrument

**say says, saying, said**
VERB If you **say** something, you speak wor

**saying sayings**
NOUN a well-known sentence or phrase tha tells you something about life

**scab scabs**
NOUN a hard, dry covering that forms over wound while it is healing

**scaffolding**
NOUN a framework of poles and boards tha is used by workmen to stand on while the are working on the outside of a building

**scald scalds, scalding, scalded**
VERB **1** If you **scald** yourself, you burn yourself with very hot liquid or steam.
NOUN **2** a burn caused by very hot liquid or steam

**scale scales**
NOUN **1** the size or extent of something • *Th* **scale** *of the building was enormous.*
NOUN **2** a set of marks or numbers used for measuring something
NOUN **3** The **scale** of something like a map, a plan or a model shows the relationship between the measurements represented and those in the real world. For example, a **scale** of 1:10 tells you that one centimetre on a model represents 10 centimetres in real life.

→ Have a look at the illustration for **map**

NOUN **4** one of the small, hard pieces of skir covering the body of a fish or a reptile

→ Have a look at the illustration for **fish**

NOUN **5** a series of musical notes going upwards or downwards in a particular ord
PLURAL NOUN **6 Scales** are a piece of equipment used for weighing things or people.

**alene**

ADJECTIVE A **scalene** triangle has sides of different lengths.

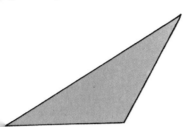

**alp scalps**

NOUN the skin under the hair on your head

**amper scampers, scampering, scampered**

VERB If you **scamper**, you run quickly and lightly.

**ampi**

PLURAL NOUN large prawns, often eaten fried in breadcrumbs

**an scans, scanning, scanned**

VERB **1** If you **scan** something, you look at every part of it carefully.
VERB **2** If you **scan** a piece of writing, you look at it quickly but not in detail.
VERB **3** If a machine **scans** something, it examines it with a beam of light or X-rays.
NOUN **4** an examination of part of the body with X-ray or laser equipment

**andal scandals**

NOUN **1** a situation or event that people think is shocking and immoral
NOUN **2** gossip about bad things that can ruin a person's reputation

**anner scanners**

NOUN a machine that is used to examine, identify or record things by using a beam of light or an X-ray

**apegoat scapegoats**

NOUN If someone is made a **scapegoat**, they are blamed for something, although it may not be their fault.

**ar scars, scarring, scarred**

NOUN **1** a mark left on your skin after a wound has healed ● *She had a scar over her eye.*
VERB **2** If an injury **scars** you, it leaves a mark on your skin for ever.

**scarce scarcer, scarcest**

ADJECTIVE If something is **scarce**, there is not very much of it.

**scare scares, scaring, scared**

VERB **1** If something **scares** you, it frightens you.
NOUN **2** something that gives you a fright

**scarecrow scarecrows**

NOUN an object shaped like a person and put in a field to scare birds away from the crops

**scarf scarfs or scarves**

NOUN a piece of cloth worn round your neck or head to keep you warm

**scarlet**

NOUN **1** a bright red colour
ADJECTIVE **2** having a bright red colour

**scary scarier, scariest**

ADJECTIVE (*informal*) frightening ● *The film was so scary I hid behind the sofa.*

**scatter scatters, scattering, scattered**

VERB **1** When you **scatter** things, you throw or drop them so they spread over a large area.
VERB **2** If a group of people or animals **scatter**, they suddenly move off in different directions.

**scavenge scavenges, scavenging, scavenged**

VERB If a human or other animal **scavenges** for things, they search for them among waste and rubbish.

**scavenger scavengers**

NOUN a person or animal that searches for things among waste and rubbish

**scenario scenarios**

NOUN **1** the way in which a situation might develop in the future ● *That is the worst possible scenario!*
NOUN **2** a piece of writing that gives an outline of the story in a film

**scene scenes**

NOUN part of a play or film in which a series of events happen in one place

**scenery**

NOUN **1** In the countryside, you can refer to everything you see as the **scenery**.
NOUN **2** In a theatre, the **scenery** is the painted cloth on the stage that makes it seem like a particular place.

a
b
c
d
e
f
g
h
i
j
k
l
m
n
o
p
q
r
s
t
u
v
w
x
y
z

**353**

**scent** scents
NOUN a smell, especially a pleasant one

**sceptic** sceptics
NOUN someone who does not believe things easily

---

**PRONUNCIATION TIP**
This word is pronounced **skep**-tik.

---

**schedule** schedules
NOUN a list of events or things you have to do, and the times at which each thing should be done or will happen

**scheme** schemes, scheming, schemed
NOUN **1** a plan or arrangement
VERB **2** When people **scheme**, they make secret plans.

**scholar** scholars
NOUN **1** a person who studies an academic subject and knows a lot about it
NOUN **2** In South African English, a **scholar** is a school pupil.

**scholarship** scholarships
NOUN If you win a **scholarship** to a school or university, your studies are paid for by the school or university, or by some other organisation.

**school** schools
NOUN a place where children are educated

**science** sciences
NOUN the study of living things, materials and physical processes such as forces, electricity, sound and light

**science fiction**
NOUN stories about travelling through space, and imaginary events happening in the future or in other worlds

**scientist** scientists
NOUN someone who studies science or is an expert in science

**scissors**
PLURAL NOUN a cutting tool with two sharp blades

**scold** scolds, scolding, scolded
VERB If you **scold** someone, you tell them off.

**scone** scones
NOUN a small cake made from flour and fat, and usually eaten with cream and jam

**scoop** scoops, scooping, scooped
VERB **1** If you **scoop** something up, you it up using a spoon or the palm of your hand.
NOUN **2** an object like a large spoon that is used for picking up food such as ice cream

**scooter** scooters
NOUN **1** a small, light motorcycle
NOUN **2** a simple cycle that a child rides, with two wheels and a narrow platform standing on while pushing the ground w one foot

**scope**
NOUN **1** the opportunity or freedom to do something
NOUN **2** the extent of something • *That sub is beyond the **scope** of this lesson.*

**scorch** scorches, scorching, scorched
VERB If you **scorch** something, you burn i slightly.

**score** scores, scoring, scored
VERB **1** If you **score** in a game, you get a goal, a run or a point.
NOUN **2** the number of goals, runs or point obtained by the two opponents in a game
NOUN **3** the written version of a piece of music which shows the parts for each musician

**scornful**
ADJECTIVE If you are **scornful** of something someone, you think very little of them and show very little respect for them.

**scorpion** scorpions
NOUN an animal that looks like a small lobster. It has a long tail with a poisonous sting on the end.

**scour** scours, scouring, scoured
VERB **1** If you **scour** a place, you look all ov it in order to find something.
VERB **2** If you **scour** something like a pan, you clean it by rubbing it hard with something rough.

**scout** scouts, scouting, scouted
NOUN **1** A **Scout** is a boy who is a member of the **Scout** Association, an organisation for boys that aims to develop character an responsibility.
NOUN **2** someone who is sent on ahead to g information about something
VERB **3** If you **scout** around for something, you look around for it.

**wl scowls, scowling, scowled**

VERB **1** If you **scowl**, you frown because you
re angry.
OUN **2** an angry expression

**abble scrabbles, scrabbling, crabbled**

RB If you **scrabble** at something, you
rape at it with your hands.

**amble scrambles, scrambling, crambled**

ERB **1** If you **scramble** over something,
ou climb over it using your hands to
elp you.
ERB **2** When you **scramble** eggs, you mix
hem up and cook them in a pan.
OUN **3** a motorcycle race over rough
round

**ap scraps, scrapping, scrapped**

OUN **1** a very small piece of something
OUN **2** unwanted or waste material
OUN **3** (*informal*) If you get into a **scrap**, you
et into a fight.
ERB **4** If you **scrap** something, you get rid
of it.

**rapbook scrapbooks**

OUN a book with blank pages that you
can fill with photographs or cuttings that
nterest you

**rape scrapes, scraping, scraped**

VERB **1** If you **scrape** something off a
surface, you remove it by pulling a rough or
sharp object over it.
VERB **2** If you **scrape** past something, you
pass very close to it.

**ratch scratches, scratching, scratched**

VERB **1** If you **scratch** something, you make
a small cut or mark on it with something
sharp.
VERB **2** If you **scratch**, you rub your skin with
your nails because it is itching.
NOUN **3** a small cut or mark on the surface of
something

**rawl scrawls, scrawling, scrawled**

VERB **1** If you **scrawl** something, you write it
in a careless and untidy way.
NOUN **2** careless and untidy writing

**ream screams, screaming, screamed**

VERB **1** If you **scream**, you shout or cry in a
loud, high-pitched voice.
NOUN **2** a loud, high-pitched cry

**screech screeches, screeching, screeched**

VERB **1** If a person, animal or machine
**screeches**, they make an unpleasant, high-
pitched noise.
NOUN **2** an unpleasant high-pitched noise

**screen screens, screening, screened**

NOUN **1** a vertical surface on which a picture
can be shown, such as a phone, computer
or television **screen**

→ Have a look at the illustration for
**computer**

NOUN **2** a panel used to separate different
parts of a room, or to protect or hide
something
VERB **3** If a doctor **screens** you for a disease,
they test to see if you have it.

**screenplay screenplays**

NOUN the script of a film

**screw screws, screwing, screwed**

NOUN **1** a small, sharp piece of metal with
a spiral groove cut into it, used for fixing
things together or for fixing something to a
wall using a twisting action
VERB **2** If you **screw** something onto
something else, you fix it there by twisting it
round and round, or by using a screw. ● *He*
***screwed*** *the top on the ink bottle.*

**screw up**

VERB If you **screw up** paper or cloth, you
twist it or squeeze it into a tight ball.

**screwdriver screwdrivers**

NOUN a tool for putting in or taking out
screws

**scribble scribbles, scribbling, scribbled**

VERB **1** If you **scribble** something, you write
it quickly and untidily.
VERB **2** To **scribble** also means to make
meaningless marks. ● *When Caroline was
three she* ***scribbled*** *on a wall.*

**script scripts**

NOUN the written version of a play or film

**scripture scriptures**

NOUN sacred writings, especially the Bible

**scroll scrolls, scrolling, scrolled**

NOUN **1** a long roll of paper or parchment
with writing on it
VERB **2** When you **scroll** text on a computer
screen, you move it up or down to see the
text that is not visible on the screen.

a
b
c
d
e
f
g
h
i
j
k
l
m
n
o
p
q
r
s
t
u
v
w
x
y
z

**scrounge** scrounges, scrounging, scrounged

VERB (*informal*) If you **scrounge** something, you get it by asking for it rather than by earning or buying it.

**scrub** scrubs, scrubbing, scrubbed

VERB **1** If you **scrub** something, you clean it by rubbing it very hard, especially with a brush and water.

NOUN **2** ground covered with bushes and small trees

**scruffy** scruffier, scruffiest

ADJECTIVE untidy

**scrum** scrums

NOUN When rugby players form a **scrum**, they form a group and push against each other with their heads down in an attempt to get the ball.

**scuba diving**

NOUN the sport of swimming underwater with special breathing equipment

---

**WORD HISTORY**

an abbreviation for *self-contained underwater breathing apparatus*

---

**scuffle** scuffles, scuffling, scuffled

VERB **1** When people **scuffle**, they have a short, rough fight.

NOUN **2** a short, rough fight

**sculptor** sculptors

NOUN someone who makes sculptures

**sculpture** sculptures

NOUN a work of art made by shaping or carving stone, clay or wood

**scum**

NOUN a layer of dirty froth on the surface of a liquid

**scurry** scurries, scurrying, scurried

VERB If you **scurry**, you run with quick, short steps.

**scuttle** scuttles, scuttling, scuttled

VERB **1** If a person or an animal **scuttles**, they run with short, quick steps.

VERB **2** To **scuttle** a ship means to sink it deliberately by making holes in the bottom.

NOUN **3** a container for coal

**scythe** scythes

NOUN a tool with a long handle and a curved blade used for cutting grass or grain

**sea** seas

NOUN one of the areas of salty water that cover much of the Earth's surface • *They swam in the warm **sea**.*

**seafood**

PLURAL NOUN fish or shellfish from the sea eaten as food

**seagull** seagulls

NOUN a common white, grey and black bir that lives near the sea

**seahorse** seahorses

NOUN a small fish that swims upright, with head that looks rather like a horse's head

**seal** seals, sealing, sealed

NOUN **1** a fish-eating mammal with flippers that lives partly on land and partly in the s

NOUN **2** something fixed over the opening o a container that prevents anything gettin in or out, and which must be broken befor the container can be opened

VERB **3** If you **seal** an envelope, you stick down the flap.

**seam** seams

NOUN **1** a line of stitches joining two pieces of cloth

NOUN **2** a long, narrow layer of coal beneat the ground

**search** searches, searching, searched

VERB **1** If you **search** for something, you look for it very thoroughly. • *I spent an hou **searching** for my glasses.*

VERB **2** If a person is **searched**, their body and clothing are examined to see if they a hiding anything.

NOUN **3** an attempt to find something • *I found my purse after a long **search**.*

**search engine** search engines

NOUN a service on the internet which lets yo search for information

**searchlight** searchlights

NOUN a light with a powerful beam that car be turned in different directions

**seashore**

NOUN the land along the edge of the sea

**seasick**

ADJECTIVE feeling sick because of the movement of a boat

**seaside**

NOUN a place by the sea, especially where people go on holiday

**son seasons, seasoning, seasoned**
NOUN **1** one of the periods into which a year
is divided and which have their own typical
weather conditions. The **seasons** are
spring, summer, autumn and winter.
VERB **2** If you **season** food, you add salt,
pepper, herbs or spices to it.

**asoning seasonings**
NOUN something with a strong taste, like
salt, pepper or spices, used to add flavour
to food

**at seats**
NOUN something you can sit on

**at belt seat belts**
NOUN a strap that you put around your body
for safety when you are travelling in a car,
coach or aircraft

**aweed**
NOUN plants that grow in the sea

**cluded**
ADJECTIVE quiet and hidden from view • *We
found a lovely **secluded** beach.*

**cond seconds**
ADJECTIVE **1** The **second** item in a series is the
one that you count as number two. It can be
written as 2$^{nd}$.
NOUN **2** one of the sixty parts that a minute is
divided into

**econdary**
ADJECTIVE **1** Something **secondary** is less
important than something else.
ADJECTIVE **2** **Secondary** education is
education for pupils between the ages of 11
and 18.

**econdary school secondary schools**
NOUN a school for pupils aged between 11
and 18

**econd-hand**
ADJECTIVE Something that is **second-hand**
has already been owned by someone else.

**econd person**
NOUN In grammar, you use the **second person**
*you* when you speak or write to someone
directly, for example, *you said, you are.*

**ecret secrets**
ADJECTIVE **1** Something that is **secret** is known
to only a small number of people and hidden
from everyone else. • *a **secret** meeting*
NOUN **2** something known to only a small
number of people and hidden from everyone
else

**secretary secretaries**
NOUN a person employed by an organisation
to keep records, write letters and do office
work

**secretive**
ADJECTIVE **Secretive** people tend to hide their
feelings and intentions, and like to keep
things secret.

**sect sects**
NOUN a group of people who have special or
unusual religious beliefs

**section sections**
NOUN one of the parts that something is
divided into

**secure secures, securing, secured**
VERB **1** If you **secure** something, you make it
safe or fix it firmly.
ADJECTIVE **2** If something is **secure**, it is safe
from harm.

**security**
NOUN all the things you do to make sure that
you and your property are safe

**sedimentary**
ADJECTIVE formed from fragments of many
layers of shell or rock

**see sees, seeing, saw, seen**
VERB **1** If you **see** something, you look at it or
notice it with your eyes.
VERB **2** If you **see** something, you understand
it or realise what it means. • *I **see** what you
mean.*
VERB **3** If you **see** that something happens,
you make sure that it is done.

**seed seeds**
NOUN the part of a plant that can grow into a
new plant of the same type
→ Have a look at the illustration for **plant**

**seek seeks, seeking, sought**
VERB (*formal*) If you **seek** something, you try
to find it.

**seem seems, seeming, seemed**
VERB If something **seems** to be the case, it
appears to be the case, or you think it is the
case.

**seen**
VERB the past participle of **see**

**seep seeps, seeping, seeped**
VERB If a liquid or gas **seeps**, it flows very
slowly.

a
b
c
d
e
f
g
h
i
j
k
l
m
n
o
p
q
r
s
t
u
v
w
x
y
z

357

A
B
C
D
E
F
G
H
I
J
K
L
M
N
O
P
Q
R
S
T
U
V
W
X
Y
Z

**seesaw seesaws**

NOUN a long plank supported in the middle, so that one person can sit on either end and each can move up and down

**seethe seethes, seething, seethed**

VERB **1** When a liquid **seethes**, it boils or bubbles.

ADJECTIVE **2** If you are **seething**, you are very angry.

**segment segments**

NOUN **1** one part of something

NOUN **2** The **segments** of an orange or grapefruit are the sections you can divide it into.

**segregate segregates, segregating, segregated**

VERB To **segregate** two groups of people means to keep them apart from each other.

**seize seizes, seizing, seized**

VERB If you **seize** something, you grab it firmly.

**seldom**

ADVERB not very often ● *They **seldom** watch television.*

**select selects, selecting, selected**

VERB If you **select** something, you choose it.

**self selves**

NOUN your own personality or nature that makes you different from anyone else

**self-conscious**

ADJECTIVE Someone who is **self-conscious** is easily embarrassed, and worried about what other people think of them. ● *She was **self-conscious** when the teacher asked her to read her poem.*

**self-defence**

NOUN the use of special physical techniques to protect yourself when someone attacks you

**selfie selfies**

NOUN (*informal*) a photograph taken by pointing a camera at yourself

**selfish**

ADJECTIVE caring only about yourself, and not about other people

**self-service**

ADJECTIVE A **self-service** shop or restaurant is one where you serve yourself.

**sell sells, selling, sold**

VERB If you **sell** something, you let someo have it in return for money.

**Sellotape**

NOUN (trademark) a transparent sticky tape

**semaphore**

NOUN a system of signalling by holding fla out with your arms in different positions show letters of the alphabet

**semi-**

PREFIX You add **semi-** to the beginning of c word to mean half or partly. For example, **semi**circle is half of a circle.

**semicircle semicircles**

NOUN a half of a circle, or something with this shape

**semicircular**

ADJECTIVE having the shape of a half circle

**semicolon semicolons**

NOUN the punctuation mark (;) is used to separate different parts of a sentence or to show a pause

**semidetached**

ADJECTIVE A **semidetached** house is joined another house on one side.

**semifinal semifinals**

NOUN one of the two matches or races in a competition that are held to decide who w compete in the final

**send sends, sending, sent**

VERB **1** When you **send** something to someone, you arrange for it to be delivered to them.

VERB **2** If a person **sends** someone somewhere, they tell them to go there.

**senile**

ADJECTIVE If old people become **senile**, they become confused and cannot look after themselves.

**nior seniors**

ADJECTIVE **1** A **senior** official or employee has one of the highest and most important jobs in an organisation.

NOUN **2** If you are someone's **senior**, you are older than they are, or in a more important position.

**nior citizen senior citizens**

NOUN an elderly person, especially one receiving a pension

**nsation sensations**

NOUN **1** a feeling that you have

NOUN **2** If something causes a **sensation**, it causes great interest and excitement.

**nsational**

ADJECTIVE **1** (*informal*) extremely good
• *The concert was sensational.*

ADJECTIVE **2** causing great excitement or interest

**ense senses**

NOUN **1** the physical abilities of sight, hearing, smell, touch and taste • *I have a good sense of smell.*

NOUN **2** a feeling • *a sense of guilt*

NOUN **3** the ability to think and behave sensibly

PHRASE **4** If something **makes sense**, you can understand it or it seems sensible.

**enseless**

ADJECTIVE **1** Something **senseless** has no reason to it. • *The violence of the hooligans was senseless.*

ADJECTIVE **2** If someone is **senseless**, they are unconscious.

**ensible**

ADJECTIVE showing good sense and judgment

**sensitive**

ADJECTIVE **1** If you are **sensitive**, you understand other people's feelings.

| SYNONYM: perceptive |

ADJECTIVE **2** If you are **sensitive** about something, you are easily worried or upset about it.

| SYNONYM: touchy |

ADJECTIVE **3** easily affected or harmed by something • *My skin is sensitive to the sun.*

**sent**

VERB the past tense and past participle of **send**

**sentence sentences, sentencing, sentenced**

NOUN **1** a group of words that make a statement, question or command. When written down, a **sentence** begins with a capital letter and ends with a full stop.

NOUN **2** In a law court, a **sentence** is a punishment given to someone who has been found guilty.

VERB **3** When a guilty person is **sentenced**, they are told officially what their punishment will be.

**sentimental**

ADJECTIVE **1** having an exaggerated feeling of tenderness or sadness

ADJECTIVE **2** having something to do with a person's feelings

**sentry sentries**

NOUN a soldier who keeps watch and guards a camp or building

**separate separates, separating, separated**

ADJECTIVE **1** If something is **separate** from something else, the two things are not connected.

VERB **2** If you **separate** people or things, you cause them to be apart from each other.

VERB **3** If people or things **separate**, they move away from each other.

---

LANGUAGE TIP
There are two *as* in *separate*.

---

**September**

NOUN the ninth month of the year. **September** has 30 days.

---

WORD HISTORY
from the Latin word *septem* meaning seven, because it was the seventh month of the Roman calendar

---

**septic**

ADJECTIVE If a wound becomes **septic**, it becomes infected by harmful bacteria.

**sequel sequels**

NOUN A **sequel** to a book or film is another book or film that continues the story.

**sequence sequences**

NOUN **1** a number of events coming one after the other

NOUN **2** the order in which things are arranged or happen • *Put the pictures in sequence to tell the story.*

a
b
c
d
e
f
g
h
i
j
k
l
m
n
o
p
q
r
s
t
u
v
w
x
y
z

**359**

**serene**

ADJECTIVE peaceful and calm

**sergeant** **sergeants**

NOUN a rank in the police force, the army or the air force

**serial** **serials**

NOUN a story that is broadcast or published in a number of parts over a period of time

**series**

NOUN **1** a number of things coming one after the other

NOUN **2** A radio or television **series** is a set of programmes with the same title.

NOUN **3** A **series** circuit is an electric circuit in which the current passes through each element in order.

**serious**

ADJECTIVE **1** A **serious** problem or situation is very bad and worrying.

ADJECTIVE **2** **Serious** matters are important and should be thought about carefully.

ADJECTIVE **3** If you are **serious** about something, you really mean it.

ADJECTIVE **4** People who are **serious** are thoughtful, quiet and do not laugh much.

**sermon** **sermons**

NOUN a talk on a religious or moral subject given as part of a church service

**serpent** **serpents**

NOUN (*literary*) a snake

**servant** **servants**

NOUN someone who is employed to work in another person's house

**serve** **serves, serving, served**

VERB **1** If you **serve** food or drink to people, you give it to them.

VERB **2** When someone **serves** customers in a shop, bar or restaurant, they help them and supply them with what they want.

• *The shop was very busy so we had to wait for the assistant to serve us.*

VERB **3** In some games, such as tennis, when you **serve** you start the game by hitting the ball to your opponent.

**server** **servers**

NOUN part of a computer network which does a particular task, for example storing information, for all or part of the network

**service** **services**

NOUN **1** a system organised to provide something for the public • *The bus service from our village into town is very good.*

NOUN **2** Motorway **services** consist of a pe[tro]l station, toilets, a shop and a restaurant.

NOUN **3** If your car has a **service**, it is checked over and repaired if it is broken o[r] damaged.

NOUN **4** a religious ceremony

**session** **sessions**

NOUN the period during which an activity takes place

**set** **sets, setting, set**

VERB **1** When something such as jelly or concrete **sets**, it changes from a liquid in[to] a solid.

NOUN **2** a group of things that go together

NOUN **3** In mathematics, a **set** is a collectio[n] of numbers that are treated as a group.

NOUN **4** In tennis, a **set** is a group of six or more games.

VERB **5** If you **set** your watch or clock, you adjust it for a particular time.

ADJECTIVE **6** If you do something at a **set** tim[e] it is fixed at that time and does not change

**settee** **settees**

NOUN a long comfortable seat for two or three people to sit on

SYNONYM: sofa

**setting** **settings**

NOUN The **setting** of something like a play or a story is its surroundings, and where it happens.

**settle** **settles, settling, settled**

VERB **1** If you **settle** something, you decide on it or sort it out. • *Let's settle this argumen[t] as quickly as possible.*

VERB **2** If you **settle** in a place, you make it your home.

VERB **3** If you **settle**, or **settle** down, you relax and make yourself comfortable.

VERB **4** If snow or dust **settles**, it sinks slowl[y] down and comes to rest.

**settlement** **settlements**

NOUN a place where people have settled and made their homes

**seven**

NOUN **Seven** is the number 7.

**seventeen**

NOUN **Seventeen** is the number 17.

**venteenth seventeenths**

OUN **1** one of seventeen equal parts of omething

DJECTIVE **2** The **seventeenth** item in a eries is the one that you count as number eventeen.

**venth sevenths**

OUN **1** one of seven equal parts of omething. It can be written as ½.

DJECTIVE **2** The **seventh** item in a series is he one that you count as number seven. It an be written as 7ᵗʰ.

**ventieth seventieths**

OUN **1** one of seventy equal parts of omething

DJECTIVE **2** The **seventieth** item in a series is he one that you count as number seventy.

**venty**

OUN **Seventy** is the number 70.

**ver severs, severing, severed**

ERB If you **sever** something, you cut it off or ut right through it.

RONUNCIATION TIP

his word rhymes with "never".

**veral**

DJECTIVE used to refer to a small number of eople or things ● There were **several** blue oxes on the table.

**vere**

DJECTIVE **1** extremely bad or serious

DJECTIVE **2** strict or harsh

RONUNCIATION TIP

his word is pronounced with suh-**veer**.

**w sews, sewing, sewed, sewn**

ERB When you **sew** something, you use a eedle and thread to make or mend it.

**wage**

OUN dirty water and waste that is carried way in drains from buildings

**wer sewers**

OUN a series of pipes and drains that carries way dirty water and waste from buildings

**x sexes**

OUN **1** one of the two groups, male and emale, into which animals, including umans, are divided

OUN **2** the physical activity by which people nd animals produce young

**sexism**

NOUN the belief that one gender is less intelligent or less able than the other, or in some way not as good as the other

**sexist sexists**

ADJECTIVE **1** believing that one gender is less intelligent or less good at doing something than the other

NOUN **2** someone who believes that one gender is less intelligent or less good at doing something than the other

**shabby shabbier, shabbiest**

ADJECTIVE Something or someone who is **shabby** looks old and ragged.

**shack shacks**

NOUN a small, roughly built hut

**shade shades, shading, shaded**

NOUN **1** an area of darkness and coolness that sunshine does not reach

NOUN **2** the different forms of a colour. For example, olive green is a **shade** of green.

NOUN **3** an object that decreases or shuts out light, such as a lampshade

VERB **4** If you **shade** a person or a thing, you protect them from the sun's heat or light.

**shadow shadows, shadowing, shadowed**

NOUN **1** the dark shape formed when an opaque object stops light from reaching a surface

VERB **2** When you **shadow** someone, you follow them and watch them closely.

**shady shadier, shadiest**

ADJECTIVE A **shady** place is sheltered from the sunlight by trees or buildings.

**shaft shafts**

NOUN **1** A **shaft** in a mine or for a lift is a passage that goes straight down.

NOUN **2** a beam of light

NOUN **3** In a machine, the **shaft** is a rod that turns in order to transmit power or movement.

**shaggy shaggier, shaggiest**

ADJECTIVE covered with thick, long, untidy hair

**shake shakes, shaking, shook, shaken**

VERB **1** If you **shake** something, you move it quickly from side to side or up and down.

VERB **2** If something **shakes**, it moves from side to side or up and down with small, quick movements.

VERB **3** When you **shake** your head, you move it from side to side in order to say no.

a
b
c
d
e
f
g
h
i
j
k
l
m
n
o
p
q
r
s
t
u
v
w
x
y
z

NOUN **4** If you give something a **shake**, you shake it.

PHRASE **5** When you **shake hands** with someone, you grasp their hand in yours as a way of greeting them.

## shaky shakier, shakiest
ADJECTIVE rather weak, shaking and unsteady • *The foal got up on **shaky** legs.*

## shall should
VERB used with *I* and *we* to refer to the future • *I **shall** go shopping tomorrow.* • *I **should** wait till next week to open my birthday present.*

## shallow shallower, shallowest
ADJECTIVE not deep • *The water here is quite **shallow**.*

## shame
NOUN **1** the feeling of guilt or embarrassment you get when you know you have done something wrong or foolish
NOUN **2** If you say something is a **shame**, you mean you are sorry about it. • *It's a **shame** you can't come round to tea.*

## shampoo shampoos
NOUN a soapy liquid used for washing your hair

---

**WORD HISTORY**
from the Hindi word *champna* meaning press or massage

---

## shamrock shamrocks
NOUN a plant with three round leaves on each stem, which is the national emblem of Ireland

---

**WORD HISTORY**
from Irish Gaelic *seamrog* meaning little clover

---

## shanty shanties
NOUN **1** a small, rough hut
NOUN **2** A sea **shanty** is a song sailors used to sing.

## shape shapes
NOUN **1** The **shape** of something is the form or pattern of its outline, for example whether it is round or square. • *The chocolates came in a box in the **shape** of a heart.*
NOUN **2** something with a definite form, for example a circle or square

## share shares, sharing, shared
VERB **1** If two people **share** something, the both use it, do it, or have it. • *We **shared** bar of chocolate.*
NOUN **2** A **share** of something is a portion it. • *I want a fair **share** of the cake.*

### share out
VERB If you **share out** something, you g it out equally among a group of people • *They **shared out** the food between ther*

## shark sharks
NOUN a large, powerful fish, usually with t fins on its back and rows of sharp teeth

## sharp sharper, sharpest
ADJECTIVE **1** A **sharp** object has an edge or point that is good for cutting or piercing things.
ADJECTIVE **2** A **sharp** change is sudden and noticeable. • *There was a **sharp** rise in temperature after the sun came up.*
ADJECTIVE **3** A **sharp** taste is sour.
ADJECTIVE **4** Someone who is **sharp** can pick up ideas very quickly.
ADJECTIVE **5** A **sharp** pain is strong and sudden.

## sharpen sharpens, sharpening, sharpened
VERB If you **sharpen** an object such as a knife, you make its edge or point sharper.

## shatter shatters, shattering, shattere
VERB If something **shatters**, it breaks into a lot of small pieces. • *The glass **shattered** when it hit the floor.*

## shave shaves, shaving, shaved
VERB When someone **shaves**, they remove hair with a razor from part of their body.

## shavings
PLURAL NOUN small, fine pieces of wood that have been cut off a larger piece

## shawl shawls
NOUN a large piece of cloth worn round a woman's head or shoulders, or used to wr a baby in

## she
PRONOUN **She** is used to refer to a woman o girl who has already been mentioned.

## sheaf sheaves
NOUN **1** a bundle of papers
NOUN **2** a bundle of ripe corn

## shear shears, shearing, sheared, shor
VERB When someone **shears** a sheep, they cut the wool off it.

**ears**

PLURAL NOUN **Shears** are a tool like a large pair of scissors, used especially for cutting hedges.

**eath sheaths**

NOUN a cover for the blade of a knife or a sword

**e'd**

a contraction of *she had* or *she would*

**ed sheds, shedding, shed**

NOUN **1** a small building used for storing things, especially in a garden
VERB **2** When an animal **sheds** hair or skin, some of it comes off.
VERB **3** If you **shed** tears, you cry.

**een**

NOUN a gentle shine on the surface of something

**eep**

NOUN a mammal kept on farms for its meat and wool

---

LANGUAGE TIP
The plural of *sheep* is *sheep*.

---

**eepdog sheepdogs**

NOUN a breed of dog often used for controlling sheep

**eepish**

ADJECTIVE If you look **sheepish**, you look shy or embarrassed.

**eer sheerer, sheerest**

ADJECTIVE **1** A **sheer** cliff or drop is vertical.
ADJECTIVE **2** complete and total • *sheer exhaustion*
ADJECTIVE **3** **Sheer** fabrics are very light and delicate.

**eet sheets**

NOUN **1** a large rectangular piece of cloth used to cover a bed
NOUN **2** a rectangular piece of paper

**eikh sheikhs**

NOUN an Arab chief or ruler

---

PRONUNCIATION TIP
This word rhymes with "make".

---

WORD HISTORY
from Arabic *shaykh* meaning old man

---

**elf shelves**

NOUN a flat piece of wood, metal or glass fixed to a wall or a cabinet or cupboard and used for putting things on

**she'll**

a contraction of *she will* or *she shall*

**shell shells**

NOUN **1** the hard covering of an egg or nut
NOUN **2** the hard, protective covering on the back of a tortoise, snail or crab

**shellfish shellfish** or **shellfishes**

NOUN a small sea creature with a shell

**shelter shelters, sheltering, sheltered**

NOUN **1** a small building made to protect people from bad weather or danger • *We waited in the bus **shelter**.*
NOUN **2** If a place gives **shelter**, it protects you from bad weather or danger.
VERB **3** If you **shelter** in a place, you stay there and are safe and protected.
VERB **4** To **shelter** someone or something means to protect them from bad weather or danger.

**shepherd shepherds**

NOUN a person who looks after sheep

**sheriff sheriffs**

NOUN **1** in America, a person elected to enforce the law in a county
NOUN **2** in Scotland, the senior judge of a county or district
NOUN **3** in Australia, an officer of the Supreme Court who does certain paperwork

**sherry sherries**

NOUN a kind of strong wine

**she's**

a contraction of *she is* or *she has*

**shield shields, shielding, shielded**

NOUN **1** a large piece of a strong material like metal or plastic that soldiers or police officers carry to protect themselves
VERB **2** If you **shield** someone or something, you protect them from something. • *He **shielded** his eyes from the sun with his hand.*

**shift shifts, shifting, shifted**

VERB **1** If you **shift** something, you move it.
VERB **2** If something **shifts**, it moves.
NOUN **3** a set period during which people work • *the night **shift***

**shilling shillings**

NOUN a coin that was once used in Britain, Australia and New Zealand. There were 20 **shillings** in a pound.

a
b
c
d
e
f
g
h
i
j
k
l
m
n
o
p
q
r
s
t
u
v
w
x
y
z

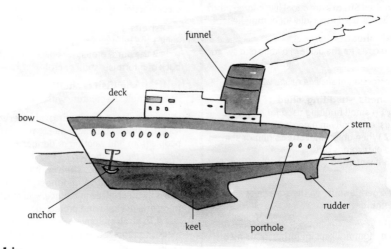

funnel

deck

bow

stern

anchor

keel

porthole

rudder

### ship

**shimmer** shimmers, shimmering, shimmered

VERB **1** If something **shimmers**, it shines with a faint, flickering light.

NOUN **2** a faint, flickering light

**shin** shins

NOUN the front part of your leg between your knee and your ankle

**shine** shines, shining, shone or shined

VERB **1** When something **shines**, it is bright because it gives out or reflects light.

VERB **2** If you **shine** a torch or lamp somewhere, you point it there so that it becomes light.

VERB **3** If you **shine** your shoes, you polish them.

**shingle**

NOUN small pebbles on the seashore

**shingles**

PLURAL NOUN a disease that causes a painful red rash, especially around the waist

**shiny** shinier, shiniest

ADJECTIVE **Shiny** things are bright and look as if they have been polished.

**ship** ships, shipping, shipped

NOUN **1** a large boat that carries passengers or cargo

VERB **2** If people or things are **shipped** somewhere, they are transported there by ship.

→ Have a look at the illustration

**shipwreck** shipwrecks; shipwrecked

NOUN **1** When there is a **shipwreck**, a ship destroyed in a storm or an accident at sea

NOUN **2** the remains of a ship that has bee damaged or sunk

ADJECTIVE **3** If someone is **shipwrecked**, the survive a shipwreck and manage to reach land.

**shipyard** shipyards

NOUN a place where ships are built and repaired

**shirk** shirks, shirking, shirked

VERB If you **shirk** a task, you try to avoid doing it.

**shirt** shirts

NOUN a piece of clothing with a collar, sleeves and buttons down the front, worn on the upper part of the body

**shiver** shivers, shivering, shivered

VERB When you **shiver**, you tremble slight because you are cold or scared.

**shoal** shoals

NOUN a large group of fish swimming together

**ock shocks, shocking, shocked**
NOUN **1** a sudden upsetting experience
VERB **2** If something **shocks** you, it
upsets you because it is unpleasant and
unexpected.

**ocking**
ADJECTIVE **1** Something that shocks people is
**shocking**.
ADJECTIVE **2** (*informal*) very bad • *The weather
has been shocking*.

**oddy shoddier, shoddiest**
ADJECTIVE badly made or done

**oe shoes**
NOUN a strong covering for each of your feet.
**Shoes** cover most of your foot, but not your
ankle.

**oelace shoelaces**
NOUN a cord for fastening a shoe

**one**
VERB the past tense and past participle of
**shine**

**ook**
VERB the past tense of **shake**

**oot shoots, shooting, shot**
VERB **1** If someone **shoots** a person or an
animal, they injure or kill them by firing a
gun at them.
VERB **2** When a film is **shot**, it is filmed.

**ooting star shooting stars**
NOUN a meteor

**op shops, shopping, shopped**
NOUN **1** a place where things are sold
NOUN **2** a place where a particular type of
work is done • *a bicycle repair shop*
VERB **3** When you **shop**, you go to the shops
to buy things.

**opkeeper shopkeepers**
NOUN someone who owns or manages a
small shop

**opping**
NOUN Your **shopping** is the goods you have
bought in a shop.

**ore shores**
NOUN the land along the edge of a sea, lake
or wide river

**ort shorter, shortest**
ADJECTIVE **1** not lasting very long
ADJECTIVE **2** small in length, distance or height
ADJECTIVE **3** If you are **short** of something, you
do not have enough of it.

ADJECTIVE **4** If a name is **short** for another
name, it is a quick way of saying it. • *her
friend Kes (**short** for Kesewa)*

**shortage shortages**
NOUN If there is a **shortage** of something,
there is not enough of it.

**shortcut shortcuts**
NOUN **1** a quicker way of getting somewhere
than the usual route
NOUN **2** a quicker way of doing something
than the usual way

**shorten shortens, shortening,
shortened**
VERB If you **shorten** something, you make it
shorter.

ANTONYM: lengthen

**shorthand**
NOUN a way of writing in which signs
represent words or syllables. It is used to
write down quickly what someone is saying.

**shortly**
ADVERB soon • *I'll be there shortly.*

**shorts**
PLURAL NOUN trousers with legs that stop at or
above the knee

**short-sighted**
ADJECTIVE If you are **short-sighted**, you
cannot see things clearly when they are far
away.

**shot shots**
VERB **1** the past tense of **shoot**
NOUN **2** the act of firing a gun
NOUN **3** In football, golf, tennis and other
ball games, a **shot** is the act of kicking or
hitting the ball.
NOUN **4** a photograph or short film sequence

**should**
VERB **1** You use **should** to say that
something ought to happen. • *Kylie should
have done better.*
VERB **2** You also use **should** to say that you
expect something to happen. • *We should
have heard by now.*
VERB **3** **Should** is used in questions where
you are asking someone for advice about
what to do. • *Should we tell her about it?*

**shoulder shoulders**
NOUN Your **shoulders** are the parts of your
body between your neck and the tops of
your arms.

a
b
c
d
e
f
g
h
i
j
k
l
m
n
o
p
q
r
s
t
u
v
w
x
y
z

**365**

**shouldn't**
VERB a contraction of *should not*

**shout** **shouts, shouting, shouted**
NOUN **1** a loud call or cry
VERB **2** If you **shout** something, you say it very loudly.

**shove** **shoves, shoving, shoved**
VERB **1** If you **shove** someone or something, you push them roughly.
NOUN **2** a rough push

**shovel** **shovels, shovelling, shovelled**
NOUN **1** a tool like a spade, with the sides curved up, used for moving earth or snow
VERB **2** If you **shovel** earth or snow, you move it with a shovel.

**show** **shows, showing, showed, shown**
VERB **1** If you **show** someone something, you let them see it.
VERB **2** If you **show** someone how to do something, you demonstrate it to them.
• *Jake **showed** me how to make a chocolate cake.*
VERB **3** If something **shows**, you can see it.
VERB **4** If you **show** someone to a room or seat, you lead them there.
NOUN **5** a form of entertainment at the theatre or on television • *My favourite talk **show** is on TV tonight.*
NOUN **6** a display or exhibition • *a flower **show***

**show off**
VERB (*informal*) If someone is **showing off**, they are trying to impress people.

**shower** **showers, showering, showered**
NOUN **1** a device that sprays you with water so that you can wash yourself
NOUN **2** If you have a **shower**, you wash yourself by standing under a **shower**.
NOUN **3** a short period of rain
VERB **4** If you are **showered** with a lot of things, they fall on you like rain.

**showroom** **showrooms**
NOUN a shop where goods such as cars or electrical items are displayed for customers to look at

**shrank**
VERB the past tense of **shrink**

**shrapnel**
NOUN small pieces of metal scattered from an exploding shell

WORD HISTORY
named after General Henry *Shrapnel* (1761–1842), who invented it

**shred** **shreds, shredding, shredded**
VERB **1** If you **shred** something, you cut or tear it into very small pieces.
NOUN **2** a small, narrow piece of paper or material

**shrew** **shrews**
NOUN a small mouse-like mammal with a long pointed nose

**shrewd** **shrewder, shrewdest**
ADJECTIVE Someone who is **shrewd** makes good judgments and uses their common sense.

**shriek** **shrieks, shrieking, shrieked**
NOUN **1** a high-pitched cry or scream
VERB **2** If you **shriek**, you make a high-pitched cry or scream.

**shrill** **shriller, shrillest**
ADJECTIVE A **shrill** sound is unpleasantly hi-pitched and piercing.

**shrimp** **shrimps**
NOUN a small edible shellfish with a long t and many legs

**shrine** **shrines**
NOUN a place of worship connected with a sacred person or object

**shrink** **shrinks, shrinking, shrank, shrunk**
VERB If something **shrinks**, it becomes smaller.

**shrinkage**
NOUN the amount by which something shrinks

**shrivel** **shrivels, shrivelling, shrivelled**
VERB When something **shrivels**, it become dry and withered.

**shrub** **shrubs**
NOUN a bushy plant with woody stems

**shrug** **shrugs, shrugging, shrugged**
VERB If you **shrug** your shoulders, you rais them slightly as a sign that you do not know or do not care about something.

**shrunk**
VERB the past participle of **shrink**

A B C D E F G H I J K L M N O P Q R S T U V W X Y Z

**udder shudders, shuddering, shuddered**

VERB **1** If you **shudder**, you tremble with fear or horror.

VERB **2** If a machine or vehicle **shudders**, it shakes violently.

NOUN **3** a shiver of fear or horror

**uffle shuffles, shuffling, shuffled**

VERB **1** If you **shuffle**, you walk without lifting your feet off the ground properly, so that they drag.

VERB **2** If you **shuffle** a pack of cards, you mix them up before you begin a game.

**ut shuts, shutting, shut**

VERB **1** If you **shut** something, you close it.

ADJECTIVE **2** If something is **shut**, it is closed.

**utter shutters**

NOUN **1** a screen that can be closed over a window

NOUN **2** the device in a camera that opens and closes to let light onto the film

**uttle shuttles**

ADJECTIVE **1** A **shuttle** service is an air, bus or train service that makes frequent journeys between two places.

NOUN **2** a type of American spacecraft

**uttlecock shuttlecocks**

NOUN the feathered object that players hit over the net in the game of badminton

**y shyer, shyest**

ADJECTIVE A **shy** person is quiet and uncomfortable in the company of other people.

**bling siblings**

NOUN (formal) Your **siblings** are your brothers and sisters.

**WORD HISTORY**

from Old English sibling meaning relative

**ck sicker, sickest**

ADJECTIVE **1** If you are **sick**, you are ill.

ADJECTIVE **2** If you feel **sick**, you feel as if you are going to vomit.

ADJECTIVE **3** If you are **sick**, you vomit.

**ckness sicknesses**

NOUN an illness or disease

**de sides, siding, sided**

NOUN **1** a position to the left or right of something • There were trees on both **sides** of the road.

NOUN **2** The **sides** of something are its outside surfaces, or edges, that are not at the top, bottom, front or back. • There is a label on the **side** of the box.

NOUN **3** The **sides** of an area, surface or object are its different surfaces or edges. • Write on one **side** of the paper.

NOUN **4** Your **sides** are the parts of your body from your armpits down to your hips.

NOUN **5** The two **sides** in a war, argument or relationship are the two people or groups involved. • Whose **side** are you on?

ADJECTIVE **6** situated on a side of a building or vehicle • the **side** door

VERB **7** If you side with someone, you support them in a quarrel or an argument.

**sideways**

ADVERB moving or facing towards one side • I took a step **sideways**.

**siding sidings**

NOUN a short railway track beside the main tracks, where engines and carriages are left when not in use

**siege sieges**

NOUN a military operation in which an army surrounds a place to stop food or help from reaching the people inside

**sieve sieves, sieving, sieved**

NOUN **1** a tool made of mesh, used for sifting or straining things

VERB **2** If you **sieve** a powder or liquid, you pass it through a sieve to get rid of lumps and make it smooth.

**sift sifts, sifting, sifted**

VERB If you **sift** a powdery substance like flour or sugar, you pass it through a sieve to remove lumps.

**sigh sighs, sighing, sighed**

VERB When you **sigh**, you let out a deep breath, usually because you are tired, sad or relieved.

**sight sights**

NOUN **1** being able to see

NOUN **2** something you see • The sunset was a beautiful **sight**.

PLURAL NOUN **3** **Sights** are interesting places that tourists visit.

**sightseeing**

NOUN visiting the interesting places that tourists usually visit

a
b
c
d
e
f
g
h
i
j
k
l
m
n
o
p
q
r
s
t
u
v
w
x
y
z

**367**

## sign signs, signing, signed
NOUN **1** a mark or symbol that always has a particular meaning, for example in mathematics or music • *a plus **sign***
NOUN **2** a board or notice with words, a picture or a symbol on it, giving information or a warning • *a stop **sign***
VERB **3** If you **sign** a document, you write your name on it by hand, in the way you usually write it.

## signal signals
NOUN **1** a gesture, sound or action that is meant to give a message to someone
NOUN **2** A railway **signal** is a piece of equipment beside the track that tells train drivers whether or not to stop.

## signature signatures
NOUN If you write your **signature**, you write your name by hand in the way you usually write it.

## significant
ADJECTIVE **1** A **significant** amount is large enough to be noticed and to matter. • *A **significant** number of people can't read.*
ADJECTIVE **2** Something that is **significant** is important and means something.

## sign language
NOUN a way of communicating using your hands, used especially by deaf people

## signpost signposts
NOUN a road sign with information on it, such as the name of a town and how far away it is

## Sikh Sikhs
NOUN a person who believes in Sikhism, an Indian religion that separated from Hinduism in the 16th century and which teaches that there is only one God

## silence
NOUN When there is **silence**, there is no sound.

SYNONYM: quietness

## silent
ADJECTIVE **1** If you are **silent**, you are not saying anything.
ADJECTIVE **2** When something is **silent**, it makes no noise.

## silhouette silhouettes
NOUN the dark outline of a shape against a light background

## silicon
NOUN an element found in sand, clay and stone. It is used to make glass and parts of computers.

## silk silks
NOUN fine, soft cloth made from threads produced from silkworm cocoons

## sill sills
NOUN a strip of stone, wood or metal underneath a window or a door

## silly sillier, silliest
ADJECTIVE foolish or childish

## silver
NOUN a valuable greyish-white metal used for making jewellery and ornaments

## similar
ADJECTIVE If one thing is **similar** to another, they are quite like each other.

## simile similes
NOUN an expression in which a person or thing is described as being similar to someone or something else. An example of a **simile** is *she runs like a deer* and *he's as white as a sheet*.

## simmer simmers, simmering, simmered
VERB When food **simmers**, it cooks gently, just below boiling point.

## simple simpler, simplest
ADJECTIVE **1** Something that is **simple** is easy to understand or do.
ADJECTIVE **2** plain in style

## simplify simplifies, simplifying, simplified
VERB If you **simplify** something, you make simple or easy to understand.

## simply
ADVERB in a simple way

## simultaneous
ADJECTIVE Things that are **simultaneous** happen at the same time.

## sin sins, sinning, sinned
NOUN **1** wicked behaviour, particularly if it breaks a religious or moral law
VERB **2** To **sin** means to do something wicked

## since
PREPOSITION **1** from a particular time until now • *I've been waiting **since** half past three.*
ADVERB **2** from a particular time until now • *They met at school and have been friends ever **since**.*
CONJUNCTION **3** because • *I had a drink, **since** was feeling thirsty.*

**ncere**

ADJECTIVE If you are **sincere**, you are genuine and truly mean what you say.

**ncerely**

ADVERB used to show that you genuinely mean or feel something • *"Well done!" he said sincerely.*

**ing sings, singing, sang, sung**

VERB 1 When you **sing**, you make musical sounds with your voice, usually with words that fit a tune.

VERB 2 When birds or insects **sing**, they make pleasant and tuneful sounds.

**inge singes, singeing, singed**

VERB If you **singe** something, you burn it slightly so that it goes brown but does not catch fire.

**ingle singles**

ADJECTIVE 1 only one and not more • *A single copy of the book was on sale in the shop.*

ADJECTIVE 2 People who are **single** are not married.

ADJECTIVE 3 A **single** bed or bedroom is for one person.

NOUN 4 A **single**, or a **single** ticket, is a ticket for a journey to a place but not back again.

NOUN 5 a recording of one or two short pieces of music

**ingular**

NOUN In grammar, the **singular** is the form of a word that means just one person or thing.

ANTONYM: plural

**inister**

ADJECTIVE Something or someone **sinister** seems harmful or evil.

WORD HISTORY
from Latin *sinister* meaning left-hand side, because the left side was considered unlucky

**sink sinks, sinking, sank, sunk**

NOUN 1 a fixed basin with taps supplying water, usually in a kitchen or bathroom

VERB 2 If something **sinks**, it moves downwards, especially through water.

**sip sips, sipping, sipped**

VERB If you **sip** a drink, you take small mouthfuls.

**sir**

NOUN 1 (*formal*) a polite way to address a man

NOUN 2 **Sir** is the title of a knight or baronet.

**siren sirens**

NOUN a warning device, for example on an ambulance, that makes a loud, wailing noise • *The fire engines switched on their sirens as they raced to the fire.*

**sister sisters**

NOUN Your **sister** is a girl or woman who has the same parents as you.

**sister-in-law sisters-in-law**

NOUN Someone's **sister-in-law** is the sister of their husband or wife, or the wife of one of their siblings.

**sit sits, sitting, sat**

VERB When you **sit**, you rest your bottom on something such as a chair or the floor. • *We sat on the bench at the bus stop.*

**site sites**

NOUN 1 a piece of ground where something happens or will happen • *the site for the fairground*

NOUN 2 a place on the internet where you can find out about a particular subject or person

**sitting room sitting rooms**

NOUN a room with comfortable chairs for relaxing in

**situated**

ADJECTIVE in a particular place • *The cottage was situated on the edge of a forest.*

**situation situations**

NOUN 1 what is happening in a particular place at a particular time

NOUN 2 The **situation** of a town or a building is its surroundings and its position.

**six**

NOUN **Six** is the number 6.

**sixteen**

NOUN **Sixteen** is the number 16.

**sixteenth sixteenths**

NOUN 1 one of sixteen equal parts of something

ADJECTIVE 2 The **sixteenth** item in a series is the one that you count as number sixteen.

a
b
c
d
e
f
g
h
i
j
k
l
m
n
o
p
q
r
s
t
u
v
w
x
y
z

**369**

**sixth** sixths

NOUN **1** one of six equal parts of something. It can be written as ⅙.

ADJECTIVE **2** The **sixth** item in a series is the one that you count as number six. It can be written as 6$^{th}$.

**sixtieth** sixtieths

NOUN **1** one of sixty equal parts of something

ADJECTIVE **2** The **sixtieth** item in a series is the one that you count as number sixty.

**sixty**

NOUN **Sixty** is the number 60.

**size** sizes

NOUN **1** The **size** of something is how big it is.

NOUN **2** a standard measurement for clothes, shoes and other objects

**sizzle** sizzles, sizzling, sizzled

VERB If something **sizzles**, it makes a hissing sound. • The sausages **sizzled** in the frying pan.

**skate** skates, skating, skated

NOUN **1** Skates are ice **skates** or roller **skates**.

VERB **2** If you **skate**, you move about wearing skates.

**skateboard** skateboards

NOUN a narrow board on wheels, that you stand on and ride for fun

**skateboarding**

NOUN the activity of standing and riding on a skateboard

**skeleton** skeletons

NOUN the framework of bones in your body

→ Have a look at the illustration

**sketch** sketches, sketching, sketched

NOUN **1** a quick, rough drawing

VERB **2** If you **sketch** something, you draw it quickly and roughly.

**sketchy** sketchier, sketchiest

ADJECTIVE If something is **sketchy**, it has little detail. • The map showing how to get to the new house was **sketchy**.

**ski** skis, skiing, skied

NOUN **1** Skis are long pieces of wood, metal or plastic that you fasten to special boots so you can move easily on snow.

VERB **2** When you **ski**, you move on snow wearing skis, especially as a sport.

**WORD HISTORY**

from Old Norse skith meaning snowshoes

**skid** skids, skidding, skidded

VERB **1** If someone or something **skids**, they slide accidentally.

NOUN **2** a skidding movement

**skilful**

ADJECTIVE having a lot of skill

**skilfully**

ADVERB in a way that shows you have a lot of skill

**skill** skills

NOUN **1** the knowledge and ability that enable you to do something well

NOUN **2** a type of work or technique that needs special training and knowledge

• I would like to learn some new **skills**.

**skim** skims, skimming, skimmed

VERB **1** If you **skim** something from the surface of a liquid, you remove it.

VERB **2** If something **skims** a surface, it moves lightly, smoothly and quickly over it.

• seagulls **skimming** the waves

**skin** skins

NOUN **1** the natural covering of a person or animal

NOUN **2** the outer covering a fruit or vegetable

**skinny** skinnier, skinniest

ADJECTIVE thin

**skip** skips, skipping, skipped

VERB **1** When you **skip**, you jump lightly from one foot to the other, often over a rope.

VERB **2** If you **skip** something, you miss it out.

• Amy **skipped** the part with the long words.

**skipper** skippers

NOUN (informal) the captain of a ship or boat

**skirt** skirts

NOUN a piece of clothing that fastens at a woman's or girl's waist and hangs down over her legs

**skittle** skittles

NOUN **1** a wooden or plastic object, shaped like a bottle, that people try to knock down with a ball

NOUN **2** Skittles is a game in which players roll a ball and try to knock down objects called skittles.

# SKELETON

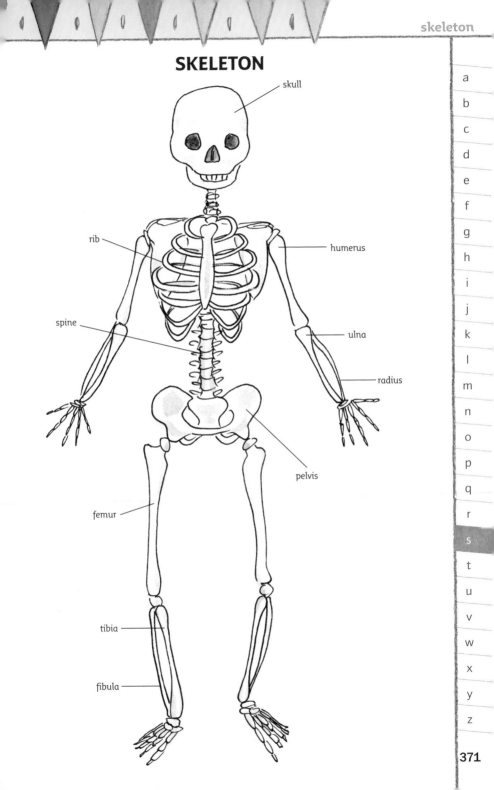

skull

rib

humerus

spine

ulna

radius

pelvis

femur

tibia

fibula

**skull skulls**
NOUN the bony part of your head that surrounds your brain
→ Have a look at the illustration for **skeleton**

**skunk skunks**
NOUN a small black and white animal from North America that gives off an unpleasant smell if it is frightened

**sky skies**
NOUN the space around the Earth that you can see when you look upwards

**Skype Skypes, Skyping, Skyped**
VERB If you **Skype** someone, you call them over the internet, usually with a video connection. • I **Skyped** Emma while she was in America.

**skyscraper skyscrapers**
NOUN a very tall building

**slab slabs**
NOUN a thick, flat piece of something, such as stone

**slack slacker, slackest**
ADJECTIVE Something that is **slack** is loose and not firmly stretched or pulled tight.

**slam slams, slamming, slammed**
VERB If you **slam** something, such as a door, or if it **slams**, it shuts with a loud bang.

**slang**
NOUN very informal words and expressions

**slant slants, slanting, slanted**
VERB 1 If something **slants**, it slopes.
NOUN 2 a slope or a leaning position

**slap slaps, slapping, slapped**
VERB 1 If you **slap** someone, you hit them with the palm of your hand.
NOUN 2 If you give someone a **slap**, you slap them.

**slash slashes, slashing, slashed**
VERB 1 If someone **slashes** something, they make a long, deep cut in it.
NOUN 2 a long, deep cut

**slate slates**
NOUN 1 a dark grey rock that splits easily into thin layers
NOUN 2 **Slates** are small, flat pieces of slate used for covering roofs.

**slaughter slaughters, slaughtering, slaughtered**
VERB 1 To **slaughter** farm animals means to kill them for meat.

VERB 2 To **slaughter** animals or people means to kill a large number of them unjustly or cruelly.
NOUN 3 the killing of many people or anima

**slave slaves, slaving, slaved**
NOUN 1 someone who is owned by another person and must work for them
VERB 2 If you **slave** over something, you wo very hard at it.

**slay slays, slaying, slew, slain**
VERB (literary) To **slay** someone means to kil them.

**sledge sledges**
NOUN a vehicle on runners used for travellin over snow

**sledgehammer sledgehammers**
NOUN a large, heavy hammer

**sleek sleeker, sleekest**
ADJECTIVE If something such as hair is **sleek**, it is smooth and shiny.

**sleep sleeps, sleeping, slept**
VERB When you **sleep**, you close your eyes and your whole body rests.

**sleepily**
ADJECTIVE in a way that shows you are tired and feel like sleeping

**sleepless**
ADJECTIVE unable to sleep or without sleep
• I had a **sleepless** night last night.

**sleepy sleepier, sleepiest**
ADJECTIVE tired and feeling like sleeping

**sleet**
NOUN a mixture of rain and snow

**sleeve sleeves**
NOUN The **sleeves** of a piece of clothing are the parts that cover your arms. • a shirt with long **sleeves**

**sleigh sleighs**
NOUN a sledge pulled by animals

**slender**
ADJECTIVE slim

**slept**
VERB the past tense and past participle of **sleep**

**slice slices, slicing, sliced**
NOUN 1 A **slice** of cake, bread or other food is a piece of it cut from a larger piece.
VERB 2 If you **slice** food, you cut it into thin pieces.

**slice** *verb* **3** To **slice** through something means to cut or move through it quickly, like a knife.
● *The ship **sliced** through the water.*

**slick** slicker, slickest; slicks
ADJECTIVE **1** A **slick** action is done quickly and smoothly.
NOUN **2** An oil **slick** is a layer of oil floating on the surface of the sea or a lake.

**slide** slides, sliding, slid
VERB When something **slides**, it moves smoothly over or against something else.
● *She **slid** the door open.*

**slight** slighter, slightest
ADJECTIVE **1** small in amount ● *a **slight** dent in the car*
ADJECTIVE **2** A **slight** person has a slim, small body.

**slim** slimmer, slimmest
ADJECTIVE **1** A **slim** person is thin.
ADJECTIVE **2** A **slim** object is fairly thin.
● *a **slim** book*
ADJECTIVE **3** If there is only a **slim** chance that something will happen, there is only a small chance that it will happen.

**slime**
NOUN an unpleasant, thick, slippery substance

**sling** slings, slinging, slung
VERB **1** (*informal*) If you **sling** something somewhere, you throw it there.
VERB **2** If you **sling** a rope between two points, you attach it so that it hangs loosely between them.
NOUN **3** a piece of cloth tied round a person's neck to support a broken or injured arm

**slip** slips, slipping, slipped
VERB **1** If you **slip**, you accidentally lose your balance.
VERB **2** If you **slip** somewhere, you go there quickly and quietly.
NOUN **3** a small mistake
NOUN **4** a small piece of paper

**slipper** slippers
NOUN **Slippers** are loose, soft shoes that you wear indoors.

**slippery**
ADJECTIVE smooth, wet or greasy, and difficult to hold or walk on

**slit** slits
NOUN a long cut or narrow opening

**slither** slithers, slithering, slithered
VERB To **slither** somewhere means to move there by sliding along the ground in an uneven way. ● *The snake **slithered** away.*

**sliver** slivers
NOUN a small, thin piece of something

**slog** slogs, slogging, slogged
VERB **1** If you **slog** at something, you work hard at it.
NOUN **2** a piece of hard work or effort

**slogan** slogans
NOUN a short, easily-remembered phrase used in advertising or by a political party

SYNONYMS: catch phrase, motto

WORD HISTORY
from Scottish Gaelic *sluagh-ghairm* meaning war cry

**slope** slopes, sloping, sloped
NOUN **1** a flat surface that is at an angle, so that one end is higher than the other
VERB **2** If a surface **slopes**, it is at an angle.

**sloppily**
ADVERB carelessly or badly

**sloppy** sloppier, sloppiest
ADJECTIVE **1** liquid and spilling easily
ADJECTIVE **2** careless or badly done
ADJECTIVE **3** sentimental

**slot** slots
NOUN a narrow opening in a machine or container for pushing something into

**sloth** sloths
NOUN a South and Central American animal that moves very slowly and hangs upside down from the branches of trees

**slouch** slouches, slouching, slouched
VERB If you **slouch**, you stand or sit with your shoulders and head drooping forwards.

**slow** slower, slowest; slows, slowing, slowed
ADJECTIVE **1** moving, happening or doing something with very little speed
ADJECTIVE **2** If a clock or watch is **slow**, it shows a time earlier than the correct one.
VERB **3** If something **slows**, or you **slow** it, it moves or happens more slowly.
**slow down**
VERB If something **slows down** or something **slows** it **down**, it moves or happens more slowly.

**slug slugs**
NOUN a small, slow-moving animal with a slimy body, like a snail without an outer shell

**sluggish**
ADJECTIVE moving slowly and without much energy

**slum slums**
NOUN a poor, run-down area of a city or town

**slumber slumbers, slumbering, slumbered**
NOUN **1** (*literary*) sleep
VERB **2** (*literary*) When you **slumber**, you sleep.

**slump slumps, slumping, slumped**
VERB If you **slump** somewhere, you fall or sit down heavily.

**slush**
NOUN melting snow

**sly slyer** or **slier, slyest** or **sliest**
ADJECTIVE **1** A **sly** person is cunning and good at deceiving people.
ADJECTIVE **2** A **sly** expression or remark shows that you know something other people do not know.

**smack smacks, smacking, smacked**
VERB **1** If you **smack** someone, you hit them with your open hand.
NOUN **2** If you give someone a **smack**, you smack them.

**small smaller, smallest**
ADJECTIVE not large in size, number or amount

**smart smarter, smartest**
ADJECTIVE **1** A **smart** person is clean and neatly dressed.
ADJECTIVE **2** clever ● *That's a smart idea.*

**smartphone smartphones**
NOUN a mobile phone that can send emails and access the internet

**smash smashes, smashing, smashed**
VERB **1** If you **smash** something, you break it into a lot of pieces by hitting it or dropping it.
VERB **2** If someone or something **smashes** through something, such as a fence, they go through it by breaking it.
VERB **3** To **smash** against something means to hit it with great force. ● *A huge wave smashed against the boat.*

**smear smears, smearing, smeared**
NOUN **1** a dirty, greasy mark on a surface
VERB **2** If something **smears** something els it leaves a dirty or greasy mark by rubbing against it.

**smell smells, smelling, smelled** or **sme**
VERB **1** When you **smell** something, you notice it with your nose.
VERB **2** If something **smells**, it gives out an odour that people notice.
NOUN **3** Your sense of **smell** is your ability to smell things.
NOUN **4** an odour or scent, especially an unpleasant one

LANGUAGE TIP
You can write either *smelled* or *smelt* as the past form of *smell*.

**smile smiles, smiling, smiled**
VERB When you **smile**, you are happy. Your lips curve upwards at the edges and open a little.

**smirk smirks, smirking, smirked**
VERB When you **smirk**, you smile in a sneering, unpleasant way.

**smog**
NOUN a mixture of smoke and fog that occur in some industrial cities

WORD HISTORY
from a combination of *smoke* and *fog*

**smoke smokes, smoking, smoked**
NOUN **1** a mixture of gases and small bits of solid material sent into the air when something burns

→ Have a look at the illustration for **volcanc**

VERB **2** If something is **smoking**, smoke is coming from it.
VERB **3** When someone **smokes** a cigarette, cigar or pipe, they suck smoke from it into their mouth and blow it out again.

**smooth smoother, smoothest; smooths, smoothing, smoothed**
ADJECTIVE **1** A **smooth** surface has no roughness and no holes in it.

ANTONYM: rough

ADJECTIVE **2** A **smooth** liquid or mixture has no lumps in it.
VERB **3** If you **smooth** something, you move your hands over it to make it smooth and flat.

**smoothie** smoothies
NOUN a thick drink made mainly from crushed fruit • *a strawberry and banana smoothie*

**smother** smothers, smothering, smothered
VERB **1** If you **smother** a fire, you cover it with something to put it out.
VERB **2** To **smother** a person means to cover their face with something so that they cannot breathe.

**smoulder** smoulders, smouldering, smouldered
VERB When something **smoulders**, it burns slowly, producing smoke but no flames.

**smudge** smudges, smudging, smudged
NOUN **1** a dirty or blurred mark or a smear on something
VERB **2** If you **smudge** something, you make it dirty or messy by touching it or rubbing it. • *Be careful you don't **smudge** the ink!*

**smug** smugger, smuggest
ADJECTIVE Someone who is **smug** is very pleased with how good or clever they are, and is self-satisfied in an unpleasant way.

**smuggle** smuggles, smuggling, smuggled
VERB To **smuggle** goods means to take them in or out of a country secretly and against the law.

**snack** snacks
NOUN **1** a small, quick meal
NOUN **2** something eaten between meals

**snag** snags, snagging, snagged
NOUN **1** a small problem • *We seem to have hit a **snag**.*
VERB **2** If you **snag** your clothes, you catch them on something sharp.

**snail** snails
NOUN a small, slow-moving animal with a long, shiny body and a shell on its back

**snake** snakes
NOUN a long, thin reptile with scales and no legs

**snap** snaps, snapping, snapped
VERB **1** If something **snaps**, it breaks suddenly with a sharp noise.
VERB **2** If an animal **snaps** at you, it shuts its jaws together quickly as if it is going to bite you.
NOUN **3** an informal photograph

**snare** snares, snaring, snared
NOUN **1** a trap for catching birds or small animals
VERB **2** To **snare** an animal or bird means to catch it using a snare.

**snarl** snarls, snarling, snarled
VERB **1** When an animal **snarls**, it bares its teeth and makes a fierce, growling noise.
VERB **2** If you **snarl**, you say something in a fierce, angry way.
NOUN **3** the noise an animal makes when it snarls

**snatch** snatches, snatching, snatched
VERB **1** If you **snatch** something, you reach out for it quickly and grab it.
NOUN **2** A **snatch** of conversation or song is a very small piece of it

**sneak** sneaks, sneaking, sneaked
VERB If you **sneak** somewhere, you go there quietly, trying not to be seen or heard.

**sneaky** sneakier, sneakiest
ADJECTIVE dishonest or deceitful

**sneer** sneers, sneering, sneered
VERB If you **sneer** at someone or something, you show by what you say that you think they are stupid or inferior.

**sneeze** sneezes, sneezing, sneezed
VERB **1** When you **sneeze**, you suddenly take a breath and blow it noisily down your nose, because there is a tickle in your nose or you have a cold.
NOUN **2** the action or sound of sneezing

**sniff** sniffs, sniffing, sniffed
VERB When you **sniff**, you breathe in air through your nose hard enough to make a sound.

**snigger** sniggers, sniggering, sniggered
VERB If you **snigger**, you laugh quietly and disrespectfully.

**snip** snips, snipping, snipped
VERB If you **snip** something, you make small, quick cuts in it or through it.

**sniper** snipers
NOUN a person who shoots at people from a hiding place

**snivel** snivels, snivelling, snivelled
VERB When someone **snivels**, they cry and sniff in an irritating way.

a
b
c
d
e
f
g
h
i
j
k
l
m
n
o
p
q
r
s
t
u
v
w
x
y
z

375

## snob snobs

NOUN **1** someone who admires people considered to be socially superior and looks down on people considered to be socially inferior

NOUN **2** someone who believes that they are better than other people

## snobbery

NOUN behaviour or an attitude that shows you think you are better than other people and have a higher social class than they do

## snooker

NOUN a game played on a large table covered with smooth, green cloth. Players score points by hitting differently coloured balls into pockets using a long stick called a cue.

## snoop snoops, snooping, snooped

VERB (*informal*) If you **snoop**, you secretly look round a place to find out things.

## snooze snoozes, snoozing, snoozed

VERB **1** (*informal*) If you **snooze**, you sleep lightly for a short time, especially during the day.

NOUN **2** (*informal*) a short, light sleep

## snore snores, snoring, snored

VERB When a sleeping person **snores**, they make a loud noise each time they breathe.

## snorkel snorkels, snorkelling, snorkelled

NOUN **1** a tube you can breathe through when you are swimming just under the surface of the sea

VERB **2** If you **snorkel**, you swim underwater using a snorkel.

## snorkelling

NOUN the activity of swimming just under the surface of water, using a tube you can breathe through

## snout snouts

NOUN An animal's **snout** is its nose.

## snow snows, snowing, snowed

NOUN **1** soft, white flakes of ice that fall from the sky in cold weather

VERB **2** When it **snows**, snow falls from the sky.

## snowball snowballs

NOUN a ball of snow for throwing

## snowboard snowboards

NOUN a board you stand on to slide across snow

## snowboarding

NOUN the activity of standing on a board to slide across snow

## snowflake snowflakes

NOUN a flake of snow

## snowman snowmen

NOUN a pile of snow shaped like a person

## snowstorm snowstorms

NOUN a storm with snow falling

## snub snubs, snubbing, snubbed

VERB **1** If you **snub** someone, you behave rudely towards them, especially by making an insulting remark or ignoring them.

ADJECTIVE **2** A **snub** nose is short and turned-up

## snug

ADJECTIVE **1** A **snug** place is warm and comfortable.

ADJECTIVE **2** If you are **snug**, you are warm and comfortable.

ADJECTIVE **3** If something is a **snug** fit, it fits very closely.

## snuggle snuggles, snuggling, snuggled

VERB If you **snuggle** somewhere, you cuddle up more closely to something or someone.

## so

ADVERB **1** also • *She laughed, and* **so** *did the teacher.*

ADVERB **2** very • *You are* **so** *funny.*

CONJUNCTION **3** therefore, for that reason • *I was cold,* **so** *I put on a coat.*

## soak soaks, soaking, soaked

VERB **1** If you **soak** something, or leave it to **soak**, you put it in a liquid and leave it there for some time.

VERB **2** When a liquid **soaks** something, it makes it very wet.

VERB **3** When something **soaks** up a liquid, the liquid is drawn up into it. • *The cloth* **soaked** *up the spilt milk.*

## soap soaps

NOUN a substance used with water for washing yourself • *a bar of* **soap**

## soap opera soap operas

NOUN a popular television drama serial about people's daily lives

---

**WORD HISTORY**

so called because soap manufacturers were often sponsors of these

**oar soars, soaring, soared**
VERB If something **soars** into the air, it rises high into it.

**ob sobs, sobbing, sobbed**
VERB When someone **sobs**, they cry noisily, gulping in short breaths.

**ober soberer, soberest**
ADJECTIVE **1** not drunk
ADJECTIVE **2** serious and thoughtful

**occer**
NOUN a game played by two teams of eleven players kicking a ball in an attempt to score goals

**ociable**
ADJECTIVE **Sociable** people are friendly and enjoy talking to other people.

SYNONYM: friendly

**ocial**
ADJECTIVE **1** to do with society or life within a society • *women from similar **social** backgrounds*
ADJECTIVE **2** to do with leisure activities that involve meeting other people • *We should organise more **social** events.*

**ocial media**
NOUN You can refer to websites and computer programs that you use to communicate with other people as **social media**.

**ocial networking site social networking sites**
NOUN a website that lets people connect, chat and share pictures and videos

**society societies**
NOUN **1** the community of people in a particular country or region
NOUN **2** an organisation for people who have the same interests

**sock socks**
NOUN a piece of clothing that covers your foot and ankle

**socket sockets**
NOUN **1** a place on a wall or on a piece of electrical equipment into which you can put a plug or bulb
NOUN **2** any hollow part of something, or an opening into which another part fits
• *eye **sockets***

**sofa sofas**
NOUN a long comfortable seat, with a back and arms, for two or more people

**WORD HISTORY**
from Arabic *suffah* meaning an upholstered raised platform

**soft softer, softest**
ADJECTIVE **1** not hard, stiff or firm • *a **soft** towel*
ADJECTIVE **2** very gentle • *a **soft** breeze*

**soften softens, softening, softened**
VERB When you **soften** something, you make it softer.

**software**
NOUN computer programs

**soggy soggier, soggiest**
ADJECTIVE unpleasantly wet

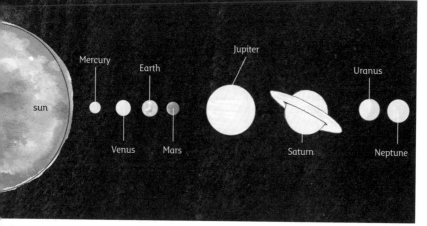

**solar system**

a
b
c
d
e
f
g
h
i
j
k
l
m
n
o
p
q
r
s
t
u
v
w
x
y
z

soil **soils, soiling, soiled**

NOUN **1** the top layer of the land surface of the earth, in which plants can grow

→ Have a look at the illustration for **photosynthesis**

VERB **2** If you **soil** something, you make it dirty.

solar

ADJECTIVE to do with the sun • **solar** energy

solar system

NOUN the sun and all the planets, comets and asteroids that orbit round it

→ Have a look at the illustration

sold

VERB the past tense and past participle of **sell**

soldier **soldiers**

NOUN a person in an army

sole **soles**

NOUN The **sole** of your foot or shoe is the underneath part.

solemn

ADJECTIVE serious rather than cheerful

solicitor **solicitors**

NOUN a lawyer who gives legal advice and prepares legal documents and cases

solid **solids**

NOUN **1** a substance that is not a liquid or gas. The particles in a **solid** are close together and cannot move around.

→ Have a look at the illustration for **state of matter**

NOUN **2** an object that is hard or firm

ADJECTIVE **3** You say that something is **solid** when it does not have any space in it.
• a **solid** steel bar

ADJECTIVE **4** A **solid** shape is a three-dimensional shape such as a cylinder.

solidify **solidifies, solidifying, solidified**

VERB If something **solidifies**, it changes from a liquid into a solid.

solitary

ADJECTIVE alone

solo **solos**

NOUN **1** a piece of music played or sung by one person alone

ADJECTIVE **2** A **solo** performance or activity is done by one person alone.

ADVERB **3** alone • to sail **solo** around the world

solstice **solstices**

NOUN one of two times in the year when th sun is at its furthest point south or north the equator

solubility

NOUN the ability of a substance to dissolve

soluble

ADJECTIVE able to be dissolved in a liquid
• **soluble** aspirin

solution **solutions**

NOUN **1** a way of dealing with a problem or difficult situation

NOUN **2** the answer to a riddle or a puzzle

NOUN **3** a liquid in which a solid substance has been dissolved

solve **solves, solving, solved**

VERB If you **solve** a problem or a question, you find a solution or answer to it.

SYNONYM: work out

sombre

ADJECTIVE **1** **Sombre** colours are dark and dull.

ADJECTIVE **2** A **sombre** person is serious, sa or gloomy.

some

ADJECTIVE **1** You use **some** to refer to a quantity or number when you are not stating the exact quantity or number.
• There's **some** money on the table.

PRONOUN **2** You use **some** to refer to a quantity or number when you are not stating the exact quantity or number.
• When the berries were ripe, we picked **some**.

somebody

PRONOUN some person

somehow

ADVERB **1** You use **somehow** to say that yo do not know how something was done or will be done. • You'll find a way of doing it **somehow**.

ADVERB **2** You use **somehow** to say that yo do not know the reason for something.
• **Somehow** it didn't feel quite right.

someone

PRONOUN You use **someone** to refer to a person without saying exactly who you mean. • I need **someone** to help me.

**somersault somersaults, somersaulting, somersaulted**
NOUN **1** a forwards or backwards roll in which the head is placed on the ground and the body is brought over it
VERB **2** If you **somersault**, you perform a somersault.

**something**
PRONOUN You use **something** to refer to anything that is not a person, without saying exactly what it is. • *There was* **something** *wrong.*

**sometimes**
ADVERB occasionally, rather than always or never

**somewhere**
ADVERB **1** **Somewhere** is used to refer to a place without stating exactly where it is.
• *a flat* **somewhere** *in the city*
ADVERB **2** **Somewhere** is used when giving an approximate amount, number or time.
• *It was* **somewhere** *between four and five o'clock.*

**son sons**
NOUN a person's male child

**song songs**
NOUN **1** a piece of music with words that are sung to the music
NOUN **2** singing • *I was woken by the bird* **song** *early in the morning.*

**sonnet sonnets**
NOUN a poem with 14 lines that rhyme according to fixed patterns

**soon sooner, soonest**
ADVERB If something is going to happen **soon**, it will happen in a very short time.

**soot**
NOUN black powder that rises in the smoke from a fire

**soothe soothes, soothing, soothed**
VERB **1** If you **soothe** someone who is angry or upset, you make them calmer.
VERB **2** Something that **soothes** pain makes the pain less severe.

**sooty**
ADJECTIVE covered in a black powder that has come from the smoke from a fire

**sophisticated**
ADJECTIVE **1** A **sophisticated** person is experienced in social situations and able to talk easily about anything.

SYNONYMS: cultured, urbane

ADJECTIVE **2** Something **sophisticated** is made using advanced and complicated methods, or is able to do advanced and complicated things. • *a* **sophisticated** *new telescope*

SYNONYM: highly developed

**sorcerer sorcerers**
NOUN someone in stories who performs magic by using the power of evil spirits

**sore sorer, sorest; sores**
ADJECTIVE **1** If part of your body is **sore**, it causes you pain and is uncomfortable.
• *I have a cough and a* **sore** *throat.*

SYNONYMS: painful, sensitive, tender

NOUN **2** a painful place where your skin has become infected

**sorrow sorrows**
NOUN deep sadness or regret

**sorry sorrier, sorriest**
ADJECTIVE If you are **sorry** about something, you feel sadness, regret or sympathy because of it.

**sort sorts, sorting, sorted**
NOUN **1** Different **sorts** of something are different types of it.

SYNONYM: kind

VERB **2** If you **sort** things, you arrange them into different groups.
**sort out**
VERB If you **sort out** a problem or misunderstanding, you find a solution to it.

**SOS**
NOUN a signal appealing urgently for help from someone whose life is in danger. **SOS** stands for Save Our Souls.

**sought**
VERB the past tense and past participle of **seek**

**soul souls**
NOUN the spiritual part of a person that some people think continues after the body is dead

a
b
c
d
e
f
g
h
i
j
k
l
m
n
o
p
q
r
s
t
u
v
w
x
y
z

**379**

**sound** sounds, sounding, sounded

NOUN **1 Sound** is everything that can be heard.

NOUN **2** something particular that you hear • the **sound** of a door opening

VERB **3** If something **sounds**, or if you **sound** it, it makes a noise. • He **sounded** his horn to warn them.

**sound effect** sound effects

NOUN **Sound effects** are added to films or plays to make them sound more life-like.

**soundproof** soundproofs, soundproofing, soundproofed

ADJECTIVE **1** If a room is **soundproof**, sound cannot get into it or out of it.

VERB **2** To **soundproof** something means to make it soundproof.

**soup** soups

NOUN liquid food made by boiling meat, fish or vegetables in water

**sour**

ADJECTIVE **1** If something is **sour**, it has a sharp, acid taste like lemons or vinegar.

ADJECTIVE **2** If milk is **sour**, it is no longer fresh.

**source** sources

NOUN The **source** of something is the person, place or thing that it originally comes from. • the **source** of the river

**south**

NOUN one of the four main points of the compass. If you face the point where the sun rises, **south** is on your right. The abbreviation for **south** is S.

→ Have a look at the illustration for **compass point**

**south-east**

NOUN a point halfway between south and east. The abbreviation for **south-east** is SE.

→ Have a look at the illustration for **compass point**

**southern**

ADJECTIVE in or from the south

**south-west**

NOUN a point halfway between south and west. The abbreviation for **south-west** is SW.

→ Have a look at the illustration for **compass point**

**souvenir** souvenirs

NOUN something you keep to remind you of holiday, place or event

**sovereign** sovereigns

NOUN **1** a king, queen or royal ruler of a country

NOUN **2** In the past, a **sovereign** was a British gold coin worth one pound.

**sow** sows, sowing, sowed, sown

NOUN **1** a female pig

VERB **2** If you **sow** seeds, you put them in th ground so they can grow.

PRONUNCIATION TIP
The noun ryhmes with "cow". The verb rhymes with "go".

**soya**

NOUN a protein derived from **soya** beans. **Soya** beans are used to make **soya** flour, margarine, oil and milk.

**space** spaces

NOUN **1** the area that is empty or available a place, building or container

NOUN **2** the area beyond the Earth's atmosphere surrounding the stars and planets

NOUN **3** a gap between two things

**spacecraft** spacecraft

NOUN a vehicle for travelling in outer space

**spaceship** spaceships

NOUN a spacecraft

**spacesuit** spacesuits

NOUN protective clothing that astronauts wear in outer space

**spacious**

ADJECTIVE having or providing a lot of space

**spade** spades

NOUN **1** a tool with a flat metal blade and a long handle used for digging

NOUN **2** **Spades** is one of the four suits in a pack of playing cards. It is marked by a black symbol in the shape of a heart-shap leaf with a stem.

**spaghetti**

NOUN long, thin pieces of pasta

WORD HISTORY
the plural of the Italian word spaghetto meaning string

**span** spans, spanning, spanned

NOUN **1** a period of time ● *looking back over a* **span** *of 40 years*

NOUN **2** the total length of something from one end to the other ● *Seagulls have a large wing* **span**.

NOUN **3** Your **span** is the distance from the top of your thumb to the top of your little finger when your hand is stretched.

VERB **4** If something **spans** a particular length of time, a distance or a gap, it stretches across it. ● *The bridge* **spanned** *the width of the river.*

**spaniel** spaniels

NOUN a breed of dog with long ears and silky fur

**spank** spanks, spanking, spanked

VERB If a child is **spanked**, it is punished by being slapped, usually on the leg or bottom.

**spanner** spanners

NOUN a tool with a specially shaped end that fits round a nut to turn it

**spare** spares, sparing, spared

ADJECTIVE **1** extra, or kept to be used when it is needed ● *There is a* **spare** *tyre in the boot of the car.*

VERB **2** If you **spare** something for a particular purpose, you make it available. ● *Can you* **spare** *the time to help me later?*

VERB **3** If someone is **spared** an unpleasant experience, they are prevented from suffering it.

**spark** sparks

NOUN a tiny, bright piece of burning material thrown up by a fire

**sparkle** sparkles, sparkling, sparkled

VERB If something **sparkles**, it shines with a lot of small, bright points of light.

SYNONYMS: glitter, twinkle

**sparrow** sparrows

NOUN a common, small bird with brown and grey feathers

**sparse** sparser, sparsest

ADJECTIVE small in number or amount and spread out over an area

**spatter** spatters, spattering, spattered

VERB If something **spatters** a surface, it covers it with small drops of liquid.

**spawn** spawns, spawning, spawned

NOUN **1** a jelly-like substance containing the eggs of fish or amphibians

VERB **2** When fish or amphibians **spawn**, they lay their eggs.

**speak** speaks, speaking, spoke, spoken

VERB **1** When you **speak**, you use your voice to say words.

SYNONYMS: say, talk, utter

VERB **2** If you **speak** a foreign language, you know it and can use it.

**speaker** speakers

NOUN **1** a person who is speaking or making a speech

NOUN **2** the part of a radio or stereo system from which the sound comes

**spear** spears, spearing, speared

NOUN **1** a weapon consisting of a long pole with a sharp point

VERB **2** To **spear** something means to pierce it with a spear or other pointed object.

**special**

ADJECTIVE Someone or something **special** is different from other people or things, often in a way that makes it more important or better than others.

**specialist** specialists

NOUN an expert in a particular subject

**species**

NOUN a group of plants or animals that have the same main features and are able to breed with each other

LANGUAGE TIP
The plural of *species* is *species*.

**specimen** specimens

NOUN an example or small amount of something that gives an idea of what the whole is like ● *a* **specimen** *of your writing*

**speck** specks

NOUN **1** a very small stain

NOUN **2** a very small amount of something

**speckled**

ADJECTIVE Something that is **speckled** is covered in small marks or spots.

**spectacle** spectacles

NOUN **1** a grand and impressive event or performance

PLURAL NOUN **2** Someone's **spectacles** are their glasses.

a b c d e f g h i j k l m n o p q r s t u v w x y z

## spectacular
ADJECTIVE very impressive or dramatic

## spectator spectators
NOUN a person who watches an event or a show

## spectrum spectra or spectrums
NOUN the range of different colours produced when light passes through a prism or a drop of water. A rainbow shows the colours in a **spectrum**.

## speech speeches
NOUN **1** the ability to speak or the act of speaking

NOUN **2** a formal talk given to an audience

NOUN **3** In grammar, direct **speech** is speech which is reported by using the exact words that the speaker used. Indirect or reported **speech** tells you what someone said, but does not use the person's actual words.

## speech bubble speech bubbles
NOUN a line around words, used in comic strips or cartoons to show what characters are saying

## speechless
ADJECTIVE unable to speak

## speech marks
PLURAL NOUN punctuation marks (" " ' ') used in written texts to show when someone is speaking

## speed speeds, speeding, sped or speeded
NOUN **1** the rate at which something moves or happens

NOUN **2** very fast movement or travel

VERB **3** If you **speed** somewhere, you move or travel there quickly.

VERB **4** Someone who is **speeding** is driving a vehicle faster than the legal speed limit.

## speedboat speedboats
NOUN a fast motorboat

## speedometer speedometers
NOUN the instrument in a vehicle which shows how fast the vehicle is moving

→ Have a look at the illustration for **car**

## spell spells, spelling, spelt or spelled
VERB **1** When you **spell** a word, you name or write its letters in order.

NOUN **2** a short period of something • We expect a **spell** of good weather.

NOUN **3** words or rhymes used to perform magic

## spellbound
ADJECTIVE If you are **spellbound**, you are so fascinated by something that you cannot think of anything else.

## spellcheck spellchecks, spellchecking, spellchecked
VERB If you **spellcheck** a document, you ru a program over it to find any words that have not been spelt correctly.

## spelling spellings
NOUN the correct order of letters in a word

## spend spends, spending, spent
VERB **1** When you **spend** money, you buy things with it. • By lunchtime, I had **spent** a my money.

VERB **2** If you **spend** time or energy, you use it. • She **spends** hours working in the garden.

## sphere spheres
NOUN a perfectly round object, such as a ba

## spherical
ADJECTIVE shaped like a sphere

## sphinx sphinxes
NOUN In mythology, the **sphinx** was a monst with a person's head and a lion's body.

## spice spices
NOUN a substance obtained from a plant, often in the form of a powder or a seed, an added to food to give it flavour

## spicy spicier, spiciest
ADJECTIVE strongly flavoured with spices

**ɔider spiders**
NOUN a small animal with eight legs. Some **spiders** spin webs to catch insects for food, others hunt.

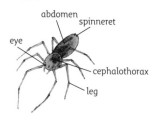

**ɔike spikes**
NOUN something long and sharply pointed. Runners often have **spikes** on the soles of their shoes to stop them slipping.

**ɔill spills, spilling, spilled or spilt**
VERB If you **spill** something, or if it **spills**, it accidentally falls or runs out of a container.

---

LANGUAGE TIP
You can write either *spilled* or *spilt* as the past form of *spill*.

---

**ɔin spins, spinning, spun**
VERB **1** If someone or something **spins**, it turns quickly around a central point.
• *The Earth **spins** on its own axis.*
NOUN **2** a rapid turn around a central point

**ɔinach**
NOUN a vegetable with large green leaves

**ɔine spines**
NOUN **1** the row of bones down the middle of your back
➔ Have a look at the illustration for **skeleton**

SYNONYM: backbone

NOUN **2** a spike on a plant or an animal
• *Porcupines are covered in **spines**.*
NOUN **3** the part of a book where the pages are joined together

**ɔiral spirals**
NOUN **1** a continuous curve that winds round and round, with each curve moving further out or further up
ADJECTIVE **2** in the shape of a spiral

**ɔire spires**
NOUN the pointed structure on top of a steeple

**spirit spirits**
NOUN **1** the part of you that is not physical and that is connected with the way you are
NOUN **2** a ghost or supernatural being
NOUN **3** liveliness, energy and self-confidence

**spiritual**
ADJECTIVE **1** to do with people's thoughts and beliefs, rather than their bodies and physical surroundings
ADJECTIVE **2** to do with people's religious beliefs

**spit spits, spitting, spat**
VERB **1** If you **spit**, you forcefully send saliva out of your mouth.
NOUN **2** saliva
NOUN **3** a long piece of metal or wood that you push through meat so that it can be hung over a fire to cook
NOUN **4** a long, flat, narrow piece of land sticking out into the sea

**spite**
NOUN **1** the desire to deliberately hurt or upset somebody
PHRASE **2 In spite of** is used to begin a statement that makes the rest of what you are saying seem surprising. • ***In spite of** the rain, they watched the fireworks outside.*

**spiteful**
ADJECTIVE A **spiteful** person does or says nasty things to people to hurt them.

**spitefully**
ADVERB in a nasty way that is intended to hurt or upset someone

**splash splashes, splashing, splashed**
VERB **1** If you **splash** around in water, you make the water fly around in a noisy way.
NOUN **2** the sound made when something hits or falls into water

**splendid**
ADJECTIVE very good or very impressive

**splint splints**
NOUN a straight piece of metal or wood that is tied to a broken arm or leg to stop it moving

**splinter splinters, splintering, splintered**
NOUN **1** a thin, sharp piece of wood or glass that has broken off a larger piece
VERB **2** If something **splinters**, it breaks into thin, sharp pieces.

**split splits, splitting, split**
VERB If something **splits**, or if you **split** it, it divides into two or more parts.

a
b
c
d
e
f
g
h
i
j
k
l
m
n
o
p
q
r
s
t
u
v
w
x
y
z

**383**

## split second **split seconds**
NOUN an extremely short period of time

## splutter **splutters, spluttering, spluttered**
VERB **1** If you **splutter**, you speak in a confused way because you are embarrassed or angry.
VERB **2** If someone or something **splutters**, they make a series of short, coughing, spitting noises.

## spoil **spoils, spoiling, spoiled** or **spoilt**
VERB **1** To **spoil** something means to damage it or stop it being successful or satisfactory. ● *My holiday was* **spoiled** *by rain.*
VERB **2** To **spoil** children means to give them everything they want, making them selfish.

---

LANGUAGE TIP
You can write either *spoiled* or *spoilt* as the past form of *spoil*.

---

## spoilsport **spoilsports**
NOUN someone who spoils other people's fun

## spoke **spokes**
NOUN **1** The **spokes** of a wheel are the bars that connect the hub to the rim.

→ Have a look at the illustration for **bicycle**

VERB **2** the past tense of **speak**

## spoken
VERB the past participle of **speak**

## sponge **sponges**
NOUN **1** a soft, natural or man-made material with lots of small holes, used for washing yourself
NOUN **2** an animal found in the sea that has a body made up of many cells
NOUN **3** a soft, light cake or pudding

## spongy **spongier, spongiest**
ADJECTIVE soft and full of small holes

## sponsor **sponsors, sponsoring, sponsored**
VERB **1** If an organisation **sponsors** something, such as an event or someone's training, it gives money to pay for it.
VERB **2** If you **sponsor** someone who is doing something for charity, you agree to give them a sum of money for the charity if they manage to do it.
NOUN **3** a person or organization that sponsors something or someone

## spontaneous
ADJECTIVE not planned or arranged

## spontaneously
ADVERB in a way that is not planned or arranged

## spooky **spookier, spookiest**
ADJECTIVE frightening and creepy

## spoon **spoons**
NOUN an object shaped like a small shallow bowl with a long handle, used for eating, stirring and serving food

## spore **spores**
NOUN **Spores** are cells produced by some plants and bacteria which can develop into new plants or bacteria.

## sport **sports**
NOUN games and other enjoyable activities that need physical effort and skill

## spot **spots, spotting, spotted**
NOUN **1** a small, round, coloured area on a surface
NOUN **2** a pimple on a person's skin
NOUN **3** a small amount of something
NOUN **4** a particular place
VERB **5** If you **spot** something, you suddenly see it.
PHRASE **6** If you do something **on the spot**, you do it immediately.

## spotless
ADJECTIVE perfectly clean

## spotlight **spotlights**
NOUN a powerful light that can be directed light up a small area ● *stage* **spotlights**

## spotty **spottier, spottiest**
ADJECTIVE marked with spots

## spouse **spouses**
NOUN Someone's **spouse** is the person they are married to.

## spout **spouts, spouting, spouted**
VERB **1** When liquid or flame **spouts** out of something, it shoots out in a long stream.
NOUN **2** a tube or opening from which liquid can pour
VERB **3** When someone **spouts** what they have learned, they say it in a boring way.

## sprain **sprains, spraining, sprained**
VERB **1** If you **sprain** a joint, you accidentally damage it by twisting it violently.
NOUN **2** the injury caused by spraining a joint

## sprang
VERB the past tense of **spring**

**rawl sprawls, sprawling, sprawled**
VERB 1 If you **sprawl** somewhere, you sit or lie there with your legs and arms spread out.
• *She **sprawled** on the bed reading her book.*
VERB 2 A place that **sprawls** is spread out over a large area.

**ray sprays, spraying, sprayed**
NOUN 1 many small drops of liquid splashed or forced into the air
NOUN 2 a liquid kept under pressure in a container
VERB 3 If you **spray** a liquid over something, you cover it with drops of the liquid.
• *We **sprayed** the dry lawn with water from the hose pipe.*

**read spreads, spreading, spread**
VERB 1 If you **spread** a substance on a surface, you put a thin layer of it on the surface. • ***Spread** the butter on the bread before you make the sandwich.*
VERB 2 If you **spread** something out, you open it out or arrange it so that it can be seen or used easily. • *He **spread** the map out on his knees.*
VERB 3 If something **spreads**, it gradually reaches more people. • *The news **spread** quickly.*

**readsheet spreadsheets**
NOUN a computer program that is used for displaying and dealing with numbers

**rightly sprightlier, sprightliest**
ADJECTIVE lively and active

**ring springs, springing, sprang, sprung**
NOUN 1 the season between winter and summer, when most plants start to grow
NOUN 2 a coil of wire that returns to its original shape after being pressed or pulled
NOUN 3 a place where water naturally comes up through the ground
VERB 4 If you **spring**, you jump upwards or forwards.

**pringboard springboards**
NOUN a springy board on which a gymnast or diver jumps to gain height

**pringbok springboks**
NOUN a small South African antelope that moves in leaps

**prinkle sprinkles, sprinkling, sprinkled**
VERB If you **sprinkle** a liquid or powder over something, you scatter it over it.

**sprint sprints, sprinting, sprinted**
NOUN 1 a short, fast race
VERB 2 If you **sprint**, you run fast over a short distance.

**sprout sprouts, sprouting, sprouted**
VERB 1 When something **sprouts**, it starts to grow.
VERB 2 If things **sprout** up, they appear very quickly.
NOUN 3 an abbreviation of *Brussels sprout*

**sprung**
VERB the past participle of **spring**

**spun**
VERB the past tense and past participle of **spin**

**spur spurs, spurring, spurred**
VERB 1 If you **spur** someone on, you encourage them.
NOUN 2 a sharp device worn on the heel of a rider's boot to urge the horse to go faster

**spurt spurts, spurting, spurted**
NOUN 1 a jet of liquid or flame
NOUN 2 a sudden increase in speed
VERB 3 If a liquid **spurts**, it gushes in a sudden stream. • *Water **spurted** out of the hose.*

**spy spies, spying, spied**
NOUN 1 a person sent to find out secret information about a country or organisation
VERB 2 Someone who **spies** tries to find out secret information about another country or organisation.
VERB 3 If you **spy** on someone, you watch them secretly.

**squabble squabbles, squabbling, squabbled**
VERB 1 When people **squabble**, they quarrel about something unimportant.
NOUN 2 a quarrel

**squad squads**
NOUN a small group of people chosen to do a particular activity

**squadron squadrons**
NOUN a section of one of the armed forces, especially the air force

WORD HISTORY
from Italian *squadrone* meaning soldiers drawn up in a square formation

**squalid**
ADJECTIVE dirty, untidy and in bad condition

**squander** squanders, squandering, squandered

VERB If you **squander** money or resources, you waste them.

**square** squares

NOUN **1** a plane shape with four equal sides and four right angles

NOUN **2** In a town or city, a **square** is a flat, open area with buildings or streets around the edge.

ADJECTIVE **3** shaped like a **square**

ADJECTIVE **4 Square** is used after units of length when you are giving the length of each side of something that is square in shape. ● *two pieces of wood 4 inches* **square**

ADJECTIVE **5** A **square** number is a number like 4, 16 or 25 which is the prodcut of a number multiplied by itself. The **square** root of a number like 16 is the number which is multiplied by itself, in this case 4.

**WORD HISTORY**
from Latin *quadra* meaning square

**squash** squashes, squashing, squashed

VERB If you **squash** something, you press it so that it becomes flat or loses its shape.

**squat** squats, squatting, squatted, squatter, squattest

VERB **1** If you **squat** down, you crouch, balancing on your feet with your legs bent.

VERB **2** A person who **squats** in an unused building lives there without permission and without paying.

ADJECTIVE **3** short and thick

**squawk** squawks, squawking, squawked

VERB **1** When a bird **squawks**, it makes a loud, harsh noise.

NOUN **2** a loud, harsh noise made by a bird

**squeak** squeaks, squeaking, squeaked

VERB **1** If something or someone **squeaks**, they make a short, high-pitched sound.

NOUN **2** a short, high-pitched sound

**squeal** squeals, squealing, squealed

VERB **1** When things or people **squeal**, the make long, high-pitched sounds.

NOUN **2** a long, high-pitched sound

**squeamish**

ADJECTIVE easily upset by unpleasant sights situations

**squeeze** squeezes, squeezing, squeez

VERB **1** When you **squeeze** something, yo press it firmly from two sides.

VERB **2** If you **squeeze** somewhere, you fo yourself into a small space or through a gap.

VERB **3** If you **squeeze** something somewhere, you force it into a small spac

**squelch** squelches, squelching, squelched

VERB If something **squelches**, it makes a wet, sucking sound.

**squid** squids

NOUN an animal that lives in the sea, with long, soft body and ten limbs

**squiggle** squiggles

NOUN a wiggly line

**squint** squints, squinting, squinted

VERB **1** If you **squint**, you screw up your ey to look at something.

NOUN **2** If someone has a **squint**, their eye look in different directions from each othe

**squirm** squirms, squirming, squirmed

VERB If you **squirm**, you wriggle and twist your body about, usually because you are nervous or embarrassed.

**squirrel** squirrels

NOUN a small, furry rodent with a long, bushy tail

**squirt** squirts, squirting, squirted

VERB **1** If a liquid **squirts**, or you **squirt** it, it comes out of a narrow opening in a thin fast stream.

NOUN **2** a thin, fast stream of liquid

**stab** stabs, stabbing, stabbed

VERB To **stab** someone means to wound them by pushing a knife into their body.

**stable** stables

NOUN **1** a building in which horses are kept

ADJECTIVE **2** Something that is **stable** cannot be moved or shaken.

ADJECTIVE **3** If someone is **stable**, they are level-headed and dependable.

**ack stacks, stacking, stacked**
NOUN **1** a pile of things, one on top of the other
VERB **2** If you **stack** items, you pile them up neatly.

**adium stadiums**
NOUN a sports ground with rows of seats around it for spectators

**aff staffs**
NOUN the people who work for an organisation

**ag stags**
NOUN an adult male deer

**age stages, staging, staged**
NOUN **1** In a theatre, the **stage** is the raised platform where the actors or entertainers perform.
VERB **2** If someone **stages** a play or event, they organise it or present it.

**agger staggers, staggering, staggered**
VERB **1** If you **stagger**, you walk unsteadily, for example because you are ill.
VERB **2** If something **staggers** you, it amazes you.
VERB **3** If events are **staggered**, they are arranged so that they do not all happen at the same time.

**agnant**
ADJECTIVE **Stagnant** water is still rather than flowing, and is often smelly and dirty.

**ain stains**
NOUN a mark on something that is difficult or impossible to clean off

**air stairs**
NOUN one of a set of steps, usually inside a building going from one floor to another
● *He walked slowly up the **stairs**.*

**aircase staircases**
NOUN a set of stairs

**ake stakes, staking, staked**
PHRASE **1** If something is **at stake**, it might be lost or damaged if something else is not successful. ● *The cup was **at stake** if he missed the goal.*
VERB **2** If you say you would **stake** your money, life or reputation on the result of something, you mean you would risk it.

**stalactite stalactites**
NOUN a stony spike hanging down like an icicle from the ceiling of a cave

stalactite

stalagmite

**stalagmite stalagmites**
NOUN a pointed piece of rock standing on the floor of a cave

**stale staler, stalest**
ADJECTIVE **Stale** food or air is no longer fresh.

SYNONYMS: fusty, musty, old

**stalk stalks, stalking, stalked**
NOUN **1** The **stalk** of a flower or leaf is its stem.
VERB **2** To **stalk** a person or an animal means to follow them quietly in order to catch, kill or observe them. ● *The cat is **stalking** the bird in the garden.*

**stall stalls, stalling, stalled**
NOUN **1** a large table displaying goods for sale or information
PLURAL NOUN **2** In a theatre, the **stalls** are the seats at the lowest level, in front of the stage.
VERB **3** When a vehicle **stalls**, the engine suddenly stops.

**stallion stallions**
NOUN an adult male horse that can be used for breeding

**stamen stamens**
NOUN the part of a flower that produces pollen

→ Have a look at the illustration for **flower**

**stamina**
NOUN the physical or mental energy needed to do something for a very long time
● *Running a marathon takes determination and **stamina**.*

a
b
c
d
e
f
g
h
i
j
k
l
m
n
o
p
q
r
s
t
u
v
w
x
y
z

A
B
C
D
E
F
G
H
I
J
K
L
M
N
O
P
Q
R
S
T
U
V
W
X
Y
Z

**388**

**stammer** stammers, stammering, stammered

VERB **1** When someone **stammers**, they speak with difficulty, repeating words and sounds and hesitating.

NOUN **2** Someone who has a **stammer** tends to stammer when they speak.

**stamp** stamps, stamping, stamped

NOUN **1** a small piece of paper that you stick on a letter or parcel before posting it, to prove that you have paid the postage

VERB **2** To **stamp** a piece of paper means to make a mark on it using a small block with a pattern cut into it. • *He* ***stamped*** *her passport.*

VERB **3** If you **stamp**, you lift your foot and put it down hard on the ground.

**stamp out**

VERB To **stamp out** something means to put an end to it. • *We must try to* ***stamp out*** *this kind of behaviour.*

**stampede** stampedes, stampeding, stampeded

VERB **1** When a group of animals **stampede**, they rush forward in a wild, uncontrolled way.

NOUN **2** a group of animals stampeding

**stand** stands, standing, stood

VERB **1** If you are **standing**, you are upright with your weight on your feet.

VERB **2** If something **stands** somewhere, that is where it is. • *The house* ***stands*** *on top of a hill.*

VERB **3** If you cannot **stand** someone or something, you do not like them at all.

VERB **4** If you **stand** in an election, you are a candidate.

NOUN **5** A **stand** at a sports ground is a building where people can watch what is happening.

**stand up**

VERB When you **stand up**, you get into a standing position.

**standard** standards

NOUN **1** how good something is

NOUN **2** an officially agreed level against which things can be measured or judged

**standstill**

NOUN a complete stop

**stank**

VERB the past tense of **stink**

**stanza** stanzas

NOUN a verse of a poem

**staple** staples, stapling, stapled

NOUN **1** a small piece of wire that holds sheets of paper firmly together. You inser with a device called a stapler.

VERB **2** If you **staple** sheets of paper, you fasten them together with staples.

**star** stars

NOUN **1** a large ball of burning gases in sp that appears as a point of light in the sky night. Our sun is a **star**.

NOUN **2** a shape with several points, usuall five or six, sticking out in a regular patter

NOUN **3** a famous actor, sports player or musician

**starboard**

ADJECTIVE The **starboard** side of a ship is the right-hand side when you are facing the fro

**starch** starches

NOUN **1** a substance found in foods such as bread, rice, pasta and potatoes that gives you energy

NOUN **2** a substance used for stiffening fab

**stare** stares, staring, stared

VERB **1** If you **stare** at something, you look it for a long time.

NOUN **2** a long, fixed look at something

**starfish** starfishes or starfish

NOUN a star-shaped animal found in the se that has five pointed limbs

**starling** starlings

NOUN a common European bird with shiny dark feathers

**start** starts, starting, started

VERB **1** If you **start** something, you begin it.

NOUN **2** The **start** of something is the point or time at which it begins.

**startle** startles, startling, startled

VERB If something sudden and unexpected **startles** you, it surprises you and gives you a slight fright.

**starve** starves, starving, starved

VERB If people are **starving**, they are suffering from a serious lack of food and a likely to die.

**ate states, stating, stated**
NOUN **1** The **state** of something or someone is their condition, or how they are.
NOUN **2** Some countries are divided into regions called **states** that make some of their own laws.
NOUN **3** You can call the government and the officials of a country the **state**. • *Carmen received a pension from the **state**.*
VERB **4** If you **state** something, you say it or write it clearly, especially in a formal way. • *Please **state** your name and address.*

**atement statements**
NOUN something you say or write that gives information in a formal way

**ate of matter states of matter**
NOUN one of the forms of matter, for example solid, liquid or gas

gas
solid
liquid

**tatic**
ADJECTIVE **1** never moving or changing • *The temperature is fairly **static**.*
NOUN **2** an electrical charge caused by friction

**tation stations**
NOUN **1** a building where trains or buses stop to let passengers on and off
NOUN **2** A building that is used by people such as the police and fire brigade. • *police **station***

**tationary**
ADJECTIVE not moving • *a **stationary** car*

SYNONYM: motionless

**tationery**
NOUN paper, pens and other writing equipment

**tatistics**
PLURAL NOUN facts worked out by looking at information that is given in numbers • *They gathered **statistics** about journeys to school.*

**statue statues**
NOUN a sculpture, often of a person

**stay stays, staying, stayed**
VERB **1** If you **stay** in one place, you do not move away from it.
VERB **2** If you **stay** with a friend, you spend time with them as a visitor.

**steady steadier, steadiest**
ADJECTIVE firm and not moving about • *She made sure the ladder was **steady** before she climbed up it.*

SYNONYMS: firm, secure, stable

**steak steaks**
NOUN a large, good-quality piece of beef or fish

**steal steals, stealing, stole, stolen**
VERB If someone **steals** something, they take it without permission and without meaning to return it.

**steam**
NOUN the hot vapour formed when water boils • *The **steam** rose into the air.*

**steam-engine steam-engines**
NOUN any engine that is powered by steam

**steel**
NOUN a very strong metal made mainly from iron

**steel band steel bands**
NOUN a group of people who play music on special metal drums

**steep steeper, steepest**
ADJECTIVE A **steep** slope rises sharply and is difficult to go up.

**steeple steeples**
NOUN a tall, pointed structure above a church roof

**steer steers, steering, steered**
VERB When someone **steers** a vehicle or boat, they control it so that it goes in the direction they want.

**steering wheel steering wheels**
NOUN the wheel inside a car or other vehicle which the driver holds when he or she is driving
→ Have a look at the illustration for **car**

a
b
c
d
e
f
g
h
i
j
k
l
m
n
o
p
q
r
s
t
u
v
w
x
y
z

**stem** stems

NOUN the thin, usually upright, part of a plant that grows above the ground and on which the leaves and flowers grow

→ Have a look at the illustration for **flower**

**stencil** stencils, stencilling, stencilled

NOUN 1 a thin sheet of card, metal or plastic with a pattern cut out of it. The pattern can be copied onto another surface by painting over the **stencil**.

VERB 2 If you **stencil** a design onto a surface, you create it using a stencil.

**step** steps, stepping, stepped

NOUN 1 the movement of lifting your foot and putting it down again when you are walking, running or dancing

NOUN 2 one of the places at different levels that you put your feet on when you go up and down a ladder or stairs

VERB 3 If you **step** in a particular direction, you take a step there.

**stepbrother** stepbrothers

NOUN the son of someone's stepmother or stepfather

**stepchild** stepchildren

NOUN a stepdaughter or stepson

**stepdaughter** stepdaughters

NOUN someone's daughter by their wife's or husband's previous marriage

**stepfather** stepfathers

NOUN a man who is married to your mother but who is not your natural father

**stepmother** stepmothers

NOUN a woman who is married to your father but who is not your natural mother

**stepsister** stepsisters

NOUN the daughter of someone's stepmother or stepfather

**stepson** stepsons

NOUN someone's son by their wife's or husband's previous marriage

**stereo** stereos

NOUN a piece of equipment that reproduces sound from records, tapes or CDs, directing the sound through two speakers

**stereotype** stereotypes

NOUN a simplified way people think of a particular type of person or thing • the **stereotype** of the polite, industrious Japanese

**sterile**

ADJECTIVE 1 clean and free from germs

ADJECTIVE 2 unable to have children or reprod▪

**sterility**

NOUN 1 the quality that something has wh▪ it is clean and free from germs

NOUN 2 **Sterility** is when someone is unab▪ to have children or reproduce.

**sterling**

NOUN the money system of Great Britain

**stern** sterner, sternest

ADJECTIVE 1 very serious and strict

NOUN 2 the back part of a ship

→ Have a look at the illustration for **ship**

**stethoscope** stethoscopes

NOUN a device used by doctors to listen to a patient's heart and breathing, made of earpieces connected to a hollow tube and small disc

**stew** stews, stewing, stewed

NOUN 1 a dish of small pieces of savoury foo▪ cooked together slowly in a liquid

VERB 2 If you **stew** meat, vegetables or fruit▪ you cook them slowly in a liquid.

**WORD HISTORY**

from Middle English *stuen* meaning to take ▪ very hot bath

**steward** stewards

NOUN 1 a person who works on a ship or plane looking after passengers and serving▪ meals

NOUN 2 a person who helps to direct the public at events such as a race or a concert

**stick** sticks, sticking, stuck

NOUN 1 a long, thin piece of wood

VERB 2 If you **stick** a long or pointed object into something, you push it in.

VERB 3 If you **stick** one thing to another, you▪ attach it with glue or tape.

VERB 4 If something **sticks**, it becomes fixed or jammed.

**stick out**

VERB If something **sticks out**, it projects from something else.

**stick up for**

VERB (*informal*) If you **stick up for** someone or something, you support or defend them.

**sticker** stickers

NOUN a label with words or pictures on it for sticking on something

**sticky stickier, stickiest**
ADJECTIVE If something is **sticky**, it is covered with a substance that can stick to other things.

**stiff stiffer, stiffest**
ADJECTIVE **1** Something that is **stiff** is firm and not easily bent. • *a stiff piece of card*
ADJECTIVE **2** If you feel **stiff**, your muscles or joints ache when you move.
ADJECTIVE **3** **Stiff** behaviour is formal, and not friendly or relaxed.
ADJECTIVE **4** difficult or severe • *It was a stiff competition.*

**stifle stifles, stifling, stifled**
VERB **1** If you feel **stifled**, you feel you cannot breathe properly.
VERB **2** If you **stifle** something, you stop it happening. • *She stifled a yawn.*
ADJECTIVE **3** **Stifling** heat is very hot and makes it difficult to breathe. • *The atmosphere in the greenhouse was stifling.*

**stigma stigmas**
NOUN the top of the centre part of a flower which takes in pollen
→ Have a look at the illustration for **flower**

**stile stiles**
NOUN a step built in a hedge or wall so that people can climb over or through it

**still stiller, stillest**
ADVERB **1** You say **still** when something is the same as it was before. • *I've still got a headache.*
ADVERB **2** even then • *I've worked all day and there's still more to do.*
ADJECTIVE **3** If someone or something is **still**, they stay in the same position without moving.
ADJECTIVE **4** When the air is **still**, there is no wind.
ADJECTIVE **5** A **still** drink is not fizzy.

**stilts**
PLURAL NOUN **1** long poles on which people balance or walk
PLURAL NOUN **2** long poles on which houses are sometimes built

**stimulate stimulates, stimulating, stimulated**
VERB **1** To **stimulate** something means to encourage it to begin or develop.
• *to stimulate interest*
SYNONYM: inspire

VERB **2** If something **stimulates** you, it interests and excites you.
SYNONYM: inspire

**sting stings, stinging, stung**
VERB **1** If an animal or plant **stings** you, it pricks your skin and hurts.
VERB **2** If a part of your body **stings**, you feel a sharp, tingling pain there.

**stink stinks, stinking, stank, stunk**
VERB **1** Something that **stinks** smells very unpleasant.
NOUN **2** a very unpleasant smell

**stir stirs, stirring, stirred**
VERB **1** When you **stir** a liquid, you move it around using a spoon or a stick.
VERB **2** If someone **stirs**, they move slightly, or start to move after sleeping or being still.
• *It was very noisy but the baby didn't stir.*

**stirrup stirrups**
NOUN one of the two metal loops hanging by leather straps from a horse's saddle, that you put your feet in when riding

**stitch stitches, stitching, stitched**
VERB **1** When you **stitch** pieces of material together, you use a needle and thread to sew them together.
NOUN **2** one of the pieces of thread that can be seen where material has been sewn
NOUN **3** one of the pieces of thread that can be seen where skin has been sewn together to heal a wound • *He had eleven stitches in his lip.*
NOUN **4** a sharp pain you feel in your side after running

**stoat stoats**
NOUN a small wild mammal with a long body, brown fur and a black-tipped tail

**stock stocks**
NOUN **1** the total amount of goods a shop has for sale
NOUN **2** If you have a **stock** of things, you have a supply ready for use.

**stocking stockings**
NOUN one of a pair of long pieces of fine, stretchy fabric that cover a woman's leg and foot

**stole stoles**
VERB **1** the past tense of **steal**
NOUN **2** a shawl to cover a woman's shoulders

**stolen**
VERB the past participle of **steal**

a
b
c
d
e
f
g
h
i
j
k
l
m
n
o
p
q
r
s
t
u
v
w
x
y
z

**391**

## stomach stomachs

NOUN **1** the organ inside your body where food is digested

→ Have a look at the illustration for **organ**

NOUN **2** the front part of your body below your waist

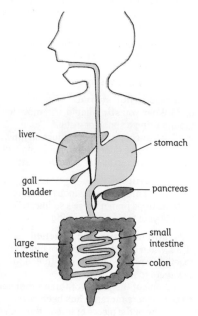

liver
stomach
gall bladder
pancreas
large intestine
small intestine
colon

## stone stones

NOUN **1** the hard solid substance found in the ground and used for building

NOUN **2** a small piece of rock

NOUN **3** a unit of weight equal to 14 pounds or about 6·35 kilograms

## stony stonier, stoniest

ADJECTIVE **Stony** ground has many stones in it.

## stood

VERB the past tense and past participle of **stand**

## stool stools

NOUN a seat with legs but no back or arms

## stoop stoops, stooping, stooped

VERB **1** If you **stoop**, you bend your body forwards.

VERB **2** If you would not **stoop** to something, you would not disgrace yourself by doing it.

## stop stops, stopping, stopped

VERB **1** If you **stop** doing something, you no longer do it.

VERB **2** If an activity **stops**, it comes to an en

VERB **3** If you **stop** something, you prevent from happening or continuing.

VERB **4** If people or things that are moving **stop**, they no longer move.

NOUN **5** a place where a bus, train or other vehicle stops to let passengers on and off

## stopwatch stopwatches

NOUN a watch that can be started and stoppe that is used to time things such as races

## storage

NOUN **1** the keeping of something somewhe until it is needed

NOUN **2** the process of storing data in a computer

## store stores, storing, stored

NOUN **1** a shop

NOUN **2** a supply of something that is kept until it is needed

NOUN **3** a place where things are kept while they are not used

VERB **4** When you **store** something somewher you keep it there until it is needed.

## storey storeys

NOUN one of the floors or levels of a building

## stork storks

NOUN a very large white and black bird with long red legs and a long bill. **Storks** live mainly near water in Eastern Europe and Africa.

## storm storms, storming, stormed

NOUN **1** a period of bad weather, when there is heavy rain, a strong wind and often thunder and lightning

VERB **2** If soldiers **storm** a defended place, they make a surprise attack on it.

NOUN **3** If there is a **storm** of protest, many people complain loudly.

## story stories

NOUN a telling of events, real or imaginary, spoken or written

## stout stouter, stoutest

ADJECTIVE **1** rather fat

ADJECTIVE **2** thick, strong and sturdy

● **stout** walking shoes

## stove stoves

NOUN a piece of equipment for heating a room or for cooking ● She warmed the milk on the **stove**.

## straddle straddles, straddling, straddled

VERB If you **straddle** something, you stand or sit with your legs either side of it.

**straight** **straighter, straightest**
ADJECTIVE **1** continuing in the same direction without curving or bending ● *a **straight** road*
ADJECTIVE **2** A **straight** angle is an angle of 180°.
ADJECTIVE **3** honest and direct ● *a **straight** answer*
ADVERB **4** immediately and directly ● *We will go **straight** to school.*
ADVERB **5** If you stand up **straight**, you stand upright.

**straighten** **straightens, straightening, straightened**
VERB If you **straighten** something, you make it straight.

**straightforward**
ADJECTIVE **1** easy to understand
ADJECTIVE **2** honest and truthful

**strain** **strains, straining, strained**
ADJECTIVE **1** If you feel **strained**, you feel tense and anxious.
NOUN **2** If a **strain** is put on something, it is affected by a strong force that may damage it.
VERB **3** If you **strain** a muscle, you use it too much and injure it so that it is painful.
VERB **4** If you **strain** food or a mixture, you separate the solid parts from the liquid parts, for example by putting it through a sieve.

**strait** **straits**
NOUN a narrow strip of sea between two pieces of land, that connects two larger areas of sea

**stranded**
ADJECTIVE If someone or something is **stranded**, they are stuck somewhere and cannot leave. ● ***stranded** on the rocks*

**strange** **stranger, strangest**
ADJECTIVE **1** unusual or unexpected ● *a **strange** dream*
ADJECTIVE **2** not known, seen or experienced before ● *She was all alone in a **strange** country.*

**stranger** **strangers**
NOUN someone you have never met before

**strangle** **strangles, strangling, strangled**
VERB To **strangle** someone means to kill them by squeezing their throat to stop them breathing.

**strap** **straps**
NOUN a narrow piece of leather or cloth, used to fasten or hold things together

**strategy** **strategies**
NOUN a plan for achieving something

**stratosphere**
NOUN the layer of the Earth's atmosphere which lies between 10 and 50 kilometres above the Earth

**straw** **straws**
NOUN **1** a hollow tube of paper or plastic that you use to suck a drink into your mouth
NOUN **2** the dry, yellowish stalks of some crops

**strawberry** **strawberries**
NOUN a small red fruit with tiny seeds in its skin

**stray** **strays, straying, strayed**
VERB **1** When people or animals **stray**, they wander away from where they should be.
VERB **2** If your thoughts **stray**, you stop concentrating.
ADJECTIVE **3** A **stray** dog or cat is one that has wandered away from where it lives.
NOUN **4** a stray dog or cat

**streak** **streaks**
NOUN a long, narrow mark or stain

**stream** **streams, streaming, streamed**
NOUN **1** a small river
NOUN **2** You can refer to a steady flow of something as a **stream**. ● *a constant **stream** of children*
VERB **3** If something **streams**, it flows fast, without stopping. ● *Rain **streamed** down the windscreen.*

**streamer** **streamers**
NOUN a long piece of paper or ribbon used as a decoration

**street** **streets**
NOUN a road in a town or village, usually with buildings along it

**strength**
NOUN how strong or powerful someone or something is

SYNONYMS: might, force, power

**strenuous**
ADJECTIVE involving a lot of effort or energy

**stress** **stresses, stressing, stressed**
NOUN **1** worry and nervous tension

SYNONYMS: anxiety, pressure, strain

VERB **2** If you **stress** a point, you emphasise it and draw attention to how important it is.

a
b
c
d
e
f
g
h
i
j
k
l
m
n
o
p
q
r
s
t
u
v
w
x
y
z

**393**

A
B
C
D
E
F
G
H
I
J
K
L
M
N
O
P
Q
R
S
T
U
V
W
X
Y
Z

### stretch stretches, stretching, stretched
VERB **1** If you **stretch** something soft or elastic, you pull it to make it longer or bigger.
VERB **2** Something that **stretches** over an area covers the whole of that area. • *Forests stretched the length of the valley.*
VERB **3** When you **stretch**, you move part of your body as far away from you as you can.
NOUN **4** an area of something • *This is a quiet stretch of beach.*

### stretcher stretchers
NOUN a long piece of material with a pole along each side, used to carry an injured person

### strict stricter, strictest
ADJECTIVE **1** Someone who is **strict** controls other people very firmly.
ADJECTIVE **2** exact or complete • *We were given strict instructions.*

### stride strides, striding, strode, stridden
VERB **1** If you **stride** along, you walk quickly with long steps.
NOUN **2** a long step

### strike strikes, striking, struck
VERB **1** If you **strike** something, you hit it with a lot of force.
VERB **2** If workers **strike**, they refuse to work because they want better working conditions or more money.
VERB **3** If you **strike** a match, you make a flame by rubbing it against something rough.

### striking
ADJECTIVE very noticeable because of being unusual or attractive

### string strings
NOUN **1** thin rope made of twisted threads
NOUN **2** a row or series of similar things • *a string of islands*

### strip strips, stripping, stripped
NOUN **1** a long, narrow piece of something
VERB **2** If you **strip**, you take off all your clothes.

### stripe stripes
NOUN a long, thin line of colour

### strode
VERB the past tense of **stride**

### stroke strokes, stroking, stroked
VERB **1** If you **stroke** something, you move your hand smoothly and gently over it.
NOUN **2** The **strokes** of a brush or pen are the movements that you make with it.
NOUN **3** If someone has a **stroke**, a blood vessel in the brain bursts or gets blocked, possibly causing death or paralysis.
NOUN **4** a style of swimming • *My best stroke is the front crawl.*

### stroll strolls, strolling, strolled
VERB **1** If you **stroll** along, you walk slowly a relaxed way.

SYNONYMS: amble, saunter

NOUN **2** a slow, pleasurable walk

SYNONYMS: amble, saunter

### strong stronger, strongest
ADJECTIVE **1** Someone who is **strong** has a lo of physical power.
ADJECTIVE **2** You also say that someone is **strong** when they are confident and have courage.
ADJECTIVE **3** **Strong** objects are able to withstand rough treatment, and are not easily damaged.
ADJECTIVE **4** great or intense • *a strong wind*

### struck
VERB the past tense and past participle of **strike**

### structure structures
NOUN **1** The **structure** of something is the way it is made, built or organised.
NOUN **2** something that has been built or put together

### struggle struggles, struggling, struggled
VERB **1** If you **struggle** to do something difficult, you try hard to do it.
VERB **2** When people **struggle**, they twist and move violently to get free of something or someone.
NOUN **3** Something that is a **struggle** is difficult to achieve and takes a lot of effort.

### stubble
NOUN **1** the short stalks remaining in the ground after a crop is harvested
NOUN **2** If a man has **stubble** on his face, he has very short hair growing there because he has not shaved recently.

### stubborn
ADJECTIVE Someone who is **stubborn** is determined not to change the way they think or how they do things.

SYNONYM: obstinate

**uck**

ADJECTIVE **1** If something or someone is **stuck**, they cannot be moved.

ADJECTIVE **2** If you are **stuck**, you cannot go on with your work because you are finding it too difficult.

VERB **3** the past tense and past participle of **stick**

**ud studs**

NOUN **1** a small piece of metal, or other material, fixed into something • *Rachel wore gold **studs** in her ears.*

NOUN **2** A male horse or other animal that is kept for **stud** is kept for breeding purposes.

NOUN **3** a place where horses are kept and bred

**cudent students**

NOUN a person studying at a university, college or school

**cudio studios**

NOUN **1** a room where an artist works

NOUN **2** a room containing special equipment where records, films, or radio or television programmes are made

**cudious**

ADJECTIVE Someone who is **studious** studies hard or is fond of studying.

**cudy studies, studying, studied**

VERB **1** If you **study** a particular subject, you spend time learning about it.

VERB **2** If you **study** something, you look at it carefully.

NOUN **3** a room for studying or working in

**cuff stuffs, stuffing, stuffed**

NOUN **1** You can refer to a substance or a group of things as **stuff**. • *She spread out her **stuff** on top of the table.*

VERB **2** If you **stuff** something somewhere, you push it there quickly and carelessly.

VERB **3** If you **stuff** something, you fill it with something else. • *Mum **stuffed** the turkey.*

**cuffy stuffier, stuffiest**

ADJECTIVE **1** If it is **stuffy** in a room, there is not enough fresh air.

ADJECTIVE **2** boring and old-fashioned

**cumble stumbles, stumbling, stumbled**

VERB **1** If you **stumble** while you are walking or running, you trip and nearly fall.

VERB **2** If you **stumble** when you are speaking, you hesitate or make mistakes.

**cump stumps, stumping, stumped**

NOUN **1** a small part of something that is left when the rest has gone • *a tree **stump***

NOUN **2** In cricket, the **stumps** are the three upright wooden sticks that support the bails, forming the wicket.

VERB **3** If a question or problem **stumps** you, you cannot think of an answer or solution.

**stun stuns, stunning, stunned**

VERB **1** If you are **stunned**, or something **stuns** you, you are very shocked by it.

VERB **2** If something **stuns** a person or an animal, it knocks them unconscious.

**stung**

VERB the past tense and past participle of **sting**

**stunk**

VERB the past participle of **stink**

**stunt stunts**

NOUN an unusual or dangerous and exciting thing that someone does to get publicity or as part of a performance

**stupid stupider, stupidest**

ADJECTIVE If you are **stupid**, you are not sensible and do not make wise decisions.

**sturdy sturdier, sturdiest**

ADJECTIVE strong, firm and well built

**stutter stutters, stuttering, stuttered**

NOUN **1** Someone who has a **stutter** finds it difficult to speak smoothly and often repeats the beginning of words.

VERB **2** When someone **stutters**, they hesitate or repeat sounds when speaking.

**sty sties**

NOUN a hut with a yard where pigs are kept on a farm

**style styles**

NOUN **1** how something is done, made, said or written • *The food was cooked in Cantonese **style**.*

NOUN **2** A person or place that has **style** is smart, elegant and fashionable.

**sub-**

PREFIX You add **sub-**to the beginning of a word to mean below or beneath. For example, something that is **sub**standard is below the required standard, and a **sub**heading comes somewhere below a main heading.

**subheading subheadings**

NOUN a title to a part of a larger section of a book. A chapter may have several sections in it, each with a **subheading**.

a
b
c
d
e
f
g
h
i
j
k
l
m
n
o
p
q
r
s
t
u
v
w
x
y
z

**395**

**subject** subjects, subjecting, subjected

NOUN **1** The **subject** of a book, programme or conversation is the thing or person it is about. ● *Horses are the **subject** of this book.*
NOUN **2** something that you learn about ● *Maths is my favourite **subject**.*
NOUN **3** The **subjects** of a country are the people who live there.
NOUN **4** In grammar, the **subject** is the word or words representing the person or thing doing the action. For example, in the sentence *My cat keeps catching birds*, *my cat* is the **subject**.
VERB **5** If you **subject** someone to something, you make them experience it.

PRONUNCIATION TIP
The noun is pronounced **sub**-jekt. The verb is pronounced sub-**jekt**.

**submarine** submarines
NOUN a type of ship that can travel beneath the surface of the sea

**submerge** submerges, submerging, submerged
VERB To **submerge** means to go beneath the surface of a liquid, or to push something beneath the surface of a liquid.

**submit** submits, submitting, submitted
VERB **1** If you **submit** to something or someone, you give in to them.
VERB **2** If you **submit** something like a report or an essay, you hand it in.

**subscribe** subscribes, subscribing, subscribed
VERB If you **subscribe** to something, you regularly pay a sum of money to be a member of something or to receive a magazine.

**subside** subsides, subsiding, subsided
VERB **1** If something **subsides**, it sinks.
VERB **2** To **subside** is to become quiet or back to normal after a fuss.

**substance** substances
NOUN anything that is a solid, a powder, a liquid or a paste

SYNONYM: material

**substantial**
ADJECTIVE **1** very large in degree or amount
ADJECTIVE **2** large and strongly built

**substitute** substitutes, substituting, substituted
VERB **1** If you **substitute** one thing for another, you use it instead of the other thing.

NOUN **2** If one thing is a **substitute** for another, it is used instead of it or put in its place.

SYNONYMS: alternative, replacement

**subtitle** subtitles
NOUN A film or television programme with **subtitles** has the speech, or a translation of it, printed at the bottom of the screen.

**subtle** subtler, subtlest
ADJECTIVE very fine, delicate or small in degree

**subtract** subtracts, subtracting, subtracted
VERB If you **subtract** one number from another, you take away the first number from the second.

**subtraction**
NOUN the process of taking one number away from another

**suburban**
ADJECTIVE to do with the outskirts of a town or city

**subway** subways
NOUN **1** a footpath that goes underneath a road
NOUN **2** an underground railway

**succeed** succeeds, succeeding, succeeded
VERB **1** If you **succeed**, you manage to do what you are trying to do.

ANTONYM: fail

VERB **2** If one person **succeeds** another, they come after them and take their place.

**success** successes
NOUN the achievement of something you have been trying to do

**successful**
ADJECTIVE having success

**succession** successions
NOUN **1** a number of things happening one after the other
NOUN **2** When someone becomes the next person to have an important position, you can call this event their **succession**.

**such**
ADVERB **1** You can use **such** to emphasise something. ● *He's **such** a nice boy.*
ADJECTIVE **2** the same kind or similar ● *I have never seen **such** flowers.*
PHRASE **3** You can use **such as** to introduce examples of something. ● *There were trees **such as** oak, ash and elm.*

**ıck sucks, sucking, sucked**
VERB If you **suck** something, you hold it in your mouth and pull at it with your cheeks and tongue, usually to get liquid out of it.

**ıdden**
ADJECTIVE happening quickly and unexpectedly • We heard a **sudden** cry.

**ıe sues, suing, sued**
VERB To **sue** someone means to start a legal case against them, usually to claim money from them.

**ıede**
NOUN a thin, soft leather with a velvety surface

**ıffer suffers, suffering, suffered**
VERB If you **suffer**, you feel pain or sadness.

**ıfficient**
ADJECTIVE If an amount is **sufficient**, there is enough of it available.

**ıffix suffixes**
NOUN a group of letters that is added to the end of a word to form a new word, for example -ness or -ship, which would make good into goodness and friend into friendship

**ıffocate suffocates, suffocating, suffocated**
VERB If someone **suffocates**, they die because they have no air to breathe.

**ıgar**
NOUN a sweet substance obtained from some plants and used to sweeten food and drinks

**ıggest suggests, suggesting, suggested**
VERB When you **suggest** something, you offer it as an idea.

**ıicide**
NOUN People who commit **suicide** deliberately kill themselves.

**ıit suits, suiting, suited**
NOUN **1** a matching jacket and trousers or skirt
VERB **2** If an arrangement **suits** you, it is convenient and suitable for you.
VERB **3** If a piece of clothing or a colour **suits** you, you look good when you are wearing it.
NOUN **4** A **suit** in a pack of cards is one of the sets of diamonds, clubs, hearts or spades.

**ıitable**
ADJECTIVE right or acceptable for a certain person, occasion, time or place • Many roads are not **suitable** for cycling.

**suitcase suitcases**
NOUN a case in which you carry your belongings when you are travelling

**suite suites**
NOUN **1** a set of rooms in a hotel
NOUN **2** a set of matching furniture or bathroom fittings

**sulk sulks, sulking, sulked**
VERB If you **sulk**, you show your annoyance by being silent and moody.

**sullen**
ADJECTIVE behaving in a bad-tempered and disagreeably silent way

**sulphur**
NOUN a yellow chemical used in industry and medicine. **Sulphur** burns with a very unpleasant smell.

**sultana sultanas**
NOUN a dried, seedless grape

**sum sums**
NOUN **1** an amount of money
NOUN **2** the total of numbers added together

**summarise summarises, summarising, summarised**; also spelt **summarize**
VERB If you **summarise** something, you give a short account of its main points.

**summary summaries**
NOUN a short account of the main points of something said or written

**summer summers**
NOUN the warmest season of the year, between spring and autumn

**summit summits**
NOUN the top of a mountain • The view from the **summit** was spectacular.

**summon summons, summoning, summoned**
VERB If someone **summons** you, they order you to go to them.

**sun**
NOUN **1** the star in our solar system around which the Earth and other planets travel, and that gives us heat and light

→ Have a look at the illustration for **solar system**

NOUN **2** the heat and light from the sun

→ Have a look at the illustrations at **greenhouse effect** and **photosynthesis**

a
b
c
d
e
f
g
h
i
j
k
l
m
n
o
p
q
r
s
t
u
v
w
x
y
z

**397**

**sunbathe sunbathes, sunbathing, sunbathed**
VERB When you **sunbathe**, you sit in the sun to get brown.

**sunburn**
NOUN sore red skin due to being in the sun for too long

**Sunday Sundays**
NOUN the first day of the week, coming before Monday

**sunflower sunflowers**
NOUN a tall flower with a very large, round yellow head

**sung**
VERB the past participle of **sing**

**sunglasses**
PLURAL NOUN dark glasses worn to protect your eyes from the sun

**sunk**
VERB the past participle of **sink**

**sunlight**
NOUN the light from the sun

**sunny sunnier, sunniest**
ADJECTIVE having lots of sunshine

**sunrise sunrises**
NOUN the time in the day when the sun first appears

**sunset sunsets**
NOUN the time when the sun goes down

**sunshine**
NOUN warmth and light that come from the sun

**super**
ADJECTIVE excellent, very good

**superb**
ADJECTIVE very good indeed

**superficial**
ADJECTIVE only on the surface

**superior**
ADJECTIVE **1** better or of higher quality than other similar things
ADJECTIVE **2** in a more important position than another person

**superlative superlatives**
ADJECTIVE **1** of the highest quality, the best
NOUN **2** the form of an adverb or adjective that expresses *most*. For example, the **superlative** of *hot* is *hottest*, and the **superlative** of *easy* is *easiest*.

**supermarket supermarkets**
NOUN a very large self-service shop that sells food and household goods

**supernatural**
ADJECTIVE Something that is **supernatural**, such as ghosts or witchcraft, cannot be explained by natural, scientific laws.

**supersonic**
ADJECTIVE faster than the speed of sound

---

WORD HISTORY
from Latin *super* + *sonus* meaning above sou

---

**superstar superstars**
NOUN a very famous entertainer or sportsperso

**superstitious**
ADJECTIVE People who are **superstitious** believe in things like magic and powers th bring good or bad luck.

**supervise supervises, supervising, supervised**
VERB If you **supervise** someone, you check what they are doing to make sure that the do it correctly.

**supper suppers**
NOUN a meal eaten in the evening or a snac eaten before you go to bed

**supple**
ADJECTIVE able to bend and move easily
● *Gymnasts are usually very **supple**.*

**supplement supplements, supplementing, supplemented**
VERB **1** To **supplement** something means t add something to it to improve it. ● *Many villagers **supplemented** their food supply by fishing for salmon.*
NOUN **2** something that is added to something else to improve it

**supply supplies, supplying, supplied**
VERB **1** If you **supply** someone with something, you provide them with it.
PLURAL NOUN **2 Supplies** are food and equipment for a special purpose. ● *His medical **supplies** were running low.*

**support supports, supporting, supported**
VERB **1** If something **supports** an object, it i underneath it and holding it up.
VERB **2** If you **support** a sports team, you ar a fan.
VERB **3** If you **support** someone, you give them money, help or encouragement.
NOUN **4** If you give **support** to someone, you are kind, encouraging and helpful to them.
NOUN **5** something that supports an object

**uppose** supposes, supposing, supposed
VERB If you **suppose** that something is so, you think that it is likely.

**uppress** suppresses, suppressing, suppressed
VERB If an army or government **suppresses** something, it stops people doing it.

**upreme**
ADJECTIVE greatest, best or most important

**ure** surer, surest
ADJECTIVE 1 If you are **sure** about something, you know you are right.
ADJECTIVE 2 If something is **sure** to happen, it will definitely happen.

**urf** surfs, surfing, surfed
NOUN 1 the white foam that forms on the top of waves when they break near the shore
VERB 2 When you **surf**, you ride towards the shore on top of a wave, on a special board called a surfboard.
VERB 3 When you **surf** the internet, you go from website to website reading the information.

**urface** surfaces
NOUN the top or outside area of something • The wind ruffled the **surface** of the lake.

**urge** surges, surging, surged
NOUN 1 a sudden great increase in the amount of something • After the rain there was a **surge** of water down the river.
VERB 2 If someone or something **surges**, they move suddenly and powerfully. • The crowd **surged** forward.

**urgeon** surgeons
NOUN a doctor who performs operations

**urgery** surgeries
NOUN 1 medical treatment in which part of the patient's body is cut open • He had to have **surgery** to repair his knee.
NOUN 2 a room where doctors or dentists see their patients

**urname** surnames
NOUN your last name. Members of the same family usually have the same **surname**.

**urplus** surpluses
NOUN If there is a **surplus** of something, there is more of it than is needed.

**urprise** surprises, surprising, surprised
NOUN 1 an unexpected event
NOUN 2 the feeling caused when something unexpected happens

VERB 3 If something **surprises** you, it gives you a feeling of surprise.

**surrender** surrenders, surrendering, surrendered
VERB If someone **surrenders**, they admit that they are defeated.

**surround** surrounds, surrounding, surrounded
VERB To **surround** someone or something means to be situated all around them. • The house is **surrounded** by a high fence.

**surroundings**
PLURAL NOUN the things and conditions around a person or place

**survey** surveys, surveying, surveyed
VERB 1 If you **survey** something, you look carefully at the whole of it. • They stood back and **surveyed** the scene.
VERB 2 to make a detailed inspection of something
NOUN 3 A **survey** of something, such as people's habits, is a detailed examination of it, often in a report.

PRONUNCIATION TIP
The verb is pronounced sur-**vey**. The noun is pronounced **sur**-vey.

**survival**
NOUN managing to go on living or existing in spite of danger or difficulties

**survive** survives, surviving, survived
VERB To **survive** means to continue to live or exist in spite of danger or difficulties.

**suspect** suspects, suspecting, suspected
VERB 1 If you **suspect** something, you think that it might be true.
VERB 2 If you **suspect** someone of doing something wrong, you think that they have done it.
NOUN 3 someone who is thought to be guilty of a crime

PRONUNCIATION TIP
The verb is pronounced sus-**spekt**. The noun is pronounced **suss**-pekt.

**suspend** suspends, suspending, suspended
VERB 1 to hang something up
VERB 2 to delay something for a time

**suspense**
NOUN the feeling of excitement or fear when you are waiting for something to happen

a
b
c
d
e
f
g
h
i
j
k
l
m
n
o
p
q
r
s
t
u
v
w
x
y
z

**399**

A
B
C
D
E
F
G
H
I
J
K
L
M
N
O
P
Q
R
S
T
U
V
W
X
Y
Z

**400**

### suspicion suspicions
NOUN the feeling of not trusting someone or that something is wrong

### suspicious
ADJECTIVE **1** If you are **suspicious** of someone, you do not trust them.
ADJECTIVE **2** If something is **suspicious**, it causes suspicion.

### swallow swallows, swallowing, swallowed
VERB If you **swallow** something, you make it go down your throat and into your stomach.

### swam
VERB the past tense of **swim**

### swamp swamps, swamping, swamped
NOUN **1** an area of permanently wet land
VERB **2** If something is **swamped**, it is covered or filled with water.
VERB **3** If you are **swamped** by things, you have more than you can manage.

### swan swans
NOUN a large, usually white, bird with a long neck that lives on rivers or lakes

### swap swaps, swapping, swapped
VERB If you **swap** one thing for another, you replace the first thing with the second.

SYNONYM: exchange

---

**PRONUNCIATION TIP**
This word rhymes with "stop".

---

### swarm swarms, swarming, swarmed
NOUN **1** a large group of insects flying together
VERB **2** When bees or other insects **swarm**, they fly together in a large group.
VERB **3** If a place is **swarming** with people, it is crowded with people.

### swat swats, swatting, swatted
VERB If you **swat** an insect, you hit it quickly to kill it.

### sway sways, swaying, swayed
VERB If something or someone **sways**, they lean or swing slowly from side to side.

### swear swears, swearing, swore, sworn
VERB **1** If you **swear**, you use very rude words.
VERB **2** If you **swear** to do something, you promise that you will do it.

### sweat sweats, sweating, sweated
NOUN **1** the salty liquid that comes through your skin when you are hot or afraid
VERB **2** When you **sweat**, sweat comes through your skin.

### sweater sweaters
NOUN a knitted piece of clothing covering your upper body and arms

### sweatshirt sweatshirts
NOUN a piece of clothing made of thick cotton, covering your upper body and arms

### swede swedes
NOUN a large round root vegetable with yellow flesh and a brownish-purple skin

### sweep sweeps, sweeping, swept
VERB **1** If you **sweep** the floor, you use a brush to gather up dust or rubbish from it.
VERB **2** If you **sweep** things off a surface, you push them all off with a quick, smooth movement.
VERB **3** If something **sweeps** from one place to another, it moves there very quickly.
• The boat **swept** down the river with the outgoing tide.

### sweet sweeter, sweetest; sweets
ADJECTIVE **1** tasting of sugar or honey
ADJECTIVE **2** A **sweet** sound is gentle and tuneful
ADJECTIVE **3** attractive and delightful
• He's such a **sweet** little baby.
NOUN **4** small pieces of sweet food, such as toffees, chocolates and mints
NOUN **5** something sweet that you eat at the end of a meal

SYNONYM: dessert

### sweet corn
NOUN a long stalk covered with juicy yellow seeds that can be eaten as a vegetable

### sweetheart sweethearts
NOUN You can call someone you are very fond of **sweetheart**.

### swell swells, swelling, swelled, swollen
VERB If something **swells**, it becomes larger and rounder.

### sweltering
ADJECTIVE If the weather is **sweltering**, it is very hot.

### swept
VERB the past tense and past participle of **sweep**

### swerve swerves, swerving, swerved
VERB If someone or something **swerves**, they suddenly change direction to avoid colliding with something.

### swift swifter, swiftest; swifts
ADJECTIVE **1** happening or moving very quickly
NOUN **2** a bird with narrow crescent-shaped wings

**swim swims, swimming, swam, swum**
VERB When you **swim**, you move through water by making movements with your arms and legs.

**swimming**
NOUN the act of moving through water using your arms and legs

**swimming costume swimming costumes**
NOUN a garment you wear while swimming

**swimming pool swimming pools**
NOUN an area of water made for swimming, usually a large hole that has been tiled and filled with water

**swimsuit swimsuits**
NOUN a one-piece swimming costume

**swindle swindles, swindling, swindled**
VERB **1** If someone **swindles** someone else, they trick them to obtain money or property.
NOUN **2** a trick in which someone is cheated out of money or property

**swine swine**
NOUN (*old-fashioned*) a pig

---

**LANGUAGE TIP**
The plural of *swine* is *swine*.

---

**swing swings, swinging, swung**
VERB **1** If something **swings**, or if you **swing** it, it moves repeatedly from side to side or backwards and forwards from a fixed point.
NOUN **2** a seat hanging from a frame or a branch, that moves backwards and forwards when you sit on it

**swipe swipes, swiping, swiped**
VERB **1** If you **swipe** at something, you try to hit it with a curved swinging movement.
VERB **2** If a credit card is **swiped**, it is put though an electronic machine to read it when paying.
VERB **3** If you **swipe**, you move your finger across the screen of a phone or computer.
• Simply **swipe** up to video.
VERB **4** (*informal*) If someone **swipes** something, they steal it.

**switch switches, switching, switched**
NOUN **1** a device used to control an electrical device or machine. When the **switch** is on, or closed, it completes the circuit and electricity can flow.
NOUN **2** a change
VERB **3** To **switch** to a different task or topic means to change to it.

**switch off**
VERB If you **switch off** a light or a machine, you stop it working by pressing a switch.

**switch on**
VERB If you **switch on** a light or a machine, you start it working by pressing a switch.

**switchboard switchboards**
NOUN a panel with switches on for connecting telephone lines

**swivel swivels, swivelling, swivelled**
VERB **1** to turn round on a central point
ADJECTIVE **2** A **swivel** chair or lamp is made so that you can move the main part of it while the base remains in a fixed position.

**swollen**
ADJECTIVE **1** Something that is **swollen** has swelled up.

SYNONYMS: enlarged, puffed up

VERB **2** the past participle of **swell**

**swoop swoops, swooping, swooped**
VERB To **swoop** is to move downwards through the air in a fast curving movement.

**swop swops, swopping, swopped**
VERB to swap

**sword swords**
NOUN a weapon consisting of a very long blade with a short handle

**swum**
VERB the past participle of **swim**

**swung**
VERB the past tense and past participle of **swing**

**sycamore sycamores**
NOUN a tree that has large leaves with five points, and winged seed cases

**syllable syllables**
NOUN a part of a word that contains a single vowel sound and is said as one unit • "Book" has one **syllable** and "reading" has two.

**syllabus syllabuses** or **syllabi**
NOUN the subjects that are studied for a particular course or examination

**symbol symbols**
NOUN a shape, design or idea that is used to represent something • Apple blossom is a Chinese **symbol** of peace and beauty.

→ Have a look at the illustration for **map**

a
b
c
d
e
f
g
h
i
j
k
l
m
n
o
p
q
r
s
t
u
v
w
x
y
z

## symmetrical
ADJECTIVE **Symmetrical** objects can be divided in half so that both halves match, with one half like a reflection of the other.

## symmetry
NOUN If something has **symmetry**, it is the same in both halves. The line drawn through something so that both sides of the line look exactly the same is called a line of **symmetry**.

## sympathetic
ADJECTIVE feeling sympathy or understanding for someone

## sympathy
NOUN an understanding of people's feelings and opinions, especially someone who is in difficulties

SYNONYM: compassion

## symphony **symphonies**
NOUN a piece of music for an orchestra, usually in four parts called movements

## symptom **symptoms**
NOUN something wrong with your body that is a sign of illness

## synagogue **synagogues**
NOUN a building where Jewish people meet for worship and religious instruction

## synonym **synonyms**
NOUN two words that have the same or a very similar meaning • *Speak is a **synonym** for talk.*

## synthetic
ADJECTIVE made from artificial substances rather than natural ones

## syringe **syringes**
NOUN a hollow tube with a plunger, used for drawing up or pushing out liquids. Doctors and vets use them to give injections.

## syrup **syrups**
NOUN a thick, sweet liquid made by boiling sugar with water

WORD HISTORY
from Arabic *sharab* meaning drink

## system **systems**
NOUN an organised way of doing or arranging something according to a fixed plan or set of rules

## tab **tabs**
NOUN a small extra piece that is attached to something and sticks out, for example a sticky marker that you put in a book to mark your place

## table **tables**
NOUN **1** a piece of furniture with a flat top supported by one or more legs
NOUN **2** a set of facts or figures arranged in rows or columns

## tablecloth **tablecloths**
NOUN a cloth used to cover a table and to keep it clean

## tablespoon **tablespoons**
NOUN **1** a large spoon used for serving food
NOUN **2** the amount that a **tablespoon** contains • *For this recipe you need two **tablespoons** of caster sugar.*

## tablet **tablets**
NOUN **1** medicine in a small, solid lump that you swallow

SYNONYM: pill

NOUN **2** a flat piece of stone with words carved on it
NOUN **3** a small mobile personal computer with a screen that you tap or swipe

## table tennis
NOUN a game for two or four people who use bats to hit a small ball over a net across the middle of the table

## tabloid **tabloids**
NOUN a newspaper with small pages, short news stories, and lots of photographs

## tachometer **tachometers**
NOUN the instrument in a vehicle which shows the speed of the engine

→ Have a look at the illustration for **car**

**tack** tacks, tacking, tacked
NOUN **1** a short nail with a flat top
NOUN **2** If you change **tack**, you find a different way of doing something.
VERB **3** If you **tack** something to a surface, you fix it there with a tack.
VERB **4** If you **tack** in a boat, you sail in a zigzag course to catch the wind.
VERB **5** If you **tack** a piece of fabric, you sew it with long, loose stitches.
NOUN **6** equipment for horses, such as bridles, saddles and harnesses

**tackle** tackles, tackling, tackled
VERB **1** If you **tackle** a difficult task, you start dealing with it.
VERB **2** If you **tackle** someone in a game such as hockey or soccer, you try to get the ball away from them.
NOUN **3** an attempt to get the ball away from your opponent in certain sports

**tact**
NOUN the ability to deal with people without upsetting or offending them

**tactful**
ADJECTIVE able to deal with people without upsetting or offending them

**tactfully**
ADVERB in a way that shows you are trying not to upset or offend someone

**tactic** tactics
NOUN one of the methods you use in order to achieve what you want

**tactless**
ADJECTIVE unable to deal with people without upsetting or offending them

**tadpole** tadpoles
NOUN a young frog or toad. **Tadpoles** are black with round heads and long tails, and live in water.
→ Have a look at the illustration for **frog**

WORD HISTORY
Middle English *tadde* meaning toad and *pol* meaning head

**tag** tags, tagging, tagged
NOUN **1** a small label made of cloth
NOUN **2** a game in which one person chases the other people who are playing
VERB **3** If you **tag along** behind someone, you follow and try to keep up.

**tail** tails
NOUN **1** The **tail** of an animal or bird is the part extending beyond the end of its body. For example, a fox has a bushy **tail**.
→ Have a look at the illustrations for **bird** and **fish**
NOUN **2** the end part of something
→ Have a look at the illustration for **aeroplane**
NOUN **3** When you toss a coin, the side called **tails** is the one that does not have a person's head on it.

LANGUAGE TIP
Do not confuse *tail* with *tale*.

**tailor** tailors
NOUN a person who makes, alters and repairs clothes, especially for men

**take** takes, taking, took, taken
VERB **1** If you **take** someone or something to a place, you get them there. ● She **took** the cat to the vet.
VERB **2** **Take** is used to show what activity is being done. ● Sam **took** a shower.
VERB **3** If you **take** a pill or some medicine, you swallow it.
VERB **4** When you **take** one number from another, you subtract it.
VERB **5** If you **take** a photograph, you use a camera to produce it.
**take after**
VERB If you **take after** a member of your family, you are like them in some way.
**take away**
VERB If you **take** one number **away** from another, you make one number smaller by the value of the other number. ● Seven **take away** two is five (7 − 2 = 5).
**take off**
VERB When a plane **takes off**, it goes into the air.

**takeaway** takeaways
NOUN **1** a shop or restaurant that sells hot, cooked food to be taken away and eaten elsewhere
NOUN **2** a hot cooked meal bought from a takeaway restaurant

**talcum powder**
NOUN a soft, perfumed powder to put on the skin to dry it

403

**tale tales**
NOUN a story

**LANGUAGE TIP**
Do not confuse *tale* with *tail*.

**talent talents**
NOUN the ability to do something very well

**talk talks, talking, talked**
VERB **1** When you **talk**, you say things to someone.
NOUN **2** a conversation or discussion
NOUN **3** an informal speech about something

**talkative**
ADJECTIVE If you are **talkative**, you talk a lot.
SYNONYM: chatty

**tall taller, tallest**
ADJECTIVE **1** If you are **tall**, you are more than the average height.
ADJECTIVE **2** having a particular height
• *How **tall** are you?*

**tally tallies**
NOUN an informal record that you keep as you count objects

**Talmud**
NOUN a collection of books of the ancient Jewish ceremonies and laws

**talon talons**
NOUN a sharp, hooked claw, especially of a bird of prey

**tambourine tambourines**
NOUN a percussion instrument made of a skin stretched tightly over a circular frame. It has small round pieces of metal around the edge that jangle when the **tambourine** is beaten or shaken.

**WORD HISTORY**
from Old French *tambourin* meaning little drum

**tame tamer, tamest; tames, taming, tamed**
ADJECTIVE **1** A **tame** animal is not afraid of people.
VERB **2** If you **tame** a wild animal, you train it not to be afraid of humans.

**tamper tampers, tampering, tampered**
VERB If you **tamper** with something, you interfere with it.

**tan tans, tanning, tanned**
NOUN **1** a suntan
NOUN **2** a yellowish-brown colour
VERB **3** If your skin **tans**, it goes brown in the sun.
VERB **4** When an animal's skin is **tanned**, it is turned into leather by treating it with chemicals.

**tang tangs**
NOUN a strong flavour or smell

**tangerine tangerines**
NOUN **1** a type of small sweet orange that is easy to peel
NOUN **2** a reddish-orange colour
ADJECTIVE **3** having a reddish-orange colour

**tangle tangles, tangling, tangled**
NOUN **1** a mass of things, such as hairs or fibres, that are twisted together and difficult to separate
VERB **2** If you **tangle** something, you twist it into knots.

**tank tanks**
NOUN **1** a large container for storing liquid or gas
NOUN **2** an armoured military vehicle that moves on tracks and has guns or rockets

**tanker tankers**
NOUN a ship or lorry designed to carry large quantities of gas or liquid

**tantrum tantrums**
NOUN a noisy and sometimes violent outburst of bad temper, especially by a child

**tap taps, tapping, tapped**
NOUN **1** a device for controlling the flow of gas or liquid from a pipe
VERB **2** If you **tap** something, you hit it lightly and quickly.
NOUN **3** a light hit, or its sound

**tape tapes, taping, taped**
NOUN **1** a long plastic ribbon covered with a magnetic substance and used to record sounds, pictures and computer information
NOUN **2** a cassette with magnetic **tape** wound round it • *video **tape***
NOUN **3** a strip of sticky plastic used for sticking things together
VERB **4** If you **tape** sounds or television pictures, you record them using a tape recorder or a video recorder.

**tape measure tape measures**
NOUN a long, narrow tape marked with centimetres or inches, and used for measuring

**taper tapers, tapering, tapered**
VERB Something that **tapers** becomes thinner towards one end.

**tape recorder tape recorders**
NOUN a machine that records sounds onto a special magnetic tape that can be played back later

**tapestry tapestries**
NOUN a piece of heavy cloth with designs embroidered on it

→ Have a look at the illustration

**WORD HISTORY**
from Old French *tapisserie* meaning carpeting

**tar**
NOUN a thick, black, sticky substance that is used in making roads

**tarantula tarantulas**
NOUN a large, hairy, poisonous spider

**target targets**
NOUN something you aim at when firing a weapon

**tarmac**
NOUN a mixture of tar and crushed stones, used for making road surfaces

**WORD HISTORY**
short for *tarmacadam*, from the name of John *McAdam*, the Scottish engineer who invented it

**tarnish tarnishes, tarnishing, tarnished**
VERB If metal **tarnishes**, it becomes stained and loses its shine.

**tarpaulin tarpaulins**
NOUN a sheet of heavy waterproof material used as a protective covering

**tart tarts**
NOUN **1** a pastry case, usually filled with something sweet such as fruit or jam
ADJECTIVE **2** Something **tart** has a sharp or sour taste.

**tartan tartans**
NOUN a coloured, woollen fabric from Scotland, with a special pattern of checks and stripes, depending on which clan it belongs to

a
b
c
d
e
f
g
h
i
j
k
l
m
n
o
p
q
r
s
t
u
v
w
x
y
z

**tapestry**

**task tasks**
NOUN any piece of work that has to be done

SYNONYMS: chore, duty, job

**tassel tassels**
NOUN a tuft of loose threads tied by a knot and used for decoration

**taste tastes, tasting, tasted**
NOUN 1 Your sense of **taste** is your ability to recognise the flavour of things in your mouth.
NOUN 2 The **taste** of something is its flavour.
NOUN 3 your own particular choice of things such as clothes, music and food • *Jenny and I have the same taste in music.*
VERB 4 When you can **taste** something in your mouth, you know what its flavour is like.
VERB 5 If food or drink **tastes** of something, it has that flavour.

**tasty tastier, tastiest**
ADJECTIVE Something that is **tasty** has a pleasant flavour.

**tattered**
ADJECTIVE ragged and torn

**tattoo tattoos, tattooing, tattooed**
VERB 1 If someone is **tattooed**, they have a design drawn on their skin by pricking little holes and filling them with coloured dye.
NOUN 2 a picture or design tattooed on someone's body

**taught**
VERB the past tense and past participle of **teach**

**taunt taunts, taunting, taunted**
VERB If you **taunt** someone, you tease them about their weaknesses or failures in order to make them angry or upset.

**taut**
ADJECTIVE Something that is **taut** is stretched very tight.

**tawny**
ADJECTIVE brownish-yellow

**tax taxes, taxing, taxed**
NOUN 1 an amount of money that people have to pay to the government so that it can provide public services such as health care and education
VERB 2 If a sum of money is **taxed**, a certain amount of it is paid to the government.
VERB 3 If something **taxes** you, it exhausts you and drains your energy.

**taxi taxis**
NOUN a car with a driver that you hire, usually for a short journey

**tea teas**
NOUN 1 the dried leaves of a shrub found in Asi
NOUN 2 a drink made by soaking the leaves of the tea plant in hot water
NOUN 3 a meal taken in the late afternoon o early evening

**tea bag tea bags**
NOUN a small paper packet with tea leaves in it, that you use to make a drink of tea

**teach teaches, teaching, taught**
VERB If someone **teaches** you something, they help you learn about it or show you how to do it.

SYNONYMS: educate, instruct, train

**teacher teachers**
NOUN someone who teaches at a school or college

**teak**
NOUN a hard wood that comes from a large Asian tree

**team teams**
NOUN a group of people who play together against another group in a sport or game

**team-mate team-mate**
NOUN In a game or sport, your **team-mates** are the other members of your team.

**teapot teapots**
NOUN a container in which tea is made. It has a handle, a spout and a lid.

**tear tears, tearing, tore, torn**
NOUN 1 a drop of liquid that comes out of your eyes when you cry
NOUN 2 a hole or rip that has been made in something • *There was a tear in the curtain.*
VERB 3 If you **tear** something, you damage it by pulling so that a hole or rip appears in it.

PRONUNCIATION TIP
Meaning 1 rhymes with "fear". Meanings 2 and 3 rhyme with "hair".

**tearful**
ADJECTIVE If you are **tearful**, you cry easily or you are crying.

**tease teases, teasing, teased**
VERB If someone **teases** you, they deliberately make fun of you or embarrass you.

**easpoon teaspoons**
NOUN **1** a small spoon used for stirring drinks
NOUN **2** the amount that a **teaspoon** holds
● *I have two **teaspoons** of sugar in my coffee.*

**eat teats**
NOUN **1** a nipple on a female animal
NOUN **2** a piece of rubber or plastic that is shaped like a nipple and fitted to a baby's feeding bottle

**echnical**
ADJECTIVE If something is **technical**, it is to do with machines, the way things work, and materials used in industry, transport and communications.

**echnique techniques**
NOUN a particular way of doing something

PRONUNCIATION TIP
This word is pronounced tek-**neek**.

**echnology**
NOUN practical things that have come about because of a greater understanding of science ● *New **technology** has helped us develop faster computers.*

**eddy bear teddy bears**
NOUN a soft, furry toy bear

**edious**
ADJECTIVE boring and lasting for a long time

**eenager teenagers**
NOUN a person aged between 13 and 19 years old

**eeth**
PLURAL NOUN the plural of **tooth**

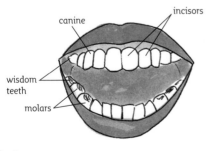

incisors
canine
wisdom teeth
molars

**tele-**
PREFIX You add **tele-**to the beginning of a word to mean at or over a distance.
● *telephone*

WORD HISTORY
from the Greek *tele* meaning far

**telecommunications**
NOUN the science and activity of sending signals and messages over long distances, for example by radio and telephone

**telegram telegrams**
NOUN a message that is sent electronically and then printed and delivered to someone's home ● *He received many letters and **telegrams** of congratulations when he won the race.*

**telegraph**
NOUN a system of sending messages over long distances using electrical or radio signals

**telephone telephones, telephoning, telephoned**
NOUN **1** a piece of electrical or electronic equipment for talking directly to someone who is in a different place
VERB **2** If you **telephone** someone, you speak to them using a telephone.

**telescope telescopes**
NOUN a long instrument, shaped like a tube, that contains lenses. When you look through it with one eye, distant objects appear larger and nearer.

**televise televises, televising, televised**
VERB If an event is **televised**, it is filmed and shown on television.

**television televisions**
NOUN a piece of electronic equipment that receives pictures and sounds transmitted over a distance

**tell tells, telling, told**
VERB **1** If you **tell** someone something, you let them know about it.
VERB **2** If you **tell** someone to do something, you order them to do it.

**telly tellies**
NOUN an abbreviation of *television*

**temper**
NOUN **1** Your **temper** is the mood you are in and the way you are feeling, whether you are irritable and angry or calm and peaceful. ● *I started the day in a bad **temper**.*
PHRASE **2** If you **lose your temper**, you become very angry.

**temperamental**
ADJECTIVE Someone who is **temperamental** changes their mood often and suddenly.

**temperature temperatures**

NOUN **1** how hot or cold something is • *There was a sudden drop in* **temperature** *once the sun had gone down.*

NOUN **2** Your **temperature** is the temperature of your body. The normal body **temperature** for humans is 37°C. • *His* **temperature** *continued to rise.*

**temple temples**

NOUN **1** a building used for the worship of a god in various religions

NOUN **2** the part on either side of your head between your forehead and your ear

**tempo tempos** or **tempi**

NOUN The **tempo** of a piece of music is its speed.

**temporary**

ADJECTIVE lasting for only a short time

**tempt tempts, tempting, tempted**

VERB **1** If you **tempt** someone, you try to persuade them to do something by offering them something they want.

ADJECTIVE **2** If something is **tempting**, it is attractive and difficult to resist.

**ten**

NOUN **Ten** is the number 10.

**tenancy tenancies**

NOUN the period of time that someone pays rent to live in a house or to use land or buildings

**tenant tenants**

NOUN someone who pays rent for the place they live in, or for land or buildings that they use

**tend tends , tending, tended**

VERB **1** If something **tends** to happen, it usually happens.

VERB **2** If you **tend** something or someone, you look after them. • *Bob* **tended** *the plants.*

**tendency tendencies**

NOUN the way a person or a thing is likely to behave or has a habit of behaving • *She has a* **tendency** *to write messily.*

**tender tenderer, tenderest**

ADJECTIVE **1** Someone who is **tender** is gentle and caring.

SYNONYMS: affectionate, gentle, loving

ADJECTIVE **2 Tender** food is easy to cut and chew.

ANTONYM: tough

ADJECTIVE **3** If a part of your body is **tender**, it is painful and sore.

**tendon tendons**

NOUN **Tendons** are like strong cords. They hold your muscles and bones together.

**tennis**

NOUN a game played by two or four players on a rectangular court. The players hit a ball over a central net.

**tense tenser, tensest; tenses, tensing, tensed**

ADJECTIVE **1** If you are **tense**, you feel worried and unable to relax.

NOUN **2** The **tense** of a verb shows whether it is in the past, present or future.

VERB **3** If you **tense** your muscles, you tighten them up.

**tension tensions**

NOUN the feeling of nervousness or worry that you have when something dangerous or important is happening

**tent tents**

NOUN a shelter made of fabric held up by poles and pinned down at the bottom with pegs and ropes

**tentacle tentacles**

NOUN the long, bending parts of an animal, such as an octopus, that it uses to feel and hold things

**tenth tenths**

NOUN **1** one of ten equal parts of something. It can be written as 1/10.

ADJECTIVE **2** The **tenth** item in a series is the one that you count as number ten. It can be written as 10th.

**tepid**

ADJECTIVE **Tepid** liquid is only slightly warm.

**term terms**

NOUN **1** one of the periods of time that each year is divided into at a school or college

NOUN **2 Terms** are words that relate to a particular subject, for example, medical **terms**, legal **terms** and scientific **terms**.

NOUN **3 Terms** are the conditions of an agreement. • *He made a list of* **terms** *for doing the job.*

NOUN **4** If you are on good **terms** with someone, you get on well with them.

**erminal terminals**
NOUN **1** a place where vehicles, passengers or goods begin or end a journey
NOUN **2** a keyboard and screen connected to a main computer
ADJECTIVE **3** A **terminal** illness or disease cannot be cured and gradually causes death.

**WORD HISTORY**
from Latin *terminus* meaning end

**erminate terminates, terminating, terminated**
VERB When you **terminate** something, or it **terminates**, it stops or ends.

**errace terraces**
NOUN **1** a row of houses joined together
NOUN **2** a flat area of stone next to a building, where people can sit

**errapin terrapins**
NOUN a small North American freshwater turtle

**WORD HISTORY**
an American Indian word

**errible**
ADJECTIVE **1** serious and unpleasant • *He had a* **terrible** *illness.*
ADJECTIVE **2** very bad or of poor quality • *That is a* **terrible** *haircut.*

**errier terriers**
NOUN a breed of small dog

**WORD HISTORY**
from Old French *chien terrier* meaning earth dog, because they were originally bred to hunt animals living in holes in the ground, such as rabbits and badgers

**errific**
ADJECTIVE **1** very pleasing or impressive • *That was a* **terrific** *film.*
ADJECTIVE **2** very great or strong • *There is a* **terrific** *wind blowing down on the beach.*

**errify terrifies, terrifying, terrified**
VERB If something **terrifies** you, it makes you feel extremely frightened.

**erritory territories**
NOUN The **territory** of a country is the land that it controls.

**error terrors**
NOUN great fear or panic

**terrorism**
NOUN the use of violence for political purposes

**test tests, testing, tested**
VERB **1** When you **test** something, you try it to find out what it is, what condition it is in, or how well it works.
VERB **2** To **test** someone means to ask them questions to find out how much they know.
NOUN **3** a set of questions or tasks given to someone to find out what they know or can do

**test tube test tubes**
NOUN a small cylindrical glass container that is used in chemical experiments

**tetanus**
NOUN a painful infectious disease caused by germs getting into wounds

**tether tethers, tethering, tethered**
VERB **1** If you **tether** an animal, you tie it to something such as a post.
NOUN **2** a rope for tying an animal to something such as a post

**tetrahedron tetrahedrons or tetrahedra**
NOUN a solid shape with four triangular faces

**text texts, texting, texted**
NOUN **1** the written part of a book, rather than the pictures or the index
NOUN **2** short for **text message**
VERB **3** If you **text** someone, you send them a text message.

a b c d e f g h i j k l m n o p q r s t u v w x y z

**409**

## textbook **textbooks**
NOUN a book about a particular subject for students to use

## textile **textiles**
NOUN a woven cloth or fabric

## text message **text messages**
NOUN a written message sent using a mobile phone

## texture **textures**
NOUN the way something feels when you touch it ● *Silk has a very smooth, soft* **texture**.

## than
PREPOSITION **1** You use **than** when you compare one thing with another. ● *She is bigger* **than** *her sister.*
CONJUNCTION **2** You use **than** when you compare one thing with another.
● *He should have helped her more* **than** *he did.*

## thank **thanks, thanking, thanked**
VERB When you **thank** someone, you show that you are pleased or grateful for something that they have done for you.

## thank you
INTERJECTION You say **thank you** to show that you are grateful to someone for something.

## that **those**
ADJECTIVE **1 That** is used when you are talking about someone or something that is a distance away from you. ● *Look at that* **tree** *over there.*
PRONOUN **2 That** is used when you are referring to someone or something you have already mentioned. ● **That** *is the film I want to see.*
CONJUNCTION **3 That** is used to introduce a fact, a statement or a result. ● *His writing was so bad* **that** *nobody could read it.*

## thaw **thaws, thawing, thawed**
VERB **1** When snow or ice **thaws**, it melts.
VERB **2** When you **thaw** frozen food, or when it **thaws**, it defrosts.

## the
ADJECTIVE called the definite article. You use **the** in front of a noun when you are referring to something in particular.
● *That's* **the** *chair I bought yesterday.*

## theatre **theatres**
NOUN **1** a building where plays and other shows are performed on a stage
NOUN **2** a room in a hospital where operations are carried out

## theatrical
ADJECTIVE involving or performed in the theatre

## theft **thefts**
NOUN the crime of stealing
> SYNONYM: robbery

## their
ADJECTIVE **Their** refers to something belonging to people or things, other than yourself or the person you are talking to, that have already been mentioned. ● *The children had been playing football, and* **their** *shirts were dirty.*

**LANGUAGE TIP**
Do not confuse *their* with *there* or *they're*.

## theirs
PRONOUN **Theirs** refers to something belonging to people or things, other than yourself or the person you are talking to, that have already been mentioned. ● *The children said that the ball that came over the wall was* **theirs**.

## them
PRONOUN **Them** refers to things or people, other than yourself or the person you are talking to, that have already been mentioned. ● *She took her gloves off and put* **them** *in a drawer.*

## theme **themes**
NOUN a main idea in a piece of writing, painting, film or music ● *The main* **theme** *of the book is growing up.*

## themselves
PRONOUN **Themselves** is used when people, other than yourself or the person you are talking to, do an action and are affected by it. ● *They enjoyed* **themselves** *at the fair.*

## then
ADVERB after that; next ● *He put on his shoes and* **then** *went for a walk.*

## theology
NOUN the study of religion and God

## theory **theories**
NOUN an idea or set of ideas that is meant to explain something

## therapist **therapists**
NOUN someone whose job is to give a specific treatment for a mental or physical illness

**therapy**

NOUN the treatment of a mental or physical illness

**there**

ADVERB in that place or to that place • *He's sitting over **there**.* • *We decided to go **there** after school.*

LANGUAGE TIP

Do not confuse *there* with *their* or *they're*.

**therefore**

ADVERB as a result • *I worked hard and **therefore** I won a prize.*

**thermal**

ADJECTIVE **1** to do with or caused by heat
ADJECTIVE **2 Thermal** clothing is specially designed to keep you warm in cold weather.

**thermometer thermometers**

NOUN an instrument for measuring the temperature of a room or a person's body

**thermos**

NOUN (trademark) a container used to keep drinks hot or cold

**thermostat thermostats**

NOUN a device used to control temperature, for example on a central heating system

**thesaurus thesauruses**

NOUN a reference book in which words with similar meanings are grouped together

**these**

ADJECTIVE **1 These** means the ones here, not a different ones. • ***These** bananas look good.*
PRONOUN **2 These** means the ones here, not a different ones. • *Have you seen **these**?*

**they**

PRONOUN **They** refers to people or things that have already been mentioned.
• *I saw Tom and Ben. **They** were looking in a shop window.*

**they'd**

a contraction of *they had* or *they would*

**they'll**

a contraction of *they will* or *they shall*

**they're**

a contraction of *they are*

LANGUAGE TIP

Do not confuse *they're* with *their* or *there*.

**they've**

a contraction of *they have*

**thick thicker, thickest**

ADJECTIVE **1** Something **thick** has a large distance between its two sides. • *I'd like a **thick** slice of bread and butter.*

ANTONYM: thin

ADJECTIVE **2** If you want to know how **thick** something is, you want to know the measurement between its two sides. • *How **thick** is this wall?*

ANTONYM: thin

ADJECTIVE **3** close together and in a large number • *She has **thick**, dark hair.*
ADJECTIVE **4 Thick** liquids contain little water and do not flow easily. • *The **thick** soup was very filling.*

ANTONYM: thin

**thicken thickens, thickening, thickened**

VERB If you **thicken** something, or if it **thickens**, it becomes thicker. • *Stir the custard in the pan until it **thickens**.*

**thickness thicknesses**

NOUN how thick something is

**thief thieves**

NOUN a person who steals

**thigh thighs**

NOUN the top part of your leg, between your knee and your hip

**thimble thimbles**

NOUN a small metal or plastic cap that you put on the end of your finger to protect it from the needle when you are sewing

**thin thinner, thinnest**

ADJECTIVE **1** Something that is **thin** is much narrower than it is long.

ANTONYM: thick

ADJECTIVE **2** A **thin** person or animal has very little fat on their body.
ADJECTIVE **3 Thin** liquids contain a lot of water and flow easily.

ANTONYM: thick

**thing things**

NOUN an object rather than a plant, animal or person

411

**think** thinks, thinking, thought
VERB **1** When you **think** about ideas or problems, you use your mind to sort them out.
VERB **2** If you **think** something, you believe it is true. • *I **think** she's got a bike for her birthday.*
VERB **3** If you **think** of something, you remember it or it comes into your mind.
VERB **4** If you are **thinking** of doing something, you might do it.

**third** thirds
NOUN **1** one of three equal parts of something. It can be written as ⅓.
ADJECTIVE **2** The **third** item in a series is the one that you count as number three. It can be written as 3ʳᵈ.

**third person**
NOUN In grammar, the **third person** is *he, she, it* or *they*.

**thirst**
NOUN If you have a **thirst**, you feel the need to drink something.

**thirstily**
ADVERB in a way that shows you are thirsty

**thirsty** thirstier, thirstiest
ADJECTIVE If you are **thirsty**, you feel as if you need to drink something.

**thirteen**
NOUN **Thirteen** is the number 13.

**thirteenth** thirteenths
NOUN **1** one of thirteen equal parts of something.
ADJECTIVE **2** The **thirteenth** item in a series is the one that you count as number thirteen.

**thirtieth** thirtieths
NOUN **1** one of thirty equal parts of something.
ADJECTIVE **2** The **thirtieth** item in a series is the one that you count as number thirty.

**thirty**
NOUN **Thirty** is the number 30.

**this** those
ADJECTIVE **1** This means the one here, not a different one. • ***This** food looks nice.*
PRONOUN **2** This means the one here, not a different one. • *Have you seen **this**?*

**thistle** thistles
NOUN a wild plant with prickly-edged leaves and purple flowers

**thorn** thorns
NOUN one of many sharp points growing on the stems of some plants. For example, brambles have many **thorns**.

**thorough**
ADJECTIVE done very carefully and completely

**thoroughly**
ADVERB **1** very carefully so that you do not miss anything • *He washed his hands **thoroughly**.*
ADVERB **2** completely • *She was **thoroughly** ashamed of what she'd done.*

**those**
PRONOUN **1** **Those** is used when you are referring to people or things you have already mentioned. • ***Those** are the shoes I was talking about.*
ADJECTIVE **2** **Those** is used when you are talking about people or things that are a distance away from you. • *Look at those **trees** over there.*

**though**
CONJUNCTION **1** despite the fact that • *She felt better, **though** her cough was still bad.*
CONJUNCTION **2** You can use **though** to mean if. • *Try to look as **though** you're working.*

**PRONUNCIATION TIP**
This word rhymes with "show".

**thought** thoughts
VERB **1** the past tense and past participle of **think**
NOUN **2** the activity of thinking • *She was lost in **thought**.*

**thoughtful**
ADJECTIVE **1** If you are **thoughtful**, you are quiet and serious.
ADJECTIVE **2** A **thoughtful** person thinks of what other people need and what they would like.

**thoughtfully**
ADVERB **1** in a way that shows you are thinking about something
ADVERB **2** in a kind way that shows you are thinking of what other people need and would like

**thoughtless**
ADJECTIVE A **thoughtless** person does not care or think about other people's needs.

**thousand** thousands
NOUN A **thousand** is the number 1000.

**housandth thousandths**

NOUN **1** one of a thousand equal parts of something. It can be written as ¹⁄₁₀₀₀.
ADJECTIVE **2** The **thousandth** item in a series is the one that you count as number one thousand. It can be written as 1000ᵗʰ.

**hrash thrashes, thrashing, thrashed**

VERB **1** To **thrash** someone is to beat them by hitting them with something like a stick or a whip.
VERB **2** If you **thrash** someone in a contest or fight, you defeat them completely.
VERB **3** If you **thrash**, or **thrash** about, you move about wildly and violently.

**hread threads**

NOUN **1** a long, fine piece of cotton, silk, nylon or wool
NOUN **2** a number of messages on the internet from different people about one particular subject ● *I saw the post but didn't read the **thread** below it.*

**hreadbare**

ADJECTIVE Fabric or clothes that are **threadbare** are old and worn thin.

**hreat threats**

NOUN **1** a warning that someone will harm you if you do not do what they want
NOUN **2** a danger or something that might cause harm

**hreaten threatens, threatening, threatened**

VERB If you **threaten** someone, you tell them that you intend to harm them in some way.

**hree**

NOUN **Three** is the number 3.

**hree-dimensional**

ADJECTIVE A **three-dimensional** object or shape is not flat, but has height or depth as well as length and width.

**hrew**

VERB the past tense of **throw**

**hrill thrills, thrilling, thrilled**

NOUN **1** a sudden feeling of great excitement, pleasure or fear
VERB **2** If something **thrills** you, it gives you a feeling of great pleasure and excitement.

**hrilled**

ADJECTIVE extremely pleased and excited

**hriller thrillers**

NOUN a book, film or play that tells an exciting story about dangerous or mysterious events

**thrilling**

ADJECTIVE exciting and very interesting

**thrive thrives, thriving, throve or thrived**

VERB to grow strongly and healthily, or to prosper

**throat throats**

NOUN **1** the back of your mouth and the top part of the tubes inside your neck that lead to your stomach and lungs
NOUN **2** the front part of a human or other animal's neck

→ Have a look at the illustration for **bird**

**throb throbs, throbbing, throbbed**

VERB If something **throbs**, it beats or vibrates with a strong, regular rhythm. ● *My finger **throbbed** after I trapped it in the door.*

**throne thrones**

NOUN a ceremonial chair used by a king or queen on important official occasions

**throng throngs, thronging, thronged**

NOUN **1** a large crowd of people ● *There was a **throng** of fans waiting at the stage door.*
VERB **2** If people **throng** somewhere, or **throng** a place, they go there in great numbers. ● *Hundreds of royal admirers **thronged** to see the procession.*

**throttle throttles, throttling, throttled**

VERB If a person **throttles** someone, they kill or injure them by squeezing their throat.

SYNONYM: strangle

**through**

PREPOSITION If you move **through** something, you go from one side of it to the other. ● *We followed the path **through** the woods.*

**throughout**

PREPOSITION **1** all the way through ● *It rained heavily **throughout** the game.*
ADVERB **2** all the way through ● *The house is painted white **throughout**.*

**throw throws, throwing, threw, thrown**

VERB When you **throw** something you let it go with a quick movement of your arm, so that it moves through the air.

SYNONYMS: chuck, fling, toss

**throw away**

VERB If you **throw away** something that you do not want, you get rid of it, usually by putting it in the rubbish bin.

**thrush thrushes**

NOUN a small brown songbird

a
b
c
d
e
f
g
h
i
j
k
l
m
n
o
p
q
r
s
t
u
v
w
x
y
z

A
B
C
D
E
F
G
H
I
J
K
L
M
N
O
P
Q
R
S
**T**
U
V
W
X
Y
Z

**thrust** thrusts, thrusting, thrust
VERB If you **thrust** something somewhere, you move or push it there quickly and with a lot of force.

**thud** thuds, thudding, thudded
VERB **1** to fall heavily
NOUN **2** the dull sound of something heavy falling

**thug** thugs
NOUN a very rough and violent person

**WORD HISTORY**
from Hindi *thag* meaning thief

**thumb** thumbs
NOUN the short, thick, jointed part on the side of your hand, similar to a finger but lower down

**thump** thumps, thumping, thumped
VERB **1** If you **thump** someone or something, you hit them hard with your fist.
VERB **2** When your heart **thumps**, it beats strongly and quickly.
NOUN **3** a hard hit
NOUN **4** a fairly loud, dull sound

**thunder**
NOUN the loud, rumbling noise that you hear from the sky during some storms, often after a flash of lightning

**thunderstorm** thunderstorms
NOUN a storm with thunder and lightning

**Thursday**
NOUN the fifth day of the week, coming between Wednesday and Friday

**WORD HISTORY**
from Old English *Thursdæg* meaning Thor's day; Thor was the Norse god of thunder

**tick** ticks, ticking, ticked
NOUN **1** a written mark to show that something is correct
VERB **2** If you **tick** something written on a piece of paper, you put a tick next to it.
VERB **3** When a clock **ticks**, it makes a regular clicking noise as it works.

**ticket** tickets
NOUN a piece of paper or card which shows that you have paid for a journey or have paid to go into a place • *Don't lose your bus ticket.*

**tickle** tickles, tickling, tickled
VERB When you **tickle** someone, you move your fingers lightly over their body in order to make them laugh.

**tidal wave** tidal waves
NOUN a very large wave, often caused by an earthquake, that flows onto the land and destroys things

**tide** tides
NOUN the regular change in the level of the sea on the shore

**tidy** tidier, tidiest; tidies, tidying, tidied
ADJECTIVE **1** Something that is **tidy** is neat and arranged in an orderly way.
ADJECTIVE **2** Someone who is **tidy** always keeps their things neat.
VERB **3** If you **tidy** a place, you make it neat by putting things in their proper place.

**tie** ties, tying, tied
VERB **1** If you **tie** one thing to another, you fasten it using cord of some kind.
VERB **2** If you **tie** a piece of cord or cloth, you fasten the ends together in a knot or bow.
NOUN **3** a long, narrow piece of cloth worn around the neck under a shirt collar, and tied in a knot at the front

**tiger** tigers
NOUN a large wild cat that has an orange-coloured coat with black stripes

**tight** tighter, tightest
ADJECTIVE **1** If clothes are **tight**, they fit you very closely.
ADVERB **2** If you hold **tight**, you hold on very firmly.

**tighten** tightens, tightening, tightened
VERB **1** If you **tighten** something like a rope or a chain, you pull it until it is straight and firmly stretched.
VERB **2** If you **tighten** something like a screw or a knot, you fasten or fix it more firmly.

**tightrope** tightropes
NOUN a tightly-stretched rope on which an acrobat balances and performs tricks

**tights**
PLURAL NOUN a piece of clothing made of thin, stretchy material that fits closely round a person's hips, legs and feet

**tile** tiles, tiling, tiled
NOUN **1** a flat, rectangular piece of something, such as slate, carpet or baked clay, that is used to cover surfaces
VERB **2** If you **tile** a surface, you fix tiles to it.

**ill tills, tilling, tilled**
NOUN **1** a drawer or box in a shop where money is kept, usually in a cash register
PREPOSITION **2** up to a certain time • *You can stay up **till** nine o'clock.*
CONJUNCTION **3** If something does not happen **till** a particular time, it does not happen before that time and only starts happening at that time. • *You can't go out to play **till** you've finished your homework.*
VERB **4** If someone **tills** the soil, they plough it.

**iller tillers**
NOUN a handle fixed to the top of the rudder on a boat. It turns the rudder and steers the boat.

**ilt tilts, tilting, tilted**
VERB If you **tilt** an object, you move it so that one end or side is higher than the other.

**imber timbers**
NOUN **1** wood that has been cut and prepared ready for building and making furniture
NOUN **2** The **timbers** of a ship or house are the large pieces of wood that have been used to build it.

**ime times, timing, timed**
NOUN **1** what we measure in minutes, hours, days, weeks and years
NOUN **2** a particular point in the day • *What **time** is it?*
NOUN **3** a particular period in history
VERB **4** If you **time** something like a race, you measure how long it takes.

**imes**
PLURAL NOUN multiplied by • *Two **times** three is six (2 × 3 = 6).*

**imetable timetables**
NOUN **1** a plan of the times when particular activities or jobs should be done
NOUN **2** a list of the times when particular trains, boats, buses or aircraft arrive and depart

**imid**
ADJECTIVE If you are **timid**, you are shy and lacking in confidence.
ANTONYM: bold

**in tins**
NOUN **1** a soft, silvery-white metal
NOUN **2** a metal container that is filled with food and then sealed in order to keep the food fresh
NOUN **3** a small metal container that may have a lid

**tingle tingles, tingling, tingled**
VERB When a part of your body **tingles**, you feel a slight prickling sensation there.

**tinkle tinkles, tinkling, tinkled**
VERB Something that **tinkles** makes a light, ringing sound.

**tinsel**
NOUN long threads with strips of shiny paper attached, used as a decoration at Christmas

**tint tints**
NOUN a shade of a particular colour, particularly a pale one

**tiny tinier, tiniest**
ADJECTIVE extremely small

**tip tips, tipping, tipped**
NOUN **1** the point or the very end of something
NOUN **2** a small gift of money given to someone like a waiter, who has done a service for you
NOUN **3** a place where rubbish is left
NOUN **4** a piece of useful information or advice
VERB **5** If you **tip** something, you tilt or overturn it. • *When he jumped up, he **tipped** the chair over.*
VERB **6** If you **tip** something somewhere, you pour it quickly and carelessly, or you empty it from a container. • *When they had finished the washing up, they **tipped** the water out of the bowl.*

**tiptoe tiptoes, tiptoeing, tiptoed**
VERB If you **tiptoe** somewhere, you walk there very quietly on your toes.

**tire tires, tiring, tired**
VERB **1** If something **tires** you, it makes you use a lot of energy so that you want to rest or sleep afterwards.
VERB **2** If you **tire** of something, you become bored with it.

**tired**
ADJECTIVE **1** feeling as if you want to rest or sleep
ADJECTIVE **2** If you are **tired** of something, you are bored with it. • *I'm **tired** of watching television. Can we do something else?*

**tiredness**
NOUN the feeling you have when you want to rest or sleep

**tissue tissues**
NOUN a small piece of soft paper that you use as a handkerchief

a
b
c
d
e
f
g
h
i
j
k
l
m
n
o
p
q
r
s
t
u
v
w
x
y
z

**title titles**

NOUN the name of something such as a book, play, film or piece of music

**to**

PREPOSITION **1** towards

PREPOSITION **2** used to compare units • *There are 100 centimetres **to** a metre.*

PREPOSITION **3** compared with or rather than • *I prefer fruit **to** chocolate.*

PREPOSITION **4** used to indicate the limit of something • *I am allowed to spend up **to** an hour watching television each night.*

ADVERB **5** if you push something like a door **to**, you close it but do not shut it completely

---

**LANGUAGE TIP**

Do not confuse *to* with *too* or *two*.

**toad toads**

NOUN an animal similar to a frog, but with drier skin and living more on land and less in the water

**toadstool toadstools**

NOUN a type of fungus similar to a mushroom and often poisonous

**toast toasts, toasting, toasted**

NOUN **1** slices of bread made brown and crisp by cooking them at a high temperature

VERB **2** If you **toast** bread, you cook it at a high temperature so that it becomes brown and crisp.

**toaster toasters**

NOUN an electrical device for toasting bread

**tobacco**

NOUN the dried leaves of a plant called **tobacco**. People smoke it in pipes, cigarettes and cigars.

**toboggan toboggans, tobogganing, tobogganed**

NOUN **1** a flat seat with two wooden or metal runners, used for sliding over the snow

SYNONYM: sledge

VERB **2** If you **toboggan**, you use a toboggan to slide over the snow.

SYNONYM: sledge

**today**

NOUN **1** the day that is happening now

ADVERB **2** on the day that is happening now • *How are you feeling **today**?*

**toddler toddlers**

NOUN a small child who has just learned to walk

**toe toes**

NOUN **1** one of the five movable parts at the end of your foot

NOUN **2** the part of a shoe or sock that covers the end of your foot

**toffee toffees**

NOUN a sticky, chewy sweet made by boiling sugar and butter together with water

**toga togas**

NOUN a long, loose robe worn in ancient Rome

**together**

ADVERB **1** If people do something **together**, they do it with each other.

ADVERB **2** If two things happen **together**, they happen at the same time.

ADVERB **3** If things are joined, mixed or fixed **together**, they are put with each other.

**toil toils, toiling, toiled**

VERB **1** If you **toil**, you work very hard.

NOUN **2** very hard work

**toilet toilets**

NOUN **1** a large bowl, connected to the drains, which you use to get rid of waste from your body

SYNONYM: lavatory

NOUN **2** a small room containing a toilet

SYNONYM: lavatory

**token tokens**

NOUN **1** a piece of paper or card that is worth a particular amount of money and can be exchanged for goods • *I got a book **token** for my birthday.*

NOUN **2** a flat round piece of metal or plastic that can sometimes be used instead of money • *Some of the phones only take **tokens**.*

NOUN **3** a sign or symbol of something • *We bought her some flowers as a **token** of our thanks.*

**told**

VERB the past tense and past participle of **tell**

**tolerate tolerates, tolerating, tolerated**

VERB If you **tolerate** something, you put up with it even though you do not like it.

**mato tomatoes**
NOUN a small, round, red fruit used as a vegetable and eaten cooked or raw

**mb tombs**
NOUN a large grave where one or more people are buried

**morrow**
NOUN **1** the day after today
ADVERB **2** on the day after today • *I'm staying home **tonight**.*

LANGUAGE TIP
*Tomorrow* has one *m* and two *r*s.

**on tons**
NOUN a unit of weight equal to 2240 pounds or about 1016 kilograms

**one tones**
NOUN **1** a particular quality that a sound has • *the clear **tone** of the bell*
NOUN **2** a shade of a colour

**ongs**
PLURAL NOUN two long, narrow pieces of metal joined together at one end. You press the pieces together to pick up objects.

**ongue tongues**
NOUN the soft part in your mouth that you can move and use for tasting, licking and speaking

**ongue twister tongue twisters**
NOUN a sentence or a rhyme that is very difficult to say

**onight**
NOUN **1** the evening or night that will come at the end of today
ADVERB **2** on the evening or night that will come at the end of today • *What will we learn **tomorrow**?*

**onne tonnes**
NOUN a unit of weight equal to 1000 kilograms

**onsil tonsils**
NOUN one of the two small, soft lumps at the back of your throat

**onsillitis**
NOUN a painful swelling of your tonsils caused by an infection

**oo**
ADVERB **1** also or as well • *She was there **too**.*
ADVERB **2 Too** shows that there is more of something than you want. • *I've had **too** much to eat.*

LANGUAGE TIP
Do not confuse *too* with *to* or *two*.

**took**
VERB the past tense of **take**

**tool tools**
NOUN any hand-held piece of equipment that you use to help you do a particular kind of work

**tooth teeth**
NOUN one of the hard, white bony parts in your mouth that you use for biting and chewing food

**toothache**
NOUN a pain in one of your teeth

**toothbrush toothbrushes**
NOUN a brush for cleaning your teeth

**toothpaste**
NOUN the substance that you use with a toothbrush to clean your teeth

**top tops**
NOUN **1** the highest point of something • *There was snow on the mountain **top**.*
NOUN **2** the upper side of something • *There was a vase of flowers on the table **top**.*
NOUN **3** a piece of clothing that you wear on the top half of your body
NOUN **4** a toy that can be made to spin
ADJECTIVE **5** The **top** thing of a series of things is the highest one. • *the **top** floor of the building*

**topic topics**
NOUN a particular subject that you write about or discuss

**topical**
ADJECTIVE to do with things that are happening now

**Torah**
NOUN Jewish law and teaching

**torch torches**
NOUN a small electric light carried in the hand and powered by batteries

WORD HISTORY
from Old French *torche* meaning handful of twisted straw, which was set on fire and held up to provide light

**tore**
VERB the past tense of **tear**

417

**torment** **torments, tormenting, tormented**
NOUN **1** great pain or unhappiness
VERB **2** If something **torments** you, it causes you great unhappiness.
VERB **3** If someone **torments** you, they keep deliberately annoying you.

**torn**
VERB the past participle of **tear**

**tornado** **tornadoes** or **tornados**
NOUN a violent storm with strong circular winds around a funnel-shaped cloud

**torpedo** **torpedoes, torpedoing, torpedoed**
NOUN **1** a tube-shaped bomb that travels underwater and explodes when it hits a target
VERB **2** If a ship is **torpedoed**, it is hit, and usually sunk, by a torpedo.

**torrent** **torrents**
NOUN a very strong stream or fall of water
• *The rain fell in a **torrent**.*

**torrential**
ADJECTIVE **Torrential** rain pours down very fast and in great quantities.

**tortoise** **tortoises**
NOUN a slow-moving reptile with a hard shell over its body into which it can pull its head and legs for protection

**torture** **tortures, torturing, tortured**
VERB If someone **tortures** another person, they deliberately cause them great pain, usually as a punishment or to get information from them.

**toss** **tosses, tossing, tossed**
VERB **1** If you **toss** something somewhere, you throw it there lightly and carelessly.
VERB **2** If you **toss** a coin, you decide something by throwing a coin into the air and guessing which side will face upwards when it lands.

**total** **totals, totalling, totalled**
NOUN **1** the number you get when you add several numbers together
VERB **2** If you **total** amounts, you add them together to find the total.
ADJECTIVE **3** complete

**toucan** **toucans**
NOUN a large tropical bird with a large, colourful beak

**touch** **touches, touching, touched**
VERB **1** If you **touch** something, you put your fingers or hand on it.
VERB **2** When two things **touch**, they come into contact.
VERB **3** If something **touches** you, it affects your emotions. • *The sad story **touched** us a*
NOUN **4** Your sense of **touch** is your ability to feel things by touching them.

**touchdown** **touchdowns**
NOUN the landing of an aircraft or spacecra

**touchy** **touchier, touchiest**
ADJECTIVE sensitive and easily offended

**tough** **tougher, toughest**
ADJECTIVE **1** A **tough** person is strong and ab to put up with things that are difficult.
ADJECTIVE **2** Something that is **tough** is stror and difficult to break or damage.
ADJECTIVE **3** **Tough** food is difficult to cut and chew.

ANTONYM: tender

**tour** **tours, touring, toured**
NOUN **1** a long journey during which you vis several places
NOUN **2** a short trip round a place such as a city or a famous building
VERB **3** If you **tour** a place, you go on a journey or a trip round it.

**tourist** **tourists**
NOUN someone who is travelling on holiday

**tournament** **tournaments**
NOUN a competition in which many players or teams compete in a series of games or contests

**tow** **tows, towing, towed**
VERB **1** If a vehicle **tows** another vehicle, it pulls it along behind it.
NOUN **2** To give a vehicle a **tow** is to pull it along behind.

**towards**
PREPOSITION If you go **towards** something, you move in its direction.

**wel towels**
NOUN a piece of thick, soft cloth that you use to dry yourself with

**wer towers**
NOUN a tall, narrow building, sometimes attached to a larger building such as a castle or church

→ Have a look at the illustrations for **castle** and **turbine**

**wn towns**
NOUN a place with many streets and buildings where people live and work

**xic**
ADJECTIVE poisonous

**y toys**
NOUN something to play with

**ace traces, tracing, traced**
VERB **1** If you **trace** something like a drawing, you copy it by drawing on thin paper over the top, which you can see through.
VERB **2** If you **trace** something, you find it after looking for it. • *Scientists **traced** the origin of the disease.*
NOUN **3** a tiny amount of something or a small mark

**rack tracks, tracking, tracked**
NOUN **1** a narrow road or path
NOUN **2** a strip of ground with rails on it that a train travels along
NOUN **3** a piece of ground, shaped like a ring, that horses, cars or athletes race around
VERB **4** If you **track** someone or something, you follow them by following the marks they leave as they pass.

**rackpad trackpads**
NOUN a flat smooth area on the keyboard of some computers that you slide your finger over in order to move the cursor

→ Have a look at the illustration for **computer**

**racksuit tracksuits**
NOUN a loose, warm suit of trousers and a top, worn for outdoor sports

**ractor tractors**
NOUN a vehicle with large rear wheels, that is used on farms for pulling machinery and other heavy loads

**trade trades**
NOUN the activity of buying, selling or exchanging goods or services between people or countries

SYNONYM: business

**trademark trademarks**
NOUN a name or symbol that a manufacturer always uses on its products. **Trademarks** are usually protected by law so that no one else can use them.

**trade union trade unions**
NOUN an organisation of workers that tries to improve the pay and conditions of its members

**tradition traditions**
NOUN a custom or belief that has existed for a long time and been passed down through the generations without changing

WORD HISTORY
from Latin *traditio* meaning a handing down

**traditional**
ADJECTIVE **1** passed down from one generation to the next
ADJECTIVE **2** having existed or gone on for a long time

**traffic**
NOUN all the vehicles, ships, aircraft or people moving along a route at a particular time

**traffic lights**
PLURAL NOUN a set of lights used to control traffic at road junctions

**traffic warden traffic wardens**
NOUN an official whose job is to make sure that vehicles are not parked in the wrong place or for longer than is allowed

**tragedy tragedies**
NOUN **1** a very sad or disastrous event or situation, especially one in which people are killed
NOUN **2** a serious story or play that usually ends with the death of the main character

**tragic**
ADJECTIVE very sad and distressing, usually involving death, destruction or disaster

**trail trails**
NOUN **1** a rough path across open country or through forests
NOUN **2** a series of marks or other signs left by someone or something as they move along • *He left a **trail** of mud behind him.*

a
b
c
d
e
f
g
h
i
j
k
l
m
n
o
p
q
r
s
t
u
v
w
x
y
z

**419**

**trailer trailers**
NOUN **1** a small vehicle that can be loaded with things and pulled behind a car or lorry
NOUN **2** a series of short pieces taken from a film or television programme in order to advertise it

**train trains, training, trained**
NOUN **1** a number of carriages or trucks that are pulled by a railway engine along railway lines
VERB **2** If you **train**, you learn how to do a particular job.
VERB **3** If you **train**, or someone **trains** you, for a sports match or a race, you prepare for it by doing exercises.

**trainers**
PLURAL NOUN special shoes worn for running and other sports

**traitor traitors**
NOUN someone who betrays their country or the group that they belong to

**tram trams**
NOUN a passenger vehicle that runs on rails along the street and is powered by electricity from an overhead wire

**tramp tramps, tramping, tramped**
NOUN **1** a person who has no home, no job, and very little money
NOUN **2** a long country walk
VERB **3** If you **tramp** from one place to another, you walk with slow, heavy footsteps.

**trample tramples, trampling, trampled**
VERB If you **trample** on something, you tread heavily on it so that it is damaged.

**trampoline trampolines**
NOUN a piece of gymnastic equipment made of a large piece of strong cloth held tight by springs in a frame, on which a gymnast bounces

**trance trances**
NOUN If someone is in a **trance**, they seem to be asleep, but they can still see, hear, answer questions and obey orders.

**trans-**
PREFIX You add **trans-** to a word to mean across, through or beyond. For example, **trans**atlantic means across or beyond the Atlantic Ocean.

**transaction transactions**
NOUN a business deal that involves buying and selling something

**transatlantic**
ADJECTIVE used to describe something that crosses the Atlantic Ocean or is on the other side of it

**transfer transfers, transferring, transferred**
VERB **1** If you **transfer** something from one place to another, you move it there.
NOUN **2** a piece of paper with a design or drawing on one side that can be ironed or pressed onto another surface, such as cloth, paper or china

**transform transforms, transforming, transformed**
VERB If you **transform** something, or it **transforms**, it changes completely.

**transfusion transfusions**
NOUN a process in which blood donated by a healthy person is injected into the body of another person who needs it because they are badly injured or ill

**transistor transistors**
NOUN **1** a small electrical device in something such as a television or radio, which is used to control electric currents
NOUN **2** a small portable radio

**translate translates, translating, translated**
VERB If you **translate** something that someone has said or written, you say it or write it in a different language.

**translucent**
ADJECTIVE If something is **translucent**, it allows the light to shine through and appears to glow.

**transmit transmits, transmitting, transmitted**
VERB **1** When a message or an electronic signal is **transmitted**, it is sent by radio waves.
VERB **2** If you **transmit** something, you send it to a different place.
VERB **3** If you **transmit** a disease, you pass it on to other people.

**transmitter transmitters**
NOUN a device for sending radio messages

**transparency**
NOUN the quality that an object or substance has when you can see through it

**ansparent**

ADJECTIVE If an object or substance is **transparent**, you can see through it.

SYNONYMS: clear, see-through

**anspiration**

NOUN the evaporation of water from a plant's leaves, stem or flowers

→ Have a look at the illustration for **water cycle**

**ansplant transplants, transplanting, transplanted**

VERB 1 To **transplant** something living, like a plant or an organ, means to remove it from one place and put it in another.

NOUN 2 an operation where an organ, such as a heart or a kidney, is taken from one person and put into another

**ansport transports, transporting, transported**

VERB 1 If you **transport** someone or something, you take them from one place to another.

NOUN 2 the name for vehicles you travel in
● Cars and planes are forms of **transport**.

**ap traps, trapping, trapped**

NOUN 1 a piece of equipment or a hole that is dug to catch animals

NOUN 2 a plan to trick, capture or cheat a person

VERB 3 If you **trap** animals, you catch them using a trap.

VERB 4 If you **trap** someone, you trick, capture or cheat them.

**rapeze trapezes**

NOUN a bar hanging from two ropes on which acrobats and gymnasts swing and perform skilful movements

**rapezium trapeziums**

NOUN a plane shape with two parallel sides of different lengths

**rash**

NOUN rubbish

**raumatic**

ADJECTIVE A **traumatic** experience is very upsetting and causes great stress.

**ravel travels, travelling, travelled**

VERB 1 If you **travel**, you go from one place to another.

NOUN 2 the journeys that people make

**trawler trawlers**

NOUN a fishing boat that pulls a wide net behind it to catch fish

**tray trays**

NOUN a flat piece of wood, metal or plastic used for carrying things on

**treacherous**

ADJECTIVE 1 disloyal and untrustworthy

ADJECTIVE 2 dangerous or unreliable

**treacle**

NOUN a thick, sweet syrup used to make cakes and toffee

**tread treads, treading, trod, trodden**

VERB 1 If you **tread** on something, you walk on it or step on it.

NOUN 2 The **tread** of a tyre or shoe is the pattern of ridges on it that stops it slipping.

NOUN 3 the part of a staircase or ladder that you put your foot on

**treason**

NOUN the crime of betraying your country, for example by helping its enemies

**treasure treasures, treasuring, treasured**

NOUN 1 a collection of gold, silver, jewels or other precious objects, especially one that has been hidden

NOUN 2 a valuable object, such as a work of art

VERB 3 If you **treasure** something, you look after it carefully because it is important to you. ● She **treasured** the shells she had collected on her holiday.

**treasury treasuries**

NOUN 1 a place where treasure is stored

NOUN 2 The **Treasury** is the government department that looks after a country's finances.

**treat treats, treating, treated**

NOUN 1 If you give someone a **treat**, you buy or arrange something special for them that they will enjoy.

VERB 2 When a doctor **treats** a patient or an illness, he or she gives them medical care and attention.

VERB 3 If you **treat** someone or something in a particular way, you behave that way towards them.

**treaty treaties**

NOUN a written agreement between countries, in which they agree to do something or to help each other

a
b
c
d
e
f
g
h
i
j
k
l
m
n
o
p
q
r
s
t
u
v
w
x
y
z

**421**

### treble **trebles, trebling, trebled**
VERB **1** If something **trebles**, or is **trebled**, it becomes three times greater in number or amount.
NOUN **2 Treble** the amount of something is three times the amount.

### tree **trees**
NOUN a large plant with a hard trunk, branches and leaves

### trek **treks, trekking, trekked**
VERB **1** If you **trek** somewhere, you go on a long and difficult journey to get there.
NOUN **2** a long and difficult journey, especially one made on foot

**WORD HISTORY**
an Afrikaans word

### tremble **trembles, trembling, trembled**
VERB If you **tremble**, you shake slightly, usually because you are frightened or cold.

### tremendous
ADJECTIVE **1** large or impressive ● *It was a* **tremendous** *performance.*
ADJECTIVE **2** (*informal*) very good or pleasing ● *The game was* **tremendous** *fun.*

### tremor **tremors**
NOUN **1** a small earthquake
NOUN **2** a slight, uncontrollable shaking movement

### trench **trenches**
NOUN a long narrow channel or ditch dug into the ground

### trend **trends, trending, trended**
NOUN **1** a general direction in which something is moving
NOUN **2** a fashion
VERB **3** If you say a topic or name is **trending** on social media, you mean that a lot of people are discussing it.

### trendy **trendier, trendiest**
ADJECTIVE (*informal*) fashionable

### trespass **trespasses, trespassing, trespassed**
VERB If you **trespass** on someone's land or property, you go onto it without their permission.

### trial **trials**
NOUN **1** a legal process in which a court listens to evidence to decide whether a person is innocent or guilty of a crime
NOUN **2** a type of experiment in which someone or something is tested to see how well they perform

### triangle **triangles**
NOUN **1** a plane shape with three straight sides
NOUN **2** a percussion instrument consisting of a thin steel bar bent in the shape of a triangle. It produces a note when struck with a small metal rod.

### triangular
ADJECTIVE shaped like a triangle

### tribal
ADJECTIVE to do with a tribe

### tribe **tribes**
NOUN a group of people of the same race, who have the same customs, religion, beliefs, language or land

### tributary **tributaries**
NOUN a stream or river that flows into a larger river

### tribute **tributes**
NOUN something said or done to show admiration and respect for someone

### trick **tricks, tricking, tricked**
VERB **1** If someone **tricks** you, they deceive you.
NOUN **2** an action done to deceive someone
NOUN **3** a clever or skilful action that is done in order to entertain people ● *a card* **trick**

### trickle **trickles, trickling, trickled**
VERB When a liquid **trickles**, it flows slowly in a thin stream.

### tricky **trickier, trickiest**
ADJECTIVE difficult to do or deal with

### tricycle **tricycles**
NOUN a vehicle similar to a bicycle but with three wheels, two at the back and one at the front

### tried
VERB the past tense and past participle of **try**

**ifle trifles**

NOUN **1** a cold pudding made of layers of sponge cake, fruit, jelly and custard

NOUN **2** something unimportant or of little value

**rigger triggers**

NOUN the small lever on a gun that is pulled in order to fire it

**rillion trillions**

NOUN A **trillion** is one million million, which is written as 1,000,000,000,000.

**rim trims, trimming, trimmed; trimmer, trimmest**

VERB **1** If you **trim** something, you cut small amounts off it to make it more tidy.

ADJECTIVE **2** neat and tidy

NOUN **3** If something is given a **trim**, it is cut a little.

NOUN **4** a decoration along the edges of something • *a coat with a velvet* **trim**

**rinket trinkets**

NOUN a cheap ornament or piece of jewellery

**rio trios**

NOUN **1** a group of three musicians who sing or play together

NOUN **2** a piece of music written for three instruments or singers

**rip trips, tripping, tripped**

NOUN **1** a journey made to a place

VERB **2** If you **trip**, or **trip over**, you catch your foot on something and fall over.

VERB **3** If you **trip** someone, or **trip** them **up**, you make them fall over by making them catch their foot on something.

**riple triples, tripling, tripled**

ADJECTIVE **1** made of three things or three parts

VERB **2** If you **triple** something, or if it **triples**, it becomes three times greater in number or size.

**riplet triplets**

NOUN one of three children born at the same time to the same mother

**ripod tripods**

NOUN a stand with three legs used to support something like a camera or telescope

**triumph triumphs, triumphing, triumphed**

NOUN **1** a great success or achievement

NOUN **2** a feeling of great satisfaction when you win or achieve something

VERB **3** If you **triumph**, you win a victory or succeed in overcoming something.

**triumphant**

ADJECTIVE If you are **triumphant**, you feel very happy because you have won a victory or achieved something.

**trivial**

ADJECTIVE unimportant

**trod**

VERB the past tense of **tread**

**trodden**

VERB the past participle of **tread**

**troll trolls**

NOUN an imaginary creature in Scandinavian mythology, that is either a dwarf or a giant and lives in caves or mountains

**trolley trolleys**

NOUN **1** a basket or cart on wheels, in which you can carry your shopping or luggage

NOUN **2** a small table on wheels, used to serve food and drink

**trombone trombones**

NOUN a brass wind instrument with a U-shaped tube that you slide to produce different notes

**troop troops, trooping, trooped**

PLURAL NOUN **1 Troops** are soldiers.

NOUN **2** A **troop** of people or animals is a group of them.

VERB **3** If people **troop** somewhere, they go there in a group.

**trophy trophies**

NOUN a cup or shield given as a prize to the winner of a competition

**tropic tropics**

NOUN The **tropics** are the hottest regions of the world, that lie on either side of the equator.

→ Have a look at the illustration for **equator**

**tropical**

ADJECTIVE belonging to or typical of the tropics

**trot trots, trotting, trotted**

VERB **1** When a horse **trots**, it runs with short steps, lifting its feet quite high off the ground.

VERB **2** If you **trot**, you run slowly with small steps.

a
b
c
d
e
f
g
h
i
j
k
l
m
n
o
p
q
r
s
t
u
v
w
x
y
z

A
B
C
D
E
F
G
H
I
J
K
L
M
N
O
P
Q
R
S
T
U
V
W
X
Y
Z

**trouble** **troubles, troubling, troubled**
NOUN **1** a difficulty or problem

SYNONYM: worry

PHRASE **2** If you are **in trouble**, someone is angry with you because of something you have done wrong.
VERB **3** If something **troubles** you, it worries or bothers you.
VERB **4** If you **trouble** someone, you worry or bother them.

**trough** **troughs**
NOUN a long, narrow container from which animals drink or feed

**trousers**
PLURAL NOUN a piece of clothing for the lower half of your body, from the waist down, covering each leg separately

**trout**
NOUN a type of edible freshwater fish

LANGUAGE TIP
The plural of *trout* can be either *trout* or *trouts*, but *trout* is more common.

**trowel** **trowels**
NOUN **1** a garden tool like a small spade, used for planting or weeding
NOUN **2** a small, flat spade used by builders for spreading cement and mortar

**truant** **truants**
NOUN a child who stays away from school without permission

**truce** **truces**
NOUN an agreement between two people or groups to stop fighting for a short time

**truck** **trucks**
NOUN a large motor vehicle used for carrying heavy loads

**trudge** **trudges, trudging, trudged**
VERB **1** If you **trudge**, you walk with slow, heavy steps.
NOUN **2** a slow, tiring walk

**true** **truer, truest**
ADJECTIVE **1** A **true** story or statement is based on facts and is not invented.

SYNONYMS: accurate, correct, factual

PHRASE **2** If something **comes true**, it actually happens. • *I hope your wish comes true.*

**trumpet** **trumpets**
NOUN a wind instrument made of a narrow brass tube that widens at the end into a bell-like shape

**truncheon** **truncheons**
NOUN a short, thick stick that police officers carry as a weapon

**trunk** **trunks**
NOUN **1** the main stem of a tree from which the branches and roots grow
NOUN **2** the long, flexible nose of an elephant
NOUN **3** a large, strong case or box with a hinged lid, used for storing things
NOUN **4** In American English, the **trunk** of a car is the boot, a covered space at the back or front that is used for luggage.
NOUN **5** the main part of your body, excluding your arms, legs and head
PLURAL NOUN **6** A man's **trunks** are his bathing pants or shorts.

**trust** **trusts, trusting, trusted**
VERB **1** If you **trust** someone, you believe that they are honest and reliable, and will treat you fairly.
VERB **2** If you **trust** someone to do something, you believe they will do it.
NOUN **3** the feeling that someone can be trusted
NOUN **4** the responsibility you have to people who trust you

**trustworthy**
ADJECTIVE A **trustworthy** person is responsible and reliable, and you know that they will do what they say they will do.

**truth** **truths**
NOUN the facts about something, rather than things that are imagined or invented

**truthful**
ADJECTIVE A **truthful** person is honest and tells the truth.

**try** **tries, trying, tried**
VERB **1** If you **try** to do something, you make an effort to do it.
VERB **2** If you **try** something, you use it, taste it or experiment with it to see how good or suitable it is.
VERB **3** When a court **tries** a person, they listen to evidence to decide if that person is guilty of a crime.
VERB **4** A person who **tries** your patience is extremely irritating and difficult.
NOUN **5** an attempt to do something

tsunami

NOUN **6** A **try** in rugby is when a player scores by carrying the ball over the opponents' goal line and putting it on the ground.

**try on**
> VERB If you **try on** a piece of clothing, you wear it to see if it fits you or if it looks nice.

**T-shirt** **T-shirts**; also spelt **tee shirt**
NOUN a simple short-sleeved cotton shirt with no collar

**tsunami** **tsunamis**
NOUN a very large wave, often caused by an earthquake, that flows onto the land and destroys things

**tub** **tubs**
NOUN a wide, circular container

**tuba** **tubas**
NOUN a large brass musical instrument that can produce very low notes

**tube** **tubes**
NOUN a hollow cylinder made of metal, plastic, rubber or other material

**tuck** **tucks, tucking, tucked**
VERB **1** If you **tuck** a piece of fabric into or under something, you push the loose ends inside or under it to make it tidy.
VERB **2** If you **tuck** into a meal, you eat eagerly and with pleasure.
VERB **3** If you **tuck** someone up in bed, you put the bedclothes snugly round them.

**Tuesday**
NOUN the third day of the week, coming between Monday and Wednesday

**tuft** **tufts**
NOUN A **tuft** of something, such as hair or grass, is a bunch of it growing closely together.

**tug** **tugs, tugging, tugged**
VERB **1** If you **tug** something, you give it a quick, hard pull.
NOUN **2** a small, powerful boat that tows large ships

**tulip** **tulips**
NOUN a brightly coloured spring flower

**tumble** **tumbles, tumbling, tumbled**
VERB If you **tumble**, you fall with a rolling or bouncing movement.

**tumbler** **tumblers**
NOUN a drinking glass with no handle or stem

**tumour** **tumours**
NOUN an abnormal growth in the body

**tuna**
NOUN a large, edible fish that lives in warm seas

LANGUAGE TIP
The plural of *tuna* can be either *tuna* or *tunas*, but *tuna* is more common.

a b c d e f g h i j k l m n o p q r s t u v w x y z

## tune tunes
NOUN a series of musical notes arranged in a particular way

## tunnel tunnels
NOUN a long underground passage
• a railway **tunnel**

## turban turbans
NOUN a long piece of cloth worn wound round the head, especially by a Hindu, Muslim or Sikh man

## turbine turbines
NOUN a machine or engine powered by a stream of air, gas, water or steam

**WORD HISTORY**
from Latin *turbo* meaning whirlwind

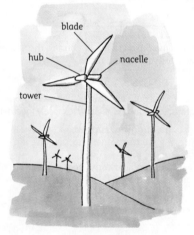

blade
hub
nacelle
tower

## turf
NOUN short, thick, even grass and the layer of soil beneath it

## turkey turkeys
NOUN a large bird kept for its meat

## turn turns, turning, turned
VERB **1** When you **turn**, you move so that you are facing or going in a different direction.
VERB **2** When you **turn** something, or when it **turns**, it moves so that it faces in a different direction or is in a different position. • She **turned** the key in the lock.
VERB **3** When something **turns**, or **turns into** something else, it becomes something different, or has a different appearance or quality. • The leaves **turned** brown in autumn.

NOUN **4** If it is your **turn** to do something, you do it next.
VERB **5** If you **turn down** something, you refuse it. • I was not hungry, so I **turned down** the chips.
VERB **6** If you **turn up** the television, for example, you increase the volume.
VERB **7** If someone **turns up**, they arrive.

## turnip turnips
NOUN a round root vegetable with a white or yellow skin

## turquoise
NOUN **1** light bluish-green
NOUN **2** A light bluish-green stone used in jewellery.

## turret turrets
NOUN a small, narrow tower on top of a larger tower or other building, such as a castle

→ Have a look at the illustration for **castle**

## turtle turtles
NOUN a large reptile with flippers for swimming and a thick shell covering its body. It lays its eggs on land but lives the rest of its life in the sea.

## tusk tusks
NOUN one of the pair of long, curving, pointed teeth of an elephant, wild boar or walrus

## tutor tutors
NOUN a private teacher or a teacher at a college or university

## TV
NOUN an abbreviation of *television*

## tweed tweeds
NOUN a thick woollen cloth. Someone wearing **tweeds** is wearing a **tweed** suit.

## tweet tweets, tweeting, tweeted
NOUN **1** a short, high-pitched sound made by a small bird
NOUN **2** a short message on the Twitter website
VERB **3** If you **tweet**, or **tweet** something, you put a short message on the Twitter website.

## tweezers
PLURAL NOUN a small tool with two arms that can be closed together to grip something. **Tweezers** are used for pulling out hairs or picking up small objects.

**welfth twelfths**

NOUN **1** one of twelve equal parts of something. It can be written as ½₁₂.

ADJECTIVE **2** The **twelfth** item in a series is the one that you count as number twelve. It can be written as 12ᵗʰ.

**welve**

NOUN **Twelve** is the number 12.

**wentieth twentieths**

NOUN **1** one of twenty parts of something. It can be written as ½₀.

ADJECTIVE **2** The **twentieth** item in a series is the one that you count as number twenty. It can be written as 20ᵗʰ.

**wenty**

NOUN **Twenty** is the number 20.

**wice**

ADVERB two times

**widdle twiddles, twiddling, twiddled**

VERB If you **twiddle** something, you turn it quickly round and round or over and over.

**wig twigs**

NOUN a small branch on a tree or bush

**wilight**

NOUN the time after sunset when it is just getting dark

**win twins**

NOUN If two people are **twins**, they have the same mother and were born on the same day.

**winkle twinkles, twinkling, twinkled**

VERB Something that **twinkles** shines with little flashes of light.

SYNONYMS: glitter, sparkle

**twirl twirls, twirling, twirled**

VERB If you **twirl** something, you make it spin round quickly.

**twist twists, twisting, twisted**

VERB **1** When you **twist** something, you turn the two ends in opposite directions.

VERB **2** If you **twist** part of your body, you injure it by turning it too sharply or in an odd direction.

**two**

NOUN **Two** is the number 2.

LANGUAGE TIP
Do not confuse *two* with *to* or *too*.

**two-dimensional**

ADJECTIVE A **two-dimensional** object or shape is flat.

**tying**

VERB the present participle of **tie**

**type types, typing, typed**

NOUN **1** If something is the same **type** as something else, they belong to the same group and have many things in common.

SYNONYMS: kind, sort

VERB **2** If you **type** something, you use a typewriter or computer to write it.

**typewriter typewriters**

NOUN a machine with keys that are pressed to write numbers and letters on a page

**typhoon typhoons**

NOUN a very violent tropical storm

WORD HISTORY
from Chinese *tai fung* meaning great wind

**typical**

ADJECTIVE Something that is **typical** of a person or animal is usual and what is to be expected of them.

**tyrannosaurus tyrannosauruses**

NOUN a very large meat-eating dinosaur that walked upright on its back legs

**tyrant tyrants**

NOUN a person who treats the people they have power over with cruelty

**tyre tyres**

NOUN a thick ring of rubber fitted round each wheel of a vehicle and filled with air

→ Have a look at the illustrations for **bicycle** and **car**

a
b
c
d
e
f
g
h
i
j
k
l
m
n
o
p
q
r
s
t
u
v
w
x
y
z

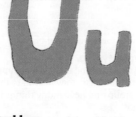

**udder** **udders**

NOUN the bag-like part of a cow, goat or ewe from which milk comes

**UFO** **UFOs**

NOUN an abbreviation of *unidentified flying object*. **UFOs** are objects seen in the skies, which some people believe come from other planets because they cannot be identified.

**ugly** **uglier, ugliest**

ADJECTIVE very unattractive or unpleasant

**ulcer** **ulcers**

NOUN a sore area on the skin or inside the body, that can take a long time to heal

**ultimate**

ADJECTIVE **1** final
NOUN **2** the best example of something

**ultraviolet light**

NOUN **Ultraviolet light** is not visible to the human eye. It is a form of radiation that causes your skin to tan in sunlight.

**umbrella** **umbrellas**

NOUN a folding frame covered in fabric and attached to a long stick, which you can open over you to protect you from the rain

**umpire** **umpires, umpiring, umpired**

NOUN **1** The **umpire** in a cricket or tennis match is the person who makes sure that the game is played fairly and the rules are not broken.
VERB **2** If a person **umpires** a game, they are the umpire.

**un-**

PREFIX You add **un-** to the beginning of a word to mean not. For example, **un**common means not common, and **un**likely means not likely.

**unable**

ADJECTIVE If you are **unable** to do something you cannot do it.

ANTONYM: able

**unanimous**

ADJECTIVE A **unanimous** decision or vote has the agreement of everyone involved.

**unaware**

ADJECTIVE not aware

**unbearable**

ADJECTIVE Something **unbearable** is so painful or upsetting that you feel that you cannot bear or endure it.

**unbelievable**

ADJECTIVE **1** very surprising or wonderful
ADJECTIVE **2** so unlikely that it is hard to believe

**uncanny**

ADJECTIVE strange and mysterious

**uncertain**

ADJECTIVE If you are **uncertain** about something, you are not sure about it.

SYNONYM: doubtful

**uncertainty**

NOUN the feeling you have when you are not sure about something

SYNONYM: doubt

**uncle** **uncles**

NOUN Your **uncle** is the brother of your mother or father, or the husband of your aunt.

**WORD HISTORY**
from Latin *avunculus* meaning mother's brother

**uncomfortable**

ADJECTIVE **1** If you are **uncomfortable**, your body is not relaxed or comfortable.
ADJECTIVE **2** If something like a chair or a piece of clothing is **uncomfortable**, it is not comfortable to sit in or to wear.
ADJECTIVE **3** If you feel **uncomfortable** in a situation, you feel worried or nervous.

**uncommon**

ADJECTIVE not common

**unconscious**

ADJECTIVE If someone is **unconscious**, they are unable to see, feel or hear anything that is going on. This is usually because they have fainted or been badly injured.

**uncover uncovers, uncovering, uncovered**
VERB **1** to take the cover off something
VERB **2** to find out a secret or discover something

**under**
PREPOSITION **1** below or beneath
PREPOSITION **2** less than • *children under the age of 14*
PREPOSITION **3** controlled or ruled by • *The soldiers were under his command.*
PREPOSITION **4** If something like a building is **under** construction, or **under** repair, it is in the process of being built or repaired.

**under-**
PREFIX You add **under-** at the beginning of a word to mean beneath or below. For example, if you **under**estimate an amount, you estimate it below what it really is.

**undercarriage undercarriages**
NOUN the part of an aircraft, including the wheels, that supports the aircraft when it is on the ground
→ Have a look at the illustration for **aeroplane**

**underestimate underestimates, underestimating, underestimated**
VERB **1** If you **underestimate** someone, you do not realise how much they can do.
VERB **2** If you **underestimate** something, you do not realise how big it is or how long it will take.

**undergo undergoes, undergoing, underwent, undergone**
VERB If you **undergo** something, you experience it or are subjected to it. • *She underwent an operation to remove her tonsils.*

**underground**
ADJECTIVE **1** below the surface of the ground
NOUN **2** a railway system in which trains travel in tunnels below the ground

**undergrowth**
NOUN small plants growing under trees

**underline underlines, underlining, underlined**
VERB If you **underline** a word or sentence, you draw a line under it.

**undermine undermines, undermining, undermined**
VERB **1** If you **undermine** a person's efforts or plans, you weaken them.
VERB **2** To **undermine** something is to make a hollow or tunnel beneath it. When

the sea **undermines** a cliff, for example, it gradually wears away the base and weakens it.

**underneath**
PREPOSITION below or beneath • *He wore a white shirt underneath a blue sweater.*

**underpants**
PLURAL NOUN a piece of men's underwear worn under trousers

**underpass underpasses**
NOUN a place where one road or path goes under another

**underprivileged**
ADJECTIVE **Underprivileged** people have less money and fewer opportunities than other people.

**understand understands, understanding, understood**
VERB **1** If you **understand** what someone says, or what you read, you know what it means.
VERB **2** If you **understand** how something works, you know how it works.
VERB **3** If you **understand** someone, you know them well and think you know why they behave the way they do.

**understudy understudies**
NOUN someone who has learnt the lines of a part in a play, and plays the part when the main actor or actress cannot perform

**undertake undertakes, undertaking, undertook, undertaken**
VERB If you **undertake** to do something, you agree to do it.

**undertaker undertakers**
NOUN someone whose job is to prepare bodies for burial and arrange funerals

**underwater**
ADVERB **1** below the surface of the water • *Submarines can travel fast underwater.*
ADJECTIVE **2** happening or used below the surface of the water • *The divers used underwater cameras.*

**underwear**
NOUN Your **underwear** is the clothing you wear next to your skin under your other clothes.

**undo undoes, undoing, undid, undone**
VERB **1** If you **undo** something like a knot, you loosen or unfasten it.
VERB **2** If you **undo** something that has been done, you reverse or remove the effects of it.

a
b
c
d
e
f
g
h
i
j
k
l
m
n
o
p
q
r
s
t
**u**
v
w
x
y
z

**429**

**undress** undresses, undressing, undressed
VERB If you **undress**, you take your clothes off.

**unearth** unearths, unearthing, unearthed
VERB If you **unearth** something, you dig it up or discover it.

**uneasy** uneasier, uneasiest
ADJECTIVE anxious or worried

**unemployed**
ADJECTIVE An **unemployed** person has no job.

**uneven**
ADJECTIVE An **uneven** surface is not level or smooth.

**unexpected**
ADJECTIVE Something **unexpected** is surprising because it was not thought likely to happen.

**unfair**
ADJECTIVE Something **unfair** does not seem right, reasonable or fair.

**unfold** unfolds, unfolding, unfolded
VERB 1 If you **unfold** something that is folded, such as a map, you open it out.
VERB 2 When a story **unfolds**, it gradually becomes clear.

**unfollow** unfollows, unfollowing, unfollowed
VERB If you **unfollow** someone on a social media website, you choose to stop looking at the messages and pictures that they post.

**unfortunate**
ADJECTIVE unlucky

**unfriend** unfriends, unfriending, unfriended
VERB If you **unfriend** someone, you stop being their friend on a social media website.

**unfriendly**
ADJECTIVE not friendly

**ungrateful**
ADJECTIVE not grateful

**unhappy** unhappier, unhappiest
ADJECTIVE sad, not happy

**unhealthy**
ADJECTIVE not healthy

**unicorn** unicorns
NOUN an imaginary animal that looks like a white horse with a straight horn growing from its forehead

**WORD HISTORY**
from Latin *unicornis* meaning having one hor

**uniform** uniforms
NOUN a special set of clothes worn by people at work or school

**WORD HISTORY**
from Latin *uniformis* meaning of one kind

**unify** unifies, unifying, unified
VERB If several things, especially countries, are **unified**, they join together to make one

**uninhabited**
ADJECTIVE An **uninhabited** place is a place where nobody lives.

**uninterested**
ADJECTIVE not interested • *I am totally **uninterested** in football.*

**union** unions
NOUN an organisation of workers that aims to improve the working conditions, pay and benefits of its members

**unique**
ADJECTIVE Something that is **unique** is the only one of its kind.

**WORD HISTORY**
from Latin *unicus* meaning one and only

**unisex**
ADJECTIVE designed to suit either men or women

**unison**
NOUN If a group of people does something in **unison**, they all do it together at the same time.

**WORD HISTORY**
from Latin *unisonus* meaning making the same musical sound

**unit** units
NOUN 1 one single, complete thing
NOUN 2 a term used to describe a fixed quantity or measurement • *A centimetre is a **unit** of length.*

**unite** unites, uniting, united
VERB If a number of people **unite**, they join together and act as a group.

**universal**
ADJECTIVE concerning or relating to everyone and everything

**universe** universes
NOUN everything that exists, including the whole of space, all the stars and the planets

WORD HISTORY
from Latin *universum* meaning whole world

**university** universities
NOUN a place where students study for degrees ● *My brother goes to **university** later this year.*

**unkempt**
ADJECTIVE untidy and not looked after properly

WORD HISTORY
from Old English *uncembed* meaning not combed

**unjust**
ADJECTIVE not fair ● *The group campaigns against **unjust** laws.*

**unkind**
ADJECTIVE rather cruel, not kind

**unknown**
ADJECTIVE If someone or something is **unknown**, people do not know about them or have not heard of them.

**unleaded**
ADJECTIVE **Unleaded** petrol does not contain any lead, and is less harmful to the atmosphere than petrol that does contain lead.

**unless**
CONJUNCTION You use **unless** to introduce the only circumstances in which something may or may not happen or is not true. ● *The team will play tomorrow **unless** it is raining.* ● *I won't go **unless** you ask me.*

**unlike**
ADJECTIVE **1** If one thing is **unlike** another, the two things are different.
PREPOSITION **2** not like ● *Unlike me, she hates chocolate.*

**unlikely** unlikelier, unlikeliest
ADJECTIVE not likely to happen or be true

**unload** unloads, unloading, unloaded
VERB to take things out of or off a container, a vehicle or a trailer

**unlock** unlocks, unlocking, unlocked
VERB When you **unlock** something, you open it by turning a key in the lock.

**unlucky** unluckier, unluckiest
ADJECTIVE If you are **unlucky**, you are unfortunate and have bad luck.

ANTONYMS: fortunate, lucky

**unnatural**
ADJECTIVE not natural or normal

**unnecessary**
ADJECTIVE not necessary

**unoccupied**
ADJECTIVE A house that is **unoccupied** has no one living in it.

**unpack** unpacks, unpacking, unpacked
VERB When you **unpack**, you take everything out of a suitcase, bag or box.

**unpleasant**
ADJECTIVE **1** Something **unpleasant** is not enjoyable and may make you uncomfortable or upset.
ADJECTIVE **2** An **unpleasant** person is unfriendly or rude.

**unplug** unplugs, unplugging, unplugged
VERB If you **unplug** something, you take the plug out of the socket to disconnect it from the electricity supply.

**unpopular**
ADJECTIVE not liked very much

**unravel** unravels, unravelling, unravelled
VERB **1** If you **unravel** threads that are knitted or tangled, you undo or untangle them.
VERB **2** If you **unravel** a mystery, you solve it.

**unreal**
ADJECTIVE existing only in the imagination, not real

**unreasonable**
ADJECTIVE not reasonable or fair

**unroll** unrolls, unrolling, unrolled
VERB If you **unroll** something that has been rolled up, you open it and make it flat.

**unruly**
ADJECTIVE badly behaved and difficult to control

**unsafe**
ADJECTIVE not safe

a b c d e f g h i j k l m n o p q r s t u v w x y z

**431**

**unscrew** **unscrews, unscrewing, unscrewed**

VERB If you **unscrew** something, you remove it by turning it or by removing the screws that are holding it.

**unselfish**

ADJECTIVE An **unselfish** person is not selfish and is concerned about other people's needs.

**unsteady**

ADJECTIVE If you are **unsteady**, you are not steady and have difficulty balancing.

**unsuccessful**

ADJECTIVE If you are **unsuccessful**, you do not manage to succeed in what you are trying to do.

**unsuitable**

ADJECTIVE Things that are **unsuitable** are not right or suitable for a particular purpose.

**untidy** **untidier, untidiest**

ADJECTIVE not tidy

**untie** **unties, untying, untied**

VERB If you **untie** something that has been tied, you unfasten or undo it.

**until**

PREPOSITION **1** If something happens **until** a particular time, it happens before that time and stops at that time. ● *The shops stay open **until** eight o'clock on Thursdays.*

PREPOSITION **2** If something does not happen **until** a particular time, it does not happen before that time and only starts happening at that time. ● *It didn't rain **until** the middle of the afternoon.*

CONJUNCTION **3** If something does not happen **until** a particular time, it does not happen before that time and only starts happening at that time. ● *You can't go out on your bike **until** you've finished cleaning your room.*

**untrue**

ADJECTIVE not true

**unusual**

ADJECTIVE Something that is **unusual** is not usual and does not happen very often.

**unwell**

ADJECTIVE If you are **unwell**, you are ill.

**unwilling**

ADJECTIVE If you are **unwilling** to do something, you do not want to do it.

**unwillingly**

ADVERB in a way that shows you do not want to do something

**unwind** **unwinds, unwinding, unwound**

VERB **1** If you **unwind** something that was wound into a ball or around something else you undo it.

VERB **2** If you **unwind** after working hard, you relax.

**unwrap** **unwraps, unwrapping, unwrapped**

VERB If you **unwrap** something, you take off the paper or other wrapping that is around it

**up**

PREPOSITION **1** towards or in a higher place ● *They went **up** the stairs to bed.*

ADVERB **2** towards or in a higher place ● *Keep your head **up**.*

ADVERB **3** If an amount of something goes **up**, it increases.

PREPOSITION **4** If you go **up** the road, you go along it.

ADJECTIVE **5** If you are **up**, you are not in bed.

**upbringing**

NOUN the way you have been brought up, and how your parents have taught you to behave

**upheaval** **upheavals**

NOUN a sudden big change that causes a lot of disturbance

**uphill**

ADVERB If you go **uphill**, you go up a hill or a slope.

**upholstery**

NOUN the soft covering on chairs and sofas that makes them comfortable

**upload** **uploads, uploading, uploaded**

VERB When you **upload** a computer file or program, you put it onto a computer or the internet.

**upon**

PREPOSITION on or on top of

**upper**

ADJECTIVE The **upper** of two things is the top or higher one. ● *the **upper** deck of the bus*

**upper-case**

ADJECTIVE Upper-case letters are written as capitals. For example, A, H, L and P are all **upper-case** letters.

**upright**

ADJECTIVE **1** Something or someone that is **upright**, is standing up straight or vertically, rather than bending or lying down.

ADJECTIVE **2** An **upright** person is decent and honest.

A B C D E F G H I J K L M N O P Q R S T U V W X Y Z

**uproar**

NOUN a lot of shouting and noise, often because people are angry

SYNONYMS: commotion, pandemonium

WORD HISTORY
from Dutch *oproer* meaning revolt

**upset upsets, upsetting, upset**

ADJECTIVE **1** unhappy and disappointed

VERB **2** If something **upsets** you, it makes you feel worried or unhappy.

VERB **3** If you **upset** something, you knock it over or spill it accidentally.

NOUN **4** A stomach **upset** is a slight stomach illness.

**upside down**

ADJECTIVE **1** the wrong way up • *She was* **upside down** *on the climbing frame.*

ADJECTIVE **2** If a place is **upside down**, it is very untidy.

**upstairs**

ADVERB **1** If you go **upstairs**, you go up to a higher floor.

ADJECTIVE **2** on a lower floor

**upthrust**

NOUN **Upthrust** is the force that pushes an object up and makes it seem to lose weight in a liquid or gas.

**up-to-date**

ADJECTIVE If something is **up-to-date**, it is modern or is the newest thing of its kind.

**upwards**

ADVERB going towards a higher place

**uranium**

NOUN a radioactive metallic element used to make nuclear energy and weapons

**urban**

ADJECTIVE to do with towns or cities rather than the country

WORD HISTORY
from Latin *urbs* meaning city

**urge urges, urging, urged**

NOUN **1** If you have an **urge** to do something, you very much want to do it.

VERB **2** If you **urge** someone to do something, you try to persuade and encourage them to do it.

**urgent**

ADJECTIVE If something is **urgent**, it needs to be dealt with immediately.

**urine**

NOUN the waste liquid that you get rid of from your body when you go to the toilet

**URL URLs**

NOUN A website's **URL** is its address on the internet. **URL** is an abbreviation for *uniform resource locator.*

**us**

PRONOUN A speaker or writer uses **us** to mean himself or herself and one or more other people.

**USB USBs**

NOUN a place on a computer where you can attach another piece of equipment, for example a printer or a memory stick

→ Have a look at the illustration for **computer**

**use uses, using, used**

VERB **1** If you **use** something, you do something with it that helps you to do a job or sort out a problem.

NOUN **2** the purpose or value of something, and the way it is used

PRONUNCIATION TIP
The verb is pronounced **yooz**. The noun is pronounced **yooss**.

**used**

VERB **1** If something **used to** happen, it happened before but does not happen now. • *We* **used to** *fish in this stream.*

ADJECTIVE **2** If you are **used to** something, you are familiar with it and have often experienced it.

VERB **3** the past tense and past participle of **use**

ADJECTIVE **4** A **used** item has already belonged to someone else.

PRONUNCIATION TIP
Meanings 1 and 2 are pronounced **yoosst**. Meanings 3 and 4 are pronounced **yoozd**.

**useful**

ADJECTIVE If something is **useful**, you can use it to help you in some way.

**useless**

ADJECTIVE Something that is **useless** is no good for anything.

### user-friendly
ADJECTIVE If something is **user-friendly**, it is easy to understand and use. ● *the most **user-friendly** camera available*

### usher ushers
NOUN a person who shows people where to sit at the theatre or cinema

### usual
ADJECTIVE **1** Something **usual** is expected and happens often.
PHRASE **2** If something happens **as usual**, it happens as you would expect, and is not surprising because it often happens that way.

### utensil utensils
NOUN a tool ● *A whisk is a kitchen **utensil**.*

### utility utilities
NOUN a service that is useful for everyone, such as water and gas supplies

### utter utters, uttering, uttered
VERB **1** When you **utter** sounds, you make or say them.
ADJECTIVE **2** complete or total ● *This is **utter** nonsense.*

### vacant
ADJECTIVE If something is **vacant**, it is not being used or no one is in it. ● *I couldn't find a **vacant** seat on the train.*

### vacation vacations
NOUN a holiday

### vaccinate vaccinates, vaccinating, vaccinated
VERB If someone **vaccinates** you, they give you an injection to protect you against a disease.

---
**PRONUNCIATION TIP**
This word is pronounced **vak**-si-nayt.

---

### vacuum vacuums, vacuuming, vacuumed
NOUN **1** a completely empty space containing no matter, solid, liquid or gas
VERB **2** If you **vacuum** something, you clean it using a vacuum cleaner.

---
**WORD HISTORY**
from Latin *vacuum* meaning empty space

---

### vacuum cleaner vacuum cleaners
NOUN an electrical device that sucks up dust and dirt from the floor

### vagina vaginas
NOUN A woman's **vagina** is the passage that leads from the outside of her body to her womb.

### vague vaguer, vaguest
ADJECTIVE not clear, definite or certain ● *They could see the **vague** outline of the mountains in the distance.*

SYNONYM: unclear

---
**PRONUNCIATION TIP**
This word is pronounced **vayg**.

---

### vaguely
ADVERB in a way that is not clear, definite or certain

**vain vainer, vainest**
ADJECTIVE **1** A **vain** person is too proud of their looks, intelligence or other good qualities.
ADJECTIVE **2** A **vain** attempt to do something is an unsuccessful attempt.

**valentine valentines**
NOUN **1** someone you love and send a card to on Saint **Valentine's** Day, February 14th
NOUN **2** a card you send to someone you love on Saint **Valentine's** Day

WORD HISTORY
Saint *Valentine* was a third-century martyr

**valiant**
ADJECTIVE brave and courageous

**valid**
ADJECTIVE A **valid** ticket or document is legal and accepted by people in authority.

**valley valleys**
NOUN a long stretch of land between hills, often with a river flowing through it

**valuable**
ADJECTIVE of great worth or very important ● *The diamond ring was very **valuable**.*

**value values, valuing, valued**
NOUN **1** the importance or usefulness of something
NOUN **2** the amount of money that something is worth
VERB **3** If you **value** something, you think it is important and valuable.

**valve valves**
NOUN **1** a device attached to a pipe or tube that controls the flow of gas or liquid
NOUN **2** a small flap in your heart or in a vein that controls the flow and direction of blood

**vampire vampires**
NOUN In horror stories, **vampires** come out of graves at night and suck people's blood.

**van vans**
NOUN a vehicle for carrying goods

**vandal vandals**
NOUN someone who deliberately damages or destroys things, particularly public property

**vandalise vandalises, vandalising, vandalised**; also spelt **vandalize**
VERB to deliberately damage or destroy things, particularly public property

**vandalism**
NOUN damage that someone deliberately causes to public or private property

**vanilla**
NOUN a flavouring used in food such as ice cream. It comes from the pod of a tropical plant.

**vanish vanishes, vanishing, vanished**
VERB If something **vanishes**, it disappears or does not exist any more.

**vapour**
NOUN a mass of tiny drops of water or other liquids in the air, which looks like mist

WORD HISTORY
from Latin *vapor* meaning steam

**variable variables**
NOUN a symbol such as *x* which can stand for any one of a set of values

**variety varieties**
NOUN a number of different kinds of similar things ● *There was a **variety** of food from different countries on the menu.*
SYNONYMS: assortment, range

**various**
ADJECTIVE of several different types ● *trees of **various** sorts*
SYNONYMS: different, miscellaneous

**varnish varnishes, varnishing, varnished**
NOUN **1** a liquid which, when painted onto a surface such as wood, gives it a hard, clear, shiny finish
VERB **2** If you **varnish** something, you paint it with varnish.

**vary varies, varying, varied**
VERB If something **varies**, it changes and is not always the same.

**vase vases**
NOUN a jar or other container for putting cut flowers in

**vast**
ADJECTIVE extremely large

**vat vats**
NOUN a large container used for storing liquids

**435**

## VAT

NOUN an abbreviation of *value-added tax*, which is a tax you pay on things you buy

## vault **vaults, vaulting, vaulted**

NOUN **1** a strong secure room where valuables are stored, often underneath a building, or where people are buried underneath a church

NOUN **2** an arched roof, often found in churches

VERB **3** If you **vault** over something, you jump over it using your hands or a pole to help.

## VDU

NOUN an abbreviation of *visual display unit*, which is a monitor screen for computers

## veal

NOUN the meat from a calf

## Veda

NOUN the collection of ancient sacred writings of the Hindu religion

## vegetable **vegetables**

NOUN **Vegetables** are plants or parts of plants that can be eaten. Peas, carrots, cabbage and potatoes are **vegetables**.

## vegetarian **vegetarians**

NOUN a person who does not eat meat, poultry or fish

## vegetation

NOUN the plants growing in a particular area

## vehicle **vehicles**

NOUN a machine, often with an engine, such as a car, bus or lorry, used for moving people or goods from one place to another

## veil **veils**

NOUN a piece of thin, soft cloth that women sometimes wear over their heads and faces

## vein **veins**

NOUN Your **veins** are the tubes in your body through which your blood flows to your heart.

## velvet

NOUN a very soft material that has a thick layer of short threads on one side

## venison

NOUN the meat from a deer

## Venn diagram **Venn diagrams**

NOUN a diagram using circles to show how sets of things relate to each other. **Venn diagrams** are used in mathematics.

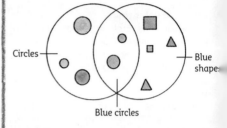

Circles — — Blue shapes

Blue circles

## venom

NOUN the poison of a snake, scorpion or spider

**WORD HISTORY**
from Latin *venenum* meaning love potion or poison

## venomous

ADJECTIVE A **venomous** snake, scorpion or spider is poisonous.

## vent **vents**

NOUN an opening in something, especially to let out smoke or gas

→ Have a look at the illustration for **volcano**

## ventilate **ventilates, ventilating, ventilated**

VERB If you **ventilate** a place, you allow fresh air to move freely through it.

## venture **ventures, venturing, ventured**

NOUN **1** something new that you do which involves some sort of risk

VERB **2** If you **venture** somewhere that might be dangerous, you go there.

## veranda **verandas**; also spelt **verandah**

NOUN a platform with a roof that is fixed to the outside wall of a house at ground level. It is often made of wood.

## verb **verbs**

NOUN In grammar, a **verb** is a word that expresses actions and states, for example *be*, *become*, *take* and *run*.

## verbal

ADJECTIVE spoken rather than written

## verdict **verdicts**

NOUN In a law court, a **verdict** is the decision reached by the judge or jury about whether a prisoner is guilty or not guilty.

**verge verges**
NOUN the narrow strip of grassy ground at the side of a road ● *We walked along the verge.*

**verify verifies, verifying, verified**
VERB If you **verify** something, you check that it is true or correct.

**verruca verrucas**
NOUN a small, hard, infectious growth that you can get on the sole of your foot

**versatile**
ADJECTIVE If someone or something is **versatile**, they have many different skills or uses.

**versatility**
NOUN the quality that someone or something has when they have many different skills or uses

**verse verses**
NOUN 1 another word for **poetry**
NOUN 2 one part of a poem, song or chapter of the Bible

**version versions**
NOUN A **version** of something is a form of it that is different in some way from earlier or later forms.

**versus**
PREPOSITION **Versus** means against, and is used to show that two people or teams are competing against each other.

**vertebra vertebrae**
NOUN one of the bones that make up your backbone

**vertebrate vertebrates**
NOUN an animal with a backbone

**vertex vertices**
NOUN the highest point of a hill, or a corner of a two-dimensional or three-dimensional shape

**vertical**
ADJECTIVE Something that is **vertical** is in an upright position or points straight up.

**very**
ADVERB **Very** is used before words to emphasise them. ● *I had a very bad dream.*

SYNONYMS: extremely, greatly, really

**vessel vessels**
NOUN 1 a ship or large boat
NOUN 2 a container for liquids
NOUN 3 one of the tubes in an animal or a plant that carries blood or other liquid around the body

**vest vests**
NOUN a piece of underwear worn on the top half of the body for warmth

WORD HISTORY
from Latin *vestis* meaning clothing

**vet vets**
NOUN a doctor for animals. **Vet** is an abbreviation of *veterinary surgeon.*

**veteran veterans**
NOUN 1 a person with a lot of experience of something, or who has been involved in something for a long time
NOUN 2 someone who has served in the armed forces, particularly during a war ● *My uncle is a Gulf War veteran.*

**via**
PREPOSITION If you go to one place **via** another, you travel through that other place to get to your destination.

WORD HISTORY
from Latin *via* meaning way or road

**viaduct viaducts**
NOUN a high bridge that carries a road or railway across a valley

**vibrate vibrates, vibrating, vibrated**
VERB If something **vibrates**, it moves a tiny amount backwards and forwards very quickly.

**vibration vibrations**
NOUN tiny, very fast backward and forward movements ● *Crayfish can detect weak vibrations in the water.*

**vicar vicars**
NOUN a priest in the Church of England

**vice vices**
NOUN a bad habit, such as being greedy or smoking

**vice versa**
ADVERB the other way around

**vicinity vicinities**
NOUN an area round something ● *She was seen in the vicinity of the school.*

**vicious**
ADJECTIVE cruel and violent

**victim victims**
NOUN someone who has been harmed or injured by someone or something

a b c d e f g h i j k l m n o p q r s t u v w x y z

**victor** victors
NOUN the winner of a contest or battle

**victory** victories
NOUN a success in a battle or competition

SYNONYMS: conquest, triumph, win

**video** videos, videoing, videoed
NOUN **1** a sound and picture recording that can be played back on a television set
NOUN **2** the recording and showing of films and events using a **video** recorder, tape and a television set
NOUN **3** a video recorder ● Set the **video** to record a programme at eight o'clock.
VERB **4** If you **video** something, you record it on video tape to watch later.

WORD HISTORY
from Latin *videre* meaning to see

**video game** video games
NOUN a game that can be played by using an electronic control to move symbols on a screen

**view** views
NOUN **1** everything you can see from a particular place
NOUN **2** If something you post on a website has a certain number of **views**, then people have looked at it that number of times.
NOUN **3** Your **view** is your opinion.

**viewer** viewers
NOUN one of the people who watch something, especially a television programme

**viewpoint** viewpoints
NOUN Your **viewpoint** is your attitude towards something.

**vigilance**
NOUN **Vigilance** is watching carefully what is happening so that you will notice any danger or trouble.

**vigilant**
ADJECTIVE careful and alert to danger or trouble

**vigilantly**
ADVERB in a careful way so that you notice any danger or trouble

**vigorous**
ADJECTIVE energetic or enthusiastic

**villa** villas
NOUN a house, especially a pleasant holiday home in a country with a warm climate

**village** villages
NOUN a collection of houses and other buildings in the countryside

→ Have a look at the illustration for **map**

WORD HISTORY
from Old French *ville* meaning farm

**villain** villains
NOUN someone who harms others or breaks the law

SYNONYMS: criminal, rogue

**vine** vines
NOUN a climbing plant, especially one that produces grapes

**vinegar**
NOUN a sharp-tasting liquid made from sour wine and used for flavouring food

WORD HISTORY
from French *vin aigre* meaning sour wine

**vineyard** vineyards
NOUN an area of land where grapes are grown for making wine

**vintage**
ADJECTIVE **1** A **vintage** wine is a good quality wine made in a particular year.
ADJECTIVE **2** A **vintage** car is one made between 1918 and 1930.

**vinyl**
NOUN a strong plastic used to make things such as furniture and floor coverings

**viola** violas
NOUN a musical instrument like a violin, but larger and with a lower pitch

**violence**
NOUN **1** behaviour that is intended to hurt or kill
NOUN **2** force that does harm or damage ● The **violence** of the storm surprised everyone.

**violent**
ADJECTIVE **1** behaving in a way that is intended to hurt or kill someone
ADJECTIVE **2** having a lot of force that causes damage ● a **violent** storm

**violet violets**
NOUN **1** a plant with dark purple flowers
NOUN **2** a bluish-purple colour
ADJECTIVE **3** having a bluish-purple colour

**violin violins**
NOUN a musical instrument with four strings that is held under the chin and played with a bow

**VIP**
NOUN an abbreviation of *very important person*
• The **VIPs** had the best seats at the concert.

**viper vipers**
NOUN a type of poisonous snake

**viral**
ADJECTIVE **1** A **viral** infection or disease is caused by a virus.
PHRASE **2** If a film clip, story, picture or message **goes viral**, it spreads quickly because people share it on social media and send it to each other.

**virtual**
ADJECTIVE almost exactly the same as the real thing, especially when created by a computer

**virtual reality**
NOUN an environment or image that has been created by a computer and looks real to the person using it

**virtue virtues**
NOUN **1** moral goodness
NOUN **2** a good quality in someone's character

**virus viruses**
NOUN **1** a tiny organism that can cause disease
NOUN **2** A disease caused by a virus can be called a **virus**.
NOUN **3** a program that damages the information stored in a computer system

**visible**
ADJECTIVE able to be seen

**vision visions**
NOUN **1** the ability to see
NOUN **2** a picture of something in your mind or imagination

**visit visits, visiting, visited**
VERB **1** If you **visit** someone, you go to see them and spend time with them.
VERB **2** If you **visit** a place, you go to see it.
NOUN **3** a trip to see a person or place

**visor visors**
NOUN **1** a transparent, movable shield attached to a helmet, which can be pulled down to protect the eyes or face
NOUN **2** a shade to protect your eyes from the sun

**visual**
ADJECTIVE to do with sight and seeing

**vital**
ADJECTIVE necessary or very important
SYNONYM: essential

**vitality**
NOUN People who have **vitality** are energetic and lively.

**vitamin vitamins**
NOUN one of a group of substances you need to have in your diet in order to stay healthy. For example, **vitamin** C is found in oranges.

**vivid**
ADJECTIVE very bright in colour or clear in detail

**vivisection**
NOUN the use of living animals for medical research

**vixen vixens**
NOUN a female fox

**vlog vlogs**
NOUN a set of videos, often about a particular subject, that someone posts on the internet
• She has her own beauty **vlog**.

**vlogger vloggers**
NOUN someone who regularly posts a vlog

**vocabulary vocabularies**
NOUN **1** the total number of words someone knows in a particular language
NOUN **2** all the words in a language

**vocal**
ADJECTIVE to do with or involving the use of the human voice

**vocation vocations**
NOUN **1** If you have a **vocation**, you want very much to do a particular job, especially one that involves helping other people.
NOUN **2** a profession or career

**voice voices**
NOUN Your **voice** is what you hear when you speak or sing.

## volcano

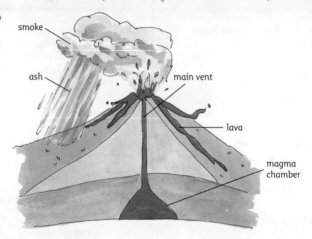

smoke

ash

main vent

lava

magma chamber

**void** voids

NOUN a very large empty space or deep hole

**volcano** volcanoes

NOUN a mountain with an opening at the top called a crater, from which lava, gas and ash sometimes erupt

→ Have a look at the illustration

WORD HISTORY
named after *Vulcan*, the Roman god of fire

**vole** voles

NOUN a small mammal like a mouse with a short tail, which lives in fields and near rivers

**volley** volleys

NOUN 1 A **volley** of shots or missiles is a lot of them fired or thrown at the same time.
NOUN 2 In tennis, a **volley** is a stroke in which the player hits the ball before it bounces.

**volleyball**

NOUN a game in which two teams hit a ball back and forth over a high net with their hands. The ball is not allowed to bounce on the ground.

**volt** volts

NOUN the unit used to measure the voltage of a battery

WORD HISTORY
named after Alessandro *Volta* who invented the electric battery

**voltage** voltages

NOUN the measure of how much electrical current a battery can push through an electric circuit

**volume** volumes

NOUN 1 the amount of space something contains or occupies
NOUN 2 The **volume** of a radio, TV or record player is how loud it is.
NOUN 3 a book, or one of a series of books

**voluntarily**

ADVERB If you do something **voluntarily** you do it because you want to do it, not because you are paid or told to do it.

**voluntary**

ADJECTIVE Something **voluntary** is done because you want to do it, not because you are paid or told to do it.

**volunteer** volunteers, volunteering, volunteered

NOUN 1 someone who does work that they are not paid for
VERB 2 If you **volunteer** to do something, you offer to do it without expecting any reward.

**vomit** vomits, vomiting, vomited

VERB If you **vomit**, food and drink comes back up from your stomach and out through your mouth.

**vote** votes, voting, voted

NOUN 1 Someone's **vote** is their choice in an election, or at a meeting where decisions are taken.
VERB 2 When people **vote**, they show their choice or opinion, usually by writing on a piece of paper or by raising their hand.

**voucher** vouchers

NOUN a piece of paper that can be used instead of money to pay for something

**vow** **vows, vowing, vowed**
VERB **1** If you **vow** to do something, you make a promise to do it.
NOUN **2** a promise

**vowel** **vowels**
NOUN **1** a sound made without your tongue touching the roof of your mouth or your teeth
NOUN **2** In the English language the letters a, e, i, o and u are **vowels**.

**voyage** **voyages**
NOUN a long journey on a ship or in a spacecraft

**vulgar**
ADJECTIVE rude or offensive

**vulnerable**
ADJECTIVE without protection and easily hurt or damaged

SYNONYM: defenceless

**vulture** **vultures**
NOUN a large bird that lives in hot countries and eats the flesh of dead animals

**waddle** **waddles, waddling, waddled**
VERB to walk with short, quick steps, swaying slightly from side to side • *A duck **waddled** past.*

**wade** **wades, wading, waded**
VERB If you **wade**, you walk through water or mud.

**wafer** **wafers**
NOUN a thin, crisp biscuit, often eaten with ice cream

**waffle** **waffles, waffling, waffled**
VERB **1** When someone **waffles**, they talk or write a lot without being clear or without saying anything of importance.
NOUN **2** a thick, crisp pancake with squares marked on it, often eaten with syrup poured over it

**wag** **wags, wagging, wagged**
VERB **1** When a dog **wags** its tail, it shakes it repeatedly from side to side.
VERB **2** If you **wag** your finger, you move it repeatedly up and down.

**wage** **wages**
NOUN the regular payment made to someone each week for the work they do

**wagon** **wagons**; also spelt **waggon**
NOUN a strong four-wheeled cart for carrying heavy loads. **Wagons** are usually pulled by horses or tractors.

**wail** **wails, wailing, wailed**
VERB If a person or an animal **wails**, they cry or moan loudly.

**waist** **waists**
NOUN the middle part of your body where it narrows slightly above your hips

**waistcoat** **waistcoats**
NOUN a sleeveless piece of clothing, usually worn over a shirt and under a jacket

a
b
c
d
e
f
g
h
i
j
k
l
m
n
o
p
q
r
s
t
u
v
w
x
y
z

**441**

**wait** **waits, waiting, waited**

VERB **1** If you **wait**, you spend time in a place or a situation, usually doing little or nothing, before something happens.

VERB **2** to serve people food and drinks as a waiter or waitress

NOUN **3** A **wait** is a period of time before something happens.

**waiter** **waiters**

NOUN a man who works in a restaurant, serving people with food and drink

**waitress** **waitresses**

NOUN a woman who works in a restaurant, serving people with food and drink

**wake** **wakes, waking, woke, woken**

VERB When you **wake**, or when something **wakes** you, you become conscious again after being asleep.

**walk** **walks, walking, walked**

VERB **1** When you **walk**, you move along by putting one foot in front of the other on the ground.

NOUN **2** If you go for a **walk**, you go from one place to another on foot.

**wall** **walls**

NOUN **1** a narrow structure of brick or stone built round a garden or building

NOUN **2** one of the four sides of a room

**wallaby** **wallabies**

NOUN a marsupial that looks like a small kangaroo

WORD HISTORY

from *wolaba*, an Australian Aboriginal word

**wallet** **wallets**

NOUN a small, flat, folding case made of leather or plastic, used for holding paper money and sometimes credit cards

**wallpaper** **wallpapers**

NOUN thick coloured or patterned paper that comes in rolls, for pasting onto the walls of rooms to decorate them

**walnut** **walnuts**

NOUN **1** a nut that you can eat. It has a wrinkled shape and a hard, round, light-brown shell.

NOUN **2** the tree on which walnuts grow. The wood from these trees is often used for making expensive furniture.

**walrus** **walruses**

NOUN an animal that lives in the sea. It looks like a large seal with a tough skin, coarse whiskers and two tusks.

**waltz** **waltzes, waltzing, waltzed**

NOUN **1** a dance that has a rhythm of three beats to the bar

VERB **2** If you **waltz** with someone, you dance a waltz with them.

**wand** **wands**

NOUN a long, thin rod used by magicians when they perform magic tricks, and by fairies in stories

**wander** **wanders, wandering, wandered**

VERB If you **wander** in a place, you walk around in a casual way.

**want** **wants, wanting, wanted**

VERB **1** If you **want** something, you feel that you would like to have it or do it.

VERB **2** to need something

**wanted**

ADJECTIVE being looked for, especially by the police as a suspected criminal

**war** **wars**

NOUN a period of fighting between countries or states, when weapons are used and many people may be killed

**ward** **wards**

NOUN **1** a long room with beds in for patients in a hospital

NOUN **2** a child who is looked after by a guardian rather than their parents

**warden** **wardens**

NOUN **1** a person in charge of a place like a park or a block of flats, or an institution like a prison or a hostel

NOUN **2** an official who makes sure that certain laws or rules are obeyed

**wardrobe** **wardrobes**

NOUN a tall cupboard in which you can hang your clothes

WORD HISTORY

from Old French *warder* meaning to guard robes and *robes* meaning clothing

**warehouse** **warehouses**

NOUN a large building where goods are stored

**warm** warmer, warmest; warms, warming, warmed
ADJECTIVE **1** Something that is **warm** has some heat, but not enough to be hot.
ADJECTIVE **2 Warm** clothes or blankets are made of material that protects you from the cold.
VERB **3** If you **warm** something, you heat it up gently so that it stops being cold.

**warm-blooded**
ADJECTIVE A **warm-blooded** animal has quite a high body temperature which does not change according to the surrounding temperature.

**warn** warns, warning, warned
VERB If you **warn** someone, you tell them that they may be in danger or in trouble.

**warning** warnings
NOUN something said or written to warn someone of a possible danger or problem

**warp** warps, warping, warped
VERB If something **warps**, or is **warped**, it becomes bent and twisted, usually because of heat or dampness.

**warrant** warrants
NOUN a special document that gives someone permission to do something • *The police had a **warrant** to search the house for evidence.*

**warren** warrens
NOUN an area of ground where there are many rabbit burrows

**warrior** warriors
NOUN a fighting man or soldier

**wart** warts
NOUN a small, hard growth on the skin

**wary** warier, wariest
ADJECTIVE If you are **wary** of something or someone, you are not sure about them, so you are cautious.

**was**
VERB a past tense of **be**

**wash** washes, washing, washed
VERB **1** If you **wash** something, you clean it with water and soap.
VERB **2** If you **wash**, you clean yourself using soap and water.

**wash up**
VERB If you **wash up**, you wash the dishes, pans and cutlery used in preparing and eating a meal.

**washable**
ADJECTIVE able to be washed without being damaged

**washing**
NOUN clothes that need to be washed or that have been washed

**washing machine** washing machines
NOUN a machine for washing clothes

**washing-up**
NOUN the task of washing plates, cutlery and pots after a meal

**wasp** wasps
NOUN a flying insect with yellow and black stripes across its body, which can sting

**waste** wastes, wasting, wasted
VERB **1** If you **waste** time, money or energy, you use too much of it on something that is not important or that you do not need.
NOUN **2** using more money or some other resource than you need to
NOUN **3** rubbish or other material that is no longer wanted, or that is left over

**watch** watches, watching, watched
NOUN **1** a small clock, usually worn on a strap on a person's wrist
VERB **2** If you **watch** something, you look at it for some time and pay attention to what is happening.

**watch out**
VERB **1** If you **watch out** for something or someone, you keep alert to see if they are near you.
VERB **2** If you tell someone to **watch out**, you are warning them to be careful.

**water** waters, watering, watered
NOUN **1** a clear, colourless, tasteless liquid that falls from clouds as rain

→ Have a look at the illustration for **photosynthesis**

VERB **2** If you **water** a plant, you pour water into the soil around it.
VERB **3** If your eyes or mouth **water**, they produce tears or saliva. • *My mouth started **watering** when I smelled Mum's baking.*

**watercolour** watercolours
NOUN **1** a type of paint that is mixed with water and used for painting pictures
NOUN **2** a picture that has been painted using watercolours

a
b
c
d
e
f
g
h
i
j
k
l
m
n
o
p
q
r
s
t
u
v
w
x
y
z

**443**

A
B
C
D
E
F
G
H
I
J
K
L
M
N
O
P
Q
R
S
T
U
V
W
X
Y
Z

## water cycle

NOUN the continuous circulation of water throughout the Earth through evaporation, condensation, precipitation and transpiration

→ Have a look at the illustration

## waterfall **waterfalls**

NOUN water from a stream or river as it flows over rocks or the edge of a steep cliff and falls to the ground below

## waterlogged

ADJECTIVE Something that is **waterlogged** is so wet that it cannot soak up any more water.

## watermark **watermarks**

NOUN **1** a mark showing the level of water
NOUN **2** a faint design in some types of paper which you can see if you hold it up to the light

## waterproof

ADJECTIVE Something that is **waterproof** does not let water pass through it. • *We put on our **waterproof** jackets as it was raining.*

## watertight

ADJECTIVE Something that is **watertight** does not allow water to pass in or out.

## waterworks

NOUN the place where the public supply of water is stored and cleaned, and from where it is supplied to our homes

## watt **watts**

NOUN a unit of measurement of electrical power

**PRONUNCIATION TIP**
This word is pronounced **wot**.

**WORD HISTORY**
Named after James *Watt* (1736–1819) who invented the steam engine

## wave **waves, waving, waved**

VERB **1** If you **wave** your hand, you move it from side to side, usually to say hello or goodbye.
VERB **2** If you **wave** something, you hold it up and move it from side to side. • *People in the crowd were **waving** flags.*
NOUN **3** a ridge of water on the surface of the sea caused by wind or by tides
NOUN **4** the form in which some types of energy, such as heat, light or sound, travel

## wax **waxes**

NOUN **1** a solid, slightly shiny substance made of fat or oil, that melts easily and is used to make candles and polish
NOUN **2** the sticky yellow substance in your ears

## way **ways**

NOUN **1** The **way** of doing something is how you do it.
NOUN **2** The **way** to a place is how you get there.

## WC **WCs**

NOUN an abbreviation of *water closet*. It is used on plans and signs to show where the toilet is located.

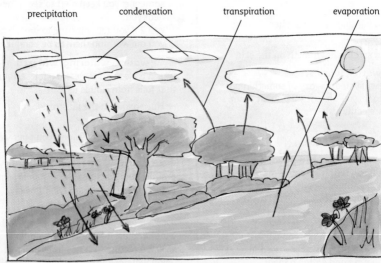

precipitation    condensation    transpiration    evaporation

water cycle

**we**

PRONOUN **We** refers to the person writing or talking and one or more other people.

**weak** weaker, weakest

ADJECTIVE If someone is **weak**, they do not have much strength or energy.

**wealth**

NOUN a large amount of money or property that someone owns

**wealthy** wealthier, wealthiest

ADJECTIVE Someone who is **wealthy** has a lot of money.

**weapon** weapons

NOUN an object used to hurt or kill people in a fight or war

**wear** wears, wearing, wore, worn

VERB When you **wear** something, such as clothes, make-up or jewellery, you have them on your body or face.

wear out

VERB When something **wears out**, or when you **wear** it **out**, it is used so much that it becomes thin, weak and no longer usable.

**wearily**

ADVERB in a way that shows you are very tired

**weariness**

NOUN the feeling you have when you are very tired

**weary** wearier, weariest

ADJECTIVE If you are **weary**, you are very tired.

**weasel** weasels

NOUN a small wild mammal with a long, thin body and short legs

**weather**

NOUN the conditions of sunshine, rain, wind or snow at a particular time in a particular place

**weave** weaves, weaving, wove, woven

VERB **1** If you **weave** something like cloth or a basket, you make it by crossing threads or grasses over and under each other. Cloth is often **woven** using a machine called a loom.
VERB **2** If you **weave** your way, you move from side to side past people and other obstacles.

**web** webs

NOUN a fine net of threads that a spider makes from a sticky substance that it produces in its body

**Web**

NOUN short for **World Wide Web**

**webbed**

ADJECTIVE **Webbed** feet have skin joining the toes together, like ducks' feet.

**webcam** webcams

NOUN a camera that sends pictures over the internet

a
b
c
d
e
f
g
h
i
j
k
l
m
n
o
p
q
r
s
t
u
v
w
x
y
z

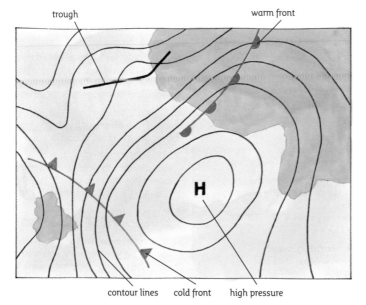

**weather map**

A
B
C
D
E
F
G
H
I
J
K
L
M
N
O
P
Q
R
S
T
U
V
**W**
X
Y
Z

**website** websites
NOUN a place on the internet where you can find out about a particular subject or person

**we'd**
a contraction of *we had* or *we would*

**wedding** weddings
NOUN a marriage ceremony

**wedge** wedges, wedging, wedged
VERB **1** If you **wedge** something somewhere, you make it stay there by holding it tightly, or by fixing something next to it to stop it from moving.
NOUN **2** a piece of something such as wood, metal or rubber with one thin edge and one thick edge, used to hold something still • *I put a **wedge** under the door to keep it open.*
NOUN **3** a piece of something that has a thick triangular shape • *I cut a **wedge** of cheese.*

**Wednesday**
NOUN the fourth day of the week, coming between Tuesday and Thursday

**WORD HISTORY**
Wednesday was the day the Anglo-Saxons honoured their god *Odin* or *Woden*

**weed** weeds, weeding, weeded
NOUN **1** a wild plant growing somewhere it is not wanted
VERB **2** If you **weed** an area of ground, you remove the weeds from it.

**week** weeks
NOUN **1** a period of seven days, especially one beginning on a Sunday and ending on a Saturday
NOUN **2** the part of a week that does not include Saturday and Sunday

**weekday** weekdays
NOUN any day except Saturday and Sunday

**weekend** weekends
NOUN Saturday and Sunday.

**weekly**
ADJECTIVE **1** happening or appearing once every week • *We do the **weekly** shopping every Thursday.*
ADVERB **2** once every week • *The bins are emptied **weekly**.*

**weep** weeps, weeping, wept
VERB If someone **weeps**, they cry.

**weigh** weighs, weighing, weighed
VERB **1** If something **weighs** a particular amount, that is how heavy it is.

VERB **2** If you **weigh** something, you find out how heavy it is by using scales.

**weight** weights
NOUN the heaviness of something

**weightless**
ADJECTIVE A person or object is **weightless** when they are in space and, because the Earth's gravity does not affect them, they float around.

**weir** weirs
NOUN a low dam built across a river to raise the water level, control the flow of water, or change the direction of the water

**WORD HISTORY**
from Old English *wer* meaning river-dam or enclosure for fish

**weird** weirder, weirdest
ADJECTIVE strange or odd

**welcome** welcomes, welcoming, welcomed
VERB **1** If you **welcome** a visitor, you greet them in a friendly way when they arrive.
GREETING **2 Welcome** can be said as a greeting to a visitor who has just arrived.
ADJECTIVE **3** If someone is **welcome** at a place, they will be accepted there in a friendly way.

**WORD HISTORY**
from Old English *wilcuma* meaning welcome guest

**weld** welds, welding, welded
VERB If you **weld** two pieces of metal together, you join them by heating their edges and pressing them together.

**welfare**
NOUN The **welfare** of a person or group is their health, comfort and happiness.

**welfare state**
NOUN a system in which the government uses money from taxes to provide health care and education, and to give benefits to certain people

**we'll**
a contraction of *we will* or *we shall*

**well** better, best; wells
ADJECTIVE **1** If you are **well**, you are healthy.
ADVERB **2** If you do something **well**, you do it to a high standard.
NOUN **3** a hole in the ground with water or oil at the bottom

**wellington wellingtons**
NOUN a long waterproof rubber boot. The word 'welly' is often used for short.

---

**WORD HISTORY**
named after the Duke of *Wellington*

---

**went**
VERB the past tense of **go**

**wept**
VERB the past tense and past participle of **weep**

**we're**
a contraction of *we are*

**were**
VERB a past tense of **be**

**west**
NOUN one of the four main points of the compass. The sun sets in the **west**. The abbreviation for **west** is W.

→ Have a look at the illustration for **compass point**

**western westerns**
ADJECTIVE **1** in or from the west
NOUN **2** a film or book about the west of America in the nineteenth and early twentieth centuries

**wet wetter, wettest; wets, wetting, wet or wetted**
ADJECTIVE **1** covered or soaked with water or other liquid
ADJECTIVE **2 Wet** weather is rainy. • *It's so **wet** today.*
VERB **3** If you **wet** something, you make it wet.

**we've**
a contraction of *we have*

**whale whales**
NOUN a very large sea mammal that breathes out water through a hole on the top of its head

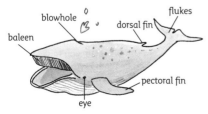

blowhole
flukes
dorsal fin
baleen
pectoral fin
eye

**wharf wharves or wharfs**
NOUN a platform beside a river or the sea, where ships load and unload

**what**
ADJECTIVE **1 What** is used in questions.
• *What time is it?*
ADJECTIVE **2** You use **what** to emphasise a comment. • *What excellent work!*
PHRASE **3** You use **what about** to show that you are making a suggestion or a question.
• *What about the homework from last night?*
PRONOUN **4** refers to information about something • *I really have no idea **what** you mean.*

**whatever**
PRONOUN **1** anything or everything of a particular type
CONJUNCTION **2** You use **whatever** to mean no matter what. • *I will go **whatever** happens.*

**wheat**
NOUN a cereal plant grown for its grain that is used to make flour

**wheel wheels, wheeling, wheeled**
NOUN **1** a circular object that turns on a rod attached to its centre. **Wheels** are fixed underneath vehicles so that they can move along.

→ Have a look at the illustrations for **bicycle** and **car**

VERB **2** If you **wheel** something somewhere, you push it along on wheels.

**wheelbarrow wheelbarrows**
NOUN a small cart with a single wheel at the front, pushed along by two handles at the back. It is used by people such as gardeners and builders.

**wheelchair wheelchairs**
NOUN a chair with large wheels, for use by people who find walking difficult or impossible

**wheeze wheezes, wheezing, wheezed**
VERB If someone **wheezes**, they breathe with difficulty, making a whistling sound.

**when**
ADVERB **1** You use **when** to ask at what time something will happen or how long ago it has happened. • *When shall I see you?*
CONJUNCTION **2** You use **when** to refer to a certain time. • *I had fun **when** I was on holiday.*

a b c d e f g h i j k l m n o p q r s t u v w x y z

**447**

A
B
C
D
E
F
G
H
I
J
K
L
M
N
O
P
Q
R
S
T
U
V
**W**
X
Y
Z

**whenever**
CONJUNCTION at any time, or every time that something happens • *I go to the park **whenever** I can.*

**where**
ADVERB **1** You use **where** to ask which place something is in, is from, or is going to. • ***Where** are we?*
CONJUNCTION **2** You use **where** to refer to a place in which something or someone is. • *You do not know **where** we live.*

**wherever**
CONJUNCTION in, at or to any place or situation • *Alex heard the same thing **wherever** he went.*

**whether**
CONJUNCTION You use **whether** when you are talking about two or more things to choose from. • *I don't know **whether** that's true or false.*

**which**
ADJECTIVE **1** You use **which** to talk or ask about alternatives. • ***Which** girl is your sister?*
PRONOUN **2** **Which** shows the thing you are talking about or gives more detail about it. • *The book **which** is on the table is mine.*

**whichever**
PRONOUN You use **whichever** when talking about different possibilities. • *You can have cake or chocolate, **whichever** you prefer.*

**whiff** whiffs
NOUN a slight smell of something • *I caught a **whiff** of her perfume as she passed.*

**while**
CONJUNCTION **1** If something happens **while** something else is happening, the two things happen at the same time. • *Mum went to the café **while** I had my lesson.*
CONJUNCTION **2** **While** can be used to mean but or although. • *I like dogs, **while** my brother prefers cats.*
NOUN **3** a period of time • *a little **while** earlier*

**whim** whims
NOUN a sudden wish or desire

SYNONYM: impulse

**whimper** whimpers, whimpering, whimpered
VERB When children or animals **whimper**, they make soft, low, unhappy sounds.

**whine** whines, whining, whined
VERB **1** If a person or an animal **whines**, the make a long, high-pitched noise, especially one that sounds sad or unpleasant.
VERB **2** If someone **whines** about something they complain about it in an annoying way.

**whip** whips, whipping, whipped
NOUN **1** a long, thin piece of leather or rope attached to a handle
VERB **2** To **whip** a person or animal means to hit them with a whip.

**whirl** whirls, whirling, whirled
VERB When something **whirls**, or when you **whirl** it round, it turns or spins round very fast.

**whirlpool** whirlpools
NOUN a small area in a river or the sea where the water is moving quickly round and round in a circle so that objects floating near it are pulled into its centre

**whirlwind** whirlwinds
NOUN a tall column of air that spins round and round very fast

**whirr** whirrs, whirring, whirred
VERB When something like a machine **whirrs**, it makes a continuous buzzing sound.

**whisk** whisks, whisking, whisked
VERB **1** If you **whisk** eggs or cream, you stir air into them quickly.
VERB **2** If you **whisk** something somewhere, you move it there quickly.
NOUN **3** a kitchen utensil for whisking things

**whisker** whiskers
NOUN **1** The **whiskers** of an animal such as a cat are the long, stiff hairs near its mouth.
NOUN **2** You can refer to the hair on a man's face, especially on his cheeks, as his **whiskers**.

**whisky** whiskies
NOUN a strong alcoholic drink made from grain such as barley

**whisper** whispers, whispering, whispered
VERB When you **whisper**, you talk very quietly and softly.

**whistle** whistles, whistling, whistled
VERB **1** When you **whistle**, you make a high-pitched sound by forcing your breath out between your lips. • *He **whistled** a tune.*
VERB **2** If something **whistles**, it makes a loud, high sound. • *The kettle **whistled**.*

NOUN **3** a small metal tube that you blow into to produce a whistling sound

## white whiter, whitest; whites

NOUN **1** the lightest possible colour, like milk or fresh snow
NOUN **2** The **white** of an egg is the clear liquid around the yolk.
ADJECTIVE **3** having the lightest possible colour
ADJECTIVE **4** **White** coffee contains milk or cream.

## whiteboard whiteboards

NOUN **1** a shiny white board that you can write on and then wipe clean
NOUN **2** a large screen that shows computer images which can be moved or altered by a pen, a finger or a stylus • *The teacher wrote the answer on the* ***whiteboard***.

## who

PRONOUN **1** You use **who** when you are asking about someone's identity. • ***Who*** *are you?*
PRONOUN **2** You use **who** to refer to the person you are talking about. • *I know you are the one* ***who*** *was in trouble yesterday.*

## whoever

PRONOUN **Whoever** means the person who.
• ***Whoever*** *wants to can go on the excursion.*

## whole wholes

NOUN **1** The **whole** of something is all of it.
• *We were abroad the* ***whole*** *of the summer.*
ADJECTIVE **2** all of something • *He ate the* ***whole*** *cake.*
ADJECTIVE **3** A **whole** number an exact number such as 1, 7, and 24, rather than a number with fractions or decimals.
ADVERB **4** in one piece • *He swallowed the sweet* ***whole***.

## wholemeal

ADJECTIVE **Wholemeal** flour is made from the whole grain of the wheat plant, including the husk.

## wholesale

ADVERB **1** If a shopkeeper buys his or her goods **wholesale**, he or she buys large amounts of them cheaply before selling them on to his or her customers.

ANTONYM: retail

ADJECTIVE **2** You can use **wholesale** to describe something unpleasant that is done to a large extent. • *the* ***wholesale*** *destruction of villages*

## wholesome

ADJECTIVE healthy or good for you

## who's

a contraction of *who is* or *who has*

LANGUAGE TIP
Do not confuse *who's* with *whose*.

## whose

PRONOUN **1** You use **whose** to ask who something belongs to. • ***Whose*** *shoe is this?*
PRONOUN **2** **Whose** gives information about something belonging to the person or things just mentioned. • *She is the pupil* ***whose*** *poem won the prize.*

LANGUAGE TIP
Do not confuse *whose* with *who's*.

## why

PRONOUN **1** You use **why** when you are asking about the reason for something. • ***Why*** *did you do that?*
ADVERB **2** You use **why** when you are talking about the reason for something.
• *I wondered* ***why*** *he did that.*

## wick wicks

NOUN the cord that burns in the middle of a candle

## wicked

ADJECTIVE **1** very bad

SYNONYMS: evil, sinful

ADJECTIVE **2** mischievous in an amusing or attractive way

WORD HISTORY
from Old English *wicca* meaning witch

## wicker

NOUN things made of reed or cane woven together, such as baskets or furniture

## wicket wickets

NOUN **1** one of the two sets of stumps and bails at which the bowler aims the ball in cricket
NOUN **2** The grass between the **wickets** in cricket is also called the **wicket**.

## wide wider, widest

ADJECTIVE **1** measuring a large distance from one side to the other
ADJECTIVE **2** measuring a certain amount from one side to the other • *The pool is 10 metres* ***wide***.
ADJECTIVE **3** If there is a **wide** variety, range or selection of something, there are many different kinds of it.

a b c d e f g h i j k l m n o p q r s t u v w x y z

A
B
C
D
E
F
G
H
I
J
K
L
M
N
O
P
Q
R
S
T
U
V
W
X
Y
Z

ADVERB **4** If you open or spread something **wide**, you open it as far as you can. • *Open your mouth* **wide**.

**widow** widows
NOUN a woman whose spouse has died

**widower** widowers
NOUN a man whose spouse has died

**width** widths
NOUN The **width** of something is how wide it is from one side to the other.

**wife** wives
NOUN Someone's **wife** is the woman they are married to.

**Wi-Fi**
NOUN a system of accessing the internet from machines such as laptop computers that are not physically connected to a network

**wig** wigs
NOUN a covering of artificial hair worn over someone's own hair to change their appearance or to hide their baldness

WORD HISTORY
short for *periwig*, from Italian *perrucca* meaning wig

**wiggle** wiggles, wiggling, wiggled
VERB If you **wiggle** something, you move it up and down or from side to side with small, jerky movements.

**wiggly**
ADJECTIVE A **wiggly** line has lots of curves in it.

**wigwam** wigwams
NOUN a kind of tent used by Native Americans

WORD HISTORY
from American Indian *wikwam* meaning their house

**wiki** wikis
NOUN a website that allows anyone visiting it to change or add to the material in it

**wild** wilder, wildest; wilds
ADJECTIVE **1** **Wild** animals and plants live and grow in natural surroundings and are not looked after by people.
ADJECTIVE **2** **Wild** land is natural and not used for farming.
ADJECTIVE **3** **Wild** behaviour is excited and uncontrolled.
NOUN **4** a free and natural state of living • *There are very few tigers left in the* **wild**.

**wilderness** wildernesses
NOUN an area of natural land that is not cultivated

**wildlife**
NOUN wild animals and plants

**wilful**
ADJECTIVE **1** Someone who is **wilful** is determined to get their own way.

SYNONYMS: headstrong, stubborn

ADJECTIVE **2** Something that is **wilful** is done or said deliberately. • **wilful** *damage*

**wilfully**
ADVERB **1** in a way that shows you are determined to get your own way
ADVERB **2** deliberately • *The child had been* **wilfully** *neglected.*

**will** wills
VERB **1** You use **will** to form the future tense. • *I* **will** *do the washing up after dinner.*
NOUN **2** the determination to do something
NOUN **3** a legal document in which people say what they want to happen to their money and property when they die
NOUN **4** what you choose or want to do • *Don't make them do it against their* **will**.

**willing**
ADJECTIVE If you are **willing**, you are glad and ready to do what is wanted or needed.

**willow** willows
NOUN a tree with long, thin branches and narrow leaves that often grows near water

**wilt** wilts, wilting, wilted
VERB If a plant **wilts**, it droops because it needs more water or is dying.

**wily** wilier, wiliest
ADJECTIVE clever and cunning

**wimp** wimps
NOUN (*informal*) someone who is feeble and timid

**win** wins, winning, won
VERB **1** If you **win** a fight, game or argument, you defeat your opponent.
VERB **2** If you **win** a prize, you receive it as a reward for succeeding in something.

**winch** winches, winching, winched
NOUN **1** a machine used to lift or pull heavy objects. It consists of a cylinder or wheel around which a rope or cable is wound.
VERB **2** If you **winch** an object or person somewhere, you lift, lower or pull them using a winch.

**wind** winds, winding, wound
VERB **1** If a road or river **winds**, it is not straight, but twists and turns.
VERB **2** When you **wind** something round something else, you wrap it round it several times.
VERB **3** When you **wind** a clock or machine, or **wind** it up, you turn a key or handle several times to make it work.
NOUN **4** a current of air that moves across the land and sea
ADJECTIVE **5** A **wind** instrument is a musical instrument that you play by blowing into it.

PRONUNCIATION TIP
Meanings 1, 2 and 3 rhyme with "mind".
Meanings 4 and 5 rhyme with "tinned".

**wind farm** wind farms
NOUN a place where wind turbines are used to convert the power of the wind into electricity

**windmill** windmills
NOUN a machine in a special building, for generating electricity, grinding grain or pumping water. It is powered by long arms called sails that are turned by the wind.

**window** windows
NOUN a space in a wall or roof or in the side of a vehicle, usually with glass in it so that light can pass through and people can see in or out

**windpipe** windpipes
NOUN the tube through which air travels in and out of your lungs when you breathe

**windscreen** windscreens
NOUN the glass at the front of a vehicle through which the driver looks

→ Have a look at the illustration for **car**

**windsurfer** windsurfers
NOUN someone who does the sport of moving over the surface of the sea or a lake on a board with a sail fixed to it

**windsurfing**
NOUN the sport of moving over the surface of the sea or a lake on a board with a sail fixed to it

**windy** windier, windiest
ADJECTIVE If it is **windy**, there is a lot of wind.

**wine** wines
NOUN an alcoholic drink usually made from grapes

**wing** wings
NOUN **1** A bird's or insect's **wings** are the parts of its body that it uses for flying.

→ Have a look at the illustrations for **bird** and **insect**

NOUN **2** An aeroplane's **wings** are the long, flat parts on each side that support it while it is in the air.

→ Have a look at the illustration for **aeroplane**

NOUN **3** A **wing** of a building is a part of it which sticks out from the main part.
● *The party was held in the east **wing** of the palace.*
NOUN **4** The **wings** of a car are the parts around the wheels.

→ Have a look at the illustration for **car**

NOUN **5** In a game such as football or hockey, the **left wing** and the **right wing** are the areas on the far left and the far right of the pitch.

**wink** winks, winking, winked
VERB When you **wink**, you close and open one eye very quickly, often to show that something is a joke or a secret.

**winner** winners
NOUN someone who wins something

**winter** winters
NOUN the coldest season of the year, between autumn and spring

**wipe** wipes, wiping, wiped
VERB If you **wipe** something, you rub its surface lightly with a cloth or your hand to clear off dirt or liquid.

**wire** wires, wiring, wired
NOUN **1** long, thin, bendy metal that can be used to make or fasten things, or to conduct an electric current
VERB **2** If someone **wires** something, or **wires** it up, they connect it so that electricity can pass through it.

**wireless** wirelesses
ADJECTIVE **1** If a computer network is **wireless**, it is connected by radio signals rather than cables.
NOUN **2** an old-fashioned word for **radio**

**wisdom**
NOUN a person's ability to use the things they have done and learned to give good advice or make good decisions

a
b
c
d
e
f
g
h
i
j
k
l
m
n
o
p
q
r
s
t
u
v
w
x
y
z

**451**

**wisdom tooth wisdom teeth**

NOUN Your **wisdom teeth** are large teeth at the back of your mouth that grow in when you are an adult.

→ Have a look at the illustration for **teeth**

**wise wiser, wisest**

ADJECTIVE Someone who is **wise** can use their experience and knowledge to make sensible decisions and judgements.

**wish wishes, wishing, wished**

NOUN **1** something that you want very much
NOUN **2** the act of wishing for something
VERB **3** If you **wish** something for someone, you hope that they will have it. • *I wished her good luck in her exams.*
VERB **4** If you **wish** to do something, you want to do it.
VERB **5** If you **wish** something was true, you would like it to be, but know it is not very likely.

**wisp wisps**

NOUN A **wisp** of something such as smoke or hair is a small, thin, streak or bunch of it. • *A wisp of hair fell over her eyes.*

**wispy wispier, wispiest**

ADJECTIVE forming long thin pieces or lines • *wispy hair*

**wit wits**

NOUN the ability to use words or ideas in an amusing and clever way

**witch witches**

NOUN a woman who claims to have magic powers and to be able to use them for good or evil. **Witches** are often characters in fairy stories.

---

**WORD HISTORY**
from Old English *wicca* meaning witch

**witchcraft**

NOUN the skill or art of using magic powers, especially evil ones

**with**

PREPOSITION If you are **with** someone, you are in their company. • *We went with Mum to the shops.*

**withdraw withdraws, withdrawing, withdrew, withdrawn**

VERB **1** If you **withdraw** something, you take it out. • *He withdrew the money from his bank.*
VERB **2** If you **withdraw** from something,

you do not continue with it. • *She withdrew from the race because of injury.*

**wither withers, withering, withered**

VERB If a plant **withers**, it wilts or shrivels up and dies.

**within**

PREPOSITION **1** inside, not going outside certain limits • *Stay within the school grounds.*
PREPOSITION **2** before a period of time has passed • *Bring back the book within three weeks.*

**without**

PREPOSITION **1** not having, not feeling or not showing something • *They went out without coats as it was a warm, dry day.*
PREPOSITION **2** If you do something **without** someone else, they are not with you when you do it. • *He went without me.*

**witness witnesses**

NOUN **1** someone who has seen an event, such as an accident, and can describe what happened
NOUN **2** someone who appears in a court of law to say what they know about a crime or other event

**witty wittier, wittiest**

ADJECTIVE amusing in a clever way

**wizard wizards**

NOUN a man in a fairy story who has magic powers

**wobble wobbles, wobbling, wobbled**

VERB If something **wobbles**, it shakes or moves from side to side because it is loose or unsteady.

**wok woks**

NOUN a large bowl-shaped pan used for Chinese cooking

**woke**

VERB the past tense of **wake**

**woken**

VERB the past participle of **wake**

**wolf wolves; wolfs, wolfing, wolfed**

NOUN **1** a wild animal related to the dog. **Wolves** hunt in packs and kill other animals for food.
VERB **2** (*informal*) If you **wolf** food, or **wolf** it down, you eat it up quickly and greedily.

**woman** women
NOUN an adult female human being
ANTONYM: man

**womb** wombs
NOUN A woman's **womb** is the part inside her body where her unborn baby grows.

**women**
PLURAL NOUN the plural of **woman**

**won**
VERB the past tense and past participle of **win**

**wonder** wonders, wondering, wondered
VERB 1 If you **wonder** about something, you think about it and try to guess or understand more about it.
VERB 2 If you **wonder** at something, you are amazed by it.
NOUN 3 a feeling of amazement and admiration

**wonderful**
ADJECTIVE marvellous or impressive

**won't**
VERB a contraction of *will not*

**wood** woods
NOUN 1 the substance that forms the trunks and branches of trees
NOUN 2 a large area of trees growing near each other

**wooden**
ADJECTIVE Something **wooden** is made of wood.

**woodland** woodlands
NOUN land that is mostly covered with trees

**woodlouse** woodlice
NOUN a small animal with seven pairs of legs, that lives in damp soil and rotten wood

**woodpecker** woodpeckers
NOUN a climbing bird with a long, sharp beak that it uses to drill holes in trees to find the insects that live in the bark

**woodwind**
ADJECTIVE **Woodwind** instruments are musical instruments such as flutes, oboes, clarinets and bassoons, made of wood or metal. They are played by being blown into.

**woodwork**
NOUN 1 the activity of making things out of wood
NOUN 2 the parts of a building that are made of wood

**woof** woofs
NOUN the sound a dog makes

**wool** wools
NOUN 1 the hair that grows on sheep and some other animals
NOUN 2 thread or cloth made from the wool of animals, and used to make clothes, blankets and carpets

**woollen**
ADJECTIVE made of wool

**woolly**
ADJECTIVE made of wool, or looking like wool

**word** words
NOUN 1 a single unit of language in speech or writing which has a meaning. *Bird*, *hot* and *sing* are all **words**.
PLURAL NOUN 2 The **words** of a play or song are the words you say or sing.
NOUN 3 If you give someone your **word** about something, you promise to do it.
NOUN 4 If you ask for a **word** with someone, you want to say something briefly to them.

**wore**
VERB the past tense of **wear**

**work** works, working, worked
VERB 1 People who **work** have a job that they are paid to do.
VERB 2 When you **work**, you spend time and energy doing something useful.
VERB 3 If something **works**, it does what it is supposed to do.
PHRASE 4 If something **works its way** into a certain position, it moves itself there gradually.

**work out**
VERB If you **work out** an answer to a problem, you solve it.

**workout** workouts
NOUN a session of exercise or training for the body

**workshop** workshops
NOUN a room or building that has tools or machinery in it that are used for making or repairing things

**world** worlds
NOUN 1 the planet we live on
NOUN 2 A person's **world** is the life they lead and the people they know.
NOUN 3 a particular field of activity • *He is a top player in the rugby **world**.*
PHRASE 4 If you **think the world** of someone, you like or admire them very much.

a
b
c
d
e
f
g
h
i
j
k
l
m
n
o
p
q
r
s
t
u
v
w
x
y
z

**453**

## World Wide Web

NOUN The **World Wide Web** is a system of linked documents accessed via the internet.

### worm worms

NOUN a small, thin animal without bones or legs, especially an earthworm

### worn

VERB **1** the past participle of **wear**

ADJECTIVE **2** looking old or exhausted

### worry worries, worrying, worried

VERB **1** If you **worry**, you feel anxious about a problem or about something that might happen.

NOUN **2** a problem, or something that makes you worry

### worse

ADJECTIVE **1** less good. The comparative form of *bad*. • *The team's results are **worse** this year than they were last year.*

> ANTONYM: better

ADVERB **2** less food or well. The comparative form of *bad* or *badly*. • *I feel **worse** than I did yesterday.*

> ANTONYM: better

### worship worships, worshipping, worshipped

VERB If you **worship** a god, you show your love and respect by praying or singing hymns.

### worst

ADJECTIVE **1** the least good. The superlative form of *bad*. • *It was the **worst** meal I have ever eaten.*

> ANTONYM: best

ADVERB **2** the least good or the least well. The superlative form of *bad* or *badly*. • *Rural areas were **worst** affected by the fires.*

> ANTONYM: best

### worth

ADJECTIVE **1** If something is **worth** a sum of money, it has that value.

ADJECTIVE **2** If something is **worth** doing, it deserves to be done.

### worthless

ADJECTIVE Something that is **worthless** has no use or no value.

### worthwhile

ADJECTIVE If something is **worthwhile**, it is important enough to spend time or effort doing it.

### would

VERB **1** the past tense of **will**

VERB **2** You use **would** to talk about something that was in the future the last time you were talking about it. • *We were sure it **would** be a success.*

VERB **3** You use **would** in polite questions. • ***Would** you like some lunch?*

### wouldn't

VERB a contraction of *would not*

### wound wounds, wounding, wounded

VERB **1** the past tense and past participle of **wind**

NOUN **2** an injury to part of a person's or an animal's body, especially a cut

VERB **3** If someone or something **wounds** a person or an animal, they injure them, especially with a cut.

> **PRONUNCIATION TIP**
> Meanings 1 and 2 rhyme with "sound". Meaning 3 is pronounced **woond**.

### wove

VERB the past tense of **weave**

### woven

VERB the past participle of **weave**

### wrap wraps, wrapping, wrapped

VERB If you **wrap** something, you fold cloth or paper around it.

### wrapping wrappings

NOUN material used to wrap something, such as a present

### wrath

NOUN great anger

### wreath wreaths

NOUN an arrangement of flowers and leaves, often in the shape of a circle, which is put on a grave to remember someone who has died

### wreck wrecks, wrecking, wrecked

VERB **1** To **wreck** something means to break it, destroy it or spoil it completely.

NOUN **2** a vehicle or ship that has been badly damaged, usually in an accident

### wreckage

NOUN the parts of a vehicle or ship that are left after it has been badly damaged, usually in an accident • *Divers found the **wreckage** of the ship on the seabed.*

### wren wrens

NOUN a small, brown songbird

**wrench** **wrenches, wrenching, wrenched**
VERB **1** If you **wrench** something, you give it a sudden and violent twist or pull.
VERB **2** If you **wrench** a limb or a joint, you twist and injure it.
NOUN **3** a wrenching movement
NOUN **4** a tool for gripping or tightening nuts and bolts

**wrestle** **wrestles, wrestling, wrestled**
VERB If you **wrestle** someone, or **wrestle** with them, you fight them by holding or throwing them, but not hitting them.

**wrestler** **wrestlers**
NOUN someone who takes part in a sport in which you fight someone by holding them or throwing them but not hitting them

**wretched**
ADJECTIVE very unhappy or unfortunate

**wriggle** **wriggles, wriggling, wriggled**
VERB **1** If a person or an animal **wriggles**, they twist and turn their body in a lively and excited way.
VERB **2** If you **wriggle** out of doing something that you do not want to do, you manage to avoid doing it.

**wring** **wrings, wringing, wrung**
VERB When you **wring** a wet cloth, or **wring** it out, you squeeze the water out of it by twisting it.

**wrinkle** **wrinkles, wrinkling, wrinkled**
NOUN **1** a soft fold or crease in something, especially a person's skin as they grow older
VERB **2** If something **wrinkles**, folds or creases develop in it.

**wrinkled**
ADJECTIVE Something that is **wrinkled** has wrinkles in it.

**wrist** **wrists**
NOUN the part of your body between your hand and your arm, which bends when you move your hand

**wristwatch** **wristwatches**
NOUN a watch you wear on your wrist

**write** **writes, writing, wrote, written**
VERB **1** When you **write**, you use a pencil, pen or keyboard to form letters, words or numbers on a surface. ● *I have **written** my name in the front of my book.*

VERB **2** If you **write** something such as a poem, a book or a piece of music, you think of the words or notes for yourself.
VERB **3** When you **write** to someone, you send them a letter.

**writer** **writers**
NOUN **1** a person who writes books, stories or articles as a job
NOUN **2** The **writer** of something is the person who wrote it.

**writhe** **writhes, writhing, writhed**
VERB If you **writhe**, you twist and turn your body, often because you are in pain.

**writing** **writings**
NOUN **1** something that has been written or printed
NOUN **2** Your **writing** is the way you write with a pen or pencil.

**written**
VERB the past participle of **write**

**wrong**
ADJECTIVE **1** If there is something **wrong** with an object, it is not working properly or has a fault. ● *There must be something **wrong** with the car as it will not start.*
ADJECTIVE **2** If something is **wrong**, it is not correct or truthful.

ANTONYM: right

ADJECTIVE **3** An action that is **wrong** is bad or against the law.

**wrote**
VERB the past tense of **write**

**wrung**
VERB the past tense and past participle of **wring**

a
b
c
d
e
f
g
h
i
j
k
l
m
n
o
p
q
r
s
t
u
v
w
x
y
z

## Xmas

NOUN (*informal*) Christmas

## X-ray **X-rays, X-raying, X-rayed**

NOUN **1** a type of radiation that can pass through some solid materials. **X-rays** are used by doctors to examine the bones or organs inside a person's body.

NOUN **2** a picture made by sending X-rays through someone's body in order to examine the inside of it

VERB **3** If someone **X-rays** something, they make a picture of the inside of it by passing X-rays through it.

## xylophone **xylophones**

NOUN a musical instrument made of a row of wooden bars of different lengths. It is played by hitting the bars with special hammers.

**PRONUNCIATION TIP**
This word is pronounced **ziy**-lu-fohn.

## yacht **yachts**

NOUN a boat with sails or an engine, used for racing or for pleasure trips

## yak **yaks**

NOUN a type of long-haired ox with long horns, found mainly in the mountains of Tibet

## yam **yams**

NOUN a root vegetable that grows in tropical regions

## yard **yards**

NOUN **1** a unit of length equal to 36 inches or about 91·4 centimetres

NOUN **2** a paved space with walls around it, next to a building

NOUN **3** a place where certain types of work are carried out, such as a ship**yard** or a builder's **yard**

## yarn **yarns**

NOUN **1** thread used for knitting or making cloth

NOUN **2** (*informal*) a story that someone tells, often with invented details to make it more interesting or exciting

## yawn **yawns, yawning, yawned**

VERB When you **yawn**, you open your mouth wide and take in more air than usual, often when you are tired or bored.

## year **years**

NOUN **1** a period of twelve months or 365 days (366 days in a leap year), usually measured from the first of January to the thirty-first of December. It takes a **year** for the Earth to orbit the sun.

NOUN **2** the part of a year during which something happens or is organised • *the school **year***

## yeast

NOUN a type of fungus used in baking and in making beer

**yell yells, yelling, yelled**
VERB **1** If you **yell**, you shout loudly, usually because you are angry, excited or in pain.
NOUN **2** a loud shout

**yellow yellower, yellowest**
NOUN **1** the colour of buttercups, egg yolks or lemons
ADJECTIVE **2** having the colour of buttercups, egg yolks or lemons

**yelp yelps, yelping, yelped**
VERB **1** When people or animals **yelp**, they give a sudden cry.
NOUN **2** a sudden cry

**yes**
INTERJECTION You say **yes** to agree with someone, to say that something is true or to accept something.

ANTONYM: no

**yesterday**
NOUN **1** the day before today
ADVERB **2** on the day before today • *She left* **yesterday**.

**yet**
ADVERB **1** If something has not happened **yet**, you expect it to happen in the future.
ADVERB **2** If something should not be done **yet**, it should be done later. • *Don't switch it off* **yet**.
CONJUNCTION **3** You use **yet** to introduce something that is rather surprising. • *He doesn't like maths,* **yet** *he always does well.*

**yew yews**
NOUN an evergreen tree with bright red berries

**yodel yodels, yodelling, yodelled**
VERB When someone **yodels**, they sing normal notes with high quick notes in between. You can hear this style of singing in the Swiss and Austrian Alps.

**yoga**
NOUN a Hindu form of exercise that develops the body and the mind, making you relaxed and fit

**yogurt yogurts**; also spelt **yoghurt**
NOUN a slightly sour, thick, liquid food made from milk that has had bacteria added to it

**yoke yokes**
NOUN a wooden bar laid across the necks of animals such as oxen to hold them together when they pull a plough or a cart

**yolk yolks**
NOUN the yellow part in the middle of an egg

**Yom Kippur**
NOUN an annual Jewish religious holiday, which is a day of fasting and prayers. It is also called the Day of Atonement.

**WORD HISTORY**
from Hebrew *yom* meaning day and *kippur* meaning atonement

**you**
PRONOUN **You** refers to the person or people you are talking or writing to.

**you'd**
a contraction of *you had* or *you would*

**you'll**
a contraction of *you will* or *you shall*

**young younger, youngest**
ADJECTIVE **1** A **young** person, animal or plant has not lived very long and is not yet mature.
PLURAL NOUN **2** The **young** of an animal are its babies.

**your**
ADJECTIVE belonging to you

**you're**
a contraction of *you are*

**yours**
PRONOUN belonging to you

**yourself yourselves**
PRONOUN you and only you • *Have you hurt* **yourself**?

**youth youths**
NOUN **1** Someone's **youth** is the time of their life before they are a fully mature adult.
NOUN **2** a boy or young man
NOUN **3** young people in general

**you've**
a contraction of *you have*

**yo-yo yo-yos**
NOUN a round wooden or plastic toy attached to a string. You play by making the **yo-yo** move up and down the string.

a
b
c
d
e
f
g
h
i
j
k
l
m
n
o
p
q
r
s
t
u
v
w
x
y
z

**457**

# Zz

**zany zanier, zaniest**
ADJECTIVE odd in a funny way

**WORD HISTORY**
from Italian *zanni* meaning clown

**zap zaps, zapping, zapped**
VERB (*informal*) If you **zap** someone or something in a computer game, you get rid of them.

**zeal**
NOUN eagerness and enthusiasm

**zebra zebras**
NOUN a type of African wild horse with black and white stripes

**zebra crossing zebra crossings**
NOUN part of a road marked with broad black and white stripes, where pedestrians can cross

**zero**
NOUN nought. The sign for zero is 0.

**zest**
NOUN **1** a feeling of great enjoyment and enthusiasm
NOUN **2** The **zest** of a citrus fruit such as an orange or lemon is the outside of the peel, used to flavour food and drinks.

**zestful**
ADJECTIVE exciting and lively

**zestfully**
ADVERB in an exciting and lively way

**zigzag zigzags, zigzagging, zigzagged**
NOUN **1** a line that has a series of sharp, angular bends to the right and left
VERB **2** If you **zigzag**, you move forward in a series of sharp turns to the left and right.

**zinc**
NOUN a bluish-white metal used to coat other metals to stop them rusting

**zip zips, zipping, zipped**
NOUN **1** a fastener used on clothes and bags, with two rows of metal or plastic interlocking teeth that separate or fasten together as you pull a small tag along them
VERB **2** When you **zip** something, or **zip** it up, you fasten it using a zip.

**zodiac**
NOUN a diagram used by astrologers to represent the movement of the stars. It is divided into 12 sections, each with a special name and symbol. ● *Capricorn, Gemini, Taurus and Pisces are all signs of the zodiac.*

**WORD HISTORY**
from the Greek *zoidiakos kuklos* meaning "circle of signs"

**zone zones**
NOUN an area of land or sea that is considered different from the areas around it, or is separated from the areas around it in some way

**zoo zoos**
NOUN a place where live animals are kept so that people can look at them

**zoologist zoologists**
NOUN someone who studies animals

**zoology**
NOUN the scientific study of animals

**zoom lens zoom lenses**
NOUN A **zoom lens** on a camera helps the photographer to take close-up pictures from far away.

**zucchini**
PLURAL NOUN small vegetable marrows with dark green skin. They are also called courgettes.

**WORD HISTORY**
from Italian plural of *zucchino* meaning gourd

# Word Wizard

# Word classes

## Nouns

A **noun** is a word that is used for talking about a person or thing. **Nouns** are sometimes called "naming words" because they are often the names of people, places, things and ideas, for example:

> **mum** *noun*
> **park** *noun*
> **bird** *noun*
> **happiness** *noun*

**Nouns** are very often found after the words *a* and *the* or words like *our*, *my* or *his*.

*We watched a <u>cartoon</u> on the <u>laptop</u>.*
*My <u>brother</u> is playing in the <u>park</u>.*
*What a great <u>idea</u>!*

**Proper nouns** are the names of people, places, days and months, and always start with a capital letter.

> **Emma** *noun*
> **London** *noun*
> **Friday** *noun*
> **June** *noun*

<u>John</u> lives in <u>Glasgow</u>.
*He went home on <u>Friday</u>.*

When a **noun** is used with another word or words, this can be called a **noun phrase**.

*She was wearing <u>a beautiful red dress</u>.*
<u>All the children</u> were sleeping.

## Adjectives

An **adjective** is a word that tells you more about a person or thing. **Adjectives** are often called "describing words" because they describe what something looks, feels or smells like, for example:

> **big** *adjective*
> **soft** *adjective*
> **nice** *adjective*

**Adjectives** are very often found before a noun, or after the verb *to be*.

*She lives in a <u>big</u> house.*
*The caterpillar is <u>long</u> and <u>green</u>.*

When you want to talk about something that is more than something else, you can use an **adjective** in the comparative (**-er**) or superlative (**-est**) forms.

> **bigger, biggest**
> **soft, softer**
> **nicer, nicest**

*I have the <u>nicest</u> sister in the world!*
*Yesterday was the <u>wettest</u> day of the year.*

# Verbs

A **verb** is a word that you use for saying what someone or something does. **Verbs** are often called "doing words" because they talk about an action that someone or something is doing, for example:

    **eat** *verb*
    **cry** *verb*
    **talk** *verb*

Verbs are often found after nouns, or words like *she*, *they* or *it*.

*The dog <u>barks</u> at the cat.*
*She <u>eats</u> sandwiches for lunch.*

When you want to talk about something that you are doing right now (in the present), you use the **present tense** of the verb.

*The children <u>talk</u> to each other.*
*She <u>does</u> her homework before dinner.*

When you want to talk about something that you did earlier (in the past), you use the **past tense** of the verb.

*Anna <u>cried</u> when she fell off her bike.*
*We <u>went</u> on holiday to Spain.*

You can make the **past tense** of many verbs by adding *d* or *ed* to the end of the verb, for example:

    *walk* → *walked*
    *dance* → *danced*

Sometimes you need to add another letter before the *ed* ending in the **past tense**, for example:

    *stop* → *stopped*
    *hug* → *hugged*

Some verbs have a completely different way of making the **past tense**, for example:

    *go* → *went*
    *do* → *done*
    *sing* → *sang*

The **subjunctive** is a form of the verb which is sometimes used in formal speech and writing. The most frequent usage is in the phrase "*If I were...*", for example:

*If I <u>were</u> you, I'd tell her how you feel.*
*What would you do if you <u>were</u> in my position?*

A **modal verb** is used to change the meaning of other verbs, especially when you want to talk about how certain something is, or your duty to do something, for example:

*It looks like it <u>might</u> rain today.*
*You <u>should</u> help your little brother.*

The main **modal verbs** are *will*, *would*, *can*, *could*, *may*, *might*, *shall*, *should*, *must* and *ought*.

*She <u>could</u> play the piano really well.*

# Adverbs

An **adverb** is a word that tells you more about how someone does something, for example:

**happily** *adverb*
**slowly** *adverb*
**well** *adverb*

**Adverbs** are very often found after verbs, or sometimes before adjectives.

*He walked <u>slowly</u> into the house.*
*The game was <u>really</u> exciting!*

If a word or phrase is used in the same way as an adverb to talk about how or when something is done, it is called an **adverbial**, for example:

*The bus leaves <u>in five minutes</u>.*

# Pronouns

A **pronoun** is a word you use instead of a noun to refer to someone or something, for example:

**I** *pronoun*
**you** *pronoun*
**our** *pronoun*
**them** *pronoun*

*Are <u>you</u> going to school tomorrow?*
*This is <u>our</u> first time in London.*

A **possessive pronoun** is a pronoun that you use instead of a noun and shows that something belongs to someone, for example:

*Those pens are <u>mine</u>.*

A **relative pronoun** is one of the words *that*, *who* or *which* that you use to introduce information about the person or thing being talked about, for example:

*Is there a bus <u>that</u> goes into town?*

# Prepositions

A **preposition** is a word that links a noun, pronoun or noun phrase to some other word in the sentence, for example:

**with** *preposition*
**for** *preposition*
**since** *preposition*

*Come <u>with</u> me.*
*I haven't seen my cat <u>since</u> this morning.*

**Prepositions** are very often found before a word ending in *ing*.

*Use this towel <u>for</u> drying your hands.*

# Conjunctions

A **conjunction** is a word that links two words or phrases or two parts of a sentence, for example:

**and** *conjunction*
**but** *conjunction*
**because** *conjunction*

*It's raining <u>and</u> it's very cold.*
*I left <u>because</u> I was bored.*

# Determiners

A **determiner** is a specific word you use before a noun and/or an adjective, for example:

**a** *determiner*
**the** *determiner*
**some** *determiner*
**my** *determiner*

*I had <u>an</u> apple in my lunch box.*
*Tomorrow we are getting <u>our</u> new car.*

# Plurals

A **singular** word is the word we use when there is only one of something, for example:

*a dog      the house      one child*

*She saw a <u>dog</u> in the park.*

A **plural** word is the word we use when there is more than one of something, for example:

*the dogs      two houses      some children*

*The <u>children</u> played in the garden.*

A **plural** is often made by adding *s* to a singular word, for example:

| | |
|---|---|
| singular | **duck** |
| plural | **ducks** |

*Shall we feed the <u>ducks</u>?*

Some **plurals** are made by adding *es* to the end of the singular word so that the plural is easier to say. Words which end in *ch*, *sh*, *ss*, *x* and *z* add *es*, for example:

| | | | |
|---|---|---|---|
| singular | **brush** | singular | **fox** |
| plural | **brushes** | plural | **foxes** |

*He uses different <u>brushes</u> when he's painting.*

Sometimes **plurals** are made by taking away the *y* at the end of the singular word and adding *ies*, for example:

| | |
|---|---|
| singular | **pony** |
| plural | **ponies** |

*The <u>ponies</u> were rolling around in the mud.*

Be careful: words ending in *ay* and *ey* just add *s* in the plural, for example:

| | | | |
|---|---|---|---|
| singular | **day** | singular | **key** |
| plural | **days** | plural | **keys** |

*It's three <u>days</u> until I go to Spain.*

Some words have **plurals** which look very different to the singular form, for example:

| | | | |
|---|---|---|---|
| singular | **child** | singular | **mouse** |
| plural | **children** | plural | **mice** |

*How many <u>children</u> are in the class?*

# Grammar and punctuation

**Grammar** is the way that words can be put together to make sentences. **Punctuation** is used in writing to make sense of the words that have been written. You use **punctuation** to show sentences, questions, speech and exclamations, and to help with spelling.

## Grammar terms

**active**  An **active** verb follows the usual pattern of subject – verb – object
*The school <u>arranged</u> a visit to the museum.*

**ambiguity**  If there is some **ambiguity** in a sentence, it means that there is more than one possible meaning.
*I saw a man on a hill with a telescope.*

**antonym**  Two words are **antonyms** if their meanings are opposites.

**clause**  A **clause** is a special type of phrase with a verb.

**cohesion**  A piece of writing has **cohesion** if it is clear how the meanings of its parts fit together.

**command**  A **command** is a sentence where someone is told to do something. A **command** starts with a capital letter and ends with an exclamation mark.
*Shut the door!*

**consonant**  A **consonant** is any of the letters that are not vowels (*a, e, i, o* or *u*).

**direct speech**  **Direct speech** is speech which shows the exact words that the speaker used, for example:
*"Would you like to go to the cinema?" she asked.*

**exclamation**  An **exclamation** is a sentence that shows a strong feeling. An **exclamation** starts with a capital letter and ends with an exclamation mark.
*What a rainy day!*

| | |
|---|---|
| **letter** | A **letter** is a single shape that people use in writing. Words are made when you put **letters** together in a special way.<br>*d+o+g → dog* |
| **main clause** | A **main clause** is a clause that can stand on its own.<br>*Emma likes cats.* |
| **object** | The **object** of a verb is usually the noun, noun phrase or pronoun that describes who or what is having something done to it by the verb. It normally comes after the verb.<br>*Our class made <u>puppets</u> yesterday.* |
| **passive** | The **passive** is a form of the verb that is used when the subject of the verb is the person or thing affected by the action.<br>*A visit to the museum <u>was arranged</u> by the school.* |
| **question** | A **question** is a sentence when someone asks about something. A **question** starts with a capital letter and ends with a question mark.<br>*Where are you going?* |
| **relative clause** | A **relative clause** is a kind of subordinate clause that gives you more information about a noun using *who* or *that*.<br>*There's the boy <u>who lives near to the school</u>.* |
| **sentence** | A **sentence** is a group of words that are connected to each other. **Sentences** can be short, or very long. A **sentence** starts with a capital letter and ends with a full stop.<br>*I like cats.*<br>*The girl, who had been playing in the garden, decided she was going to the park after tea.* |
| **statement** | A **statement** is the same as a **sentence**. |
| **subject** | The **subject** of a verb is usually the noun, noun phrase or pronoun that tells you who or what is doing the verb. It normally comes before the verb in the sentence, or after the verb in a question.<br>*<u>The children</u> went to the park.*<br>*What are <u>you</u> doing?* |
| **subordinate clause** | A **subordinate clause** is a clause in a sentence which adds to the information given in the main clause. It cannot usually stand alone as a sentence.<br>*They went out to play <u>as soon as the rain stopped</u>.* |

| | |
|---|---|
| **syllable** | A **syllable** is one of the "beats" that a word is broken up into: *cat* has one syllable; *parrot* has two syllables; *hippopotamus* has five syllables. |
| **synonym** | Two words are **synonyms** if they have the same meaning, or similar meanings. |
| **vowel** | A **vowel** is one of the letters *a, e, i, o* or *u*. |
| **word** | A **word** is a collection of letters that are put together to make a meaning. **Words** are usually separated from each other by spaces. *The bird sat on the branch.* |
| **word family** | The words in a **word family** are usually related to each other by their structure, grammar and meaning. |

# Punctuation marks

. You put a **full stop** at the end of a sentence.
*This is a sentence.*

? You put a **question mark** at the end of a question.
*Can you come to my party?*

, You use a **comma** to separate parts of a sentence or items on a list.
*She brought sandwiches, crisps, apples and juice to the picnic.*

! You use an **exclamation mark** at the end of a sentence to show a strong feeling, or when a command has been given.
*Wow, look how fast he's going!*

' An **apostrophe** is used in contractions, and also to show belonging.
*I don't know where my brother's toy is.*

A **colon** is used before a list and to introduce a reason or explanation.
*She used three main colours: green, blue and pink.*

A **semi-colon** is used to separate longer items in a list or to show a contrast between two parts of a sentence.
*Jack loves football; his brother hates it.*

**Speech marks** (also called **inverted commas**) show where speech begins and ends.
*"I like your hair," she said.*

**Brackets** are used to separate off extra information in a sentence – the sentence still makes sense without the information in the brackets.
*Bring some snacks (like chocolate and popcorn) to the sleepover.*

**Ellipsis** is used to show that some words are missing, to show a pause when someone is speaking, or to create a dramatic ending to a piece of writing.
*Well... I'm not really sure.*
*Two red eyes appeared in the cave...*

A **hyphen** is used to join two words together to make one word. There is no space on either side of a hyphen.
*We took our luggage to the check-in desk.*

A **dash** is a short line that is longer than a hyphen and has a space on each side of it. It is used to show a break in a sentence or in the same way that brackets are used.
*Don't leave your plate there – put it in the dishwasher!*

**Bullet points** are used to show a list of important items for discussion or action in a document.
*You will need to bring:*
- *pyjamas*
- *toiletries*
- *towel*

# Prefixes and suffixes

## Prefixes

A **prefix** is a letter or group of letters that are added to the beginning of a word to make a new word:

| | |
|---|---|
| **anti-** *meaning* opposite of, against | **anti**clockwise |
| **e-** *meaning* electronic | **e**mail |
| **ex-** *meaning* former | **ex**-husband |
| **mini-** *meaning* smaller | **mini**bus |
| **non-** *meaning* not | **non**-fiction |
| **semi-** *meaning* half | **semi**circle |
| **under-** *meaning* below | **under**ground |

There are some common prefixes that are added to words to give them the opposite meaning.

| **dis-** | agree $\longrightarrow$ **dis**agree | **im-** | possible $\longrightarrow$ **im**possible |
|---|---|---|---|
| **il-** | legal $\longrightarrow$ **il**legal | **un-** | happy $\longrightarrow$ **un**happy |

## Suffixes

A **suffix** is a letter or group of letters that are added to the end of a word to make a new word.

Some suffixes can change nouns into other nouns:

| **-ship** | friend $\longrightarrow$ friend**ship** | champion $\longrightarrow$ champion**ship** |
|---|---|---|

Some suffixes can change adjectives into adverbs:

| **-ly** | slow $\longrightarrow$ slow**ly** | happy $\longrightarrow$ happi**ly** |
|---|---|---|

Some suffixes can change verbs or adjectives into nouns:

| **-ment** | enjoy $\longrightarrow$ enjoy**ment** | argue $\longrightarrow$ argu**ment** |
|---|---|---|
| **-ness** | sad $\longrightarrow$ sad**ness** | happy $\longrightarrow$ happi**ness** |

Some suffixes can change nouns or verbs into adjectives:

| **-ful** | care $\longrightarrow$ care**ful** | wish $\longrightarrow$ wish**ful** |
|---|---|---|
| **-less** | hope $\longrightarrow$ hope**less** | help $\longrightarrow$ help**less** |